KU-741-242

ACCOUNTING AND FINANCE
AN INTRODUCTION

Pearson

At Pearson, we have a simple mission: to help people make more of their lives through learning.

We combine innovative learning technology with trusted content and educational expertise to provide engaging and effective learning experiences that serve people wherever and whenever they are learning.

From classroom to boardroom, our curriculum materials, digital learning tools and testing programmes help to educate millions of people worldwide – more than any other private enterprise.

Every day our work helps learning flourish, and wherever learning flourishes, so do people.

To learn more, please visit us at **www.pearson.com/uk**

NINTH EDITION

ACCOUNTING AND FINANCE: AN INTRODUCTION

Eddie McLaney
and
Peter Atrill

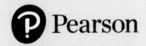 **Pearson**

Harlow, England • London • New York • Boston • San Francisco • Toronto • Sydney
Dubai • Singapore • Hong Kong • Tokyo • Seoul • Taipei • New Delhi
Cape Town • São Paulo • Mexico City • Madrid • Amsterdam • Munich • Paris • Milan

PEARSON EDUCATION LIMITED
KAO Two
KAO Park
Harlow CM17 9NA
United Kingdom
Tel: +44 (0)1279 623623
Web: www.pearson.com/uk

First published 1999 by Prentice Hill Europe (print)
Second edition published 2002 by Pearson Education Limited (print)
Third edition published 2005 (print)
Fourth edition published 2008 (print)
Fifth edition published 2010 (print)
Sixth edition published 2012 (print)
Seventh edition published 2014 (print and electronic)
Eighth edition published 2016 (print and electronic)
Ninth edition published 2018 (print and electronic)

© Prentice Hall Europe 1999 (print)
© Pearson Education Limited 2002, 2005, 2008, 2010, 2012 (print)
© Pearson Education Limited 2014, 2016, 2018 (print and electronic)

The rights of Edward McLaney and Peter Atrill to be identified as authors of this work have been
asserted by them in accordance with the Copyright, Designs and Patents Act 1988.

The print publication is protected by copyright. Prior to any prohibited reproduction, storage in a retrieval
system, distribution or transmission in any form or by any means, electronic, mechanical, recording or
otherwise, permission should be obtained from the publisher or, where applicable, a licence permitting
restricted copying in the United Kingdom should be obtained from the Copyright Licensing Agency Ltd,
Barnard's Inn, 86 Fetter Lane, London EC4A 1EN.

The ePublication is protected by copyright and must not be copied, reproduced, transferred, distributed,
leased, licensed or publicly performed or used in any way except as specifically permitted in writing
by the publishers, as allowed under the terms and conditions under which it was purchased, or as
strictly permitted by applicable copyright law. Any unauthorised distribution or use of this text may be a
direct infringement of the authors' and the publisher's rights and those responsible may be liable in law
accordingly.

All trademarks used herein are the property of their respective owners. The use of any trademark in this
text does not vest in the author or publisher any trademark ownership rights in such trademarks, nor
does the use of such trademarks imply any affiliation with or endorsement of this book by such owners.

Pearson Education is not responsible for the content of third-party internet sites.

The Financial Times. With a worldwide network of highly respected journalists, *The Financial Times*
provides global business news, insightful opinion and expert analysis of business, finance and
politics. With over 500 journalists reporting from 50 countries worldwide, our in-depth coverage of
international news is objectively reported and analysed from an independent, global perspective. To
find out more, visit www.ft.com/pearsonoffer.

ISBN: 978-1-292-20448-2 (print)
       978-1-292-20450-5 (PDF)
       978-1-292-20452-9 (ePub)

British Library Cataloguing-in-Publication Data
A catalogue record for the print edition is available from the British Library

Library of Congress Cataloging-in-Publication Data
Names: McLaney, E. J., author. | Atrill, Peter, author.
Title: Accounting and finance : an introduction / Eddie McLaney and Peter
   Atrill.
Description: Ninth Edition. | New York : Pearson, [2018] | Revised edition of
   the authors' Accounting and finance, 2016.
Identifiers: LCCN 2017051801| ISBN 9781292204482 (print) | ISBN 9781292204505
   (PDF) | ISBN 9781292204529 (ePub)
Subjects: LCSH: Accounting.
Classification: LCC HF5636 .M44 2018 | DDC 657--dc23
LC record available at https://lccn.loc.gov/2017051801

10 9 8 7 6 5 4 3 2 1
22 21 20 19 18

Cover image: © Shutterstock Premier/Allies Interactive
Print edition typeset in 9.5/12.5 pt Stone Serif ITC Pro by SPi Global
Printed and bound by L.E.G.O. S.p.A., Italy

NOTE THAT ANY PAGE CROSS REFERENCES REFER TO THE PRINT EDITION

Brief contents

Contents

Part 1 Financial accounting

5 Accounting for limited companies (2) 161

6 Measuring and reporting cash flows   203

Part 2 **Management accounting**

10 Full costing 367

Part 3 Financial management

14 Making capital investment decisions   563

15 Financing a business   614

Part 4 **Supplementary information**

Lecturer Resources

ON THE WEBSITE

For password-protected online resources tailored to support the use of this textbook in teaching, please visit **www.pearsoned.co.uk/atrillmclaney**

Preface

This text provides a comprehensive introduction to financial accounting, management accounting and core elements of financial management. It is aimed both at students who are not majoring in accounting or finance and those who are. Those studying introductory-level accounting and/or financial management as part of their course in business, economics, hospitality management, tourism, engineering or some other area should find that the book provides complete coverage of the material at the level required. Students who are majoring in either accounting or finance, should find the book useful as an introduction to the main principles, which can serve as a foundation for further study. The text does not focus on technical issues, but rather examines basic principles and underlying concepts. The primary concern throughout is the ways in which financial statements and information can be used to improve the quality of the decisions made by those who use them. To reinforce this practical emphasis, throughout the text, there are numerous illustrative extracts with commentary from real life including company reports, survey data and other sources.

The text is written in an 'open-learning' style. This means that there are numerous integrated activities, worked examples and questions through all of the chapters to help you to understand the subject fully. In framing these questions and tasks, we have tried to encourage critical thinking by requiring analysis and evaluation of various concepts and techniques. To help broaden understanding, questions and tasks often require readers to go beyond the material in the text and/or to link the current topic with material covered earlier in the book. You are encouraged to interact with the material and to check your progress continually. Irrespective of whether you are using the book as part of a taught course or for personal study, we have found that this approach is more 'user-friendly' and makes it easier for you to learn.

We recognise that most readers will not have studied accounting or finance before, and we have therefore tried to write in a concise and accessible style, minimising the use of technical jargon. We have also tried to introduce topics gradually, explaining everything as we go. Where technical terminology is unavoidable, we try to provide clear explanations. In addition, you will find all of the key terms highlighted in the text. These are then listed at the end of each chapter with a page reference. They are also listed alphabetically, with a concise definition, in the glossary given in Appendix B towards the end of the book. This should provide a convenient point of reference from which to revise.

A further consideration in helping you to understand and absorb the topics covered is the design of the text itself. The page layout and colour scheme have been carefully considered to enable easy navigation and digestion of material. The layout features a large page format, an open design, and clear signposting of the various features and assessment material.

In this ninth edition, we have taken the opportunity to make improvements suggested by students and lecturers who used the previous edition. We have, for example, substantially revised the discussion of the conceptual framework of accounting to reflect the very recent statements of the International Accounting Standards Board. We have updated and expanded the number of examples from real life and have continued to reflect the latest international rules relating to the main financial statements. To aid understanding, we have also increased the number of student progress questions (Activities) and explanatory diagrams.

We hope that you will find the book readable and helpful.

Eddie McLaney

Peter Atrill

How to use this book

We have organised the chapters to reflect what we consider to be a logical sequence and, for this reason, we suggest that you work through the text in the order in which it is presented. We have tried to ensure that earlier chapters do not refer to concepts or terms that are not explained until a later chapter. If you work through the chapters in the 'wrong' order, you will probably encounter concepts and terms that were explained previously.

Irrespective of whether you are using the book as part of a lecture/tutorial-based course or as the basis for a more independent mode of study, we advocate following broadly the same approach.

Integrated assessment material

Interspersed throughout each chapter are numerous **Activities.** You are strongly advised to attempt all of these questions. They are designed to simulate the sort of quick-fire questions that your lecturer might throw at you during a lecture or tutorial. Activities serve two purposes:

- To give you the opportunity to check that you understand what has been covered so far.
- To encourage you to think about the topic just covered, either to see a link between that topic and others with which you are already familiar, or to link the topic just covered to the next.

The answer to each Activity is provided immediately after the question. This answer should be covered up until you have deduced your solution, which can then be compared with the one given.

Towards the end of each chapter there is a **Self-assessment question.** This is more comprehensive and demanding than any of the Activities and is designed to give you an opportunity to check and apply your understanding of the core coverage of the chapter. The solution to each of these questions is provided in Appendix C at the end of the book. As with the Activities, it is important that you attempt each question thoroughly before referring to the solution. If you have difficulty with a self-assessment question, you should go over the relevant chapter again.

End-of-chapter assessment material

At the end of each chapter there are four **Review questions.** These are short questions requiring a narrative answer or discussion within a tutorial group. They are intended to help you assess how well you can recall and critically evaluate the core terms and concepts covered in each chapter. Answers to these questions are provided in the Appendix D at the end of the book. At the end of each chapter, except for Chapter 1, there are seven **Exercises.** These are mostly computational and are designed to reinforce your knowledge and understanding. Exercises are graded as 'basic', 'intermediate' and 'advanced' according to their level of difficulty. The basic and intermediate level exercises are fairly straightforward: the advanced level ones can be quite demanding but are capable of being successfully completed if you have worked conscientiously through the chapter and have attempted the basic exercises. Solutions to four of the exercises in each chapter are provided in Appendix D at the end of the book. A coloured exercise number identifies these four questions. Here, too, a thorough attempt should be made to answer each exercise before referring to the solution. Solutions to the other three exercises and to the review questions in each chapter are provided in a separate Instructors' Manual.

Content and structure

The text comprises 16 chapters organised into three core parts: financial accounting, management accounting and financial management. A brief introductory outline of the coverage of each part and its component chapters is given in the opening pages of each part.

The market research for this text revealed a divergence of opinions, given the target market, on whether or not to include material on double-entry bookkeeping techniques. So as to not interrupt the flow and approach of the financial accounting chapters, Appendix A on recording financial transactions (including Activities and three Exercise questions) has been placed in Part 4.

Acknowledgements

The publisher thanks the following reviewers for their very valuable comments on the book:

Frazer Ball
Katerina Hellström
Samuel Hinds
Eileen Roddy

Figures

Figure 5.6 from *Guidance in Strategic Report*, Financial Reporting Council, June 2014, p. 20; **Figure 10.11** from Clinton, D. and White, L. (2012) Roles and Practices in Management Accounting 2003 to 2012, *Strategic Finance*, November, pp. 37–43. Copyright 2012 by IMA®, Montvale, N.J., www.imanet.org, used with permission; **Figures 10.13, 11.4, 11.5, 13.11, 13.14** adapted from CIMA (2009) *Management Accounting Tools for Today and Tomorrow*, p. 12; **Figure 11.1** adapted from Innes, J. and Mitchell, F. (1990) *Activity Based Costing: A Review with Case Studies*, CIMA Publishing. With kind permission of Elsevier; **Figure 11.11** from Kaplan, R. and Norton, D. (1996) *The Balanced Scorecard*, Harvard Business School Press; **Figures 12.7, 12.8, 12.9, 12.11** adapted from CIMA (2009) *Management Accounting Tools for Today and Tomorrow*, p.15; **Figure 14.8** adapted *from Management Accounting Tools for Today and Tomorrow*, CIMA, July 2009, p. 18; **Figure 15.5** from *Finance and Leasing Association (FLA) Annual Review 2016*, p. 17, www.fla.org.uk; **Figure 15.15** from British Business Bank (2015), *Small Business Finance Markets 2014*.

Text

Page 13 Adapted extract from Burn-Callander, R. *Stupid errors in spreadsheets could lead to Britain's next corporate disaster*, 7 April 2015, www.telegraph.co.uk; **Pages 25-26** Extract from Ruddick, G. (2016), Rolls-Royce to scrap two divisions amid restructuring www.theguardian.com, 16 December; **Page 28** Extract from Allarey, R (2015) *This Is How Nike Managed to Clean Up Its Sweatshop Reputation* 8 June www.complex.com; **Page 29** Extract from Goyder, M. (2009) *How we've poisoned the well of wealth*, Financial Times, 15 February. Copyright The Financial Times Limited 2018. All Rights Reserved; **Page 32** Extract from BT plc, *Our business practice and code of ethics*, www.BT.com Accessed 8 November 2016; **Page 65** Extract from *2016 Brandz Top 100 Most Valuable Global Brands*, WPP and Milward Brown, www.wpp.com, 8 June 2016; **Page 68** Extract from Veolia Water UK plc Annual report 2009/10; **Page 71** Extract from Hoyle, R. (2016), *BHP Billiton Reports Worst-Ever Annual Loss*, The Wall Street Journal, www.wsj.com, 16 August; **Page 112** Extract from *European Payment Industry White Paper 2016* p.4 www.intrum.com; **Page 125** Extract from Urquhart L.(2003) *Monotub Industries in a spin as founder gets Titan for £1*, Financial Times, 23 January. Copyright The Financial Times Limited 2018. All Rights Reserved; **Page 135** Extract from Ryanair Holdings plc, Annual Report 2016, p. 144; **Pages 141-142** Extract from Mance, H. (2014) *Betfair admits to £80m payouts mistake*, Financial Times, 3 August. Copyright The Financial Times Limited 2018. All Rights Reserved; **Page 148** Extract from McCrum, D. (2016) *Vodafone joins select club on dividends*, Financial Times, 18 May. Copyright The Financial Times Limited 2018. All Rights Reserved; **Page 168** Extract from International Accounting Standards Board, www.ifrs.org; **Page 182** Extracts from Miller, H. and Pope, T. (2016) *What does the row over Google's tax bill tell us about the corporate tax system?* Institute for Fiscal Studies, 26 January; **Page 185** Adapted from the UK Corporate Governance Code, Financial Reporting Council, April 2016, pp. 5 and 6, www.frc.org.uk; **Page 189** Adapted from Cineworld Group plc, Annual Report and Accounts 2015, preamble, pp. 12 and 14.; **Pages 191-192** Extract from Waters, R. (2014) *Autonomy beset by revenues allegation*, Financial Times, 5 January. Copyright The Financial Times Limited 2018. All Rights Reserved; **Pages 194-195** Extract from Kwan Yuk, P. (2013) *Another Chinese company gets charged with fraud*, Financial Times 20 June. Copyright The Financial Times Limited 2018. All Rights Reserved; **Page 195** Extract from *Anglo Irish bank chief quits over hiding €87m loan*, www.belfasttelegraph.co.uk, 19 December 2008; **Page 196** Extract from Smith, S.(2005) *Read between the lines*, Financial Times,16 September. Copyright The Financial Times Limited 2018. All Rights Reserved; **Page 206** Extract from Johnson, L. (2013) *The most dangerous unforced errors*, Financial Times, 9 July. The Financial Times Limited 2018. All Rights Reserved; **Page 218** Extract from BP plc Annual Report 2015 www.bp.com, p. 20; **Pages 223-225** Extract from White, G. (2014), *Cash flow is king when judging a company's prospects*, Sunday Telegraph Business, 3 May; **Page 250** Extract from Wild, J. (2013), *Ryanair sees sharp fall in profits due to higher fuel costs*, Financial Times, 29 July. Copyright The Financial Times Limited 2018. All Rights Reserved; **Pages 267-268** Extract from Smith, T. (2014) *How investors ignored the warning signs at Tesco*, Financial Times, 5 September. Copyright The Financial Times Limited 2018. All Rights Reserved; **Pages 280-281** Extract from Mathurin, P.(2009) *New study re-writes the A to Z of value investing*, Financial Times, 14 August. Copyright The Financial Times Limited 2018. All Rights Reserved; **Page 298** Extract from Anderson, L. (2012), *Something for the weekend*, Financial Times, 16 November. Copyright The Financial Times Limited 2018. All Rights Reserved; **Pages 302-303** Extract from Burite, J. (2016) *Tullow Sees Opportunity Cost If Kenya-Uganda Pipeline Plan Fails*, www.bloomberg.com, 30 March; **Page 304** Extract from the FT Editorial, *UK taxpayer will lose in rush to exit*, Financial Times, 5 May 2013. Copyright The Financial Times Limited 2018. All Rights Reserved; **Page 346** Extract from Murray, D. (2016) *Record-setting wheat crop adds to international glut*, www.greatfalltribune.com, 7 August; **Page 348** Extract from Proactive investors United Kingdom (2016), *Image Scan to break even thanks to large June X-ray order*, www.proactiveinvestors.co.uk, 22 August; **Page 356** Extract from Stern, S. (2013) *Logic of outsourcing can be hard to resist*, Financial Times, 20 September. Copyright The Financial Times Limited 2018. All Rights Reserved; **Pages 402-403** Extract adapted from Jansson, E. (2008) *Flexible business models helps Spice Holdings power ahead in outsource market*, Financial Times,12 March. Copyright The Financial Times Limited 2018. All Rights Reserved; **Pages 439-440** Adapted from NatWest Bank 2013 Financial Benchmarking Report – Law firms, nw-businesssense.com; **Page 443** Extracts from Song, J. and Bradshaw, T. (2016) *Samsung recall debacle fuels brand concerns*, Financial Times, 11 October. Copyright The Financial Times Limited 2018. All Rights Reserved; **Pages 452-453** Extract from *When misuse leads to failure*, Financial Times, 24 May 2006. Copyright The Financial Times Limited 2018. All Rights Reserved; **Page 488** Extract from CIMA (2009) *Management Accounting Tools for Today and Tomorrow*, p. 15; **Page 490** Extract from CIMA (2009) *Management Accounting Tools for Today and Tomorrow*, p. 15 and McLaughlin, T, (2017), *Back to zero: Companies use 1970s budget tool to cut costs as they hunt for growth*, Reuter Business News, uk. reuter.com, 30 January; **Page 499** Extract from CIMA (2009) *Management Accounting Tools for Today and Tomorrow*, p. 15; **Pages 501-502** Extract from Timpson, J. (2011), The management column, Daily Telegraph Business, 5 June, copyright © Telegraph Media Group Limited (2011); **Page 506** Extract from CIMA (2009) *Management Accounting Tools for Today and Tomorrow*, p. 15; **Page 540** from Lucas, M., Prowle, M. and Lowth, G. (2013) *Management Accounting Practices of UK Small-medium-sized Enterprises*, CIMA, July, p. 7; **Page 584** Extract from Guthrie, J. (2016), *Kiwi combo, Lombard*, Financial Times, 9 June. Copyright The

Financial Times Limited 2018. All Rights Reserved; **Page 588** Extract from Stothard, M. (2016), Hinkley *Point is risk for overstretched EDF, warn critics*, Financial Times, 15 September. Copyright The Financial Times Limited 2018. All Rights Reserved; **Pages 602-603** Extract from *Management Accounting Tools for Today and Tomorrow*, CIMA, July 2009, p.18; **Pages 603-604** from Kingfisher plc Annual Reports 2013/14, p. 25 and 2015/16, p. 28, www.kingfisher.co.uk; **Pages 623-624** Extracts from Lewis, L. (2017) *Toshiba shares plummet on new fears over future of business*, Financial Times, 15 February. Copyright The Financial Times Limited 2018. All Rights Reserved; **Pages 626-627** Extract from Platt, E. and Hale, T. (2017), *Microsoft issues biggest bond of the year in debt market boom*, Financial Times, 30 January. Copyright The Financial Times Limited 2018. All Rights Reserved; **Page 632** Extract from Finance and Leasing Association (FLA) Annual Review 2016, p. 17, www.fla.org.uk; **Page 657** Extract from London Stock Exchange (2016), AIM Factsheet (December); **Page 660** Extracts from Bevan, K. (2016), *How to get the most from crowdfunding - and the risks to avoid*, Financial Times, 22 May. Copyright The Financial Times Limited 2018. All Rights Reserved; **Pages 695-696** Extract from Hurley, J. (2016) *Suppliers 'routinely kept waiting by supermarkets'*, www.thetimes.co.uk, 25 January; **Pages 700-701** Sky plc (2016) Annual report 2016, p. 100; **Pages 714-715** Extract from: Davies, R. and Merin, D. (2014), *Uncovering cash and insights from working capital* McKinsey and Company, July, www.mckinsey.com; **Pages 715-716** REL Consulting, The Working Capitalist – Spring 2016, p. 8, www.relconsultancy.com.

Introduction to accounting and finance

Introduction

We begin this opening chapter by considering the roles of accounting and finance. We shall then go on to identify the main users of financial information and discuss their information needs. We shall see how both accounting and finance can be valuable tools in helping users improve the quality of their decisions. In subsequent chapters, we develop this decision-making theme by examining in some detail the kinds of financial reports and methods used to aid decision making.

Since this book is mainly concerned with accounting and financial decision making for private-sector businesses, we shall devote some time to examining the business environment. We shall consider the purpose of a private-sector business, the main forms of business enterprise and the ways in which a business may be structured. We shall also consider what the key financial objective of a business is likely to be. These are all important considerations as they help to shape the kind of accounting and financial information that is produced.

Learning outcomes

When you have completed this chapter, you should be able to:

● explain the nature and roles of accounting and finance;

● identify the main users of financial information and discuss their needs;

● identify and discuss the characteristics that make accounting information useful; and

● explain the purpose of a business and describe how businesses are organised and structured.

What are accounting and finance?

Let us start by trying to understand the purpose of each. **Accounting** is concerned with *collecting, analysing* and *communicating* financial information. The ultimate aim is to help those using this information to make more informed decisions. If the financial information that is communicated were not capable of improving the quality of decisions made, there would be no point in producing it. We shall see who uses financial information, and for what kind of decisions it is useful, a little later in this chapter.

Sometimes the impression is given that the purpose of accounting is simply to prepare financial (accounting) reports on a regular basis. While it is true that accountants undertake this kind of work, it does not represent an end in itself. As already mentioned, the ultimate aim of the accountant's work is to give users better financial information on which to base their decisions. This decision-making perspective of accounting fits in with the theme of this book and shapes the way in which we deal with each topic.

Finance (or financial management), like accounting, exists to help decision makers. It is concerned with the ways in which funds for a business are raised and invested. This lies at the very heart of what business is about. In essence, a business exists to raise funds from investors (owners and lenders) and then to use those funds to make investments (in equipment, premises, inventories and so on) in order to create wealth. As businesses often raise and invest large amounts over long periods, the quality of the financing and investment decisions can have a profound impact on their fortunes.

The way in which funds are raised must fit with the particular needs of the business. An understanding of finance should help in identifying:

● the main forms of finance available;
● the costs, benefits and risks of each form of finance;
● the risks associated with each form of finance; and
● the role of financial markets in supplying finance.

Once the funds are raised, they must be invested in a way that will provide the business with a worthwhile return. An understanding of finance should also help in evaluating the risks and returns associated with an investment.

There is little point in trying to make a sharp distinction between accounting and finance. We have seen that both are concerned with the financial aspects of decision making. Furthermore, there are many overlaps and interconnections between the two areas. For example, accounting reports are a major source of information for financing and investment decisions.

Who are the users of accounting information?

For accounting information to be useful, the accountant must be clear *for whom* the information is being prepared and *for what purpose* the information will be used. There are likely to be various groups of people (known as 'user groups') with an interest in a particular organisation, in the sense of needing to make decisions about it. For the typical private-sector business, the more important of these groups are shown in Figure 1.1. Take a look at this figure and then try Activity 1.1.

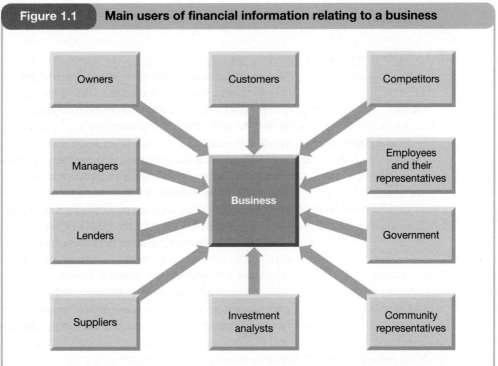

Figure 1.1   Main users of financial information relating to a business

Several user groups have an interest in accounting information relating to a business. The majority of these are outside the business but, nevertheless, have a stake in it. This is not meant to be an exhaustive list of potential users; however, the groups identified are normally the most important.

Activity 1.1

Ptarmigan Insurance plc (PI) is a large motor insurance business. Taking the user groups identified in Figure 1.1, suggest, for each group, the sorts of decisions likely to be made about PI and the factors to be taken into account when making these decisions.

Your answer may be along the following lines:

User group	Decision
Customers	Whether to take further motor policies with PI. This might involve an assessment of PI's ability to continue in business and to meet customers' needs, particularly in respect of any insurance claims made.
Competitors	How best to compete against PI or, perhaps, whether to leave the market on the grounds that it is not possible to compete profitably with PI. This might involve competitors using PI's performance in various respects as a 'benchmark' when evaluating their own performance. They might also try to assess PI's financial strength and to identify significant changes that may signal PI's future actions (for example, raising funds as a prelude to market expansion).

→

Activity 1.1 *continued*

User group	Decision
Employees	Whether to continue working for PI and, if so, whether to demand higher rewards for doing so. The future plans, profits and financial strength of the business are likely to be of particular interest when making these decisions.
Government	Whether PI should pay tax and, if so, how much, whether it complies with agreed pricing policies, whether financial support is needed and so on. In making these decisions an assessment of PI's profits, sales revenues and financial strength would be made.
Community representatives	Whether to allow PI to expand its premises and/or whether to provide economic support for the business. When making such decisions, PI's ability to continue to provide employment for the community, the extent to which it is likely to use community resources, and its likely willingness to fund environmental improvements are likely to be important considerations.
Investment analysts	Whether to advise clients to invest in PI. This would involve an assessment of the likely risks and future returns associated with PI.
Suppliers	Whether to continue to supply PI and, if so, whether to supply on credit. This would involve an assessment of PI's ability to pay for any goods and services supplied.
Lenders	Whether to lend money to PI and/or whether to require repayment of any existing loans. PI's ability to pay the interest and to repay the principal sum would be important factors in such decisions.
Managers	Whether the performance of the business needs to be improved. Performance to date would be compared with earlier plans or some other 'benchmark' to decide whether action needs to be taken. Managers may also wish to consider a change in PI's future direction. This may involve determining whether the business has the flexibility and resources to take on new challenges.
Owners	Whether to invest more in PI or to sell all, or part, of the investment currently held. This would involve an assessment of the likely risks and returns associated with PI. Owners may also be involved with decisions on rewarding senior managers. When making such a decision, the financial performance of the business would normally be considered.

Although this answer covers many of the key points, you may have identified other decisions and/or other factors to be taken into account by each group.

The conflicting interests of users

We have just seen that each user group will have its own particular interests. There is always the possibility that the interests of the various user groups will collide. The distribution of business wealth provides the most likely area for a collision to take place. Let us take the example of owners and managers. Although managers are appointed to act in the best interests of the owners, they may not always do so. Instead, they may use the wealth of the business to award themselves large pay rises, to furnish large offices or to buy expensive cars for their own use. Accounting can play an important role in monitoring and reporting how various groups benefit from the business. Thus, owners may rely on accounting information to see whether pay and benefits received by managers are appropriate and accord with agreed policies.

There is also a potential collision of interest between lenders and owners. Funds loaned to a business, for example, may not be used for their intended purpose. They may be withdrawn by the owners for their own use rather than used to expand the business as agreed. Lenders may, therefore, rely on accounting information to see whether the owners have kept to the terms of the loan agreement.

Activity 1.2

Can you think of other examples where accounting information may be relied on by a user group to see whether the distribution of business wealth is appropriate and/or in accordance with particular agreements?

Two possible examples that spring to mind are:

- employees wishing to check that they are receiving a 'fair share' of the wealth created by the business and that managers are complying with agreed profit-sharing schemes; and
- governments wishing to check that the owners of a monopoly do not benefit from excessive profits and that any pricing rules concerning the monopoly's goods or services have not been broken.

You may have thought of other examples.

How useful is accounting information?

No one would seriously claim that accounting information fully meets all of the needs of each of the various user groups. Accounting is still a developing subject and we still have much to learn about user needs and the ways in which these needs should be met. Nevertheless, the information contained in accounting reports should help users make decisions relating to the business. The information should reduce uncertainty about the financial position and performance of the business. It should help to answer questions concerning the availability of funds to pay owners a return, to repay loans, to reward employees and so on.

Typically, there is no close substitute for the information provided by the financial statements. Thus, if users cannot glean the required information from the financial statements, it is often unavailable to them. Other sources of information concerning the financial health of a business are normally much less useful.

Activity 1.3

What other sources of information might, say, an investment analyst use in an attempt to gain an impression of the financial position and performance of a business? (Try to think of at least four.) What kind of information might be gleaned from these sources?

Other sources of information available include:

- meetings with managers of the business;
- public announcements made by the business;
- newspaper and magazine articles;
- websites, including the website of the business;
- radio and TV reports;
- information-gathering agencies (for example, agencies that assess businesses' credit-worthiness or credit ratings);
- industry reports; and
- economy-wide reports.

These sources can provide information on various aspects of the business, such as new products or services being offered, management changes, new contracts offered or awarded, the competitive environment within which the business operates, the impact of new technology, changes in legislation, changes in interest rates and future levels of inflation.

The kind of information identified in Activity 1.3 is not really a substitute for accounting information. Rather, it is best used in conjunction with accounting information to provide a clearer picture of the financial health of a business.

Evidence on the usefulness of accounting

There are arguments and convincing evidence that accounting information is at least *perceived* as being useful to users. Numerous research surveys have asked users to rank the importance of accounting reports, in relation to other sources of information, for decision-making purposes. Generally, these studies have found that users rank accounting information very highly. There is also considerable evidence that businesses choose to produce accounting information that exceeds the minimum requirements imposed by accounting regulations. (For example, businesses often produce a considerable amount of accounting information for managers, which is not required by any regulations.) Presumably, the cost of producing this additional accounting information is justified on the grounds that users find it useful. Such arguments and evidence, however, leave unanswered the question of whether the information produced is actually used for decision-making purposes, that is: does it affect people's behaviour?

It is normally very difficult to assess the impact of accounting on decision making. One situation arises, however, where the impact of accounting information can be observed and measured. This is where the **shares** (portions of ownership of a business) are traded on a stock exchange. The evidence reveals that, when a business makes an announcement concerning its accounting profits, the prices at which shares are traded and the volume of shares traded often change significantly. This suggests that investors are changing their views about the future prospects of the business as a result of this new information becoming available to them and that this, in turn, leads some of them to make a decision either to buy or to sell shares in the business.

While there is evidence that accounting reports are seen as useful and are used for decision-making purposes, it is impossible to measure just how useful they really are to users. We cannot say with certainty whether the cost of producing these reports represents value for money. Accounting reports will usually represent only one input to a particular decision. The weight attached to them by the decision maker, and the resulting benefits, cannot be accurately assessed.

It is possible, however, to identify the kinds of qualities which accounting information must possess in order to be useful. Where these qualities are lacking, the usefulness of the information will be diminished. We shall now consider this point in more detail.

Providing a service

One way of viewing accounting is as a form of service. The user groups identified in Figure 1.1 can be seen as 'clients' and the accounting (financial) information produced can be seen as the service provided. The value of this service can be judged according to whether the users' information needs have been met.

To be useful, the information provided should possess certain qualities, or characteristics. In particular, it must be relevant and it must faithfully represent what it is supposed to represent. These two qualities, **relevance** and **faithful representation,** are regarded as fundamental qualities and are now explained in more detail.

- *Relevance.* Accounting information should make a difference. That is, it should be capable of influencing user decisions. To do this, it must help to *predict future events* (such as predicting the next year's profit), or help to *confirm past events* (such as establishing the previous year's profit), or do both. By confirming past events, users can check on the accuracy of their earlier predictions. This may, in turn, help them to improve the ways in which they make predictions in the future.

   We should bear in mind that accounting information often relies on the use of estimates. These can cover a wide range and may, for example, include estimates of future sales, costs and cash flows. By their very nature, however, estimates contain a degree of uncertainty.

Activity 1.4

Do you think that the use of estimates will weaken the relevance of accounting information provided to users?

Estimates will vary in the degree of uncertainty that they contain. The higher the degree of uncertainty, the less relevant estimates are likely to be.

The point raised by Activity 1.4 does not imply, however, that estimates with a high degree of uncertainty should not be reported. There may be situations where they still provide users with the most relevant information available.

To be relevant, accounting information must cross a threshold of **materiality**. An item of information should be considered material, or significant, if its omission or misstatement could alter the decisions that users make.

Activity 1.5

Do you think that information that is material for one business will also be material for all other businesses?

No. It will often vary from one business to the next. What is material will normally depend on factors such as the size of the business, the nature of the information and the amounts involved.

Ultimately, what is considered material is a matter of judgement. In making this judgement consideration should be given as to how this information is likely to be used. Where a piece of information is not material, it should not be included within the accounting reports. It will merely clutter them up and, perhaps, interfere with the users' ability to interpret them.

● *Faithful representation.* Accounting information should represent what it is supposed to represent. To do so, the information provided must reflect the *substance* of what has occurred rather than its legal form. Take, for example, a manufacturer that provides goods to a retailer on a sale-or-return basis. The manufacturer may wish to treat this arrangement as two separate transactions. Thus, a contract may be agreed for the sale of the goods and a separate contract agreed for the return of the goods, if unsold by the retailer. This may result in a sale being reported when the goods are delivered to the retailer even though they are returned at a later date. The economic substance, however, is that the manufacturer made no sale as the goods were subsequently returned. They were simply moved from the manufacturer's business to the retailer's business and then back again. Accounting reports should reflect this economic substance. To do otherwise would be misleading.

To provide a perfectly faithful representation, the information provided should be *complete.* In other words, it should incorporate everything needed for users to understand what is being portrayed. It should also be *neutral,* which means that the information should be presented and selected without bias. No attempt should be made to manipulate the information is such a way as to influence user attitudes and behaviour. Finally, it should be *free from error.* This is not the same as saying that information must be perfectly accurate; this may not be possible. We saw earlier that accounting information often contains estimates and these may turn out to be inaccurate. Nevertheless, estimates can still be faithfully represented providing they are properly described and prepared. In practice, accounting information may be unable to reflect perfectly these three aspects of faithful representation. It should aim to do so, however, insofar as possible.

Accounting information must contain *both* fundamental qualities if it is to be useful. There is little point in producing information that is relevant, but which lacks faithful representation, or producing information that is irrelevant, even if it is faithfully represented.

Further qualities

Where accounting information is both relevant and faithfully represented, there are other qualities that, if present, can *enhance* its usefulness. These are **comparability, verifiability, timeliness** and **understandability.** Each of these qualities is now considered.

- *Comparability.* Users of accounting information often want to make comparisons. They may want to compare performance of the business over time (for example, profit this year compared to last year). They may also want to compare certain *aspects* of business performance to those of similar businesses (such as the level of sales achieved during the year). Better comparisons can be made where the accounting system treats items that are basically the same in the same way and where policies for measuring and presenting accounting information are made clear.
- *Verifiability.* This quality provides assurance to users that the accounting information provided faithfully represents what it is supposed to represent. Accounting information is verifiable where different, independent experts could reach a consensus that it provides a faithful portrayal. Verifiable information tends to be supported by evidence, such as an invoice stating the cost of some item of inventories.
- *Timeliness.* Accounting information should be produced in time for users to make their decisions. A lack of timeliness will undermine the usefulness of the information. Normally, the later accounting information is produced, the less useful it becomes.
- *Understandability.* Accounting information should be set out as clearly and concisely as possible so as to help those users at whom the information is aimed.

Activity 1.6

Do you think that accounting reports should be understandable to those who have not studied accounting?

It would be very helpful if everyone could understand accounting reports. This, however, is unrealistic, as it is not normally possible to express complex financial events and transactions in simple, non-technical terms. Any attempts to do so are likely to provide a distorted picture of reality.

It is probably best that we regard accounting reports in the same way that we regard a report written in a foreign language. To understand either of these, we need to have had some preparation. When accounting reports are produced, it is normally assumed that the user not only has a reasonable knowledge of business and accounting but is also prepared to invest some time in studying the reports. Nevertheless, the onus is clearly on accountants to provide information in a way that makes it as understandable as possible to non-accountants.

It is worth emphasising that the four qualities just discussed cannot make accounting information useful. They can only enhance the usefulness of information that is already relevant and faithfully represented.

Weighing up the costs and benefits

Even though a piece of accounting information may have all the qualities described, this does not automatically mean that it should be collected and reported to users. There is still one more hurdle to jump. Consider Activity 1.7.

Activity **1.7**

Suppose an item of information is capable of being provided. It is relevant to a particular decision and can be faithfully represented. It is also comparable, verifiable and timely, and can be understood by the decision maker.

Can you think of the reason why, in practice, you might choose not to produce the information?

The reason is that you judge the cost of doing so to be greater than the potential benefit of having the information. This cost–benefit issue will limit the amount of accounting information provided.

In theory, a particular item of accounting information should only be produced if the costs of providing it are less than the benefits, or value, to be derived from its use. Figure 1.2 shows the relationship between the costs and value of providing additional accounting information.

Figure 1.2 **Relationship between costs and the value of providing additional accounting information**

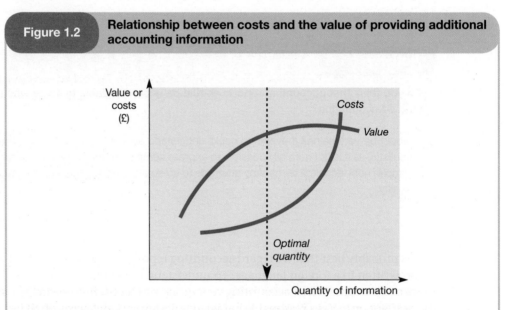

The benefits of accounting information eventually decline. The cost of providing information, however, will rise with each additional piece of information. The optimal level of information provision is where the gap between the value of the information and the cost of providing it is at its greatest.

The figure shows how the value of information received by the decision maker eventually begins to decline. This is, perhaps, because additional information becomes less relevant, or because of the problems that a decision maker may have in processing the sheer quantity of information provided. The costs of providing the information, however, will increase with each additional piece of information. The broken line indicates the point at which the gap between the value of information and the cost of providing that information is at its greatest. This represents the optimal amount of information that can be provided. This theoretical model, however, poses a number of problems in practice.

To illustrate the practical problems of establishing the value of information, let us assume that we accidently reversed our car into a wall in a car park. This resulted in a dented boot and scraped paintwork. We want to have the dent taken out and the paintwork resprayed at a local garage. We know that the nearest garage would charge £450 but we believe that other local garages may offer to do the job for a lower price. The only way of finding out the prices at other garages is to visit them, so that they can see the extent of the damage. Visiting the garages will involve using some fuel and will take up some of our time. Is it worth the cost of finding out the price for the job at the various local garages? The answer, as we have seen, is that if the cost of discovering the price is less than the potential benefit, it is worth having that information.

To identify the various prices for the job, there are several points to be considered, including:

- How many garages shall we visit?
- What is the cost of fuel to visit each garage?
- How long will it take to make all the garage visits?
- At what price do we value our time?

The economic benefit of having the information on the price of the job is probably even harder to assess. The following points need to be considered:

- What is the cheapest price that we might be quoted for the job?
- How likely is it that we shall be quoted a price cheaper than £450?

As we can imagine, the answers to these questions may be far from clear – remember that we have only contacted the local garage so far. When assessing the value of accounting information we are confronted with similar problems.

Producing accounting information can be very costly. The costs, however, are often difficult to quantify. Direct, out-of-pocket costs, such as salaries of accounting staff, are not usually a problem, but these are only part of the total costs involved. There are other costs such as the cost of users' time spent on analysing and interpreting the information provided.

Activity 1.8

What about the economic benefits of producing accounting information? Do you think it is easier, or harder, to assess the economic benefits of accounting information than to assess the costs of producing it?

It is normally much harder to assess the benefits. We saw earlier that, even if we could accurately measure the economic benefits arising from a particular decision, we must bear in mind that accounting information will be only one factor influencing that decision. Other factors will also be taken into account.

There are no easy answers to the problem of weighing costs and benefits. Although it is possible to apply some 'science' to the problem, a lot of subjective judgement is normally involved.

The qualities, or characteristics, influencing the usefulness of accounting information, which we have just discussed, are summarised in Figure 1.3.

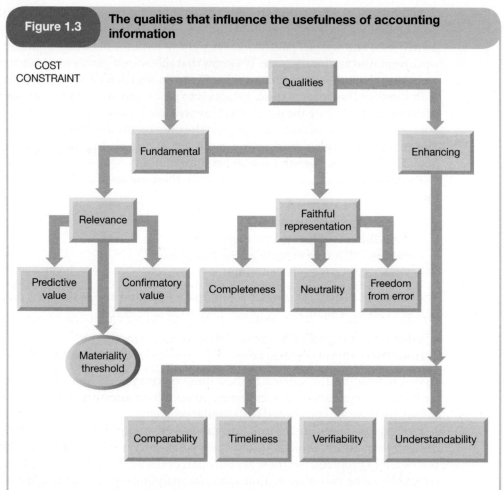

Figure 1.3 The qualities that influence the usefulness of accounting information

There are two fundamental qualities that determine the usefulness of accounting information. In addition, there are four qualities that enhance the usefulness of accounting information. The benefits of providing the information, however, should outweigh the costs.

Accounting as an information system

We have already seen that accounting can be seen as the provision of a service to 'clients'. Another way of viewing accounting is as a part of the business's total information system. Users, both inside and outside the business, have to make decisions concerning the allocation of scarce resources. To ensure that these resources are efficiently allocated, users often need financial information on which to base decisions. It is the role of the accounting system to provide this information.

The **accounting information system** should have certain features that are common to all information systems within a business. These are:

- identifying and capturing relevant information (in this case financial information);
- recording, in a systematic way, the information collected;
- analysing and interpreting the information collected; and
- reporting the information in a manner that suits the needs of users.

The relationship between these features is set out in Figure 1.4.

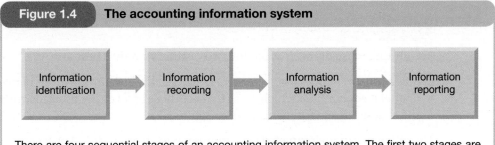

Figure 1.4   The accounting information system

| Information identification | → | Information recording | → | Information analysis | → | Information reporting |

There are four sequential stages of an accounting information system. The first two stages are concerned with preparation, whereas the last two stages are concerned with using the information collected.

Given the decision-making emphasis of this book, we shall be concerned primarily with the final two elements of the process: the analysis and reporting of financial information. We shall place much more emphasis on the way in which information is used by, and is useful to, users rather than the way in which it is identified and recorded.

Efficient accounting information systems are an essential ingredient of an efficient business. When they fail, the results can be disastrous. **Real World 1.1** describes how spreadsheets, which are widely used to prepare accounting and financial information, may introduce errors that can lead to poor financial decisions.

Real World 1.1

Systems error!

Almost one in five large businesses have suffered financial losses as a result of errors in spreadsheets, according to F1F9, which provides financial modelling and business forecasting to large businesses. It warns of looming financial disasters as 71pc of large British business always use spreadsheets for key financial decisions.

The company's new whitepaper entitled Capitalism's Dirty Secret showed that the abuse of humble spreadsheet could have far-reaching consequences. Spreadsheets are used in the preparation of British company accounts worth up to £1.9 trillion and the UK manufacturing sector uses spreadsheets to make pricing decisions for up to £170bn worth of business.

In total, spreadsheet calculations represent up to £38bn of British private sector investment decisions per year, data harvested through YouGov found. Yet 16pc of large companies have admitted finding inaccurate information in spreadsheets more than 10 times in 2014.

Grenville Croll, a spreadsheet risk expert, said of the findings: "Spreadsheets have been shown to be fallible yet they underpin the operation of the financial system. If the uncontrolled use of spreadsheets continues to occur in highly leveraged markets and companies, it is only a matter of time before another 'Black Swan' event occurs causing catastrophic loss."

The report warns that while 33pc of large businesses report poor decision-making as a result of spreadsheet problems, a third of the financial decision-makers using spreadsheets in large UK businesses are still given zero training.

Source: Adapted extract from R. Burn-Callander *Stupid errors in spreadsheets could lead to Britain's next corporate disaster*. 7 April 2015 www.telegraph.co.uk.

Management accounting and financial accounting

Accounting is usually seen as having two distinct strands. These are:

● **management accounting,** which seeks to meet the accounting needs of managers; and
● **financial accounting,** which seeks to meet those of all of the users identified earlier in the chapter except for managers (see Figure 1.1).

The difference in their targeted user groups has led to each strand of accounting developing along different lines. The main areas of difference are as follows:

● *Nature of the reports produced.* Financial accounting reports tend to be general-purpose. Although they are aimed primarily at providers of finance such as owners and lenders, they contain financial information that will be useful for a broad range of users and decisions. Management accounting reports, on the other hand, are often specific-purpose reports. They are designed with a particular decision in mind and/or for a particular manager.

● *Level of detail.* Financial accounting reports provide users with a broad overview of the performance and position of the business for a period. As a result, information is aggregated (that is, added together) and detail is often lost. Management accounting reports, however, often provide managers with considerable detail to help them with a particular operational decision.

● *Regulations.* Financial accounting reports, for many businesses and virtually all larger businesses, are subject to accounting regulations imposed by the law and accounting rule makers. These regulations often require a standard content and, perhaps, a standard format to be adopted. As management accounting reports are for internal use only, there are no regulations from external sources concerning the form and content of the reports. They can be designed to meet the needs of particular managers.

● *Reporting interval.* For most businesses, financial accounting reports are produced on an annual basis, though some large businesses produce half-yearly reports and a few produce quarterly ones. Management accounting reports will be produced as frequently as needed by managers. A sales manager, for example, may require routine sales reports on a daily, weekly or monthly basis, so as to monitor performance closely. Special-purpose reports can also be prepared when the occasion demands: for example, where an evaluation is required of a proposed investment in new equipment.

● *Time orientation.* Financial accounting reports reflect the performance and position of the business for the past period. In essence, they are backward-looking. Management accounting reports, on the other hand, often provide information concerning future performance as well as past performance. It is an oversimplification, however, to suggest that financial accounting reports never incorporate expectations concerning the future. Occasionally, businesses will release projected information to other users in an attempt to raise capital or to fight off unwanted takeover bids. Even preparation of the routine financial accounting reports typically requires making some judgements about the future (as we shall see in Chapter 3).

● *Range and quality of information.* Financial accounting reports concentrate on information that can be quantified in monetary terms. Management accounting also produces such reports, but is also more likely to produce reports that contain information of a non-financial nature, such as physical volume of inventories, number of sales orders received, number of new products launched, physical output per employee and so on. Financial accounting places greater emphasis on the use of objective, verifiable evidence when preparing reports. Management accounting reports may use information that is less objective and verifiable, but nevertheless provide managers with the information they need.

We can see from this that management accounting is less constrained than financial accounting. It may draw from a variety of sources and use information that has varying degrees of reliability. The only real test to be applied when assessing the value of the information produced for managers is whether or not it improves the quality of the decisions made.

The main differences between financial accounting and management accounting are summarised in Figure 1.5.

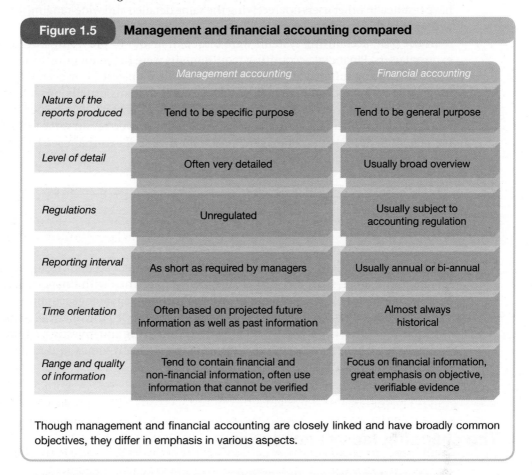

Figure 1.5 Management and financial accounting compared

	Management accounting	Financial accounting
Nature of the reports produced	Tend to be specific purpose	Tend to be general purpose
Level of detail	Often very detailed	Usually broad overview
Regulations	Unregulated	Usually subject to accounting regulation
Reporting interval	As short as required by managers	Usually annual or bi-annual
Time orientation	Often based on projected future information as well as past information	Almost always historical
Range and quality of information	Tend to contain financial and non-financial information, often use information that cannot be verified	Focus on financial information, great emphasis on objective, verifiable evidence

Though management and financial accounting are closely linked and have broadly common objectives, they differ in emphasis in various aspects.

The differences between management accounting and financial accounting suggest that there are differences in the information needs of managers and those of other users. While differences undoubtedly exist, there is also a good deal of overlap between these needs.

Activity 1.9

Can you think of any areas of overlap between the information needs of managers and those of other users? (*Hint*: Think about the time orientation and the level of detail of accounting information.)

Two points that spring to mind are:

- Managers will, at times, be interested in receiving a historical overview of business operations of the sort provided to other users.
- Other users would be interested in receiving detailed information relating to the future, such as the planned level of profits, and non-financial information, such as the state of the sales order book and the extent of product innovations.

To some extent, differences between the two strands of accounting reflect differences in access to financial information. Managers have much more control over the form and content of the information that they receive. Other users have to rely on what managers are prepared to provide or what financial reporting regulations insist must be provided. Although the scope of financial accounting reports has increased over time, fears concerning loss of competitive advantage and user ignorance about the reliability of forecast data have resulted in other users not receiving the same detailed and wide-ranging information as that available to managers.

In the past, accounting systems were biased in favour of providing information for external users. Financial accounting requirements were the main priority and management accounting suffered as a result. Survey evidence suggests, however, that this is no longer the case. Modern management accounting systems usually provide managers with information that is relevant to their needs rather than that determined by external reporting requirements. External reporting cycles, however, retain some influence over management accounting. Managers tend to be aware of external users' expectations. (See reference 1 at the end of the chapter.)

Scope of this book

This book covers both financial accounting and management accounting topics. The next six chapters (Part 1, Chapters 2 to 7) are broadly concerned with financial accounting, and the following six (Part 2, Chapters 8 to 13) with management accounting. The final part of the book (Part 3, Chapters 14 to 16) is concerned with the financial management of the business, that is, with issues relating to the financing and investing activities of the business. As we have seen, accounting information is usually vitally important for financial management decisions.

The changing face of accounting

Over the past four decades, the environment within which businesses operate has become increasingly turbulent and competitive. Various reasons have been identified to explain these changes, including:

- the increasing sophistication of customers;
- the availability of rapid and sophisticated forms of information and communication (such as the internet);
- the development of a global economy where national frontiers become less important;
- rapid changes in technology;
- the deregulation of domestic markets (for example, electricity, water and gas);
- increasing pressure from owners (shareholders) for competitive economic returns; and
- the increasing volatility of financial markets.

This new, more complex, environment has brought new challenges for managers and other users of accounting information. Their needs have changed and both financial accounting and management accounting have had to respond. To meet the changing needs of users, there has been a radical review of the kind of information to be reported.

The changing business environment has given added impetus to the search for a clear conceptual framework, or framework of principles, upon which to base financial accounting reports. Various attempts have been made to clarify their purpose and to provide a more solid foundation for the development of accounting rules. The conceptual frameworks that have been developed try to address fundamental questions such as:

- Who are the users of financial accounting information?
- What kinds of financial accounting reports should be prepared and what should they contain?
- How should items such as profit and asset values be measured?

The internationalisation of businesses has created a need for accounting rules to have an international reach. It can no longer be assumed that users of accounting information relating to a particular business are based in the country in which the business operates or are familiar with the accounting rules of that country. Thus, there has been increasing harmonisation of accounting rules across national frontiers.

Activity 1.10

How should the harmonisation of accounting rules benefit:

(a) an international investor?
(b) an international business?

(a) An international investor should benefit because accounting definitions and policies that are used in preparing financial accounting reports will not vary across countries. This should make the comparison of performance between businesses operating in different countries much easier.

(b) An international business should benefit because the cost of producing accounting reports in order to comply with the rules of different countries can be expensive. Harmonisation can, therefore, lead to significant cost savings. It may also broaden the appeal of the business among international investors. Where there are common accounting rules, they may have greater confidence to invest.

In response to criticisms that the financial reports of some businesses are opaque and difficult for users to interpret, great efforts have been made to improve reporting rules. Accounting rule makers have tried to ensure that the accounting policies of businesses are more comparable and transparent and that the financial reports provide a more faithful portrayal of economic reality.

Management accounting has also changed by becoming more outward looking in its focus. In the past, information provided to managers has been largely restricted to that collected within the business. However, the attitude and behaviour of customers and rival businesses have now become the object of much information-gathering. Increasingly, successful businesses are those that are able to secure and maintain competitive advantage over their rivals.

To obtain this advantage, businesses have become more 'customer driven' (that is, concerned with satisfying customer needs). This has led to the production of management accounting information that provides details of customers and the market, such as customer evaluation of services provided and market share. In addition, information about the costs and profits of rival businesses, which can be used as 'benchmarks' by which to gauge competitiveness, is gathered and reported.

To compete successfully, businesses must also find ways of managing costs. The cost base of modern businesses is under continual review and this, in turn, has led to the development of more sophisticated methods of measuring and controlling costs.

Why do I need to know anything about accounting and finance?

At this point you may be asking yourself, 'Why do I need to study accounting and finance? I don't intend to become an accountant!' Well, from the explanation of what accounting and finance is about, which has broadly been the subject of this chapter so far, it should be clear that the accounting/finance function within a business is a central part of its management information system. On the basis of information provided by the system, managers make decisions concerning the allocation of resources. As we have seen, these decisions may concern whether to:

● continue with certain business operations;
● invest in particular projects; or
● sell particular products.

Such decisions can have a profound effect on all those connected with the business. It is important, therefore, that *all* those who intend to work in a business should have a fairly clear idea of certain important aspects of accounting and finance. These aspects include:

● how financial reports should be read and interpreted;
● how financial plans are made;
● how investment decisions are made; and
● how businesses are financed.

Many, perhaps most, students have a career goal of being a manager within a business – perhaps a human resources manager, production manager, marketing manager or IT manager. If you are one of these students, an understanding of accounting and finance is very important. When you become a manager, even a junior one, it is almost certain that you will have to use financial reports to help you to carry out your role. It is equally certain that it is largely on the basis of financial information and reports that your performance as a manager will be judged.

As part of your management role, it is likely that you will be expected to help in forward planning for the business. This will often involve the preparation of forward-looking financial statements and setting financial targets. If you do not understand what the financial statements really mean and the extent to which the financial information is reliable, you will find yourself at a distinct disadvantage to those who do. Along with other managers, you will also be expected to help decide how the limited resources available to the business should be allocated between competing options. This will require an ability to evaluate the costs and benefits of the different options available. Once again, an understanding of accounting and finance is important to carrying out this management task.

This is not to say that you cannot be an effective and successful human resources, production, marketing or IT manager unless you are also a qualified accountant. It does mean, however, that you need to become a bit 'streetwise' in accounting and finance if you are to succeed. This book should give you that street wisdom.

Accounting for business

We have seen that the needs of the various user groups will determine the kind of accounting information to be provided. The forms of business ownership and the ways in which a business may be organised and structured, however, will partly shape these needs. In the sections that follow, we consider the business environment within which accounting information is produced. This should help our understanding of points that crop up in later chapters.

What is the purpose of a business?

Peter Drucker, an eminent management thinker, has argued that 'the purpose of business is to create and keep a customer'. (See reference 2 at the end of the chapter.) Drucker defined the purpose of a business in this way in 1967, at a time when most businesses did not adopt this strong customer focus. His view, therefore, represented a radical challenge to the accepted view of what businesses do. Fifty years on, however, his approach has become part of the conventional wisdom. It is now widely recognised that, in order to succeed, businesses must focus on satisfying the needs of the customer.

Although the customer has always provided the main source of revenue for a business, this has often been taken for granted. In the past, too many businesses have assumed that the customer would readily accept whatever services or products were on offer. When competition was weak and customers were passive, businesses could operate under this assumption and still make a profit. However, the era of weak competition has passed. Nowadays, customers have much greater choice and are much more assertive concerning their needs. They now demand higher quality services and goods at cheaper prices. They also require that services and goods be delivered faster with an increasing emphasis on the product being tailored to their individual needs. If a business cannot meet these needs, a competitor often can. Thus the business mantra for the current era is '*the customer is king*'. Most businesses now recognise this fact and organise themselves accordingly.

Real World 1.2 describes how the internet and social media have given added weight to this mantra. It points out that dissatisfied customers now have a powerful medium for broadcasting their complaints.

Real World 1.2

The customer is king

The mantra that the "customer is king" has gained even greater significance among businesses in recent years because of the rise of the internet and social media. In the past, a dissatisfied customer might tell only a few friends about a bad buying experience. As a result, the damage to the reputation of the business concerned would normally be fairly limited. However, nowadays, through the magic of the internet, several hundred people, or more, can be very speedily informed of a bad buying experience.

Businesses are understandably concerned about the potential of the internet to damage reputations, but are their concerns justified? Do customer complaints, which wing their way through cyberspace, have any real effect on the businesses concerned? A Harris Poll

Real World 1.2 *continued*

survey of 2,000 adults in the UK and US suggests they do and so businesses should be concerned. It seems that social media can exert a big influence on customer buying decisions.

The Harris Poll survey, which was conducted online, found that around 20 per cent of those surveyed use social media when making buying decisions. For those in the 18-34 age range, the figure rises to almost 40 per cent. Furthermore, 60 percent of those surveyed indicated that they would avoid buying from a business that receives poor customer reviews for its products or services.

The moral of this tale appears to be that, in this internet age, businesses must work even harder to keep their customers happy if they are to survive and prosper.

Source: Based on information in Miesbach, A.(2015) *Yes, the Customer is Still King* 30 October www.icmi.com

What kinds of business ownership exist?

The particular form of business ownership has certain implications for financial accounting and so it is useful to be clear about the main forms of ownership that can arise. There are basically three arrangements for private-sector businesses:

- sole proprietorship;
- partnership; and
- limited company.

We shall now consider these.

Sole proprietorship

Sole proprietorship, as the name suggests, is where an individual is the sole owner of a business. This type of business is often quite small in terms of size (as measured, for example, by sales revenue generated or number of staff employed); however, the number of such businesses is very large indeed. Examples of sole-proprietor businesses can be found in most industrial sectors but particularly within the service sector. Hence, services such as electrical repairs, picture framing, photography, driving instruction, retail shops and hotels have a large proportion of sole-proprietor businesses.

The sole-proprietor business is very easy to set up. No formal procedures are required and operations can often commence immediately (unless special permission is required because of the nature of the trade or service, such as running licensed premises (a pub)). The owner can decide the way in which the business is to be conducted and has the flexibility to restructure or dissolve the business whenever it suits. The law does not recognise the sole-proprietor business as being separate from the owner, so the business will cease on the death of the owner.

Although the owner must produce accounting information to satisfy the taxation authorities, there is no legal requirement to produce accounting information relating to the business for other user groups. Some user groups, however, may demand accounting information about the business and may be in a position to enforce their demands (for example, a bank requiring accounting information on a regular basis as a condition of a loan). A sole proprietor has unlimited liability which means that no distinction is made between the proprietor's personal wealth and that of the business if there are business debts to be paid.

Partnership

A **partnership** exists where two or more individuals carry on a business together with the intention of making a profit. Partnerships have much in common with sole-proprietor businesses. They are usually quite small in size (although some, such as partnerships of accountants and solicitors, can be large). They are also easy to set up, as no formal procedures are required (and it is not even necessary to have a written agreement between the partners). The partners can agree whatever arrangements suit them concerning the financial and management aspects of the business. Similarly, the partnership can be restructured or dissolved by agreement between the partners.

Activity **1.11**

What are the main advantages and disadvantages that should be considered when deciding between a sole proprietorship and a partnership?

The main advantages of a partnership over a sole-proprietor business are:

● sharing the burden of ownership;
● the opportunity to specialise rather than cover the whole range of services (for example, in a solicitors' practice each partner may specialise in a different aspect of the law); and
● the ability to raise capital where this is beyond the capacity of a single individual.

The main disadvantages of a partnership compared with a sole proprietorship are:

● the risks of sharing ownership of a business with unsuitable individuals; and
● the limits placed on individual decision making that a partnership will impose.

Partnerships are not recognised in law as separate entities and so contracts with third parties must be entered into in the name of individual partners.

Limited company

A **limited company** can range in size from quite small to very large. The number of individuals who subscribe capital and become the owners may be unlimited, which provides the opportunity to create a very large-scale business. The liability of owners, however, is limited (hence 'limited' company), which means that those individuals subscribing capital to the company are liable only for debts incurred by the company up to the amount that they have invested or agreed to invest. This cap on the liability of the owners is designed to limit risk and to produce greater confidence to invest. Without such limits on owner liability, it is difficult to see how a modern capitalist economy could operate. In many cases, the owners of a limited company are not involved in the day-to-day running of the business and will, therefore, invest in a business only if there is a clear limit set on the level of investment risk.

Note that this 'limited liability' does not apply to sole proprietors and partners. These people have a legal obligation to meet all of their business debts, if necessary using, what they may have thought of as, private assets (for example, their private houses). This ability of the owners of limited companies to limit their liability can make limited companies a more attractive way of setting up a business, compared with sole proprietorships and partnerships.

The benefit of limited liability, however, imposes certain obligations on such limited companies. To start up a limited company, documents of incorporation must be prepared that set out, among other things, the objectives of the business. Furthermore, a framework of regulations exists that places obligations on limited companies concerning the way in which they conduct their affairs. Part of this regulatory framework requires annual financial reports to be made available to owners and lenders and, usually, an annual general meeting of the owners has to be held to approve the reports. In addition, a copy of the annual financial reports must be lodged with the Registrar of Companies for public inspection. In this way, the financial affairs of a limited company enter the public domain.

With the exception of small companies, there is also a requirement for the annual financial reports to be subject to an audit. This involves an independent firm of accountants examining the annual reports and underlying records to see whether the reports provide a true and fair view of the financial health of the company and whether they comply with the relevant accounting rules established by law and by accounting rule makers. Limited companies are considered in more detail later in Chapters 4 and 5.

All of the large household-name UK businesses (Marks and Spencer, Tesco, Shell, BSkyB, Rolls-Royce, BT, easyJet and so on) are limited companies.

Activity 1.12

What are the main advantages of forming a partnership business rather than a limited liability company?

The main advantages are:

- the ease of setting up the business;
- the degree of flexibility concerning the way in which the business is conducted;
- the degree of flexibility concerning restructuring and dissolution of the business; and
- freedom from administrative burdens imposed by law (for example, the annual general meeting and the need for an independent audit).

As we have just seen, a major disadvantage of a partnership compared with a limited company is that it is not normally possible to limit the liability of all of the partners. There is, however, a hybrid form of business ownership that is referred to as a limited liability partnership (LLP). This has many of the attributes of a normal partnership but is different in that the LLP, rather than the individual partners, is responsible for any debts incurred. Accountants and solicitors often use this type of partnership.

This book concentrates on the accounting aspects of limited liability companies because they are, by far, the most important in economic terms. The early chapters will introduce accounting concepts through examples that do not draw a distinction between the different types of business. Once we have dealt with the basic accounting principles, which are the same for all three types of business, we can then go on to see how they are applied to limited companies.

How are businesses organised?

Most businesses that involve more than a few owners and/or employees are set up as limited companies. Finance will come from the owners (shareholders) both in the form of a direct cash investment to buy shares (in the ownership of the business) and through the shareholders allowing past profits, which belong to them, to be reinvested in the business. Finance will also come from lenders (banks, for example), who earn interest on their loans. Further finance will be provided through suppliers of goods and services being prepared to supply on credit.

In larger limited companies, the owners (shareholders) tend not to be involved in the daily running of the business; instead they appoint a board of directors to manage the business on their behalf. The board is charged with three major tasks:

1 setting the overall direction and strategy for the business;
2 monitoring and controlling the activities of the business; and
3 communicating with shareholders and others connected with the business.

Each board has a chairman, elected by the directors, who is responsible for running the board in an efficient manner. In addition, each board has a chief executive officer (CEO) who is responsible for running the business on a day-to-day basis. Occasionally, the roles of chairman and CEO are combined, although it is usually considered to be a good idea to separate them in order to prevent a single individual having excessive power.

The board of directors represents the most senior level of management. Below this level, managers are employed, with each manager being given responsibility for a particular part of the business's operations.

Activity 1.13

Why are most larger businesses *not* managed as a single unit by just one manager?

Three common reasons are:

● The sheer volume of activity or number of staff employed makes it impossible for one person to manage them.
● Certain business operations may require specialised knowledge or expertise.
● Geographical remoteness of part of the business operations may make it more practical to manage each location as a separate part, or set of separate parts.

The operations of a business may be divided for management purposes in different ways. For smaller businesses offering a single product or service, separate departments are often created, with each department responsible for a particular function (such as marketing, human resources and finance). The managers of each department will then be accountable to the board of directors. In some cases, individual board members may also be departmental managers.

A typical departmental structure, organised along functional lines, is shown in Figure 1.6.

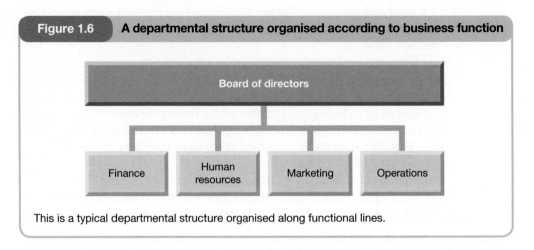

Figure 1.6   A departmental structure organised according to business function

This is a typical departmental structure organised along functional lines.

The structure set out in Figure 1.6 may be adapted according to the particular needs of the business. Where, for example, a business has few employees, the human resources function may not form a separate department but may form part of another department. Where business operations are specialised, separate departments may be formed to deal with each specialist area. Example 1.1 illustrates how Figure 1.6 may be modified to meet the needs of a particular business.

Example 1.1

Supercoach Ltd owns a small fleet of coaches that it hires out with drivers for private group travel. The business employs about 50 people. It might be departmentalised as follows:

- *marketing department,* dealing with advertising, dealing with enquiries from potential customers, maintaining good relationships with existing customers and entering into contracts with customers;
- *routing and human resources department,* responsible for the coach drivers' routes, schedules, staff duties and rotas, and problems that arise during a particular job or contract;
- *coach maintenance department,* looking after repair and maintenance of the coaches, buying spares, giving advice on the need to replace old or inefficient coaches;
- *finance department,* responsible for managing the cash flows, costing business activities, pricing new proposals, paying wages and salaries, billing and collecting amounts due from customers, processing and paying invoices from suppliers.

For large businesses that have a diverse geographical spread and/or a wide product range, the simple departmental structure set out in Figure 1.6 will usually have to be adapted. Separate divisions are often created for each geographical area and/or major product group. Each division will be managed separately and will usually enjoy a degree of autonomy. Within each division, however, departments will often be created and organised along functional lines. Some functions providing support across the various divisions, such as human resources, may be undertaken at head office to avoid duplication. The managers of each division will be accountable to the board of directors. In some cases, individual board members may also be divisional managers.

A typical divisional organisational structure is set out in Figure 1.7. Here the main basis of the structure is geographical. North division deals with production and sales in the north and so on.

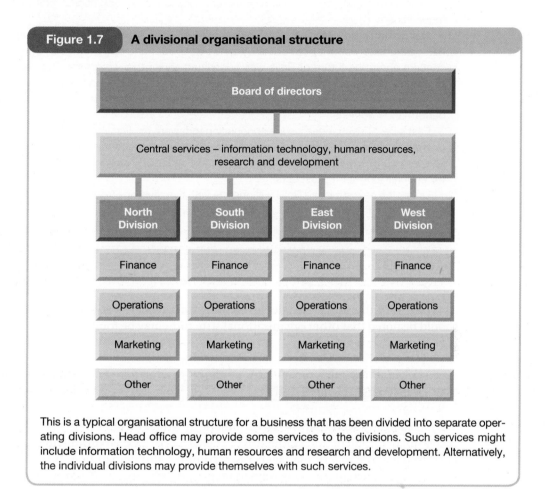

| Figure 1.7 | A divisional organisational structure |

This is a typical organisational structure for a business that has been divided into separate operating divisions. Head office may provide some services to the divisions. Such services might include information technology, human resources and research and development. Alternatively, the individual divisions may provide themselves with such services.

Once a particular divisional structure has been established, it need not be permanent. Successful businesses constantly strive to improve their operational efficiency. This could well result in revising their divisional structure. **Real World 1.3** comprises extracts from an article that describes how one well-known business has reorganised in order to simplify operations and to reduce costs.

Real World 1.3

Engineering change

The chief executive of Rolls-Royce has shaken up its senior management team and scrapped two divisions as part of his attempt to turnaround the struggling engineer. Warren East . . . will scrap the aerospace and land & sea divisions that split Rolls into two parts. . . .

The move means that Rolls will operate with five smaller businesses all reporting directly to East. The Rolls chief executive plans to bring in a chief operating officer to assist him in running the company.

→

Real World 1.3 *continued*

Rolls said the revamp will "simplify the organisation, drive operational excellence and reduce cost".

The Rolls boss is overhauling the company after it issued five profit warnings in less than two years. East wants to cut costs by between £150m and £200m a year. The level of concern about the future of Rolls was underlined earlier this week when it emerged the government has drawn up contingency plans to nationalise its nuclear submarine business or force it to merge with defence manufacturer BAE Systems in the event that the company's performance worsens.

East said: "The changes we are announcing today are the first important steps in driving operational excellence and returning Rolls-Royce to its long-term trend of profitable growth. This is a company with world-class engineering capability, strong market positions and exceptional long-term prospects."

Under the new structure Rolls will operate with five divisions from 1 January 2016 - civil aerospace, defence aerospace, marine, nuclear, and power systems.

Source: Extracts from Ruddick G. (2016) *Rolls-Royce to scrap two divisions amid restructuring*, www.theguardian.com, 16 December.

While both divisional and departmental structures are very popular in practice, it should be noted that other organisational structures may be found.

How are businesses managed?

We have already seen that the environment in which businesses operate has become increasingly turbulent and competitive. The effect of these environmental changes has been to make the role of managers more complex and demanding. It has meant that managers have had to find new ways to manage their business. This has increasingly led to the introduction of **strategic management.**

Strategic management is concerned with setting the long-term direction of the business. It involves setting long-term goals and then ensuring that they are implemented effectively. To enable the business to develop a competitive edge, strategic management focuses on doing things differently rather than simply doing things better. It should provide a business with a clear sense of purpose, along with a series of steps to achieve that purpose. The steps taken should link the internal resources of the business to the external environment of competitors, suppliers, customers and so on. This should be done in such a way that any business strengths, such as having a skilled workforce, are exploited and any weaknesses, such as being short of investment finance, are not exposed. To achieve this requires the development of strategies and plans that take account of the business's strengths and weaknesses, as well as the opportunities offered and threats posed by the external environment. Access to a new, expanding market is an example of an opportunity; the decision of a major competitor to reduce prices is an example of a threat. This topic will be considered in more depth in Chapter 12 when we consider business planning and budgeting.

Real World 1.4 provides an indication of the extent to which strategic planning is carried out in practice.

Real World 1.4

Strategic planning high on the list

A recent survey investigated the use of various management tools throughout the world. It found that strategic planning is used by more than 40 per cent of those businesses that took part. This made it the fourth most popular management tool. The survey, which is conducted annually, has placed strategic planning in first position for three of the last five years and in second position for one of those years. Figure 1.8 indicates the level of usage and satisfaction concerning this technique.

Figure 1.8   Usage and effectiveness of strategic planning

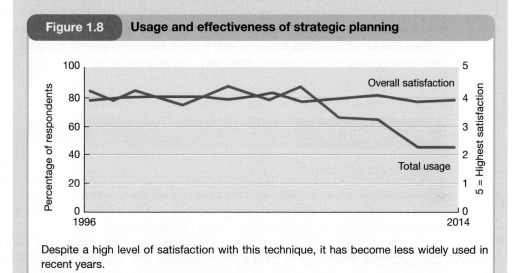

Despite a high level of satisfaction with this technique, it has become less widely used in recent years.

The results were based on a survey of 1,067 senior executives throughout the world.

Source: Rigby, D. and Bilodeau, B. (2015) *Management Tools and Trends 2015,* Bain and Company.

The quest for wealth creation

A business is normally created to enhance the wealth of its owners. Throughout this book we shall assume that this is its main objective. This may come as a surprise, as there are other objectives that a business may pursue that are related to the needs of others with a stake in the business. A business may, for example, seek to provide good working conditions for its employees, or it may seek to conserve the environment for the local community. While a business may pursue these objectives, it is normally set up primarily with a view to increasing the wealth of its owners. In practice, the behaviour of businesses over time appears to be consistent with this objective.

Within a market economy there are strong competitive forces at work that ensure that failure to enhance owners' wealth will not be tolerated for long. Competition for the funds provided by the owners and competition for managers' jobs will normally mean that the owners' interests will prevail. If the managers do not provide the expected increase in ownership wealth, the owners have the power to replace the existing management team with a new team that is more responsive to owners' needs.

Meeting the needs of other stakeholders

These points do not mean that the needs of other groups with a stake in the business, such as employees, customers, suppliers and the community, are unimportant. In fact, the opposite is true if the business wishes to survive and prosper over the longer term. For example, a business with disaffected customers may well find that they turn to another supplier, resulting in a loss of shareholder wealth. The point that modern businesses must be responsive to customer needs was discussed earlier.

Other stakeholders that contribute towards the wealth creation process must also be considered. A dissatisfied workforce can result in low productivity and strikes while dissatisfied suppliers can withhold vital supplies or give lower priority to orders received. A discontented local community can withdraw access to community resources.

Real World 1.5 describes how one well-known business came to recognise that future success depended on the support of key stakeholder groups.

Real World 1.5

The price of clothes

Nike is king. From its dominance in the athletic world, its popularity amongst consumers and being one of the most globally recognised brands, Nike is riding a wave of success that shows no signs of slowing down. But it wasn't always like that.

In the late '90s, Nike was embroiled in controversy over its reported use of sweatshops, an issue that threatened to derail Nike's popularity and undoubtedly hurt its company image. In a recent report by *Business Insider,* we're able to read just some of the things Nike has done to improve and change the way people perceive the brand. "The sweatshop perception was one of the biggest challenges Nike has faced," University of Southern California professor Jeetendr Sehdev said. "It seemed impossible they could ever shake the perception."

Nike used sweatshops. There's no denying that. BI's report mentions the 14 cents an hour earned by Indonesian workers, while also referencing a *New York Times* article from 1997 that documented abuse of workers by a Vietnamese sub-contractor. It's a part of Nike's history that the brand isn't proud of. But since then, it has doing its part in the upgrade its overseas conditions and to help make sure that the abuses of the past never occur again.

In 1998, Nike's Phil Knight helped lead the change in the company. Knight vowed Nike would be more upfront with the issues, promising to be more transparent in overseas dealings and becoming more committed to addressing and improving the issues and abuses it was confronted with and accused of. "The Nike product has become synonymous with slave wages, forced overtime, and arbitrary abuse," Knight said. "I truly believe the American consumer doesn't want to buy products made under abusive conditions."

Since then, Nike has done just that having raised minimum wage rates, improving factory conditions, and ensuring the factories have clean air. Also, Nike also publishes public reports documenting its general responsibility and factory conditions following through on the promise of being more transparent.

Source: Allarey, R (2015) This Is How Nike Managed to Clean Up Its Sweatshop Reputation, www.complex.com, 8 June.

It is clear from what we have seen that generating wealth for the owners is not the same as seeking to maximise the current year's profit. Wealth creation is concerned with the longer term. It relates not only to this year's profit but to that of future years as well. In the short term, corners can be cut and risks taken that improve current profit at the expense of future profit. **Real World 1.6** provides some examples of how emphasis on short-term profit can be very damaging.

Real World 1.6

Short-term gains, long-term problems

For many years, under the guise of defending capitalism, we have been allowing ourselves to degrade it. We have been poisoning the well from which we have drawn wealth. We have misunderstood the importance of values to capitalism. We have surrendered to the idea that success is pursued by making as much money as the law allowed without regard to how it was made.

Thirty years ago, retailers would be quite content to source the shoes they wanted to sell as cheaply as possible. The working conditions of those who produced them was not their concern. Then headlines and protests developed. Society started to hold them responsible for previously invisible working conditions. Companies like Nike went through a transformation. They realised they were polluting their brand. Global sourcing became visible. It was no longer viable to define success simply in terms of buying at the lowest price and selling at the highest.

Financial services and investment are today where footwear was thirty years ago. Public anger at the crisis will make visible what was previously hidden. Take the building up of huge portfolios of loans to poor people on US trailer parks. These loans were authorised without proper scrutiny of the circumstances of the borrowers. Somebody else then deemed them fit to be securitised and so on through credit default swaps and the rest without anyone seeing the transaction in terms of its ultimate human origin.

Each of the decision makers thought it okay to act like the thoughtless footwear buyer of the 1970s. The price was attractive. There was money to make on the deal. Was it responsible? Irrelevant. It was legal, and others were making money that way. And the consequences for the banking system if everybody did it? Not our problem.

The consumer has had a profound shock. Surely we could have expected the clever and wise people who invested our money to be better at risk management than they have shown themselves to be in the present crisis? How could they have been so gullible in not challenging the bankers whose lending proved so flaky? How could they have believed that the levels of bonuses that were, at least in part, coming out of their savings could have been justified in 'incentivising' a better performance? How could they have believed that a 'better' performance would be one that is achieved for one bank without regard to its effect on the whole banking system? Where was the stewardship from those exercising investment on their behalf?

The answer has been that very few of them do exercise that stewardship. Most have stood back and said it doesn't really pay them to do so. The failure of stewardship comes from the same mindset that created the irresponsible lending in the first place. We are back to the mindset that has allowed us to poison the well: never mind the health of the system as a whole, I'm making money out of it at the moment. Responsibility means awareness for the system consequences of our actions. It is not a luxury. It is the cornerstone of prudence.

FT   *Source*: Extracts from Goyder, M. (2009) How we've poisoned the well of wealth, *Financial Times*, 15 February. © The Financial Times Limited 2012. All Rights Reserved.

Balancing risk and return

All decision making involves the future. Financial decision making is no exception. The only thing certain about the future, however, is that we cannot be sure what will happen. Things may not turn out as planned and this risk should be carefully considered when making financial decisions.

As in other aspects of life, risk and return tend to be related. Evidence shows that returns relate to risk in something like the way shown in Figure 1.9.

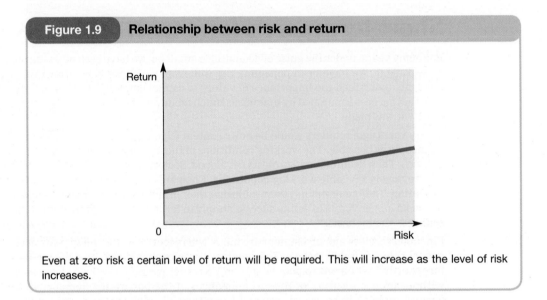

Figure 1.9 **Relationship between risk and return**

Even at zero risk a certain level of return will be required. This will increase as the level of risk increases.

Activity 1.14

Look at Figure 1.9 and state, in broad terms, where an investment in

(a) a UK government savings account, and
(b) a lottery ticket

should be placed on the risk–return line.

A UK government savings account is normally a very safe investment. Even if the government is in financial difficulties, it may well be able to print more money to repay investors. Returns from this form of investment, however, are normally very low. Investing in a lottery ticket runs a very high risk of losing the whole amount invested. This is because the probability of winning is normally very low. However, a winning ticket can produce enormous returns.

Thus, the government savings account should be placed towards the far left of the risk–return line and the lottery ticket towards the far right.

This relationship between risk and return has important implications for setting financial objectives for a business. The owners will require a minimum return to induce them to invest at all, but will require an additional return to compensate for taking risks; the higher the risk, the higher the required return. Managers must be aware of this and must strike the appropriate balance between risk and return when setting objectives and pursuing particular courses of action.

The recent turmoil in the banking sector has shown, however, that the right balance is not always struck. Some banks have taken excessive risks in pursuit of higher returns and, as a consequence, have incurred massive losses. They are now being kept afloat with taxpayers' money. **Real World 1.7** discusses the collapse of one leading bank, in which the UK government took a majority stake, and argues that the risk appetite of banks must now change.

Real World 1.7

Banking on change

The taxpayer has become the majority shareholder in the Royal Bank of Scotland (RBS). This change in ownership, resulting from the huge losses sustained by the bank, will shape the future decisions made by its managers. This does not simply mean that it will affect the amount that the bank lends to homeowners and businesses. Rather it is about the amount of risk that it will be prepared to take in pursuit of higher returns.

In the past, those managing banks such as RBS saw themselves as producers of financial products that enabled banks to grow faster than the economy as a whole. They did not want to be seen as simply part of the infrastructure of the economy. It was too dull. It was far more exciting to be seen as creators of financial products that created huge profits and, at the same time, benefited us all through unlimited credit at low rates of interest. These financial products, with exotic names such as 'collateralised debt obligations' and 'credit default swaps', ultimately led to huge losses that taxpayers had to absorb in order to prevent the banks from collapse.

Now that many banks throughout the world are in taxpayers' hands, they are destined to lead a much quieter life. They will have to focus more on the basics such as taking deposits, transferring funds and making simple loans to customers. Is that such a bad thing?

The history of banking has reflected a tension between carrying out their core functions and the quest for high returns through high risk strategies. It seems, however, that for some time to come they will have to concentrate on the former and will be unable to speculate with depositors' cash.

Source: Based on information in Robert Peston, We own Royal Bank, *BBC News*, www.bbc.co.uk, 28 November 2008.

Reasons to be ethical

The way in which individual businesses operate in terms of the honesty, fairness and transparency with which they treat their stakeholders (customers, employees, suppliers, the community, the shareholders and so on) has become a key issue. There have been many examples of businesses, some of them very well known, acting in ways that most people would regard as unethical and unacceptable. Examples of such actions include:

- paying bribes to encourage employees of other businesses to reveal information about the employee's business that could be useful;
- oppressive treatment of suppliers, for example making suppliers wait excessive periods before payment; and

- manipulating the financial statements to mislead users of them, for example to overstate profit so that senior managers become eligible for performance bonuses (known as 'creative accounting').

Despite the many examples of unethical acts that have attracted publicity over recent years, it would be very unfair to conclude that most businesses are involved in unethical activities. Nevertheless, revelations of unethical practice can be damaging to the entire business community. Lying, stealing and fraudulent behaviour can lead to a loss of confidence in business and the imposition of tighter regulatory burdens. In response to this threat, businesses often seek to demonstrate their commitment to acting in an honest and ethical way. One way in which this can be done is to produce, and adhere to, a code of ethics concerning business behaviour.

Accountants are likely to find themselves at the forefront with issues relating to business ethics. In the three examples of unethical business activity listed above, an accountant would probably have to be involved either in helping to commit the unethical act or in covering it up. Accountants are, therefore, particularly vulnerable to being put under pressure to engage in unethical acts. Some businesses recognise this risk and produce an ethical code for their accounting staff. **Real World 1.8** provides an example of one such code.

Real World 1.8

The only way is ethics

BT plc, the telecommunications business, has a code of ethics for its senior finance and accounting staff which states that they must:

- Act with honesty and integrity, including ethically handling actual or apparent conflicts of interest between their personal relationships or financial or commercial interests and their responsibilities to BT;
- Promote full, fair, accurate, timely and understandable disclosure in all reports and documents that BT files with, or submits to, the US Securities and Exchange Commission or otherwise makes public;
- Comply with all laws, rules and regulations applicable to BT and to its relationship with its shareholders;
- Report known or suspected violations of this code of ethics promptly to the chairman of the Nominating & Governance Committee; and
- Ensure that their actions comply not only with the letter but the spirit of this code of ethics and foster a culture in which BT operates in compliance with the law and BT's policies.

Source: BT plc, *Our business practice and code of ethics*, www.BT.com, accessed 8 November 2016.

Not-for-profit organisations

Although the focus of this book is accounting as it relates to private-sector businesses, there are many organisations that do not exist mainly for the pursuit of profit.

Activity (1.15)

Can you think of at least four types of organisation that are not primarily concerned with making profits?

We thought of the following:

● charities
● clubs and associations
● universities
● local government authorities
● national government departments
● churches
● trade unions.

All of these organisations need to produce accounting information for decision-making purposes. Once again, various user groups need this information to help them to make decisions. These user groups are often the same as, or similar to, those identified for private-sector businesses. They may have a stake in the future viability of the organisation and may use accounting information to check that the wealth of the organisation is being properly controlled and used in a way that is consistent with its objectives.

Real World 1.9 provides an example of the importance of accounting to relief agencies, which are, of course, not-for-profit organisations.

Real World 1.9

Accounting for disasters

In the aftermath of the Asian tsunami more than £400 million was raised from charitable donations. It was important that this huge amount of money for aid and reconstruction was used as efficiently and effectively as possible. That did not just mean medical staff and engineers. It also meant accountants.

The charity that exerts financial control over aid donations is Mango: Management Accounting for Non-Governmental Organisations (NGOs). It provides accountants in the field and it provides the back-up, such as financial training and all the other services that should result in really robust financial management in a disaster area.

The world of aid has changed completely as a result of the tsunami. According to Mango's director, Alex Jacobs, 'Accounting is just as important as blankets. Agencies have been aware of this for years. But when you move on to a bigger scale there is more pressure to show the donations are being used appropriately.'

More recently, the earthquake in Haiti led to a call from Mango for French-speaking accountants to help support the relief programme and to help in the longer-term rebuilding of Haiti.

Sources: Adapted from Bruce, R. (2005) Tsunami: finding the right figures for disaster relief, ft. com, 7 March; Bruce, R. (2006) The work of Mango: coping with generous donations, ft.com, 27 February; Grant, P. (2010) Accountants needed in Haiti, *Accountancy Age,* 5 February. © The Financial Times Limited 2012. All Rights Reserved.

Summary

The main points of this chapter may be summarised as follows:

What are accounting and finance?

- Accounting provides financial information to help various user groups make better judgements and decisions.
- Finance also helps users to make better decisions and is concerned with the financing and investing activities of the business.

Accounting and user needs

- For accounting to be useful, it must be clear *for whom* and *for what purpose* the information will be used.
- Owners, managers and lenders are important user groups but there are several others.
- Conflicts of interest between users may arise over the ways in which business wealth is generated or distributed.
- The evidence suggests that accounting is both used and useful for decision-making purposes.

Providing a service

- Accounting can be viewed as a form of service as it involves providing financial information to various users.
- To provide a useful service, accounting information must possess certain qualities, or characteristics.
- The fundamental qualities are relevance and faithful representation. Other qualities that enhance the usefulness of accounting information are comparability, verifiability, timeliness and understandability.
- Providing a service to users can be costly and financial information should be produced only if the cost of providing the information is less than the benefits gained.

Accounting information

- Accounting is part of the total information system within a business. It shares the features that are common to all information systems within a business, which are the identification, recording, analysis and reporting of information.

Management accounting and financial accounting

- Accounting has two main strands – management accounting and financial accounting.
- Management accounting seeks to meet the needs of the business's managers, and financial accounting seeks to meet the needs of providers of finance but will also be of use to other user groups.
- These two strands differ in terms of the types of reports produced, the level of reporting detail, the time orientation, the degree of regulation and the range and quality of information provided.

The changing face of accounting

- Changes in the economic environment have led to changes in the nature and scope of accounting.

- Financial accounting has improved its framework of rules and there has been greater international harmonisation of accounting rules.
- Management accounting has become more outward looking, and new methods for managing costs have emerged.

Why study accounting?

- Everyone connected with business should be a little 'streetwise' about accounting and finance. Financial information and decisions exert an enormous influence over the ways in which a business operates.

What is the purpose of a business?

- The purpose of a business is to create and keep customers.

What kinds of business ownership exist?

There are three main forms of business unit:

- sole proprietorship – easy to set up and flexible to operate but the owner has unlimited liability;
- partnership – easy to set up and spreads the burdens of ownership, but partners usually have unlimited liability and there are ownership risks if the partners are unsuitable; and
- limited company – limited liability for owners but obligations imposed on the way a company conducts its affairs.

How are businesses organised and managed?

- Most businesses of any size are set up as limited companies.
- A board of directors is appointed by owners (shareholders) to oversee the running of the business.
- Businesses are often divided into departments and organised along functional lines; however, larger businesses may be divisionalised along geographical and/or product lines.
- The move to strategic management has been caused by the changing and more competitive nature of business.

The quest for wealth creation

- The key financial objective of a business is to enhance the wealth of the owners.
- To achieve this objective, the needs of other groups connected with the business, such as employees, suppliers and the local community, cannot be ignored.
- When setting financial objectives, the right balance must be struck between risk and return.

Ethical behaviour

- Accounting staff may be put under pressure to commit unethical acts.
- Many businesses produce a code of ethical conduct to help protect accounting staff from this risk.

Not-for-profit organisations

- These produce accounting information for decision-making purposes.
- They have user groups that are similar to, or the same as, those of private-sector businesses.

Key terms

For definitions of these terms, see Appendix B.

accounting *p. 2*
finance *p. 2*
shares *p. 6*
relevance *p. 7*
faithful representation *p. 7*
materiality *p. 7*
comparability *p. 8*
verifiability *p. 8*
timeliness *p. 8*

understandability *p. 8*
accounting information
    system *p. 12*
management accounting *p. 14*
financial accounting *p. 14*
sole proprietorship *p. 20*
partnership *p. 21*
limited company *p. 21*
strategic management *p. 26*

References

1 Dugdale, D., Jones, C. and Green, S. (2006) *Contemporary Management Accounting Practices in UK Manufacturing,* CIMA/Elsevier.

2 Drucker, P. (1967) *The Effective Executive,* Heinemann.

Further reading

If you would like to explore the topics covered in this chapter in more depth, we recommend the following:

Drury, C. (2015) *Management and Cost Accounting,* 9th edn, Cengage Learning, Chapter 1.

Elliot, B. and Elliot, J. (2015) *Financial Accounting and Reporting,* 17th edn, Pearson, Chapter 11.

McLaney, E. (2018) *Business Finance: Theory and Practice,* 11th edn, Pearson, Chapters 1 and 2.

Scott, W. (2014) *Financial Accounting Theory,* 7th edn, Pearson, Chapters 1–3.

Review questions

Solutions to these questions can be found at the back of the book on pp. 786–787.

1.1 What, in economic principle, should determine what accounting information is produced? Should economics be the only issue here? (Consider who the users of accounting information are.)

1.2 Identify the main users of accounting information for a university. For what purposes would different user groups need information? Is there a major difference in the ways in which accounting information for a university would be used compared with that of a private-sector business?

1.3 Management accounting has been described as 'the eyes and ears of management'. What do you think this expression means?

1.4 Financial accounting statements tend to reflect past events. In view of this, how can they be of any assistance to a user in making a decision when decisions, by their very nature, can only be made about future actions?

PART 1

Financial accounting

We saw in Chapter 1 that accounting has two distinct strands: financial accounting and management accounting. Part 1 of this book deals with the former. In this part, we introduce the three major financial statements:

● the statement of financial position;
● the income statement; and
● the statement of cash flows.

In Chapter 2, we provide an overview of these three statements and then go on to examine the first of them, the statement of financial position, in some detail. This examination will include an explanation of the main accounting conventions used when preparing the statement. These accounting 'conventions' are generally accepted rules that have evolved to help deal with practical problems experienced by preparers and users of the statement.

In Chapter 3, we examine the second of the major financial statements, the income statement. Here we discuss important issues such as how profit is measured and the point at which it should be recognised. Once again, we consider the main accounting conventions used when preparing this financial statement.

In the UK, the limited company is the most important form of business unit and in Chapters 4 and 5 we examine its main features. From an accounting viewpoint, there is no essential difference between a limited company and any other type of business unit. There are, however, points of detail that must be understood. Chapter 4 examines the nature of limited companies, the way in which they are financed and the accounting issues that relate specifically to this form of business. Chapter 5 considers the duty of directors of a limited company to account to its owners and to others, and the regulatory framework imposed on limited companies. Some additional reports prepared by large limited companies are also considered.

Chapter 6 deals with the last of the three financial statements, the statement of cash flows. This sets out the inflows and outflows of cash during a reporting period. In this chapter, we shall see that making profit is not enough. A business must also be able to generate sufficient cash to pay its obligations. The statement of cash flows helps users to assess its ability to do this.

When taken together, the three financial statements provide useful information about a business's performance and position for a particular period. We can, however, gain even more helpful insights about the business by using financial ratios and other techniques. By combining two figures from the financial statements in the form of a ratio, and then comparing the result with a similar ratio for, say, another business, we may have a useful basis for assessing financial health. In Chapter 7, we consider various financial ratios and other techniques that can be used for this purpose.

CHAPTER 2

Measuring and reporting financial position

Introduction

We begin this chapter by taking an overview of three major financial statements that form the core of financial accounting. We examine the relationship between these financial statements and consider how each one contributes towards an assessment of the overall financial position and performance of a business.

Following this overview, we shall undertake a more detailed examination of one of these financial statements: the statement of financial position. We identify its key elements and consider the interrelationships between these elements. We also consider the main accounting conventions, or rules, that are followed when preparing the statement of financial position.

We saw in Chapter 1 that accounting information should be useful to those seeking to make decisions about a business. We end the chapter by considering the value of the statement of financial position for decision-making purposes.

Learning outcomes

When you have completed this chapter, you should be able to:

- explain the nature and purpose of the three major financial statements;

- prepare a simple statement of financial position and interpret the information that it contains;

- discuss the accounting conventions underpinning the statement of financial position; and

- discuss the uses and limitations of the statement of financial position for decision-making purposes.

The major financial statements – an overview

The major financial accounting statements aim to provide a picture of the financial position and performance of a business. To achieve this, a business's accounting function will normally produce three financial statements on a regular, recurring basis. These three statements are concerned with answering the following questions relating to a particular period:

● What cash movements took place?
● How much wealth was generated?
● What is the accumulated wealth of the business at the end of the period and what form does it take?

To address each of these questions, there is a separate financial statement. The financial statements are:

● the **statement of cash flows;**
● the **income statement** (also known as the profit and loss account); and
● the **statement of financial position** (also known as the balance sheet).

Together they provide an overall picture of the financial health of the business.

Perhaps the best way to introduce these financial statements is to look at Example 2.1 which considers a very simple business. From this we shall be able to see the sort of information that each of the statements can usefully provide. It is, however, worth pointing out that, while a simple business is our starting point, the principles for preparing the financial statements apply equally to the largest and most complex businesses. This means that we shall frequently encounter these principles again in later chapters.

Example 2.1

Paul was unemployed and unable to find a job. He therefore decided to embark on a business venture. With Christmas approaching, he decided to buy gift wrapping paper from a local supplier and to sell it on the corner of his local high street. He felt that the price of wrapping paper in the high street shops was unreasonably high. This provided him with a useful business opportunity.

He began the venture with £40 of his own money, in cash. On Monday, Paul's first day of trading, he bought wrapping paper for £40 and sold three-quarters of it for £45 cash.

● **What cash movements took place in Paul's business during Monday?**
For Monday, a *statement of cash flows* showing the cash movements (that is, cash in and cash out) for the day can be prepared as follows:

Statement of cash flows for Monday

	£
Cash introduced (by Paul)	40
Cash from sales of wrapping paper	45
Cash paid to buy wrapping paper	(40)
Closing balance of cash	45

The statement shows that Paul placed £40 cash into the business. The business received £45 cash from customers, but paid £40 cash to buy the wrapping paper. This left £45 of cash by Monday evening. Note that we are taking the standard approach found in the financial statements of showing figures to be deducted (in this case the £40 paid out) in brackets. We shall take this approach consistently throughout the chapters dealing with financial statements.

● **How much wealth (that is, profit) was generated by the business during Monday?**

An *income statement* can be prepared to show the wealth generated (profit) on Monday. The wealth generated arises from trading and will be the difference between the value of the sales made and the cost of the goods (that is, wrapping paper) sold.

Income statement for Monday

	£
Sales revenue	45
Cost of goods sold ($^3/_4$ of £40)	(30)
Profit	15

Note that it is only the cost of the wrapping paper *sold* that is matched against (and deducted from) the sales revenue in order to find the profit, not the whole of the cost of wrapping paper acquired. Any unsold inventories (also known as *stock)* will be charged against the future sales revenue that it generates. In this case the cost of the unsold inventories is $^1/_4$ of £40 = £10.

● **What is the accumulated wealth on Monday evening and what form does it take?**

To establish the accumulated wealth at the end of Monday's trading, we can draw up a *statement of financial position* for Paul's business. This statement will also list the forms of wealth held at the end of that day.

Statement of financial position as at Monday evening

	£
Cash (closing balance)	45
Inventories of goods for resale $^1/_4$ of £40)	10
Total assets	55
Equity	55

Note the terms 'assets' and 'equity' that appear in this statement. 'Assets' are business resources (things of value to the business) and include cash and inventories. 'Equity' is the word used in accounting to describe the investment, or stake, of the owner(s) – in this case Paul – in the business. Both of these terms will be discussed in some detail a little later in this chapter. Note that the equity on Monday evening was £55. This represented the £40 that Paul put in to start the business, plus Monday's profit (£15) – profits belong to the owner(s).

Let us now continue by looking at what happens on the following day.

On Tuesday, Paul bought more wrapping paper for £20 cash. He managed to sell all of the new inventories and all of the earlier inventories, for a total of £48.

→

The statement of cash flows for Tuesday will be as follows:

Statement of cash flows for Tuesday

	£
Opening balance (from Monday evening)	45
Cash from sales of wrapping paper	48
Cash paid to buy wrapping paper	(20)
Closing balance	73

The income statement for Tuesday will be as follows:

Income statement for Tuesday

	£
Sales revenue	48
Cost of goods sold (£20 + £10)	(30)
Profit	18

The statement of financial position as at Tuesday evening will be:

Statement of financial position as at Tuesday evening

	£
Cash (closing balance)	73
Inventories	–
Total assets	73
Equity	73

We can see that the total business wealth has increased to £73 by Tuesday evening. This represents an increase of £18 (that is, £73 − £55) over Monday's figure – which, of course, is the amount of profit made during Tuesday, as shown in the income statement.

We can see from the financial statements in Example 2.1 that each statement provides part of a picture of the financial performance and position of the business. We begin by showing the cash movements. Cash is a vital resource that is necessary for any business to function effectively. It is required to meet debts that become due and to acquire other resources (such as inventories). Cash has been described as the 'lifeblood' of a business.

Reporting cash movements alone, however, is not enough to portray the financial health of the business. To find out how much profit was generated, we need an income statement. It is important to recognise that cash and profits rarely move in unison. During Monday, for example, the cash balance increased by £5, but the profit generated, as shown in the income statement, was £15. The cash balance did not increase in line with profit because part of the wealth (£10) was held in the form of inventories.

The statement of financial position that was drawn up as at the end of Monday's trading provides an insight into the total wealth of the business. This wealth can be held in various forms. For Paul's business, wealth is held in the form of cash and inventories. This means that, when drawing up the statement of financial position, both forms will be listed. For a large business, many other forms of wealth may be held, such as property, equipment, motor vehicles and so on.

Activity 2.1

On Wednesday, Paul bought more wrapping paper for £46 cash. However, it was raining hard for much of the day and sales were slow. After Paul had sold half of his total inventories for £32, he decided to stop trading until Thursday morning.

Have a go at drawing up the three financial statements for Paul's business for Wednesday.

Statement of cash flows for Wednesday

	£
Opening balance (from the Tuesday evening)	73
Cash from sales of wrapping paper	32
Cash paid to buy wrapping paper	(46)
Closing balance	59

Income statement for Wednesday

	£
Sales revenue	32
Cost of goods sold ($\frac{1}{2}$ of £46)	(23)
Profit	9

Statement of financial position as at Wednesday evening

	£
Cash (closing balance)	59
Inventories (1/2 of £46)	23
Total assets	82
Equity	82

Note that the total business wealth has increased by £9 (that is, the amount of Wednesday's profit) even though the cash balance has declined. This is because the business is holding more of its wealth in the form of inventories rather than cash, compared with the position on Tuesday evening.

By Wednesday evening, the equity stood at £82. This arose from Paul's initial investment of £40, plus his profits for Monday (£15), Tuesday (£18) and Wednesday (£9). This represents Paul's total investment in his business at that time. The equity of most businesses will similarly arise from injections of funds by the owner plus any accumulated profits.

We can see that the income statement and statement of cash flows are both concerned with measuring flows (of wealth and cash respectively) during a particular period. The statement of financial position, however, is concerned with the financial position at a particular moment in time. Figure 2.1 illustrates this point.

The three financial statements discussed are often referred to as the **final accounts** of the business.

For external users of the financial statements (that is, virtually all users except the managers of the business concerned), these statements are normally backward-looking because they are based on information concerning past events and transactions. This can be useful in providing feedback on past performance and in identifying trends that provide clues to future performance. However, the statements can also be prepared using projected data

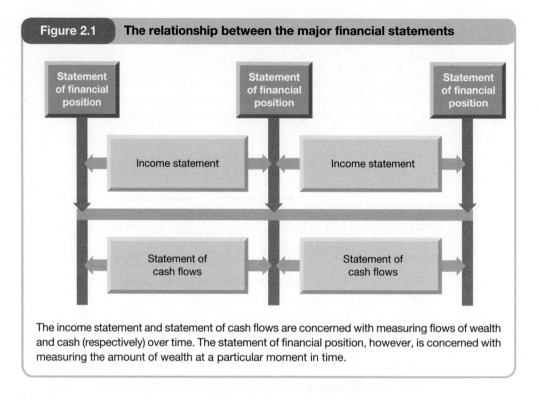

Figure 2.1 **The relationship between the major financial statements**

The income statement and statement of cash flows are concerned with measuring flows of wealth and cash (respectively) over time. The statement of financial position, however, is concerned with measuring the amount of wealth at a particular moment in time.

to help assess likely future profits, cash flows and so on. Normally, this is done only for management decision-making purposes.

Now that we have an overview of the financial statements, we shall consider each one in detail. The remainder of this chapter is devoted to the statement of financial position.

The statement of financial position

We saw a little earlier that this statement shows the forms in which the wealth of a business is held and how much wealth is held in each form. It also shows the sources of funding for that wealth. We can, however, be more specific about the nature of this statement by saying that it sets out the **assets** of a business, on the one hand, and the **claims** against the business, on the other. Before looking at the statement of financial position in more detail, we need to be clear about what these terms mean.

Assets

As asset is essentially a resource held by a business. To qualify as an asset for inclusion in the statement of financial position, however, the particular resource must possess the following three characteristics:

● *It must be an economic resource.* This type of resource confers a right, of the business, of the potential to receive economic benefits. This right is usually established through legal ownership or through a contractual agreement (for example, leasing equipment). The right must, however, entitle the business to receive economic benefits that are not equally available to others. To illustrate this point, let us consider the right to use public goods such as the road system, GPS satellites or official statistics. Although these resources may provide economic benefits to the business, others can receive the same benefits at no great cost. The right to benefit from these public goods is not, therefore, an economic resource of the business that is recognised in a conventionally drawn up statement of financial position.

Potential benefits flowing from an economic resource may take various forms depending on how the resource is used.

Activity 2.2

What forms might these benefits take? Try to think of at least two forms.

Benefits flowing from an economic resource may take the following forms:

- cash generated by using it to produce goods or services;
- cash received from the proceeds of its sale;
- the value received when exchanged for another economic resource or when used to satisfy claims against the business;
- cash generated from renting or leasing it; and/or
- the value received when used as security for a loan.

You may have thought of others.

Note that an economic resource need only have the potential to generate benefits. These benefits need not be certain or even probable. Where, however, there is a very low probability that economic benefits will flow, the information is unlikely to be relevant to users and so the resource may not be included as an asset in the statement of financial position.

- *The economic resource must be under the control of the business.* This means that the business has the capacity to decide how it should be used and is entitled to any benefits flowing from its use. Again, control is often established through legal ownership or through contractual agreement. It can, however, be established through other means, such as through the ability to prevent others gaining access to business know-how. The transaction, or other event, giving rise to control must have already occurred. As a result, the business will already possess the ability to control the resource.
- *The economic resource must be capable of measurement in monetary terms.* Unless the resource can be measured in monetary terms, with a reasonable degree of certainty, it will not be recognised as an asset on the statement of financial position. Take for example, the title of a magazine (such as *Hello!* or *Vogue*) that was created by its publisher. While it may be extremely valuable to the publishing business, its value cannot be established with reasonable certainty. It will not, therefore, appear as an asset in the statement of financial position as the valuation produced will have little relevance to user needs.

Note that all three of the characteristics identified must exist if a resource is to qualify for recognition. This will strictly limit the resources that are regarded as assets for inclusion in the statement of financial position. Once included, an asset will continue to be recognised until the economic benefits are exhausted, or the business disposes of it.

Figure 2.2 summarises the above discussion in the form of a decision chart.

Figure 2.2	Identifying an asset for inclusion in the statement of financial position

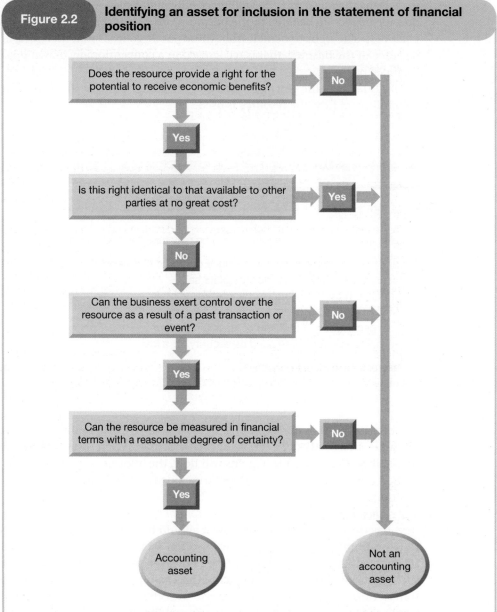

Only resources that have the characteristics identified may be included in the statement of financial position of the business concerned.

Activity 2.3

Indicate which of the following items could appear as an asset on the statement of financial position of a business. Explain your reasoning in each case.

1 £1,000 owed to the business by a credit customer who is unable to pay.
2 A patent, bought from an inventor, that gives the business the right to produce a new product. Production of the new product is expected to increase profits over the period during which the patent is held.

3 A recently hired new marketing director who is confidently expected to increase profits by over 30 per cent during the next three years.
4 A recently purchased machine that will save the business £10,000 each year. It is already being used by the business but it has been acquired on credit and is not yet paid for.

Your answer should be along the following lines:

1 Under normal circumstances, a business would expect a customer to pay the amount owed. Such an amount is therefore typically shown as an asset under the heading **'trade receivables'** (or 'debtors'). However, in this particular case, the customer is unable to pay. As a result, the item lacks the potential to provide future economic benefits and the £1,000 owing would not be regarded as an asset. Debts that are not paid are referred to as *bad debts*.
2 The patent would have all the characteristics identified and would, therefore, be regarded as an asset.
3 The new marketing director would not be considered as an asset. One argument in support of this position is that the business does not have rights of control over the director. Nevertheless, it may have control over the services that the director provides. Even if these services become the focus of attention, however, it is usually impossible to measure them in monetary terms with any degree of certainty.
4 The machine has the characteristics identified and so would be considered an asset even though it is not yet paid for. Once the business has contracted to buy the machine, and has accepted it, it gains ownership even though payment is still outstanding. (The amount outstanding would be shown as a claim, as we shall see shortly.)

The sorts of items that often appear as assets in the statement of financial position of a business include:

● property;
● plant and equipment;
● fixtures and fittings;
● patents and trademarks;
● trade receivables (debtors); and
● investments outside the business.

Activity 2.4

Can you think of two additional items that might appear as assets in the statement of financial position of a typical business?

You may be able to think of a number of other items. Two that we have met so far, because they were held by Paul's wrapping paper business (in Example 2.1), are inventories and cash.

Note that an asset does not have to be a physical item – it may be a non-physical one that gives a right to certain benefits. Assets that have a physical substance and can be touched (such as inventories) are referred to as **tangible assets.** Assets that have no physical substance but which, nevertheless, provide expected future benefits (such as patents) are referred to as **intangible assets.**

Claims

A claim is an obligation of the business to provide cash, or some other form of benefit, to an outside party. It will normally arise as a result of the outside party providing assets for use by the business. There are essentially two types of claim against a business:

- **Equity.** This represents the claim of the owner(s) against the business. This claim is sometimes referred to as the *owner's capital.* Some find it hard to understand how the owner can have a claim against the business, particularly when we consider the example of a sole-proprietor-type business, like Paul's, where the owner *is,* in effect, the business. For accounting purposes, however, a clear distinction is made between the business and the owner(s). The business is viewed as being quite separate from the owner. It is seen as a separate entity with its own separate existence. This means that, when financial statements are prepared, they relate to the business rather than to the owner(s). Viewed from this perspective, any funds contributed by the owner will be seen as coming from outside the business and will appear as a claim against the business in its statement of financial position.
- **Liabilities.** Liabilities represent the claims of other parties, apart from the owner(s). They involve an obligation to transfer economic resources (usually cash) as a result of past transactions or events. Liabilities normally arise when individuals or organisations supply goods and services, or lend money, to the business.

Once a liability has been incurred by a business, it will remain an obligation until it is settled.

Now that the meanings of the terms *assets, equity* and *liabilities* have been established, we can consider the relationship between them. This relationship is quite straightforward. If a business wishes to acquire assets, it must raise the necessary funds from somewhere. It may raise these funds from the owner(s), or from other outside parties, or from both. Example 2.2 illustrates this relationship.

Example 2.2

Jerry and Company is a new business that was created by depositing £20,000 in a bank account on 1 March. This amount was raised partly from the owner (£6,000) and partly from borrowing (£14,000). Raising funds in this way will give rise to a claim on the business by both the owner (equity) and the lender (liability). If a statement of financial position of Jerry and Company is prepared following these transactions, it will appear as follows:

Jerry and Company
Statement of financial position as at 1 March

	£
ASSETS	
Cash at bank	20,000
Total assets	20,000
EQUITY AND LIABILITIES	
Equity	6,000
Liabilities – borrowing	14,000
Total equity and liabilities	20,000

We can see from the statement of financial position that the total claims (equity and liabilities) are the same as the total assets. Thus:

$$\text{Assets} = \text{Equity} + \text{Liabilities}$$

This equation – which we shall refer to as the *accounting equation* – will always hold true. Whatever changes may occur to the assets of the business or the claims against it, there will be compensating changes elsewhere that will ensure that the statement of financial position always 'balances'. By way of illustration, consider the following transactions for Jerry and Company:

2 March	Bought a motor van for £5,000, paying by cheque.
3 March	Bought inventories (that is, goods to be sold) on one month's credit for £3,000. (This means that the inventories were bought on 3 March, but payment will not be due to be made to the supplier until 3 April.)
4 March	Repaid £2,000 of the amount borrowed, to the lender, by cheque.
6 March	Owner introduced another £4,000 into the business bank account.

A statement of financial position may be drawn up after each day in which transactions have taken place. In this way, we can see the effect of each transaction on the assets and claims of the business. The statement of financial position as at 2 March will be:

Jerry and Company
Statement of financial position as at 2 March

	£
ASSETS	
Cash at bank (20,000 − 5,000)	15,000
Motor van	5,000
Total assets	20,000
EQUITY AND LIABILITIES	
Equity	6,000
Liabilities – borrowing	14,000
Total equity and liabilities	20,000

As we can see, the effect of buying the motor van is to decrease the balance at the bank by £5,000 and to introduce a new asset – a motor van – to the statement of financial position. The total assets remain unchanged. It is only the 'mix' of assets that has changed. The claims against the business remain the same because there has been no change in the way in which the business has been funded.

The statement of financial position as at 3 March, following the purchase of inventories, will be:

Jerry and Company
Statement of Financial Position as at 3 March

	£
ASSETS	
Cash at bank	15,000
Motor van	5,000
Inventories	3,000
Total assets	23,000
EQUITY AND LIABILITIES	
Equity	6,000
Liabilities – borrowing	14,000
Liabilities – trade payable	3,000
Total equity and liabilities	23,000

The effect of buying inventories has been to introduce another new asset (inventories) to the statement of financial position. Furthermore, the fact that the goods have not yet been paid for means that the claims against the business will be increased by the £3,000 owed to the supplier, who is referred to as a **trade payable** (or trade creditor) on the statement of financial position.

Activity 2.5

Try drawing up a statement of financial position for Jerry and Company as at 4 March.

The statement of financial position as at 4 March, following the repayment of part of the borrowing, will be:

Jerry and Company
Statement of financial position as at 4 March

	£
ASSETS	
Cash at bank (15,000 − 2,000)	13,000
Motor van	5,000
Inventories	3,000
Total assets	21,000
EQUITY AND LIABILITIES	
Equity	6,000
Liabilities – borrowing (14,000 − 2,000)	12,000
Liabilities – trade payable	3,000
Total equity and liabilities	21,000

The repayment of £2,000 of the borrowing will result in a decrease in the balance at the bank of £2,000 and a decrease in the lender's claim against the business by the same amount.

Activity 2.6

Try drawing up a statement of financial position as at 6 March for Jerry and Company.

The statement of financial position as at 6 March, following the introduction of more funds, will be:

Jerry and Company
Statement of financial position as at 6 March

	£
ASSETS	
Cash at bank (13,000 + 4,000)	17,000
Motor van	5,000
Inventories	3,000
Total assets	25,000
EQUITY AND LIABILITIES	
Equity (6,000 + 4,000)	10,000
Liabilities – borrowing	12,000
Liabilities – trade payable	3,000
Total equity and liabilities	25,000

The introduction of more funds by the owner will result in an increase in the equity of £4,000 and an increase in the cash at bank by the same amount.

This example (Jerry and Company) illustrates the point that the accounting equation (assets equals equity plus liabilities) will always hold true. It reflects the fact that, if a business wishes to acquire more assets, it must raise funds equal to the cost of those assets. The funds raised must be provided by the owners (equity), or by others (liabilities), or by a combination of the two. This means that the total cost of assets acquired should always equal the total equity plus liabilities.

It is worth pointing out that businesses do not normally draw up a statement of financial position after each day, as shown in the example. We have done this to illustrate the effect on the statement of financial position of each transaction. In practice, a statement of financial position for a business is usually prepared at the end of a defined period. The period over which businesses measure their financial results is usually known as the **reporting period,** but it is sometimes called the 'accounting period' or 'financial period'.

Determining the length of the reporting period will involve weighing up the costs of producing the information against the perceived benefits of having that information for decision-making purposes. In practice, the reporting period will vary between businesses; it could be monthly, quarterly, half-yearly or annually. For external reporting purposes, an annual reporting period is the norm (although certain businesses, typically larger ones, report more frequently than this). For internal reporting purposes to managers, however, more frequent (perhaps monthly) financial statements are likely to be prepared.

The effect of trading transactions

In the example (Jerry and Company), we showed how various types of transactions affected the statement of financial position. However, one very important type of transaction – trading transactions – has yet to be considered. To show how this type of transaction affects the statement of financial position, let us return to Jerry and Company.

Example 2.2 *(continued)*

The statement of financial position that we drew up for Jerry and Company as at 6 March was as follows:

Jerry and Company
Statement of financial position as at 6 March

	£
ASSETS	
Cash at bank	17,000
Motor van	5,000
Inventories	3,000
Total assets	25,000
EQUITY AND LIABILITIES	
Equity	10,000
Liabilities – borrowing	12,000
Liabilities – trade payable	3,000
Total equity and liabilities	25,000

On 7 March, the business managed to sell all of the inventories for £5,000 and received a cheque immediately from the customer for this amount. The statement of financial position on 7 March, after this transaction has taken place, will be:

Jerry and Company
Statement of financial position as at 7 March

	£
ASSETS	
Cash at bank (17,000 + 5,000)	22,000
Motor van	5,000
Inventories (3,000 − 3,000)	–
Total assets	27,000
EQUITY AND LIABILITIES	
Equity (10,000 + (5,000 − 3,000))	12,000
Liabilities – borrowing	12,000
Liabilities – trade payable	3,000
Total equity and liabilities	27,000

We can see that the inventories (£3,000) have now disappeared from the statement of financial position, but the cash at bank has increased by the selling price of the inventories (£5,000). The net effect has therefore been to increase assets by £2,000 (that is, £5,000 less £3,000). This increase represents the net increase in wealth (the profit) that has arisen from trading. Also note that the equity of the business has increased by £2,000, in line with the increase in assets. This increase in equity reflects the fact that wealth generated, as a result of trading or other operations, will be to the benefit of the owners and will increase their stake in the business.

Activity 2.7

What would have been the effect on the statement of financial position if the inventories had been sold on 7 March for £1,000 rather than £5,000?

The statement of financial position on 7 March would then have been:

Jerry and Company
Statement of financial position as at 7 March

	£
ASSETS	
Cash at bank (17,000 + 1,000)	18,000
Motor van	5,000
Inventories (3,000 − 3,000)	–
Total assets	23,000
EQUITY AND LIABILITIES	
Equity (10,000 + (1,000 − 3,000))	8,000
Liabilities – borrowing	12,000
Liabilities – trade payable	3,000
Total equity and liabilities	23,000

As we can see, the inventories (£3,000) will disappear from the statement of financial position but the cash at bank will rise by only £1,000. This will mean a net reduction in assets of £2,000. This reduction represents a loss arising from trading and will be reflected in a reduction in the equity of the owners.

What we have just seen means that the accounting equation can be extended as follows:

$$\text{Assets (at the end of the period)} = \text{Equity (amount at the start of the period} + \text{Profit (or − Loss) for the period)} + \text{Liabilities (at the end of the period)}$$

(This is assuming that the owner makes no injections or withdrawals of equity during the period.)

Any funds introduced or withdrawn by the owners also affect equity. If the owners withdrew £1,500 for their own use, the equity of the owners would be reduced by £1,500. If these drawings were in cash, the cash balance would decrease by £1,500 in the statement of financial position.

Like all items in the statement of financial position, the amount of equity is cumulative. This means that any profit not taken out as drawings by the owner(s) remains in the business. These retained (or 'ploughed-back') earnings have the effect of expanding the business.

Classifying assets

In the statement of financial position, assets and claims are usually grouped into categories. This is designed to help users, as a haphazard listing of these items could be confusing. Assets are usually categorised as being either current or non-current.

Current assets

Current assets are basically assets that are held for the short term. To be more precise, they are assets that meet any of the following conditions:

- they are held for sale or consumption during the business's normal operating cycle;
- they are expected to be sold within a year after the date of the relevant statement of financial position;
- they are held principally for trading; and/or
- they are cash, or near cash such as easily marketable, short-term investments.

The operating cycle of a business, mentioned above, is the time between buying and/ or creating a product or service and receiving the cash on its sale. For most businesses, this will be less than a year. (It is worth mentioning that sales made by most businesses, retailers being the exception, are made on credit. The customer pays some time after the goods are received or the service is rendered.)

The most common current assets are inventories, trade receivables (amounts owed by customers for goods or services supplied on credit) and cash. For businesses that sell goods, rather than render a service, the current assets of inventories, trade receivables and cash are interrelated. They circulate within a business as shown in Figure 2.3. We can see that cash can be used to buy inventories, which are then sold on credit. When the credit customers (trade receivables) pay, the business receives an injection of cash and so on.

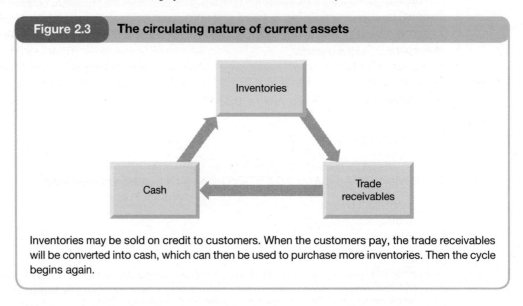

| Figure 2.3 | The circulating nature of current assets |

Inventories may be sold on credit to customers. When the customers pay, the trade receivables will be converted into cash, which can then be used to purchase more inventories. Then the cycle begins again.

For purely service businesses, the situation is similar, except that inventories are not involved.

Non-current assets

Non-current assets (also called *fixed assets*) are simply assets that do not meet the definition of current assets. They tend to be held for long-term operations. Non-current assets may be either tangible or intangible. Tangible non-current assets normally consist of **property, plant and equipment.** We shall refer to them in this way from now on. This is a rather broad term that includes items such as land and buildings, machinery, motor vehicles and fixtures and fittings.

The distinction between those assets continuously circulating (current) and those used for long-term operations (non-current) may help when assessing the mix of assets held. Most businesses need a certain amount of both types of asset to operate effectively.

Activity 2.8

Can you think of two examples of assets that may be classified as non-current assets for an insurance business?

Examples of assets that may be defined as being non-current are:

● property
● furniture
● motor vehicles
● computers
● computer software
● reference books.

This is not an exhaustive list. You may have thought of others.

The way in which a particular asset is classified (that is, between current and non-current) may vary according to the nature of the business. This is because the *purpose* for which the asset is held may vary. For example, a motor van retailer will normally hold inventories of the motor vans for sale; it would, therefore, classify them as part of the current assets. On the other hand, a business that buys one of these vans to use for delivering its goods to customers (that is, as part of its long-term operations) would classify it as a non-current asset.

Activity 2.9

The assets of Kunalun and Co., a large advertising agency, are as follows:

● cash at bank
● fixtures and fittings
● office equipment
● motor vehicles
● property
● computers
● work in progress (that is, partly completed work for clients).

Which of these do you think should be defined as non-current assets and which as current assets?

Your answer should be as follows:

Non-current assets	Current assets
Fixtures and fittings	Cash at bank
Office equipment	Work in progress
Motor vehicles	
Property	
Computers	

Classifying claims

As we have already seen, claims are normally classified into equity (owner's claim) and liabilities (claims of outsiders). Liabilities are further classified as either current or non-current.

Current liabilities

Current liabilities are basically amounts due for settlement in the short term. To be more precise, they are liabilities that meet any of the following conditions:

- they are expected to be settled within the business's normal operating cycle;
- they exist principally as a result of trading;
- they are due to be settled within a year after the date of the relevant statement of financial position; and/or
- there is no right to defer settlement beyond a year after the date of the relevant statement of financial position.

Non-current liabilities

Non-current liabilities represent amounts due that do not meet the definition of current liabilities and so represent longer-term liabilities.

Activity 2.10

Can you think of one example of a current liability and one of a non-current liability?

An example of a current liability would be amounts owing to suppliers for goods supplied on credit (**trade payables**) or a bank overdraft (a form of short-term bank borrowing that is repayable on demand). An example of a non-current liability would be long-term borrowings.

It is quite common for non-current liabilities to become current liabilities. For example, borrowings to be repaid 18 months after the date of a particular statement of financial position will normally appear as a non-current liability. Those same borrowings will, however, appear as a current liability in the statement of financial position as at the end of the following year, by which time they would be due for repayment after six months.

This classification of liabilities between current and non-current helps to highlight those financial obligations that must soon be met. It may be useful to compare the amount of current liabilities with the amount of current assets (that is, the assets that either are cash or will turn into cash within the normal operating cycle). This should reveal whether the business is able to cover its maturing obligations.

The classification of liabilities between current and non-current also helps to highlight the proportion of total long-term finance that is raised through borrowings rather than equity. Where a business relies on long-term borrowings, rather than relying solely on funds provided by the owner(s), the financial risks increase. This is because borrowing brings a commitment to make periodic interest payments and capital repayments. The business may be forced to stop trading if this commitment cannot be fulfilled. Thus, when raising long-term finance, the right balance must be struck between long-term borrowings and owner's equity. We shall consider this issue in more detail later in Chapter 7. In that chapter, we shall also look at other relationships between items appearing in the financial statement, for example the relationship between current assets and current liabilities, mentioned above.

Statement layouts

Having looked at the classification of assets and liabilities, we shall now consider the layout of the statement of financial position. Although there is an almost infinite number of ways in which the same information on assets and claims could be presented, we shall consider two basic layouts. The first of these follows the style that we adopted with Jerry and Company earlier (see pages 48–52). A more comprehensive example of this style is shown in Example 2.3.

Example 2.3

Brie Manufacturing
Statement of financial position as at 31 December 2017

	£000
ASSETS	
Non-current assets	
Property	45
Plant and equipment	30
Motor vans	19
	94
Current assets	
Inventories	23
Trade receivables	18
Cash at bank	12
	53
Total assets	147
EQUITY AND LIABILITIES	
Equity	60
Non-current liabilities	
Long-term borrowings	50
Current liabilities	
Trade payables	37
Total equity and liabilities	147

The non-current assets have a total of £94,000 which, together with the current assets total of £53,000, gives a total of £147,000 for assets. Similarly, the equity totals £60,000 which, together with the £50,000 for non-current liabilities and £37,000 for current liabilities, gives a total for equity and liabilities of £147,000.

Within each category of asset (non-current and current) shown in Example 2.3, the items are listed in reverse order of liquidity (nearness to cash). Thus, the assets that are furthest from cash come first and the assets that are closest to cash come last. In the case of non-current assets, property is listed first as this asset is usually the most difficult to turn into cash and motor vans are listed last as there is usually a ready market for them. In the case of current assets, we have already seen that inventories are converted to trade receivables and then trade receivables are converted to cash. As a result, under the heading of current assets, inventories are listed first, followed by trade receivables and finally cash itself. This ordering of assets will occur irrespective of the layout used.

Note that, in addition to a grand total for assets held, subtotals for non-current assets and current assets are shown. Subtotals are also used for non-current liabilities and current liabilities when more than one item appears within these categories.

A slight variation from the layout illustrated in Example 2.3 is as shown in Example 2.4.

Example 2.4

Brie Manufacturing
Statement of financial position as at 31 December 2017

	£000
ASSETS	
Non-current assets	
Property	45
Plant and equipment	30
Motor vans	19
	94
Current assets	
Inventories	23
Trade receivables	18
Cash at bank	12
	53
Total assets	147
LIABILITIES	
Non-current liabilities	
Long-term borrowings	(50)
Current liabilities	
Trade payables	(37)
Total liabilities	(87)
Net assets	60
EQUITY	60

We can see that the total liabilities are deducted from the total assets. This derives a figure for net assets – which is equal to equity. Using this format, the basic accounting equation is rearranged so that:

$$\text{Assets} - \text{Liabilities} = \text{Equity}$$

This rearranged equation highlights the fact that equity represents the residual interest of the owner(s) in the assets of the business, after deducting all liabilities.

Figure 2.4 summarises the two types of layout discussed in this section.

Figure 2.4   **Layouts for the statement of financial position**

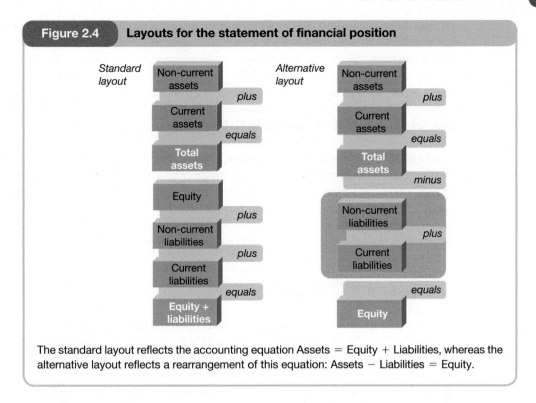

The standard layout reflects the accounting equation Assets = Equity + Liabilities, whereas the alternative layout reflects a rearrangement of this equation: Assets − Liabilities = Equity.

The layout shown in Example 2.3 is very popular in practice and will be used throughout the book.

Capturing a moment in time

As we have already seen, the statement of financial position reflects the assets, equity and liabilities of a business at *a specified point in time.* It has been compared to a photograph. A photograph 'freezes' a particular moment in time and will represent the situation only at that moment. Hence, events may be quite different immediately before and immediately after the photograph was taken. When examining a statement of financial position, therefore, it is important to establish the date for which it has been drawn up. This information should be prominently displayed in the heading to the statement, as shown above in Example 2.4. When we are trying to assess current financial position, the more recent the statement of financial position date, the more helpful it is likely to be.

A business will normally prepare a statement of financial position as at the close of business on the last day of its annual reporting period. In the UK, businesses are free to choose the date of the end of their reporting period and, once chosen, it will only normally change under exceptional circumstances. When making a decision on which year-end date to choose, commercial convenience can often be a deciding factor. For example, a business operating in the retail trade may choose to have a year-end date early in the calendar year (for example, 31 January) because trade tends to be slack during that period and more staff time is available to help with the tasks involved in the preparation of the annual financial statements (such as checking the amount of inventories held ('stocktaking')). Since trade is slack, it is also a time when the amount of inventories held by the retail business is likely to be unusually low as compared with other times of the year. Thus, the statement of financial position, though showing a fair view of what it purports to show, may show a picture of what is not typically the position of the business over the rest of the year.

The role of accounting conventions

Accounting has a number of conventions, or rules, that have evolved over time. They have evolved to deal with practical problems experienced by preparers and users of financial statements, rather than to reflect some theoretical ideal. In preparing the statements of financial position earlier in this chapter, we have followed various **accounting conventions,** although they have not been explicitly mentioned. We shall now identify and discuss the main conventions that we have applied.

Business entity convention

For accounting purposes, the business and its owner(s) are treated as being quite separate and distinct. This is why owners are treated as being claimants against their own business in respect of their investment. The **business entity convention** must be distinguished from the legal position that may exist between businesses and their owners. For sole proprietorships and partnerships, the law does not make any distinction between the business and its owner(s). For limited companies, on the other hand, there is a clear legal distinction between the business and its owners. (As we shall see in Chapter 4, the limited company is regarded as having a separate legal existence.) For accounting purposes, these legal distinctions are irrelevant and the business entity convention applies to all businesses.

Historic cost convention

The **historic cost convention** holds that the value of assets shown on the statement of financial position should be based on their historic cost (that is, acquisition cost). The use of historic cost means that problems of measurement reliability are minimised, as the amount paid for a particular asset is often a matter of demonstrable fact. Reliance on opinion is avoided, or at least reduced, which should enhance the credibility of the information in the eyes of users. A key problem, however, is that the information provided may not be relevant to user needs. Even quite early in the life of some assets, historic costs may become outdated compared to current market values. This can be misleading when assessing current financial position.

Many argue that recording assets at their current value would provide a more realistic view of financial position and would be relevant for a wide range of decisions. A system of measurement based on current value does, however, bring its own problems. The term 'current value' can be defined in different ways. It can be defined broadly as either the current replacement cost or the current realisable value (selling price) of an asset. These two types of valuation may result in quite different figures being produced to represent the current value of an item. Furthermore, the broad terms 'replacement cost' and 'realisable value' can be defined in different ways. We must therefore be clear about what kind of current value accounting we wish to use.

Activity 2.11 illustrates some of the problems associated with current value accounting.

Activity (2.11)

Plumber and Company has a fleet of motor vans that are used for making deliveries to customers. The owners want to show these vans on the statement of financial position at their current values rather than at their historic cost. They would like to use either current replacement cost (based on how much would have to be paid to buy vans of a similar type, age and condition) or current realisable value (based on how much a motor van dealer would pay for the vans, if the business sold them).

Why is the choice between the two current valuation methods important? Why would both current valuation methods present problems in establishing reliable values?

The choice between the two current valuation methods is important because the values derived under each method are likely to be quite different. Normally, replacement cost values for the motor vans will be higher than their current realisable values.

Establishing current values will usually rely on opinions, which may well vary from one dealer to another. Thus, instead of a single, unambiguous figure for, say, the current replacement cost for each van, a range of possible current replacement costs could be produced. The same problem will arise when trying to establish the current realisable value for each van.

We should bear in mind that the motor vans discussed in Activity 2.11 are less of a problem than are many other types of asset. There is a ready market for motor vans, which means that a value can be obtained by contacting a dealer. For a custom-built piece of equipment, however, identifying a replacement cost or, worse still, a selling price, could be very difficult.

Where the current values of assets are based on the opinion of managers of the business, there is a greater risk that they will lack credibility. Some form of independent valuation, or verification, may therefore be required to reassure users.

Despite the problems associated with current values, they are increasingly used when reporting assets in the statement of financial position. This has led to a steady erosion in the importance of the historic cost convention. Thus, many businesses now prepare financial statements on a modified historic cost basis. We shall consider the valuation of assets in more detail a little later in the chapter.

Prudence convention

In broad terms, the **prudence convention** holds that caution should be exercised when preparing financial statements. This may not seem to be a contentious issue: it would, after all, be difficult to argue that an incautious approach should be taken. Nevertheless, the prudence convention has excited much debate over the years. The root cause has been the way in which the convention is often applied. It can be used to support a bias towards the understatement of financial strength: that is, the understatement of assets and profit and the overstatement of liabilities.

Those who support this approach to prudence argue that it is better to understate than to overstate financial strength. They make the point that, by overstating financial strength, users of financial statements may be misled into making poor decisions.

Activity (2.12)

What sort of poor decisions may be made as a result of overstating the financial strength of a business? Try to think of at least three.

Examples of poor decisions may include:

- excessive amounts being paid out of profits to the owners, thereby, depleting their equity and undermining the financial health of the business;
- excessive bonuses being paid to managers based on overstated profits;
- new owners paying more to acquire a part, or the whole, of a business than is justified; and
- lenders providing funds to a business based on a rosier picture of financial strength than is warranted by the facts.

You may have thought of others.

A bias towards the understatement of financial strength evolved in order to counteract the excessive optimism of managers. However, just as overstatement can lead to poor decisions being made, understatement can lead to the same. It may, for example, result in existing owners selling their business too cheaply, lenders refusing a loan application based on a distorted picture of financial strength and so on.

The systematic bias towards understatement just described clashes with the need for *neutrality* in preparing financial statements.

Activity (2.13)

In Chapter 1, we discussed neutrality as a desirable element of one of the major qualitative characteristics of financial information. Can you remember which one?

Neutrality is one of three elements needed to ensure faithful representation. (The other two elements are completeness and freedom from error.)

Neutrality, by definition, requires that financial statements are not slanted or weighted so as to present either a favourable or unfavourable picture to users. To accommodate the concept of neutrality, therefore, prudence must be interpreted and applied in a different way than has occurred in the past. Adopting a cautious approach to preparing financial statements can no longer be used to justify the deliberate understatement of financial strength.

Going concern convention

Under the **going concern convention,** the financial statements should be prepared on the assumption that a business will continue operations for the foreseeable future, unless there is evidence to the contrary. In other words, it is assumed that there is no intention, or need, to sell off the non-current assets of the business.

Where a business is in financial difficulties, however, non-current assets may have to be sold to repay those with claims against the business. The realisable (sale) value of many non-current assets is often much lower than the values reported in the statement of financial position. In the event of a forced sale of assets, therefore, significant losses might arise. These losses must be anticipated and fully reported when, but only when, a business's going concern status is called into question.

Dual aspect convention

The **dual aspect convention** asserts that each transaction has two aspects, both of which will affect the statement of financial position. This means that, for example, the purchase of a computer for cash results in an increase in one asset (computer) and a decrease in another (cash). Similarly, the repayment of borrowings results in the decrease in a liability (borrowings) and the decrease in an asset (cash).

Activity 2.14

What are the two aspects of each of the following transactions?

1 Purchasing £1,000 of inventories on credit.
2 Owner withdrawing £2,000 in cash.
3 Paying a supplier £1,000 for inventories bought on credit a few weeks earlier.

Your answer should be as follows:

1 Inventories increase by £1,000, trade payables increase by £1,000.
2 Equity reduces by £2,000, cash reduces by £2,000.
3 Trade payables reduce by £1,000, cash reduces by £1,000.

Recording the dual aspect of each transaction ensures that the statement of financial position will continue to balance.

Figure 2.5 summarises the main accounting conventions that exert an influence on what appears on the of the statement of financial position.

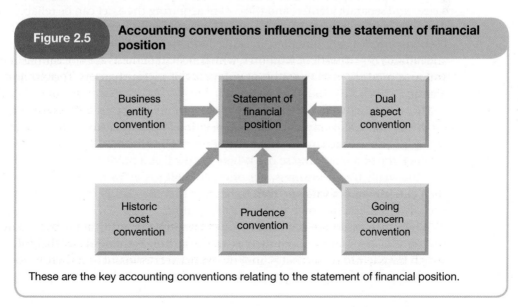

Figure 2.5 **Accounting conventions influencing the statement of financial position**

These are the key accounting conventions relating to the statement of financial position.

Money measurement

We saw earlier that an economic resource will only normally be regarded as an asset, for inclusion in the statement of financial position, where it can be measured with a reasonable degree of certainty. Unless this can be achieved, any measure provided is unlikely to be relevant to user needs.

Various resources of a business fail to meet this measurement criterion and so are excluded from the statement of financial position.

Activity 2.15

Can you identify any of these resources? Try to think of at least two.

They may include:

- human resources;
- business reputation;
- business location; and/or
- customer and supplier relationships.

From time to time, attempts are made to try to measure and report these resources so as to provide a more complete picture of financial position. However, they usually garner little support. Measures with a high degree of uncertainty produce inconsistency in reporting and create doubts in the minds of users. As a result, the integrity and credibility of financial statements can be undermined.

Let us now move on to discuss some key economic resources that normally pose measurement problems.

Goodwill and brands

Some intangible non-current assets are similar to tangible non-current assets: they have a clear and separate identity and the cost of acquiring the asset can be reliably measured. Examples normally include patents, trademarks, copyrights and licences. Other intangible non-current assets, however, are quite different. They lack a clear and separate identity and reflect a hotchpotch of attributes, which are part of the essence of the business. Goodwill and product brands are often examples of assets that lack a clear and separate identity.

The term '**goodwill**' is often used to cover various attributes such as the quality of the products, the skill of employees and the relationship with customers. The term 'product brands' is also used to cover various attributes, such as the brand image, the quality of the product, the trademark and so on. Where goodwill and product brands have been generated internally by the business, it is often difficult to determine their cost or to measure their current market value or even to be clear that they really exist. They are, therefore, excluded from the statement of financial position.

When such assets are acquired through an 'arm's-length transaction', however, the problems of uncertainty about their existence and measurement are resolved. (An arm's-length transaction is one that is undertaken between two unconnected parties.) If goodwill is acquired, when taking over another business, or if a business acquires a particular product brand, from another business, these items will be separately identified and a price agreed for them. Under these circumstances, they can be regarded as assets (for accounting purposes) by the business that acquired them and included in the statement of financial position.

To agree a price for acquiring goodwill or product brands means that some form of valuation must take place and this raises the question as to how it is done. Usually, the valuation will be based on estimates of future earnings from holding the asset – a process that is fraught with difficulties. Nevertheless, a number of specialist businesses now exist that are prepared to take on this challenge. **Real World 2.1** shows how one specialist business ranked and valued the top ten brands in the world for 2016.

Real World 2.1

Brand leaders

Millward Brown Optimor, part of WPP marketing services group, produces an annual report which ranks and values the top world brands. For 2016, the top ten brands are as follows:

Ranking	Brand	Value ($m)
1	Google	229,198
2	Apple	228,460
3	Microsoft	121,824
4	AT&T	107,387
5	Facebook	102,551
6	Visa	100,800
7	Amazon	98,988
8	Verizon	93,220
9	McDonalds	88,654
10	IBM	86,206

We can see that the valuations placed on the brands owned are quite staggering. It is also interesting to note that technology businesses dominate the rankings.

Source: 2016 Brandz Top 100 Most Valuable Global Brands, WPP and Millward Brown, www.wpp.com, 8 June 2016.

Human resources

Attempts have been made to place a monetary measurement on the human resources of a business, but without any real success. There are, however, certain limited circumstances in which human resources are measured and reported in the statement of financial position. Professional football clubs provide an example of where these circumstances normally arise. While football clubs cannot own players, they can own the rights to the players' services. Where these rights are acquired by compensating other clubs for releasing the players from their contracts with those other clubs, an arm's-length transaction arises and the amounts paid provide a reliable basis for measurement. This means that the rights to services can be regarded as an asset of the club for accounting purposes (assuming, of course, the player will bring benefits to the club).

Real World 2.2 describes how one leading club reports its investment in players on the statement of financial position.

Real World 2.2

Spurs players appear on the team sheet and on the statement of financial position

Tottenham Hotspur Football Club (Spurs) has acquired several key players as a result of paying transfer fees to other clubs. In common with most UK football clubs, Spurs reports the cost of acquiring the rights to the players' services on its statement of financial position. The club's statement as at 30 June 2015 shows the total cost of registering its squad of players at almost £208 million. The club treats a proportion of each player's transfer fee as an expense each year. The exact proportion depends on the length of the particular player's contract.

The £208 million does not include 'home-grown' players such as Harry Kane, Tom Carroll and Josh Onomah, because Spurs did not pay a transfer fee for them and so no clear-cut value can be placed on their services. During the year to 30 June 2015, the club was active in the transfer market and spent more than £37 million on acquiring new players, including Eric Dier from Sporting Lisbon and Ben Davies and Michel Vorm from Swansea City. Several players also left the club during the year, including Sandro, Michael Dawson and Kyle Naughton.

The item of players' registrations is shown as an intangible asset in the statement of financial position as it is the rights to services, not the players, that are the assets. It is shown net of depreciation (or amortisation as it is usually termed for intangible non-current assets). The carrying amount at 30 June 2015 was more than £108 million and represented almost 27 per cent of Spurs' total assets, as shown in the statement of financial position.

Source: Tottenham Hotspur plc Annual Report 2015.

Monetary stability

When using money as the unit of measurement, we normally fail to recognise the fact that it will change in value over time, despite the fact that in the UK, and throughout much of the world, inflation has been a persistent problem. This has meant that the value of money has declined in relation to other assets. In past years, high rates of inflation have resulted in statements of financial position, which were prepared on a historic cost basis, reflecting figures for assets that were much lower than if current values were employed. Rates of inflation have been relatively low in recent years and so the disparity between historic cost values and current values has been less pronounced. Nevertheless, it can still be significant. The problem of inflation has added fuel to the more general debate concerning how to measure asset values in the statement of financial position. It is to the issue of valuing assets that we now turn.

Valuing assets

We saw earlier that, when preparing the statement of financial position, the historic cost convention is normally applied for the reporting of assets. This point requires further explanation as, in practice, things are a little more complex than this. Large businesses throughout much of the world adhere to asset valuation rules set out in International Financial Reporting Standards. We shall now consider the key valuation rules.

Non-current assets

Non-current assets have useful lives that are either *finite* or *indefinite.* Those with a finite life provide benefits to a business for a limited period of time, whereas those with an indefinite life provide benefits without a foreseeable time limit. This distinction between the two types of non-current assets applies to both tangible and intangible assets.

Initially, non-current assets are recorded at their historic cost, which will include any amounts spent on getting them ready for use.

Non-current assets with finite lives

Benefits from assets with finite useful lives will be used up over time as a result of market changes, wear and tear and so on. The amount used up, which is referred to as *depreciation* (or *amortisation*, in the case of intangible non-current assets), must be measured for each reporting period for which the assets are held. Although we shall leave a detailed examination of depreciation until Chapter 3, we need to know that when an asset has been depreciated, this must be reflected in the statement of financial position.

The total depreciation that has accumulated over the period since the asset was acquired must be deducted from its cost. This net figure (that is, the cost of the asset less the total depreciation to date) is referred to as the *carrying amount.* It is sometimes also known as *net book value* or *written-down value.* The procedure just described is not really a contravention of the historic cost convention. It is simply recognition of the fact that a proportion of the historic cost of the non-current asset has been consumed in the process of generating, or attempting to generate, benefits for the business.

Activity 2.16

Try to identify *two* non-current assets with a finite useful life that can be classified as:

1 tangible and
2 intangible?

Tangible assets normally considered to have a finite life include:

- machinery and equipment;
- motor vehicles; and
- computers.

Intangible assets normally considered to have a finite life include:

- patents (many patents are granted for a period of 20 years);
- leases taken out on assets (such as a property); and
- licences (such as a taxi licence).

Non-current assets with indefinite useful lives

Benefits from assets with indefinite lives may, or may not, be used up over time. Property, in the form of land, is usually an example of a tangible non-current asset with an indefinite life. Purchased goodwill could be an example of an intangible one, though this is not always the case. These assets are not subject to routine depreciation each reporting period.

Fair values

Initially, non-current assets of all types (tangible and intangible) are recorded at cost. Subsequently, however, an alternative form of measurement may be allowed. Non-current assets may be recorded using **fair values** provided that these values can be measured reliably. Fair values are market based. They represent the selling price that can be obtained in an orderly transaction under current market conditions. The use of fair values, rather than cost, provides users with more up-to-date information, which may be more relevant to their needs. It may also place the business in a better light, as assets such as property may have increased significantly in value over time. Increasing the statement of financial position value of an asset does not, of course, make that asset more valuable. Perceptions of the business may, however, be altered by such a move.

One consequence of upwardly revaluing non-current assets with finite lives is that the depreciation charge will be increased. This is because the depreciation charge is based on the new (increased) value of the asset.

Real World 2.3 shows the effect of the revaluation of non-current assets on the financial position of one large business.

Real World 2.3

Rising asset levels

During the year to 31 March 2010, Veolia Water UK plc, which owns Thames Water, changed its policy on the valuation of certain types of non-current assets. These assets included land and buildings, infrastructure assets and vehicles, plant and machinery. The business switched from the use of historic cost to the use of fair values and independent qualified valuers carried out a revaluation exercise.

The effect of this policy change was to report a revaluation gain of more than £436 million during the year. There was a 40 per cent increase in owners' (shareholders') equity, which was largely due to this gain.

Source: Veolia Water UK plc Annual Report 2009/10.

Activity 2.17

Refer to the statement of financial position of Brie Manufacturing shown earlier in Example 2.4 (page 58). What would be the effect of revaluing the property to a figure of £110,000 in the statement of financial position? Show the revised statement.

The effect on the statement of financial position would be to increase the figure for property to £110,000 and the gain on revaluation (that is, £110,000 − £45,000 = £65,000) would be added to equity, as it is the owner(s) who will have benefited from the gain. The revised statement of financial position would therefore be as follows:

Brie Manufacturing
Statement of financial position as at 31 December 2017

	£000
ASSETS	
Non-current assets	
Property	110
Plant and equipment	30
Motor vans	19
	159
Current assets	
Inventories	23
Trade receivables	18
Cash at bank	12
	53
Total assets	212
EQUITY AND LIABILITIES	
Equity (60 + 65)	125
Non-current liabilities	
Long-term borrowings	50
Current liabilities	
Trade payables	37
Total equity and liabilities	212

Once non-current assets are revalued, the frequency of revaluation becomes an important issue. Reporting assets on the statement of financial position at out-of-date revaluations is the worst of both worlds. It lacks the objectivity and verifiability of historic cost; it also lacks the realism of current values. Thus, where fair values are used, revaluations should be frequent enough to ensure that the carrying amount of the revalued asset does not differ materially from its true fair value at the statement of financial position date.

When an item of property, plant or equipment (a tangible asset) is revalued on the basis of fair values, all assets within that particular group must be revalued. It is not therefore acceptable to revalue some items of property but not others. Although this rule provides some degree of consistency within a particular group of assets, it does not prevent the statement of financial position from containing a mixture of valuations.

Intangible assets are not usually revalued to fair values. This is because an active market is required to determine fair values. For most intangible assets, an active market does not exist. A few intangible assets, however, such as transferable taxi licences, fishing licences and production quotas, provide the exception.

It has been argued that recent emphasis on the use of fair values in accounting has resulted in the exercise of prudence becoming less important. **Real World 2.4** comprises extracts from an article by John Kay which explains why this change has taken place. The article, which is well worth reading in full, is highly critical of the change.

> **Real World 2.4**
>
> # It's really not fair
>
> Once upon a time, values were based on cost, unless assets were no longer worth their cost, in which case they had to be written down.
>
> A bird in the hand was worth more than any number in the bush: only when the bird emerged from the bush were you permitted to count it at all.
>
> Like finance, however, accounting became cleverer, and worse. By the 1980s accounting had become the principal means by which UK graduates prepared for business. Many of these trainees found jobs in the finance sector; others took jobs in non-financial business – and, since they were smart, many rose to senior positions. Young accountants were smarter, greedier, less schooled in prudence and better schooled in economics. "Fair value" increasingly replaced conservatism (prudence) as a guiding principle. But this route to the "true and fair view" – the traditional holy grail of the accountant – often led to an outcome that was just the opposite of fair.
>
> FT *Source*: Extracts from Kay, J. (2015) Playing dice with your money, ft.com, 4 September.
> © The Financial Times Ltd 2015. All Rights Reserved.

The impairment of non-current assets

All types of non-current asset are at risk of suffering a significant fall in value. This may be caused by changes in market conditions, technological obsolescence and so on. In some cases, this results in the carrying amount of the asset being higher than the amount that could be recovered from the asset; either through its continued use or through its sale. When this occurs, the asset value is said to be impaired and the general rule is to reduce the carrying amount on the statement of financial position to the recoverable amount. Unless this is done, the asset value will be overstated. The amount by which the asset value is reduced is known as an **impairment loss.** (This type of impairment in value should not be confused with routine depreciation of assets with finite lives.)

> **Activity** **(2.18)**
>
> With which of the ideas discussed earlier in the chapter is this accounting treatment of impaired assets consistent?
>
> The answer is prudence, which requires that we should adopt a cautious approach when preparing financial statements. The value of assets should not be overstated in the statement of financial position.

Real World 2.5 provides an example of where one large mining business recently incurred large impairment losses on the value of its assets.

Real World 2.5

All going impaired shape

BHP Billiton Ltd., the world's No. 1 miner by market value, recorded its worst-ever annual loss as US$7.7 billion in impairment losses exacerbated a deep slump in commodity prices.

Melbourne, Australia-based BHP reported a net loss of $6.39 billion for the 12 months through June, compared with a year-earlier net profit of $1.91 billion. Underlying profit, stripping out one-time charges, slumped 81% to $1.22 billion. As recently as 2011, annual profits topped $20 billion.

The loss deepens the gloom in the global mining sector, which has responded to global economic uncertainty and low prices for commodities from copper to iron ore by closing mines, laying off workers and slashing returns for investors.

BHP's earnings also took hits from problems not shared by many of its mining peers: a deadly disaster at an iron-ore mine in Brazil and weak oil and natural-gas markets. Those enormous charges were largely against the Brazilian venture and U.S. onshore energy assets–$2.2 billion and $4.9 billion, respectively. BHP's petroleum business, intended to help it through bad times in metals markets, lost $7.72 billion after its write-downs.

BHP Billiton's annual loss was the first at group level since it was formed in 2001 through a merger of Australia's BHP Ltd. and U.K.-based Billiton PLC.

Source: Extract from Hoyle, R. (2016) BHP Billiton Reports Worst-Ever Annual Loss, *The Wall Street Journal*, www.wsj.com, 16 August.

Intangible non-current assets with indefinite useful lives must be tested for impairment as at the end of each reporting period. Other non-current assets, however, must also be tested where events suggest that impairment has taken place.

Activity 2.19

Why might it be a good idea to have impairment tests carried out by independent experts?

Impairment tests involve making judgements about the appropriate value to place on assets. Employing independent valuers to make these judgements will normally give users greater confidence in the information reported. There is always a risk that managers will manipulate impairment values to portray a picture that they would like users to see.

When a non-current asset with a finite useful life has its value impaired, the future, periodic, depreciation expense for that asset will be based on the new (lower) impaired value.

Inventories

It is not only non-current assets that run the risk of a significant fall in value. The inventories of a business could also suffer this fate as a result of changes in market taste, obsolescence, deterioration, damage and so on. Where a fall in value means that the amount likely to be recovered from the sale of the inventories will be lower than their cost, this loss must be reflected in the statement of financial position. Thus, if the net realisable value (that is, selling price less any selling costs) falls below the historic cost of inventories held, the former should be used as the basis of valuation. This reflects, once again, the influence of prudence in preparing the statement of financial position.

Real World 2.6 reveals how one well-known business wrote down some of its inventories.

Real World 2.6

Next to nothing

The fashion and home furnishing retailer Next plc saw some of its inventories fall in value during the year ended 30 January 2016. This led to a reported loss of £103.7 million, which represented the difference between their cost and net realisable value. (However, the operating profit for the year was £867.2 million overall.) To see this in context, the value of inventories held at the year-end was £486.5 million and the cost of inventories treated as an expense during the year was £1,474.6 million. In the previous year, there was a reported loss of £100.9 million for the same reason. Inventories held at the end of January 2015 were valued at £416.8 million and inventories treated as an expense during that year was £1,452.7 million.

The fashion business, particularly women's fashion, is very fast moving and so losses from holding such inventories are not altogether surprising.

Source: Information taken from Next plc Annual Report and Accounts for the year ended 25 January 2016, pp. 92, 94, 105.

The published financial statements of large businesses will normally show the basis on which inventories are valued. **Real World 2.7** shows how one business reports this information.

Real World 2.7

Reporting inventories

The 2015/16 annual report of Ted Baker plc, a leading designer clothes brand, includes the following explanation concerning inventories:

> Inventories and work in progress are stated at the lower of cost and net realisable value. Cost includes materials, direct labour and inward transportation costs. Net realisable value is based on estimated selling price, less further costs expected to be incurred to completion and disposal. Provision is made for obsolete, slow moving or defective items where appropriate.

Source: Ted Baker plc Annual Report and Accounts 2015/16, p. 76.

Meeting user needs

The statement of financial position is the oldest of the three main financial statements and may help users in the following ways:

- *It provides insights about how the business is financed and how its funds are deployed.* The statement of financial position shows how much finance the owners contribute and how much is contributed by outside lenders. It also shows the different kinds of assets acquired and how much is invested in each kind.
- *It can provide a basis for assessing the value of the business.* Since the statement of financial position lists, and places a value on, the various assets and claims, it can provide a starting point for assessing the value of the business. We have seen earlier, however, that accounting rules may result in assets being shown at their historic cost, which may vary quite considerably from the current valuation, and that the restrictive definition of assets may completely exclude certain business resources from the statement of financial position.
- *Relationships between assets and claims can be assessed.* It can be useful to look at relationships between various statement of financial position items, for example the relationship between how much wealth is tied up in current assets and how much is owed in the short term (current liabilities). From this relationship, we can see whether the business has sufficient short-term assets to cover its maturing obligations. We shall look at this and other relationships between statement of financial position items in some detail in Chapter 7.
- *Performance can be assessed.* The effectiveness of a business in generating wealth can usefully be assessed against the amount of investment that was involved. Thus, the relationship between profit earned during a period and the value of the net assets invested can be helpful to many users, particularly owners and managers. This and similar relationships will also be explored in detail in Chapter 7.

Once armed with the insights that a statement of financial position can provide, users are better placed to make investment and other decisions. **Real World 2.8** shows how a small business was able to obtain a loan because its bank was impressed by its strong statement of financial position.

Real World 2.8

A sound education

Sandeep Sud is a qualified solicitor who also runs a school uniform business based in Hounslow, in partnership with his parents. The business, which has four full-time employees, uses its statement of financial position to gauge how it is progressing. The statement has also been a key factor in securing a bank loan for the improvement and expansion of the business premises.

According to Sandeep,

Having a strong statement of financial position helped when it came to borrowing. When we first applied for a refurbishment loan we couldn't provide up-to-date accounts to the bank manager. This could have been a problem, but we quickly got our accounts in order and the loan was approved straight away. Because our statement of financial position was strong, the bank thought we were a good risk. Although we decided not to draw down on the loan – because we used cash-flow instead – it did open our eyes to the importance of a strong statement of financial position.

Source: Adapted from 'Balance sheets: the basics', www.businesslink.gov.uk, accessed 14 April 2010.

Self-assessment question 2.1

The following information relates to Simonson Engineering as at 30 September 2017:

	£
Plant and equipment	25,000
Trade payables	18,000
Short-term borrowings	26,000
Inventories	45,000
Property	72,000
Long-term borrowings	51,000
Trade receivables	48,000
Equity at 1 October 2016	117,500
Cash in hand	1,500
Motor vehicles	15,000
Fixtures and fittings	9,000
Profit for the year to 30 September 2017	18,000
Drawings for the year to 30 September 2017	15,000

Required:

(a) Prepare a statement of financial position for the business as at 30 September 2017 using the standard layout illustrated in Example 2.3.

(b) Comment on the financial position of the business based on the statement prepared in (a).

(c) Show the effect on the statement of financial position shown in (a) of a decision to revalue the property to £115,000 and to recognise that the net realisable value of inventories at the year end is £38,000.

The solution to this question can be found in at the back of the book on pp. 765–766.

Summary

The main points of this chapter may be summarised as follows:

The major financial statements

- There are three major financial statements: the statement of cash flows, the income statement and the statement of financial position.

- The statement of cash flows shows the cash movements over a particular period.

- The income statement shows the wealth (profit) generated over a particular period.

- The statement of financial position shows the accumulated wealth at a particular point in time.

The statement of financial position

- The statement of financial position sets out the assets of the business, on the one hand, and the claims against those assets, on the other.

- Assets are resources of the business that have certain characteristics, such as the potential to provide future economic benefits.

- Claims are obligations on the part of the business to provide cash, or some other benefit, to outside parties.
- Claims are of two types: equity and liabilities.
- Equity represents the claim(s) of the owner(s) and liabilities represent the claims of others.
- The statement of financial position reflects the accounting equation:

$$\text{Assets} = \text{Equity} + \text{Liabilities}$$

Classification of assets and liabilities

- Assets are normally categorised as being current or non-current.
- Current assets are cash or near cash or are held for sale or consumption in the normal course of business, or for trading, or for the short term.
- Non-current assets are assets that are not current assets. They are normally held for the long-term operations of the business.
- Liabilities are normally categorised as being current or non-current liabilities.
- Current liabilities represent amounts due in the normal course of the business's operating cycle, or are held for trading, or are to be settled within a year of, or cannot be deferred for at least a year after, the end of the reporting period.
- Non-current liabilities represent amounts due that are not current liabilities.

Statement of financial position layouts

- The standard layout begins with assets at the top of the statement of financial position and places equity and liabilities underneath.
- A variation of the standard layout also begins with the assets at the top of the statement of financial position, but then the non-current and current liabilities are deducted from the total assets figure to arrive at a net assets figure. Equity is placed underneath.

Accounting conventions

- Accounting conventions are the rules of accounting that have evolved to deal with practical problems experienced by those preparing financial statements.
- The main conventions relating to the statement of financial position include the business entity, historic cost, prudence, going concern and dual aspect conventions.

Money measurement

- Using money as the unit of measurement limits the scope of the statement of financial position.
- Certain resources such as goodwill, product brands and human resources are difficult to measure. An 'arm's-length transaction' is normally required before such assets can be reliably measured and reported on the statement of financial position.
- Money is not a stable unit of measurement – it changes in value over time.

Asset valuation

- The initial treatment is to show non-current assets at historic cost.
- Fair values may be used rather than historic cost, provided that they can be reliably obtained. This is rarely possible, however, for intangible non-current assets.

- Non-current assets with finite useful lives should be shown at cost (or fair value) less any accumulated depreciation (amortisation).
- Where the value of a non-current asset is impaired, it should be written down to its recoverable amount.
- Inventories are shown at the lower of cost or net realisable value.

The usefulness of the statement of financial position

- The statement of financial position shows how finance has been raised and how it has been deployed.
- It provides a basis for valuing the business, though it can only be a starting point.
- Relationships between various statement of financial position items can usefully be explored.
- Relationships between wealth generated and wealth invested can be a helpful indicator of business effectiveness.

Key terms

For definitions of these terms, see Appendix B.

statement of cash flows *p. 40*
income statement *p. 40*
statement of financial position *p. 40*
final accounts *p. 43*
assets *p. 44*
claims *p. 44*
trade receivable *p. 47*
tangible asset *p. 47*
intangible asset *p. 47*
equity *p. 48*
liability *p. 48*
reporting period *p. 51*
current asset *p. 54*
non-current (fixed) asset *p. 54*

property, plant and equipment *p. 54*
current liability *p. 56*
non-current liability *p. 56*
trade payable *p. 56*
accounting convention *p. 60*
business entity convention *p. 60*
historic cost convention *p. 60*
prudence convention *p. 61*
going concern convention *p. 62*
dual aspect convention *p. 63*
goodwill *p. 64*
fair value *p. 68*
impairment loss *p. 70*

Further reading

If you would like to explore the topics covered in this chapter in more depth, we recommend the following:

Elliott, B. and Elliott, J. (2015) *Financial Accounting and Reporting,* 17th edn, Pearson, Chapters 17, 19 and 20.

International Accounting Standards Board, *2016 A Guide through IFRS Standards (Green Book),* IAS 16 *Property, Plant and Equipment* and IAS 38 *Intangible Assets.*

KPMG, *Insights into IFRS,* 13th edn, Sweet and Maxwell, 2016/17, Sections 3.2, 3.3, 3.8 and 3.10 (a summarised version of this is available free at www.kpmg.com).

Melville, A. (2015) *International Financial Reporting: A Practical Guide,* 5th edn, Pearson, Chapters 5–7.

Review questions

Solutions to these questions can be found at the back of the book on pp. 787–788.

2.1 An accountant prepared a statement of financial position for a business. In this statement, the equity of the owner was shown next to the liabilities. This confused the owner, who argued, 'My equity is my major asset and so should be shown as an asset on the statement of financial position.' How would you explain this misunderstanding to the owner?

2.2 'The statement of financial position shows how much a business is worth.' Do you agree with this statement? Explain the reasons for your response.

2.3 What is meant by the accounting equation? How does the form of this equation differ between the two statement of financial position layouts mentioned in the chapter?

2.4 From time to time, there have been attempts to place a value on the 'human assets' of a business in order to derive a figure that can be included on the statement of financial position. Do you think humans should be treated as assets? Would 'human assets' meet the conventional definition of an asset for inclusion on the statement of financial position?

Exercises

Solutions to exercises with coloured numbers can be found at the back of the book on pp. 801–803.

Basic-level exercises

2.1 On Thursday, the fourth day of his business venture, Paul, the street trader in wrapping paper (see earlier in the chapter, pp. 40–43), bought more inventories for £53 cash. During the day he sold inventories that had cost £33 for a total of £47.

Required:
Draw up the three financial statements for Paul's business venture for Thursday.

2.2 The equity of Paul's business belongs to him because he is the sole owner of the business. Can you explain how the figure for equity by Thursday evening has arisen? You will need to look back at the events of Monday, Tuesday and Wednesday (pp. 40–43) to do this.

Intermediate-level exercises

2.3 While on holiday, Helen had her credit cards and purse stolen from the beach while she was swimming. She was left with only £40, which she had kept in her hotel room, but she had three days of her holiday remaining. She was determined to continue her holiday and decided to make some money to enable her to do so. She decided to sell orange juice to holidaymakers using the local beach. On the first day, she bought 80 cartons of orange juice at £0.50 each for cash and sold 70 of these at £0.80 each. On the following day, she bought 60 cartons at £0.50 each for cash and sold 65 at £0.80 each. On the third and final day, she bought another 60 cartons at £0.50 each for cash. However, it rained and, as a result, business was poor. She managed to sell 20 at £0.80 each but sold off the rest of her inventories at £0.40 each.

Required:
Prepare an income statement and statement of cash flows for each day's trading and prepare a statement of financial position at the end of each day's trading.

2.4 On 1 March, Joe Conday started a new business. During March he carried out the following transactions:

1 March	Deposited £20,000 in a newly opened business bank account.
2 March	Bought fixtures and fittings for £6,000 cash and inventories £8,000 on credit.
3 March	Borrowed £5,000 from a relative and deposited it in the bank.
4 March	Bought a motor car for £7,000 cash and withdrew £200 in cash for his own use.
5 March	Bought a further motor car costing £9,000. The motor car bought on 4 March was given in part exchange at a value of £6,500. The balance of the purchase price for the new car was paid in cash.
6 March	Conday won £2,000 in a lottery and paid the amount into the business bank account. He also repaid £1,000 of the borrowings.

Required:
Draw up a statement of financial position for the business at the end of each day.

2.5 The following is a list of assets and claims of a manufacturing business at a particular point in time:

	£
Short-term borrowings	22,000
Property	245,000
Inventories of raw materials	18,000
Trade payables	23,000
Plant and equipment	127,000
Loan from Manufacturing Finance Co. (long-term borrowing)	100,000
Inventories of finished goods	28,000
Delivery vans	54,000
Trade receivables	34,000

Required:
Write out a statement of financial position in the standard format incorporating these figures. (*Hint*: There is a missing item that needs to be deduced and inserted.)

Advanced-level exercises

2.6 The following is a list of the assets and claims of Crafty Engineering as at 30 June last year:

	£000
Trade payables	86
Motor vehicles	38
Long-term borrowing (loan from Industrial Finance Company)	260
Equipment and tools	207
Short-term borrowings	116
Inventories	153
Property	320
Trade receivables	185

Required:
(a) Prepare the statement of financial position of the business as at 30 June last year from the information provided, using the standard layout. (*Hint:* There is a missing item that needs to be deduced and inserted.)
(b) Discuss the significant features revealed by this financial statement.

2.7 The statement of financial position of a business at the start of the week is as follows:

	£
ASSETS	
Property	145,000
Furniture and fittings	63,000
Inventories	28,000
Trade receivables	33,000
Total assets	269,000
EQUITY AND LIABILITIES	
Equity	203,000
Short-term borrowing (bank overdraft)	43,000
Trade payables	23,000
Total equity and liabilities	269,000

During the week the following transactions take place:

(a) Sold inventories for £11,000 cash; these inventories had cost £8,000.
(b) Sold inventories for £23,000 on credit; these inventories had cost £17,000.
(c) Received cash from trade receivables totalling £18,000.
(d) The owners of the business introduced £100,000 of their own money, which was placed in the business bank account.
(e) The owners brought a motor van, valued at £10,000, into the business.
(f) Bought inventories on credit for £14,000.
(g) Paid trade payables £13,000.

Required:
Show the statement of financial position after all of these transactions have been reflected.

CHAPTER 3

Measuring and reporting financial performance

Introduction

In this chapter, we continue our examination of the major financial statements by looking at the income statement. This statement was briefly considered in Chapter 2, but we shall now look at it in some detail. We shall see how it is prepared and how it links with the statement of financial position. We shall also consider some of the key measurement problems to be faced when preparing the income statement.

Learning outcomes

When you have completed this chapter, you should be able to:

- discuss the nature and purpose of the income statement;

- prepare an income statement from relevant financial information and interpret the information that it contains;

- discuss the main recognition and measurement issues that must be considered when preparing the income statement; and

- explain the main accounting conventions underpinning the income statement.

The income statement

Businesses exist for the primary purpose of generating wealth, or **profit.** The income statement – or profit and loss account, as it is sometimes called – measures and reports how much profit a business has generated over a period. It is, therefore, an immensely important financial statement for many users.

To measure profit, the total **revenue** generated during a particular period must be identified. Revenue is simply a measure of the inflow of economic benefits arising from the ordinary operations of a business. These benefits result in either an increase in assets (such as cash or amounts owed to the business by its customers) or a decrease in liabilities. Different forms of business activities generate different forms of revenue. Some examples of the different forms that revenue can take are as follows:

- sales of goods (for example, by a manufacturer);
- fees for services (for example, of a solicitor);
- subscriptions (for example, of a club); and
- interest received (for example, on an investment fund).

Real World 3.1 shows the various forms of revenue generated by a leading football club.

Real World 3.1

Gunning for revenue

Arsenal Football Club generated total revenue of £353 million for the year ended 31 May 2016. Like other leading clubs, it relies on various forms of revenue to sustain its success. Figure 3.1 shows the contribution of each form of revenue for the year.

Figure 3.1   Arsenal's revenue for the year ended 31 May 2016

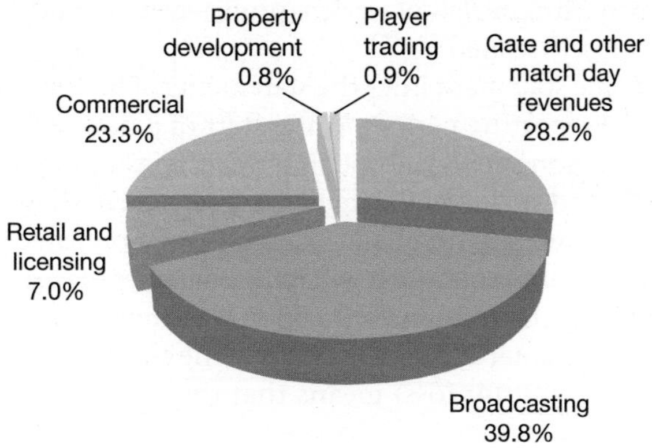

Gate receipts and broadcasting are Arsenal's main forms of revenue for 2016. These account for around two-thirds of the total revenue generated. Revenue during the year from player trading was insignificant.

Source: Based on information in Arsenal Holdings plc Statement of Accounts and Annual Report 2015/2016, p. 48.

The total expenses relating to each period must also be identified. An **expense** is really the opposite of revenue. It is a measure of the outflow of economic benefits for a financial period. This outflow results in either a decrease in assets (such as cash) or an increase in liabilities (such as amounts owed to suppliers). Expenses are normally incurred in the process of generating revenue or, at least, in attempting to generate it. The nature of the business will again determine the type of expenses that will be incurred. Examples of some of the more common types of expense are:

- the cost of buying or making the goods that are sold during the period concerned – known as **cost of sales** or *cost of goods sold*;
- salaries and wages;
- rent;
- motor vehicle running expenses;
- insurance;
- printing and stationery;
- heat and light; and
- telephone and postage.

The income statement simply shows the total revenue generated during a particular reporting period and deducts from this the total expenses incurred in generating that revenue. The difference between the total revenue and total expenses will represent either profit (if revenue exceeds expenses) or loss (if expenses exceed revenue). Therefore:

> **Profit (or loss) for the period = Total revenue for the period − Total expenses incurred in generating that revenue**

Different roles

The income statement and the statement of financial position are not substitutes for one another. Rather, they perform different roles. The statement of financial position sets out the wealth held by the business at a single moment in time, whereas the income statement is concerned with the *flow* of wealth (profit) over a period of time. The two statements are, however, closely related.

The income statement links the statements of financial position at the beginning and the end of a reporting period. At the start of a new reporting period, the statement of financial position shows the opening wealth position of the business. At the end of that reporting period, an income statement is prepared to show the wealth generated over that period. A statement of financial position is then prepared to reveal the new wealth position at the end of the period. It will reflect changes in wealth that have occurred since the previous statement of financial position was drawn up.

We saw in Chapter 2 (pages 51–53) that the effect on the statement of financial position of making a profit (or loss) means that the accounting equation can be extended as follows:

> **Assets (at the end of the period) = Equity (amount at the start of the period)**
> **+ Profit (or − Loss) for the period)**
> **+ Liabilities (at the end of the period)**

(This is assuming that the owner makes no injections or withdrawals of equity during the period.)

Activity (3.1)

Can you recall from Chapter 2 how a profit, or loss, for a period is shown in the statement of financial position?

It is shown as an adjustment to owners' equity. Profit is added and a loss is subtracted.

The accounting equation can be further extended to:

Assets (at the end of the period) = Equity (amount at the start of the period)
+ (Sales revenue − Expenses)(for the period)
+ Liabilities (at the end of the period)

In theory, it is possible to calculate the profit (or loss) for the period by making all adjustments for revenue and expenses through the equity section of the statement of financial position. However, this would be rather cumbersome. A better solution is to have an 'appendix' to the equity section, in the form of an income statement. By deducting expenses from revenue for the period, the income statement derives the profit (or loss) by which the equity figure in the statement of financial position needs to be adjusted. This profit (or loss) figure represents the net effect of trading for the period. Through this 'appendix', users are presented with a detailed and more informative view of performance.

Income statement layout

The layout of the income statement will vary according to the type of business to which it relates. To illustrate an income statement, let us consider the case of a retail business (that is, a business that buys goods in their completed state and resells them).

Example 3.1 sets out a typical layout for the income statement of a retail business.

Example 3.1

Better-Price Stores
Income statement for the year ended 30 June 2018

	£
Sales revenue	232,000
Cost of sales	(154,000)
Gross profit	78,000
Salaries and wages	(24,500)
Rent	(14,200)
Heat and light	(7,500)
Telephone and postage	(1,200)
Insurance	(1,000)
Motor vehicle running expenses	(3,400)
Depreciation – fixtures and fittings	(1,000)
– motor van	(600)
Operating profit	24,600
Interest received from investments	2,000
Interest on borrowings	(1,100)
Profit for the period	25,500

We saw in Chapter 2 that brackets are used to denote when an item is to be deducted. This convention is used by accountants in preference to + or − signs and will be used throughout the text.

We can see from Example 3.1 that three measures of profit have been calculated. Let us now consider each of these in turn.

Gross profit

The first part of the income statement is concerned with calculating the **gross profit** for the period. We can see that revenue, which arises from selling the goods, is the first item to appear. Deducted from this item is the cost of sales figure (also called cost of goods sold) during the period. This gives the gross profit, which represents the profit from buying and selling goods, without taking into account any other revenues or expenses associated with the business.

Operating profit

Operating expenses (overheads) incurred in running the business (salaries and wages, rent, insurance and so on) are deducted from the gross profit. The resulting figure is known as the **operating profit.** This represents the wealth generated during the period from the normal activities of the business. It does not take account of income from other activities. Better-Price Stores in Example 3.1 is a retailer, so interest received on some spare cash that the business has invested is not part of its operating profit. Costs of financing the business are also ignored in the calculation of the operating profit.

Profit for the period

Having established the operating profit, we add any non-operating income (such as interest receivable) and deduct any interest payable on borrowings to arrive at the **profit for the period** (or net profit). This final measure of wealth generated represents the amount attributable to the owner(s) and will be added to the equity figure in the statement of financial position. It is a residual: that is, the amount remaining after deducting all expenses incurred in generating the sales revenue and taking account of non-operating income and expenses.

Activity   **3.2**

Look back to Example 3.1 and assume that the income statement was prepared by a trainee accountant. Subsequent checking by the chief financial officer revealed the following errors:

1   Sales performance bonuses payable to staff amounting to £12,500 had been charged to cost of sales.
2   The depreciation charge for fixtures and fittings should be £10,000, not £1,000.
3   Stationery costing £500 had been treated as interest on borrowings.

What will be the gross profit, operating profit and profit for the period after these errors have been corrected?

Staff bonuses should be treated as part of the salaries and wages expense of the business. This means that cost of sales will decrease by £12,500 and gross profit will increase by a corresponding amount. The corrected gross profit is therefore £90,500 (that is, £78,000 + £12,500).

The operating profit and profit for the period, however, will not be affected by this correction. Although the operating expense salaries and wages will increase, this is offset by a compensating increase in gross profit.

The increase in the depreciation charge from £1,000 to £10,000 will decrease operating profit by £9,000. Furthermore, by treating stationery correctly, operating expenses will increase by £500, thereby decreasing operating profit by a corresponding amount. The corrected operating profit figure is, therefore, £15,100 (that is, £24,600 − £9,500).

Finally, the corrected profit for the period is calculated by taking the corrected operating profit £15,100, adding the interest received from investments, £2,000, and deducting the correct amount of interest on borrowing £600 (that is, £1,100 − £500) = £16,500.

Further issues

Having set out the main principles involved in preparing an income statement, we need to consider some further points.

Cost of sales

The cost of sales (or cost of goods sold) for a period can be identified in different ways. In some businesses, the cost of sales for each individual sale is identified at the time of the transaction. Each item of sales revenue is matched with the relevant cost of that sale. Many large retailers (for example, supermarkets) have point-of-sale (checkout) devices that not only record each sale but also simultaneously pick up the cost of the goods that are the subject of the particular sale. Businesses that sell a relatively small number of high-value items (for example, an engineering business that produces custom-made equipment) also tend to match sales revenue with the cost of the goods sold, at the time of sale. However, many businesses (for example, small retailers) may not find it practical to do this. Instead, they identify the cost of sales after the end of the reporting period.

To understand how this is done, we must remember that the cost of sales represents the cost of goods that were *sold* during the period rather than the cost of goods that were *bought* during the period. Part of the goods bought during the period may remain, as inventories, at the end of the period. These will normally be sold in the next period. To derive the cost of sales, we need to know the amount of opening and closing inventories for the period and the cost of goods bought during the period. Example 3.2 illustrates how the cost of sales is derived.

Example 3.2

Better-Price Stores, which we considered in Example 3.1, began the year with unsold inventories of £40,000 and during that year bought inventories at a cost of £189,000. At the end of the year, unsold inventories of £75,000 were still held by the business.

The opening (beginning of the year) inventories *plus* the goods bought during the year represent the total goods available for resale, as follows:

	£
Opening inventories	40,000
Purchases (goods bought)	189,000
Goods available for resale	229,000

The closing inventories represent that portion of the total goods available for resale that remains unsold at the end of the year. This means that the cost of goods actually sold during the year must be the total goods available for resale *less* the inventories remaining at the end of the year. That is:

	£
Goods available for resale	229,000
Closing inventories	(75,000)
Cost of sales (or cost of goods sold)	154,000

These calculations are sometimes shown on the face of the income statement as in Example 3.3.

Example 3.3

	£	£
Sales revenue		232,000
Cost of sales:		
Opening inventories	40,000	
Purchases (goods bought)	189,000	
Closing inventories	(75,000)	(154,000)
Gross profit		78,000

This is just an expanded version of the first section of the income statement for Better-Price Stores, as set out in Example 3.1. We have simply included the additional information concerning inventories balances and purchases for the year, provided in Example 3.2.

Classifying expenses

The classification of expense items is often a matter of judgement. For example, the income statement set out in Example 3.1 could have included the insurance expense with the telephone and postage expense under a single heading – say, 'general expenses'. Such decisions are normally based on how useful a particular classification will be to users. This will usually mean that expense items of material size will be shown separately. For businesses that trade as limited companies, however, rules dictate the classification of expense items for external reporting purposes. These rules will be discussed in Chapter 5.

Activity 3.3

The following information relates to the activities of H & S Retailers for the year ended 30 April 2017:

	£
Motor vehicle running expenses	1,200
Closing inventories	3,000
Rent payable	5,000
Motor vans – cost less depreciation	6,300
Annual depreciation – motor vans	1,500
Heat and light	900
Telephone and postage	450
Sales revenue	97,400
Goods purchased	68,350
Insurance	750
Loan interest payable	620
Balance at bank	4,780
Salaries and wages	10,400
Opening inventories	4,000

Prepare an income statement for the year ended 30 April 2017. (*Hint*: Not all items listed should appear on this statement.)

Your answer should be as follows:

H & S Retailers Income Statement for the year ended 30 April 2017

	£	£
Sales revenue		97,400
Cost of sales:		
Opening inventories	4,000	
Purchases	68,350	
Closing inventories	(3,000)	(69,350)
Gross profit		28,050
Salaries and wages		(10,400)
Rent payable		(5,000)
Heat and light		(900)
Telephone and postage		(450)
Insurance		(750)
Motor vehicle running expenses		(1,200)
Depreciation – motor vans		(1,500)
Operating profit		7,850
Loan interest		(620)
Profit for the period		7,230

Note that neither the motor vans nor the bank balance are included in this statement. This is because they are both assets and so are neither revenues nor expenses.

Figure 3.2 shows the layout of the income statement.

| Figure 3.2 | The layout of the income statement |

Recognising revenue

The revenue recognised should reflect the amount agreed with the customer for the transfer of goods or services. It should be recognised when the business has satisfied its obligations towards the customer. This occurs when control of the goods or services is transferred to the customer. Where control is transferred over time, the revenue should be recognised over time. This situation may arise where:

● *The customer enjoys the benefits as the business performs its obligations.* This can occur with service contracts, such as where an accounting firm undertakes employee payroll services for a large business.
● *The business creates, or improves, an asset held by the customer.* This can occur with building contracts, such as where a builder undertakes the refurbishment of a shop owned by a retailer.

- *The business creates an asset with no alternative use and the customer has agreed to pay for work carried out.* This can apply to special orders, such as where an engineering business produces specially-designed production equipment for a manufacturer.

Where revenue is recognised over time, the total amount should be spread across the reporting periods covered by the contract. In other words, part of the total contract price should be treated as revenue in each reporting period. To determine the appropriate amount for each period, we need some method of measuring progress towards transferring the goods or services. Various methods are available. Some are based on outputs, such as particular 'milestones' reached in completing the contract or the number of units produced or delivered. Others are based on inputs, such as resources consumed by the contract or hours expended by labour or by machines.

Activity 3.4

Generally speaking, are methods based on outputs or inputs likely to be more suitable in measuring progress towards transferring goods or services to customers?

Methods based on output often provide a direct measure of the value of goods or services transferred to customers. Methods based on input are less likely to do so.

Where methods based on output are unreliable, or unavailable, however, methods based on input may be chosen. There is no single correct method: it depends on the particular circumstances.

To illustrate an approach to recognising revenue over time, let us assume a manufacturer wishes to have a large factory built on its land. It enters into a contract with a builder to build the factory, which will take three years to complete. Building the factory can be broken down into the following stages:

- Stage 1 – clearing and levelling the land and putting in the foundations.
- Stage 2 – building the walls.
- Stage 3 – putting on the roof.
- Stage 4 – putting in the windows and completing all the interior work.

It is expected that Stage 1 of the contract will be completed by the end of Year 1, Stages 2 and 3 will be completed by the end of Year 2 and Stage 4 by the end of Year 3.

Normally, the manufacturer will pay a proportion of the total contract price following successful completion of each stage. This means that, once the performance obligations for a particular stage are satisfied, the builder can recognise as revenue the agreed proportion of the total contract price for that stage. Thus, the agreed proportion for completing Stage 1 will be reported as revenue in the income statement for Year 1 and so on.

Where revenue is not recognised over time, it will be recognised at the particular point in time when control is transferred. To determine when this point occurs, there are important indicators, such as when:

- physical possession passes to the customer;
- the business has the right to demand payment for the goods or services;
- the customer has accepted the goods or services;
- legal title passes to the customer; or
- significant risks and rewards of ownership passes to the customer.

Activity 3.5 provides an opportunity to apply the indicators mentioned above to a practical problem.

Activity 3.5

A manufacturer produces and sells a standard product on credit, which is transported to customers using the manufacturer's delivery vans. Managers believe there are four points in the production/selling cycle at which revenue might be recognised:

1 when the goods are produced;
2 when an order is received from a customer;
3 when the goods are passed to, and accepted by, the customer; and
4 when the cash is received from the customer.

At which of these points do you think the manufacturer should recognise revenue?

The indicators mentioned will usually point towards the third on the list: when the goods are passed to, and accepted by, the customer.

The point at which revenue is recognised can have a significant impact on reported revenues, and therefore profit, for a period. Where a credit sale transaction straddles the end of a reporting period, the point chosen for recognising revenue can determine whether it is included in the earlier reporting period or the later one.

We can see from Activity 3.5 that a sale on credit is usually recognised *before* the cash is received. This means that the total sales revenue shown in the income statement may include sales transactions for which the cash has yet to be received. The total sales revenue will often, therefore, be different from the total cash received from sales during the period. For cash sales (that is, sales where cash is paid at the same time as the goods are transferred), there will be no difference in timing between reporting sales revenue and cash received.

Activity 3.6

Although revenue for providing services is often recognised before the cash is received, there are occasions when a business demands payment before providing the service.

Can you think of any examples where cash may be demanded in advance of a service being provided? (*Hint*: Try to think of services that you may use.)

Examples of cash being received in advance of the service being provided may include:

- rent received from letting premises;
- telephone line rental charges;
- TV licence (BBC) or subscription fees (for example, Sky); and
- subscriptions received by health clubs or golf clubs.

You may have thought of others.

Recognising expenses

Having considered the recognition of revenue, let us now turn to the recognition of expenses. The **matching convention** provides guidance on this. This convention states that expenses should be matched to the revenue that they helped to generate. In other words, the expenses associated with a particular item of revenue must be taken into account in the same reporting period as that in which the item of revenue is included. We saw how this convention is applied with the costs of sales for Better-Price Stores in Example 3.2. The appropriate expense was just the cost of inventories that were sold and not the whole cost of inventories that were available for sale, during the period.

Applying this convention often means that an expense reported in the income statement for a period may not be the same as the cash paid for that item during the period. The expense reported might be either more or less than the cash paid during the period. Examples 3.4 and 3.5 illustrate this point.

When the expense for the period is more than the cash paid during the period

Example 3.4

Domestic Ltd, a retailer, sells household electrical appliances. It pays its sales staff a commission of 2 per cent of sales revenue generated. Total sales revenue for last year amounted to £300,000. This means that the commission to be paid on sales for the year will be £6,000. However, by the end of the year, the amount of sales commission actually paid was only £5,000. If the business reported this amount as the sales commission expense, it would mean that the income statement would not reflect the full expense for the year. This would contravene the matching convention because not all of the expenses associated with the revenue of the year would have been matched with it in the income statement. This will be remedied as follows:

- Sales commission expense in the income statement will include the amount paid plus the amount outstanding (that is, £6,000 = 5,000 + 1,000).
- The amount outstanding (£1,000) represents an outstanding liability at the end of the year and will be included under the heading **accrued expenses,** or 'accruals', in the statement of financial position. As this item will have to be paid within 12 months of the year-end, it will be treated as a current liability.
- The cash will already have been reduced to reflect the commission paid (£5,000) during the period.

These points are illustrated in Figure 3.3.

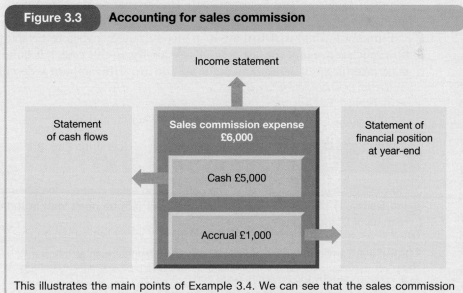

Figure 3.3   Accounting for sales commission

This illustrates the main points of Example 3.4. We can see that the sales commission expense of £6,000 (which appears in the income statement) is made up of a cash element of £5,000 and an accrued element of £1,000. The cash element appears in the statement of cash flows and the accrued

In principle, all expenses should be matched to the period in which the sales revenue to which they relate is reported. It is sometimes difficult, however, to match certain expenses to sales revenue in the same precise way that we have matched sales commission to sales revenue. For example, electricity charges incurred often cannot be linked directly to particular sales in this way. As a result, the electricity charges incurred by, say, a retailer would be matched to the *period* to which they relate. Example 3.5 illustrates this.

Example 3.5

Domestic Ltd, a retailer, has reached the end of its reporting period and has only paid for electricity for the first three quarters of the year (amounting to £1,900). This is simply because the electricity company has yet to send out bills for the quarter that ends on the same date as Domestic Ltd's year-end. The amount of Domestic Ltd's bill for the last quarter of the year is £500. In this situation, the amount of the electricity expense outstanding is dealt with as follows:

- Electricity expense in the income statement will include the amount paid, plus the amount of the bill for the last quarter of the year (that is, £1,900 + 500 = £2,400) in order to cover the whole year.
- The amount of the outstanding bill (£500) represents a liability at the end of the year and will be included under the heading 'accrued expenses' in the statement of financial position. This item would normally have to be paid within 12 months of the year-end and will, therefore, be treated as a current liability.
- The cash will already have been reduced to reflect the amount (£1,900) paid for electricity during the period.

This treatment will mean that the correct figure for the electricity expense for the year will be included in the income statement. It will also have the effect of showing that, at the end of the reporting period, Domestic Ltd owed the amount of the last quarter's electricity bill. Dealing with the outstanding amount in this way reflects the dual aspect of the item and will ensure that the accounting equation is maintained.

Domestic Ltd may wish to draw up its income statement before it is able to discover how much it owes for the last quarter's electricity. In this case, it is quite normal to make an estimate of the amount of the bill and to use this amount as described above.

Activity 3.7

How will the eventual payment of the outstanding sales commission (Example 3.4) and the electricity bill for the last quarter (Example 3.5) be dealt with in the accounting records of Domestic Ltd?

When these amounts are eventually paid, they will be dealt with as follows:

- reduce cash by the amounts paid; and
- reduce the amount of the accrued expense as shown on the statement of financial position by the same amounts.

Other expenses, apart from electricity charges, may also be matched to the period to which they relate.

Activity 3.8

Can you think of other expenses for a retailer that cannot be linked directly to sales revenue and for which matching will therefore be done on a time basis?

You may have thought of the following examples:

- rent payable;
- insurance;
- interest payable; and
- licence fees payable.

This is not an exhaustive list. You may have thought of others.

When the amount paid during the period is more than the full expense for the period

It is not unusual for a business to be in a situation where it has paid more during the year than the full expense for that year. Example 3.6 illustrates how we deal with this.

Example 3.6

Images Ltd, an advertising agency, normally pays rent for its premises quarterly in advance (on 1 January, 1 April, 1 July and 1 October). On the last day of the last reporting period (31 December), it paid the next quarter's rent (£4,000) to the following 31 March, which was a day earlier than required. This would mean that a total of five quarters' rent was paid during the year. If Images Ltd reports all of the cash paid as an expense in the income statement, this would be more than the full expense for the year. This would contravene the matching convention because a higher figure than the expenses associated with the revenue of the year would appear in the income statement.

The problem is overcome by dealing with the rental payment as follows:

- Show the rent for four quarters as the appropriate expense in the income statement (that is, 4 × £4,000 = £16,000).
- The cash (that is, 5 × £4,000 = £20,000) would already have been paid during the year.
- Show the quarter's rent paid in advance (£4,000) as a prepaid expense under assets in the statement of financial position. (The rent paid in advance will appear as a current asset in the statement of financial position, under the heading **prepaid expenses** or 'prepayments'.)

In the next reporting period, this prepayment will cease to be an asset and will become an expense in the income statement of that period. This is because the rent prepaid relates to the next period during which it will be 'used up'.

These points are illustrated in Figure 3.4.

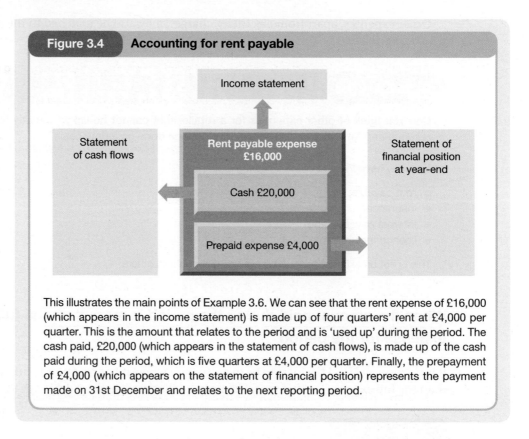

Figure 3.4   **Accounting for rent payable**

This illustrates the main points of Example 3.6. We can see that the rent expense of £16,000 (which appears in the income statement) is made up of four quarters' rent at £4,000 per quarter. This is the amount that relates to the period and is 'used up' during the period. The cash paid, £20,000 (which appears in the statement of cash flows), is made up of the cash paid during the period, which is five quarters at £4,000 per quarter. Finally, the prepayment of £4,000 (which appears on the statement of financial position) represents the payment made on 31st December and relates to the next reporting period.

In practice, the treatment of accruals and prepayments will be subject to the **materiality convention**. This convention states that, where the amounts involved are trivial, we should consider only what is expedient. This will usually mean treating an item as an expense in the period in which it is first recorded, rather than strictly matching it to the revenue to which it relates. For example, a large business may find that, at the end of a reporting period, it holds £2 worth of unused stationery. The time and effort taken to record this as a prepayment would outweigh the negligible effect on the measurement of profit or financial position. As a result, it would be treated as an expense of the current period and ignored in the following period.

Profit, cash and accruals accounting

We have seen that, normally, for a particular reporting period, total revenue is not the same as total cash received and total expenses are not the same as total cash paid. As a result, the profit for the period (that is, total revenue minus total expenses) will not normally represent the net cash generated during that period. This reflects the difference between profit and liquidity. Profit is a measure of achievement, or productive effort, rather than a measure of cash generated. Although making a profit increases wealth, cash is only one possible form in which that wealth may be held.

These points are reflected in the **accruals convention,** which asserts that profit is the excess of revenue over expenses for a period, not the excess of cash receipts over cash payments. Leading on from this, the approach to accounting that is based on the accruals convention is frequently referred to as **accruals accounting.** The statement of financial position and the income statement are both prepared on the basis of accruals accounting.

Activity 3.9

What about the statement of cash flows? Is it prepared on an accruals accounting basis?

No. The statement of cash flows simply deals with cash receipts and payments.

One major organisation, the UK government, has only recently adopted accruals accounting, despite the fact that this approach has been standard practice in all private-sector organisations, and many public-sector ones, for very many years. **Real World 3.2** is based on a *Financial Times* article that discusses the change of approach.

Real World 3.2

Casting light on the UK economy

Only recently (2014) has the UK government started using accruals accounting principles in its assessment of national output, for example, as measured by gross domestic product (GDP). Until then, it based its assessments of national economic output on a cash receipts and payments basis.

The main effect of the new accruals approach is that certain 'investments' will be recognised as such and will not simply be treated as 'expenses' in the year incurred, as they tend to be with a cash-based approach. Areas most affected by the switch to accruals accounting are:

● research and development, that is the acquisition of economically valuable knowledge;
● expenditure on weapons systems; and
● cash invested in pension schemes.

It is estimated that the effect of introducing accruals accounting will raise GDP by between 3.5 per cent and 5 per cent. Similar changes in the accounting approach taken in the United States added 3.5 per cent to its GDP.

 Source: Based on Giles, C. (2014) Accounting rules unravel the mysteries of Britain's economy, ft.com, 23 April. © The Financial Times Ltd 2014. All Rights Reserved.

Depreciation

The expense of **depreciation,** which we have already come across, requires further examination. Most non-current assets do not have a perpetual existence, but have finite, or limited, lives. They are eventually 'used up' in the process of generating revenue for the business. This 'using up' may relate to physical deterioration (as with a motor vehicle). It may, however, be linked to obsolescence (as with some IT software that is no longer useful) or the mere passage of time (as with a purchased patent, which has a limited period of validity).

In essence, depreciation is an attempt to measure that portion of the cost (or fair value) of a non-current asset that has been depleted in generating the revenue recognised during a particular period. In the case of intangibles, some people refer to the expense as **amortisation,** rather than *depreciation*.

Calculating the depreciation expense

To calculate a depreciation expense for a period, four factors have to be considered:

- the cost (or fair value) of the asset;
- the useful life of the asset;
- the residual value of the asset; and
- the depreciation method.

The cost (or fair value) of the asset

The cost of an asset will include all costs incurred by the business to bring the asset to its required location and to make it ready for use. This means that, in addition to the cost of acquiring the asset, any delivery costs, installation costs (for example, setting up a new machine) and legal costs incurred in the transfer of legal title (for example, in purchasing a lease on property) will be included as part of the total cost of the asset. Similarly, any costs incurred in improving or altering an asset to make it suitable for use will also be included as part of the total cost.

Activity 3.10

Andrew Wu (Engineering) Ltd bought a new motor car for its marketing director. The invoice received from the motor car supplier showed the following:

	£
New BMW 325i	28,350
Delivery charge	280
Alloy wheels	860
Sun roof	600
Petrol	80
Number plates	130
Road fund licence	150
	30,450
Part exchange – Reliant Robin	(1,000)
Amount outstanding	29,450

What is the total cost of the new car to be treated as part of the business's property, plant and equipment?

The cost of the new car will be as follows:

	£
New BMW 325i	28,350
Delivery charge	280
Alloy wheels	860
Sun roof	600
Number plates	130
	30,220

This cost includes delivery charges, which are necessary to bring the asset into use, and it includes number plates, as they are a necessary and integral part of the asset. Improvements (alloy wheels and sun roof) are also regarded as part of the total cost of the car. The petrol and road fund licence, however, are costs of operating the asset. These amounts will, therefore, be treated as expenses in the period in which they were incurred (although part of the cost of the licence may be regarded as a prepaid expense in the period in which it was incurred).

The part-exchange figure shown is part payment of the total amount outstanding and so is not relevant to a consideration of the total cost.

The fair value of an asset was defined in Chapter 2 as the selling price that could be obtained in an orderly transaction under market conditions. As we saw, assets may be revalued to fair value only if this can be measured reliably. Where fair values have been applied, the depreciation expense should be based on those fair values, rather than on the historic costs.

The useful life of the asset

A non-current asset has both a *physical life* and an *economic life.* The physical life will be exhausted through the effects of wear and tear and/or the passage of time. The economic life is decided by the effects of technological progress, by changes in demand or by changes in the way that the business operates. The benefits provided by the asset are eventually outweighed by the costs as it becomes unable to compete with newer assets, or becomes irrelevant to the needs of the business. The economic life of an asset may be much shorter than its physical life. For example, a computer may have a physical life of eight years and an economic life of three years.

The economic life determines the expected *useful life* of an asset for depreciation purposes. It is often difficult to estimate, however, as technological progress and shifts in consumer tastes can be swift and unpredictable.

Residual value (disposal value)

When a business disposes of a non-current asset that may still be of value to others, some payment may be received. This payment will represent the **residual value,** or *disposal value*, of the asset. To calculate the total amount to be depreciated, the residual value must be deducted from the cost (or fair value) of the asset. The likely amount to be received on disposal can, once again, be difficult to predict. The best guide is often past experience of similar assets sold.

Depreciation method

Once the amount to be depreciated (that is, the cost, or fair value, of the asset less any residual value) has been estimated, the business must select a method of allocating this depreciable amount between the reporting periods covering the asset's useful life. Although there are various ways in which this may be done, there are only two methods that are commonly used in practice.

The first of these is known as the **straight-line method.** This method simply allocates the amount to be depreciated evenly over the useful life of the asset. In other words, there is an equal depreciation expense for each year that the asset is held. Example 3.7 illustrates this.

Example 3.7

Consider the following information:

Cost of machine	£78,124
Estimated residual value at the end of its useful life	£2,000
Estimated useful life	4 years

To arrive at the depreciation expense for each year, the total amount to be depreciated must be calculated. This will be the total cost less the estimated residual value: that is, £78,124 − £2,000 = £76,124. The annual depreciation expense can then be derived by dividing the amount to be depreciated by the estimated useful life of the asset of four years. The calculation is therefore:

$$\frac{£76,124}{4} = £19,031$$

This means that the annual depreciation expense that appears in the income statement in relation to this asset will be £19,031 for each of the four years of the asset's life.

The amount of depreciation relating to the asset will be accumulated for as long as the asset continues to be owned by the business or until the accumulated depreciation amounts to the cost less residual value. This accumulated depreciation figure will increase each year as a result of the annual depreciation expense in the income statement. This accumulated amount will be deducted from the cost of the asset in the statement of financial position. At the end of the second year, for example, the accumulated depreciation will be £19,031 × 2 = £38,062. The asset details will appear on the statement of financial position as follows:

	£
Machine at cost	78,124
Accumulated depreciation	(38,062)
	40,062

As we saw in Chapter 2, this balance of £40,062 is referred to as the **carrying amount** (sometimes also known as the **written-down value** or **net book value**) of the asset. It represents that portion of the cost (or fair value) of the asset that has still to be treated as an expense (written off) in future years plus the residual value. This carrying-amount figure does not, except by coincidence, represent the current market value, which may be quite different. The only point at which the carrying amount is intended to represent the market value of the asset is at the time of its disposal. In Example 3.7, at the end of the four-year life of the machine, the carrying amount would be £2,000 – its estimated disposal value.

The straight-line method derives its name from the fact that the carrying amount of the asset at the end of each year, when plotted against time, will result in a straight line, as shown in Figure 3.5.

The second approach to calculating the depreciation expense for a period is referred to as the **reducing-balance method.** This method applies a fixed percentage rate of depreciation to the carrying amount of the asset each year. The effect of this will be high annual depreciation expenses in the early years and lower expenses in the later years. To illustrate this method, let us take the same information that was used in Example 3.7. By using a

Figure 3.5	Graph of carrying amount against time using the straight-line method

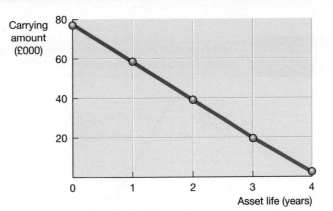

The carrying amount of the asset in Example 3.7 declines by a constant amount each year (£19,031). This is because the straight-line method provides a constant depreciation expense each year. The result, when plotted on a graph, is a straight line.

fixed percentage of 60 per cent of the carrying amount to determine the annual depreciation expense, the effect will be to reduce the carrying amount to £2,000 after four years.
The calculations will be as follows:

	£
Cost of machine	78,124
Year 1 depreciation expense (60%* of cost)	(46,874)
Carrying amount	31,250
Year 2 depreciation expense (60% of carrying amount)	(18,750)
Carrying amount	12,500
Year 3 depreciation expense (60% of carrying amount)	(7,500)
Carrying amount	5,000
Year 4 depreciation expense (60% of carrying amount)	(3,000)
Residual value	2,000

* See the box below for an explanation of how to derive the fixed percentage.

Deriving the fixed percentage

Deriving the fixed percentage to be applied requires the use of the following formula:

$$P = (1 - \sqrt[n]{R/C} \times 100\%)$$

where

P = the depreciation percentage
n = the useful life of the asset (in years)
R = the residual value of the asset
C = the cost, or fair value, of the asset.

The fixed percentage rate will, however, be given in all examples used in this book.

We can see that the pattern of depreciation is quite different between the two methods. If we plot against time the carrying amount of the asset that has been derived using the reducing-balance method, the result will be as shown in Figure 3.6.

Figure 3.6	**Graph of carrying amount against time using the reducing-balance method**

Under the reducing-balance method, the carrying amount of the asset in Example 3.7 falls by a larger amount in the earlier years than in the later years. This is because the depreciation expense is based on a fixed percentage of the carrying amount.

Activity 3.11

Assume that the machine in Example 3.7 was owned by a business that made a profit before depreciation of £40,000 for each of the four years in which the asset was held.

Calculate the profit for the business for each year under each depreciation method, and comment on your findings.

Your answer should be as follows:

Straight-line method

	(a) Profit before depreciation £	(b) Depreciation £	(a − b) Profit £
Year 1	40,000	19,031	20,969
Year 2	40,000	19,031	20,969
Year 3	40,000	19,031	20,969
Year 4	40,000	19,031	20,969

Reducing-balance method

	(a) Profit before depreciation	(b) Depreciation	(a − b) Profit
	£	£	£
Year 1	40,000	46,874	(6,874)
Year 2	40,000	18,750	21,250
Year 3	40,000	7,500	32,500
Year 4	40,000	3,000	37,000

The straight-line method of depreciation results in the same profit figure for each year of the four-year period. This is because both the profit before depreciation and the depreciation expense are constant over the period. The reducing-balance method, however, results in very different profit figures for the four years, despite the fact that in this example the pre-depreciation profit is the same each year. In the first year a loss is reported and, thereafter, a rising profit.

Although the *pattern* of profit over the four-year period will be quite different, depending on the depreciation method used, the *total* profit for the period (£83,876) will remain the same. This is because both methods of depreciating will allocate the same amount of total depreciation (£76,124) over the four-year period. It is only the amount allocated *between years* that will differ.

In practice, the use of different depreciation methods may not have such a dramatic effect on profits as suggested in Activity 3.11. This is because businesses typically have more than one depreciating non-current asset. Where a business replaces some of its assets each year, the total depreciation expense calculated under the reducing-balance method will reflect a range of expenses (from high through to low), as assets will be at different points in their economic lives. This could mean that each year's total depreciation expense may not be significantly different from that which would have been derived under the straight-line method.

Selecting a depreciation method

The appropriate depreciation method to choose is the one that reflects the consumption of economic benefits provided by the asset. Where the economic benefits are consumed evenly over time (for example, with buildings) the straight-line method is usually appropriate. Where the economic benefits consumed decline over time (for example, with certain types of machinery that lose their efficiency) the reducing-balance method may be more appropriate. Where the pattern of economic benefits consumed is uncertain, the straight-line method is normally chosen.

There is an International Financial Reporting Standard (or International Accounting Standard) to deal with the depreciation of property, plant and equipment. As we shall see in Chapter 5, the purpose of accounting standards is to narrow areas of accounting difference and to ensure that information provided to users is transparent and comparable. The relevant standard endorses the view that the depreciation method chosen should reflect the pattern of consumption of economic benefits but does not specify particular methods to be used. It states that the useful life, depreciation method and residual values for property, plant and equipment. should be reviewed at least annually and adjustments made where appropriate. For intangible non-current assets with finite lives, there is a separate standard containing broadly similar rules.

Real World 3.3 sets out the depreciation policies of one large business.

Real World 3.3

Depreciating assets

Halfords Group plc is a major retailer of automotive and cycling products. It also operates a chain of auto repair centres. The business sells exclusive and own-branded products (such as C Boardman bikes) as well as third-party branded products.

The following describes how intangible non-current assets that have been acquired are amortised (depreciated) over time.

> Amortisation is recognised in profit or loss on a straight-line basis over the estimated useful lives of intangible assets, other than goodwill, from the date that they are available for use, since this most closely reflects the expected pattern of consumption of the future economic benefits embodied in the asset. The estimated useful lives for the current and comparative periods are as follows:

- Brand names and trademarks 2 years, in respect of Autocentres, and 10 years in respect of Boardman;
- Customer relationships 5 to 15 years; and
- Favourable leases over the term of the lease.

Halford's policy for depreciating property plant and equipment is described as follows:

> Depreciation of property, plant and equipment is provided to write off the cost, less residual value, on a straight-line basis over their useful economic lives as follows:

- Leasehold premises with lease terms of 50 years or less are depreciated over the remaining period of the lease;
- Leasehold improvements are depreciated over the period of the lease to a maximum of 25 years;
- Motor vehicles are depreciated over 3 years;
- Fixtures, fittings and equipment are depreciated over 4 to 10 years according to the estimated life of the asset;
- Computer equipment is depreciated over 3 years; and
- Land is not depreciated.

Source: Extracts from Halfords Group plc Annual Report and Accounts 2016, Accounting policies, pp. 87–88.

Halfords is typical of most UK businesses in that it uses the straight-line method. The reducing-balance method is much less popular.

The approach taken to calculating depreciation is summarised in Figure 3.7.

| Figure 3.7 | Calculating the annual depreciation expense |

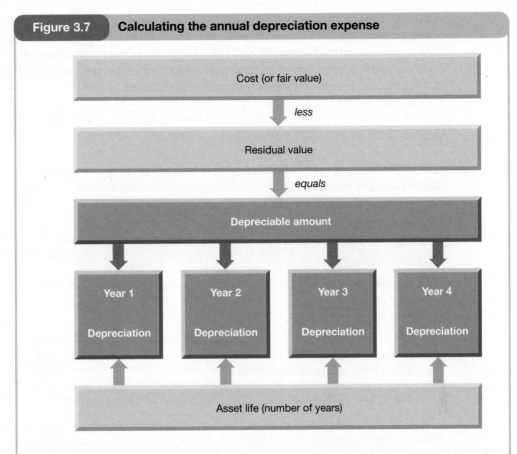

The cost (or fair value) of an asset less the residual value will represent the amount to be depreciated. This amount is depreciated over the useful life (four years in this particular case) of the asset using an appropriate depreciation method.

Impairment and depreciation

We saw in Chapter 2 that all non-current assets could be subjected to an impairment test. Where a non-current asset with a finite life has its carrying amount reduced following an impairment test, depreciation expenses for future reporting periods should be based on the impaired value.

Depreciation and asset replacement

Some appear to believe that the purpose of depreciation is to provide the funds for the replacement of a non-current asset when it reaches the end of its useful life. However, this is not the case. It was mentioned earlier that depreciation represents an attempt to allocate the cost or fair value (less any residual value) of a non-current asset over its expected useful life. The depreciation expense for a particular reporting period is used in calculating profit for that period. If a depreciation charge is excluded from the income statement, we shall not have a fair measure of financial performance. Whether or not the business intends to replace the asset in the future is irrelevant.

Where an asset is to be replaced, the depreciation expense in the income statement will not ensure that liquid funds are set aside specifically for this purpose. Although the depreciation expense will reduce profit, and therefore reduce the amount that the owners may decide to withdraw, the amounts retained within the business as a result may be invested in ways that are unrelated to the replacement of the asset.

Depreciation and judgement

From our discussions about depreciation, it is clear that accounting is not as precise and objective as it is sometimes portrayed as being. There are areas where subjective judgement is required.

Activity 3.12

What judgements must be made to calculate a depreciation expense for a period?

You may have thought of the following:

- the expected residual or disposal value of the asset;
- the expected useful life of the asset; and
- the choice of depreciation method.

Making different judgements on these matters would result in a different pattern of depreciation expenses over the life of the asset and, therefore, in a different pattern of reported profits. However, any underestimations or overestimations that are made will be adjusted for in the final year of an asset's life. As a result, the total depreciation expense (and total profit) over the asset's life will not be affected by estimation errors.

Real World 3.4 describes the effect on annual performance of extending the useful life of a non-current asset held by a well-known business.

Real World 3.4

Engineering an improvement?

BA reported a loss of £358 million for the 2008/09 financial year. This loss, however, would have been significantly higher had the business not changed its depreciation policies. The 2008/09 annual report of the business states:

> During the prior year, the Group changed the depreciation period for the RB211 engine, used on Boeing 747 and 767 fleets, from 54 months to 78 months. The change resulted in a £33 million decrease in the annual depreciation charge for this engine type.

Source: British Airways Annual Report and Accounts 2008/09, Note 15, www.britishairways.com.

Sally Dalton (Packaging) Ltd bought a machine for £40,000. At the end of its useful life of four years, the amount received on sale was £4,000. When the asset was bought the business received two estimates of the likely residual value of the asset. These were: (a) £8,000 and (b) zero.

Show the annual depreciation expenses over the four years and the total depreciation expenses for the asset under each of the two estimates. The straight-line method should be used to calculate the annual depreciation expenses.

The depreciation expense, assuming estimate (a), will be £8,000 a year (that is, (£40,000 − £8,000)/4). The depreciation expense, assuming estimate (b), will be £10,000 a year (that is, £40,000/4). As the actual residual value is £4,000, estimate (a) will lead to under-depreciation of £4,000 (that is, £8,000 − £4,000) over the life of the asset and estimate (b) will lead to over-depreciation of £4,000 (that is, £0 − £4,000). These under- and overestimations will be dealt with in Year 4.

The pattern of depreciation and total depreciation expenses will therefore be:

		Estimate	
		(a)	(b)
Year		£	£
1	Annual depreciation	8,000	10,000
2	Annual depreciation	8,000	10,000
3	Annual depreciation	8,000	10,000
4	Annual depreciation	8,000	10,000
		32,000	40,000
4	Under/(over)-depreciation	4,000	(4,000)
	Total depreciation	36,000	36,000

The final adjustment for under-depreciation of an asset is often referred to as 'loss (or deficit) on disposal of a non-current asset', as the amount actually received is less than the residual value. Similarly, the adjustment for over-depreciation is often referred to as 'profit (or surplus) on disposal of a non-current asset'. These final adjustments are normally made as an addition to the expense (or a reduction in the expense) for depreciation in the reporting period during which the asset is disposed of.

In practice, would you expect it to be more likely that the amount of depreciation would be overestimated or underestimated? **Why?**

We might expect there to be systematic overestimations of the annual depreciation expense. This is because the prudence convention tends to encourage a cautious approach to estimating the lives and residual values of assets.

Costing inventories

The cost of inventories is important in determining financial performance and position. The cost of inventories sold during a reporting period will affect the calculation of profit and the cost of inventories held at the end of the reporting period will affect the portrayal of assets held.

To calculate the cost of inventories, an assumption must be made about the physical flow of inventories through the business. This assumption need not have anything to do with how inventories *actually* flow through the business. It is concerned only with providing useful measures of performance and position.

Three common assumptions used are:

- **first in, first out (FIFO),** in which inventories are costed *as if* the earliest acquired inventories held are the first to be used;
- **last in, first out (LIFO),** in which inventories are costed *as if* the latest acquired inventories held are the first to be used; and
- **weighted average cost (AVCO),** in which inventories are costed *as if* inventories acquired lose their separate identity and go into a 'pool'. Any issues of inventories from this pool will reflect the weighted average cost of inventories held.

During a period of changing prices, the choice of assumption used in costing inventories can be important. Example 3.8 provides an illustration of how each assumption is applied and the effect of each on financial performance and position.

Example 3.8

A business that supplies grass seed to farmers and horticulturalists has the following transactions during a period:

		Tonnes	Cost/tonne £
1 May	Opening inventories	100	100
2 May	Bought	500	110
3 May	Bought	800	120
		1,400	
6 May	Sold	(900)	
	Closing inventories	500	

First in, first out (FIFO)

Using the FIFO approach, the first 900 tonnes of seed bought are treated as if these are the ones that are sold. This will consist of the opening inventories (100 tonnes), the purchases made on 2 May (500 tonnes) and some of the purchases made on 3 May (300 tonnes). The remainder of the 3 May purchases (500 tonnes) will comprise the closing inventories. This means that we have:

	Cost of sales			Closing inventories		
	Tonnes	Cost/tonne £	Total £000	Tonnes	Cost/tonne £	Total £000
1 May	100	100	10.0			
2 May	500	110	55.0			
3 May	300	120	36.0	500	120	60.0
Cost of sales			101.0	**Closing inventories**		60.0

Last in, first out (LIFO)

Using the LIFO assumption, the later purchases will be treated as if these were the first to be sold. This is the 3 May purchases (800 tonnes) and some of the 2 May purchases (100 tonnes). The earlier purchases (the rest of the 2 May purchase and the opening inventories) will comprise the closing inventories. This can be set out as follows:

	Cost of sales			Closing inventories		
	Tonnes	Cost/tonne £	Total £000	Tonnes	Cost/tonne £	Total £000
3 May	800	120	96.0			
2 May	100	110	11.0	400	110	44.0
1 May				100	100	10.0
Cost of sales			107.0	**Closing inventories**		54.0

Figure 3.8 contrasts LIFO and FIFO.

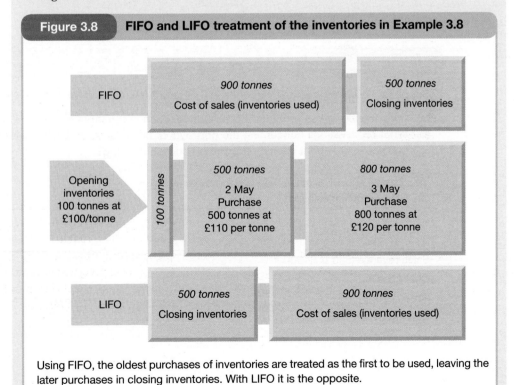

Figure 3.8   FIFO and LIFO treatment of the inventories in Example 3.8

Using FIFO, the oldest purchases of inventories are treated as the first to be used, leaving the later purchases in closing inventories. With LIFO it is the opposite.

Weighted average cost (AVCO)

Using the AVCO assumption, a weighted average cost will be determined that will be used to derive both the cost of goods sold and the cost of the remaining inventories held. This simply means that the total cost of the opening inventories and of the 2 May and 3 May purchases are added together and divided by the total number of tonnes to obtain the weighted average cost per tonne. Both the cost of sales and closing inventories values are based on that average cost per tonne. This means that we have:

	Tonnes	Cost/tonne £	Total £000
1 May	100	100	10.0
2 May	500	110	55.0
3 May	800	120	96.0
	1,400		161.0

The average cost is £161,000/1,400 = 115 per tonne.

Cost of sales			Closing inventories		
Tonnes	Cost/tonne £	Total £000	Tonnes	Cost/tonne £	Total £000
900	115	103.5	500	115	57.5

Activity 3.15

Suppose the 900 tonnes of inventories in Example 3.8 were sold for £150 per tonne.

(a) Calculate the gross profit for this sale under each of the three methods.
(b) What observations concerning the portrayal of financial position and performance can you make about each method when prices are rising?

Your answer should be along the following lines:
(a) Gross profit calculation:

	FIFO £000	LIFO £000	AVCO £000
Sales revenue (900 @ £150)	135.0	135.0	135.0
Cost of sales	(101.0)	(107.0)	(103.5)
Gross profit	34.0	28.0	31.5
Closing inventories	60.0	54.0	57.5

(b) These figures reveal that FIFO will give the highest gross profit during a period of rising prices. This is because sales revenue is matched with the earlier (and cheaper) purchases. LIFO will give the lowest gross profit because sales revenue is matched against the more recent (and dearer) purchases. The AVCO method will normally give a figure that is between these two extremes.

The closing inventories figure in the statement of financial position will be highest with the FIFO method. This is because the cost of goods still held will be based on the more recent (and dearer) purchases. LIFO will give the lowest closing inventories figure, as the goods held will be based on the earlier (and cheaper) purchases. Once again, the AVCO method will normally give a figure that is between these two extremes.

Activity 3.16

Assume that prices are falling rather than rising. How would your observations concerning the portrayal of financial performance and position be different for the various costing methods?

When prices are falling, the positions of FIFO and LIFO are reversed. FIFO will give the lowest gross profit as sales revenue is matched against the earlier (and dearer) goods bought. LIFO will give the highest gross profit as sales revenue is matched against the more recent (and cheaper) goods bought. AVCO will give a cost of sales figure between these two extremes. The closing inventories figure in the statement of financial position will be lowest under FIFO, as the cost of inventories will be based on the more recent (and cheaper) purchases. LIFO will provide the highest closing inventories figure and AVCO will provide a figure between the two extremes.

The different costing assumptions only have an effect on reported profit from one reporting period to the next. The figure derived for closing inventories will be carried forward and matched with sales revenue in a later period. If the cheaper purchases of inventories are matched to sales revenue in the current period, it will mean that the dearer purchases will be matched to sales revenue in a later period. Over the life of the business, therefore, total profit will be the same either way.

Inventories – some further issues

We saw in Chapter 2 that the convention of prudence requires that inventories be valued at the lower of cost and net realisable value. (The net realisable value of inventories is the estimated selling price less any further costs necessary to complete the goods and any costs involved in selling and distributing them.) In theory, this means that the valuation method applied to inventories could switch each year, depending on which of cost and net realisable value is the lower. In practice, however, the cost of the inventories held is usually below the current net realisable value – particularly during a period of rising prices. It is, therefore, the cost figure that will normally appear in the statement of financial position.

Activity (3.17)

Can you think of any circumstances where the net realisable value will be lower than the cost of inventories held, even during a period of generally rising prices? Try to think of at least two.

The net realisable value may be lower where:

● goods have deteriorated or become obsolete;
● there has been a fall in the market price of the goods;
● the goods are being used as a 'loss leader', that is, they are deliberately going to be sold at a price lower than their cost; and/or
● bad buying decisions have been made.

There is also an International Financial Reporting Standard that deals with inventories. It states that, when preparing financial statements for external reporting, the cost of inventories should normally be determined using either FIFO or AVCO. The LIFO assumption is not acceptable for external reporting. There is no reason, however, that a business should not apply LIFO when preparing financial statements for use by its own managers. The standard also requires the 'lower of cost and net realisable value' rule to be used and so endorses the application of the prudence convention.

Real World 3.5 sets out the inventories' costing methods used by some of the UK's leading businesses.

Real World 3.5

Counting the cost

Inventories costing methods used by some large UK businesses are as follows.

Name	Type of Business	Costing method used
J Sainsbury plc	Supermarket	AVCO
Babcock International plc	Engineering support services	FIFO
British American Tobacco plc	Tobacco manufacturer	AVCO
Premier Foods plc	Food manufacturer	FIFO
Halfords Group plc	Automotive and leisure products	AVCO
Marks and Spencer plc	Food and clothing retailer	AVCO
Diageo plc	Alcoholic beverages	AVCO
AstraZeneca plc	Pharmaceuticals	FIFO or AVCO

Source: Annual reports of the relevant businesses for 2015 or 2016.

Note that AstraZeneca plc employs more than one inventories' costing method. This presumably means that the costing method will vary according to product type, location or some other key factor.

The table simply sets out a small sample of well-known businesses and so we cannot assess the relative popularity of the FIFO and LIFO methods in practice on the basis of this.

Costing inventories and depreciation provide two examples where the **consistency convention** should be applied. This convention holds that once a particular method of accounting is selected, it should be applied consistently over time. It would not be acceptable to switch from, say, FIFO to AVCO between periods (unless exceptional circumstances make it appropriate). The purpose of this convention is to help users make valid comparisons of performance and position from one period to the next.

Activity 3.18

Reporting inventories in the financial statements provides a further example of the need to apply subjective judgement. For the inventories of a retail business, what are the main judgements that are required?

The main judgements are:

- the choice of costing method (FIFO, LIFO, AVCO); and
- deducing the net realisable value figure for inventories held.

One final point before leaving this topic. Costing inventories using FIFO, LIFO and AVCO applies to items that are interchangeable. Where they are not, as would be the case with custom-made items, the specific cost of the individual items must be used.

Trade receivables problems

We have seen that, when businesses sell goods or services on credit, revenue will usually be recognised before the customer pays the amounts owing. Recording the dual aspect of a credit sale will involve increasing sales revenue and increasing trade receivables by the amount of the revenue from the credit sale.

With this type of sale, there is always the risk that the customer will not pay the amount due. Where it becomes reasonably certain that the customer will not pay, the amount owed is considered to be a **bad debt,** which must be taken into account when preparing the financial statements.

Activity 3.19

What would be the effect on the income statement, and on the statement of financial position, of not taking into account the fact that a debt is bad?

The effect would be to overstate the assets (trade receivables) on the statement of financial position and to overstate profit in the income statement, as the revenue that has been recognised will not result in any future benefit.

To provide a more realistic picture of financial performance and position, the bad debt must be 'written off'. This will involve reducing the trade receivables and increasing expenses (by creating an expense known as 'bad debts written off') by the amount of the bad debt. The matching convention requires that the bad debt is written off in the same period as the sale that gave rise to the debt is recognised.

Note that, when a debt is bad, the accounting response is not simply to cancel the original sale. If this were done, the income statement would not be so informative. Reporting the bad debts as an expense can be extremely useful in assessing management performance.

Real World 3.6 indicates the level of bad debts incurred among small and medium size businesses European businesses.

Real World 3.6

Bad news

A survey of small and medium size businesses across 29 European countries, and generating a total of 9,440 responses, revealed the following level of bad debts within industry sectors:

Proportion of yearly revenues written-off 2015

	%
Real estate activities	1.6
Manufacturing	1.7
Accommodation and food service activities	1.8
Wholesale and retail trade	2.2
Public administration, education and human health	2.6
Professional, administrative and support service	2.7
Construction	2.7
Agriculture, forestry and fishing	2.8
Information and communication	2.9
Electricity, gas, steam and air conditioning supply	3.1
Transportation and storage	3.2
Financial and insurance activities	3.9
Mining and quarrying	4.5

Source: European Payment Industry White Paper 2016, p. 4, www.intrum.com.

Doubtful debts

At the end of a reporting period, it may not be possible to identify, with certainty, all bad debts incurred during the period. Doubts may surround certain trade receivables, but it may only be at a later date that the true position will become clear. Nevertheless, the possibility that some trade receivables will not be paid should not be ignored. It would not be prudent, nor would it comply with the need to match expenses to the period in which the associated revenue is recognised.

The business must try to determine the amount of trade receivables that, at the end of the period, are doubtful (that is, there is a possibility that they may eventually prove to be bad). This amount may be derived by examining individual trade receivables accounts or by taking a proportion (the exact proportion being based on past experience) of the total trade receivables outstanding.

Once a figure has been derived, an expense known as an **allowance for trade receivables** should be recognised. This will be shown as an expense in the income statement and deducted from the total trade receivables figure in the statement of financial position. In this way, full account is taken, in the appropriate reporting period, of those trade receivables where there is a risk of non-payment. This accounting treatment of these 'doubtful' trade receivables will be in addition to the treatment of the 'more definite' bad debts described above.

Example 3.9 illustrates the reporting of bad debts and allowances for trade receivables.

Example 3.9

Desai Enterprises had trade receivables of £350,000 outstanding at the end of the reporting period to 30 June 2017. Investigation of these trade receivables revealed that £10,000 would probably be irrecoverable and that there was doubt concerning the recoverability of a further £30,000.

Relevant extracts from the income statement for that year would be as follows:

Income statement (extracts) for the year ended 30 June 2017

	£
Bad debts written off	10,000
Allowances for trade receivables	30,000

Statement of financial position (extracts) as at 30 June 2017

	£
Trade receivables	340,000*
Allowances for trade receivables	(30,000)
	310,000

*That is, £350,000 less £10,000 irrecoverable trade receivables.

The allowances for trade receivables figure is, of course, an estimate; it is quite likely that the actual amount of trade receivables that prove to be bad will be different from the estimate. Let us say that, during the next reporting period, it was discovered that, in fact, £26,000 of the trade receivables considered doubtful proved to be irrecoverable. These trade receivables must now be written off as follows:

- reduce trade receivables by £26,000; and
- reduce allowances for trade receivables by £26,000.

However, allowances for trade receivables of £4,000 will remain. This amount represents an overestimate made when creating the allowance as at 30 June 2017. As the allowance is no longer needed, it should be eliminated. Remember that the allowance was made by creating an expense in the income statement for the year to 30 June 2017. As the expense was too high, the amount of the overestimate should be 'written back' in the next reporting period. In other words, it will be treated as revenue for the year to 30 June 2018. This will mean:

- reducing the allowances for trade receivables by £4,000; and
- increasing revenue by £4,000.

Ideally, of course, the amount should be written back to the 2017 income statement; however, it is too late to do this. At the end of the year to 30 June 2018, not only will 2017's overestimate be written back, but a new allowance should be created to take account of the trade receivables arising from 2018's credit sales that are considered doubtful.

Activity 3.20

Clayton Conglomerates had trade receivables of £870,000 outstanding at the end of the reporting period to 31 March 2016. The chief accountant believed £40,000 of those trade receivables to be irrecoverable and a further £60,000 to be doubtful. In the subsequent year, it was found that an over-pessimistic estimate of those trade receivables considered doubtful had been made and that only a further £45,000 of trade receivables had actually proved to be bad.

Show the relevant income statement extracts for both 2016 and 2017 to report the bad debts written off and the allowances for trade receivables. Also show the relevant statement of financial position extract as at 31 March 2016.

Your answer should be as follows:

Income statement (extract) for the year ended 31 March 2016

	£
Bad debts written off	40,000
Allowances for trade receivables	60,000

Income statement (extract) for the year ended 31 March 2017

	£
Allowances for trade receivables written back (revenue)	15,000

(*Note*: This figure will usually be netted off against any allowances for trade receivables created in respect of 2016.)

Statement of financial position (extract) as at 31 March 2016

	£
Trade receivables	830,000
Allowances for trade receivables	(60,000)
	770,000

Activity 3.21

The accounting treatment of bad debts and allowances for trade receivables are two further examples where judgement is needed to derive an appropriate expense figure.

What will be the effect of different judgements concerning the appropriate amount of bad debts expense and allowances for trade receivables expense on the profit for a particular period and on the total profit reported over the life of the business?

The judgement concerning whether to write off a debt as bad will affect the expenses for the period and, therefore, the reported profit. Over the life of the business, however, total reported profit would not be affected, as incorrect judgements made in one period will be adjusted for in a later period.

Suppose that a debt of £100 was written off in a period and that, in a later period, the amount owing was actually received. The increase in expenses of £100 in the period in which the bad debt was written off would be compensated for by an increase in revenue of £100 when the amount outstanding was finally received (bad debt recovered). If, on the other hand, the amount owing of £100 was never written off in the first place, the profit for the two periods would not be affected by the bad debt adjustment and would, therefore, be different – but the total profit for the two periods would be the same.

A similar situation would apply where there are differences in judgements concerning allowances for trade receivables.

Uses and usefulness of the income statement

The income statement may help in providing information on:

- *How effective the business has been in generating wealth.* Since wealth generation is the primary reason for most businesses to exist, assessing how much wealth has been created is an important issue. The income statement reveals the profit for the period, or *bottom line* as it is sometimes called. This provides a measure of the wealth created for the owners. Gross profit and operating profit are also useful measures of wealth creation.
- *How profit was derived.* In addition to providing various measures of profit, the income statement provides other information needed for a proper understanding of business performance. It reveals the level of sales revenue and the nature and amount of expenses incurred, which can help in understanding how profit was derived. The analysis of financial performance will be considered in detail in Chapter 7.

Self-assessment question 3.1

TT and Co. is a new business that started trading on 1 January 2016. The following is a summary of transactions that occurred during the first year of trading:

1   The owners introduced £50,000 of equity, which was paid into a bank account opened in the name of the business.
2   Premises were rented from 1 January 2016 at an annual rental of £20,000. During the year, rent of £25,000 was paid to the owner of the premises.
3   Rates (a tax on business premises) were paid during the year as follows:

For the period 1 January 2016 to 31 March 2016	£500
For the period 1 April 2016 to 31 March 2017	£1,200

4   A delivery van was bought on 1 January 2016 for £12,000. This is expected to be used in the business for four years and then to be sold for £2,000.
5   Wages totalling £33,500 were paid during the year. At the end of the year, the business owed £630 of wages for the last week of the year.
6   Electricity bills for the first three quarters of the year were paid totalling £1,650. After 31 December 2016, but before the financial statements had been finalised for the year, the bill for the last quarter arrived showing a charge of £620.
7   Inventories totalling £143,000 were bought on credit.
8   Inventories totalling £12,000 were bought for cash.
9   Sales revenue on credit totalled £152,000 (cost of sales £74,000).

Self-assessment question 3.1 *continued*

10 Cash sales revenue totalled £35,000 (cost of sales £16,000).
11 Receipts from trade receivables totalled £132,000.
12 Payments of trade payables totalled £121,000.
13 Van running expenses paid totalled £9,400.

At the end of the year it was clear that a credit customer who owed £400 would not be able to pay any part of the debt. All of the other trade receivables were expected to be settled in full.

The business uses the straight-line method for depreciating non-current assets.

Required:

Prepare a statement of financial position as at 31 December 2016 and an income statement for the year to that date.

The solution to this question can be found at the back of the book on pp. 767–768.

Summary

The main points of this chapter may be summarised as follows:

The income statement (profit and loss account)

- The income statement reveals how much profit (or loss) has been generated over a period and links the statements of financial position at the beginning and end of a reporting period.
- Profit (or loss) is the difference between total revenue and total expenses for a period.
- There are three main measures of profit.
  - gross profit – which is calculated by deducting the cost of sales from the sales revenue;
  - operating profit – which is calculated by deducting overheads from the gross profit;
  - profit for the period – which is calculated by adding non-operating income and deducting finance costs from the operating profit.

Expenses and revenue

- Cost of sales can be identified by matching the cost of each sale to the particular sale or by adjusting the goods bought during a period by the opening and closing inventories.
- Classifying expenses is often a matter of judgement, although there are rules for businesses that trade as limited companies.
- Revenue is recognised when a business has performed its obligations, which is when control of the goods or services is passed to the customer.
- Revenue can be recognised over a period of time or at a particular point in time.
- The matching convention states that expenses should be matched to the revenue that they help generate.

- An expense reported in the income statement may not be the same as the cash paid. This can result in accruals or prepayments appearing in the statement of financial position.
- The materiality convention states that where the amounts are immaterial, we should consider only what is expedient.
- The accruals convention states that profit = revenue − expenses (not cash receipts − cash payments).

Depreciation of non-current assets

- Depreciation requires a consideration of the cost (or fair value), useful life and residual value of an asset. It also requires a consideration of the method of depreciation.
- The straight-line method of depreciation allocates the amount to be depreciated evenly over the useful life of the asset.
- The reducing-balance method applies a fixed percentage rate of depreciation to the carrying amount of an asset each year.
- The depreciation method chosen should reflect the pattern of consumption of economic benefits of an asset.
- Depreciation allocates the cost (or fair value), less the residual value, of an asset over its useful life. It does not provide funds for replacement of the asset.

Costing inventories

- The way in which we derive the cost of inventories is important in the calculation of profit and the presentation of financial position.
- The first in, first out (FIFO) assumption is that the earliest inventories held are the first to be used.
- The last in, first out (LIFO) assumption is that the latest inventories are the first to be used.
- The weighted average cost (AVCO) assumption applies an average cost to all inventories used.
- When prices are rising, FIFO gives the lowest cost of sales figure and highest closing inventories figure and for LIFO it is the other way around. AVCO gives figures for cost of sales and closing inventories that lie between FIFO and LIFO.
- When prices are falling, the positions of FIFO and LIFO are reversed.
- Inventories are shown at the lower of cost and net realisable value.
- When a particular method of accounting, such as a depreciation method, is selected, it should be applied consistently over time.

Bad debts

- Where it is reasonably certain that a credit customer will not pay, the debt is regarded as 'bad' and written off.
- Where it is doubtful that a credit customer will pay, an allowance for trade receivables expense should be created.

Uses of the income statement

- It provides measures of profit generated during a period.
- It provides information on how the profit was derived.

Key terms

For definitions of these terms, see Appendix B.

profit *p. 81*	amortisation *p. 95*
revenue *p. 81*	residual value *p. 97*
expense *p. 82*	straight-line method *p. 97*
cost of sales *p. 82*	carrying amount *p. 98*
gross profit *p. 84*	written-down value *p. 98*
operating profit *p. 84*	net book value *p. 98*
profit for the period *p. 84*	reducing-balance method *p. 98*
matching convention *p. 90*	first in, first out (FIFO) *p. 106*
accrued expense *p. 91*	last in, first out (LIFO) *p. 106*
prepaid expense *p. 93*	weighted average cost (AVCO) *p. 106*
materiality convention *p. 94*	consistency convention *p. 111*
accruals convention *p. 94*	bad debt *p. 111*
accruals accounting *p. 94*	allowance for trade receivables *p. 113*
depreciation *p. 95*	

Further reading

If you would like to explore the topics covered in this chapter in more depth, we recommend the following:

Alexander, D. and Nobes, C. (2016) *Financial Accounting: An International Introduction,* 6th edn, Pearson, Chapters 2, 3, 9 and 10.

Elliott, B. and Elliott, J. (2015) *Financial Accounting and Reporting,* 17th edn, Pearson, Chapters 2, 8, 20 and 21.

International Accounting Standards Board, *2016 A Guide through IFRS Standards (Green Book), 2016,* IAS 2 *Inventories* and IFRS 15 *Revenue from Contracts with Customers.*

KPMG, *Insights into IFRS,* 13th edn, Sweet and Maxwell, 2016/17, Sections 3.2, 3.3, 3.8, 3.10 and 4.2 (a summarised version of this is available free at www.kpmg.com).

Review questions

Solutions to these questions can be found at the back of the book on p. 788.

3.1 'Although the income statement is a record of past achievement, the calculations required for certain expenses involve estimates of the future.' What does this statement mean? Can you think of examples where estimates of the future are used?

3.2 'Depreciation is a process of allocation and not valuation.' What do you think is meant by this statement?

3.3 What is the convention of consistency? Does this convention help users in making a more valid comparison between businesses?

3.4 'An asset is similar to an expense.' In what ways in this true or untrue?

Exercises

Solutions to exercises with coloured numbers can be found at the back of the book on pp. 804–805.

Basic-level exercises

3.1 You have heard the following statements made. Comment critically on them.

(a) 'Equity only increases or decreases as a result of the owners putting more cash into the business or taking some out.'

(b) 'An accrued expense is one that relates to next year.'

(c) 'Unless we depreciate this asset we shall be unable to provide for its replacement.'

(d) 'There is no point in depreciating the factory building. It is appreciating in value each year.'

3.2 Singh Enterprises, which started business on 1 January 2014, has a reporting period to 31 December and uses the straight-line method of depreciation. On 1 January 2014, the business bought a machine for £10,000. The machine had an expected useful life of four years and an estimated residual value of £2,000. On 1 January 2015, the business bought another machine for £15,000. This machine had an expected useful life of five years and an estimated residual value of £2,500. On 31 December 2016 the business sold the first machine bought for £3,000.

Required:
Show the relevant income statement extracts and statement of financial position extracts for the years 2014, 2015 and 2016.

3.3 The owner of a business is confused and comes to you for help. The financial statements for the business, prepared by an accountant, for the last reporting period revealed a profit of £50,000. However, during the reporting period the bank balance declined by £30,000. What reasons might explain this apparent discrepancy?

Intermediate-level exercises

3.4 Fill in the values (a) to (f) in the following table on the assumption that there were no opening balances involved.

	Relating to period		At end of period	
	Paid/received	Expense/revenue for period	Prepaid	Accruals/deferred revenues
	£	£	£	£
Rent payable	10,000	(a)	1,000	
Rates and insurance	5,000	(b)		1,000
General expenses	(c)	6,000	1,000	
Interest payable on borrowings	3,000	2,500	(d)	
Salaries	(e)	9,000		3,000
Rent receivable	(f)	1,500		1,500

3.5 Spratley Ltd is a builders' merchant. On 1 September the business had, as part of its inventories, 20 tonnes of sand at a cost of £18 per tonne and, therefore, at a total cost of £360. During the first week in September, the business bought the following amounts of sand:

	Tonnes	Cost per tonne £
2 September	48	20
4 September	15	24
6 September	10	25

On 7 September the business sold 60 tonnes of sand to a local builder.

Required:
Calculate the cost of goods sold and of the remaining inventories using the following costing methods:
(a) first in, first out
(b) last in, first out
(c) weighted average cost.

Advanced-level exercises

3.6 The following is the statement of financial position of TT and Co. (see Self-Assessment Question 3.1 on p. 115) at the end of its first year of trading:

Statement of financial position as at 31 December 2016

ASSETS	£
Non-current assets	
Property, plant and equipment:	
Delivery van at cost	12,000
Depreciation	(2,500)
	9,500
Current assets	
Inventories	65,000
Trade receivables	19,600
Prepaid expenses*	5,300
Cash	750
	90,650
Total assets	100,150
EQUITY AND LIABILITIES	
Equity	
Original	50,000
Retained earnings	26,900
	76,900
Current liabilities	
Trade payables	22,000
Accrued expenses†	1,250
	23,250
Total equity and liabilities	100,150

* The prepaid expenses consisted of rates (£300) and rent (£5,000).
†The accrued expenses consisted of wages (£630) and electricity (£620).

During 2017, the following transactions took place:

1 The owners withdrew £20,000 of equity as cash.
2 Premises continued to be rented at an annual rental of £20,000. During the year, rent of £15,000 was paid to the owner of the premises.
3 Rates on the premises £1,300 were paid for the period 1 April 2017 to 31 March 2018.
4 A second delivery van was bought on 1 January 2017 for £13,000. This is expected to be used in the business for four years and then to be sold for £3,000.
5 Wages totalling £36,700 were paid during the year. At the end of the year, the business owed £860 of wages for the last week of the year.
6 Electricity bills for the first three quarters of the year and £620 for the last quarter of the previous year were paid totalling £1,820. After 31 December 2017, but before the financial statements had been finalised for the year, the bill for the last quarter arrived showing a charge of £690.
7 Inventories totalling £67,000 were bought on credit.
8 Inventories totalling £8,000 were bought for cash.
9 Sales revenue on credit totalled £179,000 (cost £89,000).
10 Cash sales revenue totalled £54,000 (cost £25,000).
11 Receipts from trade receivables totalled £178,000.
12 Payments to trade payables totalled £71,000.
13 Van running expenses paid totalled £16,200.

The business uses the straight-line method for depreciating non-current assets.

Required:

Prepare a statement of financial position as at 31 December 2017 and an income statement for the year to that date.

3.7 The following is the income statement for Nikov and Co. for the year ended 31 December 2016, along with information relating to the preceding year.

Income statement for the year ended 31 December

	2016 £000	2015 £000
Sales revenue	420.2	382.5
Cost of sales	(126.1)	(114.8)
Gross profit	294.1	267.7
Salaries and wages	(92.6)	(86.4)
Selling and distribution costs	(98.9)	(75.4)
Rent and rates	(22.0)	(22.0)
Bad debts written off	(19.7)	(4.0)
Telephone and postage	(4.8)	(4.4)
Insurance	(2.9)	(2.8)
Motor vehicle expenses	(10.3)	(8.6)
Depreciation – delivery van	(3.1)	(3.3)
– fixtures and fittings	(4.3)	(4.5)
Operating profit	35.5	56.3
Loan interest	(4.6)	(5.4)
Profit for the year	30.9	50.9

Required:

Analyse the performance of the business for the year to 31 December 2016 in so far as the information allows.

CHAPTER 4

Accounting for limited companies (1)

Introduction

Most businesses in the UK, from the very largest to some of the very smallest, operate in the form of limited companies. Nearly three and a half million limited companies now exist, accounting for the majority of business activity and employment. The economic significance of this type of business is not confined to the UK; it can be seen in virtually all of the world's developed countries.

In this chapter, we shall consider the nature of limited companies and how they differ from sole-proprietorship businesses and partnerships. This expands on the discussion of various business forms that we met in Chapter 1. The nature of limited companies leads to a need to distinguish between various aspects of equity finance, according to how that aspect arose. This distinction is not required for other forms of business entity (sole proprietorships and partnerships). We shall examine the various elements of equity finance that a limited company may have and the restrictions that owners face when seeking to withdraw part of their equity.

The financial statements prepared for a limited company reflect certain key features of this type of business. We shall consider how the financial statements dealt with in the previous two chapters are adapted to accommodate these features. As we shall see, these adaptations relate to matters of detail rather than of underlying principle. Many large businesses operate as a group of companies rather than as a single company. We end this chapter by discussing the reasons for this and by describing the main features of financial statements prepared for groups of companies.

Learning outcomes

When you have completed this chapter, you should be able to:

- discuss the nature and financing of a limited company;

- describe the main features of the equity in a limited company and the restrictions placed on owners seeking to withdraw part of their equity;

- explain how the income statement and statement of financial position of a limited company differ in detail from those of sole proprietorships and partnerships; and

- discuss the reasons for the formation of groups of companies and the main features of financial statements prepared for groups of companies.

The main features of limited companies

Legal nature

Let us begin our examination of limited companies by discussing their legal nature. A *limited company* has been described as an artificial person that has been created by law. This means that a company has many of the rights and obligations that 'real' people have. It can, for example, enter into contracts in its own name. It can also sue other people (real or corporate) and it can be sued by them. This contrasts sharply with unincorporated businesses, such as sole proprietorships and partnerships, where it is the owner(s) rather than the business that must enter into contracts, sue and so on. This is because those businesses have no separate legal identity.

With the rare exceptions of those that are created by Act of Parliament or by Royal Charter, all UK companies are created (or *incorporated*) by registration. To create a company the person or persons wishing to create it (usually known as *promoters*) fill in a few simple forms and pay a modest registration fee. After having ensured that the necessary formalities have been met, the Registrar of Companies, a UK government official, enters the name of the new company on the Registry of Companies. Thus, in the UK, companies can be formed very easily and cheaply (for about £100).

A limited company may be owned by just one person, but most have more than one owner and some have many owners. The owners are usually known as *members* or *shareholders.* The ownership of a company is normally divided into a number of shares, each of equal size. Each owner, or shareholder, owns one or more shares in the company. Large companies typically have a very large number of shareholders. For example, at 31 March 2016, BT Group plc, the telecommunications business, had 827,000 different shareholders. These shareholders owned nearly 10 billion shares between them.

Since a limited company has its own legal identity, it is regarded as being quite separate from those that own and manage it. It is worth emphasising that this legal separateness of owners and the company has no connection with the business entity convention discussed in Chapter 2. This accounting convention applies equally to all business types, including sole proprietorships and partnerships where there is no legal distinction between the owner(s) and the business.

The legal separateness of the limited company and its shareholders leads to two important features of the limited company: perpetual life and limited liability. These are now explained.

Perpetual life

A company is normally granted a perpetual existence and so will continue even where an owner of some, or even all, of the shares in the company dies. The shares of the deceased person will simply pass to the beneficiary of his or her estate. The granting of perpetual existence means that the life of a company is quite separate from the lives of those individuals who own or manage it. It is not, therefore, affected by changes in ownership that arise when individuals buy and sell shares in the company.

Although a company may be granted a perpetual existence when it is first formed, it is possible for either the shareholders or the courts to bring this existence to an end. When this is done, the assets of the company are usually sold to generate cash to meet the outstanding liabilities. Any amounts remaining after all liabilities have been met will then be distributed between the shareholders. Shareholders may agree to end the life of a company where it has achieved the purpose for which it was formed or where they feel that the company has no real future. The courts may bring the life of a company to an end where creditors (those owed money by the company) have applied to the courts for this to be done because they have not been paid.

Where shareholders agree to end the life of a company, it is referred to as a 'voluntary liquidation'. **Real World 4.1** describes the demise of one company by this method.

Real World 4.1

Monotub Industries in a spin as founder gets Titan for £1

Monotub Industries, maker of the Titan washing machine, yesterday passed into corporate history with very little ceremony and with only a whimper of protest from minority shareholders.

At an extraordinary meeting held in a basement room of the group's West End headquarters, shareholders voted to put the company into voluntary liquidation and sell its assets and intellectual property to founder Martin Myerscough for £1 [The shares in the company were at one time worth 650p each.]

The only significant opposition came from Giuliano Gnagnatti who, along with other shareholders, has seen his investment shrink faster than a wool twin-set on a boil wash.

The not-so-proud owner of 100,000 Monotub shares, Mr Gnagnatti, the managing director of an online retailer, described the sale of Monotub as a 'free gift' to Mr Myerscough. This assessment was denied by Ian Green, the chairman of Monotub, who said the closest the beleaguered company had come to a sale was an offer for£60,000 that gave no guarantees against liabilities, which are thought to amount to £750,000.

The quiet passing of the washing machine, eventually dubbed the Titanic, was in strong contrast to its performance in many kitchens.

Originally touted as the 'great white goods hope' of the washing machine industry with its larger capacity and removable drum, the Titan ran into problems when it kept stopping during the spin cycle, causing it to emit a loud bang and leap into the air.

Summing up the demise of the Titan, Mr Green said: 'Clearly the machine had some revolutionary aspects, but you can't get away from the fact that the machine was faulty and should not have been launched with those defects.'

The usually-vocal Mr Myerscough, who has promised to pump £250,000 into the company and give Monotub shareholders £4 for every machine sold, refused to comment on his plans for the Titan or reveal who his backers were. But . . . he did say that he intended to 'take the Titan forward'.

 Source: Urquhart, L. (2003) Monotub Industries in a spin as founder gets Titan for £1, *Financial Times*, 23 January. © The Financial Times Limited 2012. All Rights Reserved.

Limited liability

Since the company is a legal person in its own right, it must take responsibility for its own debts and losses. This means that, once the shareholders have paid what they have agreed to pay for the shares, their obligation to the company, and to the company's creditors, is satisfied. Thus shareholders can limit their losses to the amount that they have paid, or agreed to pay, for their shares. This is of great practical importance to potential shareholders since they know that what they can lose, as part owners of the business, is limited.

Contrast this with the position of sole proprietors or partners. They cannot 'ring-fence' assets that they do not want to put into the business. If a sole-proprietorship or partnership business finds itself in a position where liabilities exceed the business assets, the law gives unsatisfied creditors the right to demand payment out of what the sole proprietor or partner may have regarded as 'non-business' assets. Thus the sole proprietor or partner could lose everything – house, car, the lot. This is because the law sees Jill, the sole proprietor, as being the same as Jill the private individual.

Real World 4.2 gives an example of a well-known case where the shareholders of a particular company were able to avoid any liability to those that had lost money as a result of dealing with the company.

Real World 4.2

Carlton and Granada 1 – Nationwide Football League 0

Two television broadcasting companies, Carlton and Granada, each owned 50 per cent of a separate company, ITV Digital (formerly ON Digital). ITV Digital signed a contract to pay the Nationwide Football League (in effect the three divisions of English football below the Premiership) more than £89 million on both 1 August 2002 and 1 August 2003 for the rights to broadcast football matches over three seasons. ITV Digital was unable to sell enough subscriptions for the broadcasts and so collapsed because it was unable to meet its liabilities. The Nationwide Football League tried to force Carlton and Granada (ITV Digital's only two shareholders) to meet ITV Digital's contractual obligations. It was unable to do so because the shareholders could not be held legally liable for the amounts owing.

Carlton and Granada subsequently merged into one business, but at the time of ITV Digital were two independent companies.

Activity 4.1

The fact that shareholders can limit their losses to that which they have paid, or have agreed to pay, for their shares is of great practical importance to potential shareholders.

Can you think of any practical benefit to a private-sector economy, in general, of this ability of shareholders to limit losses?

Business is a risky venture – in some cases very risky. People will usually be happier to invest money when they know the limit of their liability. If investors are given limited liability, new businesses are more likely to be formed and existing ones are likely to find it easier to raise more finance. This is good for the private-sector economy and may ultimately lead to the generation of greater wealth for society as a whole.

Although **limited liability** has this advantage to the providers of equity finance (the shareholders), it is not necessarily to the advantage of all of the others who have a stake in the business, as we saw in the case of the Nationwide Football League clubs in Real World 4.2. Limited liability is attractive to shareholders because they can, in effect, walk away from the unpaid debts of the company if their committed contribution is not enough to cover those debts. As a consequence, individuals, or businesses, may be wary of entering into a contract with a limited company. This can be a real problem for smaller, less established companies. Suppliers may insist on cash payment before delivery of goods or the rendering of a service. Alternatively, they may require a personal guarantee from a major shareholder that the debt will be paid before allowing trade credit. In this way, the supplier circumvents the company's limited liability status by demanding the personal liability of an individual. Larger, more established companies, on the other hand, find it easier to gain the confidence of suppliers.

Legal safeguards

Various safeguards exist to protect individuals and businesses contemplating dealing with a limited company. They include the requirement to indicate limited liability status in the name of the company. This should alert prospective suppliers and lenders to the potential risks involved.

A further safeguard is the restrictions placed on the ability of shareholders to withdraw their equity from the company.

Activity 4.2

Can you think why these restrictions on the withdrawal of equity are imposed?

They are designed to prevent shareholders from protecting their own investment and, as a result, leaving lenders and suppliers in an exposed position.

We shall consider this point in more detail later in the chapter.

Finally, limited companies are required to produce annual financial statements (income statements, statements of financial position and statements of cash flows) and make these publicly available. This means that anyone interested can gain an impression of the financial performance and position of the company. The form and content of the first two of these statements are considered in some detail later in the chapter and in Chapter 5. The statement of cash flows is considered in Chapter 6.

Public and private companies

When a company is registered with the Registrar of Companies, it must be registered either as a public or as a private company. The main practical difference between these is that a **public limited company** can offer its shares for sale to the general public, but a **private limited company** cannot. A public limited company must signal its status to all interested parties by having the words 'public limited company', or its abbreviation 'plc', in its name. For a private limited company, the word 'limited' or 'Ltd' must appear as part of its name.

Private limited companies tend to be smaller businesses where the ownership is divided among relatively few shareholders who are usually fairly close to one another – for example, a family company. There are vastly more private limited companies in the UK than public limited companies. Of the almost 3.5 million UK limited companies now in existence, only around 6,200 (representing 0.2 per cent of the total) are public limited companies. Figure 4.1 shows the trend in the numbers of public and private limited companies in recent years.

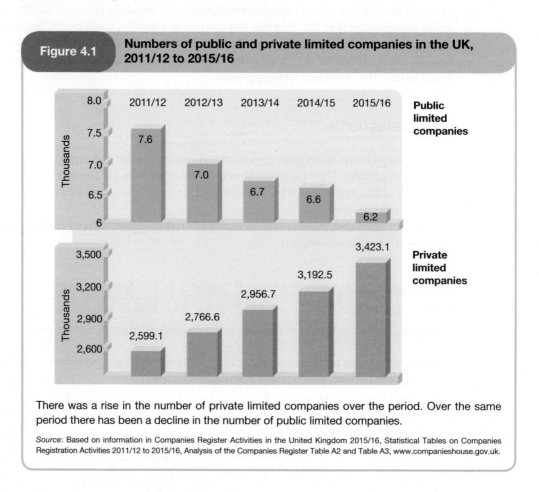

Figure 4.1	Numbers of public and private limited companies in the UK, 2011/12 to 2015/16

There was a rise in the number of private limited companies over the period. Over the same period there has been a decline in the number of public limited companies.

Source: Based on information in Companies Register Activities in the United Kingdom 2015/16, Statistical Tables on Companies Registration Activities 2011/12 to 2015/16, Analysis of the Companies Register Table A2 and Table A3, www.companieshouse.gov.uk.

Since individual public companies tend to be larger, they are often economically more important. In some industry sectors, such as banking, insurance, oil refining and grocery retailing, they are completely dominant. Although some private limited companies are large, many are little more than the vehicle through which one-person businesses operate.

Real World 4.3 shows the extent of the market dominance of public limited companies in one particular business sector.

Real World 4.3

A big slice of the market

The grocery sector is dominated by four large players: Tesco, Sainsbury, Morrison and Asda. The first three are public limited companies and the fourth, Asda, is owned by a large US public company, Wal-Mart Inc. Figure 4.2 shows the share of the grocery market of each during the 12-week period to 1 January 2017.

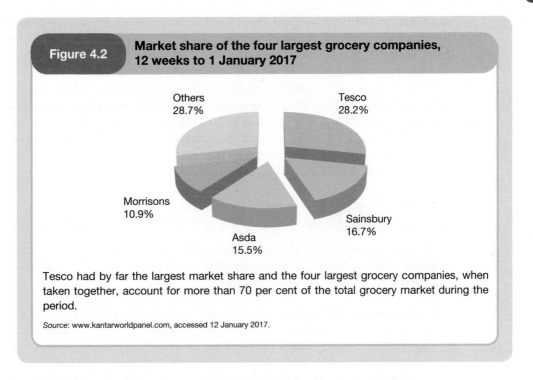

Figure 4.2 **Market share of the four largest grocery companies, 12 weeks to 1 January 2017**

Others
28.7%

Tesco
28.2%

Morrisons
10.9%

Sainsbury
16.7%

Asda
15.5%

Tesco had by far the largest market share and the four largest grocery companies, when taken together, account for more than 70 per cent of the total grocery market during the period.

Source: www.kantarworldpanel.com, accessed 12 January 2017.

Taxation

Another consequence of the legal separation of the limited company from its owners is that companies must be accountable to the tax authorities for tax on their profits and gains. This leads to the reporting of tax in the financial statements of limited companies. The charge for tax is shown in the income statement. The tax charge for a particular year is based on that year's profit. For many companies, only 50 per cent of the tax liability is due for payment during the year concerned, so the other 50 per cent will appear on the end-of-year statement of financial position as a current liability. This will be illustrated a little later in the chapter.

Companies are charged **corporation tax** on their profits and gains. It is levied on the company's taxable profit, which may differ from the profit shown on the income statement. This is because tax law does not follow normal accounting rules in every respect. Generally, however, taxable profit and accounting profit are pretty close to one another. The percentage rate of corporation tax tends to vary over time. For the corporation tax year commencing 1 April 2017, the rate is set at 19 per cent and it will remain at this rate for the following two tax years. For the tax year commencing 1 April 2020 the rate will be reduced to 18 per cent.

The tax position of companies contrasts with that of sole proprietorships and partnerships, where tax is levied not on the business but on the owner(s). This means that tax will not be reported in the financial statements of unincorporated businesses as it is a matter between the owner(s) and the tax authorities. There can be tax advantages to trading as a limited company, rather than as a sole proprietor or partner. This may partly explain the rise in popularity of private limited companies over recent years.

The role of the Stock Exchange

The London **Stock Exchange** acts as both an important *primary* and *secondary* capital market for companies. As a primary market, its function is to enable companies to raise new finance. As a secondary market, its function is to enable investors to sell their securities (including shares and loan notes) with ease. We have already seen that shares in a company may be transferred from one owner to another. The wish of some investors to sell their shares, coupled with the wish of others to buy those shares, has led to the creation of a formal market in which shares are bought and sold.

Only the shares of certain companies (*listed* companies) may be traded on the London Stock Exchange. As at 31 December 2016, just over 900 UK companies were listed. This represents only about one in 3,700 of all UK companies (public and private) and roughly one in seven public limited companies. However, many of these listed companies are massive. Nearly all of the UK businesses that are 'household names' (for example, Tesco, Next, BT, Vodafone, BP and so on) are listed companies.

Activity 4.3

As mentioned earlier, the change in ownership of shares does not directly affect a particular company. Why, in that case, do many public companies seek to have their shares traded in a recognised Stock Exchange?

Investors are generally reluctant to pledge their money unless they can see some way of turning their investment back into cash. The shares of a particular company may be valuable because it has bright prospects. Unless this value can be turned into cash, however, the benefit to investors is dubious. After all, we cannot spend shares; we normally need cash. Thus, investors are more likely to buy new shares from a company where they can liquidate their investment (turn it into cash) as and when they wish. Stock Exchanges provide the means of liquidation and, by so doing, make it easier for a company to raise new share capital.

We shall consider the role of the Stock Exchange in rather more detail in Chapter 15.

Managing a company

A limited company may have a legal personality, but it is not a human being capable of making decisions and plans about the business and exercising control over it. People must undertake these management tasks. The most senior level of management of a company is the board of directors.

Directors are elected by shareholders to manage the company on a day-to-day basis on their behalf. By law there must be at least one director for a private limited company and two for a public limited company. In a small company, the board may be the only level of management and consist of all of the shareholders. In larger companies, the board may consist of 10 or so directors out of many thousands of shareholders. (The directors are normally shareholders although they do not have to be.) Below the board of directors of the typical large company could be several layers of management comprising many thousands of people.

Financing limited companies

Equity (the owners' claim)

The equity of a sole proprietorship is normally encompassed in one figure on the statement of financial position. In the case of companies, things are a little more complicated, although the same broad principles apply. With companies, equity is divided between shares (for example, the original investment), on the one hand, and **reserves** (that is, profits and gains subsequently made), on the other. There is also the possibility that there will be more than one type of shares and of reserves. Thus, within the basic divisions of share capital and reserves, there will usually be further subdivisions. This might seem quite complicated, but we shall shortly consider the reasons for these subdivisions and all should become clearer.

The basic division

When a company is first formed, those who take steps to form it (the promoters) will decide how much needs to be raised from potential shareholders to set the company up with the necessary assets to operate. Example 4.1 illustrates this.

Example 4.1

Some friends decide to form a company to operate an office cleaning business. They estimate that the company will need £50,000 to obtain the necessary assets. Between them, they raise the cash, which they use to buy shares in the company, on 31 March 2016, with a **nominal value** (or **par value**) of £1 each.

At this point the statement of financial position of the company would be:

Statement of financial position as at 31 March 2016

	£
Net assets (all in cash)	50,000
Equity	
Share capital:	
50,000 shares of £1 each	50,000

The company now buys the necessary non-current assets (vacuum cleaners and so on) and inventories (cleaning materials) and starts to trade. During the first year, the company makes a profit of £10,000. This, by definition, means that the equity expands by £10,000. During the year, the shareholders (owners) make no drawings of their equity, so at the end of the year the summarised statement of financial position looks like this:

Statement of financial position as at 31 March 2017

	£
Net assets (various assets less liabilities*)	60,000
Equity	
Share capital:	
50,000 shares of £1 each	50,000
Reserves (revenue reserve)	10,000
Total equity	60,000

* We saw in Chapter 2 that Assets = Equity + Liabilities. We also saw that this can be rearranged so that Assets − Liabilities = Equity.

The profit is shown as a reserve, known as a **revenue reserve,** because it arises from generating revenue (making sales). Note that we do not simply merge the profit with the share capital: we must keep the two amounts separate in order to satisfy company law. There is a legal restriction on the maximum drawings of their equity (for example, as a **dividend**) that the shareholders can make. This maximum is defined by the amount of revenue reserves and so it is helpful to show these separately. We shall look at why there is this restriction, and how it works, a little later in the chapter.

Share capital

Ordinary shares

Ordinary shares represent the basic units of ownership of a business. They are issued by all companies and are often known as *equities*. Ordinary shareholders are the primary risk takers as they share in the profits of the company only after other claims have been satisfied. There are no upper limits, however, on the amount by which they may benefit. The potential rewards available to ordinary shareholders reflect the risks that they are prepared to take. Since ordinary shareholders take most of the risks, power normally rests in their hands. Usually, only the ordinary shareholders are able to vote on issues that affect the company, such as the appointment of directors.

The nominal value of such shares is at the discretion of the people who start up the company. For example, if the initial share capital is to be £50,000 this could be two shares of £25,000 each, 5 million shares of one penny each or any other combination that gives a total of £50,000. All shares must have equal value.

Activity 4.4

The initial financial requirement for a new company is £50,000. There are to be two equal shareholders. Would you advise them to issue two shares of £25,000 each? Why?

Such large-denomination shares tend to be unwieldy and difficult to sell. If one of the shareholders wished to liquidate her shareholding, she would have to find a single buyer. Where, however, the shareholding consisted of shares of smaller denomination, the price per share would be lower and the whole shareholding could probably be sold more easily to various potential buyers. It would also be possible for the original shareholder to sell just part of the shareholding and retain a part.

In practice, £1 is the normal maximum nominal value for shares. Shares of 25 pence each and 50 pence each are probably the most common. BT plc, the telecommunications business, has ordinary shares with a nominal value of 5 pence each (although their market value at 11 January 2017 was £3.97 per share).

Preference shares

In addition to ordinary shares, some companies issue **preference shares.** These shares guarantee that *if a dividend is paid,* the preference shareholders will be entitled to the first part of it up to a maximum value. This maximum is normally defined as a fixed percentage of the nominal value of the preference shares. If, for example, a company issues one million preference shares of £1 each with a dividend rate of 6 per cent, this means that the preference shareholders are entitled to receive the first £60,000 (that is,

6 per cent of £1 million) of any dividend that is paid by the company for a particular year. Any dividend payment in excess of £60,000 goes to the ordinary shareholders.

It is open to the company to issue shares of various classes – perhaps with some having unusual conditions – but in practice it is rare to find other than straightforward ordinary and preference shares. Even preference shares are not very common. Although a company may have different classes of shares with each class giving holders different rights, within each class all shares must have equal rights. The rights of the various classes of shareholders, as well as other matters relating to a particular company, are contained in that company's set of rules, known as the *memorandum and articles of association*. A copy of these rules must be lodged with the Registrar of Companies, who makes it available for inspection by the general public.

Altering the nominal value of shares

As we have already seen, the promoters of a new company may make their own choice of the nominal (par) value of the shares. This value need not be permanent. At a later date, the shareholders can decide to change it.

Suppose that a company has one million ordinary shares of £1 each and a decision is made to change the nominal value of the shares from £1 to £0.50 – in other words to halve the value. To maintain the total nominal value of the share capital intact, the company would then issue each shareholder exactly twice as many shares, each with half the original nominal value. Thus, each shareholder would retain a holding of the same total nominal value as before. This process is known, not surprisingly, as **splitting** the shares. The opposite, reducing the number of shares and increasing their nominal value per share to compensate, is known as **consolidating.** Since each shareholder would be left, after a split or consolidation, with exactly the same proportion of ownership of the company's assets as before, the process should have no effect on the total value of the shares held.

Both splitting and consolidating may be used to help make the shares more marketable. Splitting may help avoid share prices becoming too high and consolidating may help avoid share prices becoming too low. It seems that investors do not like either extreme. In addition, some Stock Exchanges do not allow shares to be traded at too low a price.

Real World 4.4 provides an example of a share consolidation by one business.

Real World 4.4

Consolidating

Pure Wafer plc, which enables semiconductor manufactures to re-use silicon test wafers, recently undertook a share consolidation. In a letter to shareholders, the chairman of the company explained the reasons for the consolidation as follows:

> The share price levels at which the Company's ordinary shares of 2 pence each are currently trading means that small absolute movements in the share price represent large percentage movements, resulting in share price volatility. The directors of the Company (the Directors) also note that the bid offer spread at these price levels can be disproportionate, to the detriment of the shareholders of the Company (the Shareholders).
>
> In addition, the Directors wish to create a more significant individual share price and a greater disparity between the share price and the nominal value of each share, to enable greater flexibility to set issue price levels (as a percentage of market price) in the context of any proposed future share issues.
>
> Accordingly, the Directors are proposing that every 10 existing ordinary shares of 2 pence each be consolidated into one ordinary share of 20 pence.

Source: Pure Wafer plc, Letter from the chairman, 30 October 2013.

Reserves

The shareholders' equity consists of share capital and reserves. As mentioned earlier, reserves are profits and gains that a company has made and which still form part of the shareholders' equity. One reason that past profits and gains may no longer continue to be part of equity is that they have been paid out to shareholders (as dividends and so on). Another reason is that reserves will be reduced by the amount of any losses that the company might suffer. In the same way that profits increase equity, losses reduce it.

Activity 4.5

Are reserves amounts of cash? Can you think of a reason why this is an odd question?

To deal with the second point first, it is an odd question because reserves are a claim, or part of one, on the assets of the company, whereas cash is an asset. So reserves cannot be cash.

Reserves are classified as either revenue reserves or **capital reserves.** In Example 4.1 we came across a revenue reserve. This reserve represents the company's retained trading profits as well as gains on the disposal of non-current assets. *Retained earnings,* as they are most often called, represent overwhelmingly the largest source of new finance for UK companies. Capital reserves arise for two main reasons:

● issuing shares at above their nominal value (for example, issuing £1 shares at £1.50); and
● revaluing (upwards) non-current assets.

Where a company issues shares at above their nominal value, UK law requires that the excess of the issue price over the nominal value be shown separately.

Activity 4.6

Can you think why shares might be issued at above their nominal value? (*Hint*: This would not usually happen when a company is first formed and the initial shares are being issued.)

Once a company has traded and has been successful, the shares would normally be worth more than the nominal value at which they were issued. If additional shares are to be issued to new shareholders to raise finance for further expansion, unless they are issued at a value higher than the nominal value, the new shareholders will be gaining at the expense of the original ones.

Example 4.2 shows how this works.

Example 4.2

Based on future prospects, the net assets of a company are worth £1.5 million. There are currently one million ordinary shares in the company, each with a nominal value of £1. The company wishes to raise an additional £0.6 million of cash for expansion and has decided to raise it by issuing new shares. If the shares are issued for £1 each (that is, 600,000 shares), the total number of shares will be

$$1.0 \text{ m} + 0.6 \text{ m} = 1.6 \text{ m}$$

and their total value will be the value of the existing net assets plus the new injection of cash:

$$£1.5 \text{ m} + £0.6 \text{ m} = £2.1 \text{ m}.$$

This means that the value of each share after the new issue will be

$$£2.1 \text{ m}/1.6 \text{ m} = £1.3125.$$

The current value of each share is

$$£1.5 \text{ m}/1.0 \text{ m} = £1.50$$

so the original shareholders will lose

$$£1.50 - £1.3125 = £0.1875 \text{ a share}$$

and the new shareholders will gain

$$£1.3125 - £1.0 = £0.3125 \text{ a share}.$$

The new shareholders will, no doubt, be delighted with this outcome; the original ones will not.

Things could be made fair between the two sets of shareholders described in Example 4.2 by issuing the new shares at £1.50 each. In this case, it would be necessary to issue 400,000 shares to raise the necessary £0.6 million. £ 1 a share of the £1.50 is the nominal value and will be included with share capital in the statement of financial position (£400,000 in total). The remaining £0.50 is a share premium, which will be shown as a capital reserve known as the **share premium account** (£200,000 in total).

It is not clear why UK company law insists on the distinction between nominal share values and the premium. In some other countries (for example, the USA) with similar laws governing the corporate sector, there is not this distinction. Instead, the total value at which shares are issued is shown as one comprehensive figure on the company's statement of financial position.

Real World 4.5 shows the equity of one very well-known business.

Real World 4.5

Flying funds

Ryanair Holdings plc, the budget airline, had the following share capital and reserves as at 31 March 2016:

	€ million
Share capital (10p ordinary shares)	7.7
Share premium	719.4
Other capital	2.3
Retained earnings	3,166.1
Other reserves	(298.7)
Total equity	3,596.8

Note how the nominal share capital figure is only a small fraction of the share premium account figure. This implies that Ryanair has issued shares at much higher prices than the 10p a share nominal value. This reflects its trading success over time. Although other reserves held by the business are negative overall, the retained earnings are huge and account for 88 per cent of the total shareholder equity.

Source: Ryanair Holdings plc, Annual Report 2016, p.144.

Bonus shares

It is always open to a company to take reserves of any kind (irrespective of whether they are capital or revenue) and turn them into share capital. This will involve transferring the desired amount from the reserve concerned to share capital and then distributing the appropriate number of new shares to the existing shareholders. New shares arising from such a conversion are known as **bonus shares.** Example 4.3 illustrates how bonus issues work.

Example 4.3

The summary statement of financial position of a company at a particular point in time is as follows:

Statement of financial position

	£
Net assets (various assets less liabilities)	128,000
Equity	
Share capital:	
50,000 shares of £1 each	50,000
Reserves	78,000
Total equity	128,000

The directors decide that the company will issue existing shareholders with one new share for every share currently owned by each shareholder. The statement of financial position immediately following this will appear as follows:

Statement of financial position

	£
Net assets (various assets less liabilities)	128,000
Equity	
Share capital:	
100,000 shares of £1 each	100,000
Reserves	28,000
Total equity	128,000

We can see that the reserves have decreased by £50,000 and share capital has increased by the same amount. To complete the transaction, 50,000 new ordinary shares of £1 each, which have been created from reserves, will be issued to the existing shareholders.

Activity 4.7

A shareholder of the company in Example 4.3 owned 100 shares before the bonus issue. How will things change for this shareholder as regards the number of shares owned and the value of the shareholding?

The answer should be that the number of shares would double, from 100 to 200. Now the shareholder owns one five-hundredth of the company (that is, 200/100,000). Before the bonus issue, the shareholder also owned one five-hundredth of the company (that is, 100/50,000). The company's assets and liabilities have not changed as a result of the bonus issue and so, logically, one five-hundredth of the value of the company should be identical to what it was before. Thus, each share is worth half as much as it used to be.

A bonus issue simply takes one part of the equity (a reserve) and puts it into another part (share capital). The transaction has no effect on the company's assets or liabilities, so there is no effect on shareholders' wealth. Issues of bonus shares have become less common in recent years, perhaps because of the lack of business profitability during the current economic climate.

Note that a bonus issue is not the same as a share split. A split does not affect the reserves.

Activity 4.8

Can you think of any reasons why a company might want to make a bonus issue if it has no economic consequence? Try to think of at least one reason.

We think that there are three possible reasons:

- *Share price.* To lower the value of each share in order to make the shares more marketable. This has a similar effect to share splitting.
- *Shareholder confidence.* To provide the shareholders with a 'feel-good factor'. It is believed that shareholders like bonus issues because they seem to make them better off, although in practice they should not affect their wealth.
- *Lender confidence.* Where reserves arising from operating profits and/or realised gains on the sale of non-current assets (revenue reserves) are used to make the bonus issue, it has the effect of taking part of that portion of the shareholders' equity that could be withdrawn by the shareholders, and locking it up. The amount transferred becomes part of the permanent equity base of the company. (We shall see a little later in this chapter that there are severe restrictions on the extent to which shareholders may make drawings from their equity.) An individual or business contemplating lending money to the company may insist that the extent that shareholders can withdraw their funds is restricted as a condition of making the loan. This point will be explained shortly.

Real World 4.6 provides an example of a bonus share issue, where it seemed that the main motive was to make the share price more manageable. The 'feel-good' factor, however, also seems to be playing a part.

Real World 4.6

Is it really a bonus?

Medusa Mining is a gold producer that is listed on various international stock markets. In 2010, it announced a one-for-ten bonus issue of shares to all shareholders of the company.

In a statement, the company said that it had achieved several significant milestones in the last calendar year and that the bonus issue was in recognition of the invaluable support the company had received from its shareholders. The bonus issue was also designed to encourage greater liquidity in Medusa shares.

Geoff Davis, managing director of Medusa, said: 'The board is extremely pleased to be in a position to reward shareholders as a result of the company having rapidly expanded its production over the last 12 months and having met all targets on time.'

Source: Adapted from Medusa Mining, www.proactiveinvestors.co.uk, 8 March 2010.

Share capital jargon

Before leaving our detailed discussion of share capital, it might be helpful to clarify some of the jargon relating to shares that is used in company financial statements.

Share capital that has been issued to shareholders is known as the **issued share capital** (or **allotted share capital**). Sometimes, but not very often, a company may not require shareholders to pay the whole amount that is due to be paid for the shares at the time of issue. This may happen where the company does not need the money all at once. Some money would normally be paid at the time of issue and the company would 'call' for further instalments until the shares were **fully paid shares.** That part of the total issue price that has been called is known as the **called-up share capital.** That part that has been called and paid is known as the **paid-up share capital.**

Borrowings

Most larger companies borrow money to supplement that raised from share issues and ploughed-back profits. Company borrowing is often on a long-term basis, perhaps on a 10-year contract. The contract, which is legally binding, will specify the rate of interest, the interest payments date and the repayment date for the amount borrowed. Lenders may be banks and other professional providers of loan finance, such as pension funds and insurance companies.

Many companies borrow in such a way that individual investors are able to lend only part of the total amount required. This is particularly the case with the larger, Stock Exchange listed, companies and involves them making an issue of **loan notes.** Although such an issue may be large, it can be taken up in small slices by private individuals and investing institutions. In some cases, these slices of loans can be bought and sold through the Stock Exchange. This means that investors do not have to wait the full term of their loan to obtain repayment. They can sell their slice of the loan to another would-be lender at intermediate points during the loan term. This flexibility can make loan notes an attractive investment to certain investors. Loan notes are often known as **loan stock** or **debentures.**

Some of the features of financing by loan notes, particularly the possibility that the loan notes may be traded on the Stock Exchange, can lead to confusing loan notes with shares. We should be clear, however, that shares and loan notes are not the same thing.

Activity 4.9

What is the essential difference in status within a company between ordinary shareholders and a loan notes holders?

Ordinary shareholders are the owners of the company who share in the profits and losses of the company. We saw earlier that they are the main risk takers and are given voting rights. Holders of loan notes are simply lenders that receive interest on their investment. They have no ownership stake in the company.

Long-term loans are usually secured on assets of the company. This would give the lender the right, if the company fails to make the contractual payments, to seize the assets concerned, sell them and use the cash to rectify this failure. A mortgage granted to a private individual buying a house or an apartment is a very common example of a secured loan.

Long-term financing of companies can be depicted as in Figure 4.3.

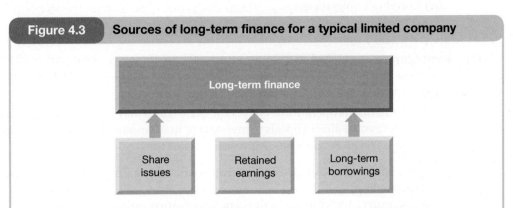

| Figure 4.3 | **Sources of long-term finance for a typical limited company** |

Companies derive their long-term finance from three sources: new share issues, retained earnings and long-term borrowings. For a typical company, the sum of the first two (jointly known as 'equity finance') exceeds the third. Retained earnings usually exceed either of the other two in terms of the amount of finance raised in most years.

It is important to the prosperity and stability of a company that it strikes a suitable balance between finance provided by the shareholders (equity) and from borrowing. This topic will be explored in Chapter 7.

Real World 4.7 shows the long-term borrowings of Rolls-Royce Holdings plc, the engine-building business, at 31 December 2015.

Real World 4.7

Borrowing at Rolls-Royce

The annual financial statements of Rolls-Royce plc set out the sources of the company's long-term borrowings (non-current liabilities). The information made available at 31 December 2015 could be summarised as:

	£m
Secured borrowings	
Lease obligations	50
Unsecured borrowings	
Loans from banks	330
6.75% notes 2019	536
2.375% notes 2020	333
2.125% notes 2021	576
3.625% notes 2025	668
3.375% notes 2026	390
	2,883

Source: Adapted from Rolls-Royce Holdings plc Annual Report and Accounts 2015 p.139, note 15.

Note the large number of sources of the company borrowings. This is typical of most large companies and probably reflects a desire to exploit all available means of raising finance, each of which may have advantages and disadvantages. Normally, a lender would accept a lower rate of interest where the loan is secured as there is less risk involved. It should be said that whether a loan to a company like Rolls-Royce is secured or unsecured is usually pretty academic. It is unlikely that such a large and profitable company would fail to meet its obligations.

Raising share capital

After an initial share issue a company may decide to make further issues of new shares in order to finance its operations. These new share issues may be carried out in various ways. They may involve direct appeals to investors or may employ the services of financial intermediaries. The most common form of share issue are:

- *rights issues* – issues made to existing shareholders, in proportion to their existing shareholding;
- *public issues* – issues made to the general investing public; or
- *private placings* – issues made to selected individuals who are usually approached and asked if they would be interested in taking up new shares.

During its lifetime, a company may use all three of these approaches to raising funds through issuing new shares (although only public companies can make appeals to the general public).

These approaches will be discussed in detail in Chapter 15.

Withdrawing equity

As we have seen, companies are legally obliged to distinguish, in the statement of financial position, between that part of the shareholders' equity that may be withdrawn and that part which may not. The withdrawable part consists of profits arising from trading and from the disposal of non-current assets. It is represented in the statement of financial position by *revenue reserves*.

Paying dividends is the most usual way of enabling shareholders to withdraw part of their equity. An alternative is for the company to buy its own shares from those shareholders wishing to sell them. This is usually known as a 'share repurchase'. The company would then normally cancel the shares concerned. Share repurchases usually involve only a small proportion of the shareholders, unlike a dividend which involves them all.

The total of revenue reserves appearing in the statement of financial position is rarely the total of all trading profits and profits on disposals of non-current assets generated by the company since it was first formed. This total will normally have been reduced by at least one of the following:

- corporation tax paid on those profits;
- any dividends paid or amounts paid to purchase the company's own shares; and
- any losses from trading and the disposal of non-current assets.

The non-withdrawable part consists of share capital plus profits arising from shareholders buying shares in the company and from upward revaluations of assets still held. It is represented in the statement of financial position by *share capital* and *capital reserves*.

Figure 4.4 shows the important division between the part of the shareholders' equity that can be withdrawn and the part that cannot.

| Figure 4.4 | Availability for withdrawal of various parts of the shareholders' equity |

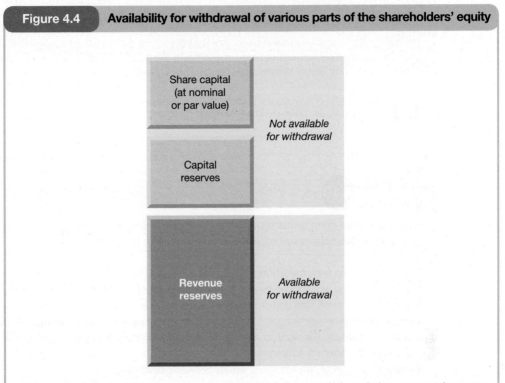

Total equity finance of limited companies consists of share capital, capital reserves and revenue reserves. Only the revenue reserves (which arise from realised profits and gains) can be used to fund a dividend or a share repurchase. In other words, the maximum legal withdrawal is the amount of the revenue reserves.

The law does not specify the size of the non-withdrawable part of shareholders' equity. However, for a company to gain the confidence of prospective lenders and suppliers, the bigger the non-withdrawable part, the better.

Real World 4.8 describes how one company contravened the rules concerning the withdrawal of equity.

| Real World 4.8 |

Ooops!

Betfair returned £80m to investors in violation of accounting rules, the gambling company has admitted. The embarrassing breach – which occurred in 2011, 2012 and 2013 before being noticed – consisted of Betfair paying out more in dividends and share buybacks than it was legally permitted to.

Betfair announced its first dividend as a public company in June 2011, partly to reassure investors who had seen the company's shares halve since its flotation six months earlier. It paid out £30m in relation to the 2011, 2012 and 2013 financial years, and also bought back £50m in shares. However, the payments did not comply with a rule change on how a company's realised profits and distributable reserves are defined.

Betfair said in its latest annual report that, 'as a result of certain changes to the technical guidance issued by the Institute of Chartered Accountants in England and Wales in October 2010, the Company did not have sufficient distributable reserves to make those distributions and so they should not have been paid by the Company to its shareholders.'

Deed polls have now been used to ensure that investors do not have to repay the dividends, and the company's annual general meeting in September will be asked to approve the cancellation of ordinary shares affected by the buyback.

 Source: Extract from Mance, H. (2014) Betfair admits to £80m payouts mistake, ft.com, 3 August. © The Financial Times Ltd 2014. All Rights Reserved.

Activity 4.10

Why are limited companies required to distinguish different parts of their shareholders' equity, whereas sole-proprietorship and partnership businesses are not?

The reason stems from the limited liability that company shareholders enjoy but which owners of unincorporated businesses do not. If a sole proprietor or partner withdraws all of the equity, the position of the lenders and credit suppliers of the business is not weakened since they can legally enforce their claims against the sole proprietor or partner as an individual. With a limited company, however, the right to enforce claims against individual owners does not exist. To protect the company's lenders and credit suppliers, therefore, the law insists that the non-withdrawable part of shareholders' equity is clearly distinguished.

Let us now look at Example 4.4 which illustrates how this protection of lenders and suppliers works.

Example 4.4

The summary statement of financial position of a company at a particular date is as follows:

Statement of financial position

	£
Total assets	43,000
Equity	
Share capital:	
20,000 shares of £1 each	20,000
Reserves (revenue)	23,000
Total equity	43,000

A bank has been asked to make a £25,000 long-term loan to the company. If the loan is granted, the statement of financial position immediately following would appear as follows:

Statement of financial position (after the loan)

	£
Total assets	68,000
Equity	
Share capital:	
20,000 shares of £1 each	20,000
Reserves (revenue)	23,000
	43,000
Non-current liability	
Borrowings – loan	25,000
Total equity and liabilities	68,000

As things stand, there are assets with a total carrying amount of £68,000 to meet the bank's claim of £25,000 It would be possible and perfectly legal, however, for the company to withdraw part of the shareholders' equity (through a dividend or share repurchase) equal to the total revenue reserves (£23,000). The statement of financial position would then appear as follows:

Statement of financial position (after withdrawal)

	£
Total assets (£68,000 − £23,000)	45,000
Equity	
Share capital:	
20,000 shares of £1 each	20,000
Reserves [revenue (£23,000 − £23,000)]	–
	20,000
Non-current liabilities	
Borrowings – bank loan	25,000
Total equity and liabilities	45,000

This leaves the bank in a very much weaker position, in that there are now total assets with a carrying amount of £45,000 to meet a claim of £25,000. Note that the difference between the amount of the borrowings (bank loan) and the total assets equals the equity (share capital and reserves) total. Thus, the equity represents a margin of safety for lenders and suppliers. The larger the amount of the equity withdrawable by the shareholders, the smaller is the potential margin of safety for lenders and suppliers.

Activity (4.11)

Can you recall the circumstances in which the non-withdrawable part of a company's capital could be reduced, without contravening the law? This was mentioned earlier in the chapter.

It can be reduced as a result of the company sustaining trading losses, or losses on disposal of non-current assets, which exceed the withdrawable amount of shareholders' equity.

The main financial statements

The financial statements of a limited company are, in essence, the same as those of a sole proprietor or partnership. There are, however, some differences of detail. We shall now consider these. Example 4.5 sets out the income statement and statement of financial position of a limited company.

Example 4.5

Da Silva plc

Income statement for the year ended 31 December 2017

	£m
Revenue	840
Cost of sales	(520)
Gross profit	320
Wages and salaries	(98)
Heat and light	(18)
Rent and rates	(24)
Motor vehicle expenses	(20)
Insurance	(4)
Printing and stationery	(12)
Depreciation	(45)
Audit fee	(4)
Operating profit	95
Interest payable	(10)
Profit before taxation	85
Taxation	(24)
Profit for the year	61

Statement of financial position as at 31 December 2017

	£m
ASSETS	
Non-current assets	
Property, plant and equipment	203
Intangible assets	100
	303
Current assets	
Inventories	65
Trade receivables	112
Cash	36
	213
Total assets	516

	£m
EQUITY AND LIABILITIES	
Equity	
Ordinary shares of £0.50 each	200
Share premium account	30
Other reserves	50
Retained earnings	25
	305
Non-current liabilities	
Borrowings	100
Current liabilities	
Trade payables	99
Taxation	12
	111
Total equity and liabilities	516

Let us now go through these statements and pick out those aspects that are unique to limited companies.

The income statement

The main points for consideration in the income statement are as follows:

Profit

We can see that, following the calculation of operating profit, two further measures of profit are shown.

- The first of these is the **profit before taxation.** Interest charges are deducted from the operating profit to derive this figure. In the case of a sole proprietor or partnership business, the income statement would end here.
- The second measure of profit is the profit for the reporting period (usually a year). As the company is a separate legal entity, it is liable to pay tax (known as corporation tax) on the profits generated. This measure of profit represents the amount that is available for the shareholders.

Audit fee

Companies beyond a certain size are required to have their financial statements audited by an independent firm of accountants, for which a fee is charged. As we shall see in Chapter 5, the purpose of the audit is to lend credibility to the financial statements. Although it is also open to sole proprietorships and partnerships to have their financial statements audited, relatively few do so. Audit fee is, therefore, an expense that is most often seen in the income statement of a company.

Figure 4.5 shows an outline of the income statement for a limited company.

Figure 4.5 **The layout of the income statement for a limited company**

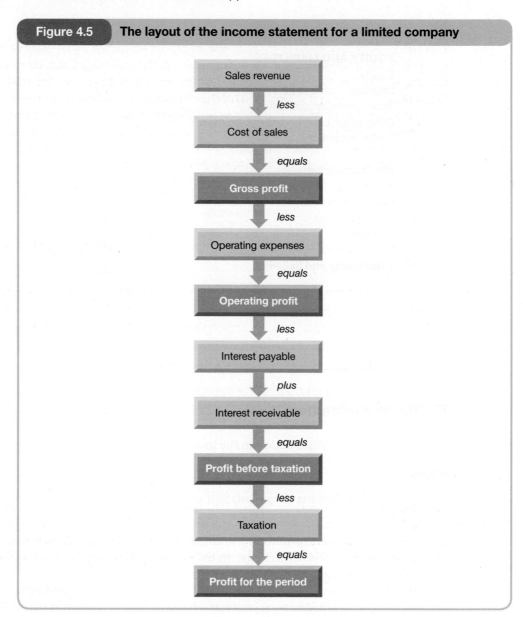

The statement of financial position

The main points for consideration in the statement of financial position are as follows:

Taxation

The amount that appears as part of the current liabilities represents 50 per cent of the tax on the profit for the year 2017. It is, therefore, 50 per cent (£12 million) of the charge that appears in the income statement (£24 million); the other 50 per cent will already have been paid. The unpaid 50 per cent will be paid shortly after the statement of financial position date. These payment dates are set down by law.

Other reserves

This will include any reserves that are not separately identified on the face of the statement of financial position. It may include a *general reserve,* which normally consists of trading profits that have been transferred to this separate reserve for reinvestment ('ploughing back') into the operations of the company. It is not necessary to set up a separate reserve for this purpose. The trading profits could remain unallocated and still swell the retained earnings of the company. It is not entirely clear why directors decide to make transfers to general reserves, since the profits concerned remain part of the revenue reserves and, as such, they still remain available for dividend.

Activity (4.12)

Can you think of a reason why the directors may wish to make a transfer to general reserves from retained earnings?

The most plausible explanation seems to be that directors feel that placing profits in a separate reserve indicates an intention to invest the funds, represented by the reserve, permanently in the company and, therefore, not to use them to pay a dividend or to fund a share repurchase.

Retained earnings appearing on the statement of financial position are, of course, also a reserve, but that fact is not indicated in its title.

Dividends

Although most companies pay dividends to shareholders, they are under no legal obligation to do so. The decision whether to pay dividends will be influenced by commercial factors such as the financial resources of the company, future commitments and shareholder expectations. It must also take account of the legal restraints on the withdrawal of equity, as discussed earlier.

Dividends are paid out of the revenue reserves and should be deducted from these reserves (usually retained earnings) when preparing the statement of financial position. Shareholders are often paid an annual dividend, perhaps in two parts. An 'interim' dividend may be paid part way through the year and a 'final' dividend shortly after the year end.

Dividends declared by the directors during the year but still unpaid at the year end *may* appear as a liability in the statement of financial position. To be recognised as a liability, however, they must be properly authorised before the year-end date. This normally means that the shareholders must approve the dividend by that date.

Large companies tend to have a clear and consistent policy towards the payment of dividends. Any change in the policy provokes considerable interest and is usually interpreted by shareholders as a signal of the directors' views concerning the future. For example, an increase in dividends may be taken as a signal from the directors that future prospects are bright: a higher dividend is seen as tangible evidence of their confidence.

Real World 4.9 provides an example of a dividend increase that was intended to be a sign of confidence in the future.

Real World 4.9

The future is bright. The future is . . . Vodafone

Vodafone, the lossmaking provider of mobile phone services, on Tuesday reported falling revenues in all the European countries where it connects calls and discloses the size of its business. Revenues from "other countries" on the continent shrank as well, in a year when sales in emerging markets failed to offset the decline. However, one announcement in the results bucked the downward trend and gave Vodafone entry to a select club: it became the 26th member of the FTSE 100 index to have increased its annual dividend for at least ten years in a row.

Never mind that most analysts do not expect the group to make profits in any of the next three years that match its 11.5 pence per share payout for 2016. It is all about the signal that dividend growth sends: 'We are confident about the future, and you can rely on us to do the right thing by shareholders.'

FT *Source*: Extract from McCrum, D. (2016) Vodafone joins select club on dividends, ft.com, 18 May. © The Financial Times Ltd 2016. All Rights Reserved.

Accounting for groups of companies

Most large businesses, including nearly all of the well-known ones, operate not as a single company but as a group of companies. In these circumstances, one company (the **parent company** (or 'parent') or **holding company**) is able to control various subsidiary companies, normally as a result of owning more than 50 per cent of their shares. Many larger businesses have numerous subsidiary companies, with each subsidiary operating some aspect of the group's activities. The reasons why many businesses operate in the form of groups include:

● a desire for each part of the business to have its own limited liability, so that financial problems in one part of a business cannot have an adverse effect on other parts; and
● an attempt to make each part of the business have some sense of independence and autonomy and, perhaps, to create or perpetuate a market image of a smaller independent business.

Each company within a group will prepare its own individual annual financial statements. The law also requires, however, that the parent company prepares **group financial statements**, also known as **consolidated financial statements**. These group financial statements amalgamate the financial statements of all of the group members. Thus, the group income statement includes the total revenue figure for all group companies to customers who are not members of the same group, the statement of financial position includes the property, plant and equipment for all group companies and so on. This means that the group financial statements will look like the financial statements of the parent company, had it owned and operated all of the assets of the business directly, instead of through subsidiary companies.

In view of what we have just seen, it may not be possible to detect whether the business operates through a single company or through a large number of subsidiaries, simply by looking at a set of group financial statements. Only by referring to the heading at the top of each statement, which should mention the word 'consolidated' or 'group', might we find this out. In many cases, however, one or two items will be reported that are peculiar to group financial statements. These items are:

- *Goodwill arising on consolidation.* This occurs when a parent acquires a subsidiary from previous owners and pays more for the subsidiary than the subsidiary's individual assets (net of liabilities) appear to be worth. This excess may represent such things as the value of a good reputation that the new subsidiary already has in the market, or the value of its having a loyal and skilled workforce. Goodwill arising on consolidation will appear as an intangible non-current asset on the group statement of financial position.
- *Non-controlling interests (NCI).* One of the principles followed when preparing group financial statements is that all of the revenue, expenses, assets, liabilities and cash flows of each subsidiary are reflected to their full extent in the group financial statements. This is true whether or not the parent owns all of the shares in each subsidiary, provided that the parent has control. (Control normally means owning more than 50 per cent of the subsidiary's ordinary shares.) Where not all of the shares are owned by the parent, the investment of those shareholders in the subsidiary, other than the parent company, appears as part of the shareholders' equity in the group statement of financial position. This shows that, although the net assets of the group are being financed mainly by the parent company's shareholders, 'outside' shareholders also finance a part. Similarly, the group income statement reflects the fact that not all of the profit of the group is attributable to the shareholders of the parent company; a part of it is attributable to the 'outside' shareholders. The interests, or claims, of outside shareholders are known as **non-controlling interests.**

Example 4.6 shows how the statement of financial position of Major plc and its subsidiary is drawn up. Note that the group statement of financial position closely resembles that of an individual company.

Example 4.6

Major plc has just bought, from the previous shareholders, 45 million (out of 60 million) ordinary shares in Minor plc, paying £75 million for them. The remaining 15 million Minor plc shares are owned by other shareholders. These shareholders are now referred to by Major plc as the non-controlling interests. Minor plc is now a subsidiary of Major plc and, as is clear from Major plc's statement of financial position, its only subsidiary company.

→

Example 4.6 *continued*

The statements of financial position of the two companies immediately following the **takeover** (that is, the acquisition of control) of Minor plc by Major plc were as follows:

Statements of financial position

	Major plc £m	Minor plc £m
ASSETS		
Non-current assets		
Property, plant and equipment	63	67
Intangible – 45 million shares in Minor plc	75	–
	138	67
Current assets		
Inventories	37	21
Trade receivables	22	12
Cash	16	2
	75	35
Total assets	213	102
EQUITY AND LIABILITIES		
Equity		
Ordinary shares of £1 each	100	60
Reserves	60	20
	160	80
Non-current liabilities		
Borrowings – loan notes	35	13
Current liabilities		
Trade payables	18	9
Total equity and liabilities	213	102

As would be normal practice, the statement of financial position of the subsidiary (Minor plc) has been revised so that the values of the individual assets are based on *fair values,* rather than what Minor plc originally paid for them. Fair values are those that would be agreed as the selling price between a buyer and a seller, both of whom are knowledgeable and willing. In this context, they probably equate to the values that Major plc would have placed on the individual tangible assets when assessing Minor plc's value.

If a statement of financial position for the group were to be drawn up immediately following the takeover, it would be as follows:

Statements of financial position of Major plc and its subsidiary

	£m
ASSETS	
Non-current assets	
Property, plant and equipment (63 + 67)	130
Intangible – goodwill (75 – ($^{45}/_{60}$ × 80))	15
	145
Current assets	
Inventories (37 + 21)	58
Trade receivables (22 + 12)	34
Cash (16 + 2)	18
	110
Total assets	255

	£m
EQUITY AND LIABILITIES	
Equity	
Ordinary shares of £1 each	100
Reserves	60
Equity attributable to equity holders of the parent	160
Non-controlling interests ($^{15}/_{60} \times 80$)	20
Total equity	180
Non-current liabilities	
Borrowings – loan notes (35 + 13)	48
Current liabilities	
Trade payables (18 + 9)	27
Total equity and liabilities	255

Note that all of the items, except two, in the group statement of financial position are simply the figures for the item concerned, in each of the two statements, added together. This is despite the fact that Major plc owns only three-quarters of the shares of Minor plc. The logic of group financial statements is that if the parent owns enough shares to control its subsidiary, all of the subsidiary's assets and claims should be reflected on the group statement of financial position.

As we have seen, there are two exceptions to this approach: goodwill and non-controlling interests. Goodwill is simply the excess of what Major paid for the shares over their fair value. Major plc bought 45 million of 60 million shares, paying £75. According to Minor plc's statement of financial position, there were net assets (non-current and current assets, less current and non-current liabilities) of £80 million.

Activity 4.13

Can you figure out how much Major plc paid for goodwill?

Major plc paid £75 million for £60 million (that is, $^{45}/_{60} \times$ £80 million) of net assets – an excess of £15 million. This is the goodwill amount.

The excess represents the goodwill element and is usually referred to as 'goodwill arising on consolidation'. This asset is seen as being the value of a loyal workforce, a regular and profitable customer base and so on, that a new business setting up would not have. The relevant International Financial Reporting Standard (IFRS 3) demands that goodwill be reviewed at least annually: if its value has been impaired, it must be written down to the lower value.

The NCI take account of the fact that, although Major plc may control all of the assets and liabilities of Minor plc, it only provides the equity finance for three-quarters of them. The other quarter, £20 million (that is, $^{15}/_{60} \times$ £80 million), is still provided by share-holders in Minor plc, other than Major plc. (Note that IFRS 3 allows an alternative method of calculating goodwill on consolidation and NCI for reporting purposes, but this is beyond the scope of this chapter.)

Example 4.7 shows the income statement of Major plc and its subsidiary (Minor plc) for the first year following the takeover. As with the statement of financial position, the various revenue and expense figures are simply the individual figures for each company added together. The non-controlling interests figure (£2 million) represents $^{15}/_{60}$ of the after-tax profit of Minor plc, which is assumed to be £8 million.

Example 4.7

Income statement for the first year

	£m
Revenue	123
Cost of sales	(56)
Gross profit	67
Administration expenses	(28)
Distribution expenses	(9)
Profit before tax	30
Taxation	(12)
Profit for the year	18
Attributable to:	
Equity holders of the parent	16
Non-controlling interests	2
	18

Self-assessment question 4.1

The summarised statement of financial position of Dev Ltd at a particular point in time is as follows:

Statement of financial position

	£
Net assets (various assets less liabilities)	235,000
Equity	
Share capital: 100,000 shares of £1 each	100,000
Share premium account	30,000
Revaluation reserve	37,000
Retained earnings	68,000
Total equity	235,000

Required:

(a) Without any other transactions occurring at the same time, the company made a one-for-five rights share issue at £2 per share payable in cash. This means that each shareholder was offered one share for every five already held. All shareholders took up their rights. Immediately afterwards, the company made a one-for-two bonus issue. Show the statement of financial position immediately following the bonus issue, assuming that the directors wanted to retain the maximum dividend payment potential for the future.

(b) Explain what external influence might cause the directors to choose not to retain the maximum dividend payment possibilities.

(c) Show the statement of financial position immediately following the bonus issue, assuming that the directors wanted to retain the *minimum* dividend payment potential for the future.

(d) What is the maximum dividend that could be paid before and after the events described in (a) if the minimum dividend payment potential is achieved?

(e) Lee owns 100 shares in Dev Ltd before the events described in (a). Assuming that the net assets of the company have a value equal to their carrying amount on the statement of financial position, show how these events will affect Lee's wealth.

(f) Looking at the original statement of financial position of Dev Ltd, shown above, what four things do we know about the company's status and history that are not specifically stated on the statement of financial position?

The solution to this question can be found at the back of the book on pp. 768–769.

Summary

The main points of this chapter may be summarised as follows:

Main features of a limited company

- It is an artificial person created by law.
- It has a separate life to its owners and is granted a perpetual existence.
- It must take full responsibility for its own debts and losses, but its owners are granted limited liability.
- To safeguard those dealing with a limited company, limited liability status is included as part of the business name, restrictions are placed on the ability of owners to withdraw equity and annual financial statements are made publicly available.
- A public company can offer its shares for sale to the public; a private company cannot.
- A limited company is governed by a board of directors elected by the shareholders.

Financing the limited company

- The share capital of a company can be of two main types: ordinary shares and preference shares.
- Holders of ordinary shares (equities) are the main risk takers and are given voting rights; they form the backbone of the company.
- Holders of preference shares are given a right to a fixed dividend before ordinary shareholders receive a dividend.
- Reserves are profits and gains made by the company and form part of the ordinary shareholders' claim.
- Borrowings provide another major source of finance.

Share issues

- Bonus shares are issued to existing shareholders when part of the reserves of the company is converted into share capital. No funds are raised.

- Shares may be issued for cash through a rights issue, a public issue or a public placing.
- The shares of a public company may be traded on the London Stock Exchange.

Withdrawing equity

- Reserves are of two types: revenue reserves and capital reserves.
- Revenue reserves arise from trading profits and from realised profits on the sale of non-current assets.
- Capital reserves arise from the issue of shares above their nominal value or from the upward revaluation of non-current assets.
- Revenue reserves can be withdrawn as dividends by the shareholders whereas capital reserves normally cannot.

Financial statements of limited companies

- The financial statements of limited companies are based on the same principles as those of sole-proprietorship and partnership businesses. However, there are some differences in detail.
- The income statement has two measures of profit displayed after the operating profit figure: profit before taxation and profit for the year.
- The income statement also shows audit fees and tax on profits for the year.
- The statement of financial position will show any unpaid tax and any unpaid, but authorised, dividends as current liabilities.
- The share capital plus the reserves make up 'equity'.

Groups of companies

- Parent companies are required to produce group financial statements incorporating the results of all companies controlled by the parent.
- A group statement of financial position is prepared by adding like items of assets and liabilities based on 'fair values' together, as if all of the trading is undertaken through the parent company.
- A 'goodwill arising on consolidation' figure often emerges in the group statement of financial position.
- Where the parent does not own all of the shares of each subsidiary, a non-controlling interests (NCI) figure will appear in the statement of financial position, representing the outside shareholders' investment.
- A group income statement is drawn up following similar logic to that applied to the group statement of financial position.

Key terms

For definitions of these terms, see Appendix B.

limited liability *p. 126*	**bonus share** *p. 136*
public limited company *p. 127*	**issued share capital** *p. 138*
private limited company *p. 127*	**allotted share capital** *p. 138*
corporation tax *p. 129*	**fully paid share** *p. 138*
Stock Exchange *p. 129*	**called-up share capital** *p. 138*
director *p. 130*	**paid-up share capital** *p. 138*
reserve *p. 131*	**loan note** *p. 138*
nominal value *p. 131*	**loan stock** *p. 138*
par value *p. 131*	**debenture** *p. 138*
revenue reserve *p. 132*	**profit before taxation** *p. 145*
dividend *p. 132*	**parent company** *p. 148*
ordinary share *p. 132*	**holding company** *p. 148*
preference share *p. 132*	**group financial statement** *p. 148*
splitting *p. 133*	**consolidated financial statement** *p. 148*
consolidating *p. 133*	**non-controlling interest** *p. 149*
capital reserve *p. 134*	**takeover** *p. 150*
share premium account *p. 135*	

Further reading

If you would like to explore the topics covered in this chapter in more depth, we recommend the following:

Elliott, B. and Elliott, J. (2015) *Financial Accounting and Reporting,* 17th edn, Pearson, Chapters 12 and 22.

Alexander, D., Britton, A., Jorissen, A., Hoogendorn, M. and Van Mourik, C. (2014) *International Financial Reporting and Analysis,* Cengage Learning EMEA, 6th edn, Chapter 10.

Melville, A. (2016) *International Financial Reporting: A Practical Guide,* 5th edn, Pearson, Chapter 1.

Thomas, A. and Ward, A. M., (2015) *Introduction to Financial Accounting,* 8th edn, McGraw-Hill Education, Chapters 28 and 29.

Review questions

Solutions to these questions can be found at the back of the book on p. 789.

4.1 How does the liability of a limited company differ from the liability of a real person, in respect of amounts owed to others?

4.2 Some people are about to form a company, as a vehicle through which to run a new business. What are the advantages to them of forming a private limited company rather than a public one?

4.3 What is a reserve? Distinguish between a revenue reserve and a capital reserve.

4.4 What is a preference share? Compare the main features of a preference share with those of

(a) an ordinary share; and
(b) loan notes.

Exercises

Solutions to exercises with coloured numbers can be found at the back of the book on pp. 805–807.

Basic-level exercises

4.1 Comment on the following quote:

'Limited companies can set a limit on the amount of debts that they will meet. They tend to have reserves of cash as well as share capital, and they can use these reserves to pay dividends to the shareholders. Many companies have preference shares as well as ordinary shares. The preference shares give a guaranteed dividend. The shares of many companies can be bought and sold on the Stock Exchange. Shareholders selling their shares can represent a useful source of new finance to the company.'

4.2 Comment on the following quotes:

(a) 'Bonus shares increase the shareholders' wealth because, after the issue, they have more shares, but each one of the same nominal value as they had before.'
(b) 'By law, once shares have been issued at a particular nominal value, they must always be issued at that value in any future share issues.'
(c) 'By law, companies can pay as much as they like by way of dividends on their shares, provided that they have sufficient cash to do so.'
(d) 'Companies do not have to pay tax on their profits because the shareholders have to pay tax on their dividends.'

4.3 Briefly explain each of the following expressions that you have seen in the financial statements of a limited company:

(a) dividend
(b) audit fee
(c) share premium account.

Intermediate-level exercises

4.4 Iqbal Ltd started trading on 1 July 2012. During the first five years of trading, the following occurred:

Year ended 30 June	Trading profit/ (loss)	Profit/(loss) on sale of non-current assets	Upward revaluation of non-current assets
	£	£	£
2013	(15,000)	–	–
2014	8,000	–	10,000
2015	15,000	5,000	–
2016	20,000	(6,000)	–
2017	22,000	–	–

Required:

Assume that the company paid the maximum legal dividend each year. Under normal circumstances, how much would each year's dividend be?

4.5 Hudson plc's outline statement of financial position as at a particular date was as follows:

	£m
Net assets (assets less liabilities)	72
Equity	
Ordinary shares	40
General reserve	32
Total equity	72

The directors made a one-for-four bonus issue, immediately followed by a one-for-four rights issue at a price of £1.80 per share.

Required:

Show the statement of financial position of Hudson plc immediately following the two share issues.

Advanced-level exercises

4.6 The following is a draft set of simplified financial statements for Pear Limited for the year ended 30 September 2017.

Income statement for the year ended 30 September 2017

	£000
Revenue	1,456
Cost of sales	(768)
Gross profit	688
Salaries	(220)
Depreciation	(249)
Other operating costs	(131)
Operating profit	88
Interest payable	(15)
Profit before taxation	73
Taxation at 30%	(22)
Profit for the year	51

Statement of financial position as at 30 September 2017

	£000
ASSETS	
Non-current assets	
Property, plant and equipment:	
Cost	1,570
Depreciation	(690)
	880
Current assets	
Inventories	207
Trade receivables	182
Cash at bank	21
	410
Total assets	1,290
EQUITY AND LIABILITIES	
Equity	
Share capital	300
Share premium account	300
Retained earnings at beginning of year	104
Profit for year	51
	755
Non-current liabilities	
Borrowings (10% loan notes repayable 2018)	300
Current liabilities	
Trade payables	88
Other payables	20
Taxation	22
Borrowings (bank overdraft)	105
	235
Total equity and liabilities	1,290

The following information is available:

1 Depreciation has not been charged on office equipment with a carrying amount of £100,000 This class of assets is depreciated at 12 per cent a year using the reducing-balance method.

2 A new machine was purchased, on credit, for £30,000 and delivered on 29 September 2017 but has not been included in the financial statements. (Ignore depreciation.)

3 A sales invoice to the value of £18,000 for September 2017 has been omitted from the financial statements. (The cost of sales figure is stated correctly.)

4 A dividend of £25,000 had been approved by the shareholders before 30 September 2017, but was unpaid at that date. This is not reflected in the financial statements.

5 The interest payable on the loan notes for the second half-year was not paid until 1 October 2017 and has not been included in the financial statements.

6 An allowance for trade receivables is to be made at the level of 2 per cent of trade receivables.

7 An invoice for electricity to the value of £2,000 for the quarter ended 30 September 2017 arrived on 4 October 2017 and has not been included in the financial statements.

8 The charge for taxation will have to be revised to take account of any amendments to the taxable profit arising from items 1 to 7. Make the simplifying assumption that tax is payable shortly after the end of the year, at the rate of 30 per cent of the profit before tax.

Required:

Prepare a revised set of financial statements for the year ended 30 September 2017 incorporating the additional information in 1 to 8 above. (Work to the nearest £1,000.)

4.7 Rose Limited is a wholesaler and retailer of high-quality teas and coffees. Approximately half of sales are on credit. Abbreviated and unaudited financial statements are as follows:

Rose Limited

Income statement for the year ended 31 March 2017

	£000
Revenue	12,080
Cost of sales	(6,282)
Gross profit	5,798
Labour costs	(2,658)
Depreciation	(625)
Other operating costs	(1,003)
Operating profit	1,512
Interest payable	(66)
Profit before taxation	1,446
Taxation	(434)
Profit for the year	1,012

Statement of financial position as at 31 March 2017

	£000
ASSETS	
Non-current assets	2,728
Current assets	
Inventories	1,583
Trade receivables	996
Cash	26
	2,605
Total assets	5,333
EQUITY AND LIABILITIES	
Equity	
Share capital (50p shares, fully paid)	750
Share premium	250
Retained earnings	1,468
	2,468
Non-current liabilities	
Borrowings – secured loan notes (2020)	300
Current liabilities	
Trade payables	1,118
Other payables	417
Tax	434
Borrowings – overdraft	596
	2,565
Total equity and liabilities	5,333

Since the unaudited financial statements for Rose Limited were prepared, the following information has become available:

1 An additional £74,000 of depreciation should have been charged on fixtures and fittings.
2 Invoices for credit sales on 31 March 2017 amounting to £34,000 have not been included; cost of sales is not affected.
3 Trade receivables totalling £21,000 are recognised as having gone bad, but they have not yet been written off.
4 Inventories which had been purchased for £2,000 have been damaged and are unsaleable. This is not reflected in the financial statements.
5 Fixtures and fittings to the value of £16,000 were delivered just before 31 March 2017, but these assets were not included in the financial statements and the purchase invoice had not been processed.
6 Wages for Saturday-only staff, amounting to £1,000, have not been paid for the final Saturday of the year. This is not reflected in the financial statements.
7 Tax is payable at 30 per cent of profit before taxation. Assume that it is payable shortly after the year-end.

Required:

Prepare revised financial statements for Rose Limited for the year ended 31 March 2017, incorporating the information in 1 to 7 above. (Work to the nearest £1,000.)

CHAPTER 5

Accounting for limited companies (2)

Introduction

Over the years, the published annual financial reports of companies have greatly increased in scope. In order to examine their content, we begin the chapter by identifying their core components. We then go on to discuss the main sources of accounting rules governing published financial statements. A detailed consideration of the accounting rules is beyond the scope of this book; however, the key rules that shape the form and content of the published financial statements are discussed. We also discuss the conceptual framework that underpins these rules.

Corporate governance, which concerns the way in which companies are directed and controlled, has become an important issue. In recent years, strenuous efforts have been made to improve standards of corporate governance, particularly for large listed companies. In this chapter, we consider the framework of rules that has been created to try to protect the interests of shareholders. We also discuss how corporate governance issues are reported.

Annual financial reports place increasing emphasis on the need for directors to report and comment on the performance and position of the company. UK law now requires the inclusion of a directors' report and a strategic report as part of the published annual financial reports. In this chapter, we examine the nature and content of both of these reports.

Despite the proliferation of accounting rules and the increase in published financial information available, the quality of some annual financial reports has caused concern. We end the chapter by looking at some well-publicised accounting scandals and the problem of creative accounting.

Learning outcomes

When you have completed this chapter, you should be able to:

- discuss both the framework of regulation and the conceptual framework that help to shape the form and content of annual financial statements;

- prepare a statement of financial position, statement of comprehensive income and statement of changes in equity in accordance with International Financial Reporting Standards;

- explain the principles upon which corporate governance rules are based and describe the main features of the corporate governance statement;

- describe the role and content of the directors' report and the strategic report; and

- discuss the threat posed by creative accounting and describe the main methods used to distort the fair presentation of position and performance.

The framework of annual financial reports

In the UK, limited companies were first required by law to publish (make public) financial information about themselves during the nineteenth century. Since then, there has been a trend towards ever greater disclosure within annual financial reports. Various reasons have been suggested for this trend. They include the increasing complexity of business, the increasing sophistication of users and an increasing recognition that other groups, apart from shareholders, have a stake in the success of a business. The annual financial reports of companies now go way beyond simply presenting the main financial statements. They cover a very wide range of information and their boundaries are becoming ever more difficult to establish.

In addition to financial information, annual financial reports often contain information relating to social matters (such as community involvement) and to environmental matters (such as carbon emissions). This has led to a growing debate as to whether such information should be included. The key questions raised include: 'Does this information really fit with the objectives of financial reporting? Should more appropriate forms of reporting be devised to convey this information?'

Whatever the outcome of this debate, its very existence has exposed the need for a more coherent reporting framework. A useful starting point in the search for such a framework is to try to identify the core components of financial reports. It has been suggested that three core components have evolved in practice. (See reference 1 at the end of the chapter.) These are set out in Figure 5.1.

Figure 5.1   The core components of financial reports

Financial statements	Corporate governance	Management commentary
The main financial statements, prepared in accordance with generally agreed accounting rules, along with explanatory notes.	Reports to shareholders on the way in which the directors have managed and controlled the business.	Contextual information to help understand the financial statements. This information both supplements and complements the financial statements.

In the sections that follow, we consider each of these three components in turn. We should bear in mind, however, that these are not clearly distinguished in the financial reports. In practice, the information is often poorly organised and overlaps occur.

The directors' duty to account

For most large companies, it is not possible for all shareholders to be involved in the management of the company. Instead, they appoint directors to act on their behalf. This separation of ownership from day-to-day control creates a need for directors to be accountable for their stewardship (management) of the company's assets. To fulfil this need, the directors must prepare financial statements that provide a fair representation of the financial position and performance of the business. This means that they must select appropriate accounting policies, make reasonable accounting estimates and adhere to all relevant accounting rules when preparing the statements. To avoid misstatements in the financial statements, whether from fraud or error, the directors must also maintain appropriate internal control systems.

Each of the company's shareholders has the right to be sent a copy of the financial statements produced by the directors. These statements must also be made available to the general public. This is achieved by the company submitting a copy to the Registrar of Companies, which is then available for public inspection. All London Stock Exchange listed companies must also publish its financial statements on its website.

Activity 5.1

It can be argued that the publication of financial statements is vital to a well-functioning private sector. Why might this be the case?

There are at least two reasons:

- Unless shareholders receive regular information about the performance and position of a business, they will have problems in appraising their investment. Under these circumstances, they would probably be reluctant to invest.
- Unless suppliers of labour, goods, services and finance, particularly those supplying credit (loans) or goods and services on credit, receive information about a company's financial health they may be reluctant to engage in commercial relationships. The fact that a company has limited liability increases the risks involved in dealing with it.

In both cases, the functioning of the private sector of the economy will be adversely affected by the absence of financial statements.

The need for accounting rules

If we accept the need for directors to prepare and publish financial statements, we should also accept the need for a framework of rules concerning how these statements are prepared and presented. Without rules, there is a much greater risk that unscrupulous directors will adopt accounting policies and practices that portray an unrealistic view of financial health. There is also a much greater risk that the financial statements will not be comparable over time or with those of other businesses. Accounting rules can narrow areas of differences and reduce the variety of accounting methods. This should help ensure that all businesses treat similar transactions in a similar way.

Example 5.1 illustrates the problems that may arise where businesses can exercise choice over the accounting policies used.

Example 5.1

Rila plc and Pirin plc are both wholesalers of electrical goods. Both commenced trading on 1 March 2016 with an identical share capital. Both acquired identical property, plant and equipment on 1 March and both achieved identical trading results during the first year of trading. The following financial information relating to both businesses is available:

	£m
Ordinary £1 shares fully paid on 1 March 2016	60
Non-current assets (at cost) acquired on 1 March 2016	40
Revenue for the year to 28 February 2017	100
Purchases of inventories during the year to 28 February 2017	70
Expenses for the year to 28 February 2017 (excluding depreciation)	20
Trade receivables as at 28 February 2017	37
Trade payables as at 28 February 2017	12
Cash as at 28 February 2017	5

The non-current assets held by both businesses are leasehold buildings that have five years left to run on the lease. Inventories for both businesses have been valued at the year-end at £16 million on a FIFO basis and £12 million on a LIFO basis.

When preparing their financial statements for the first year of trading,

- Rila plc decided to write off the cost of the leasehold premises at the end of the lease period. Pirin plc adopted the straight-line basis of depreciation for the leasehold buildings.
- Rila plc adopted the FIFO method of inventories valuation and Pirin plc adopted the LIFO method.

The income statements and the statements of financial position for the two businesses, ignoring taxation, will be as follows:

Income statements for the year to 28 February 2017

	Rila plc £m	Pirin plc £m
Revenue	100	100
Cost of sales:		
Rila plc (£70m − £16m)	(54)	
Pirin plc (£70m − £12m)		(58)
Gross profit	46	42
Expenses (excluding depreciation)	(20)	(20)
Depreciation:		
Rila plc	(−)	
Pirin plc (£40m/5)		(8)
Profit for the year	26	14

Statements of financial position as at 28 February 2017

	Rila plc £m	Pirin plc £m
ASSETS		
Non-current assets		
Property, plant and equipment at cost	40	40
Accumulated depreciation	(–)	(8)
	40	32
Current assets		
Inventories	16	12
Trade receivables	37	37
Cash	5	5
	58	54
Total assets	98	86
EQUITY AND LIABILITIES		
Equity		
Share capital	60	60
Retained earnings	26	14
	86	74
Current liabilities		
Trade payables	12	12
Total equity and liabilities	98	86

Although the two businesses are identical in terms of funding and underlying trading performance, the financial statements create an impression that the financial health of each business is quite different. The accounting policies selected by Rila plc help to portray a much rosier picture. We can see that Rila plc reports a significantly higher profit for the year and higher assets at the year-end.

Depreciation and inventories valuation are not the only areas where choices might be exercised. Nevertheless, they illustrate the potential impact of different accounting choices over the short term.

Accounting rules should help to provide greater confidence in the integrity of financial statements. This, in turn, may help a business to raise funds and to build stronger relationships with customers and suppliers. Users of accounting reports must, however, be realistic about what can be achieved through regulation. Problems of manipulation and of concealment can still occur even within a highly regulated environment and examples of both will be considered later in the chapter. The scale of these problems, however, should be reduced where there is a practical set of rules.

Even with a set of rules, problems of comparability can also still arise because accounting is not a precise science. Judgements and estimates must be made when preparing financial statements, and these may hinder comparisons. Furthermore, no two businesses are identical (unlike the companies in Example 5.1) and accounting policies may vary between businesses for valid reasons.

Sources of accounting rules

Recent years have seen increasing trends towards the internationalisation of business and the integration of financial markets. These trends have helped to strengthen the case for the international harmonisation of accounting rules. By adopting a common set of rules, users of financial statements should be better placed to compare the financial health of companies based in different countries. It should also relieve international companies of some of the burden of preparing financial statements. Different financial statements will no longer have to be prepared to comply with the rules of the various countries in which a particular company operates.

The International Accounting Standards Board (IASB) is an independent body that is at the forefront of the move towards harmonisation. The Board, which is based in the UK, is dedicated to developing a single set of high-quality, global accounting rules. These are designed to provide transparent and comparable information in financial statements. The rules, which are known as **International Accounting Standards** (IASs) or **International Financial Reporting Standards** (IFRSs), deal with key issues such as:

- what information should be disclosed;
- how information should be presented;
- how assets should be valued; and
- how profit should be measured.

Activity 5.2

We have already come across some IASs and IFRSs in earlier chapters. Try to recall at least two topics where financial reporting standards were mentioned.

We came across financial reporting standards when considering:

- the valuation and impairment of assets (Chapter 2);
- depreciation and impairment of non-current assets (Chapter 3); and
- the valuation of inventories (Chapter 3).

The growing authority of the IASB

Several important developments have greatly increased the authority of the IASB in recent years. The first major boost came when the European Commission required nearly all companies listed on the stock exchanges of EU member states to adopt IFRSs for reporting periods commencing on or after 1 January 2005. As a result, nearly 7,000 companies in 25 different countries switched to IFRSs. This was followed in 2006 by the IASB and the US Financial Accounting Standards Board (FASB) agreeing a roadmap for convergence between IFRSs and US accounting rules. More recently, however, the FASB has backtracked somewhat from this initial enthusiasm for convergence. Despite the US equivocation on convergence, the authority of the IASB has gone from strength to strength. A recent survey of 140 countries revealed that 116 countries, or 83 per cent of those surveyed, now require the use of IFRSs for all, or most, public companies. The 116 adopting countries represent 58 per cent of the world's gross domestic product. On the other hand, the four most populous counties (China, India, Indonesia and the USA) and the three countries with the largest economies (China, Japan and the USA) have yet to adopt IFRSs. (See reference 2 at the end of the chapter.)

Non-listed UK companies are not required to adopt IFRSs but have the option to do so. It is possible, however, that IFRSs will eventually become a requirement for all UK companies.

Adopting IFRSs

The EU requirement to adopt IFRSs, mentioned earlier, overrides any laws in force in member states that could either hinder or restrict compliance with them. The ultimate aim is to achieve a single framework of accounting rules for companies from all member states. The EU recognises that this will be achieved only if individual governments do not add to the requirements imposed by the various IFRSs. Thus, it seems that accounting rules developed within individual EU member countries will eventually disappear. For the time being, however, the EU accepts that the governments of member states may need to impose additional disclosures for some corporate governance matters and regulatory requirements.

In the UK, company law requires disclosure relating to various corporate governance issues. There is, for example, a requirement to disclose details of directors' remuneration in the published financial statements, which goes beyond anything required by IFRSs. Furthermore, the Financial Conduct Authority (FCA), in its role as the UK listing authority, imposes rules on Stock Exchange listed companies. These include the requirement to publish a condensed set of interim (half-yearly) financial statements in addition to the annual financial statements. (Interim statements are not required by the IASB although, if they are prepared, there is an appropriate standard.)

Figure 5.2 sets out the main sources of accounting rules for Stock Exchange listed companies.

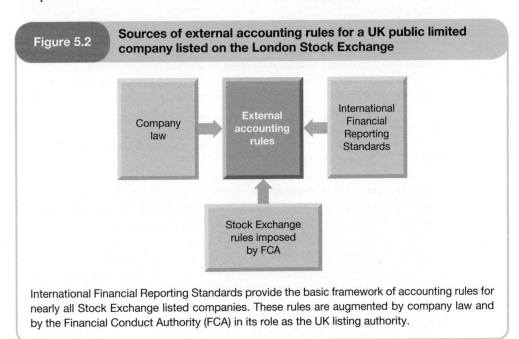

Figure 5.2 Sources of external accounting rules for a UK public limited company listed on the London Stock Exchange

International Financial Reporting Standards provide the basic framework of accounting rules for nearly all Stock Exchange listed companies. These rules are augmented by company law and by the Financial Conduct Authority (FCA) in its role as the UK listing authority.

Real World 5.1 provides a list of IASB standards that were in force as at 1 January 2017. It gives some idea of the range of topics that are covered. The IASB has an ambitious agenda and so significant changes to this list are likely to occur in the future.

Real World 5.1

International standards

The following is a list of the International Accounting Standards (IASs) and International Financial Reporting Standards (IFRSs) in force as at 1 January 2017. (The latter term is used for standards issued from 2003 onwards.) Several standards have been issued and subsequently withdrawn, which explains the gaps in the numerical sequence. In addition, several have been revised and reissued.

IAS 1	*Presentation of Financial Statements*
IAS 2	*Inventories*
IAS 7	*Statement of Cash Flows*
IAS 8	*Accounting Policies, Changes in Accounting Estimates and Errors*
IAS 10	*Events after the Reporting Period*
IAS 12	*Income Taxes*
IAS 16	*Property, Plant and Equipment*
IAS 19	*Employee Benefits*
IAS 20	*Accounting for Government Grants and Disclosure of Government Assistance*
IAS 21	*The Effects of Changes in Foreign Exchange Rates*
IAS 23	*Borrowing Costs*
IAS 24	*Related Party Disclosures*
IAS 26	*Accounting and Reporting by Retirement Benefit Plans*
IAS 27	*Separate Financial Statements*
IAS 28	*Investments in Associates and joint ventures*
IAS 29	*Financial Reporting in Hyperinflationary Economies*
IAS 32	*Financial Instruments: Presentation*
IAS 33	*Earnings per Share*
IAS 34	*Interim Financial Reporting*
IAS 36	*Impairment of Assets*
IAS 37	*Provisions, Contingent Liabilities and Contingent Assets*
IAS 38	*Intangible Assets*
IAS 39	*Financial Instruments: Recognition and Measurement*
IAS 40	*Investment Property*
IAS 41	*Agriculture*
IFRS 1	*First-time Adoption of International Financial Reporting Standards*
IFRS 2	*Share-based Payment*
IFRS 3	*Business Combinations*
IFRS 4	*Insurance Contracts*
IFRS 5	*Non-current Assets Held for Sale and Discontinued Operations*
IFRS 6	*Exploration for and Evaluation of Mineral Resources*
IFRS 7	*Financial Instruments: Disclosures*
IFRS 8	*Operating Segments*
IFRS 9	*Financial Instruments*
IFRS 10	*Consolidated Financial Statements*
IFRS 11	*Joint Arrangements*
IFRS 12	*Disclosure of Interests in Other Entities*
IFRS 13	*Fair Value Measurement*
IFRS 14	*Regulatory Deferral Accounts*
IFRS 15	*Revenue from Contracts with Customers*
IFRS 16	*Leases*

Source: International Accounting Standards Board, www.ifrs.org.

Presenting the financial statements

Now that we have gained an impression of the sources of rules affecting limited companies, let us turn our attention to the main rules to be followed in the presentation of financial statements. We shall focus on the IASB rules and, in particular, those contained in IAS 1 *Presentation of Financial Statements*. This standard is very important as it sets out the structure and content of financial statements and the principles to be followed in preparing these statements.

It might be helpful to have a set of the most recent financial statements of a Stock Exchange listed company available as you work through this section. They should all be available on the internet. Select a listed company that interests you and go to its website.

The financial statements identified in IAS 1 are as set out in Figure 5.3.

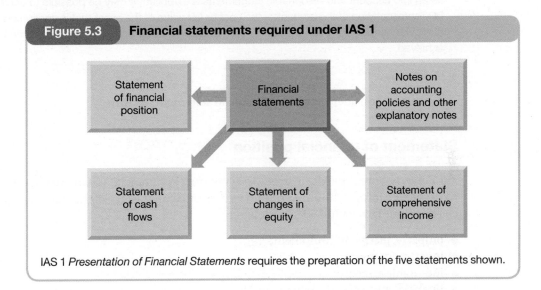

Figure 5.3   Financial statements required under IAS 1

IAS 1 *Presentation of Financial Statements* requires the preparation of the five statements shown.

The standard states that these financial statements should normally cover a one-year period and should be accompanied by comparative information for the previous year. Thus, at the end of each reporting period companies should normally produce two of each of the statements, plus the related notes. In practice, virtually all companies satisfy this requirement by showing the equivalent figures for the previous year in a separate column in the current year's statements.

Comparative narrative information should also be provided if needed for a better grasp of current period results – for example, as background to an ongoing legal dispute.

Fair representation

Before we consider the financial statements in detail, it is important to emphasise that the standard requires that they provide a fair representation of a company's financial position, financial performance and cash flows. There is a presumption that this will be achieved where they are drawn up in accordance with the various IASB standards that are currently in force. It is only in very rare circumstances that compliance with a standard would not result in a fair representation of the financial health of a company. Where the financial statements have been prepared in accordance with IASB standards, this should be clearly stated in the notes.

Activity 5.3

IAS 1 says that the financial statements are required to show a 'fair representation' of financial health. It does not say that the statements should show a 'correct' or an 'accurate' representation of financial health. Why, in your opinion, does it not use those words? (*Hint*: Think of depreciation of non-current assets.)

Accounting can never really be said to be 'correct' or 'accurate' as these words imply that there is a precise value that an asset, claim, revenue or expense could have. This is simply not true in many, if not most, cases.

Depreciation provides a good example of where 'correct' or 'accurate' would not be appropriate. The annual depreciation expense is based on judgements about the future concerning the expected useful life and residual value of an asset. If all relevant factors are taken into account and reasonable judgements are applied, it may be possible to achieve a fair representation of the amount of the cost or fair value of the asset that is consumed for a particular period. However, a uniquely correct figure for depreciation for a period cannot be achieved.

Let us now consider each of the financial statements in turn.

Statement of financial position

IAS 1 does not prescribe the format (or layout) for this financial statement but does set out the *minimum* information that should be presented on the face of the statement of financial position. This includes the following:

● property, plant and equipment;
● investment property;
● intangible assets;
● financial assets (such as shares and loan notes of other companies held as assets);
● inventories;
● trade and other receivables;
● cash and cash equivalents;
● trade and other payables;
● provisions (a provision is a liability that is of uncertain timing or amount – such as a possible obligation arising from a legal case against the company that has yet to be determined);
● financial liabilities (other than payables and provisions shown above);
● tax liabilities; and
● issued share capital and reserves (equity).

Additional information should be also shown where it is relevant to an understanding of the financial position of the business.

The standard requires that, on the statement of financial position, a distinction is normally made between current assets and non-current assets and between current liabilities and non-current liabilities. However, for certain types of business, such as financial institutions, the standard accepts that it may be more appropriate to order items according to their liquidity (that is, their nearness to cash).

Some of the assets and claims listed above may have to be sub-classified to comply with particular standards or because of their size or nature. Thus, sub-classifications are required for assets such as property, plant and equipment, trade receivables and inventories as well as for claims such as provisions and reserves. Certain details relating to share capital, such as the number of issued shares and their nominal value, must also be shown. To avoid cluttering up the statement of financial position, however, this additional information can be shown in the notes. In practice, most companies use notes for this purpose.

Statement of comprehensive income

This statement extends the conventional income statement to include certain other gains and losses that affect shareholders' equity. It may be presented either in the form of a single statement or as two separate statements, comprising an income statement and a **statement of comprehensive income.**

Again the format of the statement of comprehensive income is not prescribed, but IAS 1 sets out the *minimum* information to be presented on the face of the statement. This includes:

- revenue;
- finance costs;
- profits or losses arising from discontinued operations;
- tax expense;
- profit or loss;
- each component of other comprehensive income classified by its nature;
- any share of the comprehensive income of associates or joint ventures; and
- total comprehensive income (that is, the net figure taking account of all of the revenues and expenses in this list).

The standard makes it clear that further items should be shown on the face of the income statement where they are relevant to an understanding of performance. If, for example, a business's inventories are destroyed as a result of a flood, the cost of the flood damage should be shown as a separate item in the statement.

As a further aid to understanding, all material expenses should be separately disclosed. However, they need not be shown on the face of the income statement: they can appear in the notes to the financial statements. The kind of material items that may require separate disclosure include:

- write-down of inventories to net realisable value;
- write-down of property, plant and equipment;
- disposals of investments;
- restructuring costs;
- discontinued operations; and
- litigation settlements.

This is not an exhaustive list and, in practice, other material expenses may require separate disclosure.

The standard suggests two possible ways in which expenses can be presented on the face of the income statement. Expenses can be presented either:

- according to their nature, for example as depreciation, employee expenses and so on; or
- according to business functions, such as administrative activities and distribution (where, for example, depreciation of delivery lorries will be included in distribution expenses).

The choice between the two possible ways of presenting expenses will depend on which one will provide the more relevant and reliable information, in the directors' opinion.

To understand what other information must be presented in this statement, apart from that already contained in a conventional income statement, we should remember that, broadly, the conventional income statement shows all *realised* gains and losses for the period. It also includes some unrealised losses (that is, losses relating to assets still held). However, unrealised gains, and some unrealised losses, do not pass through the income statement, but go directly to a reserve. We saw, in an earlier chapter, an example of an unrealised gain (which, therefore, would not have passed through the conventional income statement).

Activity 5.4

Can you remember what this example was?

The example that we met earlier is where a business revalues its land and buildings. The gain arising is not shown in the conventional income statement, but is transferred to a revaluation reserve, which forms part of the equity. (We met this example in Activity 2.17 on page 68.)

Land and buildings are not the only assets to which this rule relates, but these types of asset, in practice, provide the most common examples of unrealised gains.

An example of an unrealised gain, or loss, that has not been mentioned so far, arises from exchange differences when the results of foreign operations are translated into UK currency. Any gain, or loss, usually bypasses the income statement and is taken directly to a currency translation reserve.

A weakness of conventional accounting is that there is no robust principle that can be applied to determine precisely what should, and what should not, be included in the income statement. For example, losses arising from the impairment of non-current assets normally appear in the income statement. On the other hand, losses arising from translating the carrying amount of assets expressed in an overseas currency (because they are owned by an overseas branch) do not. There is no real difference in principle between the two types of loss, but the difference in treatment is ingrained in conventional accounting practice.

The statement of comprehensive income includes *all* gains and losses for a period and so will also take unrealised gains into account as well as any remaining unrealised losses. It extends the conventional income statement by including these items immediately beneath the measure of profit for the year. An illustration of this statement is shown in Example 5.2. Here, expenses are presented according to business function and comparative figures for the previous year are shown alongside the figures for the current year.

Example 5.2

Malik plc
Statement of comprehensive income for the year ended 30 June 2017

	2017 £m	2016 £m
Revenue	100.6	97.2
Cost of sales	(60.4)	(59.1)
Gross profit	40.2	38.1
Other income	4.0	3.5
Distribution expenses	(18.2)	(16.5)
Administration expenses	(10.3)	(11.2)
Other expenses	(2.1)	(2.4)
Operating profit	13.6	11.5
Finance charges	(2.0)	(1.8)
Profit before tax	11.6	9.7
Tax	(2.9)	(2.4)
Profit for the year	8.7	7.3
Other comprehensive income		
Revaluation of property, plant and equipment	20.3	6.6
Foreign currency translation differences for foreign operations	12.5	4.0
Tax on other comprehensive income	(6.0)	(2.6)
Other comprehensive income for the year, net of tax	26.8	8.0
Total comprehensive income for the year	35.5	15.3

This example adopts a single-statement approach to presenting comprehensive income. The alternative two-statement approach simply divides the information shown into two separate parts. The income statement, which is the first statement, begins with the revenue and ends with the profit for the reporting period. The statement of comprehensive income, which is the second statement, begins with the profit for the reporting period and ends with the total comprehensive income.

Statement of changes in equity

The **statement of changes in equity** aims to help users to understand the changes in share capital and reserves that took place during the reporting period. It reconciles the figures for these items at the beginning of the period with those at the end. This is achieved by showing the effect on the share capital and reserves of total comprehensive income as well as the effect of share issues and purchases during the period. The effect of dividends during the period may also be shown in this statement, although dividends can be shown in the notes instead.

To see how a statement of changes in equity may be prepared, let us consider Example 5.3.

Example 5.3

At 1 January 2016 Miro plc had the following equity:

Miro plc

	£m
Share capital (£1 ordinary shares)	100
Revaluation reserve	20
Translation reserve	40
Retained earnings	150
Total equity	**310**

During 2016, the company made a profit for the year from normal business operations of £42 million and reported an upward revaluation of property, plant and equipment of £120 million (net of any tax payable if the unrealised gains were realised). A loss on exchange differences on translating the results of foreign operations of £10 million was also reported. To strengthen its financial position, the company issued 50 million ordinary shares during the year at a premium of £0.40. Dividends for the year were £27 million.

This information for 2016 can be set out in a statement of changes in equity as follows:

Statement of changes in equity for the year ended 31 December 2016

	Share capital	Share premium	Revaluation reserve	Translation reserve	Retained earnings	Total
	£m	£m	£m	£m	£m	£m
Balance as at 1 January 2016	100	–	20	40	150	310
Changes in equity for 2016						
Issue of ordinary shares[1]	50	20	–	–	–	70
Dividends[2]	–	–	–	–	(27)	(27)
Total comprehensive income for the year[3]	–	–	120	(10)	42	152
Balance at 31 December 2016	150	20	140	30	165	505

[1] The premium on the share price is transferred to a specific reserve.
[2] We have chosen to show dividends in the statement of changes in equity rather than in the notes. They represent an appropriation of equity and are deducted from retained earnings.
[3] The effect of each component of comprehensive income on the various elements of shareholders' equity must be separately disclosed. The revaluation gain and the loss on translating foreign operations are each allocated to a specific reserve. The profit for the year is added to retained earnings.

Statement of cash flows

The statement of cash flows should help users to assess the ability of a company to generate cash and to assess the company's need for cash. The presentation requirements for this statement are set out in IAS 7 *Statement of Cash Flows,* which we shall consider in some detail in the next chapter.

Notes

The notes play an important role in helping users to understand the financial statements. They will normally contain the following information:

- a confirmation that the financial statements comply with relevant IFRSs;
- a summary of the measurement bases used and other significant accounting policies applied (for example, the basis of inventories valuation);
- supporting information relating to items appearing on the statement of financial position, the statement of comprehensive income, the statement of changes in equity and the statement of cash flows; and
- other significant disclosures such as future contractual commitments that have not been recognised and financial risk management objectives and policies.

General points

The standard provides support for three key accounting conventions when preparing the financial statements. These are:

- the going concern convention;
- the accruals convention (except for the statement of cash flows); and
- the consistency convention.

These conventions were discussed in Chapters 2 and 3.

Finally, to improve the transparency of financial statements, the standard states that:

- offsetting liabilities against assets, or expenses against income, is not allowed. Thus it is not acceptable, for example, to offset a bank overdraft against a positive bank balance (where a company has both); and
- material items must be shown separately.

The need for a conceptual framework

In Chapters 2 and 3 we came across various accounting conventions such as the prudence, historic cost and going concern conventions. These were developed as a practical response to particular problems that were confronted when preparing financial statements. They have stood the test of time and are still of value to preparers today. However, they do not provide, and were never designed to provide, a **conceptual framework,** or framework of principles, to guide the development of financial statements. As we grapple with increasingly complex financial reporting problems, the need to have a sound understanding of *why* we account for things in a particular way becomes more pressing. Knowing *why* we account, rather than simply *how* we account, is vital if we are to improve the quality of financial statements.

In recent years, much effort has been expended in various countries, including the UK, to develop a clear conceptual framework that will guide us in the development of accounting. This framework should provide clear answers to such fundamental questions as:

- Who are the main users of financial statements?
- What is the purpose of financial statements?
- What qualities should financial information possess?

- What are the main elements of financial statements?
- How should these elements be defined, recognised and measured?

If these questions can be answered, accounting rule makers, such as the IASB, will be in a stronger position to identify best practice and to develop more coherent rules. This should, in turn, increase the credibility of financial reports in the eyes of users. It may even help reduce the possible number of rules.

Activity 5.5

Can you think how it may help reduce the number of rules required?

Some issues may be resolved by reference to the application of general principles rather than by the generation of further rules.

The IASB framework

The quest for a conceptual framework began in earnest in the 1970s when the Financial Accounting Standards Board (FASB) in the USA devoted a large amount of time and resources to this task. It resulted in a broad framework, which other rule-making bodies, including the IASB, then drew upon to develop their own frameworks.

The IASB framework was first produced in 1989 and has since provided guidance for the development of International Financial Reporting Standards. Many of the standards that pre-dated the framework have now been replaced or revised. The IASB framework has itself, however, been revised, with the most recent revision occurring in 2017.

The Conceptual Framework for Financial Reporting, as it is called, asserts that the objective of general-purpose financial reporting is '*to provide financial information about the reporting entity that is useful to existing and potential investors, lenders and other creditors in making decisions about providing resources to the entity*'. Note that it is the providers of finance that are seen as the primary users of general-purpose financial reports. This is because investors, lenders and other creditors largely rely on these reports to make their investment decisions. While other users may find general-purpose financial reports useful, the reports are not aimed at them. The IASB framework emphasises that financial reports alone cannot meet the needs of the primary users and that other sources of information, such as that relating to the economy, political events, industry changes and so on, should also be used.

The IASB framework sets out the qualitative characteristics that make financial statements useful. These are the same as those we considered in Chapter 1.

Activity 5.6

Can you recall what these qualitative characteristics are?

The fundamental characteristics identified are relevance and faithful representation: it is these characteristics that make information useful. Characteristics that enhance the quality of financial reports are comparability, timeliness, verifiability and understandability. These are regarded as desirable but, in the absence of relevance and faithful representation, they cannot make information useful.

The framework acknowledges that producing financial information incurs costs, which must be justified by the benefits provided.

The IASB framework identifies two important accounting conventions: going concern and accruals. It states that financial statements should normally be prepared on the assumption that a business is a going concern. If this assumption cannot be applied, a different basis of reporting will be required. This will affect the valuation of assets held. The framework supports the accruals convention, which is seen as a better means of assessing past and future performance than reliance on cash receipts and payments. Nevertheless, information on cash flows is also considered useful for assessing financing and investing activities, liquidity and solvency.

The IASB framework goes on to identify the main elements of financial statements. Those relating to the measurement of financial position are assets, liabilities and equity. Those relating to the measurement of performance are income and expense. Each of these elements is defined and the definitions provided are similar to those discussed in Chapters 2 and 3.

The IASB framework identifies the historic cost measurement basis as well as current value-based measures, such as fair value. There is no attempt, however, to support a particular measurement basis. The framework simply states that, when deciding upon a suitable measurement basis, the qualitative characteristics of financial information (relevance, faithful representation and so on) should be used as a guide. In addition, the cost constraint must also be taken into account. The IASB framework recognises that, sometimes, more than one measurement basis may be needed to provide relevant information concerning an asset, liability, income or expense. In most cases, this can be done by using one measurement basis in the financial statements and the other(s) in the supporting notes. Other information appearing in the notes should include the nature and risks associated with items appearing in the financial statements along with any methods, judgements and assumptions used in their presentation.

The IASB framework does not have the same legal status as the IASB standards. Nevertheless, it offers guidance for dealing with accounting issues, particularly where no relevant financial reporting standard exists. Managers are required to consider the framework when dealing with issues that fall outside the scope of existing standards.

Overall, the broad principles contained within the IASB framework appear to enjoy widespread acceptance. There has been some criticism, mainly from academics, that the framework is really a descriptive document and fails to provide any theoretical underpinning to the financial statements. It has also been suggested that the framework is too broad in nature to provide useful guidance for developing financial reporting standards, or to deal with emerging accounting issues. Nevertheless, these criticisms have not sparked major controversies.

There has been more lively debate, however, over more detailed issues. In particular, the IASB has been criticised for failing to give sufficient weight to the role of prudence in financial reporting. The recently revised framework has clarified the IASB position on this matter. It acknowledges the importance of adopting a cautious approach but makes it clear that this should support the concept of neutrality in preparing financial statements. (We may recall from Chapter 2 that, in practice, prudence has often led to the understating of the financial strength of a business.)

It is worth noting that in 2004, the IASB and FASB embarked on a joint project to produce a common conceptual framework. The aim was to underpin the financial reporting standards of both bodies, which would represent a major step towards convergence. The IASB and FASB completed the first phase of this project in 2010. In 2016, however, it was announced that the joint project was no longer being pursued and that the two bodies were working independently.

The auditors' role

Shareholders are required to elect a qualified and independent person or, more usually, a firm to act as **auditors.** The auditors' main duty is to report whether, in their opinion, the financial statements do what they are supposed to do, namely to show a true and fair view of the financial performance, position and cash flows of the company. To form such an opinion, auditors must carefully scrutinise the financial statements and the underlying evidence upon which they are based. In particular, they will examine the accounting principles followed, the accounting estimates made and the robustness of the company's internal control systems. The auditors' opinion must be included with the financial statements sent to the shareholders and to the Registrar of Companies.

The relationship between the shareholders, the directors and the auditors is illustrated in Figure 5.4. This shows that the shareholders elect the directors to act on their behalf, in the day-to-day running of the company. The directors are then required to 'account' to the shareholders on the performance, position and cash flows of the company, on an annual basis. The shareholders also elect auditors, whose role it is to give the shareholders an independent, professional view of the truth and fairness of the financial statements prepared by the directors.

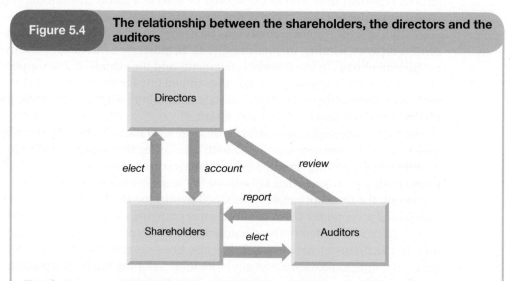

| Figure 5.4 | The relationship between the shareholders, the directors and the auditors |

The directors are appointed by the shareholders to manage the company on the shareholders' behalf. The directors are required to report each year to the shareholders, principally by means of financial statements, on the company's performance, position and cash flows. To give greater confidence in the statements, the shareholders also appoint auditors to investigate the reports and to express an opinion on their reliability.

Segmental financial reports

Most large businesses are engaged in a number of different operations, with each having its own levels of risk, growth and profitability. Information relating to each type of business operation, however, is normally added together (aggregated) in the financial statements so as to provide an overall picture of the financial performance and position of the business as a whole. For example, the revenue figure at the top of the income statement represents all of the business's revenues added together. This will be true even where the revenues come from quite different activities. Although this aggregation of information can help to provide a clearer broad picture, it can make it difficult to undertake comparisons over time or between businesses. Some idea of the range and scale of the various types of operation must be gained for a proper assessment of financial health. Thus, to undertake any meaningful analysis of financial performance and position, it is usually necessary to disaggregate (break down) the information contained within the financial statements. This disaggregated information is disclosed in **segmental financial reports.**

By breaking down the financial information according to each type of business operation, or operating segment, we can evaluate the relative risks and profitability of each segment and make useful comparisons with other businesses or other operating segments. We can also see the trend of performance for each operating segment over time and so determine more accurately the likely growth prospects for the business as a whole. We should be able to assess more easily the impact on the overall business of changes in market conditions relating to particular operating segments.

Disclosure of information relating to the performance of each segment may also help to improve the efficiency of the business by keeping managers on their toes. Operating segments that are performing poorly will be revealed and this should put pressure on managers to take corrective action. Finally, where an operating segment has been sold, the shareholders will be better placed to assess the wisdom of the managers' decision to sell it.

Segmental reporting rules

An IASB standard (IFRS 8 *Operating Segments*) requires listed companies to disclose information about their various operating segments. Defining an operating segment, however, can be a tricky business. The IASB has opted for a 'management approach', which means that an operating segment is defined by reference to how management has segmented the business for internal reporting and monitoring purposes. Thus, how the business is divided into segments, for the purposes of managing them, defines a segment, under the standard, for that particular business. An operating segment is, therefore, defined as a part of the business that:

- generates revenues and expenses;
- has its own separate financial statements; and
- has its results regularly reviewed for resource-allocation and assessment purposes.

Not all parts of the business will meet the criteria identified. The headquarters of the business ('head office'), for example, is unlikely to do so.

Activity (5.7)

What do you think are the main advantages of adopting the management approach?

Under the management approach, shareholders will receive reports that are similar to the internal reports produced for management. This means that they can assess business performance from the same viewpoint as management. It should also mean that businesses will avoid additional, perhaps heavy, reporting costs, as the information will already have been produced.

There are, of course, other ways of identifying an operating segment. One approach would be to define a segment according to the industry to which it relates. This, however, may lead to endless definition and classification problems.

To be reported separately, an operating segment must be of significant size. This normally means that it must account for 10 per cent or more of the combined revenue, profits or assets of the entire business. A segment that does not meet this size threshold may be combined with other similar segments to produce a reportable segment, or separately reported despite its size, at the directors' discretion. If neither of these options is chosen, it should be reported with other segments under a separate category of 'all other segments'.

Segmental disclosure

Financial information to be disclosed includes some profit (/loss) measure (for example, operating profit) for each segment, along with the following income statement items, provided that they are regularly reported to management:

- revenue, distinguishing between revenue from external customers and revenue from other segments of the business;
- interest revenue and interest expense;
- depreciation and other material non-cash items;
- material items of income and expense;
- any profit (loss) from associate companies or joint ventures; and
- corporation tax (where it is separately reported for a segment).

The business must also disclose the total assets for each segment and, if they are reported to management, the total liabilities. Any additions to non-current assets during the period must also be reported. Where these items are not regularly reported to management, they need not be included in the segmental report that appears in the business's annual report.

Example 5.4 provides an illustrative segmental financial report for a business.

Example 5.4

Goya Plc
Segmental report for the year ended 31 May 2017

	Publishing £m	Film-making £m	All other £m	Totals £m
Revenue from external customers	150	200	25	375
Inter-segment revenue	20	10	–	30
Interest revenue	10	–	–	10
Interest expense	–	15	–	15
Depreciation	40	20	5	65
Reportable segment profit	15	19	4	38
Other material non-cash items:				
Impairment of assets	–	10	–	10
Reportable segment assets	60	80	12	152
Expenditures for reportable				
segment non-current assets	12	18	2	32
Reportable segment liabilities	25	32	4	61

We can see that information relating to each segment as well as a combined total for all operating segments is shown.

Key items, which include revenues, profits, assets and liabilities, must be reconciled with the corresponding amounts for the business as a whole. For example, Goya plc's income statement should show revenue of £375 million for the business as a whole. When carrying out a reconciliation, we should bear in mind that:

- inter-segment revenues should be eliminated as no transaction with external parties occurs – only sales to customers outside the business are deemed to be sales of the business as a whole;
- any profit arising from inter-segment transfers should also be eliminated; and
- assets and liabilities that have not been allocated to a particular segment should be taken into account.

The last item normally refers to assets and liabilities relating to business-wide activities. Thus, head office buildings may provide an example of unallocated assets, and staff pension liabilities may provide an example of unallocated liabilities.

IFRS 8 requires certain non-financial information concerning segments to be disclosed, including the basis for identifying operating segments and the types of products and services that each segment provides. It also requires disclosure of business-wide information such as geographical areas of operations and reliance on major customers.

Segmental reporting problems

When preparing segmental reports, various problems can arise, not least of which is that of identifying a segment. We have already seen that the relevant IFRS identifies operating segments according to the internal reporting and monitoring procedures of the business. While this may be the most practical course of action, comparisons between segments in other businesses may be impossible because of the different ways in which they are defined.

Another problem may arise where there is a significant amount of sales between operating segments. Where this occurs, the **transfer price** of the goods or services between segments can have a substantial impact on the reported profits of each segment. (The transfer price is the price at which sales are made between different segments of the business.) A potential risk is that revenues and profits will be manipulated for each segment through the use of particular transfer pricing policies.

Activity 5.8

Why might a business wish to manipulate revenues and profits in this way?

Where a business operates in different countries, it may try to report high profits in a country that has low tax rates and to report low profits (or even losses) in a country with high tax rates.

Real World 5.2 contains extracts from an Institute for Fiscal Studies paper on how tax authorities around the world are finding it increasingly difficult to deal with the transfer pricing policies that businesses adopt.

Real World 5.2

Try googling 'transfer pricing'

Corporate tax has rarely excited the imagination of the public as much as in recent years. This week Google has become the latest company to attract widespread anger over the amount of tax it has paid in the UK. The sense that there are some big, profitable companies paying relatively little in corporate tax has led many to try to allocate blame. Are multinationals simply behaving badly? Is HMRC (the UK tax authority) cutting sweetheart deals with favoured companies? Have politicians failed in their task of writing the tax rules?

The most important question relates to what we're trying to tax. The current tax rules are *not* designed to tax the profits from UK sales. They're certainly not designed to tax either revenue or sales generated in the UK. They are instead designed to tax that part of a firm's profit that arises from value created in the UK. That is the principle underlying all corporate tax regimes across the OECD. The trouble is that calculating how much profit arises from value added in any individual country can be very tricky, and is often open to honest dispute.

Multinationals operate across tax jurisdictions and create profits from activities in many countries. Working out how to allocate profits to different jurisdictions is difficult. In practice, countries have long agreed to divvy up profits according to where the underlying value was created. But there is often no single 'correct' answer to how much profit should be taxed in the UK. For example: if a worker in the UK and a worker in Ireland collaborate in arranging and concluding a sale, or in designing a new product, or writing a piece of software, how much of resulting income should be attributed to UK activities?

The tax rules seek to provide an answer to this. Transfer pricing rules dictate the prices that a firm can charge for a transaction – including payments for services or for the use of ideas – that happens between two parts of the same firm that are located in different tax jurisdictions. These are the rules that determine taxable profit allocation. Yet the rules can never be detailed enough to set out what the outcome should be in every possible case. This creates room for disagreement over what the tax rules mean. This is why HMRC is often engaged with multinationals about how much tax they pay: not because they are busy cutting special deals, but because they are trying to apply the tax rules in a consistent manner.

Multinationals are in a good position to be able to employ hordes of tax advisors that help them to conclude any uncertainty in way that leads to lower tax bills, and to take advantage of any loopholes to avoid tax. Some of those loopholes are well known and many exist in other countries' tax regimes. For example, the well documented "Double Irish" refers to differences between Irish and US tax laws that allow US multinationals to shift profits out of Ireland to tax havens such as Bermuda. These kinds of gaps in tax systems can create opportunities for tax avoidance on a grand scale. There is literally nothing the UK government can do unilaterally about some of these loopholes.

Source: Extracts from Miller, H. and Pope, T. (2016) *What does the row over Google's tax bill tell us about the corporate tax system?* Institute for Fiscal Studies, 26 January.

IFRS 8 recognises the impact of transfer pricing policies on segmental revenues and profit by stating that the basis for accounting for transactions between segments must be disclosed.

A third problem is that some expenses and assets may relate to more than one operating segment and their allocation between segments may vary between businesses. Again, this may hinder comparisons of segmental profits and profitability between businesses.

Corporate governance

In recent years, the issue of **corporate governance** has generated much debate. The term is used to describe the ways in which companies are directed and controlled. The issue of corporate governance is important because, with larger companies, those who own the company (that is, the shareholders) are usually divorced from the day-to-day control of the business. The shareholders employ directors to manage the company for them. Given this position, it may seem reasonable to assume that the best interests of shareholders will guide the directors' decisions. In practice, however, this is not always the case. The directors may be more concerned with pursuing their own interests, such as increasing their pay and 'perks' (such as expensive motor cars, overseas visits and so on) and improving their job security and status. As a result, a conflict can occur between the interests of shareholders and the interests of directors.

Where directors pursue their own interests at the expense of the shareholders, there is clearly a problem for the shareholders. It may also be a problem, however, for society as a whole.

Activity 5.9

Can you think of a reason why directors pursuing their own interests may be a problem for society as a whole?

If shareholders feel that their funds are likely to be mismanaged, they will be reluctant to invest. This can have severe economic repercussions.

A shortage of funds will mean that companies can make fewer investments. It may also mean an increase in the costs of finance as businesses compete for what little funds are available. Thus, a lack of concern for shareholders can have a profound effect on the performance of individual companies and, with this, the health of the economy.

To avoid these problems, most competitive market economies have a framework of rules to help monitor and control the behaviour of directors. These rules are usually based around three guiding principles:

- *Disclosure.* This lies at the heart of good corporate governance. Adequate and timely disclosure can help shareholders to judge the performance of the directors. Where performance is considered unsatisfactory this will be reflected in the price of shares. Changes should then be made to ensure the directors regain the confidence of shareholders.
- *Accountability.* This involves setting out the duties of the directors and establishing an adequate monitoring process. In the UK, company law requires that the directors act in the best interests of the shareholders. This means, among other things, that they must not try to use their position and knowledge to make gains at the expense of the shareholders. The law also requires larger companies to have their annual financial statements independently audited. The purpose of an independent audit is to lend credibility to the financial statements prepared by the directors. We shall consider this point in more detail later in the chapter.
- *Fairness.* Directors should not be able to benefit from access to 'inside' information that is not available to shareholders. As a result, both the law and the Stock Exchange place restrictions on the ability of directors to buy and sell the shares of the company. This means, for example, that the directors cannot buy or sell shares immediately before the

announcement of the annual profits or before the announcement of a significant event such as a planned merger.

These principles are set out in Figure 5.5.

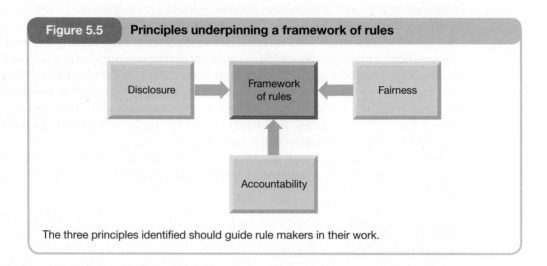

Figure 5.5 **Principles underpinning a framework of rules**

The three principles identified should guide rule makers in their work.

Strengthening the framework of rules

The number of rules designed to safeguard shareholders has increased considerably over the years. This has been in response to weaknesses in corporate governance procedures, which have been exposed through well-publicised business failures and frauds, excessive pay increases to directors and evidence that some financial reports were being 'massaged' so as to mislead shareholders.

Many believe, however, that the shareholders must shoulder some of the blame for any weaknesses. Not all shareholders in large companies are private individuals owning just a few shares each. In fact, ownership, by market value, of the shares listed on the London Stock Exchange is dominated by investing institutions such as insurance businesses, banks and pension funds, as we shall see in Chapter 15. These are often massive operations, owning large quantities of the shares of the companies in which they invest. These institutional investors employ specialist staff to manage their portfolios of shares in various companies. It has been argued that the large institutional shareholders, despite their size and relative expertise, have not been active in corporate governance matters. As a result, there has been little monitoring of directors. However, things are changing. Institutional investors, with strong encouragement from the UK government, have become more proactive in the affairs of companies in which they invest.

The UK Corporate Governance Code

In recent years there has been a real effort to address the problems of poor corporate governance. This has resulted in a code of best practice, known as the **UK Corporate Governance Code.** The UK Code sets out a number of principles underpinning its approach. **Real World 5.3** provides an outline of these.

Real World 5.3

The UK Corporate Governance Code

Key principles of the UK Code are as follows:

Leadership

- Every listed company should have a board of directors that is collectively responsible for its long-term success.
- There should be a clear division of responsibilities between the chairman, who leads the board, and the chief executive officer, who runs the company. No single person should have unbridled power.
- As part of their role as board members, non-executive directors should constructively challenge and help develop proposals on strategy.

Effectiveness

- There should be an appropriate balance of skills, experience, independence and knowledge to enable the board to carry out its duties effectively.
- Appointments to the board should be the subject of rigorous, formal and transparent procedures.
- All directors should allocate sufficient time to discharge their responsibilities.
- All board members should refresh their skills regularly and new board members should receive induction.
- The board should receive timely information that is of sufficient quality to enable it to carry out its duties.
- The board should undertake a formal and rigorous examination of its own performance each year, which will include its committees and individual directors.
- All directors should submit themselves for re-election at regular intervals, subject to satisfactory performance.

Accountability

- The board should present a balanced and understandable assessment of the company's position and future prospects.
- The board should define the company's risk appetite and tolerance and should maintain sound risk management and internal control systems.
- The board should establish formal and transparent arrangements for corporate reporting, risk management and internal control and for maintaining an appropriate relationship with the company's auditors.

Remuneration

- Remuneration levels should be designed to promote the long-term success of the company. Performance-related elements should be transparent, stretching and rigorously applied.
- There should be formal and transparent procedures for developing policy on directors' remuneration. No director should determine his or her own level of remuneration.

Relations with shareholders

- The board as a whole has a responsibility for ensuring a satisfactory dialogue with shareholders.
- The board should use general meetings to communicate with investors and to encourage their participation.

Source: Adapted from the *UK Corporate Governance Code,* Financial Reporting Council, April 2016, pp. 5 and 6, www.frc.org.uk.

The Code has the backing of the London Stock Exchange. This means that companies listed on the London Stock Exchange are expected to comply with the requirements of the Code or must give their shareholders good reason why they do not (that is, comply or explain). Failure to do one or other of these can lead to the company's shares being suspended from listing.

Activity 5.10

Why might suspension from listing be an important sanction against a non-compliant company?

A major advantage of a Stock Exchange listing is that it enables investors to sell their shares whenever they wish. A company that is suspended from listing would find it hard and, therefore, expensive to raise funds from investors because there would be no ready market for the shares.

Reporting requirements

In addition to the 'comply or explain' requirement, there are specific annual reporting requirements that must be met in order to comply with the UK Code. The more important of these include:

- a statement of how the board operates;
- names of senior directors, including the chairman, deputy chairman and chief executive, as well as names of independent, non-executive directors;
- a description of the work of key board committees – the audit committee, remuneration committee and nominations committee;
- a statement of how performance evaluation of the board, board committees and individual directors was carried out;
- a report that the board has reviewed the effectiveness of the company's risk management and internal controls systems;
- steps taken to ensure that directors understand the views of major shareholders;
- an explanation from the directors of their responsibility for preparing the accounts; and
- a statement from the directors that the business is a going concern.

Normally, this information is incorporated within a **corporate governance statement,** which forms part of the annual financial reports.

It is widely believed that the existence of the Code has improved the quality of information available to shareholders. It is also believed to have resulted in better checks on the powers of directors, and provided greater transparency in corporate affairs. However, rules can only be a partial answer. A balance must be struck between the need to protect shareholders and the need to encourage the entrepreneurial spirit of directors, which could be stifled under a welter of rules. This implies that rules should not be too tight and that means that unscrupulous directors may find ways around them.

Management commentary

A business, particularly a large business, may have very complex organisational structures, financing methods and operating systems. The financial statements must reflect these complexities if they are to provide a faithful portrayal of position and performance. As a result, they can often be lengthy, detailed and difficult to understand. To provide a clearer picture, a management commentary may be included. This can review the results and provide further information that is relevant to an understanding of performance and position.

Activity 5.11

What do you think are the main qualitative characteristics that information contained in a management commentary should possess? (*Hint*: Think back to Chapter 1.)

To be useful, the information should exhibit the characteristics for accounting information in general, which we identified in Chapter 1. Thus the information should be relevant, faithfully represented, comparable, verifiable, timely and understandable. The fact that we are often dealing with narrative information does not alter the need for these characteristics to be present.

In the UK, a management commentary has become an established part of the financial reporting landscape. In the sections below we consider two reports, the directors' report and the strategic report, which both supplement and complement the main financial statements and so form part of this commentary.

Directors' report

For many years, the directors have been required to prepare a report to shareholders relating to each financial period. The content of the **directors' report** is prescribed by law and includes assorted topics such current year's performance and position, future prospects of the business and social aspects. For companies of any size, the report must cover, amongst other things, the following matters:

- the names of those who were directors during the reporting period;
- any recommended dividend;
- the acquisition by a public limited company of its own shares;
- the involvement of employees in the affairs of the company;
- the employment and training of disabled persons;
- important events affecting the company since the year-end;
- likely future developments in the business; and
- research and development activities.

In addition to disclosing the information mentioned above, the directors' report must contain a declaration that the directors are not aware of any other information that the auditors might need in preparing their audit report. There must also be a declaration that the directors have taken steps to ensure that the auditors are aware of all relevant information. The auditors do not carry out an audit of the directors' report. However, they do check to see that the information in the report is consistent with that contained in the audited financial statements.

While the directors' report provides useful information, there is a strong case for revising its role, form and content. It contains a disjointed collection of items that lacks an underlying theme. It has become little more than a repository for miscellaneous items. The structure and presentation of the report is not tightly prescribed and so, in practice, comparisons between companies can be difficult. Furthermore, its relationship with the strategic report, which also provides additional information about the business and which we shall now discuss, is not clear.

Strategic report

Until recently, an important element of the directors' report was the *business review*. This provided largely narrative information to help assess the performance and position of the business. To give greater prominence to this element, it has been separated out and is now contained within a **strategic report.** The overall aim of the report is to help shareholders understand how well the directors have performed in promoting the success of the company. Thus, directors of all but the smallest companies are legally obliged to produce a *balanced* and *comprehensive* analysis of development and performance during the year as well as the position of the company's business at the year-end.

Activity 5.12

What do you think is meant by the terms 'balanced' and 'comprehensive' in this context?

The term 'balanced' means that both positive and negative aspects of company performance and position should be addressed and that shareholders should not be misled by the way in which the information is presented. Furthermore, there should be no omissions of important information.

The term 'comprehensive' means that *all* information needed for a proper understanding of the development, performance and position of the company should be included.

The directors must also describe the principal risks and uncertainties facing the company.

The strategic reports prepared by Stock Exchange listed companies must disclose more than those of other companies. Figure 5.6 summarises their main features.

Figure 5.6   The main features of the strategic report

Strategic management	Business environment	Business performance
How the entity intends to generate and preserve value	The internal and external environment in which the entity operates	How the entity has developed and performed and its position at the year-end
Strategy and objectives	Trends and factors	Analysis of performance and position
Business model	Principal risks and uncertainties	Key performance indicators (KPIs)
	Environmental, employee, social, community and human rights matters	Employee gender diversity

We can see that the report covers three broad areas. These are interrelated and should not be treated in isolation.

Source: Guidance in Strategic Report, Financial Reporting Council, June 2014, p. 20.

Real World 5.4 sets out the strategy, business model and key performance indicators as reported by one large business.

Real World 5.4

Showing at a cinema near you

Strategy

Cineworld Group plc operates over 200 cinemas, about half of which are in the UK and Ireland with the others mainly in Eastern Europe. It is one of the UK's largest cinema operators. Its stated aim is to 'be the best place to watch a movie' and its strategy to achieve this is to:

1   deliver a great cinema experience for all cinema goers, every time;
2   continue to expand our estate and look for profitable opportunities to grow;
3   ensure that we enhance our existing estate so we deliver a consistent level of quality across the group;
4   be leaders in the industry by offering customers the latest audio and visual technology; and
5   drive value for shareholders by delivering our growth plans in an efficient and effective way.

Business model

Its business model is summed up as follows:

Brand	We see our brands as a guarantee to the quality of the cinema experience and service our customers can always expect. We have focused brands in each territory in which we operate.
Film	Delivering a high quality film slate is one of the key external drivers of our business. Whilst we do not have control over what is in the marketplace, our close and long-standing relationships with the film distributors are fundamental to providing the best and most varied selection for our customers at the right time.
Technology	Investment in technology is central to the viewing experience we offer, but also allows us to be much more flexible in the use of our auditoriums and with our pricing policy.
Property	Nearly all of our properties are leased so that we can deploy capital into enhancing the customer experience and growing the business. Our venues are located to suit our target audiences' preferences.
Our people	Our people underpin the whole of our business model. They are the external face of our business, and are all responsible for ensuring that our customers enjoy the best possible experience during their visit to our cinemas. Promoting internal succession is a key focus across the Group.
Value	Value is generated through our focus on continually aiming to enhance revenue, profit generation and prudent cash management.

Key performance indicators (KPIs)

To monitor performance, it employs the following KPIs:

-   Admissions (number of customer visits)
-   Retail spend per person
-   Average ticket price
-   New sites
-   Total number of screens
-   Refurbishment expenditure.

Source: Adapted from Cineworld Group plc, Annual Report and Accounts 2015, preamble, pp. 12 and 14.

Activity (5.13)

Why do you think Stock Exchange listed companies are required to disclose more information about their business than other companies?

Various arguments can be made in favour of greater accountability from such companies. As their shares are frequently traded, greater transparency concerning their business operations should help investors to make more informed decisions. Share prices may, therefore, be set in a more efficient manner, which can contribute towards the smooth functioning of capital markets. In addition, Stock Exchange listed companies tend to be larger, have more economic power and have more stakeholders than other companies. Their impact on the economy and society as a whole, therefore, tends to be greater. This, in turn, creates an obligation for them to account more fully for their operations and actions.

Creative accounting

Despite the proliferation of accounting rules and the independent checks that are imposed, concerns over the quality of published financial statements surface from time to time. There are occasions when directors apply particular accounting policies, or structure particular transactions, in such a way as to portray a picture of financial health that is in line with what they want users to see, rather than what is a true and fair view of financial position and performance. Misrepresenting the performance and position of a business in this way is often called **creative accounting** and it poses a major problem for accounting rule makers and for society generally.

Activity (5.14)

Why might the directors of a company engage in creative accounting? Try to think of at least two reasons.

There are many reasons including:

- to get around restrictions (for example, to report sufficient profit to pay a dividend);
- to avoid government action (for example, the taxation of profits);
- to hide poor management decisions;
- to achieve sales revenue or profit targets, thereby ensuring that performance bonuses are paid to the directors;
- to attract new share capital or long-term borrowing by showing an apparently healthy financial position; and
- to satisfy the demands of major investors concerning levels of return.

Creative accounting methods

There are many ways in which unscrupulous directors can manipulate the financial statements. They usually involve adopting novel or unorthodox practices for reporting key elements of the financial statements, such as revenue, expenses, assets and liabilities. They may also involve the use of complicated or obscure transactions in an attempt to hide the underlying economic reality. The manipulation carried out may be designed either to bend the rules or to break them.

We shall now consider some of the more important ways in which rules may be bent or broken.

Misstating revenue

Some creative accounting methods are designed to overstate the revenue for a period. These methods often involve the early recognition of sales revenue or the reporting of sales transactions that have no real substance. **Real World 5.5** provides examples of both types of revenue manipulation.

Real World 5.5

Overstating revenue

Types of revenue manipulation include:

- *Early recognition of revenue.* A business may report the sale of goods as soon as an order has been placed, rather than when the goods are delivered to, and accepted by, the customer. This will boost current revenues and profits and is known as 'pre-dispatching'.
- *Passing goods to distributors.* A business may force its distributors to accept more goods that they can sell. This will again boost current revenues and profits and is known as 'channel stuffing' or 'trade loading'.
- *Artificial trading.* This involves businesses in the same industry selling the same items between themselves to boost sales revenue. One example is where telecoms businesses sell unused fibre optic capacity to each other. This is known as 'hollow swaps'. Another example is where energy businesses sell energy between themselves for the same price and at the same time. This is known as 'round tripping' or 'in and out trading'.

Note that artificial trading between similar businesses will inflate the sales revenue for a period but will not inflate reported profits. Nevertheless, this may still benefit the business. Sales revenue growth has become an important yardstick of performance for some investors and can affect the value they place on the business.

Source: Based on information in *The Times* (2002) 'Dirty laundry: how companies fudge the numbers', Business Section, 22 September, nisyndication.com.

The manipulation of revenue has been at the heart of many of the accounting scandals recently exposed. Given its critical role in the measurement of performance, this is, perhaps, not surprising. **Real World 5.6** discusses how the reported revenues of one UK software business have been hotly disputed. It was acquired by a US computer giant, which concluded that, as a result of this and other alleged irregularities, the price paid was far too much. It, therefore, reported a huge impairment charge soon after the acquisition.

Real World 5.6

Recomputing the numbers

Autonomy, the UK software company at the centre of massive fraud allegations, booked revenues from uncompleted transactions at the end of a number of quarters to meet sales targets, according to claims levelled in a document from the US Air Force.

The accusations, made against Autonomy founder Mike Lynch and five other former executives, contain the first details of the alleged accounting irregularities that US computer group Hewlett-Packard has said forced it to take an $8.8 billion write-off in 2012, a year after buying the UK company. Also named in the letter are two US government contractors, MicroTech and Capax Global, that acted as resellers of Autonomy's software and played a role in the disputed transactions. A representative for Mr Lynch responded that Autonomy's accounting had been in compliance with international accounting standards.

The allegations, which were first reported by the Washington Post, detail three transactions that had not been completed when Autonomy recorded revenues on them. One of the deals later fell through, while another was completed for less than the amount Autonomy recorded.

Under one of the contracts, Autonomy was said to have booked $11 milion in revenue at the end of March 2010 on a transaction involving MicroTech and an unnamed end customer. The final sale failed to materialise, with Autonomy only receiving $500,000 on the contract. After an auditor queried the large uncollected debt from MicroTech at the end of the year, according to the claims, Autonomy made a payment of $9.6 million to the contractor under the heading "Advanced technology innovation centre" and MicroTech wired back the same amount to cover some of the money it owed Autonomy.

Autonomy booked a further $15.7 million of revenue in two instalments on the final days of March and June the following year on a separate deal involving Capax, even though the ultimate sales transactions had not been completed, according to the Air Force document. The deal was later completed for $14.1 million. In the third case, a $1.95 million sale was booked in December 2010, six months before it was finalised.

FT *Source*: Extracts from Waters, R. (2014) Autonomy beset by revenues allegation, ft.com, 5 January. © The Financial Times Ltd 2014. All Rights Reserved.

Massaging expenses

Some creative accounting methods focus on the manipulation of expenses. Those expenses that rely on directors' estimates of the future or their choice of accounting policy are particularly vulnerable to manipulation.

Activity (5.15)

Can you identify the kind of expenses where the directors make estimates or choices in the ways described? Think back to Chapter 3 and try to identify at least two.

These include certain expenses that we discussed in Chapter 3, such as:

● depreciation of property, plant and equipment;
● amortisation of intangible assets, such as goodwill;
● inventories (cost of sales); and
● allowances for trade receivables.

By changing estimates about the future (for example, the useful life or residual value of an asset), or by changing accounting policies (for example, switching from FIFO to AVCO), it may be possible to derive an expense figure and, consequently, a profit figure that suits the directors.

The incorrect 'capitalisation' of expenses may also be used as a means of manipulation. This involves treating expenses as if they were amounts incurred to acquire or develop non-current assets, rather than amounts consumed during the period. The net effect of this is that the expenses will be unfairly understated and profit will, therefore, be unfairly boosted. Businesses that build their own assets are often best placed to under take this form of malpractice.

Activity 5.16

What would be the effect on the profits and total assets of a business of incorrectly capitalising expenses?

Both would be artificially inflated. Reported profits would increase because expenses would be reduced. Total assets would be increased because the expenses would be incorrectly treated as non-current assets.

Real World 5.7 provides an example of one business that paid some of its staff salaries in the form of shares in the business, rather than in cash, but failed to treat this as an expense.

Real World 5.7

Taking stock

Examples of businesses using financial engineering to boost their statements of financial position are all too easy to find. A recent one features Microsoft's takeover of Linkedin.

A possible reason that Linkedin wanting to be taken over may have been that it had been applying rather dubious approach to accounting. Employees were being remunerated by being given the business's shares rather the normal cash payments. This was being accounted for a simple share issue, rather than treating it as an expense. This led to the business's profit figure being artificially inflated to a significant extent.

This type of dubious practice is by no means restricted to Linked in. Seemingly most larger US stock market listed businesses do it. Recently, however, Facebook has shown shares, issued to employees as part of their remuneration, as an expense and the mood now seems to be to pressure businesses to do the same so that the reported profit figure is a fairer reflection of reality. Whether employees are paid in shares or in cash, it's still an expense and should be accounted for as such.

Source: Information taken from Faroohar, R. (2016), Why the creative accounting in the Microsoft-LinkedIn deal is so disturbing, *Time Magazine*, 15 June.

Concealing 'bad news'

Some creative accounting methods focus on the concealment of losses or liabilities. The financial statements can look much healthier if these can somehow be eliminated. One way of doing this is to create a 'separate' entity that will take over the losses or liabilities.

Real World 5.8 describes the, now, almost legendary, case of one large business concealing losses and liabilities.

Real World 5.8

For a very special purpose

Perhaps the most well-known case of concealment of losses and liabilities concerned the Enron Corporation. This was a large US energy business that used 'special purpose entities' (SPEs) as a means of concealment. SPEs were used by Enron to rid itself of problem assets that were falling in value, such as its broadband operations. In addition, liabilities were transferred to these entities to help Enron's statement of financial position look healthier. The company had to keep its gearing ratios (the relationship between borrowing and equity) within particular limits to satisfy credit-rating agencies and SPEs were used to achieve this. The SPEs used for concealment purposes were not independent of the company and should have been consolidated in the statement of financial position of Enron, along with their losses and liabilities.

When these, and other accounting irregularities, were discovered in 2001, there was a restatement of Enron's financial performance and position to reflect the consolidation of the SPEs, which had previously been omitted. As a result of this restatement, the company recognised $591 million in losses over the preceding four years and an additional $628 million worth of liabilities at the end of 2000.

The company collapsed at the end of 2001.

Source: William Thomas, C. (2002) The rise and fall of Enron, *Journal of Accountancy*, vol. 194, no. 3. This article represents the opinions of the author, which are not necessarily those of the Texas Society of Certified Public Accountants.

Misstating assets

There are various ways in which assets may be misstated. These include:

- using asset values that are higher than the assets' fair market values;
- capitalising costs that should have been written off as expenses, as described earlier; and
- recording assets that are not owned or which do not exist.

Real World 5.9 is adapted from an article describing how one large business is alleged to have overstated a key asset and to have misrepresented business relationships.

Real World 5.9

Counting the cash

China Media Express, a supplier of television advertising services on buses, became part of a growing list of Chinese companies accused of fraudulently misleading investors about its financial condition. The company, which is quoted on a US stock exchange has been accused by the Securities and Exchange Commission (SEC) of falsely reporting significant increases in its business operations, financial condition, and profits almost immediately upon becoming a publicly-traded company. In addition to grossly overstating its cash balances, China Media Express is also accused of falsely stating that two multi-national corporations were its advertising clients when, in fact, they were not.

The SEC alleges that, beginning in at least November 2009 and continuing thereafter, China Media materially overstated its cash balances by a range of approximately 452% to over 40,000%. For example, on March 31, 2010, China Media reported $57 million in cash on hand for the fiscal year ended December 31, 2009 when it actually had a cash balance of only $141,000. On November 9, 2010, the company issued a press release announcing a cash balance of $170 million for the period ended September 30, 2010 when it actually had a cash balance of merely $10 million.

In addition to massively overstating its cash balances, China Media is alleged to have materially misrepresented the nature of its business relationships with two multi-national corporations, claiming they were its advertising clients when, in fact, they were not.

China Media's falsely reported increases in its cash balances allowed the Company to attract investors and raise money from share sales. Between January 2010 and December 2010, a hedge fund paid China Media $53 million to purchase millions of shares in the company.

FT *Source*: Adapted from Kwan Yuk, P. (2013) Another Chinese company gets charged with fraud, ft.com, 20 June. © The Financial Times Ltd 2013. All Rights Reserved.

Inadequate disclosure

Directors may misrepresent or try to conceal certain information. This may relate to commitments made, key changes in accounting policies or estimates, significant events and so on. The information may also relate to financial transactions between the directors and the business. **Real World 5.10** provides such an example.

Real World 5.10

Banking on a loan

Anglo Irish Bank chairman Sean Fitzpatrick dramatically resigned last night, admitting he had hidden a massive €87m in loans from the bank. Mr Fitzpatrick's personal borrowings from the bank were more than twice the amount shown for loans to all thirteen directors in last year's annual accounts. Another high-profile director, Lar Bradshaw, until recently chairman of Dublin Docklands Development Authority, also resigned from the board. Anglo Irish Bank said that a loan Mr Bradshaw held jointly with Mr Fitzpatrick was temporarily transferred to another bank prior to a year end audit. "While Mr Bradshaw was unaware that this transfer took place, he believed that it was in the bank's best interest that he should resign," Anglo said. Mr Bradshaw is the former managing director of McKinsey Ireland.

As required under accounting rules, company figures showed that directors had loans of €41m from Anglo Irish. Analysts were shocked to learn last night that the true figure of directors' borrowings at present is actually €150m. Mr Fitzpatrick's €87m makes up more than half of this. A statement from the bank said Mr Fitzpatrick would move his loans to another bank, understood to be Irish Nationwide, before the end of each financial year, so that they would not be recorded by the auditors. The loans were then moved back to Anglo Irish in a practice which continued for eight years.

Source: Extract from Anglo Irish bank chief quits over hiding €87m loan, www.belfasttelegraph.co.uk, 19 December 2008.

Figure 5.7 summarises the main methods of creative accounting.

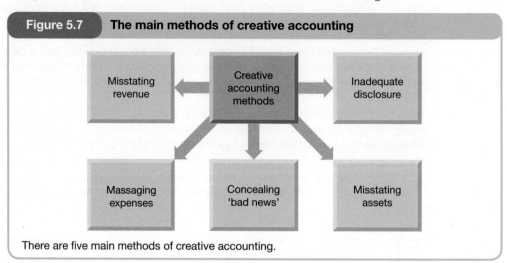

Figure 5.7   The main methods of creative accounting

There are five main methods of creative accounting.

Checking for creative accounting

When the financial statements of a business are being examined, a number of checks may be carried out to help gain a feel for their reliability. These can include checks to see whether:

- the reported profits are significantly higher than the operating cash flows for the period (as shown in the business's statement of cash flows), which may suggest that profits have been overstated;
- the tax charge is low in relation to reported profits, which may suggest, again, that profits are overstated, although there may be other, more innocent, explanations;
- the valuation methods used for assets held are based on historic cost or fair values and, if the latter approach has been used, why and how the fair values were determined;
- there have been changes in accounting policies over the period, particularly in key areas such as revenue recognition, inventories valuation and depreciation;
- the accounting policies adopted are in line with those adopted by the rest of the industry;
- the auditors' report gives a 'clean bill of health' to the financial statements; and
- the 'small print' (that is the notes to the financial statements) is being used to hide significant events or changes.

Real World 5.11 describes the emphasis that one analyst places on this last check.

Real World 5.11

Taking note

Alistair Hodgson, investment manager at private client stockbroker Pilling and Co, says "I almost look at the notes more than I look at the main figures at first. The notes tend to hold the key to anything that looks strange. I look to pick out things that the auditor has told the company to declare – the kind of thing they might not want to declare, but they have got to do so in order to make the accounts honest."

FT   *Source*: Extract from Smith, S. (2005) Read between the lines, *Financial Times*, 16 September.
© The Financial Times Limited 2012. All Rights Reserved.

Checks may also be carried out to provide confirmation of positive financial health. These may include checks to see whether:

- the business is paying increased dividends; and/or
- the directors are buying shares in the business.

Although the various checks described are useful, they cannot be used to guarantee the reliability of the financial statements. Some creative accounting practices may be very deeply seated and may go undetected for years.

Creative accounting and economic growth

Some years ago there was a wave of creative accounting scandals, particularly in the USA but also in Europe. It seems, however, that this wave has now subsided. The quality of financial reporting is improving and, it is to be hoped, trust among investors and others is being restored. As a result of the actions taken by various regulatory bodies, and by accounting rule makers, creative accounting has become a more risky and difficult process for those who attempt it. It will never disappear completely, however, and a further wave of creative accounting scandals may occur in the future.

The recent wave coincided with a period of strong economic growth and, during good economic times, investors and auditors become less vigilant. This makes it easier to manipulate the figures. We must not, therefore, become too complacent. Things may change again when we next experience a period of strong growth.

Self-assessment question 5.1

(a) You have overheard the following statements:
   1 'Dividends paid during a reporting period must be shown on the face of the Statement of changes in equity for that period.'
   2 'IAS 1 provides support for three key accounting conventions – accruals, historic cost and consistency.'
   3 'IAS 1 permits bank overdrafts to be offset against positive bank balances when preparing the statement of financial position.'

Critically comment on each of the statements.

(b) Segmental information relating to Dali plc for the year to 31 May 2017 is:

	Car parts £m	Aircraft parts £m	Boat parts £m	Total £m
Revenues from external customers	360	210	85	655
Inter-segment revenues	95	40	–	135
Interest revenue	34	–	–	34
Interest expense	–	28	8	36
Depreciation	80	55	15	150
Reportable segment profit	20	24	18	62
Other material non-cash items				
Impairment of assets	–	39	–	39
Reportable segment assets	170	125	44	339
Expenditures for reportable segment				
non-current assets	28	23	26	77
Reportable segment liabilities	85	67	22	174

Required:
Analyse the performance of each of the three main business segments of Dali plc for the year and comment on your results.

The solution to this question can be found at the end of the book on pp. 769–770.

Summary

The main points of this chapter may be summarised as follows:

Financial reporting framework

- Company annual reports have three core components: the main financial statements, corporate governance and management commentary.

Directors' duty

- Separation of ownership from day-to-day control creates a need for directors to be accountable.
- To fulfil this need, the directors have a duty to prepare and publish financial statements.
- These financial statements must provide a fair representation of the financial health of the business.

The need for accounting rules

- Accounting rules are necessary in order to avoid unacceptable accounting practices and to improve the comparability of financial statements.
- This should give greater confidence in the integrity of financial statements.

Accounting rules

- The International Accounting Standards Board (IASB) has become an important source of rules.
- Company law and the London Stock Exchange are also sources of rules for UK companies.

Presenting financial statements

- IAS 1 sets out the structure and content of financial statements.
- It requires preparation of a statement of financial position, a statement of comprehensive income, a statement of changes in equity and a statement of cash flows. In addition, explanatory notes are required.
- The financial statements must provide a fair representation of the financial health of a company and this will only normally be achieved by adherence to relevant IASB standards.
- IAS 1 sets out information to be shown in the various financial statements and some of the accounting conventions and principles to be followed in preparing the statements.

Conceptual framework

- This helps to underpin financial reporting standards.
- The IASB framework sets out the objective and primary users of general purpose financial reports, the qualitative characteristics and elements of financial statements and the different measurement bases that may be used.

The role of auditors

- Auditors are required to report to shareholders whether, in their opinion, the financial statements provide a true and fair view of the financial health of a business.

- They are elected by the shareholders and are accountable to them.

Segmental reports

- Segmental reports disaggregate information on the financial statements to help users to achieve a better understanding of financial health.
- An operating segment is defined by the IASB using the 'management approach'.
- IFRS 8 requires certain information relating to each segment to be shown.

Corporate governance

- Corporate governance issues arise because of the separation of ownership from control of the company.
- Corporate governance rules are based around the principles of disclosure, accountability and fairness.
- The UK Corporate Governance Code, which applies to UK Stock Exchange listed companies, adopts a 'comply or explain' approach.
- To comply with the UK Code, companies must fulfil specific annual reporting requirements concerning matters such as names of directors, description of the work of key committees, how board performance was evaluated and confirmation that the board has reviewed the effectiveness of management controls.

Management commentary

- Management commentary is designed to review the financial results as well as to complement and supplement the financial statements.
- The directors' report contains information of a financial and non-financial nature. It includes such diverse matters as any recommended dividend, the involvement of employees in company affairs and important events since the year-end. It is rather disjointed and lacks an underlying theme.
- The strategic report should provide a balanced and comprehensive analysis of the development and performance of the company during the year, and the position at the year-end. It should also describe the principal risks and uncertainties faced by the business.
- The strategic report of Stock Exchange listed companies must provide additional information, including the strategy business model adopted.

Creative accounting

- This involves using accounting practices to show what the directors would like users to see rather than what is a fair representation of reality.
- The main forms of creative accounting involve misstating revenues, massaging expenses, concealing bad news, misstating assets and inadequate disclosure.

Key terms

For definitions of these terms, see Appendix B.

International Accounting Standard
   p. 166

International Financial Reporting
   Standard *p. 166*

statement of comprehensive
   income *p. 171*

statement of changes in equity
   p. 173

conceptual framework *p. 175*

auditors *p. 178*

segmental financial report *p. 179*

transfer price *p. 181*

corporate governance *p. 183*

UK Corporate Governance Code
   p. 184

corporate governance statement
   p. 186

directors' report *p. 187*

strategic report *p. 188*

creative accounting *p. 190*

References

1 Financial Reporting Council (2012) *Thinking about Disclosures in a Broader Context,* Discussion paper, October.

2 Ball, R. (2016) *IFRS – ten years later,* University of Chicago, Booth School of Business essay, 26 February.

Further reading

If you would like to explore the topics covered in this chapter in more depth, we recommend the following:

Alexander, D., Britton, A., Jorissen, A., Hoogendoorn, M. and Van Mourik, C. (2014) *International Financial Reporting and Analysis,* 6th edn, Cengage Learning EMEA, Chapters 2, 3, 9 and 11.

Elliott, B. and Elliott, J. (2015) *Financial Accounting and Reporting,* 17th edn, Pearson, Chapters 9, 10 and 31.

International Accounting Standards Board, *Conceptual Framework for Financial Reporting* (September 2010).

International Accounting Standards Board, *2016 A Guide through IFRS (Green Book),* IAS 1 *Presentation of Financial Statements,* IFRS 8 *Operating Segments.*

Review questions

Solutions to these questions can be found at the back of the book on pp. 789–790.

5.1 'Searching for an agreed conceptual framework for accounting rules is likely to be a journey without an ending.' Discuss.

5.2 What problems does a user of segmental statements face when seeking to make comparisons between businesses?

5.3 Why do we need accounting rules?

5.4 What are the main methods of creative accounting?

Exercises

Solutions to exercises with coloured numbers can be sound at the back of the book in pp. 807–809.

Basic-level exercises

5.1 The size of annual financial reports published by limited companies has increased steadily over the years. Can you think of any reasons, apart from the increasing volume of accounting regulation, why this has occurred?

5.2 It has been suggested that too much information may be as bad as too little information for users of annual reports. Explain.

Intermediate-level exercises

5.3 The following information was extracted from the financial statements of I. Ching (Booksellers) plc for the year to 31 May 2017:

	£000
Finance charges	40
Cost of sales	460
Distribution expenses	110
Revenue	943
Administrative expenses	212
Other expenses	25
Gain on revaluation of property, plant and equipment	20
Loss on foreign currency translations on foreign operations	15
Tax on profit for the year	24
Tax on other components of comprehensive income	1

Required:
Prepare a statement of comprehensive income for the year ended 31 May 2017 that is set out in accordance with the requirements of IAS 1 *Presentation of Financial Statements*.

5.4 Manet plc had the following share capital and reserves as at 1 June 2016:

	£m
Share capital (£0.25 ordinary shares)	250
Share premium account	50
Revaluation reserve	120
Currency translation reserve	15
Retained earnings	380
Total equity	**815**

During the year to 31 May 2017, the company revalued property, plant and equipment upwards by £30 million and made a loss on foreign exchange translation of foreign operations of £5 million. The company made a profit for the year from normal operations of £160 million during the year and the dividend was £80 million.

Required:

Prepare a statement of changes in equity for the year ended 31 May 2017 in accordance with the requirements of IAS 1 *Presentation of Financial Statements*.

Advanced-level exercises

5.5 (a) 'The UK system of corporate governance for Stock Exchange listed companies adopts a "comply or explain" approach.' What does this mean? Set out one advantage and one disadvantage of this approach.

(b) 'The strategic report should be prepared by the company's auditors and not the directors.' Do you agree? Discuss.

5.6 You have overheard the following statements:

(a) 'The role of independent auditors is to prepare the financial statements of the company.'

(b) 'International Accounting Standards (IASs) apply to all UK companies, but London Stock Exchange listed companies must also adhere to International Financial Reporting Standards (IFRSs).'

(c) 'All listed companies in the European Union states must follow IASs and IFRSs.'

(d) 'According to IAS 1, companies' financial statements must show an "accurate representation" of what they purport to show.'

(e) 'IAS 1 leaves it to individual companies to decide the format that they use in the statement of financial position.'

(f) 'The statement of changes in equity deals with unrealised profits and gains, for example an upward revaluation of a non-current asset.'

(g) 'If a majority of the shareholders of a listed company agree, the company need not produce a full set of financial statements, but can just produce summary financial statements.'

Critically comment on each of these statements.

5.7 Segmental information relating to Turner plc for the year to 30 April 2017 is:

	Software	Electronics	Engineering	Total
	£m	£m	£m	£m
Revenues from external customers	250	230	52	532
Inter-segment revenues	45	25	–	70
Interest revenue	18	–	–	18
Interest expense	–	25	–	25
Depreciation	60	35	10	105
Reportable segment profit	10	34	12	56
Other material non-cash items:				
Impairment of assets	–	5	–	5
Reportable segment assets	140	90	34	264
Expenditures for reportable segment				
non-current assets	22	12	10	44
Reportable segment liabilities	55	38	4	97

Required:

Analyse the performance of each of the three main business segments for the year and comment on your results.

Measuring and reporting cash flows

CHAPTER 6 MEASURING AND REPORTING CASH FLOWS

The statement of cash flows

Introduction

This chapter is devoted to the first major financial statement identified in Chapter 2: the statement of cash flows. This statement reports the movements of cash during a period and the effect of these movements on the cash position of the business. It is an important financial statement because cash is vital to the survival of a business. Without cash, a business cannot operate.

In this chapter, we shall see how the statement of cash flows is prepared and how the information that it contains may be interpreted. We shall also see why the inability of the income statement to identify and explain cash flows makes a separate statement necessary.

The statement of cash flows is being considered after the chapters on limited companies because the format of the statement requires an understanding of this type of business. Most larger limited companies are required to provide a statement of cash flows for share-holders and other users as part of their annual financial reports.

Learning outcomes

When you have completed this chapter, you should be able to:

● discuss the crucial importance of cash to a business;

● explain the nature of the statement of cash flows and discuss how it can be helpful in identifying cash flow problems;

● prepare a statement of cash flows; and

● interpret a statement of cash flows.

The statement of cash flows

The statement of cash flows is a fairly late addition to the annual published financial statements. At one time, companies were only required to publish an income statement and a statement of financial position. It seems the prevailing view was that all the financial information needed by users would be contained within these two statements. This view may have been based partly on the assumption that, if a business were profitable, it would also have plenty of cash. While in the long run this is likely to be true, it is not necessarily true in the short-to-medium term.

We saw in Chapter 3 that the income statement sets out the revenue and expenses, for the period, rather than the cash inflows and outflows. This means that the profit (or loss), which represents the difference between the revenue and expenses for the period, may have little or no relation to the cash generated for the period.

To illustrate this point, let us take the example of a business making a sale (generating revenue). This may well lead to an increase in wealth that will be reflected in the income statement. However, if the sale is made on credit, no cash changes hands – at least not at the time of the sale. Instead, the increase in wealth is reflected in another asset: an increase in trade receivables. Furthermore, if an item of inventories is the subject of the sale, wealth is lost to the business through the reduction in inventories. This means that an expense is incurred in making the sale, which will also be shown in the income statement. Once again, however, no cash changes hands at the time of sale. For such reasons, the profit and the cash generated during a period rarely go hand in hand.

Activity 6.1 helps to underline how particular transactions and events can affect profit and cash for a period differently.

Activity 6.1

The following is a list of business/accounting events. In each case, state the immediate effect (increase, decrease or none) on both profit and cash:

	Effect	
	on profit	on cash
1 Repayment of borrowings	____	____
2 Making a profitable sale on credit	____	____
3 Buying a non-current asset on credit	____	____
4 Receiving cash from a credit customer (trade receivable)	____	____
5 Depreciating a non-current asset	____	____
6 Buying some inventories for cash	____	____
7 Making a share issue for cash	____	____

You should have come up with the following:

	Effect	
	on profit	on cash
1 Repayment of borrowings	none	decrease
2 Making a profitable sale on credit	increase	none
3 Buying a non-current asset on credit	none	none
4 Receiving cash from a credit customer (trade receivable)	none	increase
5 Depreciating a non-current asset	decrease	none
6 Buying some inventories for cash	none	decrease
7 Making a share issue for cash	none	increase

The reasons for these answers are as follows:

1 Repaying borrowings requires that cash be paid to the lender. This means that two figures in the statement of financial position will be affected, but none in the income statement.
2 Making a profitable sale on credit will increase the sales revenue and profit figures. No cash will change hands at this point, however.
3 Buying a non-current asset on credit affects neither the cash balance nor the profit figure.
4 Receiving cash from a credit customer increases the cash balance and reduces the credit customer's balance. Both of these figures are on the statement of financial position. The income statement is unaffected.
5 Depreciating a non-current asset means that an expense is recognised. This causes a decrease in profit. No cash is paid or received.
6 Buying some inventories for cash means that the value of the inventories will increase and the cash balance will decrease by a similar amount. Profit is not affected.
7 Making a share issue for cash increases the shareholders' equity and increases the cash balance. Profit is not affected.

From what we have seen so far, it is clear that the income statement is not the place to look if we are to gain insights about cash movements over time. We need a separate financial statement.

Why is cash so important?

It is worth asking why cash is so important. In one sense, it is just another asset that the business needs to enable it to function. Hence, it is no different from inventories or non-current assets.

The importance of cash lies in the fact that people will only normally accept cash in settlement of their claims. If a business wants to employ people, it must pay them in cash. If it wants to buy a new non-current asset, it must normally pay the seller in cash (perhaps after a short period of credit). When businesses fail, it is the lack of cash to pay amounts owed that really pushes them under. Cash generation is vital for businesses to survive and to be able to take advantage of commercial opportunities. These are the things that make cash the pre-eminent business asset. During an economic downturn, the ability to generate cash takes on even greater importance. Banks become more cautious in their lending and businesses with weak cash flows often find it difficult to obtain finance.

Real World 6.1 is taken from an article by Luke Johnson who is a 'serial entrepreneur'. Among other things, he was closely involved with taking Pizza Express from a business that owned just 12 restaurants to over 250 and, at the same time, increasing its share price from 40 pence to over £9. In the article he highlights the importance of cash flow in managing a business.

Real World 6.1

Cash flow is king

Wise entrepreneurs learn that profits are not necessarily cash. But many founders never understand this essential accounting truth. A cash flow projection is a much more important document than a profit and loss (income) statement. A lack of liquidity can kill you, whereas a company can make paper losses for years and still survive if it has sufficient cash. It is amazing how financial journalists, fund managers, analysts, bankers and company directors can still focus on the wrong numbers in the accounts – despite so many high-profile disasters over the years.

FT

Source: Extract from Johnson, L. (2013), The most dangerous unforced errors, ft.com, 9 July. © The Financial Times Ltd 2013. All Rights Reserved.

Real World 6.2 is taken from a column written by John Timpson, which appeared in the *Daily Telegraph.* Timpson is the chief executive of the successful, high street shoe repairing and key cutting business that bears his name. In the column he highlights the importance of cash reporting in managing the business.

Real World 6.2

Cash is key

Everyday the figure I look for is our bank balance. By concentrating on the cash, I can stay in control of the business.

Keeping a close eye on the cash not only gives peace of mind, it also provides the best measure of your company's performance.

The aim of the game is to make money – in other words, to create cash. The trick is to compare your bank balance with exactly the same date last year and be able to explain the difference.

My daily cash flow email compares the bank balance with the figure we forecast yesterday. I don't like surprises, but if things go awry, I want the surprise spotted straight away.

Source: Extracts from John Timpson, Ask John, *The Daily Telegraph Business*, 29 August 2016.

The main features of the statement of cash flows

The statement of cash flows summarises the inflows and outflows of cash (and cash equivalents) for a business over a period. To aid user understanding, these cash flows are divided into categories (for example, those relating to investments in non-current assets). Cash inflows and outflows falling within each category are added together to provide a total for that category. These totals are shown on the statement of cash flows and, when added together, reveal the net increase or decrease in cash (and cash equivalents) over the period.

When describing in detail how this statement is prepared and presented, we shall follow the requirements of International Accounting Standard (IAS) 7 *Statement of Cash Flows.*

A definition of cash and cash equivalents

IAS 7 defines cash as notes and coins in hand and deposits in banks and similar institutions that are accessible to the business on demand. Cash equivalents are short-term, highly liquid investments that can be readily convertible to known amounts of cash. They are also subject to an insignificant risk of changes of value. Figure 6.1 sets out this definition of cash equivalents in the form of a decision chart.

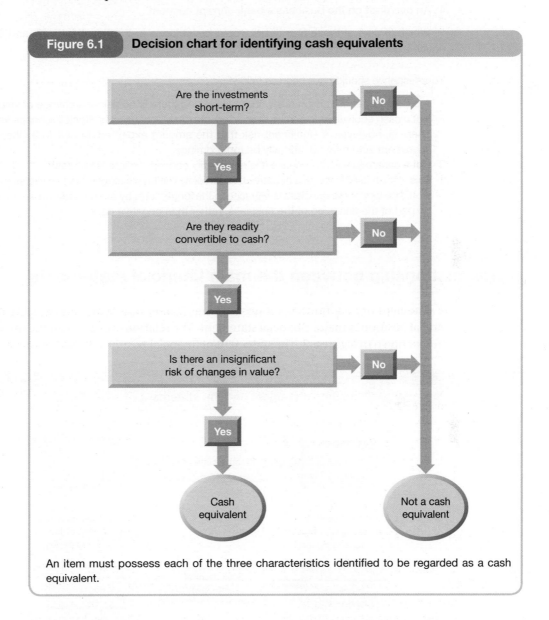

Figure 6.1   Decision chart for identifying cash equivalents

An item must possess each of the three characteristics identified to be regarded as a cash equivalent.

Activity 6.2 should clarify the types of items that fall within the definition of 'cash equivalents'.

Activity **6.2**

At the end of its reporting period, Zeneb plc's statement of financial position included the following items:

1 A bank deposit account where one month's notice of withdrawal is required.
2 Ordinary shares in Jones plc (a Stock Exchange listed business).
3 A high-interest bank deposit account that requires six months' notice of withdrawal.
4 An overdraft on the business's bank current account.

Which (if any) of these four items would be included in the figure for cash and cash equivalents?

Your response should have been as follows:

1 A cash equivalent. It is readily withdrawable and there is no risk of a change of value.
2 Not a cash equivalent. It can be converted into cash because it is Stock Exchange listed. There is, however, a significant risk that the amount expected (hoped for!) when the shares are sold may not actually be forthcoming.
3 Not a cash equivalent because it is not readily convertible into liquid cash.
4 This is cash itself, though a negative amount of it. The only exception to this classification would be where the business is financed in the longer term by an overdraft, when it would be part of the financing of the business, rather than negative cash.

The relationship between the main financial statements

The statement of cash flows is, along with the income statement and the statement of financial position, a major financial statement. The relationship between the three statements is shown in Figure 6.2. The statement of financial position shows the various assets

Figure 6.2   **The relationship between the statement of financial position, the income statement and the statement of cash flows**

```
Owners'          ────►   Income statement   ────►   Owners'
claim                                                claim

Statement of                                         Statement of
financial position                                   financial position
at the start of the                                  at the end of the
accounting period                                    accounting period

Cash             ────►   Statement of       ────►   Cash
and cash                 cash flows                  and cash
equivalents                                          equivalents
```

The statement of financial position shows the relationship, at a particular point in time, between the business's assets and claims. The income statement explains how, over a period between two statements of financial position, the equity figure in the first statement of financial position has altered as a result of trading operations. The statement of cash flows also looks at changes over the reporting period, but this statement explains the alteration in the cash (and cash equivalent) balances from the first to the second of the two consecutive statements of financial position.

(including cash) and claims (including the shareholders' equity) of the business *at a particular point in time.* The statement of cash flows and the income statement explain the *changes over a period* to two of the items in the statement of financial position. The statement of cash flows explains the changes to cash. The income statement explains changes to equity, arising from trading operations.

The layout of the statement of cash flows

As mentioned earlier, the cash flows of a business are divided into categories. The various categories and the way in which they are presented in the statement of cash flows are shown in Figure 6.3.

| Figure 6.3 | Standard presentation for the statement of cash flows |

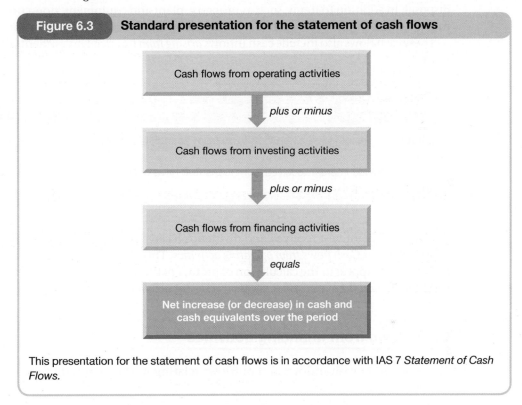

This presentation for the statement of cash flows is in accordance with IAS 7 *Statement of Cash Flows.*

Let us now consider each of the categories that has been identified.

Cash flows from operating activities

These represent the cash inflows and outflows arising from normal day-to-day trading activities, after taking account of the tax paid and financing costs (equity and borrowings) relating to these activities. The cash inflows for the period are the amounts received from trade receivables (credit customers settling their accounts) and from cash sales for the period. The cash outflows for the period are the amounts paid for inventories, operating expenses (such as rent and wages) corporation tax, interest and dividends.

Note that it is the cash inflows and outflows during a period that appear in the statement of cash flows, not revenue and expenses for that period. Similarly, tax and dividends that appear in the statement of cash flows are those actually paid during the period. Many companies pay tax on their annual profits in four equal instalments. Two of these are paid during the year concerned and the other two are paid during the following year. Thus, by the end of each year, half of the tax will have been paid and the remaining half will still be outstanding, to be paid during the following year. This means that the tax payment during a year is normally equal to half of the previous year's tax charge and half of that of the current year and it is this total that should appear in the current year's statement of cash flows.

Cash flows from investing activities

These include cash outflows to acquire non-current assets and cash inflows from their disposal. In addition to items, such as property, plant and equipment, non-current assets might include financial investments made in loans or shares in another business.

These cash flows also include cash inflows *arising from* financial investments (loans and shares).

Activity 6.3

What might be included as cash inflows from financial investments?

This can include interest received from loans that have been made and dividends received from shares in other companies.

Under IAS 7, interest received and dividends received could, if the directors chose, be classified under *Cash flows from operating activities.* This alternative treatment is available as these items appear in the calculation of profit. For the purpose of this chapter, however, we shall include them in *Cash flows from investing activities.*

Cash flows from financing activities

These represent cash inflows and outflows relating to the long-term financing of the business.

Activity 6.4

What might be included as cash inflows from financing activities?

Included here would be cash movements relating to the raising and redemption of both long-term borrowings and shares.

Under IAS 7, interest and dividends paid by the business could, if the directors chose, appear under this heading as outflows. This alternative to including them in *Cash flows from operating activities* is available as they represent a cost of raising finance. For the purpose of this chapter, however, we shall not use this alternative treatment.

Whichever treatment for interest and dividends (both paid and received) is chosen, it should be applied consistently.

Net increase or decrease in cash and cash equivalents

The final total shown on the statement will be the net increase or decrease in cash and cash equivalents over the period. It will be deduced from the totals from each of the three categories mentioned above.

The normal direction of cash flows

The effect on a business's cash and cash equivalents of activities relating to each category is shown in Figure 6.4. The arrows show the *normal* direction of cash flow for the typical, profitable, business in a typical reporting period.

Figure 6.4	Diagrammatical representation of the statement of cash flows

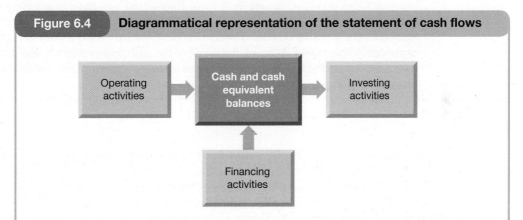

Various activities of the business each have their own effect on the total of the cash and cash equivalents, either positive (increasing the total) or negative (reducing it). The net increase or decrease in the cash and cash equivalents over a period will be the sum of these individual effects, taking account of the direction (cash in or cash out) of each activity.

Note that the direction of the arrow shows the *normal* direction of the cash flow in respect of each activity. In certain circumstances, each of these arrows could be reversed in direction.

Normally, *operating activities* provide positive cash flows and, therefore, increase the business's cash resources. For most UK businesses, cash generated from day-to-day trading, even after deducting tax, interest and dividends, is by far the most important source of new finance.

Activity 6.5

Last year's statement of cash flows for Angus plc showed a negative cash flow from operating activities. What could be the reason for this and should the business's management be alarmed by it? (*Hint*: We think that there are two broad possible reasons for a negative cash flow.)

The two reasons are:

1 The business is unprofitable. This leads to more cash being paid out to employees, to suppliers of goods and services, for interest and so on than is received from trade receivables. This should be of concern as a major expense for most businesses is depreciation. Since depreciation does not lead to a cash flow, it is not considered in *Net cash inflows from operating activities.* A negative operating cash flow might well indicate, therefore, a much larger trading loss – in other words, a significant loss of the business's wealth. This is likely to be a source of concern for management.

2 The business is expanding its activities (level of sales revenue). Although the business may be profitable, it may be spending more cash than is being generated from sales. Cash will be spent on acquiring more assets, non-current and current, to accommodate increased demand. For example, a business may need to have inventories in place before additional sales can be made. Similarly, staff will have to be employed and paid. Even when additional sales are made, they would normally be made on credit, with the cash inflow lagging behind the sales. This means that there would be no immediate cash benefit.

Expansion often causes cash flow strains for new businesses, which will be expanding inventories and other assets from zero. They would also need to employ and pay staff. To add to this problem, increased profitability may encourage a feeling of optimism, leading to a lack of attention being paid to the cash flows. This too is likely to be a cause of concern to managers. Although the cause of the cash flow problem is less disturbing than a lack of profitability, the effect could be a severe strain on cash resource and the consequent dangers of this.

Investing activities typically cause net negative cash flows. This is because many non-current assets either wear out or become obsolete and need to be replaced. Businesses may also expand their asset base. Non-current assets may, of course, be sold, which would give rise to positive cash flows. In net terms, however, the cash flows are normally negative, with cash spent on new assets far outweighing that received from the sale of old ones.

Financing activities can go in either direction, depending on the financing strategy at the time. Since businesses seek to expand, however, there is a tendency for these activities to result in cash inflows rather than cash outflows.

Real World 6.3 shows the summarised statement of cash flows of Tesco plc, the UK-based supermarket company.

Real World 6.3

Cashing in

A summary of the statement of cash flows for the business for the year ended 25 February 2017 shows the cash flows of the business under each of the headings described above.

Summary group statement of cash flows for the year ended 25 February 2017

	£m
Cash generated from operations	2,558
Interest paid	(522)
Corporation tax paid	(47)
Net cash generated from operating activities	1,989
Net cash generated from investing activities	279
Net cash used in financing activities	(1,387)
Net increase in cash and cash equivalents	881

Source: Adapted from Tesco plc, Annual Report and Financial Statements 2017, p. 90, www.tescoplc.com.

As we shall see shortly, more detailed information under each of the main headings is provided in the statement of cash flows presented to shareholders and other users.

Preparing the statement of cash flows

Deducing net cash flows from operating activities

As we have seen, the first category within the statement of cash flows is the *Cash flows from operating activities*. There are two approaches that can be taken to deriving this figure: the **direct method** and the **indirect method**.

The direct method

The direct method involves an analysis of the cash records of the business for the period, identifying all payments and receipts relating to operating activities. These receipts and payments are then summarised to provide the total figures for inclusion in the statement of cash flows. Since accounting records are normally computerised, this is a fairly simple matter. Nevertheless, very few businesses adopt the direct method.

The indirect method

The indirect method is a much more popular approach. It relies on the fact that, sooner or later, sales revenue gives rise to cash inflows and expenses give rise to outflows. This means that the figure for profit for the year will be linked to the net cash flows from operating activities. Since businesses have to produce an income statement, the information that it contains can be used as a starting point to deduce the cash flows from operating activities.

With credit sales, the cash receipt arises at some point after the sale is made. Thus, sales made towards the end of the current reporting period may result in the cash being received after the end of the period. The income statement for the current period will include all sales revenue generated during that period. Where cash relating to those sales is received after the end of the period, it will be included in the statement of cash flows for the following period. While profit for the period will not normally equal the net cash inflows from operating activities, there is a clear link between them. This means that we can deduce the cash inflows from sales if we have the relevant income statement and statements of financial position, as we shall see in Activity 6.6.

Activity 6.6

What information contained within the income statement and statement of financial position for a business can help us deduce the cash inflows from sales?

The income statement tells us the sales revenue figure. The statement of financial position will tell us how much was owed in respect of credit sales at the beginning and end of the reporting period (trade receivables).

If we adjust the sales revenue figure by the increase or decrease in trade receivables over the period, we deduce the cash from sales for the period. Example 6.1 shows how this is done.

Example 6.1

The sales revenue figure for a business for the year was £34 million. The trade receivables totalled £4 million at the beginning of the year, but had increased to £5 million by the end of the year.

Basically, the trade receivables figure is dictated by sales revenue and cash receipts. It is increased when a sale is made and decreased when cash is received from a credit customer. If, over the year, the sales revenue and the cash receipts had been equal, the beginning-of-year and end-of-year trade receivables figures would have been equal. Since the trade receivables figure increased, it must mean that less cash was received than sales revenues were made. In fact, the cash receipts from sales must have been £33 million (that is, $34 - (5 - 4)$).

Put slightly differently, we can say that as a result of sales, assets of £34 million flowed into the business. If £1 million of this went to increasing the asset of trade receivables, this leaves only £33 million that went to increase cash.

The same general point is true in respect of nearly all of the other items that are taken into account in deducing the operating profit figure. The main exception is depreciation. This expense is not normally associated with any movement in cash during that same period.

All of this means that we can take the *profit before taxation* (that is, the profit after interest but before taxation) for the year, add back the depreciation and interest expense charged in arriving at that profit, and adjust this total by movements in inventories, trade (and other) receivables and payables. If we then go on to deduct payments made during the reporting period for taxation, interest on borrowings and dividends, we have the net cash from operating activities. Example 6.2 illustrates this process.

Example 6.2

The relevant information from the financial statements of Dido plc for last year is as follows:

	£m
Profit before taxation (after interest)	122
Depreciation charged in arriving at profit before taxation	34
Interest expense	6
At the beginning of the year:	
Inventories	15
Trade receivables	24
Trade payables	18

	£m
At the end of the year:	
Inventories	17
Trade receivables	21
Trade payables	19

The following further information is available about payments during last year:

	£m
Taxation paid	32
Interest paid	5
Dividends paid	9

The cash flow from operating activities is derived as follows:

	£m
Profit before taxation (after interest)	122
Depreciation	34
Interest expense	6
Increase in inventories (17 − 15)	(2)
Decrease in trade receivables (21 − 24)	3
Increase in trade payables (19 − 18)	1
Cash generated from operations	164
Interest paid	(5)
Taxation paid	(32)
Dividends paid	(9)
Net cash from operating activities	118

As we can see, the net increase in **working capital*** (that is, current assets less current liabilities) as a result of trading was £162 million (that is, 122 + 34 + 6). Of this, £2 million went into increased inventories. More cash was received from trade receivables than sales revenue was made. Similarly, less cash was paid to trade payables than purchases of goods and services on credit. Both of these had a favourable effect on cash. Over the year, therefore, cash increased by £164 million. When account was taken of the payments for interest, tax and dividends, the net cash from operating activities was £118 million (inflow).

Note that we needed to adjust the profit before taxation (after interest) by the depreciation and interest expenses to derive the profit before depreciation, interest and taxation.

*Working capital is a term widely used in accounting and finance, not just in the context of the statement of cash flows. We shall encounter it several times in later chapters.

Activity **6.7**

In deriving the cash generated from operations, we add the depreciation expense for the period to the profit before taxation. Does this mean that depreciation is a source of cash?

No. Depreciation is a not source of cash. The periodic depreciation expense is irrelevant to cash flow. Since the profit before taxation is derived *after* deducting the depreciation expense for the period, we need to eliminate the impact of depreciation by adding it back to the profit figure. This will give us the profit before tax *and before* depreciation, which is what we need.

We should be clear why we add back an amount for interest at the start of the derivation of cash flow from operating activities only to deduct an amount for interest further down. The reason is that the first is the *interest expense* for the reporting period, whereas the second is the amount of *cash paid out for interest* during that period. These may well be different amounts, as was the case in Example 6.2.

The indirect method of deducing the net cash flow from operating activities is summarised in Figure 6.5.

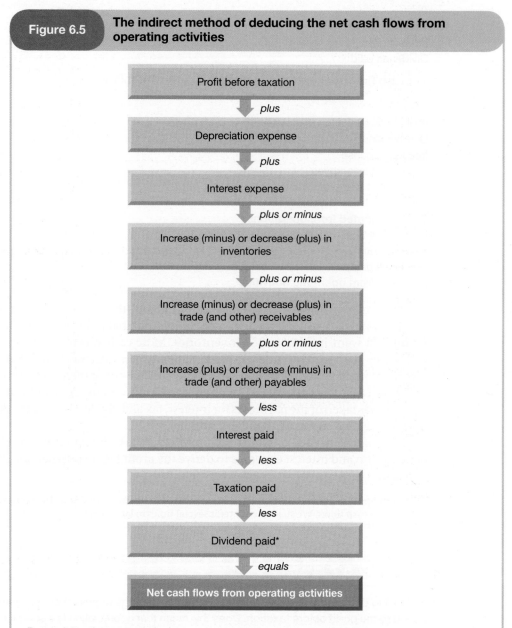

Figure 6.5	**The indirect method of deducing the net cash flows from operating activities**

Determining the net cash from operating activities firstly involves adding back the depreciation and the interest expense to the profit before taxation. Next, adjustment is made for increases or decreases in inventories, receivables and payables. Lastly, cash paid for interest, taxation and dividends is deducted.

* Note that dividends could alternatively be included under the heading 'Cash flows from financing activities'.

Activity 6.8

The relevant information from the financial statements of Pluto plc for last year is as follows:

	£m
Profit before taxation (after interest)	165
Depreciation charged in arriving at operating profit	41
Interest expense	21
At the beginning of the year:	
Inventories	22
Trade receivables	18
Trade payables	15
At the end of the year:	
Inventories	23
Trade receivables	21
Trade payables	17

The following further information is available about payments during last year:

	£m
Taxation paid	49
Interest paid	25
Dividends paid	28

What figure should appear in the statement of cash flows for *Net cash from operating activities*?

Cash flow from operating activities:

	£m
Profit before taxation (after interest)	165
Depreciation	41
Interest expense	21
Increase in inventories (23 − 22)	(1)
Increase in trade receivables (21 − 18)	(3)
Increase in trade payables (17 − 15)	2
Cash generated from operations	225
Interest paid	(25)
Taxation paid	(49)
Dividends paid	(28)
Net cash from operating activities	123

Real World 6.4 explains how one well-known business uses operating cash flow as a performance target.

Real World 6.4

Turning energy into cash

BP plc, the energy business, is one of a number of businesses that frames one of its key financial performance targets in terms of operating cash flows. Its performance over the five years ending 31 December 2015 is set out in Figure 6.6.

| Figure 6.6 | BP plc operating cash flows 2011–2015 |

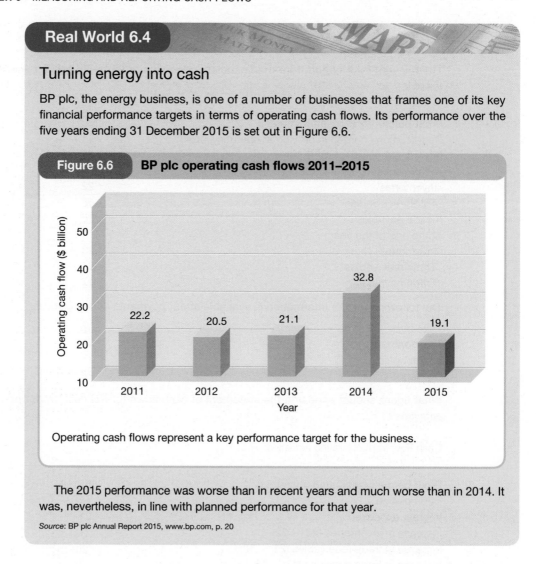

Operating cash flows represent a key performance target for the business.

The 2015 performance was worse than in recent years and much worse than in 2014. It was, nevertheless, in line with planned performance for that year.

Source: BP plc Annual Report 2015, www.bp.com, p. 20

Before we move on to consider other areas of the statement of cash flows, it is useful to emphasise an important point. The fact that we can work from the profit before taxation to derive the net cash flows from operating activities should not lead us to conclude that these two figures are broadly in line. Typically, adjustments made to the profit figure to derive net cash flows from operating activities are significant in size.

Deducing the other areas of the statement of cash flows

Deriving the cash flows from investing and financing activities is much easier than deriving *Net cash flows from operating activities*. It largely involves a comparison of the opening and closing statements of financial position to detect movements in non-current assets, non-current liabilities and equity over the period. We show how this is done in Example 6.3, which prepares a complete statement of cash flows.

Example 6.3

Torbryan plc's income statement for the year ended 31 December 2016 and the statements of financial position as at 31 December 2015 and 2016 are as follows:

Income statement for the year ended 31 December 2016

	£m
Revenue	576
Cost of sales	(307)
Gross profit	269
Distribution expenses	(65)
Administrative expenses	(26)
	178
Other operating income	21
Operating profit	199
Interest receivable	17
Interest payable	(23)
Profit before taxation	193
Taxation	(46)
Profit for the year	147

Statements of financial position as at 31 December 2015 and 2016

	2015 £m	2016 £m
ASSETS		
Non-current assets		
Property, plant and equipment		
Land and buildings	241	241
Plant and machinery	309	325
	550	566
Current assets		
Inventories	44	41
Trade receivables	121	139
	165	180
Total assets	715	746
EQUITY AND LIABILITIES		
Equity		
Called-up ordinary share capital	150	200
Share premium account	–	40
Retained earnings	26	123
	176	363
Non-current liabilities		
Borrowings – loan notes	400	250
Current liabilities		
Borrowings (all bank overdraft)	68	56
Trade payables	55	54
Taxation	16	23
	139	133
Total equity and liabilities	715	746

During 2016, the business spent £95 million on additional plant and machinery. There were no other non-current-asset acquisitions or disposals. A dividend of £50

Example 6.3 *continued*

million was paid on ordinary shares during the year. The interest receivable revenue and the interest payable expense for the year were each equal to the cash inflow and outflow respectively. £150 million of loan notes were redeemed at their nominal (par) value.

The statement of cash flows would be:

Torbryan plc

Statement of cash flows for the year ended 31 December 2016

	£m
Cash flows from operating activities	
Profit before taxation (after interest) (see Note 1 below)	193
Adjustments for:	
Depreciation (Note 2)	79
Interest receivable (Note 3)	(17)
Interest payable (Note 4)	23
Increase in trade receivables (139 − 121)	(18)
Decrease in trade payables (55 − 54)	(1)
Decrease in inventories (44 − 41)	3
Cash generated from operations	262
Interest paid	(23)
Taxation paid (Note 5)	(39)
Dividend paid	(50)
Net cash from operating activities	150
Cash flows from investing activities	
Payments to acquire tangible non-current assets	(95)
Interest received (Note 3)	17
Net cash used in investing activities	(78)
Cash flows from financing activities	
Repayments of loan notes	(150)
Issue of ordinary shares (Note 6)	90
Net cash used in financing activities	(60)
Net increase in cash and cash equivalents	12
Cash and cash equivalents at 1 January 2016 (Note 7)	(68)
Cash and cash equivalents at 31 December 2016	(56)

To see how this relates to the cash of the business at the beginning and end of the year it can be useful to provide a reconciliation as follows:

Analysis of cash and cash equivalents during the year ended 31 December 2016

	£m
Overdraft balance at 1 January 2016	(68)
Net cash inflow	12
Overdraft balance at 31 December 2016	(56)

Notes:

1 This is simply taken from the income statement for the year.
2 Since there were no disposals, the depreciation charges must be the difference between the start and end of the year's plant and machinery (non-current assets) values, adjusted by the cost of any additions.

Example 6.3 *continued*

	£m
Carrying amount at 1 January 2016	309
Additions	95
	404
Depreciation (balancing figure)	(79)
Carrying amount at 31 December 2016	325

3 Interest receivable must be deducted to work towards what the profit would have been before it was added in the income statement, because it is not part of operations but of investing activities. The cash inflow from this source appears under the *Cash flows from investing activities* heading.

4 The interest payable expense must be taken out, by adding it back to the profit figure. We subsequently deduct the cash paid for interest payable during the year. In this case the two figures are identical.

5 Taxation is paid by many companies in instalments: 50 per cent during their reporting year and 50 per cent in the following year. As a result, the 2016 payment would have been half the tax on the 2015 profit (that is, the figure that would have appeared in the current liabilities at the end of 2015), plus half of the 2016 taxation charge (that is, $16 + (^1/_2 \times 46) = 39$). Probably the easiest way to deduce the amount paid during the year to 31 December 2016 is by following this approach:

	£m
Taxation owed at start of the year (from the statement of financial position as at 31 December 2015)	16
Taxation charge for the year (from the income statement)	46
	62
Taxation owed at the end of the year (from the statement of financial position as at 31 December 2016)	(23)
Taxation paid during the year	39

This follows the logic that if we start with what the business owed at the beginning of the year, add what was owed as a result of the current year's taxation charge and then deduct what was owed at the end, the resulting figure must be what was paid during the year.

6 The share issue raised £90 million, of which £50 million went into the share capital total on the statement of financial position and £40 million into share premium.

7 There were no 'cash equivalents', just cash (though negative).

Reconciliation of liabilities from financing activities

IAS 7 requires businesses to provide a reconciliation that shows the link between liabilities at the beginning and end of the reporting period that relate to *Cash flows from financing activities* in the statement of cash flows. This reconciliation sets out movements in liabilities, such as long-term borrowings and lease liabilities, over the reporting period. A separate reconciliation is required for each type of liability.

The reconciliation appears as a note to the statement of cash flows and is designed to help users track changes occurring in the liabilities of the business. Example 6.4 illustrates how this reconciliation may be presented.

Example 6.4

Based on the information set out in the financial statements of Torbryan plc for the financial years ended 31 December 2015 and 2016 (see Example 6.3), the following reconciliation of long-term liabilities for the year to 31 December 2016 can be carried out:

Reconciliation of liabilities from financing activities for the year to 31 December 2016

	£m
Loan notes outstanding at 1 January 2016	400
Cash paid to redeem loan notes	(150)
Loan notes outstanding at 31 December 2016	250

Activity   6.9

IAS 7 requires a statement reconciling movements in liabilities, for the reporting period, but does not require a reconciliation of movements of equity. Can you suggest why this is?

The reason is that such a statement (statement of changes in equity) is required under IAS 1 *Presentation of Financial Statements,* as we saw in Chapter 5.

What does the statement of cash flows tell us?

The statement of cash flows tells us how the business has generated cash during the period and how that cash was used. This is potentially very useful information. Tracking the sources and uses of cash over time may reveal trends that could help a user to assess likely future cash movements for the business.

Looking specifically at the statement of cash flows for Torbryan plc, in Example 6.3, we can see the following:

- Net cash flow from operations seems strong, much larger than the profit for the year, after taking account of the dividend paid. This might be expected as depreciation is deducted in arriving at profit.
- Working capital has absorbed some cash, which may indicate an expansion of activity (sales revenue) over the year. As we have only one year's income statement, however, we cannot tell whether this has occurred.
- There were net outflows of cash for investing activities, but this would not be unusual. Many types of non-current assets have limited lives and need to be replaced. Expenditure during the year was not out of line with the depreciation expense for the year, which is to be expected for a business with a regular replacement programme for its non-current assets.
- There was a major outflow of cash to redeem borrowings, which was partly offset by the proceeds of a share issue. This may well represent a change of financing strategy.

Activity   6.10

Why might this be the case? What has been the impact of these changes on the long-term financing of the business?

The financing changes, together with the retained earnings for the year, have led to a significant shift in the equity/borrowings balance.

Real World 6.5 identifies the important changes in the cash flows of Ryanair plc during the year ended 31 March 2016.

Real World 6.5

Flying high

Ryanair's summarised statement of cash flows for the year ended 31 March 2016

	€m
Net cash provided by operating activities	1,846.3
Net cash from (used in) investing activities	(283.6)
Net cash from (used in) financing activities	(1,488.1)
Net decrease in cash and cash equivalents	74.6

We can see that there was a net increase in cash and cash equivalents of €74.6 million during the year. Cash and cash equivalents increased from €1,184.6 million at 31 March 2015 to €1,259.2 million at 31 March 2016. Both, however, are very large balances and represent 10 per cent and 11 per cent, respectively, of total assets held.

The net cash inflow from operating activities during the year to 31 March 2016 was €1,846.3 million. This was higher than the previous year's figure of €1,689.4 million and significantly higher than 2014's figure of €1,044.6 million. The increase was largely due to an increase in profit after tax of €692.4 million over 2015. This increased profit did not fully show itself in the increased cash flow from operations because €317.5 million of the profit arose from what Ryanair made on disposal of its holding of shares in Aer Lingus, when International Airline Group (BA and Iberia) took over Aer Lingus. Amounts relating to disposals of financial assets are not included in cash flow from operating activities, but appear under 'investing activities' in the statement of cash flows.

The net cash outflow from investing activities during the year totalled €283.6 million, down from the previous year's figure by €2,604.6 million. Although this included an outflow of €1,217.7 million for the purchase of property, plant and equipment (mostly new aircraft and a much larger figure than in recent years), this was partly offset by the sale of the Aer Lingus shares, mentioned above. There was also a major inflow, however, of €542.3 million from financial investments with a maturity of more than three months.

The net cash outflow from financing activities was €1,488.1 million. This large outflow was made up of repayments of long-term borrowings of €384.9 million and shares repurchases of a massive €1,104.0 million.

Source: Information taken from Ryanair plc Annual Report 2016, pp. 144, 145 and 149.

Real World 6.6 is an article that discusses the usefulness of the statement of cash flows.

Real World 6.6

Using the statement of cash flows

The City cheered results from oil majors BP and Royal Dutch Shell this week, despite a slump in profitability. It's all down to cash — or, rather, better cash management. This is the ultimate test of a company's ability to create real value out of its assets.

→

For investors, cash really is king. Keeping an eye on what a business is doing with its money can give you a good handle on its prospects. So, it is vital investors are comfortable looking at how a company uses its cash — and use this information to inform their investment decisions.

Many ignore cash flow and focus on profits and revenues alone. This is a mistake. The cash flow statement is just as important as the balance sheet or income statement in a company's accounts.

With the majority of investors owning shares in oil companies for their income, good cash management is vital to keep the dividend pipe flowing. Free cash flow is very important as it is from this pot that dividends are paid.

A quick and easy way of working out an approximate free cash flow figure is to take the operating cash flow number from the cash flow statement and subtract capital expenditures. You will then have a figure which is roughly the cash generated by the company after it has invested in maintaining and growing its business.

Following a profit warning in January, Shell's new chief executive Ben van Beurden unveiled a strategy that aimed to boost its cash by managing its business better, by making investments and disposing of non-core assets.

The group's cash flow hit $14 billion (£8.3bn) in the first quarter, up 21 per cent from a year ago and more than double the $6 billion seen in the fourth quarter of 2013. This was ahead of market expectations. BP also said it was on track to meet its target of $30 billion–$31 billion in operating cash flow for the year, compared with $22 billion in 2013. Both these statements cheered City analysts.

Investors had been critical of the returns both companies have generated from their invested capital over the last few years. A similar situation has been seen in mining — a sector arguably ahead of the game when compared with oil majors. BHP reported a £7.8 billion increase in free cash flow at the interim stage, by employing a similar strategy to BP and Shell. But the oil groups' cash strategy could end up having more of an impact, because oil prices have held up significantly better than the price of metals in the last few years.

Looking at cash flows can also identify companies where the dividend outlook is negative. For example, rail and bus operator FirstGroup is expected to have negative free cash flow for a number of years. Morgan Stanley is forecasting a negative free cash flow of £82.3 million this year, rising to £90.5 million in 2015. The company cancelled its dividend last year, as it needs to use its cash to service its debt pile. It did not make an interim payment but hinted that it may make a payment alongside its final results, due to be issued on May 21.

FirstGroup's board "expects to propose a final dividend of up to £50 million for the year to 31 March 2014, as a transition to a progressive dividend policy thereafter, "it said in November. However, some in the City think that, given the state of its free cash flow, it should reconsider making any payment until it becomes cash generative.

"A significant part of FirstGroup's cash flow pressure comes from servicing debt," broker Jefferies said last month. "For us, dividends look inappropriate for now."

Of course, it is too simplistic to say that a fall in free cash flow is always a bad thing. A company may be making large investments that will provide a significant return in the future. A good recent example of this is Deutsche Telekom, which slashed its guidance for 2015 free cash flow in March. Management lowered its target of €6 billion (£4.9bn) of free cash flow next year to €4.2 billion, down from €4.6 billion in 2013.

"We could achieve our original ambition level for 2015 if we were to slam the door in the face of the customer rush in the US. That's not what we want," said Thomas Dannenfeldt, Deutsche Telekom's chief financial officer. "The market is offering us the opportunity to achieve a different ambition: value-driven customer growth in the US that translates into an increase in the value of the company."

And if a company is stopping investment in its business merely to make cash flows look better this could store up problems further down the line. There is always a judgment call for an investor to make when looking at cash movements and the market has judged that BP and Shell are now spending their money much more wisely.

Both BP and Shell – the most significant dividend payers in the FTSE 100 – appear to be taking steps in the right direction to return to sustainable dividend growth. But one swallow does not a summer make. This needs to be sustained – for the sake of income seekers across the UK and beyond.

Source: White, G. (2014) Cash flow is king when judging a company's prospects, *Sunday Telegraph Business,* 3 May.

Problems with IAS 7

IAS 7 *Statement of Cash Flows* does not enjoy universal acclaim. Its critics argue that the standard is too permissive in the description and classification of important items.

Some believe that the standard would inspire greater confidence among users if it insisted that only the direct method be used to calculate cash flows from operating activities. Supporters of the direct method argue that, being cash-based, it provides greater clarity by setting out operating cash receipts and payments. No accrual-based adjustments are made, which means that it is less susceptible to manipulation than the indirect approach. This greater transparency 'would enable the market to distinguish between the weak and the strong – the better companies would be safe, and the worse would be more exposed'. (See reference 1 at the end of the chapter.) In its defence, however, it should be said that the indirect approach may help to shed light on the quality of reported profits by reconciling profit with the net cash from operating activities for a period. A business must demonstrate an ability to convert profits into cash. Revealing the link between profits and cash is, therefore, very helpful.

Self-assessment question 6.1

Touchstone plc's income statements for the years ended 31 December 2015 and 2016 and statements of financial position as at 31 December 2015 and 2016 are as follows:

Income statements for the years ended 2015 and 2016

	2015 £m	2016 £m
Revenue	173	207
Cost of sales	(96)	(101)
Gross profit	77	106
Distribution expenses	(18)	(20)
Administrative expenses	(24)	(26)
Other operating income	3	4
Operating profit	38	64
Interest payable	(2)	(4)
Profit before taxation	36	60
Taxation	(8)	(16)
Profit for the year	28	44

→

Self-assessment question 6.1 *continued*

Statements of financial position as at 31 December 2015 and 2016

	2015 £m	2016 £m
ASSETS		
Non-current assets		
Property, plant and equipment		
Land and buildings	94	110
Plant and machinery	53	62
	147	172
Current assets		
Inventories	25	24
Treasury bills (short-term investments)	–	15
Trade receivables	16	26
Cash at bank and in hand	4	4
	45	69
Total assets	192	241
EQUITY AND LIABILITIES		
Equity		
Called-up ordinary share capital	100	100
Retained earnings	30	56
	130	156
Non-current liabilities		
Borrowings – loan notes (10%)	20	40
Current liabilities		
Trade payables	38	37
Taxation	4	8
	42	45
Total equity and liabilities	192	241

Included in 'cost of sales', 'distribution expenses' and 'administrative expenses', depreciation was as follows:

	2015 £m	2016 £m
Land and buildings	5	6
Plant and machinery	6	10

There were no non-current asset disposals in either year.

The interest payable expense equalled the cash payment made during each of the years.

The business paid dividends on ordinary shares of £14 million during 2015 and £18 million during 2016.

The Treasury bills represent a short-term investment of funds that will be used shortly in operations. There is insignificant risk that this investment will lose value.

Required:

Prepare a statement of cash flows for the business for 2016.

The solution to this question can be found at the back of the book on pp. 771–772.

Summary

The main points of this chapter may be summarised as follows:

The need for a statement of cash flows

- Cash is important because no business can operate without it.
- The statement of cash flows is specifically designed to reveal movements in cash over a period.
- Cash movements cannot be readily detected from the income statement, which focuses on revenue and expenses rather than on cash inflows and outflows.
- Profit (or loss) and cash generated for the period are rarely equal.
- The statement of cash flows is a major financial statement, along with the income statement and the statement of financial position.

Preparing the statement of cash flows

- The statement of cash flows has three major categories of cash flows: cash flows from operating activities, cash flows from investing activities and cash flows from financing activities.
- The total of the cash movements under these three categories will provide the net increase or decrease in cash and cash equivalents for the period.
- A reconciliation can be undertaken to check that the opening balance of cash and cash equivalents plus the net increase (or decrease) for the period equals the closing balance.

Calculating the cash generated from operations

- The net cash flows from operating activities can be derived by either the direct method or the indirect method.
- The direct method is based on an analysis of the cash records for the period, whereas the indirect method uses information contained within the income statement and statements of financial position.
- The indirect method takes the operating profit for the period, adds back any depreciation charge and then adjusts for changes in inventories, receivables and payables during the period.

Interpreting the statement of cash flows

- The statement of cash flows shows the main sources and uses of cash.
- Tracking the cash movements over several periods may reveal financing and investing patterns and may help predict future management action.

Reconciliation of liabilities from financing activities

- IAS 7 requires businesses to provide a reconciliation that shows the link between liabilities at the beginning and end of the reporting period that relate to *Cash flows from financing activities* in the statement of cash flows.
- The reconciliation shows how borrowings and other non-equity finance have changed over the reporting period. Each type of non-equity finance needs to be separately reconciled.

Problems with IAS 7

- IAS 7 has been criticised for being too permissive over the description and classification of important items and for allowing businesses to adopt the indirect method for determining net cash from operating activities.

Key terms

For definitions of these terms, see Appendix B.
direct method   *p. 213*   **working capital**   *p. 215*
indirect method   *p. 213*

Reference

1   Clacher, D. (2013)'Why the numbers add up for direct cash flow statements', *Financial Director,*
    17 December.

Further reading

If you would like to explore the topics covered in this chapter in more depth, we recommend the
following:

Alexander, D. and Nobes, C., (2016) *Financial Accounting: An International Introduction,* 6th edn,
    Pearson, Chapter 13.

Elliott, B. and Elliott, J., (2015) *Financial Accounting and Reporting,* 17th edn, Pearson, Chapter 5.

International Accounting Standards Board, *2016 A guide through IFRS* (Green Book) 2014, IAS 7
    Statement of Cash Flows.

KPMG (2016) *Insights into IFRS,* 13th edn, Sweet and Maxwell, Section 2.3 (a summary of this book
    is available free at www.kpmg.com).

Review questions

Solutions to these questions can be found at the back of the book on pp. 790–791.

6.1 The typical business outside the service sector has about 50 per cent more of its resources tied up in inventories than in cash, yet there is no call for a 'statement of inventories flows' to be prepared. Why is cash regarded as more important than inventories?

6.2 What is the difference between the direct and indirect methods of deducing cash generated from operations?

6.3 Taking each of the categories of the statement of cash flows in turn, in which direction would you normally expect the cash flow to be? Explain your answer.

(a) Cash flows from operating activities
(b) Cash flows from investing activities
(c) Cash flows from financing activities.

6.4 What causes the profit for the reporting period not to equal the net cash inflow?

Exercises

Solution to Exercises with coloured numbers can be found at the back of the book on pp. 809–813.

Basic-level exercises

6.1 How will each of the following events ultimately affect the amount of cash?
(a) An increase in the level of inventories
(b) A rights issue of ordinary shares
(c) A bonus issue of ordinary shares
(d) Writing off part of the value of some inventories
(e) The disposal of a large number of the business's shares by a major shareholder
(f) Depreciating a non-current asset.

6.2 The following information has been taken from the financial statements of Juno plc for last year and the year before last:

	Year before last £m	Last year £m
Operating profit	156	187
Depreciation charged in arriving at operating profit	47	55
Inventories held at end of year	27	31
Trade receivables at end of year	24	23
Trade payables at end of year	15	17

Required:
What is the figure for cash generated from the operations for Juno plc for last year?

Intermediate-level exercises

6.3   Torrent plc's income statement for the year ended 31 December 2016 and the statements of financial position as at 31 December 2015 and 2016 are as follows:

Income statement for the year ended 31 December 2016

	£m
Revenue	623
Cost of sales	(353)
Gross profit	270
Distribution expenses	(71)
Administrative expenses	(30)
Other operating income	27
Operating profit	196
Interest payable	(26)
Profit before taxation	170
Taxation	(36)
Profit for the year	134

Statements of financial position as at 31 December 2015 and 2016

	2015 £m	2016 £m
ASSETS		
Non-current assets		
Property, plant and equipment		
Land and buildings	310	310
Plant and machinery	325	314
	635	624
Current assets		
Inventories	41	35
Trade receivables	139	145
	180	180
Total assets	815	804
EQUITY AND LIABILITIES		
Equity		
Called-up ordinary share capital	200	300
Share premium account	40	–
Revaluation reserve	69	9
Retained earnings	123	197
	432	506
Non-current liabilities		
Borrowings – loan notes	250	150
Current liabilities		
Borrowings (all bank overdraft)	56	89
Trade payables	54	41
Taxation	23	18
	133	148
Total equity and liabilities	815	804

During 2016, the business spent £67 million on additional plant and machinery. There were no other non-current asset acquisitions or disposals.

There was no share issue for cash during the year. The interest payable expense was equal in amount to the cash outflow. A dividend of £60 million was paid.

Required:

Prepare the statement of cash flows for Torrent plc for the year ended 31 December 2016.

6.4 Chen plc's income statements for the years ended 31 December 2015 and 2016 and the statements of financial position as at 31 December 2015 and 2016 are as follows:

Income statements for the years ended 31 December 2015 and 2016

	2015 £m	2016 £m
Revenue	207	153
Cost of sales	(101)	(76)
Gross profit	106	77
Distribution expenses	(22)	(20)
Administrative expenses	(20)	(28)
Operating profit	64	29
Interest payable	(4)	(4)
Profit before taxation	60	25
Taxation	(16)	(6)
Profit for the year	44	19

Statements of financial position as at 31 December 2015 and 2016

	2015 £m	2016 £m
ASSETS		
Non-current assets		
Property, plant and equipment		
Land and buildings	110	130
Plant and machinery	62	56
	172	186
Current assets		
Inventories	24	25
Trade receivables	26	25
Cash at bank and in hand	19	–
	69	50
Total assets	241	236
EQUITY AND LIABILITIES		
Equity		
Called-up ordinary share capital	100	100
Retained earnings	56	57
	156	157
Non-current liabilities		
Borrowings – loan notes (10%)	40	40
Current liabilities		
Borrowings (all bank overdraft)	–	2
Trade payables	37	34
Taxation	8	3
	45	39
Total equity and liabilities	241	236

Included in 'cost of sales', 'distribution expenses' and 'administrative expenses', depreciation was as follows:

	2015 £m	2016 £m
Land and buildings	6	10
Plant and machinery	10	12

There were no non-current asset disposals in either year. The amount of cash paid for interest equalled the expense in each year. Dividends were paid totalling £18 million in each year.

Required:

Prepare a statement of cash flows for the business for 2016.

6.5 The following are the financial statements for Nailsea plc for the years ended 30 June 2016 and 2017:

Income statement for years ended 30 June

	2016	2017
	£m	£m
Revenue	1,230	2,280
Operating expenses	(722)	(1,618)
Depreciation	(270)	(320)
Operating profit	238	342
Interest payable	–	(27)
Profit before taxation	238	315
Taxation	(110)	(140)
Profit for the year	128	175

Statements of financial position as at 30 June

	2016	2017
	£m	£m
ASSETS		
Non-current assets		
Property, plant and equipment (at carrying amount)		
Land and buildings	1,500	1,900
Plant and machinery	810	740
	2,310	2,640
Current assets		
Inventories	275	450
Trade receivables	100	250
Bank	–	118
	375	818
Total assets	2,685	3,458
EQUITY AND LIABILITIES		
Equity		
Share capital (fully paid £1 shares)	1,400	1,600
Share premium account	200	300
Retained earnings	828	958
	2,428	2,858
Non-current liabilities		
Borrowings – 9% loan notes (repayable 2021)	–	300
Current liabilities		
Borrowings (all bank overdraft)	32	–
Trade payables	170	230
Taxation	55	70
	257	300
Total equity and liabilities	2,685	3,458

There were no disposals of non-current assets in either year. Dividends were paid in 2016 and 2017 of £40 million and £45 million, respectively.

Required:

Prepare a statement of cash flows for Nailsea plc for the year ended 30 June 2017.

Advanced-level exercises

6.6 The following financial statements for Blackstone plc are a slightly simplified set of published accounts. Blackstone plc is an engineering business that developed a new range of products in 2013. These products now account for 60 per cent of its sales revenue.

Income statement for the years ended 31 March

	Notes	2016 £m	2017 £m
Revenue		7,003	11,205
Cost of sales		(3,748)	(5,809)
Gross profit		3,255	5,396
Operating expenses		(2,205)	(3,087)
Operating profit		1,050	2,309
Interest payable	1	(216)	(456)
Profit before taxation		834	1,853
Taxation		(210)	(390)
Profit for the year		624	1,463

Statements of financial position as at 31 March

	Notes	2016 £m	2017 £m
ASSETS			
Non-current assets			
Property, plant and equipment	2	4,300	7,535
Intangible assets	3	–	700
		4,300	8,235
Current assets			
Inventories		1,209	2,410
Trade receivables		641	1,173
Cash at bank		123	–
		1,973	3,583
Total assets		6,273	11,818
EQUITY AND LIABILITIES			
Equity			
Share capital		1,800	1,800
Share premium		600	600
Capital reserves		352	352
Retained earnings		685	1,748
		3,437	4,500
Non-current liabilities			
Borrowings – bank loan (repayable 2021)		1,800	3,800
Current liabilities			
Trade payables		931	1,507
Taxation		105	195
Borrowings (all bank overdraft)		–	1,816
		1,036	3,518
Total equity and liabilities		6,273	11,818

Notes:

1 The expense and the cash outflow for interest payable are equal for each year.
2 The movements in property, plant and equipment during the year are:

	Land and buildings £m	Plant and machinery £m	Fixtures and fittings £m	Total £m
Cost				
At 1 April 2016	4,500	3,850	2,120	10,470
Additions	–	2,970	1,608	4,578
Disposals	–	(365)	(216)	(581)
At 31 March 2017	4,500	6,455	3,512	14,467
Depreciation				
At 1 April 2016	1,275	3,080	1,815	6,170
Charge for year	225	745	281	1,251
Disposals	–	(305)	(184)	(489)
At 31 March 2017	1,500	3,520	1,912	6,932
Carrying amount				
At 31 March 2017	3,000	2,935	1,600	7,535

3 Intangible assets represent the amounts paid for the goodwill of another engineering business acquired during the year.
4 Proceeds from the sale of non-current assets in the year ended 31 March 2017 amounted to £54 million.
5 £300 million was paid in dividends on ordinary shares in 2016, and £400 million in 2017.

Required:

Prepare a statement of cash flows for Blackstone plc for the year ended 31 March 2017. (*Hint*: A loss (deficit) on disposal of non-current assets is simply an additional amount of depreciation and should be dealt with as such in preparing the statement of cash flows.)

6.7 Simplified financial statements for York plc are:

Income statement for the year ended 30 September 2017

	£m
Revenue	290.0
Cost of sales	(215.0)
Gross profit	75.0
Operating expenses (Note 1)	(62.0)
Operating profit	13.0
Interest payable (Note 2)	(3.0)
Profit before taxation	10.0
Taxation	(2.6)
Profit for the year	7.4

Statement of financial position as at 30 September

	2016 £m	2017 £m
ASSETS		
Non-current assets (Note 4)	80.0	85.0
Current assets		
Inventories and trade receivables	119.8	122.1
Cash at bank	9.2	16.6
	129.0	138.7
Total assets	209.0	223.7
EQUITY AND LIABILITIES		
Equity		
Share capital	35.0	40.0
Share premium account	30.0	30.0
Reserves	31.0	34.9
	96.0	104.9
Non-current liabilities		
Borrowings	32.0	35.0
Current liabilities		
Trade payables	80.0	82.5
Taxation	1.0	1.3
	81.0	83.8
Total equity and liabilities	209.0	223.7

Notes:

1 Operating expenses include depreciation of £13 million and a surplus of £3.2 million on the sale of non-current assets.
2 The expense and the cash outflow for interest payable are equal.
3 A dividend of £3.5 million was paid during 2017.
4 Non-current asset costs and depreciation:

	Cost £m	Accumulated depreciation £m	Carrying amount £m
At 1 October 2016	120.0	40.0	80.0
Disposals	(10.0)	(8.0)	(2.0)
Additions	20.0	–	20.0
Depreciation	–	13.0	(13.0)
At 30 September 2017	130.0	45.0	85.0

Required:

Prepare a statement of cash flows for York plc for the year ended 30 September 2017.

CHAPTER 7

Analysing and interpreting financial statements

Introduction

In this chapter, we consider the analysis and interpretation of the financial statements discussed in Chapters 2, 3 and 6. We shall see how the use of financial (or accounting) ratios can help to assess the financial performance and position of a business. We shall also take a look at the problems encountered when applying financial ratios.

Financial ratios can be used to examine various aspects of financial health and are widely employed by external users, such as shareholders and lenders, and by managers. They can be very helpful to managers in a wide variety of decision areas, such as profit planning, pricing, working capital management and financial structure.

Learning outcomes

When you have completed this chapter, you should be able to:

- identify the major categories of ratios that can be used for analysing financial statements;

- calculate key ratios for assessing the financial performance and position of a business and explain their significance;

- discuss the use of ratios in helping to predict financial failure; and

- discuss the limitations of ratios as a tool of financial analysis.

Financial ratios

Financial ratios provide a quick and relatively simple means of assessing the financial health of a business. A ratio simply relates one figure appearing in the financial statements to another figure appearing there (for example operating profit in relation to sales revenue) or, perhaps, to some non-financial resource of the business (for example, operating profit per employee).

Ratios can be very helpful when comparing the financial health of different businesses. Differences may exist between businesses in the scale of operations. As a result, a direct comparison of, say, the operating profit generated by each business may be misleading. By expressing operating profit in relation to some other measure (for example, capital employed), the problem of scale is eliminated. This means that a business with an operating profit of £10,000 and capital employed of £100,000 can be compared with a much larger business with an operating profit of £80,000 and capital employed of £1,000,000 by the use of a simple ratio. The operating profit to capital employed ratio for the smaller business is 10 per cent (that is, (10,000/100,000) $\times$ 100%) and the same ratio for the larger business is 8 per cent (that is, (80,000/1,000,000) $\times$ 100%). These ratios can be directly compared, whereas a comparison of the absolute operating profit figures might be much less meaningful. The need to eliminate differences in scale through the use of ratios can also apply when comparing the performance of the same business from one time period to another.

By calculating a small number of ratios it is often possible to build up a revealing picture of the position and performance of a business. It is not surprising, therefore, that ratios are widely used by those who have an interest in businesses and business performance. Ratios are not difficult to calculate but they can be difficult to interpret.

Ratios help us to identify which questions to ask, rather than provide the answers. They help to highlight the financial strengths and weaknesses of a business, but cannot explain why those strengths or weaknesses exist or why certain changes have occurred. They provide a starting point for further analysis. Only a detailed investigation will reveal the underlying reasons.

Ratios can be expressed in various forms, for example as a percentage or as a proportion. The way that a particular ratio is presented will depend on the needs of those who will use the information. Although it is possible to calculate a large number of ratios, only a few, based on key relationships, tend to be helpful to a particular user. Many ratios that could be calculated from the financial statements (for example, rent payable in relation to current assets) may not be considered because there is not usually any clear or meaningful relationship between the two items.

There is no generally accepted list of ratios that can be applied to the financial statements, nor is there a standard method of calculating many ratios. Variations in both the choice of ratios and their calculation will be found in practice. It is important, therefore, to be consistent in the way in which ratios are calculated for comparison purposes. The ratios that we shall discuss are very popular – presumably because they are seen as useful for decision-making purposes.

Financial ratio classifications

Ratios tend to be grouped into categories, with each category relating to a particular aspect of financial performance or position. The following broad categories are those that are usually found in practice. There are five of them:

- *Profitability*. Businesses generally exist with the primary purpose of creating wealth for their owners. Profitability ratios provide some indication of the degree of success in achieving this. These ratios express the profit made in relation to other key figures in the financial statements or to some business resource.
- *Efficiency*. Ratios may be used to measure the efficiency with which particular resources, such as inventories or employees, have been used within the business. These ratios are also referred to as *activity* ratios.
- *Liquidity*. It is vital to the survival of a business that there are sufficient liquid resources available to meet maturing obligations (that is, amounts owing that must be paid in the near future). Liquidity ratios examine the relationship between liquid resources, or cash generated, and amounts due for payment in the near future.
- *Financial gearing*. This is the relationship between the contribution to financing a business made by the owners and the contribution made by others, in the form of loans. This relationship is important because the level of gearing has an important effect on the level of risk associated with a business. Gearing ratios help to reveal the extent to which loan finance is utilised and the consequent effect on the level of risk borne by a business.
- *Investment*. Certain ratios are concerned with assessing the returns and performance of shares in a particular business from the perspective of shareholders who are not involved with the management of the business.

These five key aspects of financial health that ratios seek to examine are summarised in Figure 7.1.

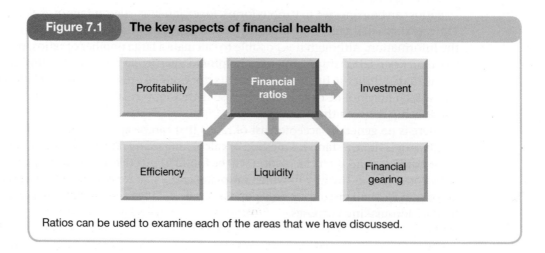

| Figure 7.1 | The key aspects of financial health |

Ratios can be used to examine each of the areas that we have discussed.

The analyst must be clear *who* the target users are and *why* they need the information. Different users of financial information are likely to have different information needs. This will, in turn, determine the ratios that they find useful. Shareholders, for example, are likely to be interested in their returns in relation to the level of risk associated with their investment. Profitability, investment and gearing ratios should, therefore, be of particular interest. Long-term lenders are likely to be concerned with the long-term viability of the business and, to assess this, profitability and gearing ratios should be of interest. Short-term lenders, such as suppliers of goods and services on credit, are likely to be interested in the ability of the business to repay the amounts owing in the short term. Liquidity ratios should, therefore, be of particular interest.

The need for comparison

Merely calculating a ratio will not tell us very much about the position or performance of a business. For example, if a ratio revealed that a retail business was generating £100 in sales revenue per square metre of floor space, it would not be possible to deduce from this information alone whether this particular level of performance was good, bad or indifferent. It is only when we compare this ratio with some 'benchmark' that the information can be interpreted and evaluated.

Activity 7.1

Can you think of any bases that could be used to compare a ratio that you have calculated from the financial statements of your business for a particular period? (*Hint*: There are three main possibilities.)

You may have thought of the following bases:

- past periods for the same business;
- similar businesses for the same or past periods; and/or
- planned performance for the business.

We shall now take a closer look at these three in turn.

Past periods

By comparing the ratio that we have calculated with the same ratio, but for a previous period, it is possible to detect whether there has been an improvement or deterioration in performance. Indeed, it is often useful to track particular ratios over time (say, five or 10 years) to see whether it is possible to detect trends. The comparison of ratios from different periods brings certain problems, however. In particular, there is always the possibility that trading conditions were quite different in the periods being compared. There is the further problem that, when comparing the performance of a single business over time, operating inefficiencies may not be clearly exposed. For example, the fact that sales revenue per employee has risen by 10 per cent over the previous period may at first sight appear to be satisfactory. This may not be the case, however, if similar businesses have shown an improvement of 50 per cent for the same period or had much better sales revenue per employee ratios to start with. Finally, there is the problem that inflation may have distorted the figures on which the ratios are based. Inflation can lead to an overstatement of profit and an understatement of asset values, as will be discussed later in the chapter.

Similar businesses

In a competitive environment, a business must consider its performance in relation to that of other businesses operating in the same industry. Survival may depend on its ability to achieve comparable levels of performance. A useful basis for comparing a particular ratio, therefore, is the ratio achieved by similar businesses during the same period. This basis is not, however, without its problems. Competitors may have different year-ends and so trading conditions may not be identical. They may also have different accounting policies, which can have a significant effect on reported profits and asset values (for example, different methods of calculating depreciation or valuing inventories). Finally, it may be difficult to obtain the financial statements of competitor businesses. Sole proprietorships and partnerships, for example, are not obliged to make their financial statements available to the public. In the case of limited companies, there is a legal obligation to do so. However, a diversified business may not provide a breakdown of activities that is sufficiently detailed to enable comparisons with other businesses. This is despite the requirement for diversified businesses to report certain information on their different segments, that we discussed in Chapter 5.

Planned performance

Ratios may be compared with targets that management developed before the start of the period under review. The comparison of actual performance with planned performance can be a useful way of assessing the level of achievement attained. Indeed, planned performance often provides the most valuable benchmark against which managers may assess their own business. However, planned performance must be based on realistic assumptions if it is to be worthwhile for comparison purposes.

Planned, or target, ratios may be prepared for each aspect of the business's activities. When developing these ratios, account will normally be taken of past performance and the performance of other businesses. This does not mean, however, that the business should seek to achieve either of these levels of performance. Neither may provide an appropriate target.

We should bear in mind that those outside the business do not normally have access to the business's plans. For such people, past performance and the performances of other, similar, businesses may provide the only practical benchmarks.

Calculating the ratios

Probably the best way to explain financial ratios is through an example. Example 7.1 provides a set of financial statements from which we can calculate important ratios.

Example 7.1

The following financial statements relate to Alexis plc, which operates a wholesale carpet business:

Statements of financial position (balance sheets) as at 31 March

	2016 £m	2017 £m
ASSETS		
Non-current assets		
Property, plant and equipment (at cost less depreciation)		
Land and buildings	381	427
Fixtures and fittings	129	160
	510	587
Current assets		
Inventories	300	406
Trade receivables	240	273
Cash at bank	4	–
	544	679
Total assets	1,054	1,266
EQUITY AND LIABILITIES		
Equity		
£0.50 ordinary shares (Note 1)	300	300
Retained earnings	263	234
	563	534
Non-current liabilities		
Borrowings – 9% loan notes (secured)	200	300
Current liabilities		
Trade payables	261	354
Taxation	30	2
Short-term borrowings (all bank overdraft)	–	76
	291	432
Total equity and liabilities	1,054	1,266

Income statements for the year ended 31 March

	2016 £m	2017 £m
Revenue (Note 2)	2,240	2,681
Cost of sales (Note 3)	(1,745)	(2,272)
Gross profit	495	409
Operating expenses	(252)	(362)
Operating profit	243	47
Interest payable	(18)	(32)
Profit before taxation	225	15
Taxation	(60)	(4)
Profit for the year	165	11

→

Statement of cash flows for the year ended 31 March

	2016 £m	2017 £m
Cash flows from operating activities		
Profit, after interest, before taxation	225	15
Adjustments for:		
Depreciation	26	33
Interest expense	18	32
	269	80
Increase in inventories	(59)	(106)
Increase in trade receivables	(17)	(33)
Increase in trade payables	58	93
Cash generated from operations	251	34
Interest paid	(18)	(32)
Taxation paid	(63)	(32)
Dividend paid	(40)	(40)
Net cash from/(used in) operating activities	130	(70)
Cash flows from investing activities		
Payments to acquire property, plant and equipment	(77)	(110)
Net cash used in investing activities	(77)	(110)
Cash flows from financing activities		
Issue of loan notes	–	100
Net cash from financing activities	–	100
Net increase in cash and cash equivalents	53	(80)
Cash and cash equivalents at start of year		
Cash/(overdraft)	(49)	4
Cash and cash equivalents at end of year		
Cash/(overdraft)	4	(76)

Notes:
1. The market value of the shares of the business at the end of the reporting period was £2.50 for 2016 and £1.50 for 2017.
2. All sales and purchases are made on credit.
3. The cost of sales figure can be analysed as follows:

	2016 £m	2017 £m
Opening inventories	241	300
Purchases (Note 2)	1,804	2,378
	2,045	2,678
Closing inventories	(300)	(406)
Cost of sales	1,745	2,272

4. At 31 March 2015, the trade receivables stood at £223 million and the trade payables at £183 million.
5. A dividend of £40 million had been paid to the shareholders in respect of each of the years.
6. The business employed 13,995 staff at 31 March 2016 and 18,623 at 31 March 2017.
7. The business expanded its capacity during the year to 31 March 2017 by setting up a new warehouse and distribution centre.
8. At 1 April 2015, the total of equity stood at £438 million and the total of equity and non-current liabilities stood at £638 million.

A brief overview

Before we start our detailed look at the ratios for Alexis plc (see Example 7.1), it is helpful to take a quick look, before calculating any ratios, at what information is obvious from the financial statements. This will usually pick up some issues that ratios may not be able to identify. It may also highlight some points that could help us in our interpretation of the ratios. Starting at the top of the statement of financial position, the following points can be noted:

- *Expansion of non-current assets.* These have increased by about 15 per cent (from £510 million to £587 million). Note 7 mentions a new warehouse and distribution centre, which may account for much of the additional investment in non-current assets. We are not told when this new facility was established, but it is quite possible that it was well into the year. This could mean that not much benefit was reflected in terms of additional sales revenue or cost saving during 2017. Sales revenue, in fact, expanded by about 20 per cent (from £2,240 million to £2,681 million); this is greater than the expansion in non-current assets.

- *Major expansion in the elements of working capital.* Inventories increased by about 35 per cent, trade receivables by about 14 per cent and trade payables by about 36 per cent between 2016 and 2017. These are major increases, particularly in inventories and payables (which are linked because the inventories are all bought on credit – see Note 2).

- *Reduction in the cash balance.* The cash balance fell from £4 million (in funds) to a £76 million overdraft between 2016 and 2017. The bank may be putting the business under pressure to reverse this, which could create difficulties.

- *Apparent debt capacity.* Comparing the non-current assets with the long-term borrowings implies that the business may well be able to offer security on further borrowing. This is because potential lenders usually look at the value of assets that can be offered as security when assessing loan requests. Lenders seem particularly attracted to land and buildings as security. For example, at 31 March 2017, non-current assets had a carrying amount (the value at which they appeared in the statement of financial position) of £587 million, but long-term borrowing was only £300 million (though there was also an overdraft of £76 million). Carrying amounts are not normally, of course, market values. On the other hand, land and buildings tend to have a market value higher than their value as shown on the statement of financial position due to a general tendency to inflation in property values.

- *Lower operating profit.* Though sales revenue expanded by 20 per cent between 2016 and 2017, both cost of sales and operating expenses rose by a greater percentage, leaving both gross profit and, particularly, operating profit massively reduced. The level of staffing, which increased by about 33 per cent (from 13,995 to 18,623 employees – see Note 6), may have greatly affected the operating expenses. (Without knowing when the additional employees were recruited during 2017, we cannot be sure of the effect on operating expenses.) Increasing staffing by 33 per cent must put an enormous strain on management, at least in the short term. It is not surprising, therefore, that the year to 31 March 2017 was not successful for the business – not, at least, in profit terms.

Having had a quick look at what is fairly obvious, without calculating any financial ratios, we shall now go on to calculate and interpret those relating to profitability, efficiency, liquidity, gearing and investment.

Profitability

The following ratios may be used to evaluate the profitability of the business:

● return on ordinary shareholders' funds
● return on capital employed
● operating profit margin
● gross profit margin.

We shall now look at each of these in turn.

Return on ordinary shareholders' funds

The **return on ordinary shareholders' funds ratio (ROSF)** compares the amount of profit for the period available to owners with their average investment in the business during that same period. The ratio (which is normally expressed in percentage terms) is as follows:

$$ROSF = \frac{\text{Profit for the year (less any preference dividend)}}{\text{Ordinary share capital + Reserves}} \times 100$$

The profit for the year (less any preference dividend) is used in calculating the ratio, because this figure represents the amount of profit that is attributable to the owners.

In the case of Alexis plc, the ratio for the year ended 31 March 2016 is:

$$ROSF = \frac{165}{(438 + 563)/2} \times 100 = 33.0\%$$

Note that, when calculating the ROSF, the average of the figures for ordinary shareholders' funds as at the beginning and at the end of the year has been used. This is because an average figure is normally more representative. The amount of shareholders' funds was not constant throughout the year, yet we want to compare it with the profit earned during the whole period. We know, from Note 8, that the amount of shareholders' funds at 1 April 2015 was £438 million. By a year later, however, it had risen to £563 million, according to the statement of financial position as at 31 March 2016.

The easiest approach to calculating the average amount of shareholders' funds is to take a simple average based on the opening and closing figures for the year. This is often the only information available, as is the case with Example 7.1. Averaging is normally appropriate for all ratios that combine a figure for a period (such as profit for the year) with one taken at a point in time (such as shareholders' funds).

Where not even the beginning-of-year figure is available, it will be necessary to rely on just the year-end figure. This is not ideal but, when this approach is consistently applied, it can still produce useful ratios.

Activity 7.2

Calculate the ROSF for Alexis plc for the year ended 31 March 2017.

The ratio for 2017 is:

$$ROSF = \frac{11}{(563 + 534)/2} \times 100 = 2.0\%$$

Broadly, businesses seek to generate as high a value as possible for this ratio. This is provided that it is not achieved at the expense of jeopardising future returns by, for example, taking on more risky activities. In view of this, the 2017 ratio is very poor by any standards; a bank deposit account will normally yield a better return. We need to find out why things went so badly wrong in the year to 31 March 2017. As we look at other ratios, we should find some clues.

Return on capital employed

The **return on capital employed ratio (ROCE)** is a fundamental measure of business performance. This ratio expresses the relationship between the operating profit generated during a period and the average long-term capital invested in the business.

The ratio is expressed in percentage terms and is as follows:

$$\text{ROCE} = \frac{\text{Operating profit}}{\text{Share capital + Reserves + Non-current liabilities}} \times 100$$

Note, in this case, that the profit figure used is the operating profit (that is, the profit *before* interest and taxation), because the ratio attempts to measure the returns to all suppliers of long-term finance before any deductions for interest payable on borrowings, or payments of dividends to shareholders, are made.

For the year to 31 March 2016, the ratio for Alexis plc is:

$$\text{ROCE} = \frac{243}{(638 + 763)/2} \times 100 = 34.7\%$$

(The capital employed figure, which is the total equity plus non-current liabilities, at 1 April 2015 is given in Note 8.)

ROCE is considered by many to be a primary measure of profitability. It compares inputs (capital invested) with outputs (operating profit) so as to reveal the effectiveness with which funds have been deployed. Once again, an average figure for capital employed should be used where the information is available.

Activity 7.3

Calculate the ROCE for Alexis plc for the year ended 31 March 2017.

The ratio for 2017 is:

$$\text{ROCE} = \frac{47}{(763 + 834)/2} \times 100 = 5.9\%$$

This ratio tells much the same story as ROSF; namely a poor performance, with the return on the assets being less than the rate that the business pays for most of its borrowed funds (that is, 9 per cent for the loan notes).

Real World 7.1 shows how financial ratios are used by businesses as a basis for setting profitability targets.

Real World 7.1

Targeting profitability

The ROCE ratio is widely used by businesses when establishing targets for profitability. These targets are sometimes made public and here are some examples:

- Barratt Developments plc, the builder, has a target ROCE on all new land acquisitions of 25 per cent.
- Greene King plc, the brewing, pub and hotel business, has a target ROCE of between 8.85 and 9.55 per cent.
- J Sainsbury plc, the supermarket business, has a minimum target ROCE of 9 per cent.
- Tate and Lyle plc, the sugar and associated products producer, has a target ROCE of between 12 and 16 per cent.
- Smurfit Kappa Group plc, the packaging manufacturer, has a target ROCE of 15 per cent.

Sources: Information taken from Key performance indicators, Barratt Developments plc, www.barrattdevelopments.com (accessed 24 January 2017); Greene King plc, Annual Report 2016, p. 62; J Sainsbury plc, Annual Report 2016, p. 73; Tate and Lyle plc, Annual Report 2016, p. 75; and Smurfit Kappa plc, Second quarter and first half 2016 results, slide 14, http://resources.smurfitkappa.com/ Resources/Documents/SKG_Q2_2016_Presentation.pdf.

Real World 7.2 provides some indication of the levels of ROCE achieved by UK businesses.

Real World 7.2

Achieving profitability

ROCE ratios for UK manufacturing and service companies for each of the six years ending in 2015 are shown in Figure 7.2.

Figure 7.2   The ROCE of UK companies

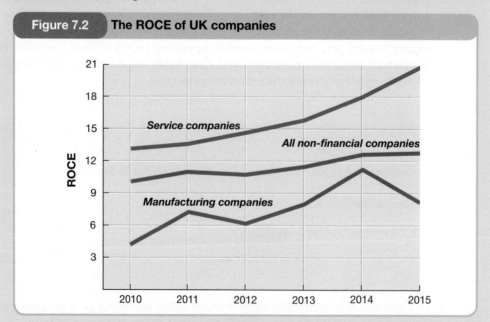

The ROCEs of manufacturing businesses have been consistently lower than those of service companies over the period. According to the Office of National Statistics, the difference between the two sectors is accounted for by the higher capital intensity of manufacturing.

Source: Figure compiled from information taken from Office of National Statistics, Profitability of UK companies October to December 2015, www.statistics.gov.uk, 6 April 2016.

Operating profit margin

The **operating profit margin ratio** relates the operating profit for the period to the sales revenue. The ratio is expressed as follows:

$$\text{Operating profit margin} = \frac{\text{Operating profit}}{\text{Sales revenue}} \times 100$$

Operating profit (that is, profit before interest and taxation) is used in this ratio as it represents the profit from trading operations before interest payable is taken into account. It is normally the most appropriate measure of operational performance, when making comparisons. This is because differences arising from the way in which the business is financed will not influence the measure.

For the year ended 31 March 2016, Alexis plc's operating profit margin ratio is:

$$\text{Operating profit margin} = \frac{243}{2,240} \times 100 = 10.8\%$$

This ratio compares one output of the business (operating profit) with another output (sales revenue). The ratio can vary considerably between types of business. Supermarkets, for example, tend to operate on low prices and, therefore, low operating profit margins. This is done in an attempt to stimulate sales and thereby increase the total amount of operating profit generated. Jewellers, on the other hand, tend to have high operating profit margins but have much lower levels of sales volume. Factors such as the degree of competition, the type of customer, the economic climate and industry characteristics (such as the level of risk) will influence the operating profit margin of a business. This point is picked up again later in the chapter.

Activity 7.4

Calculate the operating profit margin for Alexis plc for the year ended 31 March 2017.

The ratio for 2017 is:

$$\text{Operating profit margin} = \frac{47}{2,681} \times 100 = 1.8\%$$

Once again, this indicates a very weak performance compared with that of 2016. In 2016, for every £1 of sales revenue an average of 10.8p (that is, 10.8 per cent) was left as operating profit, after paying the cost of the carpets sold and other expenses of operating the business. By 2017, however, this had fallen to only 1.8p for every £1. The poor ROSF and ROCE ratios appear to have been partially, if not wholly, due to a high level of other expenses relative to sales revenue. The next ratio should provide us with a clue as to how the sharp decline in this ratio occurred.

Real World 7.3 sets out the target operating profit margins for some well-known car manufacturers.

Real World 7.3

Profit driven

- BMW has a target operating profit margin of between 8 and 10 per cent.
- Volvo has a target operating profit margin of 8 per cent by 2020.
- Nissan has a target operating profit margin of 8 per cent.
- Volkswagen has a target operating profit margin of 6 per cent.
- Daimler has a medium-term target profit margin of 9 per cent.
- Renault has set a target operating profit margin of 5 per cent.
- Ford has a long-term target of achieving an operating profit margin target of between 8 and 10 per cent.

We can see that, with the exception of Volkswagen and Renault, target operating profit margins fall within the 8 to 10 per cent range.

Sources: Fortune (2016) Here's why BMW's profit margins are falling, 4 November; Volvo pins hopes on its 'all-in car' ft.com, 17 August 2014; Greimel, H. (2016) Nissan backs off profit targets, *Autonews*, 31 July; McGee, P. (2016) VW margin target out of reach for now, admits finance chief, ft.com, 31 May; Daimler Investors relations release, www.Daimler.com/investors, 4 February 2016; European recovery lifts Renault profit despite weaker pricing, 30 July 2015, Reuters' Renault's business results improve thanks to European recovery and updated lineups, marklines.co, 14 October 2016; 'Hinrichs, J. (2016) Ford Motor Company Results, http://corporate.ford.com/content/dam/corporate/en/investors/investor-events/Press%20Releases/2016/Hinrichs-JPM-Presentation-FINAL.pdf, 9 August.

Gross profit margin

The **gross profit margin ratio** relates the gross profit of the business to the sales revenue generated for the same period. Gross profit represents the difference between sales revenue and the cost of sales. The ratio is therefore a measure of profitability in buying (or producing) and selling goods or services before any other expenses are taken into account. As cost of sales represents a major expense for many businesses, a change in this ratio can have a significant effect on the 'bottom line' (that is, the profit for the year). The gross profit margin ratio is calculated as follows:

$$\text{Gross profit margin} = \frac{\text{Gross profit}}{\text{Sales revenue}} \times 100$$

For the year ended 31 March 2016, the ratio for Alexis plc is:

$$\text{Gross profit margin} = \frac{495}{2,240} \times 100 = 22.1\%$$

Activity 7.5

Calculate the gross profit margin for Alexis plc for the year ended 31 March 2017.

The ratio for 2017 is:

$$\text{Gross profit margin} = \frac{409}{2,681} \times 100 = 15.3\%$$

The decline in this ratio means that gross profit was lower *relative* to sales revenue in 2017 than it had been in 2016. Bearing in mind that:

Gross profit = Sales revenue − Cost of sales (or cost of goods sold)

this means that cost of sales was higher *relative* to sales revenue in 2017 than in 2016. This could mean that sales prices were lower and/or that the purchase price of carpets had increased. It is possible that both sales prices and purchase prices had reduced, but the former at a greater rate than the latter. Similarly they may both have increased, but with sales prices having increased at a lesser rate than purchase prices.

Clearly, part of the decline in the operating profit margin ratio is linked to the dramatic decline in the gross profit margin ratio. Whereas, after paying for the carpets sold, for each £1 of sales revenue, 22.1p was left to cover other operating expenses in 2016, this was only 15.3p in 2017.

The profitability ratios for the business over the two years can be set out as follows:

	2016	2017
	%	%
ROSF	33.0	2.0
ROCE	34.7	5.9
Operating profit margin	10.8	1.8
Gross profit margin	22.1	15.3

Activity 7.6

What do you deduce from a comparison of the declines in the operating profit and gross profit margin ratios?

We can see that the difference in the operating profit margin was 9 per cent (that is, 10.8 per cent to 1.8 per cent), whereas that of the gross profit margin was only 6.8 per cent (that is, from 22.1 per cent to 15.3 per cent). This can only mean that operating expenses were greater compared with sales revenue in 2017 than they had been in 2016. The decline in both ROSF and ROCE was caused partly, therefore, by the business incurring higher inventories purchasing costs relative to sales revenue and partly through higher operating expenses compared with sales revenue. We need to compare each of these ratios with their planned levels, however, before we can usefully assess the business's success.

An investigation is needed to discover what caused the increases in both cost of sales and operating expenses, relative to sales revenue, from 2016 to 2017. This will involve checking on what has happened with sales and inventories prices over the two years. Similarly, it will involve looking at each of the individual areas that make up operating expenses to discover which ones were responsible for the increase, relative to sales revenue. Here, further ratios, for example, staff expenses (wages and salaries) to sales revenue, could be calculated in an attempt to isolate the cause of the change from 2016 to 2017. As mentioned earlier, the increase in staffing may well account for most of the increase in operating expenses.

Real World 7.4 discusses how some operating costs can be controlled by unusual means.

Real World 7.4

Flying more slowly

Ryanair's profits dropped sharply in the first quarter of its reporting year largely because of rising fuel costs. Europe's largest low-cost carrier by revenue said profit after tax fell 21 per cent to €78 million, in line with its forecasts. Fuel costs rose 6 per cent compared with the same period last year to make up 47 per cent of its total operating costs.

Howard Millar, chief financial officer, said the airline had looked at how to save fuel and as a result was flying its aircraft more slowly, adding about two minutes to an hour of flying time. "We're flying slightly slower, but what we're seeing is we're burning less fuel," Mr Millar said. "Fuel is our single biggest cost, so we have a proportionally bigger problem than everybody else from these higher fuel prices."

FT   Source: Extract from Wild, J. (2013) Ryanair sees sharp fall in profits due to higher fuel costs, ft.com, 29 July. © The Financial Times Ltd 2013. All Rights Reserved.

Efficiency

Efficiency ratios are used to try to assess how successfully the various resources of the business are managed. The following ratios consider some of the more important aspects of resource management:

- average inventories turnover period
- average settlement period for trade receivables
- average settlement period for trade payables
- sales revenue to capital employed
- sales revenue per employee.

We shall now look at each of these in turn.

Average inventories turnover period

Inventories often represent a significant investment for a business. For some types of business (for example, manufacturers and certain retailers), inventories may account for a substantial proportion of the total assets held (see Real World 16.1 on page 677). The **average inventories turnover period ratio** measures the average period for which inventories are being held. The ratio is calculated as follows:

$$\text{Average inventories turnover period} = \frac{\text{Average inventories held}}{\text{Cost of sales}} \times 365$$

The average inventories for the period can be calculated as a simple average of the opening and closing inventories levels for the year. In the case of a highly seasonal business, however, where inventories levels vary considerably over the year, a monthly average would be more appropriate. Such information may not, however, be available. This point concerning monthly averaging is equally relevant to any asset or claim that varies over the reporting period and would include trade receivables and trade payables.

In the case of Alexis plc, the inventories turnover period for the year ended 31 March 2016 is:

$$\text{Average inventories turnover period} = \frac{(241 + 300)/2}{1,745} \times 365 = 56.6 \text{ days}$$

(The opening inventories figure was taken from Note 3 to the financial statements.)

This means that, on average, the inventories held are being 'turned over' every 56.6 days. So, a carpet bought by the business on a particular day would, on average, have been sold about eight weeks later. A business will normally prefer a short inventories turnover period to a long one, because holding inventories has costs, for example the opportunity cost of the funds tied up. When judging the amount of inventories to carry, the business must consider such things as the likely demand for them, the possibility of supply shortages, the likelihood of price rises, the amount of storage space available, their perishability and susceptibility to obsolescence.

This ratio is sometimes expressed in terms of weeks or months rather than days: multiplying by 52 or 12, rather than 365, will achieve this.

Activity 7.7

Calculate the average inventories turnover period for Alexis plc for the year ended 31 March 2017.

The ratio for 2017 is:

$$\text{Average inventories turnover period} = \frac{(300 + 406)/2}{2,272} \times 365 = 56.7 \text{ days}$$

The inventories turnover period is virtually the same in both years.

Average settlement period for trade receivables

Selling on credit is the norm for most businesses, except for retailers, and so trade receivables tend to be a necessary evil. A business will naturally be concerned with the amount of funds tied up in trade receivables and try to keep this to a minimum. The speed of payment can have a significant effect on the business's cash flow. The **average settlement period for trade receivables ratio** indicates how long, on average, credit customers take to pay the amounts that they owe to the business. The ratio is as follows:

$$\frac{\text{Average settlement period}}{\text{for trade receivables}} = \frac{\text{Average trade receivables}}{\text{Credit sales revenue}} \times 365$$

A business will normally prefer a shorter average settlement period to a longer one as, once again, funds are being tied up that may be used for more profitable purposes. Although this ratio can be useful, it is important to remember that it produces an *average* figure for the number of days for which debts are outstanding. This average may be badly distorted by, for example, a few large customers who are very slow or very fast payers.

Since all sales made by Alexis plc are on credit, the average settlement period for trade receivables for the year ended 31 March 2016 is:

$$\text{Average settlement period for trade receivables} = \frac{(223 + 240)/2}{2,240} \times 365 = 37.7 \text{ days}$$

(The opening trade receivables figure was taken from Note 4 to the financial statements.)

Activity 7.8

Calculate the average settlement period for Alexis plc's trade receivables for the year ended 31 March 2017.

The ratio for 2017 is:

$$\text{Average settlement period for trade receivables} = \frac{(240 + 273)/2}{2,681} \times 365 = 34.9 \text{ days}$$

On the face of it, this reduction in the settlement period is welcome. It means that less cash was tied up in trade receivables for each £1 of sales revenue in 2017 than in 2016. Only if the reduction were achieved at the expense of customer goodwill or through high out-of-pocket cost might its desirability be questioned. For example, the reduction may have been due to chasing customers too vigorously or to giving large discounts to customers for prompt payment.

Average settlement period for trade payables

The **average settlement period for trade payables ratio** measures how long, on average, the business takes to pay those who have supplied goods and services on credit. The ratio is calculated as follows:

$$\text{Average settlement period for trade payables} = \frac{\text{Average trade payables}}{\text{Credit purchases}} \times 365$$

This ratio provides an average figure which, like the average settlement period for trade receivables ratio, can be distorted by the payment period for one or two large suppliers.

As trade payables provide a free source of finance for the business, it is perhaps not surprising that some businesses attempt to increase their average settlement period for trade payables. Such a policy can be taken too far, however, and can result in a loss of goodwill of suppliers.

For the year ended 31 March 2016, Alexis plc's average settlement period for trade payables is:

$$\text{Average settlement period for trade payables} = \frac{(183 + 261)/2}{1,804} \times 365 = 44.9 \text{ days}$$

(The opening trade payables figure was taken from Note 4 to the financial statements and the purchases figure from Note 3.)

Activity (7.9)

Calculate the average settlement period for trade payables for Alexis plc for the year ended 31 March 2017.

The ratio for 2017 is:

$$\text{Average settlement period for trade payables} = \frac{(261 + 354)/2}{2{,}378} \times 365 = 47.2 \text{ days}$$

There was an increase between 2016 and 2017 in the average length of time that elapsed between buying goods and services and paying for them. On the face of it, this is beneficial because the business is using free finance provided by suppliers. This may not be so, however, where it results in a loss of supplier goodwill and Alexis plc suffers adverse consequences.

Slow settlement of the amounts owed to small suppliers by their large customers has become a significant problem for many small businesses. **Real World 7.5** outlines steps that have been taken by the UK government to try to deal with this issue.

Real World 7.5

Shining a light on bad payment practice

A recent survey by the UK Federation of Small Businesses estimated that, on average, small businesses receive 30% of what they are owed by credit customers late, frequently very late.

In an attempt to deal with this, the UK government introduced a requirement that from April 2017 all large businesses will be required to make public, on a twice-yearly basis, details on their payment practices and performance. This will include publishing the average time that they take to settle amounts owed to their credit suppliers. It is believed that this transparency will put a spotlight on bad practice and lead to improved standards.

Mike Cherry, National Chairman of the Federation of Small Businesses, said:

Tackling late payments is now a key part of the government's corporate governance agenda. The comprehensive and regular duty to report is the first step to combat a business culture that feels like one where it is OK to pay small firms late. It is not OK – we estimate that 50,000 business deaths could be avoided every year, if only payments were made promptly – adding £2.5 billion to the UK economy. We need to see executive board level engagement and scrutiny of payment practices to deliver lasting cultural change.

Source: UK government press release, Boost to small businesses as payment reporting rules unveiled for large firms, Department for Business, Energy and Industrial Strategy, 2 December 2016.

In Chapter 16, we shall look in some detail at the management of the various elements of working capital, including inventories, trade receivables and trade payables. We shall consider the factors that come into play when deciding the appropriate level of each of these elements.

Sales revenue to capital employed

The **sales revenue to capital employed ratio** (or net asset turnover ratio) examines how effectively the assets of the business are being used to generate sales revenue. It is calculated as follows:

$$\text{Sales revenue to capital employed ratio} = \frac{\text{Sales revenue}}{\text{Share capital} + \text{Reserves} + \text{Non-current liabilities}}$$

Normally, a higher sales revenue to capital employed ratio is preferred to a lower one. A higher ratio tends to suggest that assets are being used more productively in the generation of revenue. However, a very high ratio may suggest that the business is 'overtrading' on its assets. In other words, it has insufficient assets to sustain the level of sales revenue achieved. We shall take a closer look at overtrading later in the chapter.

When comparing the sales revenue to capital employed ratio for different businesses, factors such as the age and condition of assets held, the valuation bases for assets and whether assets are leased or owned outright can complicate interpretation.

A variation of this formula is to use the total assets less current liabilities (which is equivalent to long-term capital employed) in the denominator (lower part of the fraction). The same result is obtained.

For the year ended 31 March 2016, this ratio for Alexis plc is:

$$\text{Sales revenue to capital employed} = \frac{2,240}{(638 + 763)/2} = 3.20 \text{ times}$$

Activity 7.10

Calculate the sales revenue to capital employed ratio for Alexis plc for the year ended 31 March 2017.

The ratio for 2017 is:

$$\text{Sales revenue to capital employed} = \frac{2,681}{(763 + 834)/2} = 3.36 \text{ times}$$

This seems to be an improvement since, in 2017, more sales revenue was being generated for each £1 of capital employed (£3.36) than was the case in 2016 (£3.20). Provided that overtrading is not an issue, and that the additional sales generate an acceptable profit, this is to be welcomed.

Sales revenue per employee

The **sales revenue per employee ratio** relates sales revenue generated during a reporting period to a particular business resource – labour. It provides a measure of the productivity of the workforce. The ratio is:

$$\text{Sales revenue per employee} = \frac{\text{Sales revenue}}{\text{Number of employees}}$$

Generally, businesses would prefer a high value for this ratio, implying that they are deploying their staff efficiently.

For the year ended 31 March 2016, the ratio for Alexis plc is:

$$\text{Sales revenue per employee} = \frac{£2,240m}{13,995} = £160,057$$

Activity 7.11

Calculate the sales revenue per employee for Alexis plc for the year ended 31 March 2017.

The ratio for 2017 is:

$$\text{Sales revenue per employee} = \frac{£2,681m}{18,623} = £143,962$$

This represents a fairly significant decline, which merits further investigation. As already mentioned, the number of employees increased quite notably (by about 33 per cent) during 2017. We need to know why this had not generated additional sales revenue sufficient to maintain the ratio at its 2016 level. It may be because the extra employees were not appointed until late in the year ended 31 March 2017.

The efficiency, or activity, ratios may be summarised as follows:

	2016	2017
Average inventories turnover period	56.6 days	56.7 days
Average settlement period for trade receivables	37.7 days	34.9 days
Average settlement period for trade payables	44.9 days	47.2 days
Sales revenue to capital employed (net asset turnover)	3.20 times	3.36 times
Sales revenue per employee	£160,057	£143,962

Activity 7.12

What do you deduce from a comparison of the efficiency ratios over the two years?

Maintaining the inventories turnover period at the 2016 level may be reasonable, although to assess whether this is a satisfactory period we need to know the planned inventories turnover period. The inventories turnover period for other businesses operating in carpet retailing, particularly those regarded as the market leaders, may have been helpful in formulating the plans. On the face of things, a shorter trade receivables settlement period and a longer trade payables settlement period are both desirable. These may, however, have been achieved at the cost of a loss of the goodwill of customers and suppliers, respectively. The increased sales revenue to capital employed ratio seems beneficial, provided the business can manage this increase. The decline in the sales revenue per employee ratio is undesirable but is probably related to the dramatic increase in the number of employees. As with the inventories turnover period, these other ratios need to be compared with planned, or target, ratios.

Relationship between profitability and efficiency

In our earlier discussions concerning profitability ratios, we saw that return on capital employed (ROCE) is regarded as a key ratio by many businesses. The ratio is:

$$\text{ROCE} = \frac{\text{Operating profit}}{\text{Long-term capital employed}} \times 100$$

where long-term capital comprises share capital plus reserves plus long-term borrowings. This ratio can be broken down into two elements, as shown in Figure 7.3. The first ratio is the operating profit margin ratio and the second is the sales revenue to capital employed (net asset turnover) ratio, both of which we discussed earlier. By breaking down the ROCE ratio in this manner, we highlight the fact that the overall return on funds employed within the business will be determined both by the profitability of sales and by efficiency in the use of capital.

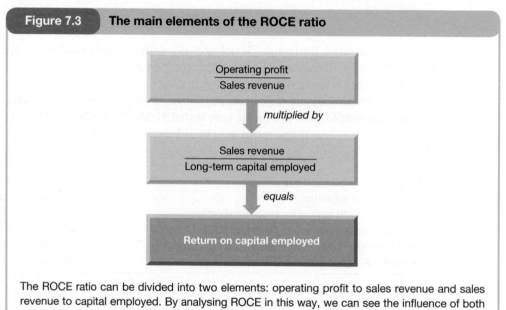

| Figure 7.3 | The main elements of the ROCE ratio |

The ROCE ratio can be divided into two elements: operating profit to sales revenue and sales revenue to capital employed. By analysing ROCE in this way, we can see the influence of both profitability and efficiency on this important ratio.

Example 7.2 looks at the return on capital of two different businesses operating in the same industry.

Example 7.2

Consider the following information, for last year, for two different businesses operating in the same industry.

	Antler plc	Baker plc
	£m	£m
Operating profit	20	15
Average long-term capital employed	100	75
Sales revenue	200	300

The ROCE for each business is identical (20 per cent). However, the manner in which that return was achieved by each business is quite different. In the case of Antler plc, the operating profit margin is 10 per cent and the sales revenue to capital employed ratio is 2 times (so, ROCE = 10% × 2 = 20%). In the case of Baker plc, the operating profit margin is 5 per cent and the sales revenue to capital employed ratio is 4 times (and so, ROCE = 5% × 4 = 20%).

Example 7.2 demonstrates that a relatively high sales revenue to capital employed ratio can compensate for a relatively low operating profit margin. Similarly, a relatively low sales revenue to capital employed ratio can be overcome by a relatively high operating profit margin. In many areas of retail and distribution (for example, supermarkets and delivery services), operating profit margins are quite low, but the ROCE can be high, provided that assets are used productively (that is, low margin, high sales revenue to capital employed).

Activity 7.13

Show how the ROCE ratio for Alexis plc can be analysed into the two elements for each of the years 2016 and 2017. What conclusions can you draw from your figures?

ROCE = Operating profit margin × Sales revenue to capital employed

2016	34.7%	10.8%	3.20
2017	5.9%	1.8%	3.36

As we can see, the relationship between the three ratios holds for Alexis plc for both years. The small apparent differences arise because the three ratios are stated here only to one or two decimal places.

In the year to 31 March 2017, the business was more effective at generating sales revenue (sales revenue to capital employed ratio increased). However, it fell well below the level needed to compensate for the sharp decline in the profitability of sales (operating profit margin). As a result, the 2017 ROCE was well below the 2016 value.

Liquidity

Liquidity ratios are concerned with the ability of the business to meet its short-term financial obligations. The following ratios are widely used:

- current ratio
- acid test ratio
- cash generated from operations to maturing obligations ratio.

These ratios will now be considered.

Current ratio

The **current ratio** compares the 'liquid' assets (that is, cash and those assets held that will soon be turned into cash) of the business with the current liabilities. The ratio is calculated as follows:

$$\text{Current ratio} = \frac{\text{Current assets}}{\text{Current liabilities}}$$

It seems to be believed by some that there is an 'ideal' current ratio (usually 2 times or 2:1) for all businesses. However, this is not the case. Different types of business require different current ratios. A manufacturing business, for example, will normally have a relatively high current ratio because it will tend to hold inventories of finished goods, raw materials and work in progress. It will also normally sell goods on credit, thereby giving rise to trade receivables. A supermarket chain, on the other hand, will have a relatively low ratio, as it will hold only fast-moving inventories of finished goods and its sales will be for cash rather than on credit (see Real World 16.1 on page 677).

The higher the current ratio, the more liquid the business is considered to be. As liquidity is vital to the survival of a business, a higher current ratio might be thought to be preferable to a lower one. If a business has a very high ratio, however, it may be that excessive funds are tied up in cash or other liquid assets and are not, therefore, being used as productively as they might otherwise be.

As at 31 March 2016, the current ratio of Alexis plc is:

$$\text{Current ratio} = \frac{544}{291} = 1.9 \text{ times (or 1.9:1)}$$

Activity 7.14

Calculate the current ratio for Alexis plc as at 31 March 2017.

The ratio for 2017 is:

$$\text{Current ratio} = \frac{679}{432} = 1.6 \text{ times (or 1.6:1)}$$

Although this is a decline from 2016 to 2017, it may not be a matter for concern. The next ratio may provide a clue as to whether there seems to be a problem.

Acid test ratio

The **acid test ratio** is similar to the current ratio, but represents a more stringent test of liquidity. For many businesses, inventories cannot be converted into cash quickly. (Note that, in the case of Alexis plc, the inventories turnover period was about 57 days in both years (see page 251).) As a result, there is a good case for excluding this particular asset.

The acid test ratio is calculated as follows:

$$\text{Acid test ratio} = \frac{\text{Current assets (excluding inventories)}}{\text{Current liabilities}}$$

As at 31 March 2016, the acid test ratio for Alexis plc is:

$$\text{Acid test ratio} = \frac{544 - 300}{291} = 0.8 \text{ times (or 0.8:1)}$$

We can see that the 'liquid' current assets do not quite cover the current liabilities, so the business may be experiencing some liquidity problems.

The minimum level for this ratio is often stated as 1.0 times (or 1:1; that is, current assets (excluding inventories) equal current liabilities). However, for many highly successful businesses, it is not unusual for the acid test ratio to be below 1.0 without causing liquidity problems (again, see Real World 16.1 on page 677).

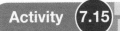

Activity 7.15

Calculate the acid test ratio for Alexis plc as at 31 March 2017.

The ratio for 2017 is:

$$\text{Acid test ratio} = \frac{679 - 406}{432} = 0.6 \text{ times}$$

The 2017 ratio is significantly below that for 2016 and may well be a cause for concern. The underlying reasons for the rapid decline in the ratio should be investigated and, if necessary, steps taken to prevent any further deterioration.

Cash generated from operations to maturing obligations ratio

The **cash generated from operations (CGO) to maturing obligations ratio** compares the cash generated from operations (taken from the statement of cash flows) with the current liabilities of the business. It provides a further indication of the ability of the business to meet its maturing obligations. The ratio is expressed as:

$$\frac{\text{Cash generated from operations}}{\text{to maturing obligations ratio}} = \frac{\text{Cash generated from operations}}{\text{Current liabilities}}$$

The higher this ratio is, the better the liquidity of the business. This ratio has the advantage over the current ratio that the operating cash flows for a period usually provide a more reliable guide to the liquidity of a business than current assets held at the statement of financial position date.

Alexis plc's ratio for the year ended 31 March 2016 is:

$$\text{Cash generated from operations to maturing obligations ratio} = \frac{251}{291} = 0.9 \text{ times}$$

This indicates that the operating cash flows for the year are not quite sufficient to cover the current liabilities at the end of the year.

Activity 7.16

Calculate the cash generated from operations to maturing obligations ratio for Alexis plc for the year ended 31 March 2017.

The ratio for 2017 is:

$$\text{Cash generated from operations to maturing obligations ratio} = \frac{34}{432} = 0.1 \text{ times}$$

This shows an alarming decline in the ability of the business to meet its maturing obligations from its operating cash flows. It confirms that liquidity is a real cause for concern.

The liquidity ratios for the two-year period may be summarised as follows:

	2016	2017
Current ratio	1.9	1.6
Acid test ratio	0.8	0.6
Cash generated from operations to maturing obligations ratio	0.9	0.1

Activity 7.17

What do you deduce from these liquidity ratios?

There has clearly been a decline in liquidity from 2016 to 2017. This is indicated by all three ratios. The most worrying is the decline in the last ratio as it reveals that the ability to generate cash from trading operations has declined significantly in relation to short-term obligations. The apparent liquidity problem may, however, be planned and short term and linked to the increase in non-current assets and number of employees. When the benefits of the expansion come on stream, liquidity may improve. On the other hand, short-term lenders and suppliers may become anxious due to the decline in liquidity. This could lead them to press for payment, which could well cause further problems.

Financial gearing

Financial gearing occurs when a business is financed, at least in part, by borrowing rather than by owners' equity. The extent to which a business is geared (that is, financed from borrowing) is an important factor in assessing risk. Borrowing involves taking on a commitment to pay interest charges and to make capital repayments. Where the borrowing is heavy, this can be a significant financial burden; it can increase the risk of the business becoming insolvent. Nevertheless, most businesses are geared to some extent. (Costain Group plc, the builders and construction business, is a rare example of a UK business with almost no borrowings.)

Given the risks involved, we may wonder why a business would want to take on gearing. One reason is that the owners have insufficient funds, so the only way to finance the business adequately is to borrow. Another reason is that gearing can be used to increase the returns to owners. This is possible provided the returns generated from borrowed funds exceed the cost of paying interest. Example 7.3 illustrates this point.

Example 7.3

The long-term capital structures of two new businesses, Lee Ltd and Nova Ltd, are as follows:

	Lee Ltd £	Nova Ltd £
£1 ordinary shares	100,000	200,000
10% loan notes	200,000	100,000
	300,000	300,000

In their first year of operations, they each make an operating profit (that is, profit before interest and taxation) of £50,000. The tax rate is 20 per cent of the profit before taxation (but after interest).

Lee Ltd would probably be considered relatively highly geared, as it has a high proportion of borrowed funds in its long-term capital structure. Nova Ltd is much lower geared. The profit available to the shareholders of each business in the first year of operations will be:

	Lee Ltd £	Nova Ltd £
Operating profit	50,000	50,000
Interest payable	(20,000)	(10,000)
Profit before taxation	30,000	40,000
Taxation (20%)	(6,000)	(8,000)
Profit for the year (available to ordinary shareholders)	24,000	32,000

The return on ordinary shareholders' funds (ROSF) for each business will be:

Lee Ltd

$$\frac{24,000}{100,000} \times 100 = 24\%$$

Nova Ltd

$$\frac{32,000}{200,000} \times 100 = 16\%$$

We can see that Lee Ltd, the more highly geared business, has generated a higher ROSF than Nova Ltd. This is despite the fact that the ROCE (return on capital employed) is identical for both businesses (that is, (£50,000/£300,000) × 100 = 16.7%).

Note that at the £50,000 level of operating profit, the shareholders of both businesses have generated higher returns as a result of gearing. If both businesses were totally financed by equity, the profit for the year (that is, after taxation) would be £40,000 (that is, £50,000 less 20 per cent taxation), giving an ROSF of 13.3 per cent (that is, £40,000/£300,000).

An effect of gearing is that returns to shareholders become more sensitive to changes in operating profits. For a highly geared business, a change in operating profits will lead to a proportionately greater change in the ROSF ratio.

Activity 7.18

Assume that the operating profit was £70,000 rather than £50,000. What would be the effect of this on ROSF?

The revised profit available to the shareholders of each business in the first year of operations will be:

	Lee Ltd £	Nova Ltd £
Operating profit	70,000	70,000
Interest payable	(20,000)	(10,000)
Profit before taxation	50,000	60,000
Taxation (20%)	(10,000)	(12,000)
Profit for the year (available to ordinary shareholders)	40,000	48,000

The ROSF for each business will now be:

Lee Ltd

$$\frac{40,000}{100,000} \times 100 = 40\%$$

Nova Ltd

$$\frac{48,000}{200,000} \times 100 = 24\%$$

We can see that for Lee Ltd, the higher-geared business, the returns to shareholders have increased by two thirds (from 24 per cent to 40 per cent), whereas for the lower-geared business, Nova Ltd, the benefits of gearing are less pronounced, increasing by only half (from 16 per cent to 24 per cent). The effect of gearing can, of course, work in both directions. So, for a highly geared business, a small decline in operating profit will bring about a much greater decline in the returns to shareholders.

The reason that gearing seems to be beneficial to shareholders is that, in practice, interest rates for borrowings tend to be low by comparison with the returns that the typical business can earn. On top of this, interest expenses are tax-deductible, in the way shown in Example 7.3 and Activity 7.18. This makes the apparent cost of borrowing quite cheap. It is debatable, however, whether low interest rates really are beneficial to shareholders. Since borrowing increases the risk to shareholders, there is a hidden cost involved. Many argue that this cost is precisely compensated by the higher returns, giving no net benefit to shareholders. In other words, the apparent benefits of higher returns from gearing are illusory. What are not illusory, however, are the benefits to shareholders from the tax-deductibility of interest payments. We shall discuss this point in a little more detail in Chapter 15.

Activity 7.19

If shareholders gain from the tax-deductibility of interest on borrowings, who loses?

The losers are the tax authority (ultimately the government) and, therefore, other taxpayers.

The effect of gearing is like that of two intermeshing cogwheels of unequal size (see Figure 7.4). The circular movement in the larger cog (operating profit) causes a more than proportionate movement in the smaller cog (returns to ordinary shareholders).

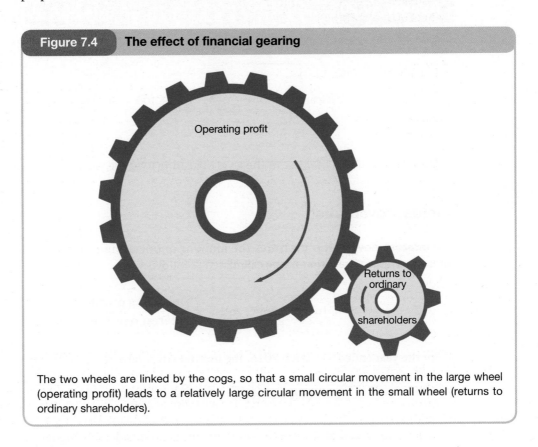

Figure 7.4   The effect of financial gearing

Operating profit

Returns to ordinary shareholders

The two wheels are linked by the cogs, so that a small circular movement in the large wheel (operating profit) leads to a relatively large circular movement in the small wheel (returns to ordinary shareholders).

Two ratios are widely used to assess gearing:

- gearing ratio
- interest cover ratio.

Gearing ratio

The **gearing ratio** measures the contribution of long-term lenders to the long-term capital structure of a business:

$$\text{Gearing ratio} = \frac{\text{Long-term (non-current) liabilities}}{\text{Share capital + Reserves +}} \times 100$$
$$\text{Long-term (non-current) liabilities}$$

As at 31 March 2016, the gearing ratio for Alexis plc is:

$$\text{Gearing ratio} = \frac{200}{(563 + 200)} \times 100 = 26.2\%$$

This is a level of gearing that would not normally be considered to be very high.

Activity (7.20)

Calculate the gearing ratio of Alexis plc as at 31 March 2017.

The ratio for 2017 is:

$$\text{Gearing ratio} = \frac{300}{(534 + 300)} \times 100 = 36.0\%$$

This is a substantial increase in the level of gearing over the year.

Interest cover ratio

The **interest cover ratio** measures the amount of operating profit available to cover interest payable. The ratio may be calculated as follows:

$$\textbf{Interest cover ratio} = \frac{\textbf{Operating profit}}{\textbf{Interest payable}}$$

For the year ended 31 March 2016, the interest cover ratio for Alexis plc is:

$$\text{Interest cover ratio} = \frac{243}{18} = 13.5 \text{ times}$$

This ratio shows that the level of operating profit is considerably higher than the level of interest payable. This means that a large fall in operating profit could occur before operating profit levels failed to cover interest payable. The lower the level of operating profit coverage, the greater the risk to lenders that interest payments will not be met. There will also be a greater risk to the shareholders that the lenders will take action against the business to recover the interest due.

Activity (7.21)

Calculate the interest cover ratio of Alexis plc for the year ended 31 March 2017.

The ratio for 2017 is:

$$\text{Interest cover ratio} = \frac{47}{32} = 1.5 \text{ times}$$

Alexis plc's gearing ratios are:

	2016	2017
Gearing ratio	26.2%	36.0%
Interest cover ratio	13.5 times	1.5 times

Activity 7.22

What do you deduce from a comparison of Alexis plc's gearing ratios over the two years?

The gearing ratio has changed significantly. This is mainly due to the substantial increase in the contribution of long-term lenders to financing the business. The gearing ratio at 31 March 2017 would not be considered very high for a business that is trading successfully. It is the low profitability that is the problem. The interest cover ratio has declined dramatically from 13.5 times in 2016 to 1.5 times in 2017. This was partly caused by the increase in borrowings in 2017, but mainly caused by the dramatic decline in profitability in that year. The situation in 2017 looks hazardous. Only a small decline in future operating profits would result in the profit being unable to cover interest payments.

Without knowledge of the planned ratios, it is not possible to reach a valid conclusion on Alexis plc's gearing.

Investment ratios

Various ratios are available that are designed to help shareholders assess the returns on their investment. The following are widely used:

- dividend payout ratio
- dividend yield ratio
- earnings per share
- cash generated from operations per share
- price/earnings ratio.

Dividend payout ratio

The **dividend payout ratio** measures the proportion of earnings paid out to shareholders in the form of dividends. The ratio is calculated as follows:

$$\text{Dividend payout ratio} = \frac{\text{Dividends announced for the year}}{\text{Earnings for the year available for dividends}} \times 100$$

In the case of ordinary shares, the earnings available for dividends will normally be the profit for the year (that is, the profit after taxation) less any preference dividends relating to the year. This ratio is normally expressed as a percentage.

For the year ended 31 March 2016, the dividend payout ratio for Alexis plc is:

$$\text{Dividend payout ratio} = \frac{40}{165} \times 100 = 24.2\%$$

Activity 7.23

Calculate the dividend payout ratio of Alexis plc for the year ended 31 March 2017.

The ratio for 2017 is:

$$\text{Dividend payout ratio} = \frac{40}{11} \times 100 = 363.6\%$$

This would normally be regarded as an alarming increase in the ratio over the two years. Paying a dividend of £40 million in 2017 would seem to be very imprudent.

The information provided by the above ratio is often expressed slightly differently as the **dividend cover ratio**. Here, the calculation is:

$$\text{Dividend cover ratio} = \frac{\text{Earnings for the year available for dividend}}{\text{Dividends announced for the year}}$$

For 2016, the ratio for Alexis plc would be 165/40 = 4.1 times. That is to say, the earnings available for dividend cover the actual dividend paid by just over four times. For 2017, the ratio is 11/40 = 0.3 times.

Dividend yield ratio

The **dividend yield ratio** relates the cash return from a share to its current market value. This can help investors to assess the cash return on their investment in the business. The ratio, expressed as a percentage, is:

$$\text{Dividend yield} = \frac{\text{Dividend per share}}{\text{Market value per share}} \times 100$$

For the year ended 31 March 2016, the dividend yield for Alexis plc is:

$$\text{Dividend yield} = \frac{0.067^*}{2.50} \times 100 = 2.7\%$$

The shares' market value is given in Note 1 to Example 7.1 (page 242).

* Dividend proposed/number of shares = 40/(300 × 2) = £0.067 dividend per share (the 300 is multiplied by 2 because they are £0.50 shares).

Activity 7.24

Calculate the dividend yield ratio for Alexis plc for the year ended 31 March 2017.

The ratio for 2017 is:

$$\text{Dividend yield} = \frac{0.067^*}{1.50} \times 100 = 4.5\%$$

* 40/(300 × 2) = £0.067.

Earnings per share

The **earnings per share (EPS) ratio** relates the earnings generated by the business, and available to shareholders, during a period to the number of shares in issue. For equity (ordinary) shareholders, the amount available will be represented by the profit for the year (profit after taxation) less any preference dividend, where applicable. The ratio for equity shareholders is calculated as follows:

$$\text{Earnings per share} = \frac{\text{Earnings available to ordinary shareholders}}{\text{Number of ordinary shares in issue}}$$

For the year ended 31 March 2016, the EPS for Alexis plc is:

$$\text{EPS} = \frac{£165m}{600m} = 27.5p$$

Many investment analysts regard the EPS ratio as a fundamental measure of share performance. The trend in earnings per share over time is used to help assess the investment potential of a business's shares. Although it is possible to make total profit increase through ordinary shareholders investing more in the business, this will not necessarily lead to an increase in the profitability *per share*.

Real World 7.6 points out the danger of placing too much emphasis on this ratio. The equity fund manager, Terry Smith, argues that, had more attention been paid to ROCE rather than EPS, investors would have spotted that all was not well with Tesco plc, the supermarket giant. He also takes to task, Warren Buffet, the legendary investor, for ignoring his own advice and investing heavily in the business.

Real World 7.6

A trolley load of problems

In his 1979 letter to shareholders, Mr Buffett stated: "The primary test of managerial economic performance is the achievement of a high earnings rate on equity capital employed (without undue leverage, accounting gimmickry, etc) and not the achievement of consistent gains in earnings per share."

This makes it all the more surprising to me that both Mr Buffett and the many acolytes who have seemingly followed him to the gates of hell in Tesco, ignored this chart:

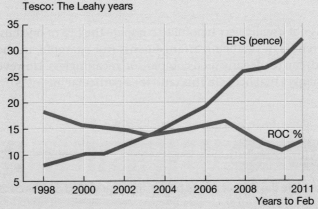

Tesco: The Leahy years

Source: Company

This is not the first such chart that I have come across in which a company reports steadily rising earnings per share (EPS), on which most analysts and "investors" focus. For them, the rise in EPS seems to have a mesmeric effect like Kaa the snake in *The Jungle Book*.

But they ignore the point that more capital is being employed to generate those earnings at ever lower returns. Add in the fact that Tesco has changed its definition of return on capital employed (ROCE) eight times during those years, and there's more than enough material to send investors running for cover – even those who have less aversion than I do to retailers.

Yet much of the commentary about what has gone wrong at Tesco focuses on Philip Clarke, who took over as chief executive from Sir Terry Leahy in 2011, as if everything was going swimmingly until then. Looking at the ROCE line in the chart it is clear that this was not the case.

Moreover, one thing to bear in mind is that if Tesco's ROCE during the Leahy years fell from a very good 19 per cent to a less than adequate 10 per cent, this is an average of returns on capital employed, which includes both capital invested years ago and more recent commitments. To drag the average ROCE down so dramatically it is likely that returns on new investments in those years were not just inadequate, but in some cases negative – as the ill-starred US expansion proved to be.

Even if return on capital employed does not have the same importance for you as it does for me, or Mr Buffett (at least in 1979), consider this: in 14 of the past 18 years (taking us back to 1997 when Sir Terry became chief executive) Tesco's free cash flow less its dividend (with free cash defined as operating cash flow less gross capital expenditure) was a negative number. In plain English, Tesco was not generating enough cash both to invest and to pay its dividend. In half of those 14 years, the proceeds of fixed asset disposals took the numbers back into the black, but that is not exactly a sustainable source of financing.

So guess what they did instead? Yes, they borrowed it. Tesco's gross debt, which was £894 million when Sir Terry took over, peaked at nearly £15.9 billion in 2009. The company spent much of its free cash on fixed-asset investment and raised debt to help pay the dividend. This is neither healthy nor sustainable, as investors in Tesco have now come to realise.

The concept that this might not be sustainable hardly requires much thought. Neither does charting the ROCE versus the growth in EPS. Yet it is evident that many investors, including it seems Mr Buffett (who has been trimming his Tesco stake in recent years) either didn't do this or ignored the results if they did. It makes me wonder what else they are ignoring.

FT

Source: Smith, T. (2014) How investors ignored the warning signs at Tesco, ft.com, 5 September. © The Financial Times Ltd 2014. All Rights Reserved.

It is not usually very helpful to compare the EPS of one business with that of another. Differences in financing arrangements (for example, in the nominal value of shares issued) can render any such comparison meaningless. However, it can be useful to monitor changes that occur in this ratio for a particular business over time.

Activity 7.25

Calculate the EPS of Alexis plc for the year ended 31 March 2017.

The ratio for 2017 is:

$$EPS = \frac{£11m}{600m} = 1.8p$$

Cash generated from operations per share

In the short term at least, cash generated from operations (found in the statement of cash flows) can provide a good guide to the ability of a business to pay dividends and to undertake planned expenditures. Many see a cash generation measure as more useful in this context than the earnings per share figure. The **cash generated from operations (CGO) per ordinary share ratio** is calculated as follows:

$$\text{Cash generated from operations per share} = \frac{\text{Cash generated from operations less preference dividend (if any)}}{\text{Number of ordinary shares in issue}}$$

For the year ended 31 March 2016, the ratio for Alexis plc is:

$$\text{CGO per share} = \frac{£251m}{600m} = 41.8p$$

Activity 7.26

Calculate the CGO per ordinary share for Alexis plc for the year ended 31 March 2017.

The ratio for 2017 is:

$$\text{CGO per share} = \frac{£34m}{600m} = 5.7p$$

There has been a dramatic decrease in this ratio over the two-year period.

Note that, for both years, the CGO per share for Alexis plc is higher than the earnings per share. This is not unusual. The effect of adding back depreciation to derive the CGO figures will often ensure that a higher figure is derived.

Price/earnings ratio

The **price/earnings (P/E) ratio** relates the market value of a share to the earnings per share. This ratio can be calculated as follows:

$$\text{P/E ratio} = \frac{\text{Market value per share}}{\text{Earnings per share}}$$

As at 31 March 2016, the P/E ratio for Alexis plc is:

$$\text{P/E ratio} = \frac{£2.50}{27.5 \, p^*} = 9.1 \text{ times}$$

* The EPS figure (27.5p) was calculated on page 267.

This ratio indicates that the market value of the share is 9.1 times the current level of earnings. It is a measure of market confidence in the future of a business. The higher the P/E ratio, the greater the confidence in the future earning power of the business and, consequently, the more investors are prepared to pay in relation to that current earning power.

Activity (7.27)

Calculate the P/E ratio of Alexis plc as at 31 March 2017.

The ratio for 2017 is:

$$\text{P/E ratio} = \frac{£1.50}{1.8p} = 83.3 \text{ times}$$

As P/E ratios provide a useful guide to market confidence about the future, they can be helpful when comparing different businesses. However, differences in accounting policies between businesses can lead to different profit and earnings per share figures. This can distort comparisons.

The investment ratios for Alexis plc over the two-year period are as follows:

	2016	2017
Dividend payout ratio	24.2%	363.6%
Dividend yield ratio	2.7%	4.5%
Earnings per share	27.5p	1.8p
Cash generated from operations per share	41.8p	5.7p
P/E ratio	9.1 times	83.3 times

Activity (7.28)

What do you deduce from the investment ratios set out above? Can you offer an explanation why the share price has not fallen as much as it might have done, bearing in mind the much poorer trading performance in 2017?

Although the EPS has fallen dramatically and the dividend payment for 2017 seems very imprudent, the share price has held up reasonably well (fallen from £2.50 to £1.50). Moreover, the dividend yield and P/E ratios have improved in 2017. This is an anomaly of these two ratios, which stems from using a forward-looking value (the share price) in conjunction with historic data (dividends and earnings). Share prices are based on investors' assessments of the business's future. It seems that the 'market' was less happy with Alexis plc at the end of 2017 than at the end of 2016. This is evidenced by the fact that the share price had fallen by £1 a share. The decline in share price, however, was less dramatic than the decline in profit for the year. This suggests that investors believe the business will perform better in the future. Perhaps they are confident that the large increase in assets and employee numbers occurring during the year to 31 March 2017 will yield benefits in the future; benefits that the business has not yet been able to generate.

Real World 7.7 provides information about the share performance of a selection of large, well-known UK businesses. This type of information is provided on a daily basis by several newspapers, notably the *Financial Times*.

Real World 7.7

Market statistics for some well-known businesses

The following data were extracted from the *Financial Times* of 28 January 2017, relating to the previous day's trading of the shares of some well-known businesses on the London Stock Exchange:

Share	Price (pence)	Change (pence)	52-week high	52-week low	Yield %	P/E	Volume (000s)
Marks and Spencer	344.00	+2.80	448.00	255.10	5.44	22.33	8,158.6
HSBC	687.60	+3.70	692.48	392.37	5.78	42.53	20,951.6
National Express	335.90	+0.20	379.10	252.81	3.17	16.07	1,018.2
Tate and Lyle	668.00	−3.50	850.00	529.00	4.19	17.13	2,014.8
Unilever	3,233.50	+42.50	3,807.50	2,869.50	3.20	22.49	2,229.0
TUI Travel	1,160.00	+8.00	1,219.00	813.00	4.18	22.35	558.1

Price   Mid-market price in pence (that is, the price midway between buying and selling price) of the shares at the end of trading on 27 January 2017.

Change   Gain or loss in the mid-market price during 27 January 2017.

High/low   Highest and lowest prices reached by the share during the 52 weeks ended on 27 January 2017.

Yield   Dividend yield, based on the most recent year's dividend and the share price at the end of 27 January 2017.

P/E   Price/earnings ratio, based on the most recent year's (after-tax) profit for the year and the share price at the end of 27 January 2017.

Volume   The number of shares (in thousands) that were bought/sold on 27 January 2017.

So, for example, for the retail business Marks and Spencer plc:

- the shares had a mid-market price of 344.00 pence each at the close of Stock Exchange trading on 27 January 2017;
- the shares had increased in price by 2.80 pence during trading on 27 January 2017;
- the shares had highest and lowest prices during the previous 52 weeks of 448.00 pence and 255.10 pence, respectively;
- the shares had a dividend yield, based on the 27 January 2017 closing price (and the dividend for the most recent year) of 5.44 per cent;
- the shares had a P/E ratio, based on the 27 January 2017 closing price (and the after-taxation earnings per share for the most recent year) of 22.33;
- during trading on 27 January 2017, 8,158,600 of the business's shares changed hands between buyers and sellers.

FT   Source: *Financial Times*, 28 January 2017, p. 21. © The Financial Times Ltd 2017. All Rights Reserved.

Real World 7.8 shows how investment ratios can vary between different industry sectors.

Real World 7.8

Yielding dividends

Investment ratios can vary significantly between businesses and between industries. To give some indication of the range of variations that occur, the average dividend yield ratios and average P/E ratios for listed businesses in 12 different industries are shown in Figures 7.5 and 7.6, respectively.

Figure 7.5 — Average dividend yield ratios for businesses in a range of industries

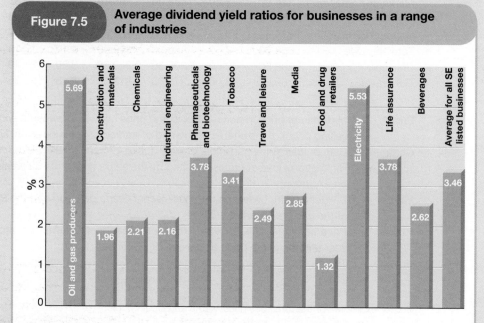

These dividend yield ratios are calculated from the current market value of the shares and the most recent year's dividend paid.

Some industries tend to pay out lower dividends than others, leading to lower dividend yield ratios. The average for all Stock Exchange listed businesses was 3.46 per cent (as is shown in Figure 7.5), but there is a wide variation, with food and drug retailers at 1.32 per cent and oil and gas producers at 5.69 per cent.

Some types of businesses tend to invest heavily in developing new products, hence their tendency to pay low dividends compared with their share prices. Some of the inter-industry differences in the dividend yield ratio can be explained by the nature of the calculation of the ratio. The prices of shares at any given moment are based on expectations of their economic futures; dividends are actual past events. A business that had a good trading year recently may have paid a dividend that, in the light of investors' assessment of the business's economic future, may be high (a high dividend yield).

Real World 7.8 continued

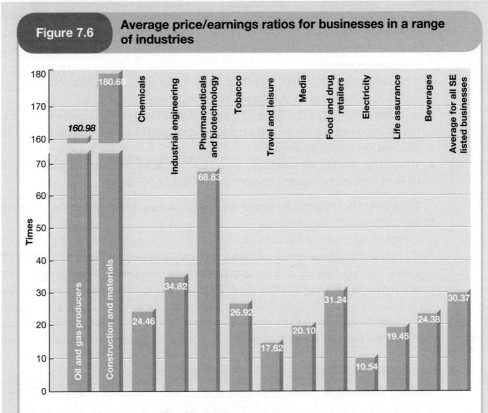

Figure 7.6 — **Average price/earnings ratios for businesses in a range of industries**

These P/E ratios are calculated from the current market value of the shares and the most recent year's earnings per share (EPS).

Businesses that have a high share price relative to their recent historic earnings have high P/E ratios. This may be because their future is regarded as economically bright, which may be the result of investing heavily in the future at the expense of recent profits (earnings). On the other hand, high P/Es also arise where businesses have recent low earnings, but investors believe that their future is brighter. The average P/E for all Stock Exchange listed businesses was 30.37 times, but the average for electricity was as low as 10.54 times and that for construction and materials as high as a remarkable 180.69 times.

FT   *Source*: Both figures are constructed from data appearing in the *Financial Times*, 28 January 2017, p. 19. © The Financial Times Limited 2017. All Rights Reserved.

Financial ratios and the problem of overtrading

Overtrading occurs where a business is operating at a level of activity that cannot be supported by the amount of finance that has been committed. This situation is often due to poor financial control over the business by its managers. The underlying reasons for over-trading are varied. It may occur:

- in young, expanding businesses that fail to prepare adequately for the rapid increase in demand for their goods or services, something which often leads to insufficient finance to fund the level of trade receivables and inventories needed to support the level of sales revenue generated;
- in businesses where the managers may have misjudged the level of expected sales demand or have failed to control escalating project costs;
- as a result of a fall in the value of money (inflation), causing more finance to have to be committed to inventories and trade receivables, even where there is no expansion in the real volume of trade; and
- where the owners are unable to inject further funds into the business themselves and/or they cannot persuade others to invest in the business.

Whatever the reason, the problems that it brings must be dealt with if the business is to survive over the longer term.

Overtrading results in liquidity problems such as exceeding borrowing limits, or slow repayment of borrowings and trade payables. The last of these can result in suppliers withholding supplies, thereby making it difficult to meet customer needs. The managers of the business might be forced to direct all of their efforts to dealing with immediate and pressing problems, such as finding cash to meet interest charges due or paying wages. Longer-term planning becomes difficult as managers spend their time going from crisis to crisis. Ultimately, the business may fail because it cannot meet its maturing obligations – it runs out of cash.

Activity (7.29)

If a business is overtrading, do you think the following ratios would be higher or lower than normally expected?

1 Current ratio
2 Average inventories turnover period
3 Average settlement period for trade receivables
4 Average settlement period for trade payables

Your answer should be as follows:

1 The current ratio would be lower than normally expected. This ratio is a measure of liquidity, and lack of liquidity is a typical symptom of overtrading.
2 The average inventories turnover period would be lower than normally expected. Where a business is overtrading, the level of inventories held will be low because of the problems of financing them. In the short term, sales revenue may not be badly affected by the low inventories levels, and therefore inventories will be turned over more quickly.
3 The average settlement period for trade receivables may be lower than normally expected. Where a business is suffering from liquidity problems, it may chase credit customers more vigorously in an attempt to improve cash flows.
4 The average settlement period for trade payables may be higher than normally expected. The business may try to delay payments to its suppliers because of the liquidity problems arising.

To deal with the overtrading problem, a business must ensure that the finance available is consistent with the level of operations. Thus, if a business that is overtrading is unable to raise new finance, it should cut back its level of operations in line with the finance available. Although this may mean lost sales and lost profits in the short term, cutting back may be necessary to ensure survival over the longer term.

Trend analysis

It is often helpful to see whether ratios are indicating trends. Key ratios can be plotted on a graph to provide a simple visual display of changes occurring over time. The trends occurring within a business may, for example, be plotted against trends for rival businesses or for the industry as a whole for comparison purposes. An example of trend analysis is shown in **Real World 7.9**.

Real World 7.9

Trend setting

| Figure 7.7 | **Current ratio of three leading businesses** |

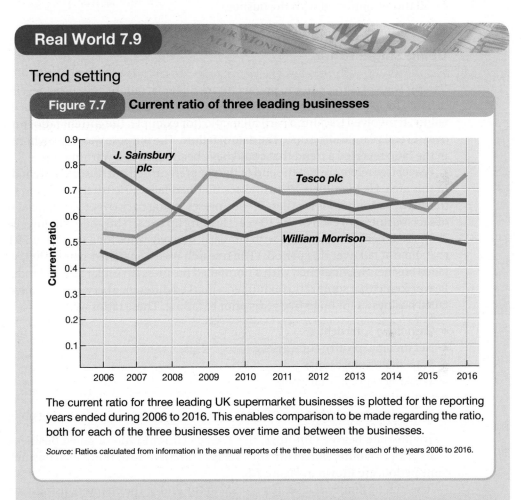

The current ratio for three leading UK supermarket businesses is plotted for the reporting years ended during 2006 to 2016. This enables comparison to be made regarding the ratio, both for each of the three businesses over time and between the businesses.

Source: Ratios calculated from information in the annual reports of the three businesses for each of the years 2006 to 2016.

In Figure 7.7, the current ratios of three of the UK's leading supermarket companies are plotted over time. We can see that the current ratios of the three businesses have tended to move closer. Tesco's ratio was lower than those of its main rivals until 2005; it then overtook Morrison and, in 2009, Sainsbury. Sainsbury's current ratio shows a fairly consistent downward path until 2010. Morrison has tended to maintain the lowest current ratio over time. With well-managed businesses like these, it is highly likely that any changes are the result of deliberate policy.

Source: Annual reports of the three businesses 2004 to 2016.

Using ratios to predict financial failure

Financial ratios, based on current or past performance, are often used to help predict the future. Normally, both the choice of ratios and the interpretation of results are dependent on the judgement and opinion of the analyst. There have been, however, attempts to develop a more rigorous and systematic approach to the use of ratios for prediction purposes. In particular, researchers have investigated the ability of ratios to predict the financial failure of a business.

By financial failure, we mean a business either being forced out of business or being severely adversely affected by its inability to meet its financial obligations. It is often referred to as 'going bust' or 'going bankrupt'. This is, of course, a likely area of concern for all those connected with the business.

Using single ratios

Various ways of using ratios to predict future financial failure have been developed. Early research focused on seeing whether a single ratio was a good or bad predictor of financial failure. It involved tracking a particular ratio (for example, the current ratio) for a business over several years leading up to the date of failure. The purpose was to see whether changes in the ratio revealed a trend that could have been taken as a warning sign.

Beaver (see reference 1 at the end of the chapter) carried out the first systematic research in this area. He identified 79 businesses that had failed. He then calculated the average (mean) of various ratios for these 79 businesses, going back over the financial statements of each business for each of the 10 years leading up to each business's failure. Beaver then compared these average ratios with similarly derived ratios for a sample of 79 businesses that did not fail over this period. (The research used a matched-pair design, where each failed business was matched with a non-failed business of similar size and industry type.) Beaver found that some ratios exhibited a marked difference between the failed and non-failed businesses for up to five years prior to failure. These ratios were:

● Cash flow/Total debt;
● Net income (profit)/Total assets;
● Total debt/Total assets;
● Working capital/Total assets;
● Current ratio: and
● No credit interval (that is, cash generated from operations to maturing obligations).

To illustrate Beaver's findings, the average current ratio of failed businesses for five years prior to failure, along with the average current ratio of non-failed businesses for the same period, are shown in Figure 7.8.

Research by Zmijewski (see reference 2 at the end of the chapter), using a sample of 72 failed and 3,573 non-failed businesses over a six-year period, found that businesses that ultimately went on to fail were characterised by lower rates of return, higher levels of gearing, lower levels of coverage for their fixed interest payments and more variable returns on shares. While we may not find these results very surprising, it is interesting to note that Zmijewski, like a number of other researchers in this area, did not find liquidity ratios particularly useful in predicting financial failure. Intuition might have led us (wrongly it seems) to believe that the liquidity ratios would have been particularly helpful in this context. As we saw earlier, however, Beaver did find the current ratio to be a useful predictor.

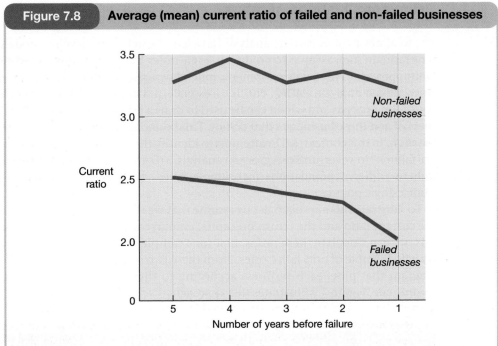

| Figure 7.8 | **Average (mean) current ratio of failed and non-failed businesses** |

The vertical scale of the graph is the average value of the current ratio for each group of businesses (failed and non-failed). The horizontal axis is the number of years before failure. Thus, Year 1 is the most recent year and Year 5 the least recent year. We can see that a clear difference between the average for the failed and non-failed businesses can be detected five years prior to the failure of the former group.

The approach adopted by Beaver and Zmijewski is referred to as **univariate analysis** because it looks at one ratio at a time. Although this approach can produce interesting results, there are practical problems associated with its use.

Activity (7.30)

Let us assume that research indicates that a particular ratio is shown to be a good predictor of failure. Can you think of a practical problem that may arise when using this ratio to predict financial failure for a particular business?

Where a particular ratio for a business differs from the average value for that same ratio for non-failed businesses, the analyst must rely on judgement to interpret whether this difference is significant. There is no clear decision rule that can be applied. Different analysts may, therefore, come to different conclusions about the likelihood of failure.

A further problem arises where more than one ratio is used to predict failure. Let us say, for example, that past research has identified two ratios as being good predictors of financial failure. When applied to a particular business, however, it may be that one ratio predicts financial failure, whereas the other does not. Given these conflicting signals, how should the analyst interpret the results?

Using combinations of ratios

The weaknesses of univariate analysis have led researchers to develop models that combine ratios in such a way as to produce a single index that can be interpreted more clearly. One approach to model development, much favoured by researchers, employs **multiple discriminate analysis (MDA)**. This is, in essence, a statistical technique that is similar to regression analysis and which can be used to draw a boundary between those businesses that fail and those businesses that do not. This boundary is referred to as the **discriminate function.** In this context, MDA attempts to identify those factors likely to influence financial failure. However, unlike regression analysis, MDA assumes that the observations come from two different populations (for example, failed and non-failed businesses) rather than from a single population. ——

To illustrate this approach, let us assume that we wish to test whether two ratios (say, the current ratio and the return on capital employed) can help to predict failure. To do this, we can calculate these ratios, first for a sample of failed businesses and then for a matched sample of non-failed ones. From these two sets of data we can produce a scatter diagram that plots each business according to these two ratios to produce a single co-ordinate. Figure 7.9 illustrates this approach.

Figure 7.9	Scatter diagram showing the distribution of failed and non-failed businesses

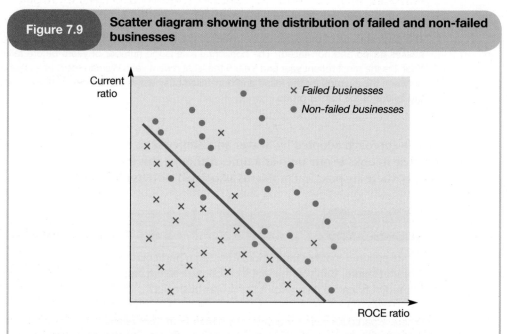

The distribution of failed and non-failed businesses is based on two ratios. The line represents a boundary between the samples of failed and non-failed businesses. Although there is some crossing of the boundary, the boundary represents the line that minimises the problem of misclassifying particular businesses.

Using the observations plotted on the diagram, we try to identify the boundary between the failed and the non-failed businesses. This is the diagonal line in Figure 7.9.

We can see that those businesses that fall below and to the left of the line are predominantly failed and those that fall to the right are predominantly non-failed ones. Note that there is some overlap between the two populations. In practice, the boundary produced is unlikely, therefore, to eliminate all errors. Some businesses that fail may fall on the non-failed businesses side of the boundary. The opposite also happens. However, the analysis will tend to minimise the misclassification errors.

The boundary shown in Figure 7.9 can be expressed in the form

$$Z = a + (b \times \text{Current ratio}) + (c \times \text{ROCE})$$

where a, b and c are all constants and b and c are weights to be attached to each ratio. A weighted average or total score (Z) is then derived. By 'constants' we mean that the same values are used for assessing each individual business. The values ascribed to these constants are those that have been found in practice to provide a Z score that most effectively is able to differentiate between the failed and the non-failed businesses. Using this model to assess a particular business's health, we would deduce the current and ROCE ratios for that business and use them in the equation above. If the resulting Z-score were to come out below a certain value, we should view that business as being at risk.

Note that this example, using the current and ROCE ratios, is purely hypothetical and only intended to illustrate the approach.

Z-score models

Altman (see reference 3 at the end of the chapter) was the first to develop a model (in 1968), using financial ratios, that was able to predict financial failure in practice. In 2000, he revised the model. In fact, the revisions necessary to make the model effective in more modern times were quite minor. Altman's revised model, the Z-score model, is based on five financial ratios and is as follows:

$$Z = 0.717a + 0.847b + 3.107c + 0.420d + 0.998e$$

where

$a =$ Working capital/Total assets
$b =$ Accumulated retained profits/Total assets
$c =$ Operating profit/Total assets
$d =$ Book (statement of financial position) value of ordinary and preference shares/Total liabilities at book (statement of financial position) value
$e =$ Sales revenue/Total assets

The weightings (or coefficients) in the above model are constants that reflect the importance to the Z-score of each of the ingredients (a to e).

In developing and revising this model, Altman carried out tests using a paired sample of failed businesses and non-failed businesses and collected relevant data for each business for five years prior to failure. He found that the model represented by the formula above was able to predict failure for up to two years before it occurred. However, the predictive accuracy of the model became weaker the longer the time before the date of the actual failure.

The ratios used in this model were identified by Altman through a process of trial and error, as there is no underlying theory of financial failure to help guide researchers in their selection of appropriate ratios. According to Altman, those businesses with a Z-score of less than 1.23 tend to fail. The lower the score the greater is the probability of failure. Those with a Z-score greater than 4.14 tend not to fail. Those businesses with a Z-score between 1.23 and 4.14 occupied a 'zone of ignorance' and were difficult to classify. However, the model was able overall to classify 91 per cent of the businesses correctly; only 9 per cent fell into the 'zone of ignorance'. Altman based his model on US businesses.

In recent years, other models, using a similar approach, have been developed throughout the world. In the UK, Taffler has developed separate Z-score models for different types of business. (See reference 4 at the end of the chapter for a discussion of the work of Taffler and others.)

The prediction of financial failure is not the only area where research into the predictive ability of ratios has taken place. Researchers have also developed ratio-based models that claim to assess the vulnerability of a business to takeover by another. This is also an area that is of vital importance to all those connected with the business.

Real World 7.10 is an article which discusses some research that showed that investing in shares in businesses with very low Z-scores is unsuccessful compared with investing in businesses with higher Z-scores. This is what we might expect to happen and provides support for the use of Z-scores in assessing the health of businesses. The research did not show, however, that the higher the Z-score, the more successful the investment.

Real World 7.10

From A to Z

Investors looking to profit during a recession should be targeting stocks [shares] with strong fundamentals, according to research by Morgan Stanley. This "value investing" approach – buying into companies where fundamental measures, such as book value and earnings, are not yet reflected in their share prices – is not new. But Morgan Stanley's analysis has found that the ability of this approach to deliver returns in downturns depends on the financial strength of the companies – in particular, the importance attached to the balance sheet [statement of financial position] by investors. "If a stock's balance sheet is weak, the valuation multiple will be of little importance at this stage in the economic cycle," says Graham Secker, Morgan Stanley strategy analyst.

He ranked a basket of European companies by their Altman Z-score – a measure of financial strength devised by US academic Edward Altman. A Z-score can be calculated for all non-financial companies and the lower the score, the greater the risk of the company falling into financial distress. When Secker compared the companies' Z-scores with their share price movements, he discovered that the companies with weaker balance sheets underperformed the market more than two thirds of the time.

Morgan Stanley also found that a company with an Altman Z-score of less than 1 tends to underperform the wider market by more than 4 per cent over the year with an associated probability of 72 per cent. "Given the poor performance over the last year by stocks with a low Altman Z-score, the results of our backtest are now even more compelling than they were 12 months ago," argues Secker. "We calculate that the median stock with an Altman Z-score of 1 or less has underperformed the wider market by 5–6 per cent per annum between 1990 and 2008."

Secker sees this as logical. In a recession, companies with balance sheets that are perceived to be weak are deemed a higher risk by lenders and face a higher cost of capital. This turns market sentiment against them and will generally lead to their share prices falling below their peers.

In 2008, the share price performance for stocks with an Altman Z-score of less than 1 was the worst since Morgan Stanley's analysis began in 1991. Under the Morgan Stanley methodology, the 2008 score is calculated using 2007 company financials. Of all the companies with a 2008 Z-score of less than 1, the median share price performance was a loss of 49 per cent, compared with a wider market fall of 42 per cent.

When compound annual growth rates since 1991 are analysed, the results are more dramatic. On average, companies with Z-scores of less than 1 saw their shares fall 4.4 per cent, compared with an average rise of 1.3 per cent for their peers. In only five of the last 18 years has a stock with an Altman score of 1 or less outperformed the market. These were generally years of strong economic growth. However, companies with the highest Z-scores aren't necessarily the best performers. During the bear market of 2000 to 2002, companies that had a Z-score above 3 fell almost twice as much as the market.

Analysts say the 2009 Z-scores, based on 2008 balance sheets, are far lower than in previous years as companies absorb the strain of the downturn in their accounts. "There's been a lot of change between 2007 and 2008 [accounting years], tightening of credit and a vast deterioration in corporate balance sheets," says Secker. "I'd expect 2009 [Z-scores] to be much worse."

Analysis by the *Financial Times* and Capital IQ, the data provider, corroborates this – showing that the 2009 scores have been badly affected by the crisis. Some 8 per cent of global companies with a market capitalisation of more than $500 million have Altman scores below 1 for 2009 – based on 2008 company financials. This is the highest percentage since 2002 and the largest annual increase since 2001 – showing the impact of the recession on the balance sheets of even the largest companies. If smaller companies were included, the results would be worse – as their earnings and market capitalisations have been affected far more.

European balance sheets were hit the hardest, with companies averaging a Z-score of 2.8, compared with 4.0 for Asia and the US, according to Capital IQ. This suggests the scores are not due to chance. A similar differential was recorded in 2001 during the last recession. On this evidence, US companies appear more resilient than their global peers in a downturn.

On a sector basis, healthcare and IT companies have the highest Z-scores. In 2008, their scores were more than three times higher than the average for the lowest-scoring sector: utilities. A similar pattern was found in 2001 – suggesting that investors may want to think twice before buying into 'defensive' utilities in a downturn.

FT *Source*: Mathurin, P. (2009) New study re-writes the A to Z of value investing, *Financial Times*, 14 August. © The Financial Times Limited 2009. All Rights Reserved.

As well as the research that we have just discussed in **Real World 7.10**, there has been a great deal of investigation, much of it by academics, into the practical effectiveness of Altman's Z-score model, or slight variations of it. These investigations have ranged over many different economies and industries. They have overwhelmingly supported the model. Its usefulness is further supported by its apparent widespread use by businesses and independent analysts for practical purposes.

Limitations of ratio analysis

Although ratios offer a quick and useful method of analysing the position and performance of a business, they are not without their problems and limitations. We shall now review some of their shortcomings.

Quality of financial statements

It must always be remembered that ratios are based on financial statements. They will, therefore, inherit the limitations of the financial statements on which they are based. In Chapter 2, we saw that one important limitation of financial statements is their failure to include all resources controlled by the business. Internally generated goodwill and brands, for example, are excluded from the statement of financial position because they fail to meet the strict definition of an asset. This means that, even though these resources may be of considerable value, key ratios such as ROSF, ROCE and the gearing ratio will fail to acknowledge their presence.

Activity (7.31)

Assume that a business has internally generated goodwill that had been created in earlier years. If this resource were introduced as a non-current asset with an indefinite life in the current statement of financial position, what would be the effect on ROSF, ROCE and the gearing ratio?

The effect of introducing internally generated goodwill will be similar to that of an asset revaluation, which we considered in Chapter 2. Total assets will increase and equity will also increase. An increase in equity will increase the denominator (lower part of the fraction) for all three ratios. This will, in turn, lead to lower ratios than would be the case if the goodwill were not introduced.

The quality of financial statements may also be undermined by deliberate attempts to make them misleading. We discussed this problem of *creative accounting* in Chapter 5.

Inflation

A persistent, albeit recently less severe, problem, in most countries is that the financial results of businesses can be distorted as a result of inflation. One effect of inflation is that the reported value of assets that have been held for any length of time may bear little relation to current values. Generally speaking, the reported value of assets will be understated in current terms during a period of inflation as they are usually reported at their original cost (less any amounts written off for depreciation). This means that comparisons, either between businesses or between periods, will be hindered. A difference in, say, ROCE may simply be due to assets, shown in one of the statements of financial position being compared, having been acquired more recently (ignoring the effect of depreciation on the asset values). Another effect of inflation is to distort the measurement of profit. In the calculation of profit, sales revenue is often matched with costs incurred at an earlier time. This is because there is often a time lag between acquiring a particular resource and using it to help generate sales revenue. For example, inventories may well be acquired several months before they are sold. During a period of inflation, this will mean that the expense may not reflect prices that are current at the time of the sale. The cost of sales figure is usually based on the historic cost of the inventories concerned. As a result, expenses will be understated in the income statement and this, in turn, means that profit will be overstated. One effect of this will be to distort the profitability ratios discussed earlier.

The restricted view given by ratios

It is important not to rely exclusively on ratios, thereby losing sight of information contained in the underlying financial statements. As we saw earlier in this chapter, some items reported in these statements can be vital in assessing position and performance. For example, the total sales revenue, capital employed and profit figures may be useful in assessing changes in absolute size that occur over time, or in assessing differences in scale between businesses. The standard ratios do not provide such information. When comparing one figure with another, ratios measure *relative* performance and position and, therefore, provide only part of the picture. When comparing two businesses, therefore, it will often be useful to assess the absolute size of profits, as well as the relative profitability of each business. For example, Business A may generate £1 million operating profit and have a ROCE of 15 per cent and Business B may generate £100,000 operating profit and have a ROCE of

20 per cent. Although Business B has a higher level of *profitability,* as measured by ROCE, it nevertheless generates lower total operating profits. This fact should not be overlooked.

The basis for comparison

We saw earlier that if ratios are to be useful they require a basis for comparison. Moreover, it is important that we compare like with like. Where the comparison is with another business, there can be difficulties. No two businesses are identical: the greater the differences between the businesses being compared, the greater are the limitations of ratio analysis. Furthermore, any differences in accounting policies, financing methods (gearing levels) and reporting year-ends will add to the problems of making comparisons between businesses.

Statement of financial position ratios

Because the statement of financial position is only a 'snapshot' of the business at a particular moment in time, any ratios based on statement of financial position figures, such as the liquidity ratios, may not be representative of the financial position of the business for the year as a whole. For example, it is common for a seasonal business to have a reporting year-end that coincides with a low point in business activity. As a result, inventories and trade receivables may be low at that time. This means that the liquidity ratios may also be low. A more representative picture of liquidity can only really be gained by taking additional measurements at other points in the year.

Real World 7.11 points out another way in which ratios are limited.

Real World 7.11

Remember, it's people that really count . . .

Lord Weinstock (1924 to 2002) was an influential industrialist whose management style and philosophy helped to shape management practice in many UK businesses. During his long and successful reign at GEC plc, a major engineering business, Lord Weinstock relied heavily on financial ratios to assess performance and to exercise control. In particular, he relied on ratios relating to sales revenue, expenses, trade receivables, profit margins and inventories turnover. However, he was keenly aware of the limitations of ratios and recognised that, ultimately, people produce profits.

In a memo written to GEC managers he pointed out that ratios are an aid to good management rather than a substitute for it. He wrote:

> The operating ratios are of great value as measures of efficiency but they are only the measures and not efficiency itself. Statistics will not design a product better, make it for a lower cost or increase sales. If ill-used, they may so guide action as to diminish resources for the sake of apparent but false signs of improvement.
>
> Management remains a matter of judgement, of knowledge of products and processes and of understanding and skill in dealing with people. The ratios will indicate how well all these things are being done and will show comparison with how they are done elsewhere. But they will tell us nothing about how to do them. That is what you are meant to do.

Source: Extract from Stephen Aris, *Arnold Weinstock and the Making of GEC* (Aurum Press, 1998), published in *The Sunday Times*, 22 February 1998, p. 3.

Self-assessment question 7.1

Both Ali plc and Bhaskar plc operate wholesale electrical stores throughout the UK. The financial statements of each business for the year ended 30 June 2017 are as follows:

Statements of financial position as at 30 June 2017

	Ali plc £m	Bhaskar plc £m
ASSETS		
Non-current assets		
Property, plant and equipment (cost less depreciation):		
Land and buildings	360.0	510.0
Fixtures and fittings	87.0	91.2
	447.0	601.2
Current assets		
Inventories	592.0	403.0
Trade receivables	176.4	321.9
Cash at bank	84.6	91.6
	853.0	816.5
Total assets	1,300.0	1,417.7
EQUITY AND LIABILITIES		
Equity		
£1 ordinary shares	320.0	250.0
Retained earnings	367.6	624.6
	687.6	874.6
Non-current liabilities		
Borrowings – loan notes	190.0	250.0
Current liabilities		
Trade payables	406.4	275.7
Taxation	16.0	17.4
	422.4	293.1
Total equity and liabilities	1,300.0	1,417.7

Income statements for the year ended 30 June 2017

	Ali plc £m	Bhaskar plc £m
Revenue	1,478.1	1,790.4
Cost of sales	(1,018.3)	(1,214.9)
Gross profit	459.8	575.5
Operating expenses	(308.5)	(408.6)
Operating profit	151.3	166.9
Interest payable	(19.4)	(27.5)
Profit before taxation	131.9	139.4
Taxation	(32.0)	(34.8)
Profit for the year	99.9	104.6

All purchases and sales were on credit. The market values of a share in Ali plc and Bhaskar plc at the end of the year were £6.50 and £8.20, respectively.

Required:

(a) For each business, calculate two ratios that are concerned with each of the following aspects:
  - profitability
  - efficiency
  - liquidity
  - gearing
  - investment
  (ten ratios in total).

  What can you conclude from the ratios that you have calculated?
(b) Calculate the Z-scores for each business using the Altman model.
(c) Comment on the Z-scores for each business and on the validity of applying the Altman model to these particular businesses.

The solution to this question can be found at the back of the book on pp. 772–773.

Summary

The main points of this chapter may be summarised as follows:

Ratio analysis

- Compares two related figures, usually both from the same set of financial statements.
- Is an aid to understanding what the financial statements really mean.
- Is an inexact science so results must be interpreted cautiously.
- Usually requires the performance for past periods, similar businesses and/or planned performance as benchmark ratios.
- Can often benefit from a brief overview of the financial statements to provide insights that may not be revealed by ratios and/or may help in the interpretation of them.

Profitability ratios

- Are concerned with effectiveness at generating profit.
- Most commonly found in practice are the return on ordinary shareholders' funds (ROSF), return on capital employed (ROCE), operating profit margin and gross profit margin.

Efficiency ratios

- Are concerned with efficiency of using assets/resources.
- Most commonly found in practice are the average inventories turnover period, average settlement period for trade receivables, average settlement period for trade payables, sales revenue to capital employed and sales revenue per employee.

Liquidity ratios

- Are concerned with the ability to meet short-term obligations.
- Most commonly found in practice are the current ratio, the acid test ratio and the cash generated to maturing obligations ratio.

Gearing ratios

- Are concerned with relationship between equity and debt financing.
- Most commonly found in practice are the gearing ratio and the interest cover ratio.

Investment ratios

- Are concerned with returns to shareholders.
- Most commonly found in practice are the dividend payout ratio, the dividend yield ratio, earnings per share (EPS), cash generated from operations per share, and the price/earnings (PIE) ratio.

Uses of ratios

- Individual ratios can be tracked to detect trends, for example by plotting them on a graph.
- Ratios can be used to detect signs of overtrading.
- Ratios can be used to predict financial failure.
- Univariate analysis uses a single ratio at a time in an attempt to predict financial failure whereas multiple discriminate analysis (MDA) combines various ratios within a model.

Limitations of ratio analysis

- Ratios are only as reliable as the financial statements from which they derive.
- Inflation can distort the information.
- Ratios give a restricted view.
- It can be difficult to find a suitable benchmark (for example, another business) to compare with.
- Some ratios could mislead due to the 'snapshot' nature of the statement of financial position.

Key terms

For definitions of these terms, see Appendix B.

References

1 Beaver, W. H. (1966) 'Financial ratios as predictors of failure', in *Empirical Research in Accounting: Selected Studies,* pp. 71–111.

2 Zmijewski, M. E. (1983) 'Predicting corporate bankruptcy: an empirical comparison of the extent of financial distress models', Research Paper, State University of New York, 1983.

3 Altman, E. I. (2000) 'Predicting financial distress of companies: revisiting the Z-score and Zeta models', New York University Working Paper, June.

4 Neophytou, E., Charitou, A. and Charalamnous, C. (2001) 'Predicting corporate failure: empirical evidence for the UK', University of Southampton Department of Accounting and Management Science Working Paper 01-173.

Further reading

If you would like to explore the topics covered in this chapter in more depth, we recommend the following:

Elliott, B. and Elliott, J. (2015) *Financial Accounting and Reporting,* 17th edn, Pearson, Chapters 28 and 29.

Penman, S. (2012) *Financial Statement Analysis and Security Valuation,* 5th edn, McGraw-Hill Irwin, Chapters 7–12.

Schoenebeck, K. and Holtzman, M. (2013) *Interpreting and Analyzing Financial Statements,* 6th edn, Pearson, Chapters 2–5.

Subramanyam K. and Wild J. (2015) *Financial Statement Analysis,* McGraw Hill Higher Education, 11th edn, Chapters 6 and 8.

Review questions

Solutions to these questions can be found at the back of the book on p. 791.

7.1 Some businesses (for example, supermarket chains) operate on a low operating profit margin. Does this mean that the return on capital employed from the business will also be low?

7.2 What potential problems arise particularly for the external analyst from the use of statement of financial position figures in the calculation of financial ratios?

7.3 Is it responsible to publish Z-scores of businesses that are in financial difficulties? What are the potential problems of doing this?

7.4 Identify and discuss three reasons why the P/E ratios of two businesses operating within the same industry may differ.

Exercises

Solutions to exercises with coloured numbers can be found at the back of the book on pp. 813–815.

Basic-level exercises

7.1 Set out below are ratios relating to three different businesses. Each business operates within a different industrial sector.

Ratio	A plc	B plc	C plc
Operating profit margin	3.6%	9.7%	6.8%
Sales to capital employed	2.4 times	3.1 times	1.7 times
Average inventories turnover period	18 days	N/A	44 days
Average settlement period for trade receivables	2 days	12 days	26 days
Current ratio	0.8 times	0.6 times	1.5 times

Required:
State, with reasons, which one of the three businesses is:
(a) A holiday tour operator
(b) A supermarket chain
(c) A food manufacturer.

7.2 Amsterdam Ltd and Berlin Ltd are both engaged in retailing, but they seem to take a different approach to it according to the following information:

Ratio	Amsterdam Ltd	Berlin Ltd
Return on capital employed (ROCE)	20%	17%
Return on ordinary shareholders' funds (ROSF)	30%	18%
Average settlement period for trade receivables	63 days	21 days
Average settlement period for trade payables	50 days	45 days
Gross profit margin	40%	15%
Operating profit margin	10%	10%
Average inventories turnover period	52 days	25 days

Required:

Describe what this information indicates about the differences in approach between the two businesses. If one of them prides itself on personal service and one of them on competitive prices, which do you think is which and why?

Intermediate-level exercises

7.3   The directors of Helena Beauty Products Ltd have been presented with the following abridged financial statements:

Helena Beauty Products Ltd
Income statement for the year ended 30 September

	2016		2017	
	£000	£000	£000	£000
Sales revenue		3,600		3,840
Cost of sales				
Opening inventories	320		400	
Purchases	2,240		2,350	
	2,560		2,750	
Closing inventories	(400)	(2,160)	(500)	(2,250)
Gross profit		1,440		1,590
Expenses		(1,360)		(1,500)
Profit		80		90

Statement of financial position as at 30 September

	2016	2017
	£000	£000
ASSETS		
Non-current assets		
Property, plant and equipment	1,900	1,860
Current assets		
Inventories	400	500
Trade receivables	750	960
Cash at bank	8	4
	1,158	1,464
Total assets	3,058	3,324
EQUITY AND LIABILITIES		
Equity		
£1 ordinary shares	1,650	1,766
Retained earnings	1,018	1,108
	2,668	2,874
Current liabilities	390	450
Total equity and liabilities	3,058	3,324

Required:

Using six ratios, comment on the profitability (three ratios) and efficiency (three ratios) of the business.

7.4 Conday and Co. Ltd has been in operation for three years and produces antique reproduction furniture for the export market. The most recent set of financial statements for the business is set out as follows:

Statement of financial position as at 30 November

	£000
ASSETS	
Non-current assets	
Property, plant and equipment (cost less depreciation)	
Land and buildings	228
Plant and machinery	762
	990
Current assets	
Inventories	600
Trade receivables	820
	1,420
Total assets	2,410
EQUITY AND LIABILITIES	
Equity	
Ordinary shares of £1 each	700
Retained earnings	365
	1,065
Non-current liabilities	
Borrowings – 9% loan notes (Note 1)	200
Current liabilities	
Trade payables	665
Taxation	48
Short-term borrowings (all bank overdraft)	432
	1,145
Total equity and liabilities	2,410

Income statement for the year ended 30 November

	£000
Revenue	2,600
Cost of sales	(1,620)
Gross profit	980
Selling and distribution expenses (Note 2)	(408)
Administration expenses	(194)
Operating profit	378
Finance expenses	(58)
Profit before taxation	320
Taxation	(95)
Profit for the year	225

Notes:

1 The loan notes are secured on the land and buildings.
2 Selling and distribution expenses include £170,000 in respect of bad debts.
3 A dividend of £160,000 was paid on the ordinary shares during the year.
4 The directors have invited an investor to take up a new issue of ordinary shares in the business at £6.40 each making a total investment of £200,000. The directors wish to use the funds to finance a programme of further expansion.

Required:

(a) Analyse the financial position and performance of the business and comment on any features that you consider significant.

(b) State, with reasons, whether or not the investor should invest in the business on the terms outlined.

Advanced-level exercises

7.5 Threads Limited manufactures nuts and bolts, which are sold to industrial users. The abbreviated financial statements for 2016 and 2017 are as follows:

Income statements for the year ended 30 June

	2016	2017
	£000	£000
Revenue	1,180	1,200
Cost of sales	(680)	(750)
Gross profit	500	450
Operating expenses	(200)	(208)
Depreciation	(66)	(75)
Operating profit	234	167
Interest	(–)	(8)
Profit before taxation	234	159
Taxation	(80)	(48)
Profit for the year	154	111

Statements of financial position as at 30 June

	2016	2017
	£000	£000
ASSETS		
Non-current assets		
Property, plant and equipment	702	687
Current assets		
Inventories	148	236
Trade receivables	102	156
Cash	3	4
	253	396
Total assets	955	1,083
EQUITY AND LIABILITIES		
Equity		
Ordinary share capital (£1 shares, fully paid)	500	500
Retained earnings	256	295
	756	795
Non-current liabilities		
Borrowings – bank loan	–	50
Current liabilities		
Trade payables	60	76
Other payables and accruals	18	16
Taxation	40	24
Short-term borrowings (all bank overdraft)	81	122
	199	238
Total equity and liabilities	955	1,083

Dividends were paid on ordinary shares of £70,000 and £72,000 in respect of 2016 and 2017, respectively.

Required:

(a) Calculate the following financial ratios for *both* 2016 and 2017 (using year-end figures for statement of financial position items):

    1 return on capital employed

    2 operating profit margin

    3 gross profit margin

    4 current ratio

    5 acid test ratio

    6 settlement period for trade receivables

    7 settlement period for trade payables

    8 inventories turnover period.

(b) Comment on the performance of Threads Limited from the viewpoint of a business considering supplying a substantial amount of goods to Threads Limited on usual trade credit terms.

7.6   Genesis Ltd was incorporated three years ago and has grown rapidly since then. The rapid rate of growth has created problems for the business, which the directors have found difficult to deal with. Recently, a firm of management consultants has been asked to help the directors to overcome these problems.

In a preliminary report to the board of directors, the management consultants state: 'Most of the difficulties faced by the business are symptoms of an underlying problem of overtrading.'

The most recent financial statements of the business are set out below.

Statement of financial position as at 31 October

ASSETS	£000	£000
Non-current assets		
Property, plant and equipment		
Land and buildings at cost	530	
Accumulated depreciation	(88)	442
Fixtures and fittings at cost	168	
Accumulated depreciation	(52)	116
Motor vans at cost	118	
Accumulated depreciation	(54)	64
		622
Current assets		
Inventories		128
Trade receivables		104
		232
Total assets		854
EQUITY AND LIABILITIES		
Equity		
Ordinary £0.50 shares		60
General reserve		50
Retained earnings		74
		184
Non-current liabilities		
Borrowings – 10% loan notes (secured)		120
Current liabilities		
Trade payables		184
Taxation		8
Short-term borrowings (all bank overdraft)		358
		550
Total equity and liabilities		854

Income statement for the year ended 31 October

	£000	£000
Revenue		1,640
Cost of sales:		
Opening inventories	116	
Purchases	1,260	
	1,376	
Closing inventories	(128)	(1,248)
Gross profit		392
Selling and distribution expenses		(204)
Administration expenses		(92)
Operating profit		96
Interest payable		(44)
Profit before taxation		52
Taxation		(16)
Profit for the year		36

All purchases and sales were on credit.
A dividend was paid during the year on ordinary shares of £4,000.

Required:
(a) Calculate and discuss five financial ratios that might be used to establish whether the business is overtrading. Do these five ratios suggest that the business is overtrading?
(b) State the ways in which a business may overcome the problem of overtrading.

7.7 The financial statements for Harridges Ltd are given below for the two years ended 30 June 2016 and 2017. Harridges Limited operates a department store in the centre of a small town.

Income statements for the years ended 30 June

	2016	2017
	£000	£000
Sales revenue	2,600	3,500
Cost of sales	(1,560)	(2,350)
Gross profit	1,040	1,150
Wages and salaries	(320)	(350)
Overheads	(260)	(200)
Depreciation	(150)	(250)
Operating profit	310	350
Interest payable	(50)	(50)
Profit before taxation	260	300
Taxation	(105)	(125)
Profit for the year	155	175

Statement of financial position as at 30 June

	2016 £000	2017 £000
ASSETS		
Non-current assets		
Property, plant and equipment	1,265	1,525
Current assets		
Inventories	250	400
Trade receivables	105	145
Cash at bank	380	115
	735	660
Total assets	2,000	2,185
EQUITY AND LIABILITIES		
Equity		
Share capital: £1 shares fully paid	490	490
Share premium	260	260
Retained earnings	350	450
	1,100	1,200
Non-current liabilities		
Borrowings – 10% loan notes	500	500
Current liabilities		
Trade payables	300	375
Other payables	100	110
	400	485
Total equity and liabilities	2,000	2,185

Dividends were paid on ordinary shares of £65,000 and £75,000 in respect of 2016 and 2017, respectively.

Required:
(a) Choose and calculate eight ratios that would be helpful in assessing the performance of Harridges Ltd. Use end-of-year values and calculate ratios for both 2016 and 2017.
(b) Using the ratios calculated in (a) and any others you consider helpful, comment on the business's performance from the viewpoint of a prospective purchaser of a majority of shares.

PART 2

Management accounting

Part 2 deals with the area known as 'management accounting' or 'managerial accounting'. This area is concerned with providing information to help managers to run the business in an efficient and effective way. The information provided is designed to help them make decisions in planning for the future and in ensuring that plans are actually achieved.

It is difficult to overstate the extent to which management accounting, and the role of the management accountant, has changed over recent times. The advance of the computer has had an enormous influence. Information technology (IT) has released the management accountant from much of the routine work associated with preparation of management accounting reports and has provided the opportunity to take a more proactive role within the business. This has led to the management accountant becoming part of the management team and, therefore, directly involved in planning and decision making.

The role of the management accountant has also changed as a result of the increasingly turbulent economic environment. Businesses must now strive harder to gain competitive advantage. As mentioned in Chapter 1, they must now be more customer-focused, more outward-looking and more orientated towards value creation in order to survive and prosper. This has meant that managers require a much broader range of information from the management accountant than in the past.

These new dimensions to the management accountant's role have implications for the kind of skills required to operate effectively. In particular, certain 'soft' skills are needed, such as interpersonal skills for working as part of an effective team and communication skills to help influence the attitudes and behaviour of others.

Through working as part of a cross-functional team, the management accountant should gain a greater awareness of strategic and operational matters and an increased understanding of the information needs of managers. This is likely to have a positive effect on the design and development of management accounting systems. We should, therefore, see increasing evidence that management accounting systems are being designed to fit the particular structure and processes of the business rather than the other way round. By participating in planning, decision making and control of the business as well as providing management accounting information for these purposes, the management accountant plays a key role in achieving the objectives of the business. It is a role that should add value to the business and improve its competitive position.

Part 2 begins with a consideration of the basics of financial decision making. The first chapter in this part, Chapter 8, deals with how we identify information that is relevant to a particular decision. In practice, managers may be confronted with a large volume of financial information and must be able to discriminate between that which is relevant to a particular decision and that which can be ignored. Unless they can do this, there is a risk of making poor decisions. Chapter 9 continues our examination of basic concepts by considering the relationship between costs, volume of activity and profit. We shall see that an understanding of this relationship can be helpful in developing plans and in making a variety of decisions. This chapter incorporates an examination of break-even analysis, which is concerned with deducing the volume of activity at which the sales revenue equals the costs incurred. At this point, neither profit nor loss is made by the activity. Knowledge of the break-even figure can be useful in assessing the degree of risk associated with business operations.

In Chapter 10 we look at how businesses have traditionally determined the full cost of each unit of their output. By 'full cost' we mean the figure that takes account of all of the costs of providing a product or service. This includes not simply those costs that are directly caused by the unit of output, but indirect costs such as rent and administrative salaries, which are also incurred in providing the product or service. This topic is continued in Chapter 11, where we consider a more recent approach to determining the full cost of a product or service. In this chapter, we also discuss the changes to the business environment that have occurred and the management accounting techniques developed to help businesses retain their competitiveness in this new environment.

Chapter 12 deals with the way in which businesses convert their objectives and long-term plans into workable short-term plans, or budgets. Budgets are an important feature of business life and so we consider the budgeting process in some detail. We shall examine the purpose of budgets and the way in which budgets are prepared. In Chapter 13, we shall see how, after the budget period, actual performance can be compared with budgeted performance. This comparison can help assess performance and identify reasons for any failure to meet budget targets. By finding out what went wrong, managers may be able to put things right for the future. The chapter concludes with a discussion of the impact of budgets on the attitudes and behaviour of managers.

CHAPTER

Making management decisions

Introduction

This chapter considers how management decisions should be made. The principles outlined provide the basis for much of the rest of the book.

Management decisions should seek to promote the objectives of the business. When considering a proposed course of action, this involves weighing the benefits and associated costs. It is important to distinguish carefully between those benefits and costs that are relevant and those that are not. As we shall see, not all benefits and costs that can be identified may be relevant to the course of action.

When making management decisions, potential risks must also be considered. This involves assessing the likelihood that and extent to which actual benefits and costs relating to a proposed course of action will not turn out as predicted. Failure to carefully weigh relevant benefits and costs, along with the risks associated with each, is likely to result in poor decisions being made.

Learning outcomes

When you have completed this chapter, you should be able to:

● define and distinguish between relevant costs, outlay costs and opportunity costs;

● identify and quantify the costs and benefits that are relevant to a particular decision and reach a conclusion on the basis of them;

● define risk and explain its importance to management decisions; and

● assess the riskiness of a particular decision.

Cost–benefit analysis

Managers tend to spend much of their time making plans and decisions. As part of this process, they try to assess the likely outcome from each course of action being considered. This involves a careful weighing of the prospective **benefits** against the **costs** involved. Benefits are those outcomes, resulting from a course of action, that help a business to achieve its objectives. Costs, on the other hand, represent the sacrifice of resources needed to achieve those benefits. For a proposed plan, or decision, to be worthwhile, the likely benefits should exceed the associated costs.

Real World 8.1 provides an interesting example of where **cost-benefit analysis** was used to evaluate a possible course of action designed to solve a serious problem faced by many businesses.

Real World 8.1

Stocktaking

Light-fingered employees are a problem for all employers, however the issue is particularly severe in the retail trade. Tatiana Sandino, an associate professor in accounting and management at Harvard Business School and co-author Clara Xiaoling Chen, an assistant professor of accountancy at the University of Illinois at Urbana-Champaign cite figures from the National Retail Security survey in the US which says that employee theft of inventories contributed to a loss of $15.9 billion in 2008.

To try to discover what might dissuade employees from stealing, the two academics wondered if higher remuneration might help. They hypothesised that higher wages might encourage employees to feel more warmly towards their employers, that these employees – if they were paid more – would be less inclined to steal because they would not want to lose their jobs and paying a larger sum in the first place would attract more honest employees.

Using two data sets and including factors such as workers' different socio-economic environments and how many people the stores employed, the authors found that paying a larger salary caused a drop in employee theft and could, in certain circumstances, make fiscal sense.

A cost–benefit analysis found that what an employer saved in cash and inventories theft covered about 39 per cent of the cost of the wage increase.

"Our study suggests that an increase in wages will decrease theft, but won't fully pay off," says Prof Sandino. The pair suggest that raising salaries might be the right course of action if other benefits – such as reduced employee turnover or higher employee productivity – account for at least 61 per cent of the wage increase.

FT *Source:* Extracts from Anderson, L. (2012) Something for the weekend, ft.com, 16 November.
© The Financial Times Limited 2012. All Rights Reserved.

To help weigh costs and benefits arising from a particular decision, it would be useful if both could be measured in monetary terms (as they were in the example discussed in Real World 8.1). This would then provide a common denominator for cost–benefit analysis. Some costs and benefits, however, may elude attempts to place a reliable monetary value on them. Take, for example, the likely problems of trying to measure the costs, in terms of loss of reputation, incurred by selling customers faulty products or the benefits accruing from steps taken to lift morale among the workforce. To add to the measurement problems, the timing and duration of these costs and benefits may be difficult to estimate.

Nevertheless, the costs and benefits just described can have a significant effect on the achievement of business objectives. They should not, therefore, be ignored or given less weight when making decisions. There is always a risk that managers will take too narrow a view and act on the basis that 'the things that count are the things that get counted'. That is, attention will be paid to those aspects where it is easy to assign a monetary value, but aspects that are difficult to value will be ignored. We shall return to this point a little later in the chapter.

What is meant by 'cost'?

The term 'cost' is a slippery concept. Although a very broad description was given earlier when discussing cost–benefit analysis, it can be defined in different ways. Managers therefore need to be clear what it means in the context of decision making. This is an important issue to which we now turn.

Identifying and measuring cost may seem, at first sight, to be pretty straightforward: it is simply the amount paid for the goods supplied or the service provided. When measuring cost *for decision-making purposes,* however, things are not quite that simple. The following activity illustrates why this is the case.

Activity 8.1

Assume that you own a motor car, for which you paid a purchase price of £5,000 – much below the current list price – at a recent car auction. You have just been offered £6,000 for this car.

What is the cost to you of keeping the car for your own use? *Note:* Ignore running costs and so on; just consider the 'capital' cost of the car.

By retaining the car, you are forgoing a cash receipt of £6,000. Thus, the real sacrifice, or cost, incurred by keeping the car for your own use is £6,000.

Any decision that the car owner in Activity 8.1 may make, with respect to the car's future, should logically take account of the figure of £6,000. This is known as the **opportunity cost** since it is the value of the opportunity forgone in order to pursue the other course of action. (In this case, the other course of action is to retain the car.)

We can see that the cost of retaining the car is not the same as the purchase price. In one sense, of course, the cost of the car is £5,000 because that is how much was paid for it. However, this cost, which for obvious reasons is known as the **historic cost,** is only of academic interest. It cannot logically ever be used to make a decision on the car's future. If we disagree with this point, we should ask ourselves how we should assess an offer of £5,500, from another person, for the car. The answer is that we should compare the offer price of £5,500 with the opportunity cost of £6,000. This should lead us to reject the second offer as it is less than the £6,000 opportunity cost. In these circumstances, it would not be logical to accept the offer of £5,500 on the basis that it was more than the £5,000 that we originally paid. The only other figure that should concern us is the value to us, in terms of pleasure, usefulness and so on, of retaining the car. If we valued this more highly than the £6,000 opportunity cost, we should reject both offers.

We may still feel, however, that the £5,000 is relevant here because it will help us in assessing the profitability of the decision. If we sold the car, we should make a profit of either £500 (£5,500 − £5,000) or £1,000 (£6,000 − £5,000) depending on which offer we accept. Since we should seek to make the higher profit, the right decision is to sell the car for £6,000. However, we do not need to know the historic cost of the car to make the right decision. What decision should we make if the car cost us £4,000 to buy? Clearly we should still sell the car for £6,000 rather than for £5,500 as the important comparison is between the offer price and the opportunity cost. We should reach the same conclusion whatever the historic cost of the car.

To emphasise the above point, let us assume that the car cost £10,000. Even in this case the historic cost would still be irrelevant. Had we just bought a car for £10,000 and found that shortly after it is only worth £6,000, we may well be fuming with rage at our mistake, but this does not make the £10,000 a **relevant cost.** The only relevant factors, in a decision on whether to sell the car or to keep it, are the £6,000 opportunity cost and the value of the benefits of keeping it. Thus, the historic cost can never be relevant to a future decision.

To say that historic cost is an **irrelevant cost** is not to say that *the effects of having incurred that cost* are always irrelevant. The fact that we own the car, and are thus in a position to exercise choice as to how to use it, is not irrelevant. It is highly relevant.

Opportunity costs are rarely taken into account in the routine accounting processes, such as recording revenues, expenses, assets and claims. This is because they do not involve any out-of-pocket expenditure. It seems that they are calculated only where they are relevant to a particular management decision. Historic costs, on the other hand, do involve out-of-pocket expenditure and are recorded. They are used in preparing the annual financial statements, such as the statement of financial position and the income statement. This is logical, however, since these statements are intended to be accounts of what has actually happened and are drawn up after the event.

Relevant costs: opportunity and outlay costs

We have just seen that, when we are making decisions concerning the future, **past costs** (that is, historic costs) are irrelevant. It is future opportunity costs and future **outlay costs** that are of concern. An opportunity cost can be defined as the value, in monetary terms, of being deprived of the next best opportunity in order to pursue the particular objective. An outlay cost is an amount of money that will have to be spent to achieve that objective. We shall shortly meet plenty of examples of both of these types of future cost.

To be relevant to a particular decision, a future outlay cost, or opportunity cost, must satisfy all three of the following criteria:

1 *It must relate to the objectives of the business*. Most businesses have enhancing owners' (shareholders') wealth as their key strategic objective. That is to say, they are seeking to become richer (see Chapter 1). Thus, to be relevant to a particular decision, a cost must have an effect on the wealth of the business.

2 *It must be a future cost*. Past costs cannot be relevant to decisions being made about the future.

3 *It must vary with the decision*. Only costs that differ between outcomes should be used to distinguish between them. Take, for example, a road haulage business that has decided that it will buy a new, additional lorry and the decision lies between two different models. The load capacity, the fuel and maintenance costs are different for each lorry. The potential costs and benefits associated with these factors are relevant items. The lorry will require a driver, so the business will need to employ one, but a suitably qualified driver could drive either lorry equally well, for the same wage. The cost of employing the driver is thus irrelevant to the decision as to which lorry to buy. This is despite the fact that this cost is a future one.

Activity 8.2

If the decision did not concern a choice between two models of lorry but rather whether to operate an additional lorry or not, would the cost of employing the additional driver be relevant?

Yes – because it would then be a cost that would vary with the decision.

Figure 8.1 sets out in diagrammatic form how we determine which costs are relevant to a particular decision.

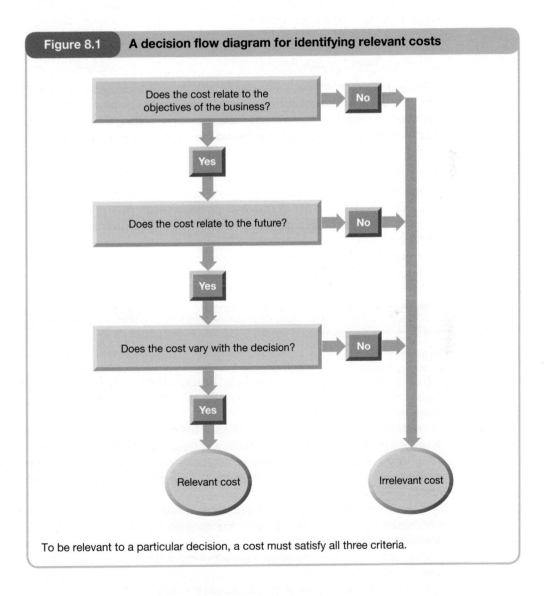

Figure 8.1   A decision flow diagram for identifying relevant costs

To be relevant to a particular decision, a cost must satisfy all three criteria.

To be relevant to a particular decision, the benefits must also satisfy all three criteria mentioned. That is, they should relate to the objectives of the business, they should relate to the future and they should vary with the decision.

Activity 8.3

A garage has a car that it bought several months ago. The car needs new tyres before it is roadworthy. A tyre fitting business has offered to fit four new tyres on the car for £400.

The garage paid £9,000 to buy the car. Without the new tyres it could be sold for an estimated £10,500. What is the minimum price at which the garage should sell the car with new tyres?

The minimum price is the amount required to cover all the relevant costs. At this price, the benefits will exactly equal the costs and so neither a profit nor loss is made. Any price that is lower than this amount will mean the wealth of the business is reduced. In this case, the minimum price is:

	£
Opportunity cost of the car	10,500
Cost of the new tyres	400
Total	10,900

The original cost of the car is irrelevant for reasons already discussed. It is the opportunity cost of the car that concerns us. In this case, it is the sales value forgone. If the new tyres are purchased, the garage will have to pay £400; but will pay nothing if they are not. The £400 is, therefore, a relevant cost as it is a future cost that varies with the decision.

It should be emphasised that the garage will not try to sell the car with its new tyres for £10,900; it will try to get as much as possible for it. Any price above the £10,900, however, will make the garage better off than would be the case if it did not buy the new tyres.

Real World 8.2 discusses the opportunity cost of two countries building separate oil pipelines rather than cooperating in a joint venture.

Real World 8.2

Benefits foregone

Tullow Oil Plc, which has oil discoveries in Uganda and Kenya, sees an opportunity cost if the two countries don't collaborate on a pipeline to ship their crude to the Indian Ocean, a company official said.

Landlocked Uganda is deciding on whether the pipeline will traverse northern Kenya's desert to a proposed port at Lamu, or south past Lake Victoria to Tanga on Tanzania's coast. While Tullow, which discovered Uganda's oil, has a seat at the talks, the pipeline decision is "above our pay grade," Tim O'Hanlon, the London-based company's vice president for African business, said in an interview.

"For us we think of it as an East African integrated regional infrastructure and the opportunity cost of Uganda and Kenya not cooperating on the pipeline is enormous," he said Wednesday in Tanzania's commercial capital, Dar es Salaam. "A joint pipeline has real tangible economic value, measurable value for individual countries Uganda and Kenya, and East Africa in general."

Tanzanian President John Magufuli said earlier this month he'd agreed with his Ugandan counterpart, Yoweri Museveni, to route the conduit via his country at a cost of about

$4 billion, with Total SA helping fund the project. Nagoya, Japan-based Toyota Tsusho Corp. estimates the Kenyan route may cost about $5 billion.

Separate Pipelines

A Ugandan decision to route the pipeline through Tanzania would probably mean Kenya would need its own facility to transport its oil, according to O'Hanlon. "We are talking about two separate pipelines or a joint pipeline through Kenya," he said.

Tullow along with Total SA and the China National Offshore Oil Corp. are developing Uganda's oil fields in the western region of Hoima. The Chinese company was awarded its production license in 2013, the only one so far issued by Uganda's government.

O'Hanlon said Tullow expects its first production in Uganda about three or four years after the company makes its final investment decision in 2017, and that it will be awarded production licenses in the next few weeks.

"It's taken time but it's going fine and it's of course one of the key issues that we have to have in place before we march into production," he said. To contact the reporter on this story:

Joseph Burite in Dar es Salaam at jburite@bloomberg.net
To contact the editors responsible for this story:
Paul Richardson at pmrichardson@bloomberg.net
Michael Gunn

Source: Direct Extract from Burite, J.,(2016) *Tullow Sees Opportunity Cost If Kenya-Uganda Pipeline Plan Fails*, www.bloomberg.com, 30 March.

Irrelevant costs: sunk costs and committed costs

A **sunk cost** is simply another way of referring to a past cost and so the terms 'sunk cost' and 'past cost' can be used interchangeably. A **committed cost** arises where an irrevocable decision has been made to incur the cost. This is often because a business has entered into a legally-binding contract. A committed cost is effectively the same as a past cost, despite the fact that payment may not be due until some point in the future. Since the business must eventually pay, the cost will not vary with the decision. Thus, as with a past cost, a committed cost can never be a relevant cost for decision-making purposes.

Activity 8.4

Past costs are irrelevant costs. Does this mean that what happened in the past is irrelevant?

No, it does not mean this. The fact that the business has an asset that it can deploy in the future is highly relevant. What is not relevant is how much it cost to acquire that asset. This point was examined in the discussion that followed Activity 8.1.

Another reason why the past is not irrelevant is that it generally – though not always – provides us with our best guide to the future. Suppose that we need to estimate the cost of doing something in the future to help us to decide whether it is worth doing. In these circumstances, our own experience, or that of others, on how much it has cost to do the thing in the past may provide us with a valuable guide to how much it is likely to cost in the future.

Real World 8.3 provides extracts from a *Financial Times* article that deals with the possible disposal by the UK government of its stake in a bank that came close to collapse during the recent recession and had to be rescued. It points out that what the government paid for its shares in the bank is a sunk cost and, therefore, an irrelevant one.

Real World 8.3

Bank transfer

Royal Bank of Scotland and George Osborne, the UK chancellor, are both eager to see the back of the other. RBS has declared that it should be healthy enough by next year for the government to start selling off its 81 per cent, and Mr Osborne has privately mooted a similar notion.

Last week, RBS displayed some encouraging signs of progress. For a long time, it seemed in such a dire state that it needed either to be fully nationalised, or split into good and bad banks and recapitalised by the taxpayer. Those risks, if not eliminated, have been reduced.

This does not mean the bank and its major shareholder can take a victory lap. RBS still has plenty of work to do, and concerns linger about whether it has fully acknowledged its bad loans. Its shares suffered when it announced its first-quarter results, revealing the rapid contraction of its investment arm.

The government must consider two factors before privatisation. The first is what price it can achieve, and whether it will match the book value paid by the Labour government in 2008. It need not get too hung up on the purchase price because that is a sunk cost. But neither should it be so enthusiastic to sell that it fails to get the best return for taxpayers.

FT *Source*: Extracts from the FT editorial, UK taxpayer will lose in rush to exit, ft.com, 5 May 2013. © The Financial Times Limited 2013. All Rights Reserved.

Sunk cost fallacy

Although we should ignore past costs when considering future courses of action, this is often easier said than done. It seems that we often display an irrational commitment to past costs. We persist in continuing along a particular path because of our previous investment of time, effort or money. The end result is often to make poor decisions about the future direction. Managers can be as guilty of this kind of behaviour as anyone else.

In behavioural economics, the refusal to abandon an attachment to an irrecoverable investment is known as the **sunk cost fallacy**. Various reasons have been suggested as to why we act in this way. In **Real World 8.4** we consider some of these.

Real World 8.4

Clinging to the past

Perhaps you have said, or heard, the following sort of comments:

'I might as well finish this book. It's not very good but I've paid for it and now I'm more than half was through.'

'I can't throw out these shoes. They are almost new and, although they hurt my feet, I paid a fortune for them'

'I really don't want to buy the car any more. However, I paid the dealer a non-refundable deposit and so I suppose I should go ahead.'

'I hate my job as an accountant but I've invested too many years of my life to achieve the qualifications just to throw it all away.'

These sort of comments show an attachment to past decisions rather than a concern for the future. They are irrational because costs previously incurred are not a good guide to maximising future utility. The investment of time, money or other resources should not be determined by what has already been spent.

Why do we do this? It may be because we suffer from *loss aversion*, which is a strong dislike of wasting resources. This is a strong negative emotion: the greater the amount wasted, the greater the suffering. The pain of incurring losses is usually much greater than the pleasure achieved by making equivalent gains. We may, therefore, stick with the book or the job in the hope that things improve in the future.

To abandon an investment may lead to feelings of regret and failure, which we may seek to avoid. It may also attract criticism. We may be blamed for giving up too easily or for making the original investment. This can make it difficult to own up to our poor decisions.. Finally we may not be able to see clearly the options available by not sticking with the investment. However, new opportunities may come into view once we have abandoned the sunk cost.

An example of the sunk cost fallacy in business occurred when the British and French governments agreed to develop the Concorde – a supersonic passenger jet. This turned out to be a very bad investment. Development costs were much higher than expected and it became clear, before the project was completed, that it would not be financially viable. Nevertheless, both governments decided to press ahead and complete the project rather than admit failure and write off the investment cost. Many believe that the decision to continue was largely determined by the costs already incurred. The Concorde was in operation from 1976 to 2003.

Source: Based on information in Leahy, R. (2014) *Letting go of sunk costs*, www.psychologytoday.com, 24 September and J. Blasingame (2011) *Beware of the Concorde fallacy*, www.forbes.com, 15 September.

Determining the relevant cost of labour and materials

Having set out the broad principles of what constitutes a relevant cost, let us now consider two key elements that go to make up the cost of a product or service – labour and materials. Determining the relevant costs of each can be quite tricky. This is because, in practice, they will vary according to the particular circumstances. By keeping in mind the principles just discussed, however, we should be able to separate the relevant costs arising from a course of action from any irrelevant costs.

Labour

The relevant cost of labour will vary according to whether the business is operating with spare capacity or whether it is operating at full capacity. In Activity 8.5, we consider the situation where a business has temporary spare capacity but does not intend to lay off its workers.

Activity 8.5

Assume the same information set out in Activity 8.3. Further assume, however, that the car also needs a replacement engine before it can be driven. It is possible to buy a reconditioned engine for £1,200, which would take seven hours to fit by a mechanic who is paid £15 an hour. The garage is currently short of work, but the owners are reluctant to lay off any mechanics or even to cut down their basic working week. This is because skilled mechanics are difficult to find and an upturn in demand for their skills is expected soon.

What is the minimum price at which the garage should sell the car with a reconditioned engine and with new tyres fitted?

Again, the minimum price is the amount required to cover the relevant costs of the job. This minimum price will now be as follows:

	£
Opportunity cost of the car	10,500
Cost of new tyres	400
Cost of the reconditioned engine	1,200
Total	12,100

The cost of the new engine is a relevant cost for the same reason as the cost of new tyres: it is a future cost that varies with the decision. If the garage decides against fitting the engine, this cost will not be incurred. The cost of labour, on the other hand, is an irrelevant cost because it does not vary with the decision. As the mechanic will still be employed even though there is no work, the garage will incur the same cost whether or not the mechanic undertakes the engine-replacement job. If this job is not undertaken, the mechanic will be paid to do nothing. The additional labour cost for this job is, therefore, zero.

Where the business is working at full capacity the relevant cost of labour will depend on whether additional workers are employed to undertake the task or whether workers currently spending time on another task are redeployed. Let us first consider the situation where additional workers are employed to carry out a specified task.

Activity 8.6

Assume exactly the same circumstances as in Activity 8.5, except that the garage is currently working at full capacity. It is possible, however, to employ a recently-retired mechanic, on a casual basis, to fit the engine. The mechanic will be employed for seven hours and will be paid £15 an hour.

What is the minimum price at which the garage should sell the car, with a reconditioned engine fitted and new tyres, under these altered circumstances?

The minimum price is:

	£
Opportunity cost of the car	10,500
Cost of new tyres	400
Cost of mechanic (7 × £15)	105
Cost of the reconditioned engine	1,200
Total	12,205

The opportunity cost of the car, the cost of the new tyres and the cost of the reconditioned engine are the same as in Activity 8.5. However, a charge for labour has now been added to obtain the minimum price. This is because it is now a future cost that varies with the decision. If the garage decides against fitting the engine, the mechanic will not be hired.

If overtime payments are made to existing workers to fit the engine, a similar situation to hiring a mechanic on a casual basis would arise. The overtime payments would be regarded as a relevant cost as they would vary with the decision.

Where a business is working at full capacity, it may be possible to redeploy the existing workforce in order to carry out a new task. This will mean that an opportunity cost is normally incurred as workers will be taken away from other revenue-generating tasks. Activity 8.7 below considers this scenario.

Activity 8.7

Assume exactly the same circumstances as in Activity 8.6, except that the garage redeploys a mechanic to carry out the engine-replacement job. This means that other work, which the mechanic would have done during the seven hours, will not be undertaken. This other work could have been charged to a customer at the rate of £60 an hour. The mechanic, however, is only paid £15 an hour.

What is the minimum price at which the garage should sell the car, with new tyres and a reconditioned engine fitted, under these circumstances?

The minimum price is:

	£
Opportunity cost of the car	10,500
Cost of new tyres	400
Opportunity cost of mechanic (7 × £60)	420
Cost of the reconditioned engine	1,200
Total	12,520

The opportunity cost of the car, the cost of the new tyres and the cost of the reconditioned engine are the same as in Activity 8.6. However, the opportunity cost of labour is now different. It is the amount sacrificed in making time available to undertake the engine-replacement job. While the mechanic is working on this job, the opportunity to do other work, for which customers would pay £420, is lost.

Note that the £15 an hour mechanic's wage is still not relevant. The mechanic will be paid £15 an hour irrespective of whether it is the engine-replacement work or some other job that is undertaken.

The points made above concerning the relevant cost of labour are summarised in Figure 8.2.

| Figure 8.2 | A decision flow diagram for identifying the relevant cost of labour |

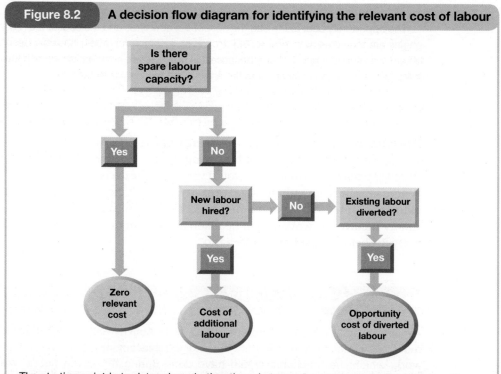

The starting point is to determine whether there is temporary spare capacity. In these circumstances, the relevant cost of labour is usually zero. Relevant labour costs often only arise where the business is operating at full capacity.

Materials

The relevant cost of materials will vary according to whether the materials are held in inventories and whether there is an intention to replace them. In Activity 8.8, the materials required for a particular job are already held in inventories, but not all need to be replaced. When attempting this activity, keep firmly in mind the principles discussed earlier.

Activity 8.8

A business is considering making a bid to undertake a contract. The contract will require the use of two types of raw material – A1 and B2. Quantities of both of these materials are held by the business. If it chose to do so, the business could sell the raw materials in their present state. All of the inventories of these two raw materials will need to be used on the contract. Information on the raw materials concerned is as follows:

Inventories item	Quantity (units)	Historic cost (£/unit)	Sales value (£/unit)	Current purchase cost (£/unit)
A1	500	5	3	6
B2	800	7	8	10

Inventories item A1 is in frequent use in the business on a variety of work.

The inventories of item B2 were bought a year ago for a contract that was abandoned. It has recently become obvious that there is no likelihood of ever using this raw material unless the contract currently being considered proceeds.

Management wishes to deduce the minimum price at which the business could undertake the contract without reducing its wealth as a result (that is, the price at which the costs are exactly equal to the benefits). This can be used as the baseline in deducing the bid price.

How much should be included in the minimum price in respect of the two inventories items detailed above?

The minimum price must cover the relevant costs. The costs to be covered by the minimum price are:

Inventories item	
A1	£6 × 500 = £3,000
B2	£8 × 800 = £6,400

We are told that the item A1 is in frequent use and so, if it is used on the contract, it will need to be replaced. The business will, therefore, have to buy 500 units additional to those which would have been required had the contract not been undertaken. The purchase cost of the materials is £6 per unit and so the relevant cost is 500 × £6.

Item B2 will never be used by the business unless the contract is undertaken. This means that if the contract is not undertaken, the only reasonable thing for the business to do is to sell the B2. If, however, the contract is undertaken and the B2 is used, it will have an opportunity cost equal to the potential proceeds from disposal, which is £8 a unit. In other words, the relevant cost will be the sales value of item B2 that has been forgone.

Note that the historic cost information about both materials is irrelevant. This will always be the case as it represents a sunk cost.

Where an item of materials is not held in inventories, it will have to be purchased specifically for the job. In this case, therefore, the purchase cost of the materials will be the relevant cost. It is a future cost that will vary with the decision.

Now have a go at Activity 8.9, which is a little more difficult than the previous activity.

Activity 8.9

HLA Ltd is in the process of preparing a quotation for a special job for a customer. The job will have the following material requirements:

Material	Units required	Units currently held in inventories			Current purchase cost (£/unit)
		Quantity held (units)	Historic cost (£/unit)	Sales value (£/unit)	
P	400	0	–	–	40
Q	230	100	62	50	64
R	350	200	48	23	59
S	170	140	33	12	49
T	120	120	40	0	68

→

Material Q is used consistently by the business on various jobs.

The business holds materials R, S and T as the result of previous overbuying. No other use (apart from this special job) can be found for R, but the 140 units of S could be used in another job as a substitute for 225 units of material V that are about to be purchased at a price of £10 a unit. Material T has no other use, it is a dangerous material that is difficult to store and the business has been informed that it will cost £160 to dispose of the material currently held.

If it chose to, the business could sell the raw materials Q, R and S already held in their present state.

What is the relevant cost of the materials for the job specified above?

The relevant cost is as follows:

	£
Material P	
This will have to be purchased at £40 a unit (400 × £40)	16,000
Material Q	
Those units already held will have to be replaced and the remaining 130 units will have to be purchased, therefore the relevant cost is (230 × £64)	14,720
Material R	
200 units of this are held and these could be sold. The relevant cost of these is the sales value forgone (200 × £23)	4,600
The remaining 150 units of R would have to be purchased (150 × £59)	8,850
Material S	
This could be sold or used as a substitute for material V.	
The existing inventories could be sold for £1,680 (that is, 140 × £12); however, the saving on material V is higher. This higher figure must be taken as the opportunity cost (225 × £10)	2,250
The remaining units of material S must be purchased (30 × £49)	1,470
Material T	
A saving on disposal will be made if material T is used	(160)
Total relevant cost	47,730

The points made above concerning the relevant cost of materials are summarised in Figure 8.3.

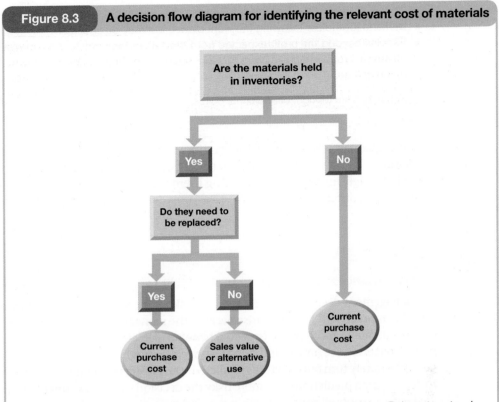

Figure 8.3   A decision flow diagram for identifying the relevant cost of materials

The starting point is to determine whether the materials are held inventories. Relevant costs arise where inventories have to be replaced or where there is an opportunity cost involved in their use. Where materials are not held in inventories, the cost of purchasing them is the relevant cost.

Non-measurable costs and benefits

It was mentioned at the beginning of the chapter that certain costs and benefits might defy measurement in monetary terms. These costs and benefits often have a broader, but less immediate, impact on the business. Ultimately, however, they are likely to affect the ability of a business to achieve its objectives.

Activity 8.10

Activities 8.5 to 8.7 were concerned with the cost of putting a car into a marketable condition. Apart from the quantifiable items mentioned, are there other costs or benefits that are difficult to quantify, but which should, nevertheless, be taken into account in making a decision as to whether to do the work?

We can think of four:

- Turning away another job in order to do the engine replacement may result in customer dissatisfaction.
- The quality of workmanship may be lower where casual labour is employed, which could damage the reputation of the business.

- Demand for the car following the work carried out may be uncertain.
- Benefits beyond the profit expected from the sale of the particular car may accrue. By offering a broader range of cars for sale, more car-buying customers may be attracted to the garage.

  You may have thought of additional points.

These 'qualitative' costs and benefits should provide a further input to the final plans or decisions. To include these costs and benefits, managers must rely on judgement when attaching weightings to them. By taking them into account, however, the final picture may be quite different compared to that provided by only the quantifiable costs and benefits.

Risk

All management decisions involve **risk.** By risk we mean the chance that things will not turn out as predicted. This may arise because the manager failed to identify, or incorrectly estimated, one or more of the expected benefits or costs. As decision making, by its very nature, relates to the future, and since managers do not have perfect powers of prediction, outcomes rarely turn out exactly as predicted. The greater the potential for actual outcomes to deviate from predictions, the more risky the decision. Some assessment of the risk associated with a proposed course of action is a vital ingredient for management decisions.

Activity 8.11 considers some of the risks that could arise from a particular decision.

Activity 8.11

Look back at Activity 8.9 (page 309). Suppose that on the basis of the estimated relevant material cost the special job went ahead. Try to think of at least three ways in which the estimated cost could prove incorrect and thereby have an adverse effect on any profit estimated from the contract.

We can think of several, including the possibility that:

- The quantity of each of the five materials required for the job (for example, 400 units of Material P) may prove to be underestimated.
- The current purchase (replacement) costs of Materials P, Q, R and S may prove to be underestimated.
- The saving on the disposal cost of Material T may prove to be overestimated.
- The current purchase (replacement) cost of Material V may prove to be overestimated.
- The sales value of Materials R and S may prove to be underestimated.

When considering HLA Ltd's decision whether to undertake the 'special job', the benefit (the price negotiated for the job) and the estimated costs should be carefully weighed. There should also be an assessment of the likelihood that and extent to which the final outcomes do not turn out as expected. Where a net financial benefit is predicted, this must be weighed against the risks that the actual benefit is lower, and/or costs higher, than expected.

There are various approaches to dealing with risk. We shall now consider one of the most popular of these.

Sensitivity analysis

Sensitivity analysis involves an examination of the key input factors affecting a management decision to see how changes in each input might influence its viability.

The starting point is to assess a project using the best available estimates for each of the key inputs to the decision (for example, sales revenue, labour cost, material cost and so on). Assuming that the outcome is positive, the estimate used for each input factor is then examined to see by how much it could change before the project becomes no longer viable for that reason alone.

Suppose that a project to make a product, which requires the purchase of a new machine, is estimated to provide a net financial benefit for a business. To carry out a sensitivity analysis on this project, we should consider each of the key input factors in turn. These factors may include:

- initial outlay for the machine;
- sales volume and selling price;
- relevant operating costs;
- life of the project; and
- the cost of financing the project.

For each input factor, we calculate the value that it could have before the financial outcome becomes negative (that is, the value at which the overall net benefit to the business is zero). The difference between the value for each factor at which the net financial benefit equals zero and its estimated value represents the 'margin of safety' for that factor. The factors affecting the sensitivity of a particular project analysis are set out in Figure 8.4.

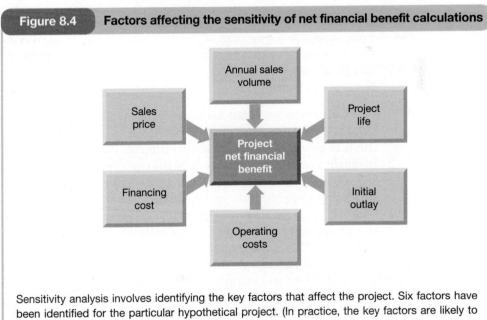

| Figure 8.4 | Factors affecting the sensitivity of net financial benefit calculations |

Sensitivity analysis involves identifying the key factors that affect the project. Six factors have been identified for the particular hypothetical project. (In practice, the key factors are likely to vary between projects.) Once identified, each factor will be examined in turn to find the value it should have for the project to have a zero net financial benefit.

As a result of carrying out a sensitivity analysis, managers are able to gain a 'feel' for the project, which otherwise might not be possible. A computer spreadsheet model of the project can be very helpful in carrying out sensitivity analysis. It then becomes easy to try various values for the input factors in order to see the effect of each.

Example 8.1 provides an illustration of a sensitivity analysis. It is straightforward enough to be undertaken without recourse to a spreadsheet model.

Example 8.1

S. Saluja (Property Developers) Ltd intends to bid at an auction, to be held today, for a large house that has fallen into disrepair. The auctioneer believes that the house will be sold for about £500,000. The business wishes to renovate the property and to divide it into nine studio apartments, to be sold for £150,000 each. The renovation will cost £800,000. There is some uncertainty over all of the input values.

To simplify matters, we shall ignore the cost of financing this project.

(a) What is the net financial benefit of the proposed project to the business?
(b) Assuming that none of the other inputs deviates from the best estimates provided:
  1 What auction price would have to be paid for the house to cause the project to have a zero net financial benefit?
  2 What renovation cost would cause the project to have a zero net financial benefit?
  3 What is the sale price of each of the apartments that would cause the project to have a zero net financial benefit?
(c) Comment on the values obtained in answering (b).

The answers to these questions are as follows:

(a) The net financial benefit of the proposed project:

	£
Sales revenue (9 × £150,000)	1,350,000
Cost of house	(500,000)
Cost of renovation	(800,000)
Net financial benefit	50,000

(b) 1 To obtain a zero net financial benefit, the auction price would have to be £50,000 higher than the current estimate – that is, a total price of £550,000. This is 10 per cent above the current estimated price.
  2 To obtain a zero net financial benefit, the cost of renovation would have to be £50,000 higher than the current estimate – that is, a total price of £850,000. This is about 6 per cent above the current estimated price.
  3 To obtain a zero net financial benefit, the selling price would have to be a total of £50,000 lower than the current estimate – that is, total revenue of £1,300,000. This is about 4 per cent below the current estimated price.
(c) These calculations indicate that the auction price would have to be about 10 per cent above the estimated price before a zero net financial benefit arises. The margin of safety is, therefore, not very high for this factor. In practice, this should not represent a real risk because the business could withdraw from the bidding if the price rises to an unacceptable level.

The other two factors represent more real risks.

Only after the project is at a very late stage can the business be sure as to what the actual price per apartment will be. It would be unusual to be able to have fixed contracts for sale of all of the apartments before the auction. The calculations show that the price of the apartments would have to fall only by about 4 per cent from the estimated price before the net financial benefit is reduced to zero. Hence, the margin of safety for this factor is very small.

Similarly, success of the project is quite sensitive to the cost of renovation: a 6 per cent increase in this factor would cause the project to be financially unsuccessful. It might be possible for the developer to enter into a binding, fixed-price contract (subject to the developer buying the house) with a suitable builder before the auction. This may be difficult to achieve, however.

It seems from the calculations that the sale price of the apartments and the renovation cost are the key sensitive factors to consider. A careful re-examination of these two factors seems appropriate before a final decision is made.

Note that, in the interests of simplicity, this example ignored the cost of financing the project. In practice, this is normally important and needs to be included. In Chapter 14, It we shall consider, in detail, how this cost is included in the decision-making process.

A slightly different form of sensitivity analysis from that just described is to pose a series of 'what if?' questions. This can help to see how possible changes to each input factor will affect the viability of the project. When considering sales, for example, the following 'what if?' questions may be asked:

- What if sales volume is 5 per cent higher than expected?
- What if sales volume is 10 per cent lower than expected?
- What if sales price is reduced by 15 per cent?
- What if sales price could be increased by 20 per cent?

While this form of sensitivity analysis also examines the effect of changes in each key factor, it does not seek to find the point at which a change makes the project no longer viable.

There are three major drawbacks with the use of sensitivity analysis:

- It does not give managers clear decision rules concerning acceptance or rejection of the project and so they must rely on their own judgement.
- It does not provide any indication of the likelihood that a particular change to an input factor will actually occur.
- It is a static form of analysis. Only one input is considered at a time, while the rest are held constant. In practice, however, it is likely that more than one input value will differ from the best estimates provided. Even so, it would be possible to deal with changes in various inputs simultaneously, were the project data put onto a spreadsheet model. This approach, where more than one variable is altered at a time, is known as **scenario building.**

Self-assessment question 8.1

JB Limited is a small specialist manufacturer of electronic components. Makers of aircraft, for both civil and military purposes, use much of its output. One of the aircraft makers has offered a contract to JB Limited for the supply, over the next 12 months, of 400 identical components. The data relating to the production of each component are as follows:

● *Material requirements:*
   3 kg of Material M1 (see note 1 below)
   2 kg of Material P2 (see note 2 below)
   1 bought-in component (part number 678) (see note 3 below)

Note 1:   Material M1 is in continuous use by the business; 1,000 kg are currently held by the business. The original cost was £4.70/kg, but it is known that future purchases will cost £5.50/kg.

Note 2:   1,200 kg of Material P2 are currently held. The original cost of this material was £4.30/kg. The material has not been required for the last two years. Its scrap value is £1.50/kg. The only foreseeable alternative use is as a substitute for Material P4 (in constant use) but this would involve further processing costs of £1.60/kg. The current cost of Material P4 is £3.60/kg.

Note 3:   It is estimated that the component (part number 678) could be bought in for £50 each.

● *Labour requirements*: each component would require five hours of skilled labour and five hours of semi-skilled. A skilled employee is available and is currently paid £14/hour. A replacement would, however, have to be obtained at a rate of £12/hour for the work that would otherwise be done by the skilled employee. The current rate for semi-skilled work is £10/hour and an additional employee could be appointed for this work.

● *General manufacturing costs*: It is JB Limited's policy to charge a share of the general costs (rent, heating and so on) to each contract undertaken at the rate of £20 for each machine hour used on the contract. If the contract is undertaken, the general costs are expected to increase as a result of undertaking the contract by £3,200.

Spare machine capacity is available and each component would require four machine hours. A price of £200 a component has been offered by the potential customer.

Required:

(a) Should the contract be accepted? Support your conclusion with appropriate figures to present to management.

(b) How sensitive is the successful financial outcome of this contract to:
   1   the price of Material M1; and
   2   the skilled labour rate (in each case taken alone and assuming that all other inputs turn out as projected)?

(c) What other factors ought management to consider that might influence the decision?

The solution to this question can be found at the back of the book on p. 774.

Summary

The main points in this chapter may be summarised as follows:

Cost–benefit analysis

- Involves a careful weighing of the costs and benefits of plans and decisions.
- To be worthwhile, benefits should exceed the associated costs.
- Not all costs and benefits can be measured in monetary terms.

Relevant and irrelevant costs

- Relevant costs must:
    - relate to the objective being pursued by the business;
    - be future costs; and
    - vary with the decision.
- Relevant costs therefore include:
    - opportunity costs; and
    - differential future outlay costs.
- Irrelevant costs therefore include:
    - all past (or sunk) costs;
    - all committed costs; and
    - non-differential future outlay costs.

Relevant cost of labour and materials

- The relevant cost of labour will vary according to whether the business is operating with spare capacity or is operating at full capacity.
- The relevant cost of materials will vary according to whether the materials are held in inventories and whether they need to be replaced.

Non-measureable costs and benefits

- Should provide an input to the final plans or decisions.
- Managers must rely on judgement when applying weights to these items.

Dealing with risk

- All decision-making involves risk: that is the likelihood that what was projected may not actually occur.
- Sensitivity analysis is an assessment, taking each input factor in turn, of how much each one can vary from estimate before a project is not viable.
- It provides useful insights to projects.
- It suffers from the following weaknesses:
    - It does not give a clear decision rule.
    - It does not indicate the likelihood of changes to an input factor actually occurring.
    - It can be rather static, but scenario building solves this problem.

Key terms

For definitions of these terms, see Appendix B.

benefit *p. 298*	**outlay cost** *p. 300*
cost *p. 298*	**sunk cost** *p. 303*
cost–benefit analysis *p. 298*	**committed cost** *p. 303*
opportunity cost *p. 299*	**sunk cost fallacy** *p. 304*
historic cost *p. 299*	**risk** *p. 312*
relevant cost *p. 300*	**sensitivity analysis** *p. 313*
irrelevant cost *p. 300*	**scenario building** *p. 315*
past cost *p. 300*	

Further reading

If you would like to explore the topics covered in this chapter in more depth, we recommend the following:

Bhimani, A., Horngren, C., Datar, S. and Rajan, M. (2015) *Management and Cost Accounting,* 6th edn, Pearson, Chapter 10.

Datar, S. and Rajan, M. (2017) *Horngren's Cost Accounting: A Managerial Emphasis,* 16th edn, Pearson, Chapter 11.

Drury, C. (2015) *Management and Cost Accounting,* 9th edn, Cengage Learning, Chapters 9 and 12.

Hilton, R. and Platt, D. (2014) *Managerial Accounting,* 10th edn, McGraw-Hill Higher Education, Chapter 14.

Review questions

Solutions to these questions can be found at the back of the book on p. 792.

8.1 To be relevant to a particular decision, a cost must have three attributes. What are they?

8.2 Distinguish between a sunk cost and an opportunity cost.

8.3 What is meant by the expression 'committed cost'? How do committed costs arise?

8.4 Following a sensitivity analysis, it appears that the success of Project X depends on the actual cost of raw materials not exceeding 10 per cent of their projected cost. It also depends on the actual sales volume not being less than 10 per cent of the projected sales volume. Does this mean that raw material cost and sales volume represent areas of equal risk for Project X?

Exercises

Solutions to exercises with **coloured numbers** can be found at the back of the book on pp. 816–818.

Basic-level exercises

8.1 Lombard Ltd has been offered a contract for which there is available production capacity. The contract is for 20,000 identical items, manufactured by an intricate assembly operation, to be produced and delivered in the next few months at a price of £80 each. The specification for one item is as follows:

Assembly labour	4 hours
Component X	4 units
Component y	3 units

There would also be the need to hire equipment, for the duration of the contract, at an outlay cost of £200,000.

The assembly is a highly skilled operation and the workforce is currently underutilised. It is the business's policy to retain this workforce on full pay in anticipation of high demand next year, for a new product currently being developed. There is sufficient available skilled labour to undertake the contract now under consideration. Skilled workers are paid £15 an hour.

Component X is used in a number of other sub-assemblies produced by the business. It is readily available. 50,000 units of Component X are currently held in inventories. Component Y was a special purchase in anticipation of an order that did not in the end materialise. It is, therefore, surplus to requirements and the 100,000 units that are currently held may have to be sold at a loss. An estimate of various values for Components X and Y provided by the materials planning department is as follows:

Component	*X*	*Y*
	£/unit	*£/unit*
Historic cost	4	10
Replacement cost	5	11
Net realisable value	3	8

It is estimated that any additional relevant costs associated with the contract (beyond the above) will amount to £8 an item.

Required:
Analyse the information and advise Lombard Ltd on the desirability of the contract.

8.2 Andrews and Co. Ltd has been invited to tender for a contract. It is to produce 10,000 metres of an electrical cable in which the business specialises. The estimating department of the business has produced the following information relating to the contract:

- *Materials:* The cable will require a steel core, which the business buys in. The steel core is to be coated with a special plastic, also bought in, using a special process. Plastic for the covering will be required at the rate of 0.10 kg/metre of completed cable.
- *Direct labour:*

Skilled:	10 minutes/metre
Unskilled:	5 minutes/metre

The business already holds sufficient of each of the materials required to complete the contract. Information on the cost of the inventories is as follows:

	Steel core £/metre	Plastic £/kg
Historic cost	1.50	0.60
Current buying-in cost	2.10	0.70
Scrap value	1.40	0.10

The steel core is in constant use by the business for a variety of work that it regularly undertakes. The plastic is a surplus from a previous contract where a mistake was made and an excess quantity ordered. If the current contract does not go ahead, this plastic will be scrapped.

Unskilled labour, which is paid at the rate of £7.50 an hour, will need to be taken on specifially to undertake the contract. The business is fairly quiet at the moment which means that a pool of skilled labour exists that will still be employed at full pay of £12 an hour to do nothing if the contract does not proceed. The pool of skilled labour is sufficient to complete the contract.

Required:

Indicate the minimum price at which the contract could be undertaken, such that the business would be neither better nor worse off as a result of doing it.

Intermediate-level exercises

8.3 SJ Services Ltd has been asked to quote a price for a special contract to render a service that will take the business one week to complete. Information relating to labour for the contract is as follows:

Grade of labour	Hours required	Basic rate/hour
Skilled	27	£24
Semi-skilled	14	£18
Unskilled	20	£14

A shortage of skilled labour means that the necessary staff to undertake the contract would have to be moved from other work that is currently yielding an excess of sales revenue over labour and other costs of £8 an hour.

Semi-skilled labour is currently being paid at semi-skilled rates to undertake unskilled work. If the relevant members of staff are moved to work on the contract, unskilled labour will have to be employed for the week to replace them.

The unskilled labour actually needed to work on the contract will be specifically employed for the week of the contract.

All labour is charged to contracts at 50 per cent above the rate paid to the employees, so as to cover the contract's fair share of the business's general costs (rent, heating and so on). It is estimated that these general costs will increase by £250 as a result of undertaking the contract.

Undertaking the contract will require the use of a specialised machine for the week. This machine is currently being hired out to another business at a weekly rental of £175 on a week-by-week contract.

To derive the above estimates, the business has had to spend £800 on a specialised study. If the contract does not proceed, the results of the study can be sold for £600.

An estimate of the contract's fair share of the business's rent is £350 a week.

Required:

Deduce the minimum price at which SJ Services Ltd could undertake the contract such that it would be neither better nor worse off as a result of undertaking it.

8.4   A business in the food industry is currently holding 2,000 tonnes of material in bulk storage. This material deteriorates with time. In the near future, it will, therefore, be necessary for it to be repackaged for sale or sold in its present form.

The material was acquired in two batches: 800 tonnes at a price of £40 a tonne and 1,200 tonnes at a price of £44 a tonne. The current market price of any additional purchases is £48 a tonne. If the business were to dispose of the material, in its present state, it could sell any quantity but for only £36 a tonne; it does not have the contacts or reputation to command a higher price.

Processing this material may be undertaken to develop either Product A or Product X. No weight loss occurs with the processing, that is, 1 tonne of the material will make 1 tonne of A or X. For Product A, there is an additional cost of £60 a tonne, after which it will sell for £105 a tonne. The marketing department estimates that a maximum of 500 tonnes could be sold in this way.

With Product X, the business incurs additional costs of £80 a tonne for processing. A market price for X is not known and no minimum price has been agreed. The management is currently engaged in discussions over the minimum price that may be charged for Product X in the current circumstances. Management wants to know the relevant cost per tonne for Product X so as to provide a basis for negotiating a profitable selling price for the product.

Required:
Identify the relevant cost per tonne for Product X, given sales volumes of X of:

(a)   up to 1,500 tonnes
(b)   over 1,500 tonnes, up to 2,000 tonnes
(c)   over 2,000 tonnes.

Explain your answer.

Advanced-level exercises

8.5   A local education authority is faced with a predicted decline in the demand for school places in its area. It is believed that some schools will have to close in order to remove up to 800 places from current capacity levels. The schools that may face closure are referenced as A, B, C and D. Their details are as follows:

- *School A* (capacity 200) was built 15 years ago at a cost of £1.2 million. It is situated in a 'socially disadvantaged' community area. The authority has been offered £14 million for the site by a property developer.
- *School B* (capacity 500) was built 20 years ago and cost £1 million. It was renovated only two years ago at a cost of £3 million to improve its facilities. An offer of £8 million has been made for the site by a business planning a shopping complex in this affluent part of the area.
- *School C* (capacity 600) cost £5 million to build five years ago. The land for this school is rented from a local business for an annual cost of £300,000. The land rented for School C is based on a 100-year lease. If the school closes, the property reverts immediately to the owner. If School C is not closed, it will require a £3 million investment to improve safety at the school.
- *School D* (800 capacity) cost £7 million to build eight years ago; last year £1.5 million was spent on an extension. It has a considerable amount of grounds, which is currently used for sporting events. This factor makes it attractive to developers, who have recently offered £9 million for the site. If School D is closed, it will be necessary to pay £1.8 million to adapt facilities at other schools to accommodate the change.

In its accounting system, the local authority depreciates non-current assets based on 2 per cent a year on the original cost. It also differentiates between one-off, large items of capital expenditure or revenue, on the one hand, and annually recurring items, on the other.

The local authority has a central staff, which includes administrators for each school costing £200,000 a year for each school, and a chief education officer costing £80,000 a year in total.

Required:

(a) Prepare a summary of the relevant cash flows (costs and revenues, relative to not making any closures) under the following options:

1 closure of D only
2 closure of A and B
3 closure of A and C.

Show separately the one-off effects and annually recurring items, rank the options open to the local authority and, briefly, interpret your answer. *Note:* Various approaches are acceptable provided that they are logical.

(b) Identify and comment on any two different types of irrelevant cost contained in the information given in the question.

(c) Discuss other factors that might have a bearing on the decision.

8.6 Rob Otics Ltd, a small business that specialises in manufacturing electronic-control equipment, has just received an inquiry from a potential customer for eight identical robotic units. These would be made using Rob Otics's own labour force and factory capacity. The product specification prepared by the estimating department shows the following:

Material and labour requirements for each robotic unit:

Component X	2 per unit
Component Y	1 per unit
Component Z	4 per unit
Assembly labour	25 hours per unit (but see below)
Inspection labour	6 hours per unit

As part of the costing exercise, the business has collected the following information:

- *Component X.* This item is normally held by the business as it is in constant demand. There are 10 units currently held which were bought for £150 a unit. The sole supplier of Component X has announced a price rise of 20 per cent, effective immediately, for any further supplies. Rob Otics has not yet paid for the items currently held.
- *Component Y.* 25 units are currently held. This component is not normally used by Rob Otics, but the units currently held are because of a cancelled order following the bankruptcy of a customer. The units originally cost the business £4,000 in total, although Rob Otics has recouped £1,500 from the liquidator of the bankrupt business. As Rob Otics can see no use for these units (apart from the possible use of some of them in the order now being considered), the finance director proposes to scrap all 25 units (zero proceeds).
- *Component Z.* This is in regular use by Rob Otics. There is none in inventories but an order is about to be sent to a supplier for 75 units, irrespective of this new proposal. The supplier charges £25 a unit on small orders but will reduce the price to £20 a unit for all units on any order over 100 units.
- *Other items.* These are expected to cost £250 in total.

Assembly labour is currently in short supply in the area and is paid at £10 an hour. If the order is accepted, all necessary labour will have to be transferred from existing work. As a result, other orders will be lost. It is estimated that for each hour transferred to this contract £38 will be lost (calculated as lost sales revenue £60, less materials £12 and labour £10). The production director suggests that, owing to a learning process, the time taken to make each unit will reduce, from 25 hours to make the first one, by one hour a unit made. (That is 25 hours to make the first one, 24 hours to make the second, 23 hours to make the third one and so on.)

Inspection labour can be provided by paying existing employees overtime which is at a premium of 50 per cent over the standard rate of £12 an hour.

When the business is working out its contract prices, it normally adds an amount equal to £20 for each assembly labour hour to cover its general costs (such as rent and electricity). To the resulting total, 40 per cent is normally added as a profit mark-up.

Required:

(a) Prepare an estimate of the minimum price that you would recommend Rob Otics Ltd to charge for the proposed contract such that it would be neither better nor worse off as a result. Provide explanations for any items included.

(b) Identify any other factors that you would consider before fixing the final price.

8.7 A business places substantial emphasis on customer satisfaction and, to this end, delivers its product in special protective containers. These containers have been made in a department within the business. Management has recently become concerned that this internal supply of containers is very expensive. As a result, outside suppliers have been invited to submit tenders for the provision of these containers. A quote of £250,000 a year has been received for a volume that compares with current internal supply.

An investigation into the internal costs of container manufacture has been undertaken and the following emerges:

(a) The annual cost of material is £120,000, according to the stores records, maintained at actual historic cost. Three-quarters (by cost) of this represents material that is regularly stocked and replenished. The remaining 25 per cent of the material cost is a special foaming chemical. This chemical is not used by the business for any other purpose than making the containers. There are 40 tonnes of this chemical currently held. It was bought in bulk for £750 a tonne. Today's replacement price for this material is £1,050 a tonne, but it is unlikely that the business could realise more than £600 a tonne if it had to be disposed of owing to the high handling costs and special transport facilities required.

(b) The annual labour cost is £80,000 for this department. Most of this cost, however, relates to casual employees or recent starters. If an outside quote were accepted, therefore, little redundancy would be payable. There are, however, two long-serving employees who would each accept as a salary £15,000 a year until they reached retirement age in two years' time.

(c) The department manager has a salary of £30,000 a year. The closure of this department would release him to take over another department for which a vacancy is about to be advertised. The salary, status and prospects are similar.

(d) A rental charge of £9,750 a year, based on floor area, is allocated to the containers department. If the department were closed, the floor space released would be used for warehousing and, as a result, the business would give up the tenancy of an existing warehouse for which it is paying £15,750 a year.

(e) The plant cost £162,000 when it was bought five years ago. Its market value now is £28,000 and it could continue for another two years, at which time its market value would have fallen to zero. (The plant depreciates evenly over time.)

(f) Annual plant maintenance costs are £9,900 and allocated general administrative costs £33,750 for the coming year.

Required:
Calculate the annual cost of manufacturing containers for comparison with the quote using relevant figures for establishing the cost or benefit of accepting the quote. Indicate any assumptions or qualifications you wish to make.

CHAPTER 9

Cost–volume–profit analysis

Introduction

This chapter considers the relationship between cost, the volume of activity and profit. We shall see how an understanding of this relationship can be used to make decisions and to assess risk, particularly within the context of short-term decisions.

The theme of Chapter 8 concerning relevant costs is further developed in this chapter. We shall take a look at circumstances where a whole class of cost – fixed cost – can be treated as irrelevant for decision-making purposes.

Learning outcomes

When you have completed this chapter, you should be able to:

- distinguish between fixed cost and variable cost and use this distinction to explain the relationship between cost, volume of activity and profit;

- prepare a break-even chart and deduce the break-even point for some activity;

- discuss the weaknesses of break-even analysis; and

- demonstrate the way in which marginal analysis can be used when making short-term decisions.

Cost behaviour

We saw in the previous chapter that cost represents the resources sacrificed to achieve benefits. Costs incurred by a business may be classified in various ways, and one useful way is according to how they behave in relation to changes in the volume of activity. Costs may be classified according to whether they:

- remain constant (fixed) when changes occur to the volume of activity; or
- vary according to the volume of activity.

These are known as **fixed costs** and **variable costs,** respectively. Thus, in the case of a restaurant, the manager's salary would normally be a fixed cost while the cost of the unprepared food would be a variable cost.

As we shall see, knowing how much of each type of cost is associated with a particular activity can be of great value to the decision maker.

Fixed cost

The way in which a fixed cost behaves can be shown by preparing a graph that plots the fixed cost of a business against the level of activity, as in Figure 9.1. The distance 0F represents the amount of fixed cost, and this stays the same irrespective of the volume of activity.

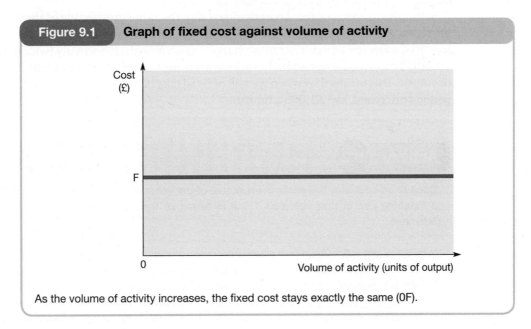

| Figure 9.1 | Graph of fixed cost against volume of activity |

As the volume of activity increases, the fixed cost stays exactly the same (0F).

Staff salaries (or wages) are often assumed to be a variable cost but, in practice, they tend to be fixed. Members of staff are not normally paid according to the volume of output and it is unusual to dismiss staff when there is a short-term downturn in activity. Where there is a long-term downturn, or at least it seems that way to management, redundancies may occur with fixedcost savings. This, is, however, true of all types of fixed cost. For example, management may also decide to close some branches to make rental cost savings.

Activity 9.1

Can you give some examples of items of cost that are likely to be fixed for a hairdressing business?

We came up with the following:

- rent;
- insurance;
- cleaning cost; and
- staff salaries.

You may have thought of others.

These items of cost are likely to be the same irrespective of the number of customers having their hair cut or styled.

There are circumstances in which the labour cost is variable (for example, where staff are paid according to how much output they produce), but this is unusual. Whether labour cost is fixed or variable will depend on the particular circumstances.

It is important to be clear that 'fixed', in this context, means only that the cost is unaffected by changes in the volume of activity. Fixed cost is likely to be affected by inflation. If rent (a typical fixed cost) goes up because of inflation, a fixed cost will have increased, but not because of a change in the volume of activity.

Similarly, the level of fixed cost does not stay the same irrespective of the time period involved. Fixed cost elements are almost always *time-based*: that is, they vary with the length of time concerned. The rental charge for two months is normally twice that for one month. Thus, fixed cost normally varies with time, but (of course) not with the volume of output. This means that when we talk of fixed cost being, say, £1,000, we must add the period concerned, say, £1,000 a month.

Activity 9.2

Does fixed cost stay the same irrespective of the volume of output, even where there is a massive rise in that volume? Think in terms of the rent cost for the hairdressing business.

In fact, the rent is only fixed over a particular range (known as the 'relevant' range). If the number of people wanting to have their hair cut by the business increased, and the business wished to meet this increased demand, it would eventually have to expand its physical size. This might be achieved by opening an additional branch, or perhaps by moving the existing business to larger accommodation. It may be possible to cope with relatively minor increases in activity by using existing space more efficiently, or by having longer opening hours. If activity continued to increase, however, increased rent charges may be inevitable.

In practice, the situation described in Activity 9.2 would look something like Figure 9.2.

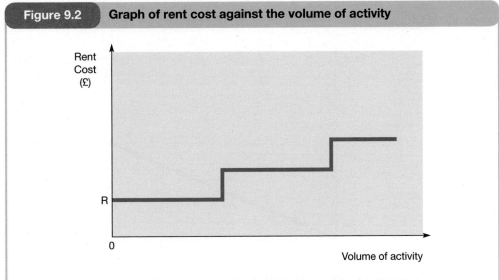

| Figure 9.2 | Graph of rent cost against the volume of activity |

As the volume of activity increases from zero, the rent (a fixed cost) is unaffected. At a particular point, the volume of activity cannot increase further without additional space being rented. The cost of renting the additional space will cause a 'step' in the rent cost. The higher rent cost will continue unaffected if volume rises further until eventually another step point is reached.

At lower volumes of activity, the rent cost shown in Figure 9.2 would be 0R. As the volume of activity increases, a point will be reached where the existing accommodation becomes inadequate. To expand the business beyond this point, larger accommodation will be needed, which will mean a sharp increase in fixed cost. Where the volume of activity continues to increase, another point will be reached where the accommodation becomes inadequate. Hence, even larger accommodation will be needed, leading to a further sharp increase in fixed cost. Elements of fixed cost that behave in this way are often referred to as **stepped fixed costs**.

Variable cost

We saw earlier that variable cost varies with the volume of activity. In a manufacturing business, for example, this would include the cost of raw materials used.

Variable cost can be represented graphically as in Figure 9.3. At zero volume of activity, the variable cost is zero. It then increases in a straight line as activity increases.

Activity 9.3

Can you think of some examples of cost elements that are likely to be variable for a hairdressing business?

We can think of a couple:

- lotions, sprays and other materials used; and
- laundry cost to wash towels used.

You may have thought of others.

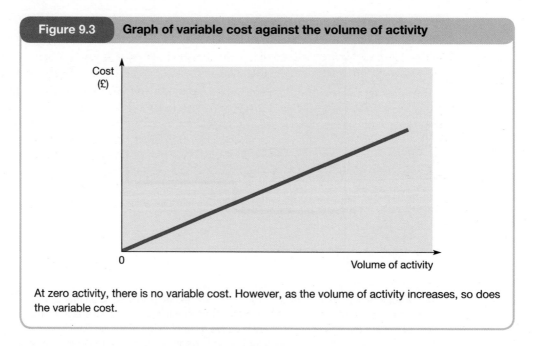

Figure 9.3   Graph of variable cost against the volume of activity

At zero activity, there is no variable cost. However, as the volume of activity increases, so does the variable cost.

As with many types of business activity, the variable cost incurred by hairdressers tends to be low in comparison with the fixed cost. Thus, fixed cost tends to make up the bulk of total cost.

The straight line for variable cost on this graph implies that this type of cost will be the same per unit of activity, irrespective of the volume of activity. We shall consider the practicality of this assumption a little later in this chapter.

Semi-fixed (semi-variable) cost

In some cases, a particular cost has an element of both fixed and variable cost. These can be described as **semi-fixed (semi-variable) costs**. An example might be the electricity cost for the hairdressing business. Some of this will be for heating and lighting, and this part is probably fixed, at least until the volume of activity increases to a point where longer opening hours or larger accommodation is necessary. The other part of the cost will vary with the volume of activity. Here we are talking about such things as power for hairdryers.

Activity   9.4

Can you suggest another cost for a hairdressing business that is likely to be semi-fixed (semi-variable)?

We thought of telephone charges for landlines. These tend to have a rental element, which is fixed, and there may also be certain calls that must be made irrespective of the volume of activity involved. However, increased business would probably lead to the need to make more telephone calls and so to increased call charges.

Analysing semi-fixed (semi-variable) costs

The fixed and variable elements of a particular cost may not always be clear. Past experience, however, can often provide some guidance. Let us again take the example of electricity. If we have data on what the electricity cost has been for various volumes of activity, say the relevant data over several three-month periods (electricity is usually billed by the quarter), we can estimate the fixed and variable elements. The easiest way to do this is to use the **high-low method**. This method involves taking the highest and lowest total electricity cost figures from the range of past quarterly data available. An assumption is then made that the difference between these two quarterly figures is caused entirely by the change in variable cost.

Example 9.1 demonstrates how the fixed and variable elements of electricity cost may be estimated using this method.

Example 9.1

Davos Ltd collected data relating to its electricity cost and volume of activity over several quarters and found the following:

	Lowest quarterly activity	Highest quarterly activity
Volume of activity	100,000 units	180,000 units
Total electricity cost	£80,000	£120,000

We can see that an increase in activity of 80,000 units (that is, from 100,000 to 180,000 units) led to an increase in total electricity cost of £40,000 (that is from £80,000 to £120,000). As it is assumed that this increase is caused by an increase in variable cost, the variable cost per unit of output must be £40,000/80,000 = £0.50 per unit.

The breakdown in total electricity cost for the highest and lowest quarters will therefore be as follows:

	Lowest quarterly activity	Highest quarterly activity
	100,000 units	180,000 units
Volume of activity	£	£
Variable cost		
100,000 × £0.50	50,000	
180,000 × £0.50		90,000
Fixed cost (balancing figure)	30,000	30,000
Total electricity cost	80,000	120,000

Activity 9.5

What do you think is the weakness of using the high–low approach?

The problem with this method is that it relies on only two points in a range of information relating to quarterly electricity charges. It ignores all other information.

A more reliable estimate of the fixed and variable cost elements can be made if the full range of electricity cost for each quarter is used in the analysis. By plotting total electricity cost against the volume of activity for each quarter, a graph that looks like the one shown in Figure 9.4 may be produced.

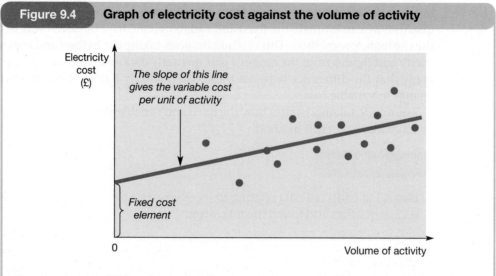

| Figure 9.4 | Graph of electricity cost against the volume of activity |

The slope of this line gives the variable cost per unit of activity

Fixed cost element

Here the electricity bill for a time period (for example, three months) is plotted against the volume of activity for that same period. This is done for a series of periods. A line is then drawn that best 'fits' the various points on the graph. From this line we can then deduce both the cost at zero activity (the fixed element) and the slope of the line (the variable element).

Each of the dots in Figure 9.4 is the electricity charge for a particular quarter plotted against the volume of activity (probably measured in terms of sales revenue) for the same quarter. The diagonal line on the graph is the *line of best fit*. This means that this was the line that best seemed (to us, at least) to represent the data. A better estimate can usually be made using a statistical technique (*least squares regression*), which does not involve drawing graphs and making estimates. In terms of accuracy, however, there is probably little practical difference between the two approaches.

From the graph we can say that the fixed element of the electricity cost is the amount represented by the vertical distance from the origin at zero (bottom left-hand corner) to the point where the line of best fit crosses the vertical axis of the graph. The variable cost per unit is the amount that the graph line rises for each increase in the volume of activity, that is, the slope of the line.

Armed with knowledge of how much each element of cost represents for a particular product or service, it is possible to make predictions regarding total and per-unit cost at various projected levels of output. This information can be very useful to decision makers. Much of the rest of this chapter will be devoted to seeing how it can be useful, starting with **break-even analysis**.

Finding the break-even point

If, for a particular product or service, we know the fixed cost for a period and the variable cost per unit, we can produce a graph like the one shown in Figure 9.5. This graph shows the total cost over the possible range of volume of activity.

Figure 9.5	Graph of total cost against volume of activity

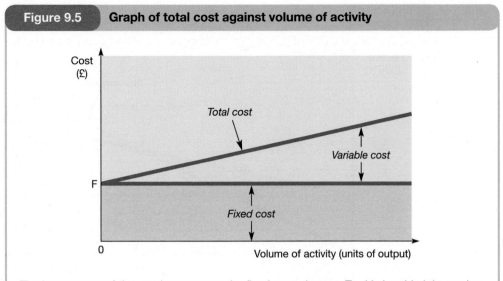

The bottom part of the graph represents the fixed cost element. To this is added the wedge-shaped top portion, which represents the variable cost. The two parts together represent total cost. At zero activity, the variable cost is zero, so total cost equals fixed cost. As activity increases so does total cost, but only because variable cost increases. We are assuming that there are no steps in the fixed cost.

The bottom part of Figure 9.5 shows the fixed cost area. Added to this is the variable cost, the wedge-shaped portion at the top of the graph. The uppermost line represents the total cost over a range of volume of activity. For any particular volume, the total cost can be measured as the vertical distance between the graph's horizontal axis and the relevant point on the uppermost line.

Logically, the total cost at zero activity is the amount of the fixed cost. This is because, even where there is nothing happening, the business will still be paying rent, salaries and so on, at least in the short term. As the volume of activity increases from zero, the fixed cost is augmented by the relevant variable cost to give the total cost.

If we take this total cost graph in Figure 9.5, and superimpose on it a line representing total revenue over the range of volume of activity, we obtain a **break-even chart**. This is shown in Figure 9.6.

Note in Figure 9.6 that, at zero volume of activity (zero sales), there is zero sales revenue. The profit (loss), which is the difference between total sales revenue and total cost, for a particular volume of activity, is the vertical distance between the total sales revenue line and the total cost line at that volume of activity. Where there is no vertical distance between these two lines (total sales revenue equals total cost) the volume of activity is at **break-even point (BEP)**. At this point, there is neither profit nor loss; that is, the activity *breaks even*. Where the volume of activity is below BEP, a loss will be incurred because total cost exceeds total sales revenue. Where the business operates at a volume of activity above BEP, there will be a profit because total sales revenue will exceed total cost. The further the volume of activity is below BEP, the higher the loss: the further above BEP it is, the higher the profit.

Deducing BEPs graphically is a laborious business. Since, however, the relationships in the graph are all linear (that is, the lines are all straight), it is easy to calculate the BEP.

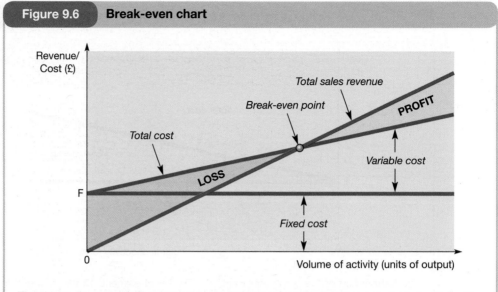

| Figure 9.6 | Break-even chart |

The sloping line starting at zero represents the sales revenue at various volumes of activity. The point at which this finally catches up with the sloping total cost line, which starts at F, is the break-even point (BEP). Below this point a loss is made, above it a profit.

We know that at BEP (but not at any other volume of activity):

$$\text{Total sales revenue} = \text{Total cost}$$

(At all other volumes of activity except the BEP, either total sales revenue will exceed total cost or the other way round. Only at BEP are they equal.) The above formula can be expanded so that:

$$\text{Total sales revenue} = \text{Fixed cost} + \text{Variable cost}$$

If we call the number of units of output at BEP *b,* then:

$$b \times \text{Sales revenue per unit} = \text{Fixed cost} + (b \times \text{Variable cost per unit})$$

so:

$$(b \times \text{Sales revenue per unit}) - (b \times \text{Variable cost per unit}) = \text{Fixed cost}$$

and:

$$b \times (\text{Sales revenue per unit} - \text{Variable cost per unit}) = \text{Fixed cost}$$

giving:

$$b = \frac{\text{Fixed cost}}{\text{Sales revenue per unit} - \text{Variable cost per unit}}$$

If we look back at the break-even chart in Figure 9.6, this formula seems logical. The total cost line starts off at point F, higher than the starting point for the total sales revenues line (zero) by amount F (the amount of the fixed cost). Because the sales revenue per unit is greater than the variable cost per unit, the sales revenue line will gradually catch up with the total cost line. The rate at which it will catch up is dependent on the relative steepness of the two lines. Bearing in mind that the slopes of the two lines are the variable cost per unit and the selling price per unit, the above equation for calculating *b* looks perfectly logical.

Although the BEP can be calculated quickly and simply without resorting to graphs, this does not mean that the break-even chart is without value. The chart shows the relationship between cost, volume and profit over a range of activity and in a form that can easily be understood by non-financial managers. The break-even chart can therefore be a useful device for explaining this relationship. Example 9.2 illustrates the use of the BEP formula.

Example 9.2

Cottage Industries Ltd makes baskets. The fixed cost of operating the workshop for a month totals £500. Each basket requires materials that cost £2 and takes one hour to make. The business pays the basket makers £10 an hour. The basket makers are all on contracts such that if they do not work for any reason, they are not paid. The baskets are sold to a wholesaler for £14 each.

What is the BEP for basket making for the business?

Solution

The BEP (in number of baskets) is:

$$BEP = \frac{\text{Fixed cost}}{(\text{Sales revenue per unit} - \text{Variable cost per unit})}$$

$$= \frac{£500}{£14 - (£2 + £10)}$$

$$= 250 \text{ baskets per month}$$

Note that the BEP must be expressed with respect to a period of time.

Real World 9.1 shows information on the BEPs of one well-known business.

Real World 9.1

BE at Ryanair

Commercial airlines seem to pay a lot of attention to their BEPs and their 'load factors', that is, their actual level of activity. Figure 9.7 shows the BEPs and load factors for Ryanair, the 'no-frills' carrier.

We can see that Ryanair made operating profits in each of the five years considered. This is because the airline's load factor was consistently greater than its BEP.

→

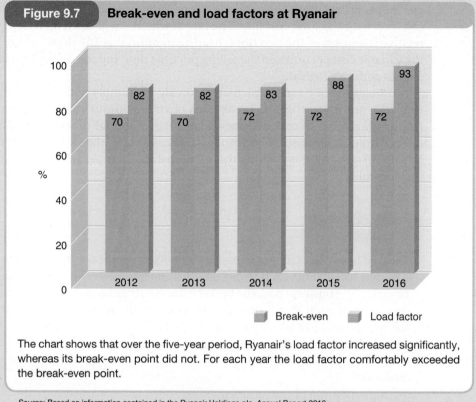

Figure 9.7   Break-even and load factors at Ryanair

The chart shows that over the five-year period, Ryanair's load factor increased significantly, whereas its break-even point did not. For each year the load factor comfortably exceeded the break-even point.

Source: Based on information contained in the Ryanair Holdings plc, Annual Report 2016.

Activity 9.6

In Real World 9.1, we saw that Ryanair's BEP varied from 70 per cent to 72 per cent over the five-year period. Why was it not the same each year?

Break-even point depends on three broad factors. These are sales revenue, variable cost and fixed cost. Each of these can vary quite noticeably from one year to another. Ryanair's sales revenue could be affected by the level of disposable income among the travelling public and/or by levels of competition from other airlines. Costs can vary from one year to another, particularly the cost of aviation fuel.

[Interestingly, Ryanair's average fuel cost was €2.07 per gallon in 2012, €2.38 in 2013, €2.45 in 2014, €2.34 in 2015 and €2.21 in 2016. It seems that this major cost for the business can vary widely from one year to the next.]

Activity 9.7

Can you think of reasons why the managers of a business might find it useful to know the BEP of some activity that they are planning to undertake?

By knowing the BEP, it is possible to compare the expected, or planned, volume of activity with the BEP and so make a judgement about risk. If the volume of activity is expected to be only just above the BEP, this may suggest that it is a risky venture. Only a small fall from the expected volume of activity could lead to a loss.

Activity 9.8

Cottage Industries Ltd (see Example 9.2) expects to sell 500 baskets a month. The business has the opportunity to rent a basket-making machine. Doing so would increase the total fixed cost of operating the workshop for a month to £3,000. Using the machine would reduce the labour time to half an hour per basket. The basket makers would still be paid £10 an hour.

(a) How much profit would the business make each month from selling baskets
  • without the machine; and
  • with the machine?
(b) What is the BEP if the machine is rented?
(c) What do you notice about the figures that you calculate?

(a) Estimated monthly profit from basket making:

	Without the machine		With the machine	
	£	£	£	£
Sales revenue (500 × £14)		7,000		7,000
Materials (500 × £2)	(1,000)		(1,000)	
Labour (500 × 1 × £10)	(5,000)			
(500 × ½ × £10)			(2,500)	
Fixed cost	(500)		(3,000)	
		(6,500)		(6,500)
Profit		500		500

(b) The BEP (in number of baskets) with the machine:

$$BEP = \frac{Fixed\ cost}{Sales\ revenue\ per\ unit\ -\ Variable\ cost\ per\ unit}$$

$$= \frac{£3,000}{£14 - (£2 + £5)}$$

$$= 429\ baskets\ a\ month$$

The BEP without the machine is 250 baskets per month (see Example 9.2).

(c) There is no difference between the two manufacturing strategies as regards to profit, at the expected sales volume. There is, however, a distinct difference between the two strategies regarding the BEP. Without the machine, the actual volume of sales could fall by 50 per cent of that expected (from 500 to 250) before the business fails to make a profit. With the machine, however, a reduction in the volume of sales of just 14 per cent (from 500 to 429) means that the business fails to make a profit. On the other hand, for each additional basket sold above the estimated 500, an additional profit of only £2 (that is, £14 − (£2 + £10)) would be made without the machine, whereas £7 (that is, £14 − (£2 + £5)) would be made with the machine. (Note how knowledge of the BEP and the planned volume of activity offers a basis for assessing the riskiness of the activity.)

Real World 9.2 reveals how ill-fated airline, Malaysian Airlines, which has failed to reach its BEP since 2010, aims to be profitable by 2018. The ways in which this is to be achieved brings into focus the relationship between cost, volume of activity and profit.

Real World 9.2

Approaching take off

Malaysian Airways has been unprofitable since 2010. To make matters worse, it suffered two air disasters during 2014, which adversely affected passenger volumes and profitability.

In an attempt to turn the business around, a new chief executive officer (CEO), Christopher Mueller, was appointed. The new CEO plans to lower costs and improve profits by:

- reducing the workforce from 20,000 employees to 14,000;
- reducing the number of flights and the size of the fleet;
- focusing on domestic and regional routes;
- stopping some long-haul, loss-making routes, for example, its only US route from Kuala Lumpur to Los Angeles; and
- renegotiating some key contracts, including some of those with airports.

These are drastic steps. However, the new CEO believes they are necessary to achieve break even and to save the business.

FT   *Source*: Information taken from McGee, P. and Parker, A. (2015) Disaster-plagued Malaysian Airways seeks break even by 2018, ft.com, 1 June. © The Financial Times Limited 2015. All Rights Reserved.

We shall take a closer look at the relationship between fixed cost, variable cost and profit together with any advice that we might give the management of Cottage Industries Ltd after we have briefly considered the notion of contribution.

Contribution

The bottom part of the break-even formula (sales revenue per unit less variable cost per unit) is known as the **contribution per unit.** Thus, for the basket-making activity, without the machine the contribution per unit is £2 and with the machine it is £7. This can be quite a useful figure to know in a decision-making context. It is called 'contribution' because it contributes to meeting the fixed cost and, if there is any excess, it then contributes to profit.

We shall see, a little later in this chapter, how knowing the amount of the contribution generated by a particular activity can be valuable in making short-term decisions of various types, as well as being useful in the BEP calculation.

Contribution margin ratio

The **contribution margin ratio** is the contribution from an activity expressed as a percentage of the sales revenue, thus:

$$\text{Contribution margin ratio} = \frac{\text{Contribution}}{\text{Sales revenue}} \times 100\%$$

Contribution and sales revenue can both be expressed in per-unit or total terms. For Cottage Industries Ltd (Example 9.2 and Activity 9.8), the contribution margin ratios are:

$$\text{Without the machine, } \frac{14 - 12}{14} \times 100\% = 14\%$$

$$\text{With the machine, } \frac{14 - 7}{14} \times 100\% = 50\%$$

The ratio can provide an impression of the degree to which sales revenue is eaten away by variable cost.

Margin of safety

The **margin of safety** is the extent to which the planned volume of output or sales lies above the BEP. To illustrate how the margin of safety is calculated, we can use the information in Activity 9.8 relating to each option.

	Without the machine (number of baskets)	*With the machine (number of baskets)*
(a) Expected volume of sales	500	500
(b) BEP	250	429
Margin of safety (the difference between (a) and (b))	250	71
Expressed as a percentage of expected volume of sales	50%	14%

The margin of safety can be used as a partial measure of risk.

Activity 9.9

What advice would you give Cottage Industries Ltd about renting the machine, on the basis of the values for margin of safety?

It is a matter of personal judgement which, in turn, is related to individual attitudes to risk, as to which strategy to adopt. Most people, however, would prefer the strategy of not renting the machine, since the margin of safety between the expected volume of activity and the BEP is much greater. Thus, for the same level of return, the risk will be lower without renting the machine.

The relative margins of safety are directly linked to the relationship between the selling price per basket, the variable cost per basket and the monthly fixed cost. Without the machine the contribution (selling price less variable cost) per basket is £2; with the machine it is £7. On the other hand, without the machine the fixed cost is £500 a month; with the machine it is £3,000. This means that, with the machine, the contributions have more fixed cost to 'overcome' before the activity becomes profitable. However, the rate at which the contributions can overcome fixed cost is higher with the machine, because variable cost is lower. Thus, one additional, or one fewer, basket sold has a greater impact on profit than it does if the machine is not rented. The contrast between the two scenarios is shown graphically in Figure 9.8.

Figure 9.8	Break-even charts for Cottage Industries Ltd's basket-making activities

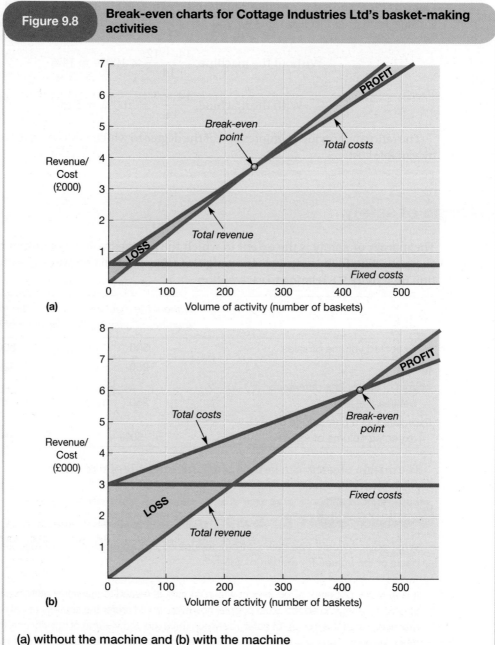

(a) without the machine and (b) with the machine

Without the machine the contribution per basket is low. Thus, each additional basket sold does not make a dramatic difference to the profit or loss. With the machine, however, the opposite is true; small increases or decreases in the sales volume will have a great effect on the profit or loss.

Real World 9.3 goes into more detail on Ryanair's margin of safety and operating profit over recent years.

Real World 9.3

Ryanair's margin of safety

As we saw in Real World 9.1, commercial airlines pay a lot of attention to BEPs. They are also interested in their margin of safety (the difference between load factor and BEP).

Figure 9.9 shows Ryanair's margin of safety and its operating profit over a five-year, period.

| Figure 9.9 | Ryanair's margin of safety |

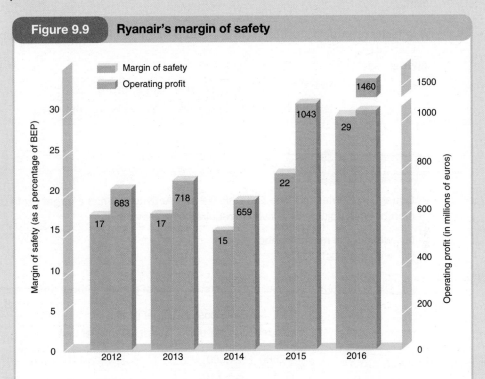

The margin of safety is expressed as the difference between the load factor and the BEP (for each year), expressed as a percentage of the BEP. Generally, the higher the margin of safety, the higher the operating profit.

We can see that, in each year, the load factor has been significantly more than the BEP. This has resulted in substantial operating profits.

Source: Based on information contained in the Ryanair Holdings plc, Annual Report 2016.

Achieving a target profit

In the same way as we can derive the number of units of output necessary to break even, we can calculate the volume of activity required to achieve a particular level of profit. We can expand the equation given in the section 'Finding the break-even point' (on p. 330) so that:

Total sales revenue = Fixed cost + Total variable cost + Target profit

If we let t be the required number of units of output to achieve the target profit, then:

$t \times$ Sales revenue per unit $=$ Fixed cost $+ (t \times$ Variable cost per unit$) +$ Target profit

so:

$(t \times$ Sales revenue per unit$) - (t \times$ Variable cost per unit$) =$ Fixed cost $+$ Target profit

and:

$t \times$ (Sales revenue per unit $-$ Variable cost per unit$) =$ Fixed cost $+$ Target profit

giving:

$$t = \frac{\text{Fixed cost} + \text{Target profit}}{\text{Sales revenue per unit} - \text{Variable cost per unit}}$$

Activity 9.10

Cottage Industries Ltd (see Example 9.2 and Activity 9.8) has a target profit of £4,000 a month. What volume of activity is required to achieve this:

(a) without the machine; and
(b) with the machine?

(a) Using the formula above, the required volume of activity without the machine:

$$\frac{\text{Fixed cost} + \text{Target profit}}{\text{Sales revenue per unit} - \text{Variable cost per unit}}$$

$$= \frac{£500 + £4,000}{£14 - (£2 + £10)}$$

$$= 2,250 \text{ baskets a month}$$

(b) The required volume of activity with the machine:

$$= \frac{£3,000 + £4,000}{£14 - (£2 + £5)}$$

$$= 1,000 \text{ baskets a month}$$

Operating gearing and its effect on profit

The relationship between fixed cost and variable cost is known as **operating gearing** (or operational gearing). An activity with a relatively high fixed cost compared with its total variable cost, at its normal level of activity, is said to have high operating gearing. Thus, Cottage Industries Ltd has higher operating gearing using the machine than it has if not using it. Renting the machine increases the level of operating gearing quite dramatically because it causes an increase in fixed cost but, at the same time, it leads to a reduction in variable cost per basket.

The reason why the word 'gearing' is used in this context is because, as with intermeshing gear wheels of different circumferences, a movement in one of the factors (volume of output) causes a more-than-proportionate movement in the other (profit) as illustrated by Figure 9.10.

Figure 9.10	The effect of operating gearing

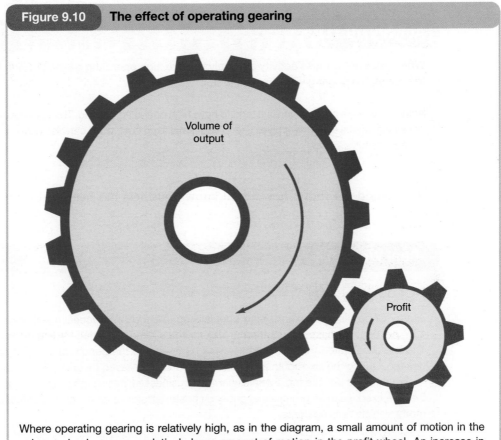

Where operating gearing is relatively high, as in the diagram, a small amount of motion in the volume wheel causes a relatively large amount of motion in the profit wheel. An increase in volume would cause a disproportionately greater increase in profit. The equivalent would also be true of a decrease in activity, however.

Increasing the level of operating gearing makes profit more sensitive to changes in the volume of activity. We can demonstrate operating gearing with Cottage Industries Ltd's basket-making activities as follows:

	Without the machine			*With the machine*		
Volume (number of baskets)	500	1,000	1,500	500	1,000	1,500
	£	£	£	£	£	£
Contributions*	1,000	2,000	3,000	3,500	7,000	10,500
Fixed cost	(500)	(500)	(500)	(3,000)	(3,000)	(3,000)
Profit	500	1,500	2,500	500	4,000	7,500

* £2 per basket without the machine and £7 per basket with it.

Note that, without the machine (lower operating gearing), a doubling of the output from 500 to 1,000 units brings a trebling of the profit. With the machine (higher operating gearing), a doubling of output from 500 units causes profit to rise by eight times. At the same time, reductions in the volume of output tend to have a more damaging effect on profit where the operating gearing is higher.

Activity (9.11)

What types of business activity are likely to have high operating gearing? (*Hint*: Cottage Industries Ltd might give you some idea.)

Activities that are capital intensive tend to have high operating gearing. This is because renting or owning capital equipment gives rise to additional fixed cost, but it can also give rise to lower variable cost.

Real World 9.4 shows how a well-known business has benefited from operating gearing.

Real World 9.4

Not down at heel

Jimmy Choo plc, the luxury brand specialising in shoes and accessories, announced a 13.7 per cent increase in operating profits for the six-month period ending 30 June 2016. The business stated that this increase was partly due to the beneficial effect of operating gearing. During the six-month period, sales revenue increased by only 3.8 per cent.

Jimmy Choo plc, like most wholesale/retail businesses, has a high proportion of its costs that are fixed, such as premises occupancy costs, employee costs, plant depreciation and motor vehicle running costs.

Source: Information from Jimmy Choo plc, Preliminary results statement for the six months ended 30 June 2016, www.jimmychooplc. com, 25 August 2016.

Profit–volume charts

A slight variant of the break-even chart is the **profit–volume (PV) chart**. A typical PV chart is shown in Figure 9.11.

The PV chart is obtained by plotting loss or profit against volume of activity. The slope of the graph is equal to the contribution per unit, since each additional unit sold decreases the loss, or increases the profit, by the sales revenue per unit less the variable cost per unit. At zero volume of activity there is no contribution, so there is a loss equal to the amount of the fixed cost. As the volume of activity increases, the amount of the loss gradually decreases until BEP is reached. Beyond BEP a profit is made, which increases as the volume of activity increases.

As we can see, the PV chart does not tell us anything not shown by the break-even chart. It does, however, highlight key information concerning the profit (loss) arising at any volume of activity. The break-even chart shows this as the vertical distance between the total cost and total sales revenue lines. The PV chart, in effect, combines the total sales revenue and total variable cost lines, which means that profit (or loss) is directly readable.

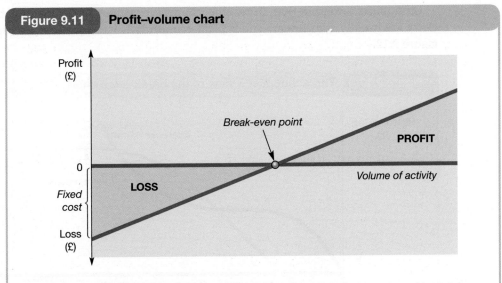

| Figure 9.11 | **Profit–volume chart** |

The sloping line is profit (loss) plotted against activity. As activity increases, so does total contribution (sales revenue less variable cost). At zero activity there is no contribution, so there will be a loss equal in amount to the total fixed cost.

The economist's view of the break-even chart

So far in this chapter we have treated all the relationships as linear – that is, all of the lines in the graphs have been straight. However, this is usually not strictly valid in practice.

Consider, for example, the variable cost line in the break-even chart; accountants would normally treat this as being a straight line. In reality, however, the line may not be straight because, at high levels of output, **economies of scale** may occur. These are cost savings arising from an increase in the volume of activity.

Activity 9.12

How might a manufacturer benefit from economies of scale relating to its raw material requirements?

Raw material (a typical variable cost) may be capable of being used more efficiently with higher volumes of activity. Furthermore, buying larger quantities of raw material makes the business eligible for bulk discounts, thereby lowering the cost.

It is possible, however, that a high volume of activity will lead to *diseconomies of scale*. In other words, it may lead to a higher variable cost per unit of output. For instance, high usage of a particular raw material may lead to shortages, which might cause higher prices to have to be paid for supplies. Where there are either economies or diseconomies of scale, the cost per unit will not be constant over all volumes of activity.

There is also a tendency for sales revenue per unit to reduce as volume is increased. To sell more of a particular product or service, it will usually be necessary to lower the price per unit.

Economists recognise that, in real life, the relationships portrayed in the break-even chart are usually non-linear. The typical economist's view of the chart is shown in Figure 9.12.

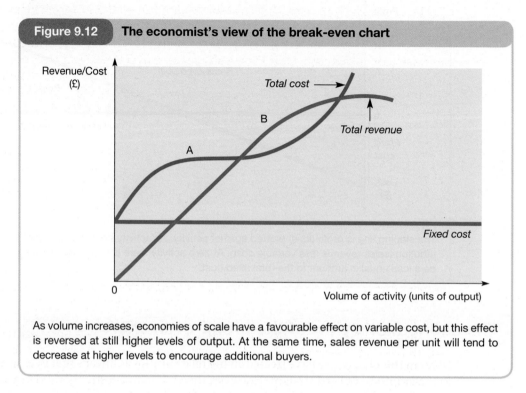

Figure 9.12 **The economist's view of the break-even chart**

As volume increases, economies of scale have a favourable effect on variable cost, but this effect is reversed at still higher levels of output. At the same time, sales revenue per unit will tend to decrease at higher levels to encourage additional buyers.

Note, in Figure 9.12, that the total variable cost line starts to rise quite steeply with volume but, around point A, economies of scale start to take effect. With further increases in volume, total variable cost does not rise as steeply because the variable cost *for each additional unit of output* is lowered. These economies of scale continue to have a benign effect on cost until a point is reached where the business is operating towards the end of its efficient range. Beyond this range, problems will emerge that adversely affect variable cost. For example, the business may be unable to find cheap supplies of the variable cost elements, as mentioned above, or may suffer production difficulties, such as machine breakdowns. As a result, the total variable cost line starts to rise more steeply.

At low levels of output, sales may be able to be made at a relatively high price per unit. To increase sales output beyond point B, however, it may be necessary to lower the average sales price per unit. This will mean that the total revenue line will not rise as steeply, and may even curve downwards. Note how this 'curvilinear' representation of the break-even chart can easily lead to the existence of more than one BEP.

Accountants justify their approach by arguing that, although the lines may not, in practice, be perfectly straight, this defect is not usually worth taking into account. This is partly because information used in the analysis is based on estimates of the future. These estimates will, inevitably, be flawed because of our inability to predict with great accuracy. It is pointless, it can be argued, to be concerned with the minor approximation of treating total cost and total revenue lines as straight. Only where significant economies or diseconomies of scale are involved should the non-linearity of variable cost be taken into account. Furthermore, for most businesses, the range of possible volumes of activity over which they operate (the **relevant range**) is quite narrow. When dealing with short distances, it may be perfectly reasonable to treat a curved line as being straight.

The problem of breaking even

Most businesses struggle to break even at some point in their life; however, for some businesses, it can be a regular occurrence. Businesses whose fortunes are linked to the **business cycle** are particularly vulnerable to this risk. The business cycle refers to the contraction and expansion in activity arising within an economy over time. Businesses operating in industries such as construction, commodities and airlines are particularly sensitive to movements in this cycle. Hence, demand for their output can vary greatly. During a downturn in economic activity, breaking even may be beyond their reach.

Real World 9.5 reveals how sensitivity analysis was used to test the sensitivity of shale oil production to changes in oil prices.

Real World 9.5

Cracking up

The oil market is becoming obsessed with a single question: when will shale crack? Not in the sense of pumping rock full of fluid until it fractures to release petroleum. But as in, when will the US shale oil industry's fracking spree finally slow down? The discussion has become more urgent since West Texas Intermediate crude tumbled below $50 a barrel.

Analysts have been slashing their oil price forecasts and examining the sensitivity of shale production to lower prices. Every dollar-per-barrel move adds or subtracts 100,000 b/d (barrels per day) from next year's US crude supply, argues Bank of America Merrill Lynch. "Within a $20 band, you get an almost 2 million b/d swing," says Francisco Blanch, the bank's global head of commodities research. Citigroup sees price swings having a modest effect on production this year. But next year US oil output could range from 9.6 million b/d if it was $40 a barrel to 12.1 million b/d at $70 barrel.

Figure 9.13	Sensitivity of US crude oil production to oil price

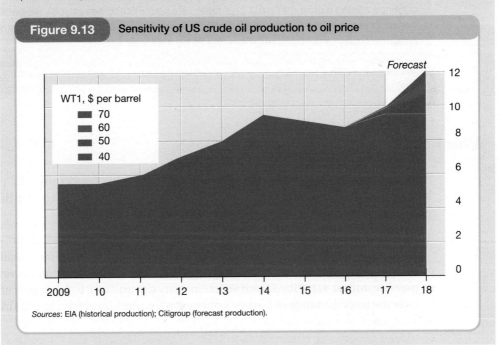

Sources: EIA (historical production); Citigroup (forecast production).

FT   *Source*: Text extracts from G. Meyer (2017) *When will the US fracking spree finally slow down?* ft.com, 7 July.

The agriculture industry can have its own cyclical pattern. Good years tend to be followed by bad years. **Real World 9.6** is an extract from an article which describes how US wheat farmers are currently finding it hard to break even.

Real World 9.6

Not reaping rewards

The US Department of Agriculture reports that global stocks of wheat will exceed international demand by more than a quarter of a billion tons this year.

"From a financial perspective, the cost of production has not gone down nearly as much as the price of grain," said Adrian Doucette, president of Stockman Bank for northcentral Montana. Stockman Bank is Montana's single largest private agricultural lending institution. "An example we had the other day was someone who cut a phenomenal yield, but their inputs were $240 an acre," Doucette said. "So when you work that backward to $4 for a bushel of wheat, you've got to have a pretty good yield to make a profit."

That means that if the farmer was lucky enough to get $4 a bushel, his crop needs to average 60 bushels an acre just to break even. The 30-year average is 36 bushels an acre as reported by Montana State University extension offices.

Figures from the Chicago Board of Trade show that between January 2011 and March 2014, U.S. wheat prices fluctuated between $5.77 and $8.67 a bushel. But for the past two years, the price has consistently remained below $5 a bushel and has now slipped below $4. On July 14, NASS predicted the open market price for wheat will continue to fall, projecting a season-ending average price of around $3.70 a bushel. At those prices, only exceptional harvests have any hope of showing a profit.

"That is a concern," Doucette said. "We're seeing a lot of deals where, given normal yields, the breakeven price is higher than the current market price. That tells me people are going to have to use up some of their equity; either in real estate or other assets if they continue raising a crop that's not profitable. We never like to see anyone go backward, but it is going to happen if break evens are above the market price. For the ones who don't have the equity to fall back on, it's going to be a difficult fall."

Source: Extract from Murray, D. (2016) *Wheat price is below break-even point: Record-setting wheat crop adds to international glut*, www.greatfalltribune.com, 7 August.

Weaknesses of break-even analysis

Although break-even analysis can provide useful insights concerning the relationship between cost, volume and profit, it does have its weaknesses. There are three general problems:

1 *Non-linear relationships.* Break-even analysis, as it is generally used, assumes that total variable cost and total revenue lines are perfectly straight when plotted against volume of output. In real life, this is unlikely to be the case. We saw earlier, however, that, in practice, minor variations from strict linearity are unlikely to be significant and that, over the relevant range of business operations, curved lines tend to be fairly straight.

2 *Stepped fixed cost.* Most types of fixed cost are not fixed over the whole range of activity. They tend to be 'stepped' in the way depicted in Figure 9.2. This means that, in practice, great care must be taken in making assumptions about fixed cost. The problem is amplified because many activities involve different types of fixed cost (for example, rent, supervisory salaries and administration cost), which are likely to have steps at different points.

3 *Multi-product businesses.* Most businesses provide more than one product (or service). This can be a problem for break-even analysis since additional sales of one product may affect sales of another of the business's products. There is also the problem of identifying the fixed cost associated with a particular product. Fixed cost may be incurred for the benefit of more than one product – for example, several products may be made in the same factory. There are ways of apportioning the fixed cost of the factory between products, but they tend to be arbitrary, which undermines the value of break-even analysis.

Activity 9.13

We saw above that, in practice, relationships between costs, revenues and volumes of activity are not necessarily straight-line ones.
  Can you think of at least three reasons, with examples, why this may be the case?

We thought of the following:

- *Economies of scale with labour.* A business may operate more economically at a higher volume of activity. For example, employees may be able to increase productivity by specialising in particular tasks.
- *Economies of scale with buying goods or services.* A business may find it cheaper to buy in goods and services where it is buying in bulk as discounts are often given.
- *Diseconomies of scale.* This may mean that the per-unit cost of output is higher at higher levels of activity. For example, it may be necessary to pay higher rates of pay to workers to recruit the additional staff needed at higher volumes of activity.
- *Lower sales prices at high levels of activity.* Some consumers may only be prepared to buy the particular product or service at a lower price. Thus, it may not be possible to achieve high levels of sales volume without lowering the price.

You may have thought of others.

Despite some practical problems, break-even analysis seems to be widely used. The media frequently refer to the BEP for businesses and other activities. Football is one example. There is often mention of the number of spectators required for a particular club to break even. Furthermore, UEFA has implemented a financial fair play rule for football clubs based on the concept of break even. Clubs participating, or wishing to participate, in its competitions must, as a minimum, balance their spending against the revenues generated over a three-year period. This is designed to prevent clubs recklessly spending money in pursuit of success and thereby placing their long-term future in jeopardy. Failure to adhere to this break-even rule can result in exclusion from UEFA competitions. **Real World 9.7** discusses an example of one such exclusion.

Real World 9.7

Penalty!

Galatasaray, the Turkish football champions, were not able to compete in either of the two competitions organised by UEFA, basically the Champions League and the Europa cup, for both the 2016/17 and 2017/18 seasons. The ban arose from the club breaching UEFA's fair play rules by overspending on staff remuneration during the previous years.

Source: Based on information in: *Champions Galatasaray get year-long ban from UEFA competitions,* www.espnfc.com, 2 March 2016.

The media also reports on particular businesses that are struggling to break even. **Real World 9.8** describes how one business is moving towards this point.

Real World 9.8

Seeing through the problem

X-ray screening supplier Image Scan Holdings Plc is on track to break even when it announces final results later this year, after the impact from a large customer order. Last June, the group reported an £800,000 order for its ThreatScan-LS1 portable X-ray systems. Image Scan expects to have realised half of this by the end of the financial year and therefore now expects to materially exceed current market expectations.

"For a company the size of Image Scan, large orders can present their own challenges. However excellent progress has been made with the planning for the recent orders and we have the commitments from our supply chain," said chairman and chief executive Bill Mawer. "I am delighted that as a consequence Image Scan will now approach break even in the current financial year".

Source: Proactive investors United Kingdom (2016) *Image Scan to break even thanks to large June X-ray order,* www.proactiveinvestors.co.uk, 22 August.

Real World 9.9 provides evidence concerning the extent to which managers use break-even analysis.

Real World 9.9

Break-even analysis in practice

A survey of management accounting practice in the USA was conducted in 2003. Nearly 2,000 businesses replied to the survey. These tended to be larger businesses, of which about 40 per cent were manufacturers and about 16 per cent financial services; the remainder were across a range of other industries.

The survey revealed that 62 per cent use break-even analysis extensively, with a further 22 per cent considering using the technique in the future.

The survey is now pretty old and covers only larger businesses. It should, therefore, be treated with caution. Nevertheless, it may provide some indication of what is current practice in the USA and elsewhere in the developed world.

A much more recent, and UK-based, survey of the practices of 11 small and medium sized businesses found a marked tendency to use break-even analysis.

Sources: Taken from the *2003 Survey of Management Accounting* by Ernst and Young, 2003; Lucas, M., Prowle, M. and Lowth, G. (2013) *Management Accounting Practices of UK Small and Medium-sized Enterprises,* CIMA, July 2013.

Using contribution to make decisions: marginal analysis

In Chapter 2, where we discussed relevant costs for decision making, we saw that, when deciding between two or more possible courses of action, *only costs that vary with the decision should be included in the analysis.* This principle can be applied to the consideration of fixed cost.

For many decisions that involve:

- relatively small variations from existing practice, and/or
- relatively limited periods of time,

fixed cost is not relevant. It will be the same irrespective of the decision made. This is because fixed cost elements cannot, or will not, be altered in the short term.

Activity 9.14

Ali plc owns a workshop from which it provides an IT repair and maintenance service. There has recently been a downturn in demand for the service. It would be possible for Ali plc to carry on the business from smaller, cheaper accommodation.

Can you think of any reasons why the business might not immediately move to smaller, cheaper accommodation?

We thought of broadly three reasons:

1. It is not usually possible to find a buyer for the existing accommodation at very short notice and it may be difficult to find an available alternative property quickly.
2. It may be difficult to move accommodation quickly where there is, say, delicate equipment to be moved.
3. Management may feel that the downturn might not be permanent and would, therefore, be reluctant to take such a dramatic step and deny itself the opportunity to benefit from a possible revival of trade.

You may have thought of others.

We shall now consider some types of decisions where fixed cost can be regarded as irrelevant. In making these decisions, we should have as our key objective the enhancement of owners' (shareholders') wealth. Since these decisions are short-term in nature, generating as much net cash inflow as possible will normally increase wealth.

In **marginal analysis** only costs and revenues that vary with the decision are considered. This means that fixed cost can usually be ignored. This is because marginal analysis is usually applied to minor alterations in the level of activity. It tends to be true, therefore, that the variable cost per unit will be equal to the **marginal cost,** which is the additional cost of producing one more unit of output. While marginal cost normally equals variable cost, there may be times when producing one more unit will involve a step in the fixed cost. If this occurs, the marginal cost is not just the variable cost; it will include the increment, or step, in the fixed cost as well.

Marginal analysis may be used in four key areas of decision making:

- pricing/assessing opportunities to enter contracts;
- determining the most efficient use of scarce resources;
- make-or-buy decisions; and
- closing or continuation decisions.

Let us consider each of these areas in turn.

Pricing/assessing opportunities to enter contracts

To understand how marginal analysis may be used in assessing an opportunity, consider the following activity.

Activity (9.15)

Cottage Industries Ltd (see Example 9.2, page 333) has spare capacity as its basket makers have some spare time. An overseas retail chain has offered the business an order for 300 baskets at a price of £13 each.

Without considering any wider issues, should the business accept the order? (Assume that the business does not rent the machine.)

Since the fixed cost will be incurred in any case, it is not relevant to this decision. All we need to do is to see whether the price offered will yield a contribution. If it will, the business will be better off by accepting the contract than by refusing it.

	£
Additional revenue per unit	13
Additional cost per unit	(12)
Additional contribution per unit	1

For 300 units, the additional contribution will be £300 (that is, 300 × £1). Since no fixed cost increase is involved, irrespective of what else is happening to the business, it will be £300 better off by taking this contract than by refusing it.

As ever with decision making, there are other factors that are either difficult or impossible to quantify. These should be taken into account before reaching a final decision. In the case of Cottage Industries Ltd's decision concerning the overseas customer, these could include the following:

- The possibility that spare capacity will have been 'sold off' cheaply when there might be another potential customer who will offer a higher price but, by that time, the capacity will be fully committed. It is a matter of commercial judgement as to how likely this will be.
- Selling the same product, but at different prices, could lead to a loss of customer goodwill. The fact that a different price will be set for customers in different countries (that is, in different markets) may be sufficient to avoid this potential problem.
- If the business is going to suffer continually from being unable to sell its full production potential at the 'usual' price, it might be better, in the long run, to reduce capacity and make fixed cost savings. Using the spare capacity to produce marginal benefits may lead to the business failing to address this issue.
- On a more positive note, the business may see this as a way of breaking into a different market. This is something that might be impossible to achieve if the business charges its usual price.

The marginal cost is the minimum price at which the business can offer a product or service for sale. It will result in the business being no better off as a result of making the sale than if it had not done so. Achieving more than this minimum price will generate a profit (an increase in owners' wealth).

A marginal cost approach to pricing would only be used where there is not the opportunity to sell at a price that will cover the full cost. In the long run, the business must more than cover all of its costs, both variable and fixed, if it is to be profitable.

Activity 9.16

A commercial aircraft is due to take off in one hour's time with 20 seats unsold. What is the minimum price at which these seats could be sold such that the airline would be no worse off as a result?

The answer is that any price above the additional cost of carrying one more passenger would represent an acceptable minimum. If there are no such costs, the minimum price is zero.

This is not to say that the airline will seek to charge the minimum price; it will presumably seek to charge the highest price that the market will bear. The fact that the market will not bear the full cost, plus a profit margin, should not, in principle, be sufficient for the airline to refuse to sell seats, where there is spare passenger capacity.

In practice, airlines are major users of a marginal costing approach. They often offer low priced tickets for off-peak travel, where there are not sufficient customers willing to pay 'normal' prices. By insisting on a Saturday stopover for return tickets, they tend to exclude 'business' travellers, who are probably forced to travel, but for whom a Saturday stopover may be unattractive. UK train operators often offer substantial discounts for off-peak travel. Similarly, hotels often charge very low rates for rooms at off-peak times. A hotel mainly used by business travellers may well offer very low room rates for Friday and Saturday occupancy.

Real World 9.10 explains how basing pharmaceutical prices that are set a little above marginal costs can be of real benefit to poorer countries and yet still be profitable for the businesses concerned.

Real World 9.10

A shot in the arm for poorer countries

The large pharmaceutical businesses ('big pharma') seem to be viewed as villains by the general public as a result of recent large increases in the prices of their drugs output. It seems, however, that big pharma businesses can be commercially successful without taking advantage of the fact that they may represent the only source of a particular drug.

In the view of the former chief executive of one big pharma business, GlaxoSmithKline (GSK) it is possible to be beneficial to people and to be profitable at the same time. Businesses cannot survive unless they make a profit. This means that everything that they do meets the marginal costs, as a minimum. For GSK, this amounts to making a 'contribution' wherever they are selling their drugs, no matter how small that contribution may be.

GSK ranks each country by a wealth measure (gross national product per head of population) and then with particular types of drug, vaccines for example, it applies a sliding scale of pricing according to the wealth measure – poorer people pay less. This tends to lead to high sales volumes for GSK, so the small contribution per sale still leads to a sustainable business model for the business.

Source: Information taken from: Mukherjee, S. (2016) *GSK's CEO Explains How Big Pharma Can Help the Poor and Still Make Money*, www.fortune.com, 2 November.

The most efficient use of scarce resources

Normally, the output of a business is determined by customer demand for the particular goods or services. In some cases, however, output will be restricted by the productive capacity of the business. Limited productive capacity might stem from a shortage of any factor of production – labour, raw materials, space, machine capacity and so on. Such scarce factors are often known as *key* or *limiting* factors.

Where productive capacity acts as a brake on output, management must decide on how best to deploy the scarce resource. That is, it must decide which products, from the range available, should be produced and how many of each should be produced. Marginal analysis can be useful to management in such circumstances. The guiding principle is that the most profitable combination of products will occur where the *contribution per unit of the scarce factor* is maximised. Example 9.3 illustrates this point.

Example 9.3

A business provides three different services, the details of which are as follows:

Service (code name)	AX107	AX109	AX220
	£	£	£
Selling price per unit	50	40	65
Variable cost per unit	(25)	(20)	(35)
Contribution per unit	25	20	30
Labour time per unit	5 hours	3 hours	6 hours

The market will take as many units of each service as can be provided, but the ability to provide the service is limited by the availability of labour, all of which needs to be skilled. Fixed cost is not affected by the choice of service provided because all three services use the same facilities.

The most profitable service is AX109 because it generates a contribution of £6.67 (£20/3) an hour. The other two generate only £5.00 each an hour (£25/5 and £30/6). So, to maximise profit, priority should be given to the production that maximises the contribution per unit of limiting factor.

Our first reaction might be that the business should provide only service AX220, as this is the one that yields the highest contribution per unit sold. If so, we would have been making the mistake of thinking that it is the ability to sell that is the limiting factor. If the above analysis is not convincing, we can take a random number of available labour hours and ask ourselves what is the maximum contribution (and, therefore, profit) that could be made by providing each service exclusively. Bear in mind that there is no shortage of anything else, including market demand, just a shortage of labour.

Activity 9.17

A business makes three different products, the details of which are as follows:

Product (code name)	B14	B17	B22
Selling price per unit (£)	25	20	23
Variable cost per unit (£)	10	8	12
Weekly demand (units)	25	20	30
Machine time per unit (hours)	4	3	4

Fixed cost is not affected by the choice of product because all three products use the same machine. Machine time is limited to 148 hours a week.

Which combination of products should be manufactured if the business is to produce the highest profit?

Product (code name)	B14	B17	B22
	£	£	£
Selling price per unit	25	20	23
Variable cost per unit	(10)	(8)	(12)
Contribution per unit	15	12	11
Machine time per unit	4 hours	3 hours	4 hours
Contribution per machine hour	£3.75	£4.00	£2.75
Order of priority	2nd	1st	3rd

Therefore produce:

20 units of product B17 using	60 hours
22 units of product B14 using	88 hours
	148 hours

This leaves unsatisfied the market demand for a further 3 units of product B14 and 30 units of product B22.

Activity 9.18

What practical steps could be taken that might lead to a higher level of contribution for the business in Activity 9.17?

The possibilities for improving matters that occurred to us are as follows:

● Consider obtaining additional machine time. This could mean obtaining a new machine, subcontracting the machining to another business or, perhaps, squeezing a few more hours a week out of the business's existing machine. Perhaps a combination of two or more of these is a possibility.

Activity 9.18 *continued*

- Redesign the products in a way that requires less time per unit on the machine.
- Increase the price per unit of the three products. This might well have the effect of dampening demand, but the existing demand cannot be met at present. It may, therefore, be more profitable, in the long run, to make a greater contribution on each unit sold than to take one of the other courses of action to overcome the problem.

Activity 9.19

Going back to Activity 9.17, what is the maximum price that the business concerned would logically be prepared to pay to have the remaining B14s machined by a subcontractor, assuming that no fixed or variable cost would be saved as a result of not doing the machining in-house?

Would there be a different maximum if we were considering the B22s?

If the remaining three B14s were subcontracted at no cost, the business would be able to earn a contribution of £15 a unit, which it would not otherwise be able to gain. Therefore, any price up to £15 a unit would be worth paying to a subcontractor to undertake the machining. Naturally, the business would prefer to pay as little as possible, but anything up to £15 would still make it worthwhile subcontracting the machining.

This would not be true of the B22s because they have a different contribution per unit; £11 would be the relevant figure in their case.

Make-or-buy decisions

Businesses are frequently confronted by the need to decide whether to produce the product or service that they sell themselves, or to buy it in from some other business. Thus, a producer of electrical appliances might decide to subcontract the manufacture of one of its products to another business, perhaps because there is a shortage of production capacity in the producer's own factory, or because it believes it to be cheaper to subcontract than to make the appliance itself.

It might just be part of a product or service that is subcontracted. For example, the producer may have a component for the appliance made by another manufacturer. In principle, there is hardly any limit to the scope of make-or-buy decisions. Virtually any part, component or service that is required in production of the main product or service, or the main product or service itself, could be the subject of a make-or-buy decision. So, for example, the human resources function of a business, which is normally performed in-house, could be subcontracted. At the same time, electrical power, which is typically provided by an outside electrical utility business, could be generated in-house. Obtaining services or products from a subcontractor is referred to as **outsourcing**.

Activity 9.20

Shah Ltd needs a component for one of its products. It can outsource production of the component to a subcontractor who will provide the components for £20 each. Shah Ltd can produce the components internally for a total variable cost of £15 per component. Shah Ltd has spare capacity.

Should the component be subcontracted or produced internally?

The answer is that Shah Ltd should produce the component internally, since the variable cost of subcontracting is greater by £5 (that is, £20 − £15) than the variable cost of internal manufacture.

Activity 9.21

Now assume that Shah Ltd (Activity 9.20) has no spare capacity, so it can only produce the component internally only by reducing its output of another of its products. While it is making each component, it will lose contributions of £12 from the other product.
   Should the component be subcontracted or produced internally?

The answer is to subcontract. In this case, both the variable cost of production and the opportunity cost of lost contributions must be taken into account. Thus, the relevant cost of internal production of each component is:

	£
Variable cost of production of the component	15
Opportunity cost of lost production of the other product	12
	27

This is obviously more costly than the £20 per component that will have to be paid to the subcontractor.

Activity 9.22

What factors, other than the immediately financially quantifiable, would you consider when making a make-or-buy decision?

We feel that there are two major factors:

1 The general problems of subcontracting, particularly
   (a) loss of control of quality; and
   (b) potential unreliability of supply.
2 Expertise and specialisation. Generally, businesses should focus on their core competences.

Picking up on the second point in Activity 9.22, it is possible for most businesses, with sufficient determination, to do virtually everything in-house. This may, however, require a level of skill and facilities that most businesses neither have nor wish to acquire. For example, while most businesses could generate their own electricity, their managements usually take the view that this is better done by a generator business. Specialists can often do things more cheaply, with less risk of things going wrong.

Real World 9.11 comprises extracts from an article that expands on the answer to Activity 9.22 in pointing out the limits to beneficial outsourcing.

Real World 9.11

Outsourcing can be neat, plausible and wrong

For every complicated problem, the journalist H.L. Mencken said, there is a solution that is neat, plausible, and wrong. When outsourcing first became a popular business practice two decades ago, some executives mistakenly believed they had found a neat solution that was plausible, and right.

While there were obvious 'cost arbitrage' savings to be made by taking a business unit out of a high-wage area and transporting the activity to an emerging market – the so-called 'lift and shift' approach – it turned out that life was more complicated than that. Outsourcing was not and is not an easy option. Contracts take a lot of managing. Cheaper will not necessarily mean more efficient, and more efficient will not necessarily mean more effective. The 'people factor' is significant. Service level agreements have to be monitored and maintained. And initial cost savings can be eroded as wages rise in rapidly developing economies.

In any case, intelligent outsourcing is no longer simply about cost savings. 'That's just "table stakes",' says Anoop Sagoo, senior managing director at Accenture, the consulting firm. 'We've moved on a long way from what people used to think about when they discussed outsourcing,' he says.

Another interesting aspect of current thinking on outsourcing is the way it forces (or should force) businesses to ask hard and fundamental questions about how they operate, and what sort of business they really are. If growth is the ultimate goal this matters. Jonathan Cooper-Bagnall, head of shared services and outsourcing at PA Consulting, says that intelligent outsourcing can provide businesses with the sort of flexibility they need to be able to compete successfully, and grow. 'In the wake of the financial crisis, some companies have cut their cost base very deep, and are not in a position to rebuild that cost base,' he says. 'So they have to use third parties in a smart way. Say you were a bank or a retailer setting up in a new market. Do you really need to build your own systems, hire all your own people?' he asks. Mr Cooper-Bagnall goes further. 'What is really core to your business? Do you need your own R&D team? Or are you really a branding company? Other people can handle logistics, procurement, do the product development – your job is to market it.' This is where the logic of outsourcing ultimately takes you. How and where do you create value?

But before selling a too optimistic version of outsourcing, Mr Cooper-Bagnall adds: 'The talent needed to run these [outsourced] operations is in short supply, and expensive. Business acumen, managing suppliers, and those other sorts of relationship skills, are rarely found in one individual. How do you find and develop people for these roles? It's not easy.' In order to avoid classic outsourcing pitfalls, it is worth asking what the common characteristics of successful attempts to outsource are.

Outsourcing is not the answer to everything. It can be taken too far. Companies can lose control – or 'sight' – of far-flung operations. And some activities will, or should, always remain core. But the logic of outsourcing can be hard to resist. And for those looking to grow quickly, flexibly and sustainably, it is an unavoidable option.

FT *Source*: Extracts from Stern, S. (2013) Logic of outsourcing can be hard to resist, ft.com, 20 September. © The Financial Times Limited 2013. All Rights Reserved.

Closing or continuation decisions

It is quite common for businesses to produce separate financial statements for each department or section, to try to assess their relative performance. Example 9.4 considers how marginal analysis can help decide how to respond where it is found that a particular department underperforms.

Example 9.4

Goodsports Ltd is a retail shop that operates through three departments, all in the same accommodation. The three departments occupy roughly equal-sized areas of the accommodation. The projected trading results for next year are:

	Total	Sports equipment	Sports clothes	General clothes
	£000	£000	£000	£000
Sales revenue	534	254	183	97
Cost	(482)	(213)	(163)	(106)
Profit/(loss)	52	41	20	(9)

It would appear that if the general clothes department were to close, the business would be more profitable, by £9,000 a year.

When the cost is analysed between that part that is variable and that part that is fixed, however, the contribution of each department can be deduced and the following results obtained:

	Total	Sports equipment	Sports clothes	General clothes
	£000	£000	£000	£000
Sales revenue	534	254	183	97
Variable cost	(344)	(167)	(117)	(60)
Contribution	190	87	66	37
Fixed cost (rent and so on)	(138)	(46)	(46)	(46)
Profit/(loss)	52	41	20	(9)

Now it is obvious that closing the general clothes department, without any other developments, would make the business worse off by £37,000 (the department's contribution). The department should not be closed, because it makes a positive contribution. The fixed cost would continue whether the department was closed or not. As can be seen from the above analysis, distinguishing between variable and fixed cost, and deducing the contribution, can make the picture much clearer.

Activity (9.23)

In considering Goodsports Ltd (in Example 9.4), we saw that the general clothes department should not be closed 'without any other developments'.

What 'other developments' could affect this decision, making continuation either more attractive or less attractive?

The things that we could think of are as follows:

- Expansion of the other departments or replacing the general clothes department with a completely new activity. This would make sense only if the space currently occupied by the general clothes department could generate contributions totalling at least £37,000 a year.
- Subletting the space occupied by the general clothes department. Once again, this would need to generate a net rent greater than £37,000 a year to make it more financially beneficial than keeping the department open.
- Keeping the department open, even if it generated no contribution whatsoever (assuming that there is no other use for the space), may still be beneficial. If customers are attracted into the shop because it has general clothing, they may then buy something from one of the other departments. In the same way, the activity of a sub-tenant might attract customers into the shop. (On the other hand, it might drive them away!)

You may have thought of others.

Figure 9.14 summarises the four key decision-making areas where marginal analysis tends to be used.

Figure 9.14 **The four key areas of decision making using marginal analysis**

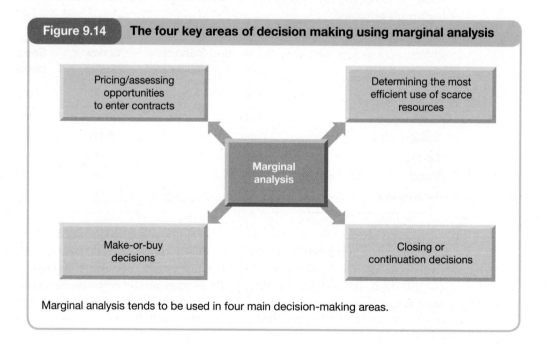

Marginal analysis tends to be used in four main decision-making areas.

Self-assessment question 9.1

Khan Ltd can render three different types of service (Alpha, Beta and Gamma) using the same staff. Various estimates for next year have been made as follows:

Service	Alpha	Beta	Gamma
Selling price (£/unit)	30	39	20
Variable material cost (£/unit)	15	18	10
Other variable costs (£/unit)	6	10	5
Share of fixed cost (£/unit)	8	12	4
Staff time required (hours)	2	3	1

Fixed cost for next year is expected to total £40,000.

Required:

(a) If the business were to render only service Alpha next year, how many units of the service would it need to provide in order to break even? (Assume for this part of the question that there is no effective limit to market size and staffing level.)

(b) If the business has limited staff hours available next year, in which order of preference would the three services come?

(c) The maximum market for next year for the three services is as follows:

Alpha	3,000 units
Beta	2,000 units
Gamma	5,000 units

Khan Ltd has a maximum of 10,000 staff hours available next year.

What quantities of each service should the business provide next year and how much profit would this be expected to yield?

The solution to this question can be found at the back of the book on p. 775.

Summary

The main points of this chapter may be summarised as follows:

Cost behaviour

- Fixed cost is independent of the level of activity (for example, rent).
- Variable cost varies with the level of activity (for example, raw materials).
- Semi-fixed (semi-variable) cost is a mixture of fixed and variable costs (for example, electricity).

Break-even analysis

- The break-even point (BEP) is the level of activity (in units of output or sales revenue) at which total cost (fixed + variable) = total sales revenue.

- Calculation of BEP is as follows:

$$\text{BEP (in units of output)} = \frac{\text{Fixed cost for the period}}{\text{Contribution per unit}}$$

- Knowledge of the BEP for a particular activity can be used to help assess risk.
- Contribution per unit = sales revenue per unit less variable cost per unit.
- Contribution margin ratio = contribution/sales revenue ($\times 100\%$).
- Margin of safety = excess of planned volume (or sales revenue) of activity over volume (or sales revenue) at BEP.
- Calculation of the volume of activity (t) required to achieve a target profit is as follows:

$$t = \frac{\text{Fixed cost} + \text{Target profit}}{\text{Sales revenue per unit} - \text{Variable cost per unit}}$$

- Operating gearing is the extent to which the total cost of some activity is fixed rather than variable.
- The profit–volume (PV) chart is an alternative approach to the break-even chart, which is probably easier to understand.
- Economists tend to take a different approach to break-even, taking account of economies (and diseconomies) of scale and of the fact that, generally, to be able to sell large volumes, price per unit tends to fall.

Weaknesses of break-even analysis

- There are non-linear relationships between cost, revenue and volume.
- There may be stepped fixed cost. Most elements of fixed cost are not fixed over all volumes of activity.
- Multi-product businesses have problems in allocating fixed cost to particular activities.

Marginal analysis (ignores fixed cost where this is not affected by the decision)

- Assessing contracts – we consider only the effect on contributions.
- Using scarce resources – the limiting factor is most effectively used by maximising its contribution per unit.
- Make-or-buy decisions – we take the action that leads to the highest total contributions.
- Closing/continuing an activity – should be assessed by net effect on total contributions.

Key terms

For definitions of these terms, see Appendix B.

fixed cost *p. 325*
variable cost *p. 325*
stepped fixed cost *p. 327*
semi-fixed (semi-variable)
  cost *p. 328*
high–low method *p. 329*
break-even analysis *p. 330*
break-even chart *p. 331*
break-even point (BEP) *p. 331*
contribution per unit *p. 336*

contribution margin ratio *p. 336*
margin of safety *p. 337*
operating gearing *p. 340*
profit–volume (PV) chart *p. 342*
economies of scale *p. 343*
relevant range *p. 344*
business cycle *p. 345*
marginal analysis *p. 349*
marginal cost *p. 349*
outsourcing *p. 354*

Further reading

If you would like to explore the topics covered in this chapter in more depth, we recommend the following:

Bhimani, A., Horngren, C., Datar, S. and Rajan, M. (2015) *Management and Cost Accounting,* 6th edn, Pearson, Chapters 8 and 9.

Burns, J., Quinn, M., Warren, L. and Oliveira, J. (2013) *Management Accounting,* McGraw-Hill Education, Chapters 11–13.

Drury, C. (2015) *Management and Cost Accounting,* 9th edn, Cengage Learning EMEA, Chapter 8.

Hilton, R. and Platt, D. (2014) *Managerial Accounting,* 10th edn, McGraw-Hill Higher Education, Chapters 6 and 7.

Review questions

Solutions to these questions can be found at the back of the book on pp. 792–793.

9.1 Define the terms *fixed cost* and *variable cost.* Explain how an understanding of the distinction between fixed cost and variable cost can be useful to managers.

9.2 What is meant by the BEP for an activity? How is the BEP calculated? Why is it useful to know the BEP?

9.3 When we say that some business activity has *high operating gearing,* what do we mean? What are the implications for the business of high operating gearing?

9.4 If there is a scarce resource that is restricting sales, how will the business maximise its profit? Explain the logic of the approach that you have identified for maximising profit.

Exercises

Solutions to exercises with coloured numbers can be found at the back of the book on pp. 818–819.

Basic-level exercises

9.1 Motormusic Ltd makes a standard model of car radio, which it sells to car manufacturers for £60 each. Next year the business plans to make and sell 20,000 radios. The business's costs are as follows:

Manufacturing	
Variable materials	£20 per radio
Variable labour	£14 per radio
Other variable costs	£12 per radio
Fixed cost	£80,000 per year
Administration and selling	
Variable	£3 per radio
Fixed	£60,000 per year

Required:

(a) Calculate the break-even point for next year, expressed both in quantity of radios and sales value.

(b) Calculate the margin of safety for next year, expressed both in quantity of radios and sales value.

9.2 Lannion and Co. is engaged in providing and marketing a standard advice service. Summarised results for the past two months reveal the following:

	October	November
Sales (units of the service)	200	300
Sales revenue (£)	5,000	7,500
Operating profit (£)	1,000	2,200

There were no price changes of any description during these two months.

Required:

(a) Deduce the BEP (in units of the service) for Lannion and Co.
(b) State why the business might find it useful to know its BEP.

Intermediate-level exercises

9.3 Gandhi Ltd renders a promotional service to small retailing businesses. There are three levels of service: the 'Basic', the 'Standard' and the 'Comprehensive'. The business plans next year to work at absolute full production capacity. Managers believe that the market will not accept more of any of the three services at the planned prices. The plans are:

Service	Number of units of the service	Selling price £	Variable cost per unit £
Basic	11,000	50	25
Standard	6,000	80	65
Comprehensive	16,000	120	90

The business's fixed cost totals £660,000 a year. Each service takes about the same length of time, irrespective of the level.

One of the accounts staff has just produced a report that seems to show that the Standard service is unprofitable. The relevant extract from the report is as follows:

Standard service cost analysis

	£	
Selling price per unit	80	
Variable cost per unit	(65)	
Fixed cost per unit	(20)	(£660,000/(11,000 + 6,000 + 16,000))
Loss	(5)	

The writer of the report suggests that the business should not offer the Standard service next year. The report goes on to suggest that, if the price of the Basic service were to be lowered, the market could be expanded.

Required:

(a) Should the Standard service be offered next year, assuming that the quantity of the other services could not be expanded to use the spare capacity?

(b) Should the Standard service be offered next year, assuming that the released capacity could be used to render a new service, the 'Nova', for which customers would be charged £75 per unit, and which would have a variable cost of £50 per unit and take twice as long per unit as each the other three services?

(c) What is the minimum price that could be accepted for the Basic service, assuming that the necessary capacity to expand it will come only from not offering the Standard service?

9.4 The management of a business is concerned about its inability to obtain enough fully trained labour to enable it to meet its present budget projection.

Service	Alpha £000	Beta £000	Gamma £000	Total £000
Variable cost:				
Materials	6	4	5	15
Labour	9	6	12	27
Expenses	3	2	2	7
Allocated fixed cost	6	15	12	33
Total cost	24	27	31	82
Profit	15	2	2	19
Sales revenue	39	29	33	101

The amount of labour likely to be available amounts to £20,000. All of the variable labour is paid at the same hourly rate. You have been asked to prepare a statement of plans, ensuring that at least 50 per cent of the budgeted sales revenues are achieved for each service and the balance of labour is used to produce the greatest profit.

Required:

(a) Prepare the statement, with explanations, showing the greatest profit available from the limited amount of skilled labour available, within the constraint stated. (*Hint*: Remember that all labour is paid at the same rate.)

(b) What steps could the business take in an attempt to improve profitability, in the light of the labour shortage?

9.5 A hotel group prepares financial statements on a quarterly basis. The senior management is reviewing the performance of one hotel and making plans for next year.

The managers have in front of them the results for this year (based on some actual results and some forecasts to the end of this year):

Quarter	Sales revenue £000	Profit/(loss) £000
1	400	(280)
2	1,200	360
3	1,600	680
4	800	40
Total	4,000	800

The total estimated number of guests (guest nights) for this year is 50,000, with each guest night being charged at the same rate. The results follow a regular pattern; there are no unexpected cost fluctuations beyond the seasonal trading pattern shown above.

For next year, management anticipates an increase in unit variable cost of 10 per cent and a profit target for the hotel of £1 million. These will be incorporated into its plans.

Required:

(a) Calculate the total variable and total fixed cost of the hotel for this year. Show the provisional annual results for this year in total, showing variable and fixed cost separately. Show also the revenue and cost per guest.

(b) 1 If there is no increase in guests for next year, what will be the required revenue rate per hotel guest to meet the profit target?

   2 If the required revenue rate per guest is not raised above this year's level, how many guests will be required to meet the profit target?

(c) Outline and briefly discuss the assumptions, that are made in typical PV or break-even analysis, and assess whether they limit its usefulness.

Advanced-level exercises

9.6 A business makes three products, A, B and C. All three products require the use of two types of machine: cutting machines and assembling machines. Estimates for next year include the following:

Product	A	B	C
Selling price (£ per unit)	25	30	18
Sales demand (units)	2,500	3,400	5,100
Material cost (£ per unit)	12	13	10
Variable production cost (£ per unit)	7	4	3
Time required per unit on cutting machines (hours)	1.0	1.0	0.5
Time required per unit on assembling machines (hours)	0.5	1.0	0.5

Fixed cost for next year is expected to total £42,000.

The business has cutting machine capacity of 5,000 hours a year and assembling machine capacity of 8,000 hours a year.

Required:

(a) State, with supporting workings, which products in which quantities the business should plan to make next year on the basis of the above information. (*Hint*: First determine which machines will be a limiting factor (scarce resource).)

(b) State the maximum price per product that it would be worth the business paying to a subcontractor to carry out that part of the work that could not be done internally.

9.7   Darmor Ltd has three products, which require the same production facilities. Information about the production cost for one unit of its products is as follows:

Product	X £	Y £	Z £
Labour: Skilled	6	9	3
Unskilled	2	4	10
Materials	12	25	14
Other variable costs	3	7	7
Fixed cost	5	10	10

All labour and materials are variable costs. Skilled labour is paid £12 an hour and unskilled labour is paid £8 an hour. All references to labour cost above are based on basic rates of pay. Skilled labour is scarce, which means that the business could sell more than the maximum that it is able to make of any of the three products.

Product X is sold in a regulated market and the regulators have set a price of £30 per unit for it.

Required:

(a) State, with supporting workings, the price that must be charged for Products Y and Z, such that the business would find it equally profitable to make and sell any of the three products.

(b) State, with supporting workings, the maximum rate of overtime premium that the business would logically be prepared to pay its skilled workers to work beyond the basic time.

CHAPTER  10

Full costing

Introduction

Full (absorption) costing is a widely used approach that takes account of all of the cost of producing a particular product or service. In this chapter, we shall see how this approach can be used to deduce the cost of some activity, such as making a unit of product (for example, a tin of baked beans), providing a unit of service (for example, a car repair) or creating a facility (for example, building a high-speed rail link from London to Birmingham).

The precise approach taken to deducing full cost will depend on whether each product or service is identical to the next or whether each job has its own individual characteristics. It will also depend on whether the business accounts for overheads on a segmental basis. We shall look at how full costing is carried out and we shall also consider its usefulness for management purposes.

This chapter considers the traditional form of full costing, which is known as absorption costing. In Chapter 11, we shall consider activity-based costing, which is a more recently developed approach.

Learning outcomes

When you have completed this chapter, you should be able to:

● deduce the full (absorption) cost of a cost unit in a single-product and a multi-product environment;

● discuss the problems of deducing full (absorption) cost in practice;

● discuss the usefulness of full (absorption) cost information to managers; and

● compare and contrast the full costing and variable costing approaches.

What is full costing?

Full cost is the total amount of resources, usually measured in monetary terms, sacrificed to achieve a given objective. Thus, if the objective is to supply a customer with a product or service, all resources sacrificed to make the product, or provide the service, are included as part of the full cost. To derive the full cost figure, the various elements of cost incurred are accumulated and then assigned to the particular product or service.

The logic of **full costing** is that the entire cost of running a facility, such as an office or factory, must be regarded as part of the cost of the output that it helps to generate. Take, for example, the rent incurred in running an architect's office. While this may not alter if the architect undertakes one more assignment, there would be nowhere to work unless the office was available. Thus, the office rent must be taken into account when calculating the full cost of providing each architectural assignment.

A **cost unit** is a unit of whatever is having its cost determined, such as an architectural assignment. Usually, it is one unit of output of a particular product or service.

Why do managers want to know the full cost?

We saw in Chapter 1 that management accounting information aims to improve the quality of managers' decisions. There are four main areas where information relating to the full cost of a business's products or services may help serve this purpose. These are:

- *Pricing and output decisions.* Having full cost information can help managers make decisions on the price to charge customers for the business's products or services. Full cost information, along with relevant information concerning prices, can also be used to determine the number of units of products or services to be produced.
- *Exercising control.* Determining the full cost of a product or service is often a useful starting point for exercising cost control. Where the reported full cost figure is considered too high, for example, individual elements of full cost may then be examined to see whether there are opportunities for savings. This may lead to re-engineering the production process, finding new sources of supply and so on. Also, budgets and plans are often expressed in full cost terms. Budgets are typically used to help managers exercise control by comparing planned (budgeted) performance, with actual performance. We shall pick up this point in later chapters, particularly Chapters 11 and 13.
- *Assessing relative efficiency.* Full cost information can help compare the cost of carrying out an activity in a particular way, or particular place, with its cost if carried out in a different way, or place. A motor car manufacturer, for example, may wish to compare the cost of building a particular model of car in one manufacturing plant, rather than in another. This could help in deciding where to locate future production.
- *Assessing performance.* Profit is an important measure of business performance. To measure the profit arising from a particular product or service, the sales revenue that it generates should be compared with the costs consumed in generating that revenue. This can help in assessing past decisions. It can also help in guiding future decisions, such as continuing with, or abandoning, the particular product or service.

Figure 10.1 shows the four uses of full cost information.

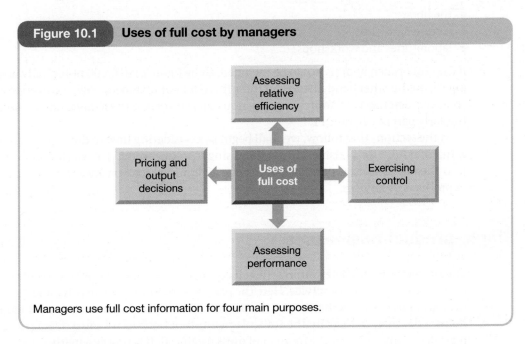

Figure 10.1 **Uses of full cost by managers**

Managers use full cost information for four main purposes.

Now let us consider **Real World 10.1**.

Real World 10.1

Costing by degrees

The University of Cambridge calculated that, for the academic year 2014/15, the average cost of educating an undergraduate student was £18,000.

This figure represents the full cost of carrying out this activity.

Source: Morgan, J. (2016) Cambridge's 'Cost of education' rises to £18K per student, *Times Higher Education Supplement*, 8 September.

When considering the information in Real World 10.1, an important question that arises is 'what does this full cost figure include?' Does it simply include the cost of the salaries earned by academics during the time spent in lectures, seminars and tutorials or does it include other things? If other costs are to be included, what are they? Would they include, for example, a charge for the costs of time spent by academics in:

- preparing materials for lectures;
- editing and updating course materials;
- preparing and marking examination papers;
- invigilation of examinations; and
- organising and visiting placements?

Would there be a charge for administrative staff carrying out teaching support activities such as:

- timetabling;
- preparing prospectuses;
- student counselling; and
- careers' advice?

Would there be a charge for the use of university facilities such as:

- the library;
- lecture halls; and
- laboratories and workshops?

If the cost of such items is not to be included, is the figure of £18,000 potentially misleading? If, on the other hand, the cost of these items is to be included, how can an appropriate charge be determined? Addressing questions such as these is the focus of this chapter and the early part of Chapter 11.

In the sections that follow, we shall begin by considering how to derive the full cost of a unit of output for a business providing a single product or service. We then go on to see how the full cost of a unit of output may be determined for a business providing a range of products or services.

Single-product businesses

The simplest case for determining the full cost per unit of output is where a business produces a single product or service. Here the production process will involve a series of continuous or repetitive activities and the output will consist of identical, or near identical, items. Logically, to identify the full cost per unit of output, we must average the total manufacturing cost over the number of units produced. It is simply a matter of adding up all of the elements of cost of production incurred in a particular period (materials, labour, rent, fuel, power and so on) and dividing this total by the total number of units of output for that period. This approach is referred to as **process costing.**

Activity 10.1

Fruitjuice Ltd began operations at the beginning of May. It has just one product, a sparkling orange drink that is marketed as 'Orange Fizz'. During May the business produced 7,300 litres of the drink. The manufacturing cost incurred was made up as follows:

	£
Ingredients (oranges, sugar, water and so on)	390
Fuel	85
Rent of factory accommodation	350
Depreciation of equipment	75
Labour	852

What is the full cost per litre of producing 'Orange Fizz' in May?

$$\text{Full cost per litre} = \text{Total manufacturing costs/Number of litres produced}$$

$$= £(390 + 85 + 350 + 75 + 852)/7,300$$

$$= 1,752/7,300$$

$$= £0.24 \text{ per litre}$$

Process-costing problems

Process costing tends to be fairly straightforward as it involves tracking the production of identical, or near identical, items. Nevertheless, problems can still arise when measuring certain elements of manufacturing cost. In the case of Fruitjuice Ltd, for example, how is the cost of depreciation deduced? It can only be an estimate and so its reliability is open to question. The cost of raw materials may also be a problem. Should we use the 'relevant' cost of the raw materials (in this case, almost certainly the replacement cost), or the actual price paid for it (historic cost)? As the cost per litre will presumably be used for decision-making purposes, replacement cost provides the more logical choice. For some reason, however, historic cost seems to be more widely used in practice.

There can also be problems in calculating how much output was produced. If making Orange Fizz is not a very fast process, some of the product will be in the process of being made at any given moment. Partially completed Orange Fizz represents **work in progress** (or work in process) that should be taken into account when calculating the total output, and cost per unit of output, for a period.

Activity 10.2

Can you think of industries where process costing may be suitable? Try to think of at least two.

Suitable industries are likely to include:

- paint manufacturing;
- chemical processing;
- oil extraction;
- plastic manufacturing;
- paper manufacturing;
- brick manufacturing;
- beverages; and
- semiconductor chips.

You may have thought of others.

Multi-product businesses

Many businesses provide products or services that are distinct rather than identical. In this situation, the process-costing approach that we used with litres of 'Orange Fizz' (Activity 10.1) would be inappropriate. While it may be appropriate to assign an average cost to each *identical* unit of output, this is not reasonable where units of output are quite different. It would be illogical, for example, to assign the same cost to each car repair carried out by a garage, irrespective of the complexity and size of the repair.

Where a business offers distinct products or services, a **job-costing** approach is normally used. This involves accumulating costs for each individual unit of output in order to determine its full cost. To understand how this can be done, we first need to understand the difference between direct and indirect cost.

Direct and indirect cost

To provide full cost information, the various elements of cost must be accumulated and then assigned to particular cost units on some reasonable basis. Where cost units are not identical, the starting point is to separate cost into two categories: direct cost and indirect cost.

- **Direct cost.** This is a cost that can be identified with specific cost units. That is to say, the cost can be traced to a particular cost unit and can be measured reliably. The main examples of a direct cost are direct materials and direct labour. Thus, in determining the cost of a car repair by a garage, both the cost of spare parts used in the repair and the cost of the mechanic's time would form part of the direct cost of that repair. Collecting elements of direct cost is a simple matter of having a cost-recording system that is capable of capturing the cost of direct materials used on each job and the cost of direct workers.
- **Indirect cost** (or **overheads**). This comprises all other elements of total cost. That is to say those items that cannot be identified with each particular cost unit (job). Thus, the amount paid to rent the garage would be an indirect cost of a particular car repair.

We shall use the terms 'indirect cost' and 'overheads' interchangeably for the remainder of this book.

Real World 10.2 gives some indication of the relative importance of direct and indirect costs in practice.

Real World 10.2

Counting the cost

A survey of 176 UK businesses operating in various industries, all with an annual turnover of more than £50 million, was conducted by Al-Omiri and Drury. They discovered that the full cost of the businesses' output on average is split between direct and indirect costs as shown in Figure 10.2.

Figure 10.2	Percentage of full cost contributed by direct and indirect cost

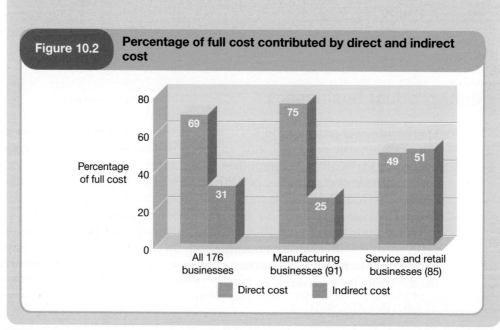

For the manufacturers, the 75 per cent direct cost was, on average, made up as follows:

	Percentage
Direct materials	52
Direct labour	14
Other direct costs	9

Source: Al-Omiri, M. and Drury, C. (2007) A survey of factors influencing the choice of product costing systems in UK organizations, *Management Accounting Research*, vol. 18, pp. 399–424.

Activity 10.3

A garage owner wishes to know the direct cost of each job (car repair) that is carried out. How might the direct cost (labour and materials) information concerning a particular job be collected?

Usually, direct workers are required to record how long was spent on each job. Thus, the mechanic doing the job would record the length of time worked on the car. The pay rates should be available. It is simply then a matter of multiplying the number of hours spent on a job by the relevant rate of pay. The stores staff would normally be required to keep a record of the cost of parts and materials used on each job.

A 'job sheet' will normally be prepared – probably on the computer – for each individual job. The quality of the information generated will rely on staff faithfully recording all elements of direct labour and materials applied to the job.

Job costing

To deduce the full cost of a particular cost unit, we first identify the direct cost of the cost unit, which is usually fairly straightforward. The next step, however, is less straightforward. We have to 'charge' each cost unit with a suitable share of indirect cost (overheads). Put another way, cost units will *absorb* overheads. This term leads to full costing also being called **absorption costing**. The absorption process is shown graphically in Figure 10.3.

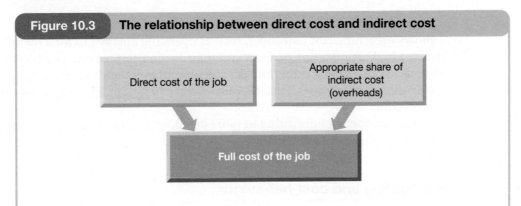

Figure 10.3   **The relationship between direct cost and indirect cost**

The full cost of any particular job is the sum of those cost elements that can be measured specifically in respect of the job (direct cost) and a share of the cost of creating the environment in which production (of an object or service) can take place, but which do not relate specifically to any particular job (indirect cost).

Activity 10.4

Sparky Ltd is a business that employs a number of electricians. The business undertakes a range of work for its customers, from replacing fuses to installing complete wiring systems in new houses.

In respect of a particular job done by Sparky Ltd, into which category (direct or indirect) would each of the following cost elements fall?

● the wages of the electrician who did the job;
● depreciation of the tools used by the electrician;
● the cost of cable and other materials used on the job; and
● rent of the building where Sparky Ltd stores its inventories of cable and other materials.

The electrician's wages earned while working on the particular job and the cost of the materials used on the job are included in direct cost. This is because we can measure how much time was spent on the particular job (and therefore its direct labour cost) and the amount of materials used (and therefore the direct material cost) in the job.

The other cost elements are included in the general cost of running the business and, as such, must form part of the indirect cost of doing the job. They cannot be directly measured in respect of the particular job.

It is important to note that whether a cost is direct or indirect depends on the item being costed – the cost objective. To refer to indirect cost without specifying the cost objective would be illogical.

Activity 10.5

Into which category, direct or indirect, would each of the elements of cost listed in Activity 10.4 fall, if we were seeking to find the cost of operating the entire business of Sparky Ltd for a month?

The answer is that all of them will form part of the direct cost, since they can all be related to, and measured in respect of, running the business for a month.

Broader-reaching cost objectives, such as operating Sparky Ltd for a month, tend to include a higher proportion of direct cost than do more limited ones, such as a particular job done by Sparky Ltd. Costing broader cost objectives is, therefore, more straightforward than costing narrower ones. This is because direct cost is normally easier to deal with than indirect cost.

Before considering full costing in more detail, let us first be clear as to how it differs from the approach discussed in the previous chapter.

Full costing and cost behaviour

We saw in Chapter 9 that the full cost of doing something (or *total cost,* as it is known in the context of marginal analysis) can be analysed between its fixed and variable elements. This is illustrated in Figure 10.4.

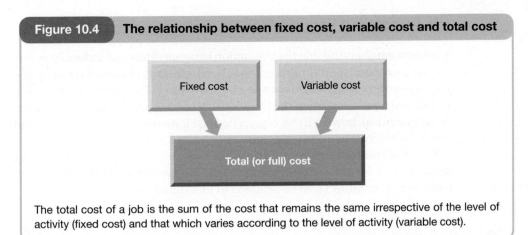

Figure 10.4 The relationship between fixed cost, variable cost and total cost

The total cost of a job is the sum of the cost that remains the same irrespective of the level of activity (fixed cost) and that which varies according to the level of activity (variable cost).

The apparent similarity of what is shown in Figure 10.4 to that shown in Figure 10.3 may create the impression that variable cost and direct cost are the same, and that fixed cost and indirect cost (overheads) are also the same. This, however, is not the case.

Fixed cost and variable cost are defined in terms of **cost behaviour** in the face of changes in the volume of activity. Direct cost and indirect cost, on the other hand, are defined in terms of the extent to which they can be identified with, and measured in respect of, particular cost units (jobs). These two sets of notions are entirely different. While a fixed cost can often be an indirect cost and a variable cost can often be a direct cost, this is far from being a hard and fast rule. Take, for example, most manufactured products. They are likely to have indirect cost, such as power for machinery, which is variable, and direct cost, such as labour, which is fixed. Thus, identifying a cost as being either indirect or direct tells us nothing about whether it is fixed or variable.

The relationship between the reaction of cost to volume changes, on the one hand, and how cost elements must be gathered to deduce the full cost for a particular job, on the other, is shown in Figure 10.5.

Total cost is the sum of direct and indirect costs. It is also the sum of fixed and variable costs. We should always bear in mind that these two facts are not connected.

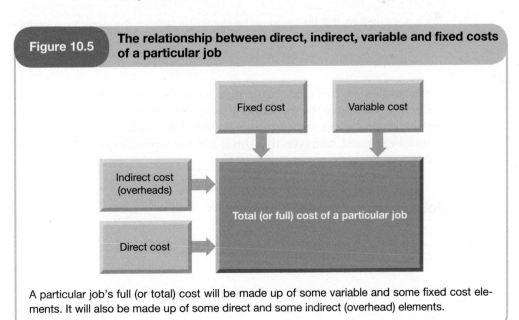

Figure 10.5 The relationship between direct, indirect, variable and fixed costs of a particular job

A particular job's full (or total) cost will be made up of some variable and some fixed cost elements. It will also be made up of some direct and some indirect (overhead) elements.

The problem of indirect cost

It is worth emphasising that the distinction between direct and indirect cost is only important in a job-costing environment, that is, where units of output differ. This distinction was of no consequence when costing a litre of 'Orange Fizz' drink (Activity 10.1) as all cost was shared equally between the individual litres of 'Orange Fizz'. Where units of output are not identical, however, this cannot be done if we wish to achieve an appropriate measure of the full cost of a particular job.

Although indirect cost must form part of the full cost of each cost unit, it cannot, by definition, be identified directly with particular cost units. This raises a major practical issue: how can indirect cost be assigned to individual cost units?

Overheads as service renderers

Indirect cost (overheads) can be viewed as rendering a service to cost units. Take, for example, a legal case undertaken by a firm of lawyers for a particular client. The legal case can be regarded as receiving a service from the office in which the work is done. It seems reasonable, therefore, to charge each case (cost unit) with a share of the cost of running the office (rent, lighting, heating, cleaning, building maintenance and so on). It also seems reasonable for this charge to be related to the amount of service received from the office.

The next step is the difficult one. How might the cost of running the office, which is a cost incurred for all the work undertaken by the firm, be divided between individual legal cases?

The easiest way would be to share this overhead cost equally between each case handled by the firm within the period. This method, however, has little to commend it.

Activity 10.6

Why would this method have little to commend it?

It is highly unlikely that the cases will be identical in terms of the extent to which they received service from the office. This is because they will differ in both size and complexity.

Where they have not received identical service, we must identify something observable and measurable about the various legal cases that allows us to distinguish between them. In practice, time spent working on each individual case by direct labour tends to be used. It must be stressed, however, that this is not the 'correct' way and it is certainly not the only way.

Job costing: a worked example

To see how job costing works, let us consider Example 10.1.

Example 10.1

Johnson Ltd provides a personal computer maintenance and repair service. It has overheads of £10,000 each month. Each month 1,000 direct labour hours are worked and charged to cost units (jobs carried out by the business). A particular PC repair undertaken by the business used direct materials costing £15. Direct labour worked on the repair was 3 hours and the wage rate is £16 an hour. Johnson Ltd charges overheads to jobs on a direct labour hour basis. What is the full (absorption) cost of the repair?

Solution

First, let us establish the **overhead absorption (recovery) rate,** that is, the rate at which individual repairs will be charged with overheads. This is £10 (that is, £10,000/1,000) per direct labour hour.

Thus, the full cost of the repair is:

	£
Direct materials	15
Direct labour (3 × £16)	48
	63
Overheads (3 × £10)	30
Full cost of the job	93

Note, in Example 10.1, that the number of labour hours (3 hours) appears twice in deducing the full cost: once to deduce the direct labour cost and a second time to deduce the overheads to be charged to the repair. These are really two separate issues, although both are based on the same number of labour hours.

Note also that, if all the jobs undertaken during the month are assigned overheads in a similar manner, all £10,000 of overheads will be charged between the various jobs. Jobs that involve a lot of direct labour will be assigned a large share of overheads. Similarly, jobs that involve little direct labour will be assigned a small share of overheads.

Activity 10.7

Can you think of reasons why direct labour hours tend to be regarded as the most logical basis for sharing overheads between cost units? Try to think of at least one.

The reasons that occurred to us are as follows:

● Large jobs should logically attract large amounts of overheads because they are likely to have been rendered more 'service' by the overheads than small ones. The length of time that they are worked on by direct labour may be seen as a rough way of measuring relative size, though other means of doing this may be found – for example, relative physical size, where the cost unit is a physical object, like a manufactured product.

Activity 10.7 continued

- Most overheads are related to time. Rent, heating, lighting, non-current asset depreciation and supervisors' and managers' salaries, which are all typical overheads, are all, more or less, time-based. That is, the overheads for one week tend to be about half of those for a similar two-week period. Thus, assigning overheads to jobs on the basis of the time the units of output benefited from the 'service' rendered by the overheads seems logical.
- Direct labour hours are capable of being measured for each job. They will normally be measured to deduce the direct labour element of cost in any case. Thus, a direct labour hour basis of dealing with overheads is practical to apply in the real world.

It cannot be emphasised enough that there is no 'correct' way to assign overheads to jobs. Overheads cannot, by definition, be easily identified with individual jobs. If, nevertheless, we wish to recognise that overheads are part of the full cost of all jobs, we must find some way of assigning a share of the total overheads to each job. In practice, the direct labour hour method seems to be the most popular way of doing so.

Real World 10.3 describes another approach to assigning overheads to jobs that was used by one well-known organisation.

Real World 10.3

Recovering costs

The UK National Health Service (NHS) calculates the cost of various medical and surgical procedures that it undertakes for its patients. In determining the costs of a procedure requiring time in hospital as an 'in patient', the NHS identifies the full cost of the particular procedure (for example, a knee replacement operation). To this it adds a share of the hospital overheads to cover the cost of the patient's stay in hospital.

Until recently, total ward overheads for a period were absorbed by dividing them by the number of 'bed days' throughout the hospital, to establish a 'bed-day rate'. A bed day is one patient spending one day occupying a bed in the hospital. The total cost of a particular patient's treatment was then calculated as:

the cost of the procedure + (the number of days the patient spent in hospital x the bed day rate)

The direct labour hour basis of absorption was not used. The bed-day rate is, however, an alternative, logical, time-based approach.

The NHS now uses a different form of full costing known as *activity-based costing*. The general principles of this method are described in Chapter 11.

Source: NHS England (2014) *NHS Better Care Better Value Indicators*, 15 May.

Activity (10.8)

Marine Suppliers Ltd undertakes a range of work, including making sails for small sailing boats on a made-to-measure basis.

The business expects the following to arise during the next month:

Direct labour cost	£60,000
Direct labour time	6,000 hours
Indirect labour cost	£9,000
Depreciation of machinery	£3,000
Rent	£5,000
Heating, lighting and power	£2,000
Machine time	2,000 hours
Indirect materials	£500
Other miscellaneous indirect production cost elements (overheads)	£200
Direct materials cost	£6,000

The business has received an enquiry about a sail. It is estimated that this particular sail will take 12 direct labour hours to make and will require 20 square metres of sail-cloth, which costs £10 per square metre.

The business normally uses a direct labour hour basis of charging indirect cost (overheads) to individual jobs.

What is the full (absorption) cost of making the sail?

The direct cost of making the sail can be identified as follows:

	£
Direct materials (20 × £10)	200.00
Direct labour (12 × (£60,000/6,000))	120.00
	320.00

To deduce the indirect cost (overhead) element that must be added to derive the full cost of the sail, we first need to total these cost elements as follows:

	£
Indirect labour	9,000
Depreciation	3,000
Rent	5,000
Heating, lighting and power	2,000
Indirect materials	500
Other miscellaneous indirect production cost (overhead) elements	200
Total indirect cost (overheads)	19,700

Since the business uses a direct labour hour basis of charging indirect cost to jobs, we need to deduce the indirect cost (or overhead) recovery rate per direct labour hour. This is simply:

£19,700/6,000 = £3.28 per direct labour hour

Thus, the full cost of the sail is expected to be:

	£
Direct materials (20 × £10)	200.00
Direct labour (12 × (£60,000/6,000))	120.00
Indirect cost (12 × £3.28)	39.36
Full cost	359.36

Figure 10.6 shows the process for applying indirect (overhead) and direct costs to the sail that was the subject of Activity 10.8.

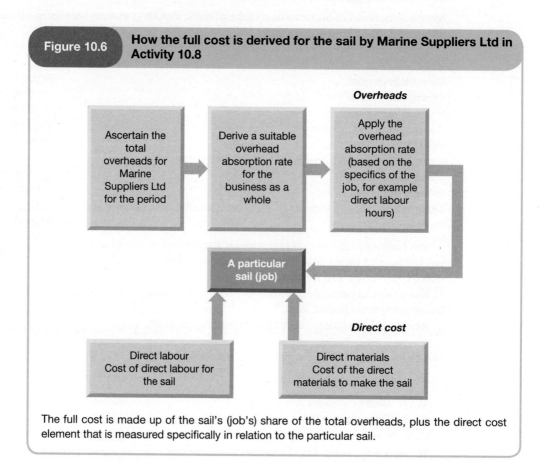

| Figure 10.6 | **How the full cost is derived for the sail by Marine Suppliers Ltd in Activity 10.8** |

Overheads

Ascertain the total overheads for Marine Suppliers Ltd for the period → **Derive a suitable overhead absorption rate for the business as a whole** → **Apply the overhead absorption rate (based on the specifics of the job, for example direct labour hours)**

A particular sail (job)

Direct cost

Direct labour Cost of direct labour for the sail

Direct materials Cost of the direct materials to make the sail

The full cost is made up of the sail's (job's) share of the total overheads, plus the direct cost element that is measured specifically in relation to the particular sail.

Activity 10.9

Suppose that Marine Suppliers Ltd (see Activity 10.8) used a machine hour basis of charging overheads to jobs. What would be the cost of the particular job if it was expected to take 5 machine hours (as well as 12 direct labour hours)?

The total overheads of the business will of course be the same irrespective of the method of charging them to jobs. Thus, the overhead recovery rate, on a machine hour basis, will be:

£19,700/2,000 = £9.85 per machine hour

The full cost of the sail is, therefore, expected to be:

	£
Direct materials (20 × £10)	200.00
Direct labour (12 × (£60,000/6,000))	120.00
Indirect cost (5 × £9.85)	49.25
Full cost	369.25

Real World 10.4 briefly describes the findings of one study, which reveals differences between larger and smaller businesses in their approach to assigning overheads.

Real World 10.4

Size matters

A questionnaire study of 272 management accountants working in UK manufacturing businesses found that a lower proportion of small and medium size (SME) businesses assigned overheads to product costs than for larger businesses. Furthermore, SMEs that did assign overhead costs used fewer overhead recovery rates when assigning overheads to product costs.

These findings might be expected given the differences between SMEs and larger businesses in resourcing levels and also, perhaps, levels of financial awareness among managers. These findings are consistent with another survey discussed in Real World 10.9.

Source: Brierley, J. (2011) A comparison of the product costing practices of large and small- to medium-sized enterprises: a survey of British manufacturing firms, *International Journal of Management*, vol. 28, pp. 184–193.

Activity 10.10

Can you think of industries or businesses where job costing may be suitable? Try to think of at least two.

Job costing may be suitable for a wide variety of industries or businesses, including:

- house building;
- civil engineering;
- accounting services;
- film making;
- interior design;
- consultancy; and
- shipbuilding.

You may have thought of others.

Selecting a basis for charging overheads

We saw earlier that there is no single correct way of charging overheads. The final choice is a matter of judgement. It seems reasonable to say, however, that the nature of the overheads should influence the basis for charging them to jobs. Where production is capital-intensive and overheads are primarily machine-based (such as depreciation, machine maintenance, power and so on), machine hours might be preferred. Otherwise direct labour hours might be chosen.

It would be irrational to choose one of these methods in preference to the other simply because it apportions either a higher or a lower amount of overheads to a particular job. The total overheads will be the same irrespective of how they are apportioned between individual jobs and so a method that gives a higher share of overheads to one particular job must give a lower share to the remaining jobs. There is one cake of fixed size: if one person receives a relatively large slice, others must on average receive relatively small slices. To illustrate further this issue of apportioning overheads, consider Example 10.2.

Example 10.2

A business, that provides a service, expects to incur overheads totalling £20,000 next month. The total direct labour time worked is expected to be 1,600 hours and machines are expected to operate for a total of 1,000 hours.

During the next month, the business expects to do just two large jobs. Information concerning each job is as follows:

	Job 1	Job 2
Direct labour hours	800	800
Machine hours	700	300

How much of the total overheads will be charged to each job if overheads are to be charged on:

(a) a direct labour hour basis; and
(b) a machine hour basis?

What do you notice about the two sets of figures that you calculate?

Solution

(a) **Direct labour hour basis**

Overhead recovery rate = £20,000/1,600 = £12.50 per direct labour hour.

Job 1	£12.50 × 800 = £10,000
Job 2	£12.50 × 800 = £10,000

(b) **Machine hour basis**

Overhead recovery rate = £20,000/1,000 = £20.00 per machine hour.

Job 1	£20.00 × 700 = £14,000
Job 2	£20.00 × 300 = £6,000

It is clear from these calculations that the total overheads charged to jobs is the same (that is, £20,000) whichever method is used. Whereas the machine hour basis gives Job 1 a higher share of these overheads than the direct labour hour method, the opposite is true for Job 2.

It is not feasible to charge overheads using one method for one job and using the other method for the other job. This would mean either total overheads would not be fully charged to the jobs, or the jobs would be overcharged with overheads. If, for example, the direct labour hour method was used for Job 1 (£10,000) and the machine hour basis was used for Job 2 (£6,000), only £16,000 of a total £20,000 of overheads would be charged to jobs. As a result, the purpose of full (absorption) costing, which is to charge *all* overhead costs to jobs carried out during the period, would not be achieved. Furthermore, if selling prices are based on full cost, there is a risk that the business would not charge high enough prices to cover all its costs.

Figure 10.7 shows the effect of the two different methods of charging overheads to Jobs 1 and 2.

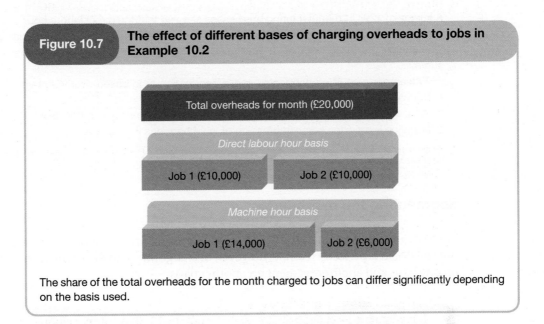

Figure 10.7 The effect of different bases of charging overheads to jobs in Example 10.2

Total overheads for month (£20,000)

Direct labour hour basis

Job 1 (£10,000)   Job 2 (£10,000)

Machine hour basis

Job 1 (£14,000)   Job 2 (£6,000)

The share of the total overheads for the month charged to jobs can differ significantly depending on the basis used.

Activity 10.11

The point was made above that it would normally be irrational to prefer one basis of charging overheads to jobs simply because it apportions either a higher or a lower amount of overheads to a particular job. This is because the total overheads are the same irrespective of the method of charging the total to individual jobs.

Can you think of any circumstances where it may not be so irrational?

This might occur where a customer has agreed to pay a price for a particular job based on full cost plus an agreed fixed percentage for profit. Here it would be beneficial to the producer for the total cost of the job to be as high as possible.

Public-sector organisations, such as central and local government, have been known to enter into such **cost-plus pricing** contracts, where the price is full cost plus a profit loading. These contracts are, however, now pretty rare as they are so open to abuse. Normally, contract prices are agreed in advance, typically in conjunction with competitive tendering.

Real World 10.5 provides some insight into the basis of overhead recovery in practice.

Real World 10.5

Overhead recovery rates in practice

A survey of 129 UK manufacturing businesses showed that the direct labour hour basis (or a close approximation to it) of charging indirect cost (overheads) to cost units was overwhelmingly the most popular. It was used by 72 per cent of the respondents to the survey.

Fifteen per cent of respondents used a 'production-time based overhead rate'. This is presumably something like a machine hour rate.

Although this survey applied only to manufacturing businesses, in the absence of other information it provides some impression of what happens in practice.

Source: Based on information taken from Brierley, J., Cowton, C. and Drury, C. (2007) Product costing practices in different manufacturing industries: a British survey, *International Journal of Management*, vol. 24, no. 4, pp. 667–675.

Segmenting the overheads

We have just seen that charging the same overheads to different jobs on different bases is not feasible. It is perfectly feasible, however, to charge one segment of the total overheads on one basis and another segment on another basis.

Activity 10.12

Taking the same business as in Example 10.2, on closer analysis we find that of the overheads that total £20,000 next month, £8,000 relates to machines (depreciation, maintenance, rent of the space occupied by the machines and so on) and the remaining £12,000 to more general overheads. The other information about the business is exactly as it was before.

How much of the total overheads will be charged to each job if the machine-related overheads are to be charged on a machine hour basis and the remaining overheads are charged on a direct labour hour basis?

Direct labour hour basis

$$\text{Overhead recovery rate} = £12,000/1,600 = £7.50 \text{ per direct labour hour}$$

Machine hour basis

$$\text{Overhead recovery rate} = £8,000/1,000 = £8.00 \text{ per machine hour}$$

Overheads charged to jobs

	Job 1 £	Job 2 £
Direct labour hour basis:		
£7.50 × 800	6,000	
£7.50 × 800		6,000
Machine hour basis:		
£8.00 × 700	5,600	
£8.00 × 300		2,400
Total	11,600	8,400

We can see from this that all the overheads of £20,000 have been charged.

Segmenting the overheads in this way is quite common. A business may be divided into separate areas for costing purposes. Overheads can then be charged differently from one area to the next, according to the nature of the work done in each.

Dealing with overheads on a cost centre basis

We saw in Chapter 1 that businesses are often divided into departments, where each department carries out a separate task. Many of these businesses charge overheads to cost units on a department-by-department basis. They do so in the belief that it will give rise to more accurate full costing information. It is probably only in a minority of cases, however, that it leads to any great improvement in accuracy. Although applying overheads on a departmental basis may not be of enormous benefit, it is probably not an expensive exercise. Cost elements are collected department by department for other purposes (particularly control) and so applying overheads on a department-by-department basis may be a fairly straightforward matter.

In Example 10.3 we see how the departmental approach to deriving full cost can be applied in a service-industry context.

Example 10.3

Autosparkle Ltd offers a motor vehicle paint-respray service. The jobs that it undertakes range from painting a small part of a saloon car, usually following a minor accident, to a complete respray of a double-decker bus.

Each job starts life in the Preparation Department, where it is prepared for the Paintshop. Here, the job is worked on by direct workers, in most cases taking some direct materials from the stores with which to treat the old paintwork and, generally, to render the vehicle ready for respraying. Thus the job will be charged with direct materials, direct labour and a share of the Preparation Department's overheads. The job then passes into the Paintshop Department, already valued at the cost that it picked up in the Preparation Department.

In the Paintshop, the staff draw direct materials (mainly paint) from the stores and direct workers spend time respraying, using sophisticated spraying apparatus as well as working by hand. So, in the Paintshop, the job is charged with direct materials, direct labour and a share of that department's overheads. The job now passes into the Finishing Department, valued at the cost of the materials, labour and overheads that it accumulated in the first two departments.

In the Finishing Department, vehicles are cleaned and polished ready to go back to the customers. Further direct labour and, in some cases, materials are added. All jobs also pick up a share of that department's overheads. The job, now complete, passes back to the customer.

Figure 10.8 shows graphically how this works for a particular job.

Example 10.3 *continued*

Figure 10.8   **A cost unit (Job A) passing through Autosparkle Ltd's process**

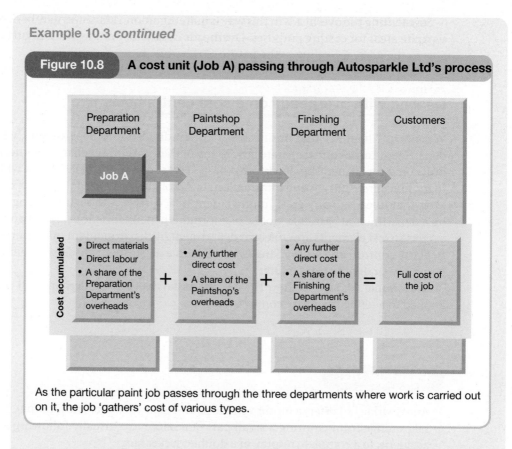

As the particular paint job passes through the three departments where work is carried out on it, the job 'gathers' cost of various types.

The approach to charging overheads to jobs (for example, direct labour hours) might be the same for all three departments, or it might be different from one department to another. It is possible that cost elements relating to the spraying apparatus dominate the Paintshop overhead cost, so the Paintshop's overheads might well be charged to jobs on a machine hour basis. The other two departments are probably labour-intensive, so that direct labour hours may be seen as being appropriate there.

The passage of a job through the departments, picking up cost as it goes, can be compared to a snowball being rolled across snow: as it rolls, it picks up more and more snow.

Where cost determination is dealt with departmentally, each department is known as a **cost centre.** This can be defined as a particular physical area or some activity or function for which the cost is separately identified. Charging direct cost to jobs in a departmental system is exactly the same as where the whole business is one single cost centre. It is simply a matter of keeping a record of:

● the number of hours of direct labour worked on the particular job and the grade of labour, where there are different grades with different rates of pay;
● the cost of the direct materials taken from stores and applied to the job; and
● any other direct cost elements, for example some subcontracted work, associated with the job.

This record keeping will normally be done cost centre by cost centre.

The total production overheads of the entire business must be broken down on a cost centre basis. That is, they must be divided between the cost centres, so that the sum of the overheads of the individual cost centres equals the overheads for the entire business. By charging all of their overheads to jobs, the cost centres will, between them, charge all of the overheads of the business to jobs.

Real World 10.6 provides an indication of the number of different cost centres that businesses tend to use in practice.

Real World 10.6

Cost centres in practice

It is usual for businesses to have several cost centres. A survey of 186 larger UK businesses involved in various activities by Drury and Tayles gave the results shown in Figure 10.9.

| Figure 10.9 | Analysis of the number of cost centres within a business |

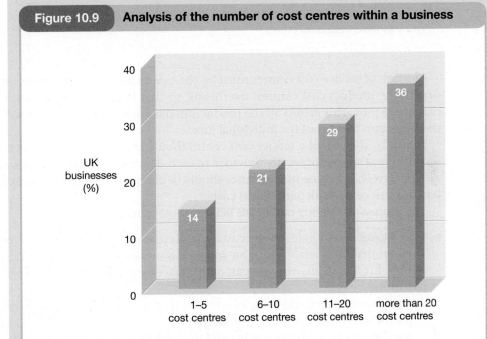

The survey of larger businesses shows, as might be expected, that they tend to have several cost centres.

We can see that 86 per cent of businesses surveyed had six or more cost centres and that 36 per cent of businesses had more than 20 cost centres. Although this is not shown in the figure, 3 per cent of businesses surveyed had a single cost centre (that is, there was a business-wide or overall overhead rate used). Clearly, businesses that deal with overheads on a business-wide basis are relatively rare.

Source: Based on information taken from Drury, C. and Tayles, M. (2006) Profitability analysis in UK organisations, *British Accounting Review*, vol. 38, no. 4, pp. 405–425.

For cost assignment purposes, we need to distinguish between **product cost centres** and **service cost centres.** Product cost centres are those in which jobs are worked on by direct workers and/or where direct materials are added. In these cost centres, jobs can be charged with a share of their overheads. The Preparation, Paintshop and Finishing Departments, discussed in Example 10.3, are all examples of product cost centres.

Activity (10.13)

Can you guess what a service cost centre is? Can you think of an example of a service cost centre for a large manufacturing business?

A service cost centre is one where no direct cost is involved. It renders a service to other cost centres. Examples include:

- cleaning;
- training;
- stores;
- maintenance;
- human resources; and
- catering.

You may have thought of others.

The cost of service cost centres must be charged to product cost centres and become part of the product cost centres' overheads, so that those overheads can, in turn, be charged to jobs. This means all the production overheads of the business will then find their way into the cost of the individual jobs.

Logically, the cost of a service cost centre should be charged to product cost centres according to the level of service provided to each. Thus, a product cost centre that incurs a higher level of machine maintenance should be charged with a larger share of the maintenance cost centre's (department's) cost.

The process of dividing overheads between cost centres is as follows:

- **Cost allocation.** Allocate indirect cost elements that are specific to particular cost centres. These are items that relate to, and are specifically measurable in respect of, individual cost centres. In other words, they are part of the direct cost of running the cost centre. Examples include:
  - salaries of indirect workers whose activities are wholly within the cost centre, for example the salary of the cost centre manager;
  - rent, where the cost centre is housed in a building for which rent can be separately identified; and
  - electricity, where it is separately metered for each cost centre.
- **Cost apportionment.** Apportion the more general overheads to the cost centres. These are overheads that relate to more than one cost centre, perhaps to all. It would include:
  - rent, where more than one cost centre is housed in the same building;
  - electricity, where it is not separately metered; and
  - salaries of cleaning staff who work in a variety of cost centres.

These overheads would be apportioned to cost centres on the basis of the extent to which each cost centre benefits from the overheads concerned. For example, the rent cost might be apportioned on the basis of the square metres of floor area occupied by each cost centre. With electricity used to power machinery, the basis of apportionment might be the level of mechanisation of each cost centre. As with charging overheads to individual jobs, there is no single 'correct' basis of apportioning general overheads to cost centres.

- Having allocated and apportioned the overhead cost to all cost centres, the total cost of service cost centres must then be apportioned to product cost centres. As we have just seen the basis used should reflect the level of service rendered by the individual service cost centre to the individual production cost centre. With the human resources cost centre (department) cost, for example, the basis of apportionment might be the number of staff in each product cost centre.

Activity 10.14

Can you think why this basis of apportionment of the human resources department may not always be suitable? What does it assume?

It assumes that the number of staff determines the amount of benefit received from the human resources cost centre. Where a particular product cost centre has severe staff problems, it may account for a huge proportion of the human resources department's time even though that cost centre may employ relatively few people.

The final total for each product cost centre will be charged to jobs as they pass through. The process of applying overheads to cost units on a cost centre (departmental) basis is shown in Figure 10.10.

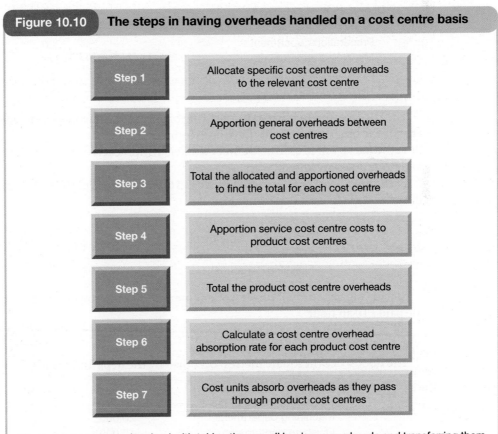

Figure 10.10 The steps in having overheads handled on a cost centre basis

Step 1 — Allocate specific cost centre overheads to the relevant cost centre

Step 2 — Apportion general overheads between cost centres

Step 3 — Total the allocated and apportioned overheads to find the total for each cost centre

Step 4 — Apportion service cost centre costs to product cost centres

Step 5 — Total the product cost centre overheads

Step 6 — Calculate a cost centre overhead absorption rate for each product cost centre

Step 7 — Cost units absorb overheads as they pass through product cost centres

There are seven steps involved with taking the overall business overheads and transferring them to their effect on individual cost units, when dealt with on a cost centre basis.

Let us now go on to consider Example 10.4, which deals with overheads on a cost centre (departmental) basis.

Example 10.4

A business consists of four cost centres:

- Preparation department
- Machining department
- Finishing department
- Human resources (HR) department.

The first three are product cost centres and the last renders a service to the other three. The level of service rendered is thought to be roughly in proportion to the number of employees in each product cost centre.

Overheads, and other data, for next month are expected to be as follows:

	£000
Rent	10,000
Electricity to power machines	3,000
Electricity for heating and lighting	800
Insurance of building	200
Cleaning	600
Depreciation of machines	2,000
Total monthly salaries of the indirect workers:	
Preparation department	200
Machining department	240
Finishing department	180
HR department	180

The HR department has a staff consisting of only indirect workers (including managers). The other departments have both indirect workers (including managers) and direct workers. There are 100 indirect workers within each of the four departments and none does any 'direct' work.

Each direct worker is expected to work 160 hours next month. The number of direct workers in each department is:

Preparation department	600
Machining department	900
Finishing department	500

Machining department direct workers are paid £12 an hour; other direct workers are paid £10 an hour.

All of the machinery is in the machining department. Machines are expected to operate for 120,000 hours next month.

The floor space (in square metres) occupied by the departments is as follows:

Preparation department	16,000
Machining department	20,000
Finishing department	10,000
HR department	2,000

Deducing the overheads, cost centre by cost centre, can be done, using a schedule, as follows:

	£000	Total £000	Prep'n £000	Mach'g £000	Fin'g £000	HR £000
Allocated cost:						
Machine power		3,000		3,000		
Machine depreciation		2,000		2,000		
Indirect salaries		800	200	240	180	180
Apportioned cost						
Rent	10,000					
Heating and lighting	800					
Insurance of buildings	200					
Cleaning	600					
Apportioned by floor area		11,600	3,867	4,833	2,417	483
Cost centre overheads		17,400	4,067	10,073	2,597	663
Reapportion HR cost by number of staff (including the indirect workers)		–	202	288	173	(663)
		17,400	4,269	10,361	2,770	–

Activity 10.15

Assume that the machining department overheads (in Example 10.4) are to be charged to jobs on a machine hour basis, but that the direct labour hour basis is to be used for the other two departments. What will be the full (absorption) cost of a job with the following characteristics?

	Preparation department	Machining department	Finishing department
Direct labour hours	10	7	5
Machine hours	–	6	–
Direct materials (£)	85	13	6

(*Hint*: This should be tackled as if each cost centre were a separate business, then departmental cost elements are added together for the job so as to arrive at the total full cost.)

First, we need to deduce the indirect (overhead) recovery rates for each cost centre:
  Preparation department (direct labour hour based):

$$\frac{£4,269,000}{600 \times 160} = £44.47$$

Machining department (machine hour based):

$$\frac{£10,361,000}{120,000} = £86.34$$

Finishing department (direct labour hour based):

$$\frac{£2,770,000}{500 \times 160} = £34.63$$

Activity 10.15 *continued*

The cost of the job is as follows:

	£	£
Direct labour:		
Preparation department (10 × £10)	100.00	
Machining department (7 × £12)	84.00	
Finishing department (5 × £10)	50.00	
		234.00
Direct materials:		
Preparation department	85.00	
Machining department	13.00	
Finishing department	6.00	
		104.00
Overheads:		
Preparation department (10 × £44.47)	444.70	
Machining department (6 × £86.34)	518.04	
Finishing department (5 × £34.63)	173.15	
		1,135.89
Full cost of the job		1,473.89

Activity 10.16

The manufacturing cost for Buccaneers Ltd for next year is expected to be made up as follows:

	£000
Direct materials:	
Forming department	450
Machining department	100
Finishing department	50
Direct labour:	
Forming department	180
Machining department	120
Finishing department	75
Indirect materials:	
Forming department	40
Machining department	30
Finishing department	10
Human resources department	10
Indirect labour:	
Forming department	80
Machining department	70
Finishing department	60
Human resources department	60
Maintenance cost	50
Rent	100
Heating and lighting	20
Building insurance	10
Machinery insurance	10
Depreciation of machinery	120
Total manufacturing cost	1,645

Activity 10.16 *continued*

The following additional information is available:

1 Each of the four departments is treated as a separate cost centre.
2 All direct labour is paid £10 an hour for all hours worked.
3 The human resources department renders services to all three of the production departments.
4 The area of the building in which the business manufactures amounts to 50,000 square metres, divided as follows:

	Sq m
Forming department	20,000
Machining department	15,000
Finishing department	10,000
Human resources department	5,000

5 The maintenance employees are expected to divide their time between the production departments as follows:

	%
Forming department	15
Machining department	75
Finishing department	10

6 Machine hours are expected to be as follows:

	Hours
Forming department	5,000
Machining department	15,000
Finishing department	5,000

On the basis of this information:

(a) Allocate and apportion overheads to the three product cost centres.
(b) Deduce overhead recovery rates for each product cost centre using two different bases for each cost centre's overheads.
(c) Calculate the full cost of a job with the following characteristics:

Direct labour hours:	
Forming department	4 hours
Machining department	4 hours
Finishing department	1 hour
Machine hours:	
Forming department	1 hour
Machining department	2 hours
Finishing department	1 hour

Activity 10.16 *continued*

Direct materials:

Forming department	£40
Machining department	£9
Finishing department	£4

Use whichever of the two bases of overhead recovery, deduced in (b), that you consider more appropriate.

(d) Explain why you consider the basis used in (c) to be the more appropriate.

(a) Overheads can be allocated and apportioned as follows:

Cost	Basis of apportionment	Total £000	Forming £000	Machining £000	Finishing £000	HR £000
Indirect materials	Specifically allocated	90	40	30	10	10
Indirect labour	Specifically allocated	270	80	70	60	60
Maintenance	Staff time	50	7.5	37.5	5	–
Rent	100					
Heat and light	20					
Buildings insurance	10					
	Area	130	52	39	26	13
Machine insurance	10					
Machine depreciation	120					
	Machine hours	130	26	78	26	–
		670	205.5	254.5	127	83
HR	Direct labour	–	39.84	26.56	16.6	(83)
		670	245.34	281.06	143.6	–

Note: The direct cost is not included in the above because it is allocated *directly* to jobs.

(b) Overhead recovery rates are as follows:

Basis 1: direct labour hours

$$\text{Forming} = \frac{\text{£245,340}}{\text{£(180,000/10)}} = \text{£13.63 per direct labour hour}$$

$$\text{Machining} = \frac{\text{£281,060}}{\text{£(120,000/10)}} = \text{£23.42 per direct labour hour}$$

$$\text{Finishing} = \frac{\text{£143,600}}{\text{£(75,000/10)}} = \text{£19.15 per direct labour hour}$$

Basis 2: machine hours

$$\text{Forming} = \frac{\text{£245,340}}{5,000} = \text{£49.07 per machine hour}$$

Activity 10.16 *continued*

$$\text{Machining} = \frac{£281,060}{15,000} = £18.74 \text{ per machine hour}$$

$$\text{Finishing} = \frac{£143,600}{£5,000} = £28.72 \text{ per machine hour}$$

(c) Full cost of job – on direct labour hour basis of overhead recovery:

	£	£
Direct labour cost (9 × £10)		90.00
Direct materials (£40 + £9 + £4)		53.00
Overheads:		
Forming (4 × £13.63)	54.52	
Machining (4 × £23.42)	93.68	
Finishing (1 × £19.15)	19.15	167.35
Full cost		310.35

(d) The reason for using the direct labour hour basis rather than the machine hour basis was that labour is more important, in terms of the number of hours applied to output, than is machine time. Strong arguments could have been made for the use of the alternative basis; certainly, a machine hour basis could have been justified for the machining department.

It may be reasonable to use one basis in respect of one product cost centre's overheads and a different one for those of another. For example, machine hours could have been used for the machining department and a direct labour hours basis for the other two.

From our discussions so far, we can see that assigning overhead costs to products is as much art as science. It is not surprising, therefore, that there have been calls for a more rigorous approach to this problem. We shall examine this point in some detail in the next chapter. In the meantime, however, take a look at **Real World 10.7**.

Real World 10.7

What do we want? When do we want it?

In 2012, a survey of 200 US management accountants revealed that all were concerned about the accuracy of the cost information produced within their business. In 2003, a similar survey was carried out, which revealed that 80 per cent of respondents felt this same concern. In both surveys, the most common reason cited was the treatment of overheads.

The degree to which greater accuracy in costing information was required by respondents from the two surveys is shown in Figure 10.11.

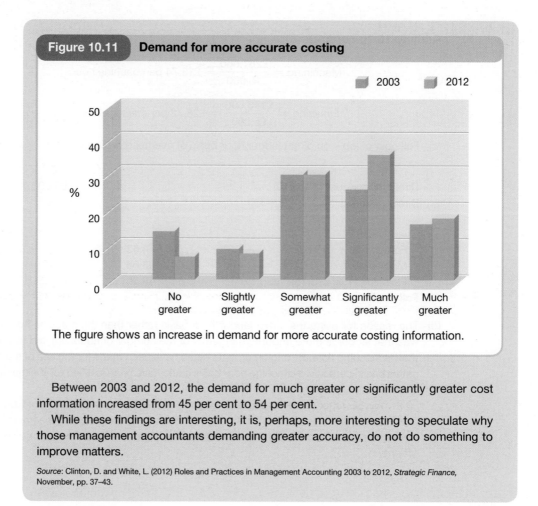

Figure 10.11   Demand for more accurate costing

The figure shows an increase in demand for more accurate costing information.

Between 2003 and 2012, the demand for much greater or significantly greater cost information increased from 45 per cent to 54 per cent.

While these findings are interesting, it is, perhaps, more interesting to speculate why those management accountants demanding greater accuracy, do not do something to improve matters.

Source: Clinton, D. and White, L. (2012) Roles and Practices in Management Accounting 2003 to 2012, *Strategic Finance*, November, pp. 37–43.

Batch costing

Many types of goods and some services are produced in a batch of identical, or nearly identical, units of output. Each batch produced, however, is distinctly different from other batches. A theatre, for example, may put on a production whose nature and cost is very different from that of other productions. On the other hand, ignoring differences in the desirability of the various types of seating, all of the individual units of output (tickets to see the production) are identical.

In these circumstances, the cost per ticket is calculated using a **batch costing** approach and involves:

- using a job-costing approach (taking account of direct and indirect costs and so on) to find the cost of mounting the production; and then
- dividing the cost of mounting the production by the expected number of tickets to be sold to find the cost per ticket.

Figure 10.12 shows the process for deriving the cost of one cost unit (product) in a batch.

Batch costing is used in a variety of industries including clothing manufacturing, engineering component manufacturing, tyre manufacturing, bakery goods and footwear manufacturing.

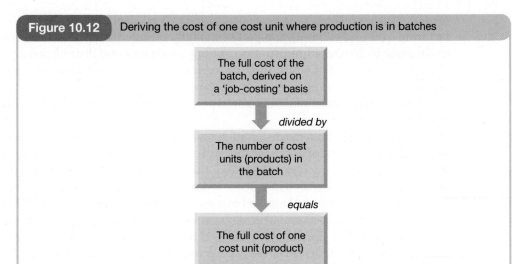

Figure 10.12 Deriving the cost of one cost unit where production is in batches

The cost for the batch is derived using a job-costing basis and this batch cost is divided by the number in the batch to determine the cost for each cost unit.

Activity 10.17

Consider the following businesses:

- a pharmaceutical manufacturer;
- a sugar refiner;
- a picture framer;
- a private hospital;
- a coal-mining business;
- an architect's office;
- a cement manufacturer; and
- an antique furniture restorer.

Try to identify, for each business, which form of full costing (process, job or batch costing) is likely to be most appropriate.

Process costing is likely to be most appropriate for the sugar refiner, the coal-mining business and the cement manufacturer. Each business is normally involved in producing identical, or near identical, items through a series of repetitive activities.

Job costing is likely to be most appropriate for the picture framer, the private hospital, the architect's office and the antique furniture restorer. Each of these businesses is normally involved in producing a customised product, or service, with each item requiring different inputs of labour, materials and so on.

Batch costing is likely to be most appropriate for the pharmaceutical manufacturer. The production process will normally involve making identical products, such as tablets and lotions, in batches, where each batch is different.

Non-manufacturing overheads

For external reporting purposes (preparing the periodic financial statements and so on), an International Financial Reporting Standard (IAS 2 *Inventories*) requires that all inventories, including work in progress, are valued at full cost. When calculating full cost, only those overheads relating to the manufacturing process should be included. Non-manu-facturing overheads do not form part of the full cost calculation. These overheads nor-mally relate to general administration, selling, marketing and distribution and must be charged to the period in which they are incurred. As mentioned above, this rule applies only for external reporting purposes, as the basis, for example, of the value at which inven-tories appear in the statement of financial position. They need not be applied for internal reporting purposes.

For managerial decision making, non-manufacturing overheads are sometimes included as part of the total cost of goods produced. To do this, an appropriate basis for assigning these overheads to products must be found. This is not an easy task and inappropriate bases are often used. One basis used in practice is direct labour hours, even though its relevance for this purpose is dubious. Another basis used involves adding an amount based on the percentage of total non-manufacturing overheads to total manufacturing costs (see refer-ence 1 at the end of the chapter). Thus, if total non-manufacturing overheads were £2.5 million and total manufacturing costs were £10 million, an additional 25 per cent (£2.5m/£10m) loading would be added as part of the total overhead cost.

Activity 10.18

What is the risk of using arbitrary bases for assigning non-manufacturing overheads?

Unless an appropriate share of non-manufacturing overheads is assigned to products, manag-ers will be provided with misleading information.

A final point worth making is that, where the cost of products includes both manufac-turing and non-manufacturing costs and things turn out as expected, selling the products at their full cost should cause the business to break even exactly. Thus, whatever profit (in total) is loaded onto full cost to set actual selling prices will result in that level of profit being earned for the period.

Real World 10.8 below describes the findings from a recent study concerning the treat-ment of non-manufacturing costs.

Real World 10.8

Adding to the cost

A questionnaire-based survey of management accountants in UK manufacturing operations found that just over half of the operating units included non-manufacturing overheads as part of the total product cost.

Results from 169 of the responses revealed that the smaller the non-manufacturing overheads, as a percentage of either total operating unit costs or total overhead costs, the more likely they were to be included as part of the total cost. This is a surprising result for which the reasons are unclear. The opposite finding might have been expected. That is, the higher the percentage of non-manufacturing overheads, the greater the likelihood that they would be included.

The study also found that other factors, such as the size of the operating units and the level of competition, had no significant effect on the decision to include non-manufacturing overheads as part of the total product cost.

Source: Brierley, J. (2015) An examination of the factors influencing the inclusion of non-manufacturing overhead costs in product costs, *International Journal of Managerial and Financial Accounting*, vol. 7, no. 2, pp. 134–150.

Full (absorption) costing and estimation errors

While deriving the full cost of some activity can be done after the work is completed, it is frequently estimated in advance. This may be because some idea of full cost is needed as a basis for setting a selling price. Estimates, however, rarely turn out to be 100 per cent accurate. Where actual outcomes differ from estimated outcomes, an over-recovery or under-recovery of overheads will normally occur. Example 10.5 illustrates how this over- or under-recovery is calculated.

Example 10.5

Downham Engineering plc produces a standard valve. At the beginning of the year, it was planned that manufacturing the valves would incur £4 million in overheads and would require 400,000 direct labour hours for the year. The business, which uses the direct labour basis of absorbing overheads, set the overhead recovery rate at (£4.0m/400,000) = £10 per direct labour hour.

At the end of the year it was found that, in producing the valves, 450,000 direct labour hours were used in the production process but that the total manufacturing overheads were as planned.

The overheads absorbed for the year can be calculated as follows:

Overheads absorbed = overhead recovery rate × actual direct labour hours

As 450,000 direct labour hours were used, the amount charged for overheads would have been:

$$450,000 \times £10 = £4.5 \text{ million}$$

By comparing the overheads incurred with the actual overheads absorbed we find that £0.5 million (that is, £4.5m − £4.0m) of overheads were 'over-recovered'.

For external reporting purposes, any under- or over-recovery of overheads is normally adjusted in the income statement. Thus, the over-recovery in Example 10.5 would normally be deducted from the cost of goods sold figure shown in the income statement for that year.

Activity 10.19

In Example 10.5, assume that, at the end of the year, it was found that 380,000 direct labour hours (instead of 450,000 hours) were actually used during the year in making the valves and that manufacturing overheads actually incurred were £4.2 million.

What adjustment should be made to the income statement for the year?

The manufacturing overheads recovered will be 380,000 × £10 = £3.8 million. The overheads incurred were £4.2 million. This means that £0.4 million (that is, £4.2m − £3.8m) has been under-recovered. This amount will be added to the cost of goods figure appearing in the income statement for the year.

Real World 10.9 is taken from the results of a survey conducted by the UK Chartered Institute of Management Accountants (CIMA) in July 2009. Broadly, the survey asked management accountants in a wide range of business types and sizes to indicate the extent to which their business used a range of management accounting techniques; 439 management accountants completed the survey. We shall be making reference to this survey on a number of occasions throughout the book. When we do, we shall refer to it as the 'CIMA survey'.

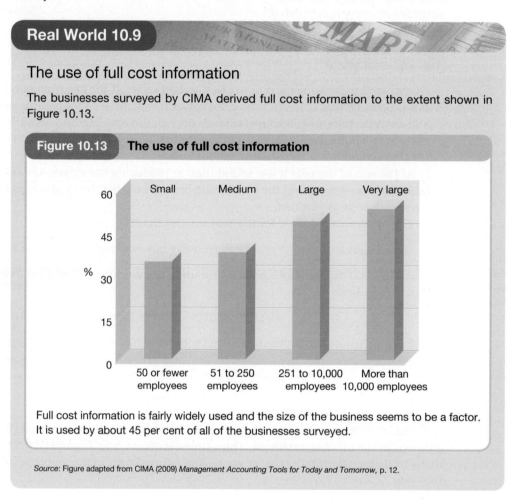

Real World 10.9

The use of full cost information

The businesses surveyed by CIMA derived full cost information to the extent shown in Figure 10.13.

Figure 10.13 | **The use of full cost information**

Full cost information is fairly widely used and the size of the business seems to be a factor. It is used by about 45 per cent of all of the businesses surveyed.

Source: Figure adapted from CIMA (2009) *Management Accounting Tools for Today and Tomorrow*, p. 12.

The CIMA survey reveals that full cost information is more widely used by larger businesses than by smaller ones. The reasons for this are not clear. It may be that larger businesses have greater resources and expertise than smaller ones. This may enable them to employ techniques that are simply not practical for smaller businesses. On the other hand, it may reflect the different types of business within each size category.

Full cost (cost-plus) pricing

A business may seek to set its selling prices by simply adding a profit loading to the full cost of a product or service. The amount of profit is often calculated as a percentage of the full (absorption) cost figure. This approach to pricing is known as cost-plus pricing.

The prices at which businesses are able to sell their output will usually be a major deter-minant of the quantity that they make available to the market. This is a perfectly logical approach. If a business charges the full cost (including non-manufacturing overheads) of its output as a selling price, the business will, in theory, break even, because the sales revenue will exactly cover all of the costs. Charging something above full cost will yield a profit. Garages carrying out vehicle repairs typically operate in this way. Solicitors and accountants doing work for clients also often use this approach.

If full cost (cost-plus) pricing is to be used, the required profit from each unit sold must be determined. This must logically be based on the total profit required for the period. In practice, this required profit is often set in relation to the amount of capital invested in the business. In other words, businesses seek to generate a target return on capital employed. It seems, therefore, that the profit loading on full cost should reflect the business's target profit and that the target should itself be based on a target return on capital employed.

Activity 10.20

A business has just completed a service job whose full cost has been calculated at £112. For the current period, the total costs (direct and indirect) are estimated at £250,000. The profit target for the period is £100,000.

Suggest a selling price for the job.

If the profit is to be earned by jobs in proportion to their full cost, then the profit for each pound of full cost must be £0.40 (that is, £100,000/250,000). Thus, the target profit on the job must be

$$£0.40 \times 112 = £44.80$$

This means that the target price for the job must be

$$£112 + £44.80 = £156.80$$

Other ways could be found for apportioning a share of profit to jobs – for example, direct labour or machine hours. Such bases may be preferred where it is believed that these factors are better representatives of effort and, therefore, profitworthiness. It is clearly a matter of judgement as to how profit is apportioned to units of output.

Price makers and price takers

Despite the logic of basing selling prices on full cost, where there is a competitive market for the product or service, it is often not possible to set prices on a cost-plus basis. The problem with cost-plus pricing is that the market may not agree with the price. Businesses will usually have to accept the price that the market is prepared to pay. A business may fairly deduce the full cost of some product and then add what might be regarded as a reasonable level of profit, only to find that a rival producer is offering a similar product for a much lower price, or that the market simply will not buy at the cost-plus price.

Most suppliers are not strong enough in the market to dictate pricing. Most are *price takers* not *price makers*. They must accept the price offered by the market or they do not sell any of their products. Cost-plus pricing may be appropriate for price makers, but it has less relevance for price takers.

Use of cost-plus information by price takers

The cost-plus price is not entirely without use to price takers. When contemplating entering a market, knowing the cost-plus price will give useful information. It will tell the price taker whether or not it can profitably enter the market. As mentioned earlier, the full cost can be seen as a long-run break-even selling price. If entering a market means that this break-even price, plus an acceptable profit, cannot be achieved, then the business might be better to stay out. Having a breakdown of the full cost may put the business in a position to examine where costs might be capable of being cut. This may enable the business to bring the full cost plus profit within a figure acceptable to the market. Here, the market would be providing the target price towards which the business can work, if it wishes to compete. We shall discuss an extension of this approach – *target costing* – in Chapter 11.

It is not necessary for a business to dominate a particular market for it to be a price maker. Many small businesses are, to some extent, price makers. This tends to be where buyers find it difficult to make clear distinctions between the prices offered by various suppliers. An example of this might be a car repair undertaken by a garage, where the nature and extent of the problem is not clear. As a result, garages normally charge cost-plus prices for car repairs.

In its 'pure' sense, cost-plus pricing implies that the seller sets the price that is then accepted by the customer. Often the price will not be finalised until after the product or service has been completed; as, for example, with a car repair or with work done by a firm of accountants. Sometimes, however, cost-plus is used as a basis of negotiating a price in advance, which then becomes the fixed price. This is often the case with contracts with central or local government departments. Typically, with such public contracts, the price is determined by competitive tendering. Here each potential supplier offers a price for which it will perform the subject of the contract and the department concerned selects the supplier offering the lowest price, subject to quality safeguards. In some cases, however, particularly where only one supplier is capable of doing the work, a fixed cost-plus approach is used.

Cost-plus is also often the approach taken when monopoly suppliers of public utility services are negotiating with the government-appointed regulator over the prices which they are legally allowed to charge their customers. For example, the UK mains water suppliers, when agreeing the prices that they can charge customers, argue their case with Ofwat, the water industry regulator, on the basis of cost-plus information.

Real World 10.10 discusses how one business sees itself as partly protected from the recession that hit the UK from 2008 as a result of having contracts with its customers on a cost-plus price basis.

Real World 10.10

Adding Spice to cost-plus pricing

Spice plc is a business that undertakes consultancy and other subcontract (outsourced) work for various UK public utilities (water and electricity suppliers). The business started when a group of managers bought Yorkshire Electricity's maintenance division to run it as a separate, independent unit.

Simon Rigby, Spice's chief executive, was very relaxed about the prospect of an economic recession. He said 'I would not wish a recession on anybody, but if we have a recession it is going to throw Spice into very sharp focus. How do you think my 10-year cost-plus contracts are going to be affected by recession? The answer is not at all.'

It must be said that Spice plc is very unusual in having so many 'cost-plus' priced contracts.

FT   *Source*: Adapted from Jansson, E. (2008) Flexible business models helps Spice Holdings power ahead in outsource market, ft.com, 12 March. © The Financial Times Limited 2012. All Rights Reserved.

Real World 10.11 considers the extent to which cost-plus pricing seems to be used in practice.

Real World 10.11

Counting the cost plus

A survey of 267 large UK and Australian businesses found broadly as follows:

- Cost plus is regarded as important in determining selling prices by most of the businesses, but many businesses only use it for a small percentage of their total sales.
- Retailers base most of their sales prices on their costs. This is not surprising; we might expect that retailers add a mark-up on their cost prices to arrive at selling prices.
- Retailers and service businesses (both financial services and others) attach more importance to cost-plus pricing than do manufacturers and others.
- Cost-plus pricing tends to be more important in industries where competition is most intense. This is perhaps surprising because we might have expected fewer 'price makers' in more competitive markets.
- The extent of the importance of cost-plus pricing seems to have nothing to do with the size of the business. We might have imagined that larger businesses would have more power in the market and be more likely to be price makers, but the evidence does not support this. The reason could be that many larger businesses are, in effect, groups of smaller businesses. These smaller subsidiaries may not be bigger players in their markets than are small independent businesses. Also, cost-plus pricing tends to be particularly important in retailing and service businesses, where many businesses are quite small.

Source: Guilding, C., Drury, C. and Tayles, M. (2005) An empirical investigation of the importance of cost-plus pricing, *Management Auditing Journal*, vol. 20, no. 2, pp. 125–137.

Full (absorption) costing and relevant costs

We saw in Chapter 2 that, for decision-making purposes, relevant costs are future costs that vary with the decision. We have also seen, however, that full costing tends to rely on past cost. Moreover, it focuses on outlay cost and overlooks opportunity costs. This appears to suggest an unbridgeable gap between the relevant cost and the full costing approaches. If this case, the usefulness of full costing for decision making is called into question.

In theory, relevant cost analysis should be used whenever a decision is needed to set a price for a product, to introduce a new product, or to stop producing an existing product. In practice, however, it may not be feasible to do this. Let us assume that a large business makes 300 separate product types. Here the range of possibilities is enormous. In addition to carrying out relevant cost analysis on each product, it could also be carried out on different combinations of two, three, four products and so on. To deal with this tsunami of possible options, full cost information, based on historic cost, can be used to act as a filter. It can direct attention to those products or services that would most benefit from relevant cost analysis. By providing an indication of the long-run average cost of each product, managers have some idea of the long-term cash outflows to be incurred. They may then decide to investigate further using relevant cost analysis.

Full (absorption) costing versus variable costing

An alternative to full (absorption) costing is **variable (marginal) costing** – which we discussed in Chapter 3. We may recall that this approach distinguishes between fixed and variable costs.

Under variable costing, income is measured in a different way to that of full costing. It will include only variable cost (that is, both variable direct and variable indirect cost) as part of the cost of the goods or service produced. Any fixed cost (that is, both fixed direct and fixed indirect cost) will be treated as a cost of the period in which it is incurred. Thus, inventories of finished products, or work in progress, carried from one accounting period to the next, is valued on the basis of their variable cost only.

As we have seen, full costing calculates product cost by taking the direct cost (whether fixed or variable) and an appropriate share of the indirect cost (whether fixed and variable) for the period in which the product is produced.

To illustrate the difference between the two costing approaches, let us consider Example 10.6.

Example 10.6

Lahore Ltd commenced operations on 1 June and makes a single product, which sells for £14 per unit. In the first two months of operations, the following results were achieved:

	June (number of units)	July (number of units)
Production output	6,000	6,000
Sales volume	4,000	5,000
Opening inventories	–	2,000
Closing inventories	2,000	3,000

Manufacturing overhead cost is £18,000 per month and direct manufacturing cost is £5 per unit. There is also a monthly fixed non-manufacturing overhead cost (marketing and administration) of £5,000. There was no work in progress at the end of either June or July. Assume for the sake of simplicity that Lahore Ltd's direct costs are all variable and its overheads are all fixed. (However, this would be very unusual in practice.)

The operating profit for each month is calculated below, first using a variable costing approach and then a full costing approach.

Variable costing

In this case, only the variable costs are charged to the units produced and all the fixed cost (manufacturing and non-manufacturing) is charged to the period. Inventories will be carried forward at their variable cost.

	June		July	
	£	£	£	£
Sales revenue				
(4,000 × £14)		56,000		
(5,000 × £14)				70,000
Opening inventories				
(2,000 × £5)	–		10,000	
Cost of units produced				
(6,000 × £5)	30,000		30,000	
Closing inventories				
(2,000 × £5)	(10,000)	(20,000)		
(3,000 × £5)			(15,000)	(25,000)
Contribution margin		36,000		45,000
Fixed cost:				
Manufacturing	(18,000)		(18,000)	
Non-manufacturing	(5,000)	(23,000)	(5,000)	(23,000)
Operating profit		13,000		22,000

Full costing

In this case, the manufacturing overhead cost becomes part of the product cost and inventories are carried forward to the next period at their full cost – that is, direct (all variable) cost plus an appropriate manufacturing overhead (all fixed) cost element. There are 6,000 units produced in each period and the fixed manufacturing overhead cost for each period is £18,000. Hence, the manufacturing overhead cost element per unit is £3 (that is, £18,000/6,000). The full cost per unit will therefore be £8 (that is, £5 + £3).

→

Example 10.6 (*continued*)

	June		July	
	£	£	£	£
Sales revenue				
(4,000 × £14)		56,000		
(5,000 × £14)				70,000
Opening inventories	–			
(2,000 × £8)			16,000	
Cost of units produced				
(6,000 × £8)	48,000		48,000	
Closing inventories				
(2,000 × £8)	(16,000)	(32,000)		
(3,000 × £8)			(24,000)	(40,000)
Gross profit		24,000		30,000
Non-manufacturing cost		(5,000)		(5,000)
Operating profit		19,000		25,000

We can see that the total operating profit over the two months is £35,000 (that is, £13,000 + £22,000) when calculated on a variable cost basis. It is £44,000 (that is, £19,000 + £25,000) when calculated on a full cost basis. The difference between the two is £9,000 (that is, £44,000 − £35,000). This difference arises from the way in which the manufacturing overhead (all fixed) cost has been dealt with. On a full cost basis, the cost of inventories at the end of July includes overheads that have yet to be treated as an expense (that is, 3,000 × £3). On a variable cost basis, however, these overheads have already been treated as an expense.

In practice, the choice of costing approach may not have such a dramatic effect on reported profit as shown in Example 10.6. Differences in operating profit shown in this example arise from the changes in inventories levels between periods – from zero at the beginning of June, to 2,000 units at the end of June, to 3,000 units by the end of July. These are significant changes in the context of a monthly output of only 6,000 units. In practice, this would be unusual. Where the same amount of inventories and work in progress are held at reporting-period ends and fixed cost remains unchanged from one reporting period to the next, reported profit will not vary between the two approaches. This is because the same amount of fixed cost will be treated as an expense in each period; all of it originating from the current period in the case of variable costing, some of it originating from past periods in the case of full costing.

It is also important to note that, over the entire life of a particular business, total operating profit will be the same whichever costing method has been applied. This is because, ultimately, all fixed costs will be charged as expenses.

Which method is better?

A key difference between the two approaches is that, under the variable costing approach, profit is influenced only by changes in sales. Profit under the full (absorption costing) approach, on the other hand, is influenced by changes in the level of both sales and production.

Activity (10.21)

Briefly explain why profit calculated under an absorption costing approach is influenced by changes in the level of production (as well as sales). Take a look at Example 10.6 to help you.

Under a variable costing approach, all fixed production costs are charged to the period in which they are incurred. Under an absorption costing approach, fixed production costs are assigned to inventories and only the fixed production costs linked to those inventories sold during the period are charged against that period's sales revenue.

Where production exceeds sales for a period, some of the fixed production costs incurred during the period will be carried forward in inventories to the next period. The larger the amount of fixed production costs carried forward, the smaller will be the amount charged against profit for the current period. Where sales exceed production, profit for the current period will be charged with fixed production costs brought forward in inventories from the previous period.

It is claimed that, by ignoring the effect of changes in the level of production, the profit calculated under variable costing is a more realistic measure of overall achievement. In a multiproduct environment, however, the profitability of each item cannot be determined unless each is assigned an appropriate share of *all* costs. After all, goods and services cannot be provided unless fixed costs are incurred in their production. This suggests that full (absorption) costing provides a more useful measure of profit, item by item.

Variable costing highlights the key relationship between costs, volume of output and profit. This can be very helpful when making a range of management decisions. Full (absorption) costing, on the other hand, tends to obscure this relationship. Under normal reporting procedures, fixed and variable costs are not separated out. It would, however, be quite possible to do this.

We saw in Chapter 9 that variable costing identifies those costs that can be avoided in the short term. This again may be helpful when making a range of management decisions. A powerful counterargument, however, is that, over the long term, all elements of cost can be avoided. For managers to focus solely on those that can be avoided over the short term (the variable costs) may be unhelpful. When making long-term planning decisions, for example, managers need to know the full cost of producing products or services.

In practice, management accountants can prepare internal financial reports using either approach. We have seen, however, that absorption costing must be used for external reporting purposes. Some businesses align their internal reporting procedures with their external reporting procedures. A potential advantage of doing so is that managers will focus on the same numbers as those presented to shareholders and lenders.

Real World 10.12 provides some indication of the extent to which variable costing is used in practice.

Real World 10.12

Variable costing in practice

A survey of 41 UK manufacturing businesses found that 68 per cent of them used a variable costing approach to management reporting.

Many would find this surprising. The requirement is for financial statements in published annual reports to be in fullcost terms. It seemed to be widely believed that this has led those businesses to use a full-cost approach for management reporting as well. This appears not to be the case, however.

It should be added that many of those that used variable costing quite possibly misused it. For example, three-quarters of those that used it treated labour cost as variable. Possibly in some cases the cost of labour is variable (with the level of activity), but it seems likely that this is not true for most of these businesses. At the same time, most of the 68 per cent treat all overheads as a fixed cost. It seems likely that, for most businesses, overheads would have a variable element.

Source: Dugdale, D., Jones, C. and Green, S. (2005) *Contemporary Management Accounting Practices in UK Manufacturing*, CIMA Research Publication, Vol. 1, No. 13.

Self-assessment question (10.1)

Hector and Co. Ltd has been invited to tender for a contract to produce 1,000 clothes hangers. The following information relates to the contract.

- *Materials:* The clothes hangers are made of metal wire covered with a padded fabric. Each hanger requires 2 metres of wire and 0.5 square metres of fabric.
- *Direct labour:* Each hanger requires 10 minutes of skilled labour and 5 minutes of unskilled labour.

The business already holds sufficient of each of the materials required to complete the contract. Information on the cost of the materials is as follows:

	Metal wire £/m	Fabric £/sq m
Historic cost	2.20	1.00
Current buying-in cost	2.50	1.10
Scrap value	1.70	0.40

The metal wire is in constant use by the business for a range of its products. The fabric has no other use for the business and is scheduled to be scrapped if the present contract does not go ahead.

Unskilled labour, which is paid at the rate of £7.50 an hour, will need to be taken on specifically to undertake the contract. The business is fairly quiet at the moment, which means that a pool of skilled labour exists that will still be employed at full pay of £12.00 an hour to do nothing if the contract does not proceed. The pool of skilled labour is sufficient to complete the contract.

The business charges jobs with overheads on a direct labour hour basis. The production overheads of the entire business for the month in which the contract will be undertaken are estimated at £50,000. The estimated total direct labour hours that will be worked are 12,500. The business tends not to alter the established overhead recovery rate to reflect increases

Self-assessment question 10.1 *continued*

or reductions to estimated total hours arising from new contracts. The total overheads are not expected to increase as a result of undertaking the contract.

The business normally adds 12.5 per cent profit loading to the job cost to arrive at a first estimate of the tender price.

Required:
(a) Price this job on a traditional job-costing basis.
(b) Indicate the minimum price at which the contract could be undertaken such that the business would be neither better nor worse off as a result of doing it.

The solution to this question can be found at the back of the book on p. 775.

Summary

The main points of this chapter may be summarised as follows:

> **Full (absorption) cost = the total amount of resources sacrificed to achieve a particular objective**

Uses of full (absorption) cost information

- Pricing and output decisions.
- Exercising control.
- Assessing relative efficiency.
- Assessing performance.

Single-product businesses – process costing

- Where all units of output are identical, the full cost can be calculated as follows:

$$\text{Cost per unit} = \frac{\text{Total cost of output}}{\text{Number of units produced}}$$

- Where there is work in progress at the end of the period, the equivalent units of output that it represents must be calculated to derive total output and cost per unit of output.

Multi-product businesses – job costing

- Where units of output are not identical, costs are divided into two categories: direct cost and indirect cost (overheads).
- Direct cost = cost that can be identified with, and measured in respect of, specific cost units (for example, labour of a garage mechanic, in relation to a particular car repair).
- Indirect cost (overheads) = cost that cannot be identified with, and measured in respect of, a particular job (for example, the rent of a garage).
- Full (absorption) cost = direct cost + indirect cost.
- Direct/indirect cost is not linked to variable/fixed cost.

- Indirect cost is difficult to assign to individual cost units – different bases are used and there is no single correct approach.
- Traditionally, indirect cost is seen as the cost of providing a 'service' to cost units.
- Time-based methods, such as the direct labour hour method, are often used to assign indirect cost to cost units in practice.

Dealing with indirect cost on a cost centre (departmental) basis

- Indirect cost (overheads) can be segmented – usually on a cost centre basis – each product cost centre has its own overhead recovery rate.
- Cost centres are areas, activities or functions for which costs are separately determined.
- Overheads must be allocated or apportioned to cost centres.
- Service cost centre cost must then be apportioned to product cost centre overheads.
- Product cost centre overheads must then be absorbed by cost units (jobs).

Batch costing

- A variation of job costing where each job consists of a number of identical (or near identical) cost units:

$$\text{Cost per unit} = \frac{\text{Cost of the batch (direct } + \text{ indirect)}}{\text{Number of units in the batch}}$$

Full cost information and relevant cost

- Full costing does not take account of relevant costs. It focuses on past costs and ignores opportunity costs.
- Relevant cost analysis can be difficult to apply in practice because of the range of possible options.
- Full costing can direct managers' attention to areas that may benefit from relevant cost analysis.

Full (absorption) costing versus variable costing

- With full costing, both fixed and variable costs are included in product cost and treated as expenses when the product is sold.
- With variable costing, only the variable product cost is linked to the products in this way. Fixed cost is treated as an expense of the period in which it was incurred.
- Variable costing tends to be more straightforward and, according to proponents, provides a more realistic measure of overall achievement.
- Proponents of full costing argue, however, that it provides a better measure of profitability, item by item. Manufacturing fixed costs are an essential ingredient of total product cost.
- Variable costing highlights the relationship between cost, volume and profit, which is obscured under a full costing system.
- Variable costing directs managers' attention to those (variable) costs that can be avoided in the short term. However, all costs can be avoided in the long term and it may be a bad idea to focus on the short term.

Key terms

For definitions of these terms, see Appendix B.

full cost   *p. 368*
full costing   *p. 368*
cost unit   *p. 368*
process costing   *p. 370*
work in progress   *p. 371*
job costing   *p. 371*
direct cost   *p. 372*
indirect cost   *p. 372*
overheads   *p. 372*
absorption costing   *p. 373*
cost behaviour   *p. 375*

overhead absorption (recovery)
  rate   *p. 377*
cost-plus pricing   *p. 383*
cost centre   *p. 386*
product cost centre   *p. 387*
service cost centre   *p. 387*
cost allocation   *p. 388*
cost apportionment   *p. 388*
batch costing   *p. 396*
variable (marginal)
  costing   *p. 404*

Reference

1   Drury, C. and Tayles, M. (1994) Product costing in UK manufacturing organisations, *European Accounting Review,* vol. 3, no. 3, pp. 443–469.

Further reading

If you would like to explore the topics covered in this chapter in more depth, we recommend the following:

Bhimani, A., Horngren, C., Datar, S. and Rajan, M. (2015) *Management and Cost Accounting,* 6th edn, Pearson, Chapters 3 and 4.

Burns, J., Quinn, M., Warren, L. and Oliveira, J. (2013) *Management Accounting,* McGraw-Hill Education, Chapters 4 and 5.

Drury, C. (2015) *Management and Cost Accounting,* 9th edn, Cengage Learning EMEA, Chapters 2–5.

Hilton, R. and Platt, D. (2014) *Managerial Accounting,* 10th edn, McGraw-Hill Higher Education, Chapters 2 and 3.

Review questions

Solutions to these questions can be found at the back of the book on pp. 793–794.

10.1 What problem does the existence of work in progress cause in process costing?

10.2 What is the point of distinguishing direct cost from indirect cost? Why is this not necessary in process-costing environments?

10.3 Are direct cost and variable cost the same thing? Explain your answer.

10.4 It is sometimes claimed that the full cost of a product or service reflects the break-even selling price. Explain what this means.

Exercises

Solutions to exercises with coloured numbers can be found at the back of the book on pp. 820–823.

Basic-level exercises

10.1 Consider this statement:

'In a job costing system, it is necessary to divide up the business into departments. Fixed costs (or overheads) will be collected for each department. Where a particular fixed cost relates to the business as a whole, it must be divided between the departments. Usually this is done on the basis of area of floor space occupied by each department relative to the entire business. When the total fixed costs for each department have been identified, this will be divided by the number of hours that were worked in each department to deduce an overhead recovery rate. Each job that was worked on in a department will have a share of fixed cost allotted to it according to how long it was worked on. The total cost for each job will therefore be the sum of the variable cost of the job and its share of the fixed cost.'

Required:

Prepare a table of two columns. In the first column you should show any phrases or sentences in the above statement with which you do not agree. In the second column you should show your reason for disagreeing with each one.

10.2 Bodgers Ltd, a business that provides a market research service, operates a job costing system. Towards the end of each financial year, the overhead recovery rate (the rate at which indirect cost will be absorbed by jobs) is established for the forthcoming year.

(a) Why does the business bother to predetermine the recovery rate in the way outlined?

(b) What steps will be involved in predetermining the rate?

(c) What problems might arise with using a predetermined rate?

10.3 Pieman Products Ltd makes road trailers to the precise specifications of individual customers. The following are predicted to occur during the forthcoming year, which is about to start:

Direct materials cost	£50,000
Direct labour cost	£160,000
Direct labour time	16,000 hours
Indirect labour cost	£25,000
Depreciation of machine	£8,000
Rent	£10,000
Heating, lighting and power	£5,000
Indirect materials	£2,000
Other indirect cost (overhead) elements	£1,000
Machine time	3,000 hours

All direct labour is paid at the same hourly rate.

A customer has asked the business to build a trailer for transporting a racing motorcycle to race meetings. It is estimated that this will require materials and components that will cost £1,150. It will take 250 direct labour hours to do the job, of which 50 will involve the use of machinery.

Required:

Deduce a logical cost for the job and explain the basis of dealing with overheads that you propose.

Intermediate-level exercises

10.4 Promptprint Ltd, a printing business, has received an enquiry from a potential customer for the quotation of a price for a job. The pricing policy of the business is based on the plans for the next financial year shown below.

	£
Sales revenue (billings to customers)	196,000
Materials (direct)	(38,000)
Labour (direct)	(32,000)
Variable overheads	(2,400)
Maintenance	(3,000)
Depreciation	(27,600)
Rent	(36,000)
Heat and light	(8,000)
Profit	49,000

A first estimate of the direct cost for the particular job is:

	£
Direct materials	4,000
Direct labour	3,600

Required:

(a) Prepare a recommended price for the job based on the plans, commenting on your method, ignoring the information given in the Appendix (below).

(b) Incorporate the effects of the information shown in the Appendix (below) into your estimates of the direct material cost, explaining any changes you consider it necessary to make to the above direct material cost of £4,000.

Appendix to Exercise 10.4

Based on historic cost, direct material cost was computed as follows:

	£
Paper grade 1	1,200
Paper grade 2	2,000
Card (zenith grade)	500
Inks and other miscellaneous items	300
	4,000

Paper grade 1 is regularly used by the business. Enough of this paper to complete the job is currently held. Because it is imported, it is estimated that if it is used for this job, a new purchase order will have to be placed shortly. Sterling has depreciated against the foreign currency by 25 per cent since the last purchase.

Paper grade 2 is purchased from the same source as grade 1. The business holds exactly enough of it for the job, but this was bought in for a special order. This order was cancelled, although the defaulting customer was required to pay £500 towards the cost of the paper. The accountant has offset this against the original cost to arrive at the figure of £2,000 shown above. This paper is rarely used and due to its special chemical coating will be unusable if it is not used on the job in question.

The card is another specialist item currently held by the business. There is no use foreseen and it would cost £750 to replace, if required. However, the inventories controller had planned to spend £130 on overprinting to use the card as a substitute for other materials costing £640.

Inks and other items are in regular use in the print shop.

10.5 Many businesses charge overheads to jobs on a cost centre basis.

Required:

(a) What is the advantage that is claimed for charging overheads to jobs on a cost centre basis and why is it claimed?
(b) What circumstances need to exist for it to make a difference to a particular job whether overheads are charged on a business-wide basis or on a cost centre basis? (Note that the answer to this part of the question is not specifically covered in the chapter. You should, nevertheless, be able to deduce the reason from what you know.)

Advanced-level exercises

10.6 Athena Ltd is an engineering business doing work for its customers to their particular requirements and specifications. It determines the full cost of each job taking a 'job-costing' approach, accounting for overheads on a cost centre (departmental) basis. It bases its prices to customers on this full cost figure. The business has two departments (both of which are cost centres): a Machining Department, where each job starts, and a Fitting Department, which completes all of the jobs. Machining Department overheads are charged to jobs on a machine hour basis and those of the Fitting Department on a direct labour hour basis. The budgeted information for next year is as follows:

Heating and lighting	£25,000	(allocated equally between the two departments)
Machine power	£10,000	(all allocated to the Machining Department)
Direct labour	£200,000	(£150,000 allocated to the Fitting Department and £50,000 to the Machining Department; all direct workers are paid £10 an hour)
Indirect labour	£50,000	(apportioned to the departments in proportion to the direct labour cost)
Direct materials	£120,000	(all applied to jobs in the Machining Department)
Depreciation	£30,000	(all relates to the Machining Department)
Machine time	20,000 hours	(all worked in the Machining Department)

Required:

(a) Prepare a statement showing the budgeted overheads for next year, analysed between the two cost centres. This should be in the form of three columns: one for the total figure for each type of overhead and one column each for the two cost centres, where each type of overhead is analysed between the two cost centres. Each column should also show the total of overheads for the year.

(b) Derive the appropriate rate for charging the overheads of each cost centre to jobs (that is, a separate rate for each cost centre).

(c) Athena Ltd has been asked by a customer to specify the price that it will charge for a particular job that will, if the job goes ahead, be undertaken early next year. The job is expected to use direct materials costing Athena Ltd £1,200, to need 50 hours of machining time, 10 hours of Machine Department direct labour and 20 hours of Fitting Department direct labour. Athena Ltd charges a profit loading of 20 per cent to the full cost of jobs to determine the selling price.

Show workings to derive the proposed selling price for this job.

10.7 Bookdon plc manufactures three products, X, Y and Z, in two product cost centres: a machine shop and a fitting section; it also has two service cost centres: a canteen and a machine maintenance section. Shown below are next year's planned production data and manufacturing cost for the business.

	X	Y	Z
Production	4,200 units	6,900 units	1,700 units
Direct materials	£11/unit	£14/unit	£17/unit
Direct labour:			
Machine shop	£6/unit	£4/unit	£2/unit
Fitting section	£12/unit	£3/unit	£21/unit
Machine hours	6 hr/unit	3 hr/unit	4 hr/unit

Planned overheads are as follows:

	Machine shop	Fitting section	Canteen	Machine maintenance section	Total
Allocated overheads	£27,660	£19,470	£16,600	£26,650	£90,380
Rent, heat and light					£17,000
Depreciation and insurance of equipment					£25,000
Additional data:					
Gross carrying amount of equipment	£150,000	£75,000	£30,000	£45,000	
Number of employees	18	14	4	4	
Floor space occupied	3,600 sq m	1,400 sq m	1,000 sq m	800 sq m	

All machining is carried out in the machine shop. It has been estimated that approximately 70 per cent of the machine maintenance section's cost is incurred servicing the machine shop and the remainder servicing the fitting section.

Required:

(a) Calculate the following planned overhead absorption rates:
   (1) A machine hour rate for the machine shop.
   (2) A rate expressed as a percentage of direct wages for the fitting section.
(b) Calculate the planned full cost per unit of Product X.

Costing and performance evaluation in a competitive environment

Introduction

In recent years, we have seen major changes in the business world, including deregulation, privatisation, the growing expectations of shareholders and the impact of new technology. These have led to a much faster-changing and more competitive environment that has radically altered the way that businesses are managed. In this chapter, we shall consider some of the management accounting techniques that have been developed to help businesses maintain their competitiveness in this new era.

We begin by considering the impact of this new environment on the full costing approach that we considered in Chapter 10. We shall see that activity-based costing, which is a development of the traditional full costing approach, takes a much more questioning, much less accepting attitude towards overheads. We shall also examine some recent approaches to costing that can help manage costs and, therefore, increase the ability of a business to compete on price.

Management accounting embraces both financial and non-financial measures and, in this chapter, we shall consider the increasing importance of non-financial measures in managing a business. These include the balanced scorecard approach, which seeks to integrate financial and non-financial measures into a framework for the achievement of business objectives.

Finally, we examine the idea of shareholder value, which has been a 'hot' issue among managers in recent years. Many leading businesses now claim that the quest for shareholder value is the driving force behind strategic and operational decisions. We shall consider what the term 'shareholder value' means and we shall look at one of the main methods of measuring shareholder value.

Learning outcomes

When you have completed this chapter, you should be able to:

● discuss the nature and usefulness of activity-based costing;

● explain how new developments such as total life-cycle costing and target costing can be used to control costs;

● discuss the importance of non-financial measures of performance in managing a business and the way in which the balanced scorecard attempts to integrate financial and non-financial measures; and

● explain the term 'shareholder value' and describe the role of EVA® in measuring and delivering shareholder value.

Cost determination in the changed business environment

Costing and pricing: the traditional way

The traditional, and still widely-used, approach to job costing developed when the notion of trying to determine the cost of industrial production first emerged. This was around the time of the UK Industrial Revolution when industry was characterised by the following:

● *Direct-labour-intensive and direct-labour-paced production.* Labour was at the heart of production. Although machinery was used, the speed of production tended to be dictated by direct labour.
● *A low level of indirect cost relative to direct cost.* Little was spent on power, heat and light, machinery (depreciation charges) and other areas typical of the indirect cost (overheads) of modern businesses.
● *A relatively uncompetitive market.* Transport difficulties, limited industrial production worldwide and a lack of knowledge by customers of competitors' prices meant that businesses could prosper without being too scientific in their costing. Typically they could simply add a margin for profit to full cost to arrive at the selling price (cost-plus pricing). Furthermore, customers would usually accept those products on offer, rather than demand precisely what they wanted.

Since overheads at that time represented a pretty small element of total cost, it was acceptable and practical to deal with them in a fairly arbitrary manner. Not too much effort was devoted to trying to control overheads because the potential rewards of better control were relatively small, certainly when compared with the benefits from firmer control of direct labour and material costs. It was also reasonable to charge overheads to individual jobs on a direct labour hour basis. Most of the overheads were incurred directly in support of direct labour: providing direct workers with a place to work, heating and lighting the workplace, employing people to supervise the direct workers and so on. Direct workers, perhaps aided by machinery, carried out all production.

At that time, service industries were a relatively unimportant part of the economy and would have largely consisted of self-employed individuals. These individuals would probably not have been interested in trying to do more than work out a rough hourly/daily rate for their time and then use this as a basis for pricing.

Costing and pricing: the new environment

In recent years, the world of industrial production has fundamentally changed. Most of it is now characterised by:

- *Capital-intensive and machine-paced production.* Machines are at the heart of much production, including both the manufacture of goods and the provision of services. Most labour supports the efforts of machines, for example, by technically maintaining them. Furthermore, machines often dictate the pace of production. According to evidence provided in Real World 10.2 (page 372), direct labour accounts on average for just 14 per cent of manufacturers' total cost.
- *A high level of indirect cost relative to direct costs.* Modern businesses tend to have very high depreciation, servicing and power costs. There are also high costs of personnel and staff welfare, which were scarcely envisaged in the early days of industrial production. At the same time, there are very low (sometimes no) direct labour costs. Although direct material cost often remains an important element of total cost, more efficient production methods lead to less waste and, therefore, to a lower total material cost, again tending to make indirect cost (overheads) more dominant. Again, according to Real World 10.2, overheads account for 25 per cent of manufacturers' total cost and 51 per cent of service sector total cost.
- *A highly competitive international market.* Production, much of it highly sophisticated, is carried out worldwide. Transport, including fast airfreight, is relatively cheap. Fax, telephone and, particularly, the internet ensure that potential customers can quickly and cheaply find the prices of a range of suppliers. Markets now tend to be highly price-competitive. Customers increasingly demand products custom made to their own requirements. This means that businesses need to know their product costs with greater accuracy. They also have to take a more careful and informed approach to pricing.
- *Short product-life cycles* Technological innovation, greater competition and more demanding customers have forced businesses to quicken the pace of new product development. Technology-based products, for example, are continually updated with improved features and faster processors. This has led to the design stage assuming greater importance and a greater need to manage costs at this stage. It is now widely recognised that the way in which products are designed will largely determine the future costs of production. Shorter product-life cycles also create a need for a business to forecast future demand with greater accuracy. This helps to ensure that products are available for sale at the time that customers demand them. Similarly, shorter product-life cycles create a need for close tracking of inventories to avoid the costs of obsolescence.

In the UK, as in many developed countries, service industries now dominate the economy, employing the great majority of the workforce and producing most of the value of productive output. Although there are still many self-employed individuals supplying services, many service providers are vast businesses.

Activity 11.1

Can you think of any service providers that are vast businesses? Try to think of at least three.

Some examples that we came up with are:

- banks
- restaurant chains
- insurance businesses
- airlines
- hotel chains
- cinema operators.

You may have thought of others.

For most of these larger service providers, the activities closely resemble modern manufacturing. They too are characterised by high capital intensity, high overheads in relation to direct costs and a competitive international market.

Cost management systems

Changes in the competitive environment mean that businesses must now manage costs more effectively. To do this, cost management systems must provide managers with the information needed. Traditional cost management systems have often proved inadequate for this task and so, in recent years, new systems have taken root. We shall look at some of these new systems shortly but, before doing so, let us consider an important reason for their development.

The problem of overheads

In Chapter 10, we considered the traditional approach to job costing (that is, deriving the full cost of a unit of output where each unit of output differs from the others). We may recall that this approach involves collecting the direct costs for each job. These are the costs that can be clearly linked to, and measured in respect of, the particular job. The indirect costs (overheads), which cannot be linked to products in the same way, are allocated, or apportioned, to product cost centres and then charged to individual jobs using appropriate overhead recovery rates. These recovery rates are typically based on direct labour hours.

In the past, this approach has worked reasonably well, largely because overhead recovery rates (that is, rates at which overheads are absorbed by jobs) were typically much lower for each direct labour hour than the wage rate paid to direct workers. We have now, however, reached the point where overheads are often far more significant. It is not unusual for overhead recovery rates to be between five and ten times the hourly wage rate. Where production is dominated by direct labour that is paid, say, £12 an hour, it may be of no great consequence to assign overheads using an overhead recovery rate of, say, £1 an hour.

It becomes much more so, however, where the overhead recovery rate is, say, £60 an hour. This can result in very arbitrary product costing. Even a small change in the amount of direct labour worked can have a huge effect on the total cost calculated for a job. This is not because direct labour is highly paid, but rather because of the effect of direct labour hours on the overhead cost loading.

Taking a closer look

The changes in the competitive environment discussed above have led to much closer attention being paid to the issue of overheads, what causes them and how they are charged to jobs. It is increasingly recognised that overheads do not just happen; something must be causing them. To illustrate this point, let us consider Example 11.1.

Example 11.1

Modern Producers Ltd has a storage area within its factory that is set aside for its inventories of finished goods. The cost of running the storage area includes a share of the factory rent and other establishment costs, such as heating and lighting. It also includes the salaries of staff employed to look after the inventories.

The business has two product lines: A and B. Product A tends to be made in small batches and low levels of finished inventories are held. The business prides itself on its ability to instantly supply Product B, in large quantities. As a consequence, most of the space in the storage area is filled with finished Product Bs, ready to be despatched once an order is received.

Traditionally, the whole cost of operating the storage area would have been treated as a part of general overheads and included in the total of overheads charged to jobs, probably on a direct labour hour basis. This means that, when assessing the cost of Products A and B, the cost of operating the storage area would have fallen on them according to the number of direct labour hours worked on manufacturing each one, a factor that has nothing to do with storage. In fact, most of the storage cost should be charged to Product B, since this product causes (and benefits from) the stores' cost much more than Product A.

Failure to account more precisely for the cost of running the storage area is masking the fact that Product B is not as profitable as it seems. It may even be creating losses as a result of the high storage cost that it causes. However, much of this cost is being charged to Product A, even though this product makes much less use of the storage area.

Activity-based costing

Activity-based costing (ABC) aims to overcome the kind of problem just described by directly tracing the cost of all activities supporting the production process (that is, the overheads) and linking those costs to particular units of output (of products or services). This is done on the basis that the particular units of output that cause the overheads are linked to them, as we just saw with stores operating costs in Example 11.1. For a manufacturing business, these support activities may include materials ordering, running machines, inspection, processing customer orders and so on. The cost of these support activities goes to make up total overhead cost. The purpose of tracing activity costs in this way is to provide a more realistic, and more finely measured, account of the overhead cost element for a particular unit of output.

To implement a system of ABC, managers must begin by carefully examining the business's operations. They will need to identify:

● each of the various support activities involved in the process of making products or providing services;
● the costs to be assigned to each support activity; and
● the factors that cause a change in the costs of each support activity, that is, the **cost drivers.**

Identifying the cost drivers is a vital element of a successful ABC system. They have a cause-and-effect relationship with activity costs and so are used as a basis for assigning support activity costs to a particular unit of output. This point is now considered in further detail.

Assigning overheads

Once the various support activities, their costs and the factors that drive these costs have been identified, ABC requires three steps:

1 Establishing an overhead **cost pool** for each support activity. There will be just one cost pool for each separate cost driver.
2 Assigning the total cost associated with each support activity to the relevant cost pool.
3 Charging the units of output with the total cost within each pool using the relevant cost driver.

Step 3, above, involves dividing the amount in each cost pool by the estimated total usage of the cost driver to derive a cost per unit of the cost driver. This unit cost figure is then multiplied by the number of units of the cost driver used by a particular unit of output, to determine the amount of overhead cost to be attached to it (or absorbed by it).

Example 11.2 should make this process clear.

Example 11.2

The management accountant at Modern Producers Ltd (see Example 11.1) has estimated that the cost of running the storage area for finished goods for next year will be £90,000. This will be the amount allocated to the 'storage area cost pool'.

It is estimated that each Product A will spend an average of one week in the storage area before being sold. With Product B, the equivalent period is four weeks. Both products are of roughly similar size and have very similar storage needs. It is felt, therefore, that the period spent in the storage area ('product weeks') is the cost driver.

Next year, 50,000 Product As and 25,000 Product Bs are expected to pass through the storage area. The estimated total usage of the cost driver will be the total number of 'product weeks' that the products will be in the storage area. For next year, this will be:

Product A	50,000 × 1 week	=	50,000
Product B	25,000 × 4 weeks	=	100,000
			150,000

Example 11.2 *continued*

The cost per unit of cost driver is the total cost of the storage area divided by the number of 'product weeks', as calculated above. This is:

$$£90,000/150,000 = £0.60$$

To determine the cost to be attached to a particular unit of each product, the figure of £0.60 must be multiplied by the number of 'product weeks' that a product stays in the storage area. Thus, each unit of Product A will be charged with £0.60 (that is, £0.60 × 1) and each Product B with £2.40 (that is, £0.60 × 4).

Benefits of ABC

Through the direct tracing of overheads to products in the way described, ABC seeks to establish a more accurate cost for each unit of product or service. This should help managers in assessing product profitability and in making decisions concerning pricing and the appropriate product mix. Other benefits, however, may also flow from adopting an ABC approach.

Activity 11.2

Can you think of any other benefits that an ABC approach to costing may provide?

By identifying the various support activities' costs and analysing what causes them to change, managers should gain a better understanding of the business. This, in turn, should help them in controlling overheads and improving efficiency. It should also help them in forward planning. They may, for example, be in a better position to assess the likely effect of new products and processes on activities and costs.

ABC and the traditional approach compared

The traditional absorption costing approach and the ABC approach have much in common. Both approaches adopt a two-stage allocation process for assigning overhead costs. With the traditional approach, overhead costs are usually first assigned to product cost centres. The costs accumulated in each cost centre are then charged to units of output using an overhead recovery rate. With the ABC approach, overhead costs are first assigned to cost pools. The costs accumulated are then charged to units of output using the cost driver rate for each activity.

At the first stage of allocation, the cost centre in traditional absorption costing and the cost pool in ABC fulfil similar roles. Both provide a location for assigning overhead costs. However, a cost centre is usually based around a department (see Example 10.3) whereas a cost pool is based around an activity (see Examples 11.1 and 11.2). At the second stage, overhead recovery rates and cost driver rates also fulfil similar roles. Both provide a means of assigning overhead costs to units of output. The two differ, however, in the way in which these costs are assigned.

The two approaches to dealing with overhead costs are illustrated in Figure 11.1.

| **Figure 11.1** | **Traditional versus activity-based costing** |

Traditional approach

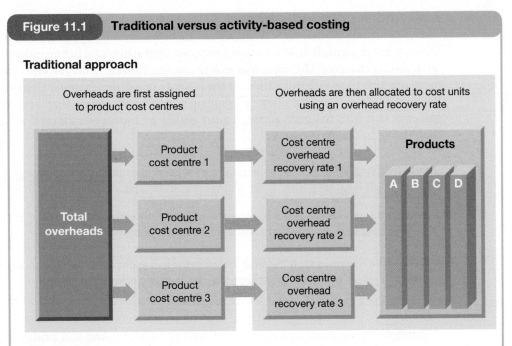

ABC approach

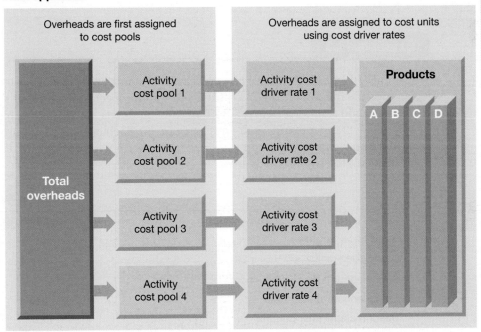

With the traditional approach, overheads are first assigned to product cost centres and then absorbed by cost units based on an overhead recovery rate (using direct labour hours worked on the cost units or some other approach) for each cost centre. With activity-based costing, overheads are assigned to cost pools and then cost units are charged with overheads to the extent that they drive the costs in the various pools.

Source: Adapted from Innes, J. and Mitchell, F. (1990) *Activity Based Costing: A Review with Case Studies,* CIMA Publishing. With kind permission of Elsevier.

ABC and service industries

Much of our discussion of ABC has concentrated on the manufacturing industry, perhaps because early users of ABC were manufacturing businesses. However, ABC may be even more relevant to service industries. In the absence of a direct material element, a service business's total cost is often largely made up of overheads. As we shall see later, there is evidence that ABC has been adopted more widely by businesses that sell services rather than those that make products.

Activity 11.3

What is the difference in the way in which direct costs are accounted for when using ABC compared to the traditional absorption costing approach?

The answer is none at all. Differences between the two approaches are only concerned with the way in which overheads are charged to jobs in order to derive the full cost.

Example 11.3 provides an example of activity-based costing and brings together the points that have been raised so far.

Example 11.3

Comma Ltd manufactures two types of Sprizzer – Standard and Deluxe. Each product requires the incorporation of a difficult-to-handle special part (one of them for a Standard and four for a Deluxe). Both of these products are made in batches (large batches for Standards and small ones for Deluxes). Each new batch requires that the production facilities are 'set up'.

Details of the two products are:

	Standard	Deluxe
Annual production and sales – units	12,000	12,000
Sales price per unit	£65	£87
Batch size – units	1,000	50
Direct labour time per unit – hours	2	$2\frac{1}{2}$
Direct labour rate per hour	£8	£8
Direct material cost per unit	£22	£32
Number of special parts per unit	1	4
Number of set-ups per batch	1	3
Number of separate material issues from stores per batch	1	1
Number of purchase orders issued per year	50	240

The business has just one cost centre.

In recent months, Comma Ltd has been trying to persuade customers who buy the Standard to purchase the Deluxe instead. An analysis of overhead costs for Comma Ltd has provided the following information:

Overhead cost analysis	£	Cost driver
Set-up cost	73,200	Number of set-ups
Special part handling cost	60,000	Number of special parts
Purchase order cost	29,000	Number of purchase orders
Material handling cost	63,000	Number of batches
Other overheads	108,000	Labour hours

We shall calculate the profit per unit and the operating profit margin for Standard and Deluxe Sprizzers, first using the traditional direct-labour-hour-based absorption of overheads, and then using activity-based costing methods.

Traditional approach

Using the traditional full (absorption) costing approach that we considered in Chapter 10, the overheads are added together and an overheads recovery rate deduced as follows:

Overheads	£
Set-up cost	73,200
Special part handling cost	60,000
Purchase order cost	29,000
Material handling cost	63,000
Other overheads	108,000
	333,200

$$\text{Overhead recovery rate} = \frac{\text{Total overheads}}{\text{Number of labour hours}}$$

$$= \frac{333,200}{54,000 \text{ [that is, } (12,000 \times 2) + (12,000 \times 2^{1}/_{2})]}$$

$$= £6.17 \text{ per hour}$$

The total cost per unit of each type of Sprizzer is calculated by adding the direct cost to the overheads cost per unit. The overheads cost per unit is calculated by multiplying the number of direct labour hours spent on the product (2 hours for each

→

Example 11.3 *continued*

Standard and 2½ hours for each Deluxe) by the overheads recovery rate calculated above. Hence:

	Standard	Deluxe
	£	£
Direct costs:		
Labour	16.00	20.00
Material	22.00	32.00
Indirect cost:		
Overheads (£6.17 per hour)	12.34	15.43
Total cost per unit	50.34	67.43

The operating profit margin is calculated as follows:

	Standard £ per unit	Deluxe £ per unit
Sales price	65.00	87.00
Total cost (see above)	50.34	67.43
Profit	14.66	19.57
Operating profit margin [(profit/sales) × 100%]	22.55%	22.49%

ABC approach

Using the ABC costing approach, the activity cost driver rates will be calculated as follows:

Overhead cost pool	Driver	(a) Standard driver volume	(b) Deluxe driver volume	(c) Total driver volume (a + b)	(d) Costs £	(e) Driver rate (d/c) £
Set-up	Set-ups per batch	12	720	732	73,200	100
Special part	Special parts per unit	12,000	48,000	60,000	60,000	1
Purchase orders	Purchase orders per year	50	240	290	29,000	100
Material handling	Number of batches	12	240	252	63,000	250
Other overheads	Labour hours	24,000	30,000	54,000	108,000	2

The activity-based costs are derived as follows:

Overhead	(f) Total costs Standard (a × e) £	(g) Total costs Deluxe (b × e) £	Unit costs Standard (f/12,000) £	Unit costs Deluxe (g/12,000) £
Set-up	1,200	72,000	0.10	6.00
Special part	12,000	48,000	1.00	4.00
Purchase orders	5,000	24,000	0.42	2.00
Material handling	3,000	60,000	0.25	5.00
Other overheads	48,000	60,000	4.00	5.00
Total overheads			5.77	22.00

The total cost per unit is calculated as follows:

	Standard £ per unit	Deluxe £ per unit
Direct costs:		
Labour	16.00	20.00
Material	22.00	32.00
Indirect cost:		
See above	5.77	22.00
Total cost per unit	43.77	74.00

The operating profit margin is calculated as follows:

	Standard £ per unit	Deluxe £ per unit
Sales price	65.00	87.00
Total cost (see above)	43.77	74.00
Profit	21.23	13.00
Operating profit margin [(profit/sales) × 100%]	32.67%	14.94%

Activity 11.4

Comment on the managerial implications for Comma Ltd of the results in Example 11.3.

The figures show that under the traditional approach the returns on sales for each product are broadly equal. However, the ABC approach shows that the Standard product is far more profitable. Hence, the business should reconsider its policy of trying to persuade customers to switch to the Deluxe product.

Benefits and costs of ABC

By adopting a more forensic approach to assigning overheads, ABC can provide a more accurate cost figure for each unit of output. This should help in assessing product profitability and in making pricing and product mix decisions. ABC can also help managers gain a better understanding of business operations. This, in turn, should help improve performance.

Despite its apparent advantages, critics point out that ABC can be a costly exercise. Setting up the costing system, as well as updating it, can consume a great deal of resources. Running an ABC system can also be complex and time consuming, particularly where business operations involve a large number of activities and cost drivers. Management reports generated from a complex costing system are also likely to be complex. If managers find these reports difficult to understand, the potential benefits of employing ABC may be lost.

Where products or services have similar levels of output involving similar activities and processes, or where overheads form a relatively low proportion of the total costs, the more accurate measurements provided by ABC are unlikely to lead to strikingly different outcomes from those obtained under the traditional approach. As a result, opportunities for better pricing, planning and cost control may be few. If this were the case, switching to an ABC system would be difficult to justify.

Measurement and tracing problems may arise with ABC. Not all costs can be easily traced to a particular activity. Nevertheless, all activity costs have to be assigned to one cost pool or another. To ensure that all these costs are taken into account, some may be assigned to cost pools on an arbitrary basis. Poor quality data on activity costs may also lead to arbitrary cost assignments. A final problem is that the relationship between activity costs and their cost drivers may be difficult to determine. Identifying a cause-and-effect relationship can be difficult where activity costs are fixed and do not change with changes in operating activities.

Finally, ABC is criticised for the same reason that traditional full costing is criticised – it does not provide relevant information for decision making. This is because it tends to use past costs and to ignore opportunity costs. Past costs, however, are irrelevant in decision making. Opportunity costs, on the other hand, are relevant and can be significant. For these reasons, some view full costing as an expensive waste of time.

ABC in practice

Real World 11.1 briefly describes how ABC is used at the Royal Mail.

Real World 11.1

Delivering ABC

Early in the 2000s, the Royal Mail adopted ABC and used it to find the cost of making postal deliveries. Royal Mail identified 340 activities that gave rise to costs, created a cost pool and identified a cost driver for each of these.

The Royal Mail continues to use an ABC approach to deriving its costs. The volume of mail is obviously a major driver of costs.

In 2013, the Royal Mail was sold by the UK government and is now in the private sector. It continues to use ABC, however,

Source: Royal Mail Group Ltd, ABC Costing Manual 2016-17, August 2016.

Real World 11.2 provides some indication of the extent to which ABC is used in practice.

Real World 11.2

ABC in practice

A survey of 176 UK businesses operating in various industries, all with annual sales revenue of more than £50 million, was conducted by Al-Omiri and Drury. This indicated that 29 per cent of larger UK businesses use ABC.

The adoption of ABC in the UK varies widely between industries, as is shown in Figure 11.2.

Figure 11.2   The percentage of businesses in different sectors that use ABC

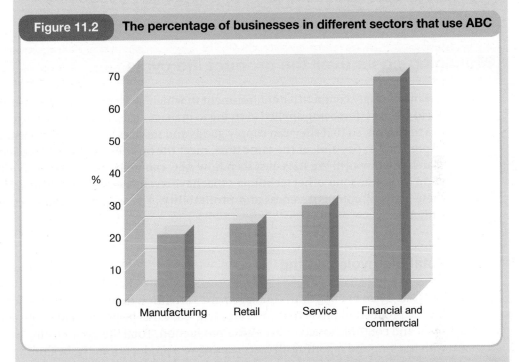

Al-Omiri and Drury took their analysis a step further by looking at the factors that apparently lead a particular business to adopt ABC. They found that businesses that used ABC tended to be:

- large;
- sophisticated, in terms of using advanced management accounting techniques generally;
- in an intensely competitive market for their products; and
- operating in a service industry, particularly in the financial services.

The 2009 CIMA survey emphatically supported the finding that larger businesses tend to use ABC more than smaller ones. It showed that only 22 per cent of businesses with fewer than 50 employees use ABC, whereas 46 per cent of businesses with more than 10,000 employees use the technique.

All of these findings are broadly in line with other recent research evidence involving businesses from around the world.

Sources: Al-Omiri, M. and Drury, C. (2007) A survey of factors influencing the choice of product costing systems in UK organisations, *Management Accounting Research*, Vol. 18, pp. 399–424; CIMA (2009) *Management Accounting Tools for Today and Tomorrow*, p. 12.

Activity 11.5

Suggest reasons why service providers, particularly those that provide financial services, are likely to be relatively major users of ABC.

Since service providers have no direct material cost, overheads often comprise a relatively large proportion of total costs. This can provide a real incentive to examine overheads more closely.

Financial services providers tend to be large and operate in a very competitive market. These are two characteristics that Al-Omiri and Drury (Real World 11.2) identified as being typical of ABC adopters.

Managing costs over the product life cycle

The increasingly competitive environment in which modern businesses operate is leading to greater effort being applied in trying to manage costs. Businesses need to keep costs to a minimum so that they can supply goods and services at a price that customers will be prepared to pay and, at the same time, meet the businesses' objectives of enhancing shareholder wealth. We have just seen how ABC can help manage costs. We shall now go on to outline some other techniques that have recently emerged in an attempt to meet these goals of competitiveness and profitability. These can be used in conjunction with ABC.

Total life-cycle costing

Total life-cycle costing draws management's attention to the fact that it is not only during the production phase that costs are incurred. Costs begin to accumulate at an earlier point and continue to accumulate after production. Total life-cycle costing is concerned with tracking and reporting all costs relating to a product from the beginning to the end of its life – which could be for a period of 20 years or more. If the revenues generated over the life cycle of the product are also tracked, its profitability can be assessed. This represents a radical departure from traditional management accounting approaches, which are normally concerned with assessing performance over periods of one year or less.

Total life-cycle costing starts from the premise that the life cycle of a product or service has three phases. These are:

1 The *pre-production phase*. This is the period that precedes production of the product or service. During this phase, research and development – both of the product or service and of the market – is conducted. The product or service is designed and so is the means of production. The phase culminates with setting up the necessary production facilities and with advertising and promotion.
2 The *production phase* comes next. During this phase the product is made and sold or the service is provided to customers. This is the phase where traditional absorption costing or ABC usually makes its biggest contribution.

3 The *post-production phase* comes last. During this phase, costs may be incurred to correct faults that arose with products or services sold (after-sales service). Since these costs may start to be incurred before the last product or service is sold, this phase will typically overlap with the production phase. During this phase, costs may also be incurred as a result of closing production at the end of the product's or service's life. Where the risk of environmental damage must be eliminated, as with an oil rig or power station, for example, these costs can be extremely high.

The total life cycle of a product or service is shown in Figure 11.3.

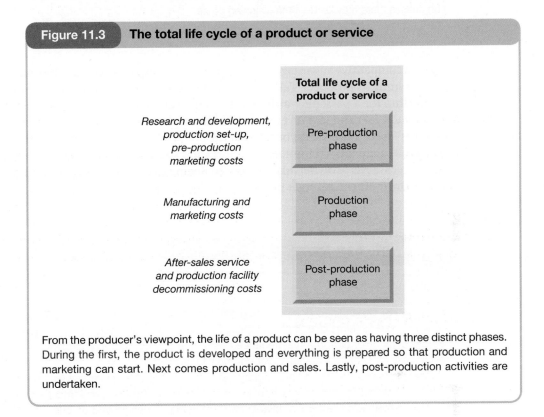

Figure 11.3   The total life cycle of a product or service

Research and development, production set-up, pre-production marketing costs → Pre-production phase

Manufacturing and marketing costs → Production phase

After-sales service and production facility decommissioning costs → Post-production phase

Total life cycle of a product or service

From the producer's viewpoint, the life of a product can be seen as having three distinct phases. During the first, the product is developed and everything is prepared so that production and marketing can start. Next comes production and sales. Lastly, post-production activities are undertaken.

For some businesses, particularly those engaged in an advanced manufacturing environment, a very high proportion (perhaps as much as 80 per cent) of the total costs incurred over the life of a particular product are either incurred, or committed, at the pre-production phase. Take the example of a car manufacturer. A significant proportion of the total life-cycle costs are incurred when designing, developing and setting up production of a new model. In addition, a commitment to incur costs during the production phase is made. This is because the design will incorporate features that lead to particular manufacturing costs. Once the design of the car has been finalised and the manufacturing plant set up, it may be too late to 'design out' a costly feature without incurring another large cost. Decisions made at the pre-production phase can also lead to a commitment to incur costs at the post-production phase. These decisions are, therefore, the most critical as they have the potential for huge cost savings at later points in time.

Activity   11.6

Can you provide an example of a decision made at the pre-production phase of a new car model that will result in costs being incurred after the manufacture of the product?

After-sales service costs may be incurred as a result of some design fault. Once the manufacturing facilities have been established, it may not be economic to revise the design but merely to deal with the problem through after-sales service procedures.

Where the manufacturing plant or production facilities are no longer needed when production ceases there may be decommissioning costs.

To gain competitive advantage, manufacturers may also try to reduce the total life-cycle costs of owning its products. Take, for example, an airplane manufacturer. The total cost of ownership for a passenger airline over its life can be extremely high. Costs include maintenance, fuel and lost revenues when the airplane is out of service. Steps to reduce these costs for customers must be taken at the pre-production phase through the development of new materials, technology, processes and so on. **Real World 11.3** shows how the total life-cycle costs of ownership influenced Boeing in the design and construction of its new 787 Dreamliner passenger plane.

Real World 11.3

Building a dream

With the 787 Dreamliner, Boeing took greater account of the cost to maintain the airplane structure and systems over their lifetimes. This resulted in the basic 787-8 airplane having 30 per cent lower airframe maintenance costs than any comparable airplane and greater availability for service than any other commercial airplane.

The new life-cycle design philosophy led to significant changes in the way the airplane is built. They include extensive use of composites in the airframe and primary structure, an electric system architecture, a reliable and maintainable design and an improved maintenance programme.

Source: Adapted from Hale, J. (2006) Boeing 787 from the ground up, *Aero Quarterly boeing.com Commercial Aeromagazine,* Issue 24, Quarter 4, pp. 17–23.

Total life-cycle costing can be used to manage costs. It was mentioned earlier that, by the start of the production phase, it may be too late to try to manage a large element of the product's or service's total life-cycle cost. With total life-cycle costing, managers will be able to see, at an early stage, the cost consequences of incorporating particular designs or particular elements into products. Where the costs are unacceptable, changes may be made. This may involve assessing the costs of alternative designs. Where a number of equally acceptable designs for a particular product are being considered, knowledge of the total life-cycle costs of each can help decide the final outcome.

Real World 11.4 provides some idea of the extent to which total life-cycle costing is used in practice.

Real World 11.4

Total (whole) life-cycle costing in practice

The 2009 CIMA survey showed that total life-cycle costing is not widely used in practice, as is shown by Figure 11.4. About 14 per cent of all of the businesses surveyed used the approach.

Figure 11.4   The use of total life-cycle costing

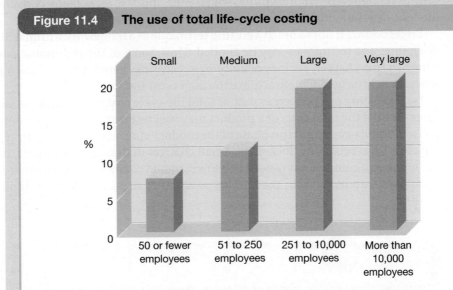

The use of total life-cycle costing is not widespread, but it tends to be much more popular with larger businesses.

Source: Adapted from CIMA (2009) *Management Accounting Tools for Today and Tomorrow*, p. 12.

Target costing

We saw in Chapter 10 that businesses may adopt a cost-plus approach to pricing. This involves totalling the costs of providing a product or service and then adding a percentage for profit to derive a selling price. Cost-plus pricing, however, is not normally suitable for businesses that operate in a highly competitive market. This is because the cost-plus price may be unacceptable to the market.

Target costing approaches the pricing decision from the opposite direction to cost-plus pricing. The starting point is to set a target price for a product based on market research, which will normally include an analysis of competitors' prices. The target profit, based on the financial objective of the business, is then deducted from the identified price. The resulting figure is the *target cost* of the product. Where the target cost is less than the current estimated cost, there will be a 'cost gap'. Efforts must then be made to bridge this gap by making the product, or rendering the service, in a way that meets the target cost.

A team of specialists, drawn from each of the main functional areas, such as design, production, purchasing and marketing, will normally be charged with achieving the target cost. However, stakeholders from outside the business, such as suppliers and customers, may also be invited to join the team. Together they will examine all aspects of the product and the production process to try to eliminate anything that does not add value. This may involve revising the design, developing more efficient means of production, and negotiating with suppliers to provide goods and services more cheaply. The process is often iterative (trial and error) and will continue until total product costs are reduced in line with the target cost figure, or it is found that the target cost figure cannot be achieved. To prevent too much time and resources being consumed in this process, deadlines may be set for reaching the target cost figure.

Target costing is not so much a costing technique as a framework within which various disciplines and techniques may be applied. Thus, some of the techniques covered elsewhere in this chapter, such as activity-based costing, benchmarking and value chain analysis, may be used to help achieve the target cost figure.

Target costing can be seen as part of total life-cycle costing. As we have seen, a large proportion of the total costs of a product may well be determined at the pre-production phase. Careful planning at this phase of the product's life may prevent future manufacturing costs from becoming 'locked in'. Small changes in design, for example, may reduce the number of components needed or allow standard components rather than specialised components to be used. In the end, these small changes may lead to significant cost savings.

Activity 11.7

Although target costing has its enthusiasts, there are potential problems with its use. Try to think of at least two of these.

Potential problems include:

- Attempts to lower costs can lead to conflict – for example, between the business and its suppliers and between the business and its employees.
- It can cause considerable stress among employees who are trying to meet target costs that are extremely difficult to achieve.
- It can be time-consuming, leading to significant delays in the launch of new products.
- It can be a costly exercise.

You may have thought of others.

Real World 11.5 indicates the level of usage of target costing. This shows quite a low level of usage in the UK. In contrast, other survey evidence shows that target costing is very widely used by Japanese manufacturing businesses.

Real World 11.5

Target practice

The 2009 CIMA survey showed that target costing is not widely used in practice, as is shown by Figure 11.5.

Target costing is used by about 16 per cent of all of the businesses surveyed.

Figure 11.5   **The use of target costing**

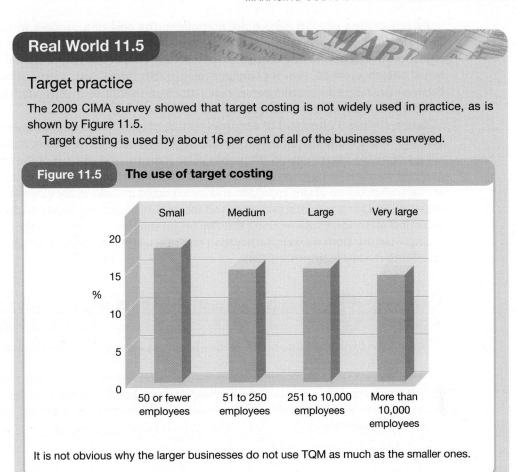

It is not obvious why the larger businesses do not use TQM as much as the smaller ones.

Source: Adapted from CIMA (2009) Management Accounting Tools for Today and Tomorrow, p. 12.

Kaizen costing

To ensure long-term competitiveness, businesses may look beyond the use of target costing at the pre-production phase of a product's life. When the production phase is reached, **kaizen costing** may be used to continue the quest for cost savings. The Japanese word 'kaizen' means 'continuous improvement', which can be accomplished through many small steps. Kaizen costing seeks to achieve cost savings through small, incremental changes on a continuous basis rather than, say, through the radical redesign of the production process on a 'one-off' basis. Since the production phase is quite late in the product life cycle (from a cost management point of view), only small cost savings can usually be made. The majority of production-phase cost savings should already have been made through target costing.

To reduce manufacturing costs, the production process is closely examined in the search for improvements. The focus is on the elimination of waste through unnecessary effort and excessive processes.

Kaizen costing aims to reduce the manufacturing cost of a product to below that incurred during the previous period. This involves target setting. A target percentage reduction in manufacturing cost is set for a period and, at the end of each period, the actual percentage reduction is compared against this target. Any significant deviation between the target and actual percentage reduction should be investigated and action taken if the target has not been reached.

Kaizen costing is often part of a broader culture of continuous improvement within a business. The underlying philosophy is that no process can ever be perfect and so there is always room for improvement. It involves close scrutiny of every part of the production process with ideas being generated as to how things can be improved. Employees are seen as vital to the success of this approach and are expected to make suggestions for eliminating waste and for improving processes and the quality of output. Unlike traditional cost reduction methods, those working directly on production or rendering the service, for example factory-floor workers, rather than engineers, accountants or managers, are seen as holding the key to improvements.

Activity 11.8

Why do you think that those on the factory floor hold the key to improvements?

Those closest to production, particularly those with 'hands-on' experience, have a more intimate knowledge of the process. They are, therefore, more likely to spot opportunities for small improvements, such as minimising the time spent going to the stores or changing a sequence of small operations.

Real World 11.6 explains how a small UK manufacturer used kaizen costing to advantage.

Real World 11.6

Thinking small pays off

John Smedley is a Derbyshire-based luxury knitwear business. The business had been experiencing trading losses, but the application of kaizen techniques returned the business to profit. The business's chief executive, Ian MacLean, explained:

> What is amazing about manufacturing is that if you squeeze a little bit more profit from each step, the overall profit gain can be very large.

Kaizen improvements were made throughout the manufacturing process. This included training production staff, so that they are able to be more flexible in the tasks they can undertake, and better management of purchasing the wool raw material. As a result productivity has already increased by 5 per cent. This has been sufficient to turn an annual £1.9 million loss to a £1.5 million profit, over a period of three years. The business's finance director believes that there remains scope to push this up by a further 8 per cent.

FT *Sources*: Taken from Moules, J. (2013) John Smedley stitches rebound into 200-year-old knitwear brand, ft.com, 11 August and Moules, J. (2014) Thinking small pays off for John Smedley, ft.com, 31 August. © The Financial Times Limited 2014. All Rights Reserved.

Other approaches to managing costs in a modern environment

Value chain analysis

To secure competitive advantage, a business must be able to perform key activities more successfully than its competitors. This means that it must either obtain some cost advantage over its competitors, or differentiate itself in some way from them. To help identify particular ways in which competitive advantage may be achieved, it is useful to analyse a business into a sequence of value-creating activities. This sequence is known as the value chain. **Value chain analysis** examines the potential for each link in the chain to add value.

For a manufacturing business, the value-creating sequence begins with the acquisition of inputs, such as raw materials and energy. It ends with the sale of completed goods and after-sales service. Value chain analysis applies equally well to service-providing businesses as to manufacturers. Service providers also have a sequence of activities leading to provision of the service to their customers. For both types of business, analysing these activities in an attempt to identify and eliminate non-value-added activities can reap significant rewards.

Figure 11.6 sets out the main 'links' in the value chain for a manufacturing business. We can see that there are five primary activities and four secondary activities. Primary activities are those involved in producing, selling, storing and distributing the product. Secondary activities provide a support role to the primary activities.

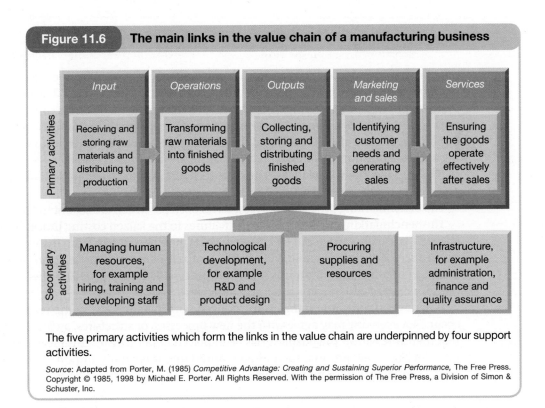

Figure 11.6   **The main links in the value chain of a manufacturing business**

The five primary activities which form the links in the value chain are underpinned by four support activities.

Source: Adapted from Porter, M. (1985) *Competitive Advantage: Creating and Sustaining Superior Performance*, The Free Press. Copyright © 1985, 1998 by Michael E. Porter. All Rights Reserved. With the permission of The Free Press, a Division of Simon & Schuster, Inc.

Each link in the value chain represents an activity that will incur costs and affect profits. Ideally, each will add value – that is, the customer will be prepared to pay more for the activity than it costs to carry out. If, however, a business is to outperform its rivals, it must ensure that the value chain is configured in such a way that it leads either to a cost advantage or to differentiation.

To achieve a cost advantage, the costs associated with each link in the chain must be identified and then examined to see whether they can be reduced or eliminated. For example, a non-value-added activity may be identified, such as the inspection of the completed product by a quality controller. The introduction of a 'quality' culture in the business could lead to much greater reliability in output quality. As a result, inspection would no longer be needed and this cost could be eliminated. To achieve differentiation from its rivals, a business must achieve uniqueness in at least one part of the value chain. A large baker, for example, may try to differentiate its products by moving production facilities to its retail shops to ensure that the products are freshly available to customers.

Value chain analysis should help managers gain a clearer view of the strengths and weaknesses of the business and help identify areas for improvement. In some cases, it may result in significant operational changes, such as the introduction of new manufacturing or service-provision technology or the development of new sales policies. In other cases, it may result in significant strategic shifts. A manufacturing business, for example, may find that it is unable to match the manufacturing costs achieved by its rivals. At the same time, it may have competitive strengths in the areas of marketing and distribution. In such circumstances, a decision may be made to focus on the business's core competencies. This may lead it to outsource the manufacturing function and to concentrate on the marketing and distribution of the goods.

Benchmarking

Benchmarking is an activity – usually a continuing one – where a business seeks to emulate a business that is 'best-in-class' in order to achieve greater success. The best-in-class business provides a standard, or benchmark, against which a business can compare its own performance. Benchmarking can also provide an insight into how performance can be improved. It can also help to avoid the pitfalls experienced by other businesses. Studying a high-performing business, and discovering the factors that lead to success, may lead to the introduction of new ideas. These could result in improved operational efficiency and greater competitive advantage.

The benchmarking process involves a series of steps, which are set out in Figure 11.7.

The benchmarking process has similar features to the kaizen costing process discussed above. It is usually carried out by a team with its members drawn from the various functional areas of the business and will usually continue over time. Furthermore, employees make a vital contribution towards the whole process. This is achieved by offering suggestions for change and by implementing the agreed changes.

Whenever significant change is introduced within a business, some resistance may occur. Not everyone may agree with the new processes, or structures, and some may feel that their role within the business has been placed under threat. This means that when introducing a new process, such as benchmarking, it is vitally important to have the strong support of senior management.

| Figure 11.7 | **The benchmarking process** |

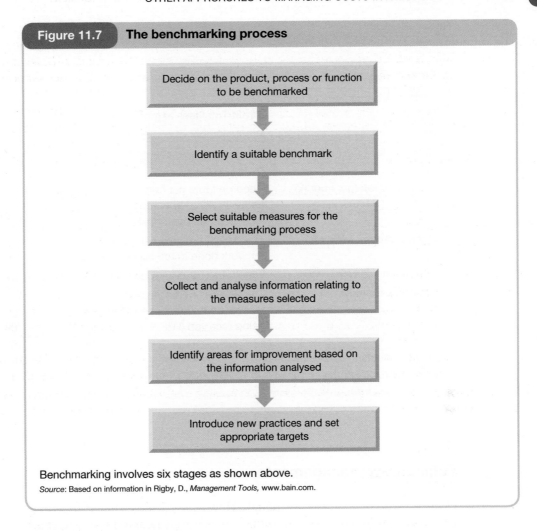

Benchmarking involves six stages as shown above.

Source: Based on information in Rigby, D., *Management Tools*, www.bain.com.

Benchmarking in practice

Real World 11.7 provides an example of how benchmarking may be used to assess the operational efficiency of law firms.

| Real World 11.7 |

Legal measures

The banking group NatWest plc undertook an analysis of the performance of 337 small to medium-sized law firms in the UK. The NatWest report covered law firms with a fee income of up to £27 million during 2012. A variety of measures were used to provide benchmarks against which operational efficiency could be compared. The main measures employed, as well as figures for the upper quartile of law firms for each measure, were:

Performance measure	Calculation of measure	Upper quartile
Fees per equity partner (£000)	Total fees earned/Number of equity (non-salaried) partners	676
Fees per fee earner (£000)	Total fees earned/Number of employees generating fees	193

Real World 11.7 *continued*

Performance measure	Calculation of measure	Upper quartile
Profit as a percentage of fees (%)	(Profit/Total fees earned) × 100%	33
Profit per equity partner (£000)	Profit/Number of equity partners	160
Chargeable hours (per year)	Number of hours charged to clients by fee earners	1,198
Recovered rate per hour (£)	Recorded rate per hour by a fee earner × the percentage of time recorded that can be billed	188
Work in progress (days)	The delay from time being recorded for work done to the bill being raised	26
Debtor days (days)	Time taken for clients to pay the bill	27
Total lock-up (days)	The delay from the time being recorded for work done to the cash being received (WIP + Debtor days)	69

For benchmarking purposes, the upper quartile figures can be used as a measure of superior performance and so provide a surrogate for best-in-class.

Source: Adapted from NatWest Bank (2013) 2013 Financial Benchmarking Report – Law firms nw-businesssense.com.

Total quality management

Quality has become a major weapon that businesses deploy when competing against their rivals. As mentioned earlier, customers increasingly demand products (both goods and services) that meet their specific requirements. One of these requirements will be that products should be of a suitable quality. This means that the products should meet customers' needs and be available at a price they are willing to pay.

This emphasis on creating quality products has led to **total quality management (TQM).** The TQM philosophy is concerned with providing products that meet, or exceed, customers' requirements all of the time. This implies that defective products should never reach the customer. Ideally, there should never be any defective production. TQM has been characterised as *getting it right first time, every time*. It aims to create a virtuous sequence of events where quality improvements lead to reduced production problems, increased customer satisfaction and increased profits.

Employee involvement at all levels within the business is essential if a quality culture is to be developed. Managers must, therefore, take steps to bring this about.

A systematic approach should be adopted for delivering quality improvements. The main steps to be taken are set out in Figure 11.8.

Figure 11.8	Delivering improvements in quality

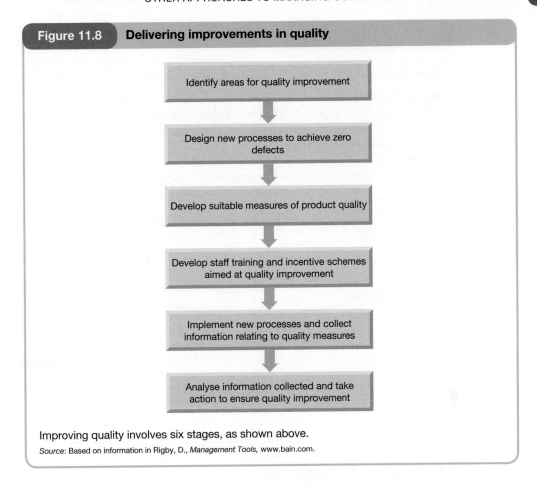

Improving quality involves six stages, as shown above.

Source: Based on information in Rigby, D., *Management Tools,* www.bain.com.

Activity 11.9

What kind of cost savings might accrue to a business that 'gets it right first time, every time'?

These might include

- savings on costs incurred in repairing reputational damage from poor quality products; and
- saving the cost of replacing or rectifying poor quality products.

Real World 11.8 provides some idea of the extent to which TQM is used in practice.

Real World 11.8

Quality practice

Bain & Company, a firm of management consultants, undertakes an annual survey of key management tools. Figure 11.9 shows the results of its 2015 survey, using a database of more than 13,000 executives worldwide, which looks at levels of usage and satisfaction with total quality management.

There has been a decline in the level of usage in recent years; however, there has been no reduction in the level of overall satisfaction.

| Figure 11.9 | The use of total quality management |

Despite consistently high levels of satisfaction, there has been a sharp decline in usage of this technique over recent years.

Source: Rigby, D. (2015) *Insights Management Tools, Total Quality Management,* Bain & Company, http://www.bain.com/publications/articles/management-tools-total-quality-management.aspx, 10 June.

Managing quality costs

A business must ensure that its products are of the right quality. This means that they must meet customer requirements concerning performance and must be technically sound. Doing this, however, will lead to costs being incurred. It has been estimated that **quality costs** can amount to up to 30 per cent of total processing costs. They tend to be incurred during the production phase of the product life cycle and fall into four main categories:

1 *Prevention costs.* These are involved with procedures to try to prevent products being produced that are not up to the required quality. Such procedures might include staff training on quality issues and investment in new equipment. Some types of prevention costs might be incurred during the *pre-production phase* of the product life cycle, where the production process could be designed in such a way as to avoid potential quality problems with the output.

2 *Appraisal costs.* These are concerned with monitoring raw materials, work in progress and finished products to ensure that they achieve the quality standards that have been set.

3 *Internal failure costs.* These include the costs of rectifying substandard products before they reach the customer as well as the costs of scrap arising from quality failures.

4 *External failure costs.* These include the costs of rectifying quality problems with products that have been passed to the customer. They also include the cost to the business of its lost reputation for quality and reliability.

These four categories of cost together comprise the total quality costs incurred by a business.

Often external failure costs are the most critical of the four categories mentioned above as they can be very costly to correct. They can also lead to lost sales and lost customer goodwill, which may put the entire future of the business at risk. **Real World 11.9** comprises extracts from a *Financial Times* article. It describes the concerns over a well-known product that was recalled by the manufacturer which cast a shadow over the entire brand.

Real World 11.9

Great balls of fire!

Samsung's Electronics' suspension of all sales and exchanges of its fire-prone Galaxy Note 7 smartphone has fuelled concerns that the spiralling safety issues and dwindling customer confidence in its flagship device may spread to the company's other consumer products. Analysts warn that damage from the recall fiasco is likely to hit Samsung's reputation as well as sales in coming months, potentially benefiting rivals such as Apple and Google just as their new devices hit the market ahead of the crucial holiday sales season.

The world's largest smartphone maker has stopped all production and sales of the Note 7 as it conducts a thorough investigation into why some replacement models, issued after an initial recall, are also catching fire. The South Korean company urged consumers to stop using the devices and asked all global partners to stop sales and exchanges of the phone during the probe.

However, analysts said it would be difficult for Samsung to regain consumer confidence any time soon, as the second withdrawal of the product in two months highlights the company's struggle to fix the problem. It has also heightened criticism that it was too quick to blame the safety issues on the original battery supplier.

Whatever the cause, the quality issues have raised concerns of "contagion" to other Samsung phones and products if the safety problem relates to components other than the battery. However, there are no signs so far that any other models have issues with overheating, and Samsung's investigation only relates to the affected Galaxy Note 7.

"Samsung's credibility is on the line. Samsung needs to make sure that consumers can trust its brand or else other products [and future products] are at risk," said Bryan Ma, analyst at IDC. Carolina Milanesi, an analyst at Creative Strategies, said Samsung should "kill" the Note product line altogether to prevent the company's broader reputation being tarnished further, with the recall "becoming such a saga". "If Samsung as a brand gets stained, that is what's going to cost them," she said. "The cost of the recall and stopping production is nothing compared to the permanent damage to the brand."

FT *Source*: Extracts from Song, J. and Bradshaw, T. (2016) Samsung recall debacle fuels brand concerns, ft.com, 11 October. © The Financial Times Limited 2016. All Rights Reserved.

Figure 11.10 summarises the main categories of total quality costs.

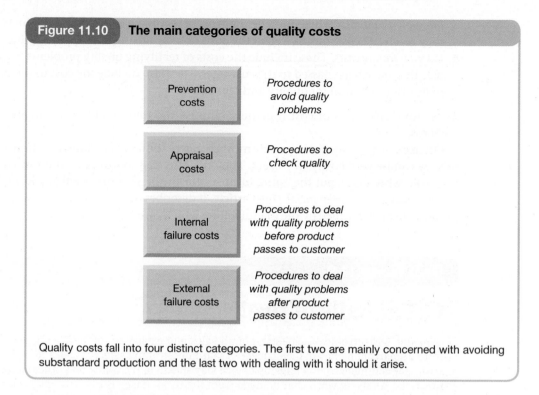

Figure 11.10 The main categories of quality costs

Quality costs fall into four distinct categories. The first two are mainly concerned with avoiding substandard production and the last two with dealing with it should it arise.

An alternative view

While the costing methods just described are used and are regarded as useful by many businesses, some believe that they fail to provide the key to successful cost management. It has been suggested that undue emphasis on costing methods, such as total life-cycle costing, is misplaced and what is really needed is for businesses to develop ways of learning and adapting to their changing environment. To manage costs successfully, businesses should continually review them in the face of new threats and pressures rather than relying on particular techniques to provide solutions.

Hopwood (see reference 1 at the end of the chapter) suggests that to transform costs over time to enable them to fit the strategic objectives, businesses do not need very sophisticated techniques or highly bureaucratic systems. Rather, they need to change the ways in which costs are viewed and dealt with. He suggests that the following broad principles should be adopted.

Spread the responsibility

Employees throughout the business should share responsibility for managing costs. Thus, design experts, engineers, store managers, sales managers and so on should all contribute towards managing costs and should see this as part of their job. The involvement of non-accountants is, of course, a feature of target costing and kaizen costing. Thus, this point already appears to be widely accepted.

Hopwood suggests that employees should be provided with a basic understanding of costing ideas, such as fixed and variable costs, relevant costs and so on, to enable them to contribute fully. As cost-consciousness permeates the business, and non-accounting employees become more involved in costing issues, the role of accountants will change. They will often facilitate, rather than initiate, cost management proposals and will become part of the multi-skilled teams engaged in creatively managing them.

Spread the word

Throughout the business, costs and cost management should become everyday topics for discussion. Managers should seize every opportunity to raise these topics with employees, as talking about costs can often lead to ideas being developed and action being taken to manage costs.

Think local

Emphasis should be placed on managing costs within specific sites and settings. Managers of departments, product lines or local offices are more likely to become engaged in managing costs if they are allowed to take initiatives in areas over which they have control. Local managers tend to have local knowledge not possessed by managers at head office. They are more likely to be able to spot cost-saving opportunities than are their more senior colleagues. Where initiatives for cost management have been developed by senior management, and are applied across the whole business, they are unlikely to have the same beneficial effect as local initiatives.

Benchmark continually

Benchmarking should be a never-ending journey. There should be regular, as well as special-purpose, reporting of cost information for benchmarking purposes. The costs of competitors may provide a useful basis for comparison, as we saw earlier. In addition, costs that may be expected as a result of moving to new technology or work patterns may be helpful.

Focus on managing costs rather than reducing them

Conventional management accounting tends to focus on cost reduction, which is, essentially, taking a short-term perspective on costs. Effective cost management, however, requires that, in some situations, costs should be increased rather than reduced.

Hopwood argues that these principles, when used in conjunction with overall financial controls, provide the best way to manage costs.

Non-financial measures of performance

Financial measures have long been seen as the most important ones for a business. They provide a valuable means of summarising and evaluating business achievement. Furthermore, the continued importance of financial measures is in no real doubt. Nevertheless, there has been increasing recognition that financial measures alone will not provide managers with sufficient information to manage a business effectively. Non-financial measures are also needed to help gain a deeper understanding of the business and to help achieve its objectives, including financial objectives.

Financial measures portray various aspects of business achievement (for example, sales revenues, profits and return on capital employed) that can help managers determine whether the business is increasing the wealth of its owners. These measures are vitally important but, in an increasingly competitive environment, managers also need to understand what *drives* the creation of wealth. These **value drivers** may be such things as employee satisfaction, customer loyalty and the level of product innovation. Often they do not lend themselves to financial measurement. Non-financial measures, however, may provide some means of assessment.

Activity (11.10)

How might we measure

(a) employee satisfaction?
(b) customer loyalty?
(c) the level of product innovation?

(a) Employee satisfaction may be measured through the use of an employee survey. This could examine attitudes towards various aspects of the job, the degree of autonomy that is permitted, the level of recognition and reward received, the level of participation in decision making, the degree of support received in carrying out tasks and so on. Less direct measures of satisfaction may include employee turnover rates and employee productivity. However, other factors may have a significant influence on these measures.

(b) Customer loyalty may be measured through the proportion of total sales generated from existing customers, the number of repeat sales made to customers, the percentage of customers renewing subscriptions or other contracts and so on.

(c) The level of product innovation may be measured through the number of innovations during a period compared to those of competitors, the percentage of sales attributable to recent product innovations, the number of innovations that are brought successfully to market and so on.

Financial measures tend to be 'lag' indicators, in that they tell us about outcomes. In other words, they measure the consequences arising from past management decisions. Non-financial measures can also act as 'lag indicators' but can, perhaps more usefully, be used as 'lead' indicators. This is because they tend to focus on those things that drive performance. If we measure changes in these value drivers, we may be able to predict changes in future financial performance. A business may find from experience, for example, that a 10 per cent decline in the level of product innovation during one period tends to lead to a 20 per cent reduction in sales revenues over the next three periods. In this case, the level of product innovation can be regarded as a lead indicator. It can tell managers that a future decline in sales is likely, unless corrective action is taken. Thus, by using this lead indicator, managers can identify key changes at an early stage and can respond quickly.

The balanced scorecard

One of the most impressive attempts to integrate the use of financial and non-financial measures has been the **balanced scorecard,** developed by Robert Kaplan and David Norton (see reference 2 at the end of the chapter). The balanced scorecard is both a management system and a measurement system. In essence, it provides a framework that translates the aims and objectives of a business into a series of key performance measures and targets. This framework is intended to make the strategy of the business more coherent by tightly linking it to particular targets and initiatives. As a result, managers should be able to see more clearly whether the objectives that have been set have actually been achieved.

The balanced scorecard approach involves setting objectives and developing appropriate measures and targets in four main areas:

1 *Financial.* This area will specify the financial returns required by shareholders and may involve the use of financial measures such as:
   ● return on capital employed;
   ● operating profit margin; and
   ● percentage sales revenue growth.
2 *Customer.* This area will specify the kind of customer and/or markets that the business wishes to service and will establish appropriate measures such as:
   ● customer satisfaction; and
   ● new customer growth levels.
3 *Internal business process.* This area will specify those business processes (for example, innovation, types of operation and after-sales service) that are important to the success of the business. It will also establish appropriate measures, such as:
   ● percentage of sales from new products;
   ● time to market for new products;
   ● product cycle times; and
   ● speed of response to customer complaints.
4 *Learning and growth.* This area will specify the kind of people, the systems and the procedures that are necessary to deliver long-term business growth. This area is often the most difficult for the development of appropriate measures. However, examples of measures may include:
   ● employee motivation;
   ● employee skills profiles; and
   ● information systems' capabilities.

These four areas are shown in Figure 11.11.

The balanced scorecard approach does not prescribe the particular objectives, measures or targets that a business should adopt; this is a matter for the individual business to decide. There are differences between businesses in terms of technology employed, organisational structure, management philosophy and business environment, so each business should develop objectives and measures that reflect its unique circumstances. The balanced scorecard simply sets out the framework for developing a coherent set of objectives for the business and for ensuring that these objectives are then linked to specific targets and initiatives.

A balanced scorecard will be prepared for the business as a whole or, in the case of large, diverse businesses, for each major division. However, having prepared an overall scorecard, it is then possible to prepare a balanced scorecard for each sub-unit, such as a department, within the business or division. Thus, the balanced scorecard approach can cascade down the business and can result in a pyramid of balanced scorecards that are linked to the 'master' balanced scorecard through an alignment of the objectives and measures employed.

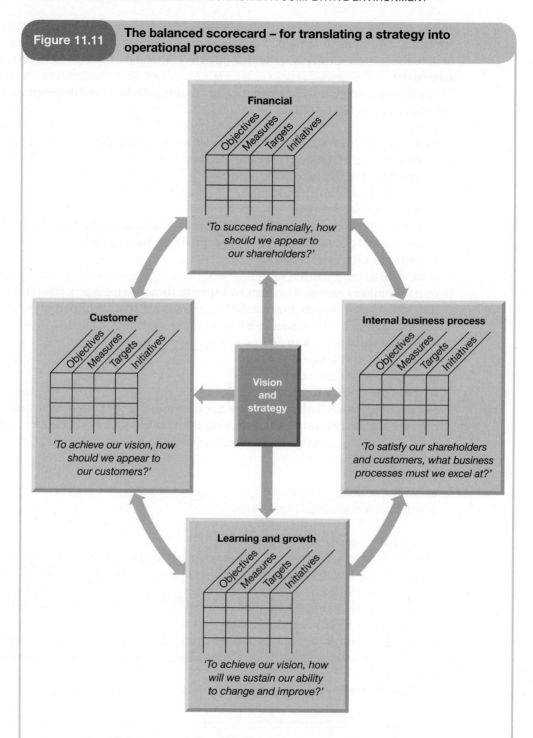

Figure 11.11 The balanced scorecard – for translating a strategy into operational processes

There are four main areas covered by the balanced scorecard. Note that, for each area, a fundamental question must be addressed. By answering these questions, managers should be able to develop the key objectives of the business. Once this has been done, suitable measures and targets can be developed that are relevant to those objectives. Finally, appropriate management initiatives will be developed to achieve the targets set.

Source: Kaplan, R. and Norton, D. (1996) *The Balanced Scorecard,* Harvard Business School Press.

Although many measures, both financial and non-financial, could be used in a balanced scorecard, only a handful should be used. According to Kaplan and Norton, a maximum of 20 measures will normally be needed to capture the factors that are critical to the success of the business. (If a business has come up with more than 20 measures, it is usually because the managers have not thought hard enough about what the key measures really are.) The key measures developed should be a mix of lagging indicators (those relating to outcomes) and lead indicators (those relating to the things that drive performance). Interestingly, Tesco plc, the UK supermarket business, operated for a number of years with a version of the balanced scorecard that had more than 40 different measures. This was abandoned in 2015 in favour of a balanced scorecard with a much more limited number of measures. The business's new CEO, Dave Lewis, felt that the older version was too complex for employees to handle.

Although the balanced scorecard employs measures across a wide range of business activity, it does not seek to dilute the importance of financial measures and objectives. In fact, the opposite is true. Kaplan and Norton insist that a balanced scorecard must reflect a concern for the financial objectives of the business. This means that measures and objectives in the other three areas identified must ultimately be related back to the financial objectives. There must be a cause-and-effect relationship. So, for example, an investment in staff development (in the learning and growth area) may lead to improved levels of after-sales service (internal business process area) which, in turn, may lead to higher levels of customer satisfaction (customer area) and, ultimately, higher sales revenues and profits (financial area). At first, cause-and-effect relationships may not be very clearly identified. However, by gathering information over time, the business can improve its understanding of the linkages and thereby improve the effectiveness of the scorecard.

Figure 11.12 shows the cause-and-effect relationship between the investment in staff development and the business's financial objectives.

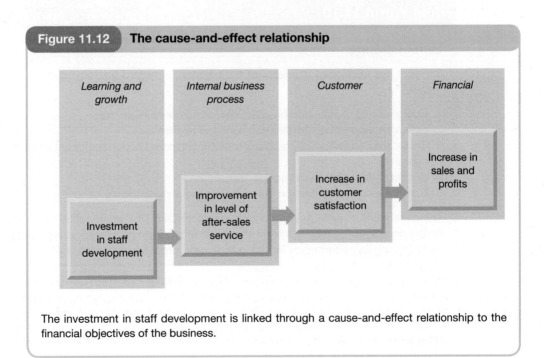

Figure 11.12   The cause-and-effect relationship

The investment in staff development is linked through a cause-and-effect relationship to the financial objectives of the business.

Activity (11.11)

Do you think the approach illustrated in Figure 11.12 is a rather cynical way of dealing with staff development? Should staff development have to be justified in terms of the financial results achieved?

This approach may seem rather cynical. However, Kaplan and Norton argue that unless this kind of link between staff development and increased financial returns can be demonstrated, managers are likely to become sceptical about the benefits of staff development and so the result may be that there will be no investment in staff.

Why is this framework referred to as a *balanced* scorecard? According to Kaplan and Norton, there are various reasons. It is because it aims to strike a balance between:

- *external* measures, relating to customers and shareholders, and *internal* measures, relating to business process, learning and growth;
- the measures that reflect *outcomes* (lag indicators) and measures that help *predict future performance* (lead indicators); and
- *hard* financial measures and *soft* non-financial measures.

It is possible to adapt the balanced scorecard to fit the needs of the particular business. Barclays plc, the UK bank, has done this as **Real World 11.10** explains.

Real World 11.10

Bank balance

Barclays has developed a version of the balance scorecard that covers five key areas, namely:

1 Customer and client – dealing with bank/customer relationships
2 Colleague – covering staff development and relations
3 Citizenship – relating to the bank's relationships with the communities in which it operates
4 Conduct – focusing on the bank's integrity
5 Company – concentrating on the bank's financial performance

The bank has just eight key performance indicators (KPIs) within these five areas. The bank's annual reports devote a large amount of space to discussing its balanced scorecard and reporting its performance for the year against target for each of the KPIs.

Source: Barclays plc, Annual Report 2015, pp. 11–16.

Real World 11.11 provides some impression of the extent to which the balanced score-card is used in practice.

Real World 11.11

A question of balance

Figure 11.13 shows the results of the Bain & Company survey (see Real World 11.8) which also looks at levels of usage and satisfaction for the balanced scorecard.

Figure 11.13 **Use of (and satisfaction with) the balanced scorecard**

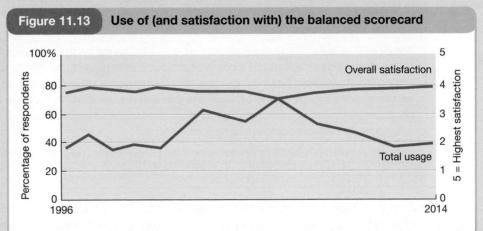

Although the level of satisfaction with this technique has been consistently high, the level of usage has varied over time.

We can see that the level of usage has risen and then fallen over the period 1996–2014. The level of satisfaction with this management tool, however, has been consistently high.

Source: Rigby, D. (2015) *Insights Management Tools, Balanced Scorecard,* Bain & Company, http://www.bain.com/publications/articles/management-tools-balanced-scorecard.aspx, 10 June, used with permissions from Bain & Company.

Real World 11.12 provides an interesting analogy with aeroplane pilots limiting themselves to just one control device.

(un)Real World 11.12

Fear of flying

Kaplan and Norton invite us to imagine the following conversation between a passenger and the pilot of a jet aeroplane during a flight:

Q: I'm surprised to see you operating the plane with only a single instrument. What does it measure?

A: Airspeed. I'm really working on airspeed this flight.

Q: That's good. Airspeed certainly seems important. But what about altitude? Wouldn't an altimeter be helpful?

(un) Real World 11.12 *continued*

A: I worked on altitude for the last few flights and I've gotten pretty good on it. Now I have to concentrate on proper airspeed.

Q: But I notice you don't even have a fuel gauge. Wouldn't that be useful?

A: You're right; fuel is significant, but I can't concentrate on doing too many things well at the same time. So on this flight I'm focusing on airspeed. Once I get to be excellent at airspeed, as well as altitude, I intend to concentrate on fuel consumption on the next set of flights.

The point they are trying to make (apart from warning against flying with a pilot like this!) is that to fly an aeroplane, which is a complex activity, a wide range of navigation instruments is required. A business, however, can be even more complex to manage than an aeroplane and so a wide range of measures, both financial and non-financial, is necessary. Reliance on financial measures is not enough and so the balanced scorecard aims to provide managers with a more complete navigation system.

Source: Kaplan, R. and Norton, D. (1996) *The Balanced Scorecard,* Harvard Business School Press. Copyright © 1996 by the Harvard Business School Publishing Corporation. All Rights Reserved. Reprinted by permission of Harvard Business School Press.

This story makes the point that concentrating on only a few areas of performance may lead to other important areas being ignored. Too narrow a focus can adversely affect behaviour and distort performance. This may, in turn, mean that the business fails to meet its strategic objectives. Perhaps we should bear in mind another apocryphal story concerning a factory, in the former communist Russia, that produced nails. The factory had its output measured according only to the weight of nails manufactured. For one financial period, it achieved its output target by producing one very large nail!

Scorecard problems

Not all attempts to embed the balanced scorecard approach within a business are successful. Why do things go wrong? It has been suggested that often too many measures are used, thereby making the scorecard too complex and unwieldy – we saw earlier that Tesco revised its version of the scorecard for this reason. It has also been suggested that managers are confronted with trade-off decisions between the four different dimensions. They struggle with this because they lack a clear compass. Imagine a manager who has a limited budget and therefore has to decide whether to invest in staff training or product innovation. If both add value to the business, which choice will be optimal?

While such problems exist, David Norton believes that there are two main reasons why the balanced scorecard fails to take root within a business, as **Real World 11.13** explains.

Real World 11.13

When misuse leads to failure

There are two main reasons why businesses go wrong with the widely used balanced scorecard, according to David Norton, the consultant who created the concept with Robert Kaplan, a Harvard Business School Professor. 'The number one cause of failure is that you don't have leadership at the executive levels of the organisation,' says Mr Norton. 'They don't embrace it and use it for managing their strategy.'

The second is that some companies treat it purely as a measurement tool, a problem he admits stems partly from its name. The concept has evolved since its inception, he says. The latest Kaplan–Norton thinking is that companies need a unit at corporate level – they call it an 'office of strategy management' – dedicated to ensuring that strategy is communicated to every employee and translated into plans, targets and incentives in each business unit and department.

Incentives are crucial, Mr Norton believes. Managers who have achieved break-throughs in performance with the scorecard say they would tie it to executive compensation sooner if they were doing it again. 'There's so much change in organisations that managers don't always believe you mean what you say. The balanced scorecard may just be "flavour of the month". Tying it to compensation shows that you mean it.'

FT *Source*: Extract from When misuse leads to failure, *Financial Times*, 24 May 2006. © The Financial Times Limited 2006. All Rights Reserved.

Norton's last point in Real World 11.13, relating to linking performance as measured by scorecard targets to management pay, has been taken up by Barclays (Real World 11.10). At Barclays part of senior management remuneration is directly dependent on scorecard performance.

Measuring shareholder value

Traditional measures of financial performance have been subject to much criticism in recent years. As a result, new measures that help to guide and assess strategic management decisions have been advocated. These new measures are based on the idea of increasing shareholder value. In this section, we shall consider one of the more popular of these measures. Before doing so, however, we shall see why increasing shareholder value is regarded as the ultimate financial objective of a business.

The quest for shareholder value

Many leading businesses now claim that the quest for shareholder value is the driving force behind their strategic and operational decisions. Let us begin, therefore, by considering what is meant by the term 'shareholder value'.

In simple terms, 'shareholder value' is about putting the needs of shareholders at the heart of management decisions. It is argued that shareholders invest in a business with a view to maximising their financial returns in relation to the risks that they are prepared to take. Since shareholders appoint managers to act on their behalf, management decisions and actions should reflect a concern for maximising shareholder returns. Although the business may have other 'stakeholder' groups, such as employees, customers and suppliers, it is the shareholders that should be seen as the most important group.

This, of course, is not a new idea. As we discussed in Chapter 1, maximising shareholder wealth is assumed to be the key objective of a business. However, not everyone accepts this. Some believe that a balance must be struck between the competing claims of the various stakeholders. A debate concerning the merits of each viewpoint is beyond the scope of this book. It is worth pointing out, however, that, in recent years, the business environment has radically changed.

In the past, shareholders have been accused of being too passive and of accepting too readily the profits and dividends that managers have delivered. This seems to have changed. Shareholders are now much more assertive and, as owners of the business, are in a position to insist that their needs are given priority. Since the 1980s, we have witnessed the deregulation and globalisation of business, as well as enormous changes in technology. The effect has been to create a much more competitive world. This has meant not only competition for products and services but also competition for funds. Businesses must now compete more strongly for shareholder funds and so must offer competitive rates of return.

Thus, self-interest may be the most powerful reason for managers to make every effort to maximise shareholder returns. If they do not, there is a risk that shareholders will either replace them with managers who will, or allow the business to be taken over by another business with managers who are dedicated to maximising shareholder returns.

How can shareholder value be created?

Creating shareholder value can be viewed as a four-stage process:

- *Stage 1*: Set objectives for the business that reflect the central importance of maximising shareholder returns. This will set a clear direction for the business.
- *Stage 2*: Establish an appropriate means of measuring the returns, or value, that have been generated for shareholders. For reasons that we shall discuss later, the traditional methods of measuring returns to shareholders are inadequate for this purpose.
- *Stage 3*: Manage the business in such a manner as to promote shareholder returns maximisation. This means setting demanding targets and then achieving them through the best possible use of resources, the use of incentive systems and the embedding of a shareholder value culture throughout the business.
- *Stage 4*: Measure the shareholder returns over a period of time to see whether the objectives have actually been achieved.

Figure 11.14 shows the shareholder value creation process.

Figure 11.14	The four-stage process for creating shareholder value

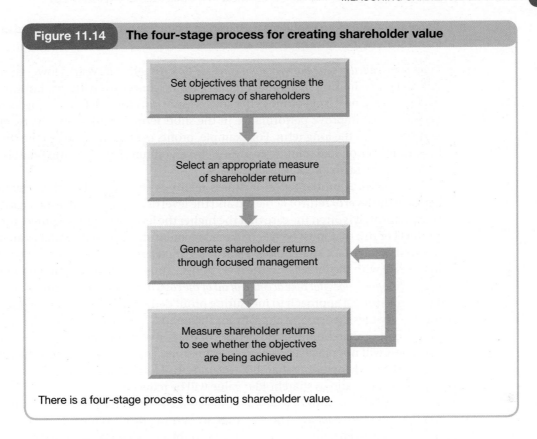

There is a four-stage process to creating shareholder value.

The need for new measures

Given a commitment to maximise shareholder returns, we must select an appropriate measure that will help us assess the returns to shareholders over time. It is argued that the traditional methods for measuring shareholder returns are seriously flawed and so should not be used for this purpose.

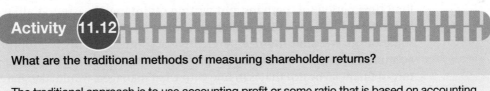

Activity 11.12

What are the traditional methods of measuring shareholder returns?

The traditional approach is to use accounting profit or some ratio that is based on accounting profit, such as return on shareholders' funds or earnings per share.

There are broadly four problems with using accounting profit, or a ratio based on profit, to assess shareholder returns. These are:

- *Profit is measured over a relatively short period of time* (usually one year). However, when we talk about maximising shareholder returns, we are concerned with maximising returns over the *long term*. Using profit as the key measure runs the risk that managers will take decisions that improve performance in the short term, but have an adverse effect on performance in the long term. For example, profits may be increased in the short term by cutting back on staff training and research expenditure. However, this type of expenditure may be vital to long-term survival.
- *Risk is ignored.* A fundamental business reality is that there is a clear relationship between the level of returns achieved and the level of risk that must be taken to achieve those returns. It is often the case that the higher the level of returns required, the higher the level of risk that must be taken. A management strategy that produces an increase in profits can reduce shareholder value if the increase in profits achieved is not commensurate with the increase in the level of risk. Thus, profit alone is not enough.
- *Accounting profit does not take account of all of the costs of the capital invested by the business.* The conventional approach to measuring profit deducts the cost of borrowing (that is, interest charges) in arriving at profit for the period, but there is no similar deduction for the cost of shareholder funds. Critics of the conventional approach point out that a business will not make a profit, in an economic sense, unless it covers the cost of all capital invested, including shareholder funds. Unless the business achieves this, it will operate at a loss and so shareholder value will be reduced.
- *Accounting profit reported by a business can vary according to the particular accounting policies that have been adopted.* The way that accounting profit is measured can vary from one business to another. Some businesses adopt a very conservative approach, which finds expression in particular accounting policies. This might include immediately treating some intangible assets (for example, research and development and goodwill) as expenses ('writing them off') rather than retaining them on the statement of financial position as assets. Similarly, the use of the reducing-balance method of depreciation (which means high depreciation charges in the early years) reduces profit in those early years.

  Businesses that adopt less conservative accounting policies would report higher profits in the early years of owning depreciating assets. Writing off intangible assets over a long time period (or, perhaps, not writing off intangible assets at all) will have this effect. So will the use of the straight-line method of depreciation. There may also be some businesses that indulge in 'creative accounting'. This is adopting particular accounting policies, or carrying out particular transactions, in a way that paints a picture of financial health that is in line with what managers would like shareholders and others to see, rather than what is a true and fair view of financial performance and position. This often involves artificially increasing the revenue figures or reducing the expense figures for a period in order to inflate profits. Creative accounting has been a major problem for accounting rule makers and for society generally.

Economic value added (EVA®)

Economic value added (EVA®) has been developed and trademarked by a US management consultancy firm, Stern Stewart. However, EVA® is based on the idea of economic profit, an idea that has been around for many years. The measure reflects the point made earlier that, for a business to be profitable in an economic sense, it must generate returns that exceed the required returns of investors. It is not enough simply to make an accounting profit, because this measure does not take full account of the returns required by investors.

EVA® indicates whether or not the returns generated exceed the required returns by investors. The formula is as follows:

$$EVA® = NOPAT - (R \times C)$$

where

NOPAT = net operating profit after tax
R = required returns of investors
C = capital invested (that is, the net assets of the business).

Only when EVA® is positive can we say that the business is increasing shareholder wealth. To maximise shareholder wealth, managers must increase EVA® by as much as possible.

Activity 11.13

Can you suggest what managers might do in order to increase EVA®? (*Hint*: Use the formula shown above as your starting point.)

The formula suggests that in order to increase EVA® managers may try to:

- increase NOPAT. This may be done either by reducing expenses or by increasing sales revenue; and/or
- reduce capital invested by using assets more efficiently. This means selling off any assets that are not generating adequate returns and investing in assets that generate a satisfactory NOPAT; and/or
- reduce the required rates of return for investors. This may be achieved by changing the capital structure in favour of borrowing (which tends to be cheaper to service than share capital). However, this strategy can create problems.

EVA® relies on conventional financial statements (income statement and statement of financial position) to measure the wealth created for shareholders. However, the NOPAT and capital figures shown on these statements are used only as a starting point. They have to be adjusted because of the problems and limitations of conventional measures. According to Stern Stewart, the major problem is that both profit and capital tend to be understated because of the conservative bias in accounting measurement.

Profit is understated as a result of judgemental write-offs (such as goodwill written off or research and development expenditure written off) and as a result of excessive provisions being created (such as an allowance for trade receivables). Both of these stem from taking an unrealistically pessimistic view of the value of some of the business's assets.

Capital can also be understated because assets are reported at their original cost (less amounts written off for depreciation and so on) which can, in some cases, produce figures considerably below current market values. In addition, certain assets, such as internally generated goodwill and brand names, are omitted from the financial statements because no external transactions have occurred.

Stern Stewart has identified more than a hundred adjustments that could be made to the conventional financial statements in order to eliminate the conservative bias. However, it is believed that, in practice, only a handful of adjustments will usually have to be made to the accounting figures of any particular business. Unless an adjustment is going to have a significant effect on the calculation of EVA®, it is really not worth making. The adjustments made should reflect the nature of the particular business. Each business is unique and so must customise the calculation of EVA® to its particular circumstances. (This aspect of EVA® can be seen either as indicating flexibility or as being open to manipulation depending on whether or not you support this measure.)

Common adjustments that have to be made include:

1 *Research and development (R&D) costs and marketing costs.* Logically these costs should be treated as an expense over the period that they benefit. Following standard accounting practice, however, tends to mean that they are often written off in the period in which they are incurred. This means that any amounts written off immediately should be added back to the assets on the statement of financial position. This will increase the figure for invested capital to be written off over time. It will also increase operating profit.

2 *Restructuring costs.* This item can be viewed as an investment in the future rather than an expense to be written off. Supporters of EVA® argue that by restructuring, the business is better placed to meet future challenges and so any amounts incurred should be added back to assets. This too will increase operating profit, where such costs are charged in deriving operating profit.

3 *Marketable investments.* Investment in shares and loan notes of other businesses are not included as part of the capital invested in the business. This is because the income from marketable investments is not included in the calculation of operating profit. (Income from this source will be added in the income statement *after* operating profit has been calculated.)

In addition to these accounting adjustments, the tax charge must be adjusted so that it is based on the operating profits for the year. This means that it should not take account of the tax charge on non-operating income, such as income from investments, or the tax allowance on interest payable.

Example 11.4 is a simple demonstration showing how EVA® may be calculated.

Example 11.4

Scorpio plc was established two years ago and has produced the following statement of financial position and income statement at the end of the second year of trading.

Statement of financial position as at the end of the second year

	£m
ASSETS	
Non-current assets	
Plant and equipment	80.0
Motor vehicles	12.4
Marketable investments	6.6
	99.0

	£m
Current assets	
Inventories	34.5
Trade receivables	29.3
Cash	2.1
	65.9
Total assets	164.9
EQUITY AND LIABILITIES	
Equity	
Share capital	60.0
Retained earnings	23.7
	83.7
Non-current liabilities	
Loan notes	50.0
Current liabilities	
Trade payables	30.3
Taxation	0.9
	31.2
Total equity and liabilities	164.9

Income statement for the second year

	£m
Sales revenue	148.6
Cost of sales	(76.2)
Gross profit	72.4
Wages	(24.6)
Depreciation of plant and equipment	(12.8)
Marketing expenses	(22.5)
Allowances for trade receivables	(4.5)
Operating profit	8.0
Income from investments	0.4
	8.4
Interest payable	(0.5)
Ordinary profit before taxation	7.9
Restructuring costs	(1.9)
Profit before taxation	6.0
Tax	(1.5)
Profit for the year	4.5

Discussions with the chief financial officer reveal the following:

1 Marketing costs relate to the launch of a new product. The benefits of the marketing campaign are expected to last for three years (including this most recent year).

2 The allowance for trade receivables was created this year and the amount is considered to be very high. A more realistic figure for the allowance would be £2.0 million.

3 Restructuring costs were incurred as a result of a collapse in a particular product market. As a result of the business restructuring, benefits are expected to flow for an infinite period.

Example 11.4 *continued*

4 The business has a 10 per cent required rate of return for investors.
5 The rate of tax on profits is 20 per cent.

The first step in calculating EVA® is to adjust the net operating profit after tax to take account of the various points revealed by the discussion with the chief financial officer. The revised figure is calculated as follows:

NOPAT adjustment

		£m
Operating profit		8.0
Tax (Note 1)		(1.6)
		6.4
EVA® adjustments (to be added back to profit)		
Marketing costs ($^2/_3 \times 22.5$)	15.0	
Excess allowance	2.5	17.5
Adjusted NOPAT		23.9

The next step is to adjust the net assets (as represented by equity and loan notes) to take account of the points revealed.

Adjusted net assets (or capital invested)

	£m	£m
Net assets (from the statement of financial position)		133.7
Marketing costs (Note 2)	15.0	
Allowance for trade receivables	2.5	
Restructuring costs (Note 3)	1.9	19.4
		153.1
Marketable investments (Note 4)		(6.6)
Adjusted net assets		146.5

Notes:

1 Tax is based on 20 per cent of the operating profits (£8.0m × 20% = £1.6m). (Tax complications, such as the difference between the tax allowance for non-current assets and the accounting charge for depreciation have been ignored.)

2 The marketing costs represent two years' benefits added back ($^2/_3 \times$ £22.5m).

3 The restructuring costs are added back to the net assets as they provide benefits over an infinite period. (Note that they were not added back to the operating profit as these costs were deducted after arriving at operating profit in the income statement.)

4 The marketable investments do not form part of the operating assets of the business. The income from these investments is not, therefore, part of the operating income.

Activity (11.14)

Can you work out the EVA® for the second year of Scorpio plc in Example 11.4?

EVA® can be calculated as follows:

$$EVA® = NOPAT - (R \times C)$$

$$= £23.9m - (10\% \times £146.5m)$$

$$= £9.3m \text{ (to one decimal place)}$$

We can see that EVA® is positive and so the business increased shareholder wealth during the year.

Although EVA® is used by many large businesses, both in the USA and Europe, it tends to be used for management purposes only: few businesses report this measure to shareholders. One business that does, however, is Whole Foods Market, a leading retailer of natural and organic foods, which operates more than 460 stores in the USA and the UK. **Real World 11.14** describes the way in which the business uses EVA® and the results of doing so.

Real World 11.14

The Whole picture

Whole Foods Market aims to improve its operations by achieving improvements to EVA®. To encourage managers along this path, an incentive plan has been introduced. The plan embraces senior executives, regional managers and store managers, and the bonuses awarded form a significant part of their total remuneration. To make the incentive plan work, measures of EVA® based on the whole business, the regional level, the store level and the team level are calculated.

EVA® is also used to evaluate capital investment decisions such as the acquisition of new stores and the refurbishment of existing stores. Unless there is clear evidence that value will be added, investment proposals are rejected. EVA® is also used to improve operational efficiency. It was mentioned earlier that one way in which EVA® can be increased is through an improvement in NOPAT. The business is, therefore, continually seeking ways to improve sales and profit margins and to bear down on costs.

Source: Based on information in www.wholefoodsmarket.com, accessed 25 October 2016.

An important advantage of the EVA® measure is the discipline to which managers are subjected as a result of the charge for capital that has been invested. Before any increase in shareholder wealth can be recognised, an appropriate deduction is made for the use of business resources. Thus, EVA® encourages managers to use these resources efficiently. Where managers are focused simply on increasing profits, there is a danger that the resources used to achieve any increase in profits will not be taken into proper account.

Self-assessment question (11.1)

Psilis Ltd makes a product in two qualities, called 'Basic' and 'Super'. The business is able to sell these products at a price that gives a standard profit mark-up of 25 per cent of full cost. Management is concerned by the lack of profit.

Full cost for one unit of a product is calculated by charging overheads to each type of product on the basis of direct labour hours. The costs are as follows:

	Basic £	Super £
Direct labour (all £10/hour)	40	60
Direct material	15	20

The total overheads are £1,000,000.

Based on experience over recent years, in the forthcoming year the business expects to make and sell 40,000 Basics and 10,000 Supers.

Recently, the business's management accountant has undertaken an exercise to try to identify activities and cost drivers in an attempt to be able to deal with the overheads on a more precise basis than had been possible before. This exercise has revealed the following analysis of the annual overheads:

Activity (and cost driver)	Cost £000	Annual number of activities		
		Total	Basic	Super
Number of machine set-ups	280	100	20	80
Number of quality-control inspections	220	2,000	500	1,500
Number of sales orders processed	240	5,000	1,500	3,500
General production (machine hours)	260	500,000	350,000	150,000
Total	1,000			

The management accountant explained the analysis of the £1,000,000 overheads as follows:

- The two products are made in relatively small batches, so that the amount of the finished product held in inventories is negligible. The Supers are made in very small batches because demand for them is relatively low. Each time a new batch is produced, the machines have to be reset by skilled staff. Resetting for Basic production occurs about 20 times a year and for Supers about 80 times: about 100 times in total. The cost of employing the machine-setting staff is about £280,000 a year. It is clear that the more set-ups that occur, the higher the total set-up costs; in other words, the number of set-ups is the factor that drives set-up costs.
- All production has to be inspected for quality, which costs about £220,000 a year. The higher specifications of the Supers mean that there is more chance that there will be quality problems. Thus the Supers are inspected in total 1,500 times annually, whereas the Basics only need about 500 inspections. The number of inspections is the factor that drives these costs.
- Sales order processing (dealing with customers' orders, from receiving the original order to despatching the products) costs about £240,000 a year. Despite the larger amount of

Self-assessment question 11.1 *continued*

Basic production, there are only 1,500 sales orders each year because the Basics are sold to wholesalers in relatively large-sized orders. The Supers are sold mainly direct to the public by mail order, usually in very small-sized orders. It is believed that the number of orders drives the costs of processing orders.

Required:
(a) Deduce the full cost of each of the two products on the basis used at present and, from these, deduce the current selling price.
(b) Deduce the full cost of each product on an ABC basis, taking account of the management accountant's recent investigations.
(c) What conclusions do you draw? What advice would you offer the management of the business?
(d) The managers of the business are concerned that sales order processing is not being carried out efficiently. They have therefore decided to benchmark this function against best practice. Produce a list of measures that might be used by the business as a basis for a benchmarking exercise. (*Hint:* In developing the measures think about the key factors of time, quality, income and cost.)
(e) The benchmarking process will be carried out by a team of staff. Set out the criteria that you feel would be appropriate to use when selecting team members.

The solution to this question can be found at the back of the book on pp. 776–778.

Summary

The main points of this chapter may be summarised as follows:

Activity-based costing (ABC)

- ABC deals with overheads (in full costing) by treating all costs as being caused or 'driven' by activities. It is claimed to be more relevant to the modern commercial environment than is the traditional approach.
- It involves identifying the support activities and their costs (overheads) and then analysing these costs to discover what drives them.
- The costs of each support activity are collected into a cost pool and the relevant cost driver is used to attach an amount of overheads from this pool to each unit of output.
- ABC should provide more accurate costs for each unit of output and should help in better control of overheads.
- ABC is, however, time-consuming and costly, and can suffer from measurement problems. It is unlikely to suit all businesses.

Total (whole) life-cycle costing

- Total life-cycle costing tracks and reports all costs relating to a product from the beginning to the end of its life.
- The life cycle of a product can be broken down into three phases: pre-production, production and post-production.

● A high proportion of costs is incurred and/or committed during the pre-production phase.

Target costing

● Target costing is a market-based approach to managing costs that is used at the pre-production phase.

● It tries to reduce costs so that an acceptable profit can be made at the target price.

● It provides a framework within which various techniques may be used to reduce costs rather than a costing method.

Kaizen costing

● Kaizen costing is concerned with continual and gradual cost reduction at the production phase.

● It involves setting targets for reductions in manufacturing costs each period and then comparing actual costs reductions against the targets.

● It is often part of a broader culture of continuous improvement within a business.

Value chain analysis

● Value chain analysis involves examining the various activities in the product life cycle to identify and try to eliminate non-value-added activities.

● Each link in the chain represents an activity that gives rise to costs. Any links in the chain that fail to add value should be evaluated critically and eliminated whenever possible.

Benchmarking

● Benchmarking attempts to emulate a successful operation carried out within, or outside, the business.

● It is normally a continuing process aimed at gaining greater operating efficiency and competitive advantage.

● It involves identifying a suitable benchmark measure for a particular product or function, collecting and analysing information relating to the measure, identifying areas for improvement and then introducing new practices and targets.

Managing quality

● The total quality management (TQM) philosophy is concerned with providing products that meet or exceed customers' requirements all of the time.

● Ensuring the quality of output will incur costs, known as *quality costs*. They can be divided into four categories: prevention costs, appraisal costs, internal failure costs and external failure costs.

● If more is spent on prevention costs, savings may be made through the reduction of appraisal costs and failure costs.

An alternative view

● Costs may be managed without using sophisticated techniques if:
  – there is a shared responsibility for managing costs;
  – discussion of costs becomes an everyday activity;
  – costs are managed locally;
  – benchmarking is used at regular intervals; and
  – the focus is on managing rather than reducing costs.

Non-financial measures of performance

- Non-financial measures are increasingly being used to manage businesses.
- The balanced scorecard is a management tool that uses financial and non-financial measures to assess progress towards objectives.
  - It has four aspects: financial, customer, internal business process and learning and growth.
  - It encourages a balanced approach to managing the business.

Value-based management

- Shareholder value is seen as the key objective of most businesses.
- One approach used to measure shareholder value is economic value added (EVA®).
- Economic value added is a means of measuring whether the returns generated by the business exceed the required returns of investors.
- $EVA^® = NOPAT - (R \times C)$

where

NOPAT = net operating profit after tax
R = required returns from investors
C = capital invested (that is, the net assets of the business).

Key terms

For definitions of these terms, see Appendix B.

activity-based costing (ABC) *p. 420*	**benchmarking** *p. 438*
cost driver *p. 421*	**total quality management**
cost pool *p. 421*	**(TQM)** *p. 440*
total life-cycle costing *p. 430*	**quality cost** *p. 442*
target costing *p. 433*	**value driver** *p. 445*
kaizen costing *p. 435*	**balanced scorecard** *p. 446*
value chain analysis *p. 437*	**economic value added (EVA®)** *p. 456*

References

1 Hopwood, A. (2002) Costs count in the strategic agenda, ft.com, 13 August.

2 Kaplan, R. and Norton, D. (1996) *The Balanced Scorecard,* Harvard Business School Press.

Further reading

If you would like to explore the topics covered in this chapter in more depth, we recommend the following:

Bhimani, A., Horngren, C., Datar, S. and Rajan, M. (2015) *Management and Cost Accounting,* 6th edn, Pearson, Chapters 11, 12 and 20.

Burns, J., Quinn, M., Warren, L. and Oliveira, J. (2013) *Management Accounting,* McGraw-Hill Education, Chapters 6 and 20.

Drury, C. (2015) *Management and Cost Accounting,* 9th edn, Cengage Learning EMEA, Chapter 21.

Hilton, R. and Platt, D. (2014) *Managerial Accounting,* 10th edn, McGraw-Hill Higher Education, Chapters 3, 5 and 15.

Review questions

Solutions to these questions can be found at the back of the book on pp. 794–795.

11.1 How does activity-based costing (ABC) differ from the traditional approach? What is the underlying difference between their philosophies?

11.2 The use of activity-based costing in helping to deduce full costs has been criticised. What has been the basis of this criticism?

11.3 What are the main categories of quality costs that a business may incur and why is it useful to categorise them?

11.4 Identify the main phases of the total life cycle of a product or service and identify the particular phase(s) for which target costing and kaizen costing are particularly appropriate.

Exercises

Solutions to exercises with coloured numbers can be found at the back of the book on pp. 823–825.

Basic-level exercises

11.1 Aires plc was recently formed and issued 80 million £0.50 shares at nominal value and loan notes that totalled £24 million. The business used the proceeds from the capital issues to purchase the remaining lease on some commercial properties. Aires plc plans to set up a wholesaling business that is expected to generate an operating profit of £12 million each year. The lease will expire in four years' time. At the end of the four years, the business will be wound up and the lease will have no residual value.

The required rate of return by investors is 12 per cent.

Required:
Calculate the expected shareholder value generated by the business in each of the four years, using the EVA® approach.

11.2 Comment critically on the following statements that you have overheard:
(a) 'The balanced scorecard is another name for the statement of financial position.'
(b) 'The financial area of the balanced scorecard is, in effect, the income statement of the business and measures the profit for the period.'
(c) 'Adopting the balanced scorecard approach means accepting a particular set of targets that were set out by Kaplan and Norton.'
(d) 'The balanced scorecard approach tends to take little notice of financial objectives.'

Intermediate-level exercises

11.3 Kaplan plc makes a range of suitcases of various sizes and shapes. There are 10 different models of suitcase produced by the business. To keep inventories of finished suitcases to a minimum, each model is made in a small batch. Each batch is costed as a separate job and the cost for each suitcase deduced by dividing the batch cost by the number of suitcases in the batch.

At present, the business derives the cost of each batch using a traditional job costing approach. Recently, however, a new management accountant was appointed, who is advocating the use of activity-based costing (ABC) to deduce the cost of the batches. The management accountant claims that ABC leads to much more reliable and relevant costs and that it has other benefits.

Required:

(a) Explain how the business deduces the cost of each suitcase at present.
(b) Explain how ABC could be applied to costing the suitcases, highlighting the differences between ABC and the traditional approach.
(c) Explain what advantages the new management accountant probably believes ABC to have over the traditional approach.

11.4 Comment critically on the following statements that you have overheard:
(a) 'Direct labour hours are the most appropriate basis to use to charge indirect cost (overheads) to jobs in the modern manufacturing environment where people are so important.'
(b) 'Activity-based costing is a means of more accurately accounting for direct labour cost.'
(c) 'Activity-based costing cannot really be applied to the service sector because the "activities" that it seeks to analyse tend to be related to manufacturing.'
(d) 'Kaizen costing is an approach where great efforts are made to reduce the costs of developing a new product and setting up its production processes.'
(e) 'Benchmarking is an approach to job costing where each direct worker keeps a record of the time spent on each job on his or her workbench before it is passed on to the next direct worker or into finished inventories (stock) stores.'

Advanced-level exercises

11.5 Badger Ltd (Badger) manufactures plastic building materials. After a recent analysis, Badger has decided to classify its products into two varieties: Largeflo and Smallflo. There are several products in each of these two categories. Largeflo are produced on large machines by a simple process. Smallflo are manufactured on small machines by a more complex process with more production stages. The previous pricing policy has been to absorb all overheads using direct labour hours to obtain total cost. Price is then calculated as total cost plus a 35 per cent mark-up.

The recent analysis has also examined overhead costs; the results are shown below. Set-up costs are incurred during the production stage for each batch. The ordering costs for bought-in parts are incurred initially for each production type.

Analysis of overhead costs

	Cost per month £	Monthly volume
Large machine cost	96,000	480 hours
Small machine cost	44,800	1,280 hours
Set-up cost	32,500	260 set-ups
Ordering bought-in parts	10,800	120 different parts
Handling charges	45,600	380 movements
Other overheads	50,300	(see below)
	280,000	

There are 4,000 direct labour hours available each month.

Details for a typical Largeflo product (one of several Largeflo products) and a typical Smallflo product (again, one of several Smallflo products) are shown overleaf.

	Largeflo	*Smallflo*
Monthly production	1,000 units	500 units
Batch size	1,000 units	50 units
Machine time per batch		
– large	100 hours	–
– small	–	25 hours
Number of bought-in parts	–	3 per product type
Set-ups	1 per batch	2 per batch
Handling charges	1 movement per batch	5 movements per batch
Materials per unit	£16	£15
Direct labour per unit	½ hour	½ hour

Direct labour is paid £16 per hour.

Required:

(a) Calculate the price for each of the Largeflo and Smallflo products detailed above, using traditional absorption costing based on direct labour hours.

(b) Calculate the price for the Largeflo and Smallflo products using activity-based costing. Assume that 'Other overheads' are allocated using direct labour hours.

(c) Outline the points that you would raise with the management of Badger in the light of your answers to (a) and (b).

(d) Outline the practical problems that may be encountered in implementing activity-based techniques and comment on how they may be overcome.

11.6 Pisces plc produced the following statement of financial position and income statement at the end of the third year of trading:

Statement of financial position as at the end of the third year

	£m
ASSETS	
Non-current assets	
Property	40.0
Machinery and equipment	80.0
Motor vans	18.6
Marketable investments	9.0
	147.6
Current assets	
Inventories	45.8
Trade receivables	64.6
Cash	1.0
	111.4
Total assets	259.0
EQUITY AND LIABILITIES	
Equity	
Share capital	80.0
Reserves	36.5
	116.5
Non-current liabilities	
Loan notes	80.0
Current liabilities	
Trade payables	62.5
	259.0

Income statement for the third year

	£m
Sales revenue	231.5
Cost of sales	(143.2)
Gross profit	88.3
Wages	(43.5)
Depreciation of machinery and equipment	(14.8)
Research and development	(40.0)
Allowance for trade receivables	(10.5)
Operating loss	(20.5)
Income from investments	0.6
	(19.9)
Interest payable	(0.8)
Normal loss before taxation	(20.7)
Restructuring costs	(6.0)
Loss before taxation	(26.7)
Tax	–
Loss for the year	(26.7)

An analysis of the underlying records reveals the following:

1 The research and development expense relates to the cost of developing a new product in the previous year. This cost is written off over a two-year period (starting last year). However, this is a prudent approach and the benefits are expected to last for 16 years.

2 The allowance for trade receivables (bad debts) was created this year and the amount of the provision is very high. A more realistic figure for the allowance would be £4 million.

3 Restructuring costs were incurred at the beginning of the year and are expected to provide benefits for an infinite period.

4 The business has a 7 per cent required rate of return for investors.

Required:
Calculate the EVA® for the business for the third year of trading.

11.7 A business manufactures refrigerators for domestic use. There are three models: Lo, Mid and Hi. The models, their quality and their price are aimed at different markets.

Product costs are computed using a blanket (business-wide) overhead rate. Products absorb overheads on a labour-hour basis. Prices as a general rule are set based on cost plus 20 per cent. The following information is provided:

	Lo	Mid	Hi
Material cost (£/unit)	25	62.5	105
Direct labour hours (per unit)	$\frac{1}{2}$	1	1
Budget production/sales (units)	20,000	1,000	10,000

The budgeted overheads for the business, for the year, amount to £4,410,000. Direct labour is costed at £8 an hour.

The business is currently facing increasing competition, especially from imported goods. As a result, the selling price of Lo has been reduced to a level that produces a very low profit margin. To address this problem, an activity-based costing approach has been suggested. The overheads have been analysed and it has been found that these are grouped around main business activities of machining (£2,780,000), logistics (£590,000) and establishment costs (£1,040,000). It is maintained that these costs could be allocated based respectively on cost drivers of machine hours, material orders and space, to reflect the use of resources in each of these areas. After analysis, the following proportionate statistics are available related to the total volume of products:

	Lo %	Mid %	Hi %
Machine hours	40	15	45
Material orders	47	6	47
Space	42	18	40

Required:

(a) Calculate for each product the full cost and selling price determined by:
    1 The original (traditional) costing method.
    2 The activity-based costing method.

(b) What are the implications of the two systems of costing in the situation given?

(c) What business/strategic options exist for the business in the light of the new information?

Budgeting

Introduction

In its 2016 annual report, BSkyB Group plc, the satellite television broadcaster, stated:

> There is a comprehensive budgeting and forecasting process, and the annual budget, which is regularly reviewed and updated, is approved by the board [of directors].

As we shall see, the practice at BSkyB is typical of businesses of all sizes.

What is a budget? What is it for? How is it prepared? Who prepares it? Why does the board regard it as important enough to consider? We shall be looking at the answers to each of these questions in the course of this chapter.

We shall see that budgets set out short-term plans to help managers run the business. They provide the means to assess whether actual performance was as planned and, if not, the reasons for this. Budgets do not exist in a vacuum; they are an integral part of a planning framework adopted by well-run businesses. To understand fully the nature of budgets we must, therefore, understand the strategic planning framework within which they are set.

The chapter begins with a discussion of the overall planning framework and then goes on to consider in detail the role that budgeting plays. We shall see that preparing budgets relies on an understanding of many of the issues relating to the behaviour of costs and full costing. These are topics that we explored in Chapters 9 and 10.

Learning outcomes

When you have completed this chapter, you should be able to:

● define a budget and show how budgets, strategic objectives and strategic plans are related;

● explain the budgeting process and the interlinking of the various budgets within the business;

- identify the uses of budgeting and construct various budgets, including the cash budget, from relevant data; and

- discuss the criticisms that are made of budgeting.

How budgets link with strategic plans and objectives

It is vital that businesses develop plans for the future. Whatever a business is trying to achieve, it is unlikely to happen unless its managers are clear what the future direction of the business should be. The development of plans involves five key steps:

1 *Establish mission, vision and objectives*
   The mission and vision statements set out the overriding purpose of the business and what it seeks to achieve. The strategic objectives state how the mission of the business can be achieved and will usually include quantifiable goals.

2 *Undertake a position analysis*
   This involves an assessment of where the business is currently placed in relation to where it wants to be, as set out in its mission, vision and strategic objectives.

3 *Identify and assess the strategic options*
   The business must explore the various ways in which it might move from where it is now (identified in Step 2) to where it wants to be (identified in Step 1).

4 *Select strategic options and formulate plans*
   This involves selecting what seems to be the best of the courses of action, or strategies, (identified in Step 3) and formulating a long-term strategic plan. This strategic plan is then normally broken down into a series of short-term plans, one for each aspect of the business. These plans are the budgets. Thus, a **budget** is a business plan for the short term – typically one year – and is expressed mainly in financial terms. Its role is to convert the strategic plans into actionable blueprints for the immediate future. Budgets will define precise targets concerning such things as:
   - cash receipts and payments;
   - sales volumes and revenues, broken down into amounts and prices for each of the products or services provided by the business;
   - detailed inventories' requirements;
   - detailed labour requirements; and
   - specific production requirements.

5 *Perform, review and control*
   Here the business pursues the budgets derived in Step 4. By comparing the actual outcome with the budgets, managers can see if things are going according to plan. Where actual performance does not match the budgets, action must be taken to exercise control.

Activity 12.1

The approach described in Step 3 suggests that managers will systematically collect information and then carefully evaluate all the options available. Do you think this is what managers really do?

In practice, managers may not be as rational and capable as implied.

To develop the point made in the answer to Activity 12.1, managers may find it difficult to handle a large amount of information covering a wide range of options. To avoid becoming overloaded, they may restrict the range of possible options and/or discard some information. Managers may also adopt a simple approach to evaluating the information resulting in poor decisions being made.

From the description of the planning process just described, we can see that the relationship between the mission, vision, strategic objectives, strategic plans and budgets can be summarised as follows:

- the mission and vision set the overall direction and, once set, this is likely to last for quite a long time – perhaps throughout the life of the business;
- the strategic objectives, which are also long-term, will translate the mission and vision into specific, often quantifiable, targets;
- the strategic plans identify how each objective will be pursued; and
- the budgets set out, in detail, the short-term plans and targets necessary to fulfil the strategic objectives.

An analogy might be found in terms of a student enrolling on a course of study. The student's mission might be to have a happy and fulfilling life. A key strategic objective flowing from this mission might be to embark on a career that will be rewarding in various ways. The particular study course might have been identified as the most effective way to work towards this objective. Successfully completing the course would then be the strategic plan. In working towards this strategic plan, passing a particular stage of the course might be identified as the target for the forthcoming year. This short-term target is analogous to the budget. Having achieved the 'budget' for the first year, the student's budget for the second year becomes passing the second stage.

Figure 12.1 shows the planning and control process in diagrammatic form.

It should be emphasised that planning (including budgeting) is the responsibility of managers rather than accountants. Although accountants play a role in the planning process, by supplying relevant information to managers and by contributing to decision making as part of the management team, they should not dominate the process. In practice, however, this often seems to occur. While accountants may be adept at dealing with financial information, managers are failing in their responsibilities if they allow them to have an excessive influence in the budgeting process.

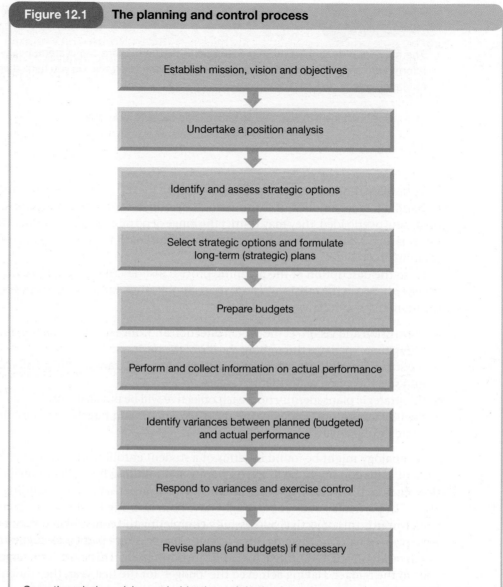

Figure 12.1 **The planning and control process**

Establish mission, vision and objectives

Undertake a position analysis

Identify and assess strategic options

Select strategic options and formulate long-term (strategic) plans

Prepare budgets

Perform and collect information on actual performance

Identify variances between planned (budgeted) and actual performance

Respond to variances and exercise control

Revise plans (and budgets) if necessary

Once the mission, vision and objectives of the business have been determined, the various strategic options available must be considered and evaluated in order to derive a strategic plan. The budget is a short-term financial plan for the business that is prepared within the framework of the strategic plan. Control can be exercised through the comparison of budgeted and actual performance. Where a significant divergence emerges, some form of corrective action should be taken. If the budget figures prove to be based on incorrect assumptions about the future, it might be necessary to revise the budget.

Time horizon of plans and budgets

Setting strategic plans is typically a major exercise performed about every five years and budgets are usually set annually for the forthcoming year. These time horizons, however, may vary according to the needs of the particular business. Those businesses involved in certain industries – say, information technology – may feel that five years is too long a planning period since new developments can, and do, occur virtually overnight. Here, a planning horizon of two or three years may be more appropriate. Similarly, a budget need not be set for one year, although this appears to be a widely used time horizon.

One business that keeps its strategic planning under more frequent review is Greene King plc, the brewery, pub and hotel business. **Real World 12.1** explains how strategic planning is a regular annual event for the business.

Real World 12.1

Strategic planning at the pub

According to its annual report, Greene King has the following approach to strategic planning:

> There is a two-day meeting of the board in February each year focusing on strategy, with the business unit managing directors and heads of the main functional areas, namely trading, marketing, HR (Human Resources) and property, attending for part thereof. The strategy sessions include an in-depth review of relevant economic factors and issues affecting the sector and management's projections for the medium term. The board then has the opportunity to agree the strategic plans across all areas for the short and medium term. Following approval of the company's strategy, budgets are prepared for the next financial year, which are reviewed and approved by the board in April. The board also has a programme to review each business unit and main functional area in detail on a regular basis, with particular focus on the achievement of strategic objectives. The relevant managing director or functional head attends such meetings to present and answer questions.

Source: Greene King plc Annual Report 2016, p. 48.

Budgets and forecasts

A budget may, as we have already seen, be defined as a business plan for the short term. Note particularly that a budget is a *plan,* not a forecast. To talk of a plan suggests an intention or determination to achieve the targets; **forecasts** tend to be predictions of the future state of the environment.

Clearly, forecasts are very helpful to the planner/budget-setter. If, for example, a reputable forecaster has predicted the number of new cars to be purchased in the UK during next year, it will be valuable for a manager in a car manufacturing business to take this into account when setting next year's sales budgets. However, a forecast and a budget are quite different.

Periodic and continual budgets

Budgeting can be undertaken on a periodic or a continual basis. A **periodic budget** is prepared for a particular period (usually one year). Managers will agree the budget for the year and then allow the budget to run its course. Although it may be necessary to revise the budget on occasions, preparing the periodic budget is, in essence, a one-off exercise during each financial year. A **continual budget,** as the name suggests, is continually updated. We have seen that an annual budget will normally be broken down into smaller time intervals (usually monthly periods) to help control the activities of the business. A continual budget will add a new month to replace the month that has just passed, thereby ensuring that, at all times, a budget for a full planning period is available. A continual budget is also referred to as a **rolling budget**.

Activity 12.2

Which method of budgeting do you think is likely to be more costly and which method is likely to be more beneficial for forward planning?

We saw that periodic budgeting is a 'one-off' exercise. It will usually take less time and effort and will, therefore, be less costly. However, as time passes, the budget period shortens and, towards the end of the financial year, managers will be working to a very short planning period indeed. Continual budgeting, on the other hand, will ensure that managers always have a full year's budget to help them make decisions. It is claimed that continual budgeting ensures that managers plan throughout the year rather than just once each year. In this way, it encourages a perpetual forward-looking attitude.

While continual budgeting encourages a forward-looking attitude, there is a danger that budgeting will become a mechanical exercise. Managers may not have time to step back from their other tasks each month and consider the future with sufficient care. Continually taking this forward-looking attitude may be difficult, therefore, to sustain.

Continual budgets do not appear to be very popular in practice. A survey of 340 senior financial staff of small, medium and large businesses in North America revealed that only 9 per cent of businesses use them (see reference 1 at the end of the chapter). However, a 2015 survey suggests that 69 per cent of businesses intend to adopt a rolling budgeting approach within the next five years. This was a survey involving over 900 finance professionals in businesses of all sizes in more than 50 countries (see reference 2 at the end of the chapter).

Activity 12.3

Can you think of any reason why most businesses prepare detailed budgets for the forthcoming year, rather than for a shorter or longer period?

The reason is probably that a year represents a long enough time for the budget preparation exercise to be worthwhile, yet short enough into the future for detailed plans to be capable of being made. As we shall see later in this chapter, the process of formulating budgets can be a time-consuming exercise, but there are economies of scale – for example, preparing the budget for the next year would not normally take twice as much time and effort as preparing the budget for the next six months.

An annual budget sets targets for the forthcoming year for all aspects of the business. It is usually broken down into monthly budgets, which define monthly targets. Indeed, in many instances, the annual budget will be built up from monthly figures. The sales staff, for example, may be required to set sales targets for each month of the budget period. These targets may well differ from month to month, particularly where there are seasonal demand variations. Other budgets will be set for each month, as we shall explain shortly.

Limiting factors

Some aspect of the business will, inevitably, stop it achieving its objectives to the maximum extent. This is often a limited ability of the business to sell its products. Sometimes, it is some production shortage (such as labour, materials or plant) that is the **limiting factor** or, linked to these, a shortage of funds. Often, production shortages can be overcome by an increase in funds – for example, more plant can be bought or leased. This is not always a practical solution, because no amount of money will buy certain labour skills or increase the world supply of some raw material.

Easing an initial limiting factor, for example a plant capacity problem, may be possible. This means that some other factor, perhaps lack of sales demand, will replace the production problem, though at a higher level of output. Ultimately, however, the business will hit a ceiling; some limiting factor will prove impossible to ease.

The limiting factor must be identified. Ultimately, most, if not all, budgets will be affected by it. If the limiting factor can be identified at the outset, all managers can be informed of the restriction early in the process. When preparing budgets, account can then be taken of it.

How budgets link to one another

A typical larger business will prepare more than one budget for a particular period. Each budget prepared will relate to a specific aspect of its operations. The ideal situation is probably that there should be a separate operating budget for each person who is in a managerial position, no matter how junior. The contents of each of the individual operating budgets will be summarised in **master budgets,** usually consisting of a budgeted income statement and statement of financial position. The cash budget is considered by some to be a third master budget.

Figure 12.2 illustrates the interrelationship and interlinking of individual operating budgets, in this particular case using a manufacturing business as an example.

The sales budget is usually the first to be prepared (at the left of Figure 12.2), as the level of sales often determines the overall level of activity for the forthcoming period. This is because sales demand is the most common limiting factor. The finished inventories requirement tends to be set by the level of sales, though it would also be dictated by the policy of the business on the level of the finished products inventories that it chooses to hold. The requirement for finished inventories will determine the required production levels, which will, in turn, dictate the requirements of the individual production departments or sections. The demands of manufacturing, in conjunction with the business's policy on how long it holds raw materials before they enter production, define the raw materials inventories budget. The purchases budget will be dictated by the materials inventories budget, which will, in conjunction with the policy of the business on taking credit from suppliers, dictate the trade payables budget. One of the determinants of the cash budget will be the trade payables budget; another will be the trade receivables budget, which itself derives, through the business's policy on settlement periods granted to credit customers, from the sales budget. Cash will also be affected by overheads and direct labour costs (themselves linked to production) and by capital expenditure. Cash will also be affected by new finance and redemption of existing sources. (This is not shown in Figure 12.2 because the diagram focuses only on budgets concerned with operational matters.)

A manufacturing business has been used as the example in Figure 12.2 simply because it has all of the types of operating budgets found in practice. Service businesses have similar budgets, but may not have inventories budgets.

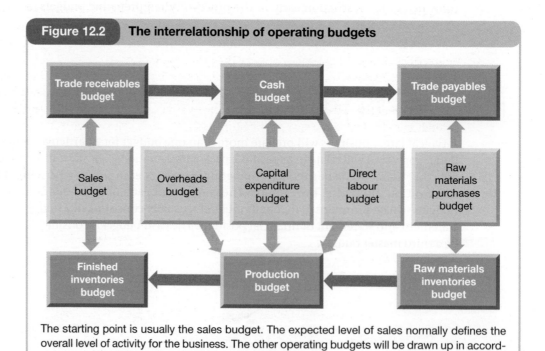

Figure 12.2 **The interrelationship of operating budgets**

The starting point is usually the sales budget. The expected level of sales normally defines the overall level of activity for the business. The other operating budgets will be drawn up in accordance with this. Thus, the sales budget will largely define the finished inventories requirements and from this we can define the production requirements and so on. This shows the interrelationship of operating budgets for a manufacturing business.

Sales demand is not always the limiting factor. Assuming that the budgeting process takes the order just described, it might be found that there is some constraint other than sales demand. The production capacity of the business may, for example, be incapable of meeting the necessary levels of output to match the sales budget for one or more months. Finding a practical way of overcoming the problem may be possible. However, it may be necessary to revise the sales budget downwards to match the production capacity.

Activity 12.4

Can you think of any ways in which a short-term shortage of production facilities of a manufacturer might be overcome?

We thought of the following:

- Raising production output in preceding months and increasing inventories ('stockpiling') to meet periods of higher demand.
- Increasing production capacity, perhaps by working overtime and/or acquiring (buying or leasing) additional plant.
- Subcontracting some production output.
- Encouraging potential customers to change the timing of their purchases by offering discounts or other special terms during the months that have been identified as quiet.

You might well have thought of other approaches.

Apart from the horizontal relationships between budgets, which we have just considered, there will often be vertical ones. Breaking down the sales budget into a number of subsidiary budgets, perhaps one for each regional sales manager, is a common approach. The overall sales budget will then be a summary of the subsidiary ones. This may apply to many other budgets, most particularly the production budget.

Figure 12.3 shows the vertical relationship of sales budgets. The business in the example has four geographical sales regions, each one the responsibility of a separate manager. Each regional manager is responsible to the overall sales manager of the business. The overall sales budget is the sum of the budgets for the four sales regions.

Figure 12.3   The vertical relationship between a business's sales budgets

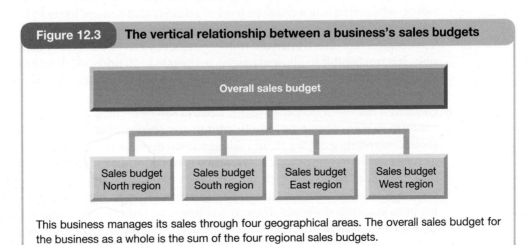

This business manages its sales through four geographical areas. The overall sales budget for the business as a whole is the sum of the four regional sales budgets.

Although sales are often managed on a geographical basis, with budgets reflecting this fact, they may be managed on some other basis. For example, a business may manage its sales according to product type, with a specialist manager for each type of product. Thus, an insurance business may have separate sales managers and, therefore, separate sales budgets, for life insurance, household insurance, motor insurance and so on. Very large businesses may even have separate product managers for each geographical region. Each manager will have a separate budget, which will combine to form the product sales budget for the business as a whole.

All of the operating budgets that we have discussed must mesh with the master budgets, that is, the budgeted income statement and statement of financial position.

How budgets help managers

Budgets are viewed as providing five key benefits. These are:

- *Promoting forward thinking and identifying short-term problems.* We have seen that a shortage of production capacity might be identified during the budgeting process. Making this discovery in good time may leave open a number of ways of overcoming the problem. If the potential production problem is picked up early enough, all of the suggestions in the answer to Activity 12.4 and, possibly, other ways of overcoming the problem can be explored. Identifying the problem early gives managers time to explore the best way of overcoming it. The best solution may only be feasible if action can be taken well in advance.

- *Improving co-ordination between the various sections of the business.* It is crucially important that the activities of the various departments and sections of the business are linked so that the activities of one are complementary to those of another. Let us take an example. The activities of the purchasing/procurement department of a manufacturing business should dovetail with the raw materials needs of the production departments. If they do not, production could run out of raw materials, which may lead to expensive production stoppages. It could also lead to excessive amounts of raw materials being purchased, resulting in unnecessary inventories holding costs.

- *Motivating managers to better performance.* Having a stated task can motivate managers to improve their performance. Simply telling managers to do their best is not very motivating, whereas setting a required level of achievement is more likely to be so. This is because it enables managers to relate their particular role to the business's objectives. Since budgets are directly derived from strategic objectives, budgeting makes this possible. It is not feasible to allow managers to operate in an unconstrained environment. Having to operate in a way that matches the goals of the business is a price of working in an effective business.

- *Providing a basis for a system of control.* **Control** can be defined as compelling events to conform to plan. This definition is valid in any context. For example, when we talk about controlling a car, we mean making the car do what we plan that it should do. If managers wish to control and monitor their own performance, and that of more junior staff, they need some yardstick against which to measure and assess performance. It may be possible to compare current performance with past performance or with what happens in another business. However, planned performance is usually the most logical yardstick. Where information concerning actual performance as well as planned performance (the budget) is available, a basis for comparison, and therefore control, is established. Since *actual* outcomes and budgeted outcomes can be stated in the same terms, making comparisons between actual and budget performance is fairly straightforward. Where actual outcomes vary from budgeted outcomes, this will be apparent. Managers can then take steps to get the business back on track. By making such comparisons, **management by exception** can be employed. This involves senior managers focusing on those areas that failed to achieve the budget (the exceptions). They need not spend much time on those that are performing well.

Effective budgets allow all managers to exercise self-control. By knowing what is expected of them and what they have actually achieved, they can assess how well they are performing and take steps to correct any failures.

We shall be looking more closely at the control aspect of budgeting in Chapter 13.

● *Providing a system of authorisation for managers to spend up to a particular limit.* Some activities (for example, staff development and research and development) are allocated a fixed amount of funds at the discretion of senior management. This provides the authority to spend.

Figure 12.4 shows the benefits of budgets in diagrammatic form.

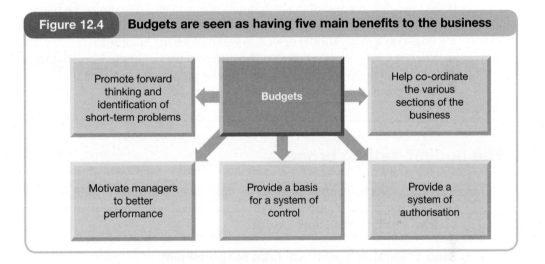

Figure 12.4   Budgets are seen as having five main benefits to the business

The following two activities pick up issues that relate to some of the uses of budgets.

Activity 12.5

The third point on the list of the benefits of budgets (motivation) implies that managers are set stated tasks. Do you think there is a danger that requiring managers to work towards such predetermined targets will stifle their skill, flair and enthusiasm?

If the budgets are set in such a way as to offer challenging yet achievable targets, the manager is still required to show skill, flair and enthusiasm. There is the danger, however, that where targets are badly set (either unreasonably demanding or too easy to achieve), they could be demotivating and have a stifling effect.

Activity 12.6

The fourth point on the list of the benefits of budgets (control) implies that current management performance is compared with some yardstick. What is wrong with comparing actual performance with past performance, or the performance of others, in an effort to exercise control?

What happened in the past, or is happening elsewhere, does not necessarily represent a sensible target for this year in this business. Considering what happened last year, and in other businesses, may help in the formulation of plans, but past events and the performance of others should not automatically be seen as the target.

The five identified benefits of budgets can conflict with one another on occasion. Using the budget as a motivational device can provide an example of this. Some businesses set budget targets at a more demanding level than managers can reasonably be expected to achieve in an attempt to get them to strive harder. For control purposes, however, the budget becomes less useful as a benchmark against which to compare actual performance. Incidentally, there is good reason to doubt the effectiveness of setting excessively demanding targets as a motivational device, as we shall see in Chapter 13.

Where a conflict arises between the different uses of budgets, managers must decide which should be given priority. They must be prepared to trade off the benefits resulting from one particular use for the benefits of another.

The budget-setting process

Budgeting is such an important area for businesses, and other organisations, that it tends to be approached in a fairly methodical and formal way. This usually involves a number of steps, which we shall now consider.

Step 1: Establish who will take responsibility

Those responsible for the budget-setting process must have real authority within the business.

Activity 12.7

Why should this be the case?

One of the crucial aspects of the process is establishing co-ordination between budgets so that the plans of one department match, and are complementary to, those of other departments. This usually requires compromise leading to the adjustment of initial budgets. This in turn means that a senior manager has to be closely involved. Only such a person will possess the influence and, where needed, formal authority to make departmental managers compromise.

A **budget committee** is usually formed to supervise and take responsibility for the budget-setting process. This committee usually includes a senior representative of most of the functional areas of the business – marketing, production, human resources and so on. Having senior staff involved in this way can help to highlight the importance that they place on budgets and the budgeting process. Often, a **budget officer** is appointed to carry out the technical tasks of the committee, or to supervise others carrying them out. Not surprisingly, given their technical expertise, accountants are often given this role.

Step 2: Communicate budget guidelines to relevant managers

Budgets are intended to be the short-term plans that seek to work towards the achievement of strategic plans and to the overall objectives of the business. It is, therefore, important that, in drawing up budgets, managers are well aware of what the strategic plans are and how the forthcoming budget period is intended to work towards them. Managers also need to be made aware of the commercial/economic environment in which they will be operating. This may include awareness of market trends, future rates of inflation, forecast changes in technology and so on. It is the budget committee's responsibility to see that managers have all the necessary information.

Step 3: Identify the key, or limiting, factor

As we saw earlier in the chapter, there will be a limiting factor that restricts the business from achieving its objectives to the maximum extent. Identifying this limiting factor at an early stage in the budget-setting process is vitally important.

Step 4: Prepare the budget for the area of the limiting factor

The limiting factor will determine the overall level of activity for the business. As we have already seen, this will often be sales output, since the ability to sell is frequently the constraint on future growth. (When discussing the interrelationship of budgets earlier in the chapter, we started with the sales budget for this reason.)

Step 5: Prepare draft budgets for all other areas

Other budgets are prepared to align with the budget for the limiting factor. In budget preparation, the computer has become an indispensable tool. Much of the work of preparing budgets is repetitive and tedious, yet the end result has to provide a reliable representation of the plans made. Computers are ideally suited to such tasks whereas human beings are not. Budgets often have to be redrafted several times because of some minor change; computers do this without complaint.

Setting individual budgets may be approached in one of two broad ways. The *top-down approach* is where the senior management of each budget area originates the budget targets, perhaps discussing them with lower levels of management and, as a result, refining them before the final version is produced. The *bottom-up approach* involves targets being fed upwards from the lowest level. For example, junior sales managers will be asked to set their own sales targets, which then become incorporated into the budgets of higher levels of management until the overall sales budget emerges.

Where the bottom-up approach is adopted, it is usually necessary to haggle and negotiate at different levels of authority to achieve agreement. Perhaps the plans of some departments do not fit with those of others or the targets set by junior managers are not acceptable to their superiors. The bottom-up approach is less popular in practice than the top-down approach (see reference 3 at the end of the chapter).

Activity 12.8

What are the advantages and disadvantages of each type of budgeting approach (bottom-up and top-down)?

The bottom-up approach allows greater involvement among managers in the budgeting process and this, in turn, may increase the level of commitment to the targets set. It also allows the business to draw more fully on the detailed knowledge and expertise of its managers. However, this can be time-consuming and may result in some managers setting themselves undemanding targets in order to have an easy life.

The top-down approach enables senior management to communicate plans to employees and to co-ordinate the activities of the business more easily. It may also help in establishing more demanding targets for managers. However, the level of commitment to the budget may be lower as many of those responsible for achieving the budgets will have been excluded from the budget-setting process.

There will be further discussion of the benefits of participation in target setting in Chapter 13.

Step 6: Review and co-ordinate budgets

The budget committee will, at this stage, review the various budgets to satisfy itself that the budgets are consistent with one another. Where there is a lack of co-ordination, steps must be taken to ensure that the budgets mesh. Since this will require that at least one budget is revised, this activity normally benefits from a consensual approach. Ultimately, however, the committee may be forced to assert its authority and insist that alterations are made.

Step 7: Prepare the master budgets

The master budgets are the budgeted income statement and budgeted statement of financial position – and, perhaps, a summarised cash budget. The individual operating budgets, which have already been prepared, should provide all the information needed to prepare the master budgets. The budget committee usually undertakes the task of preparing the master budgets.

Step 8: Communicate the budgets to all interested parties

The formally agreed operating budgets are now passed to the individual managers responsible for their implementation. This is, in effect, senior management communicating to the other managers the targets they are expected to achieve.

Step 9: Monitor performance relative to the budget

Much of the budget-setting activity will have been pointless unless each manager's actual performance is compared with the benchmark of planned performance, which is incorporated in the budget. This issue is examined in detail in Chapter 13.

The steps in the budget-setting process are shown in diagrammatic form in Figure 12.5.

| Figure 12.5 | Steps in the budget-setting process |

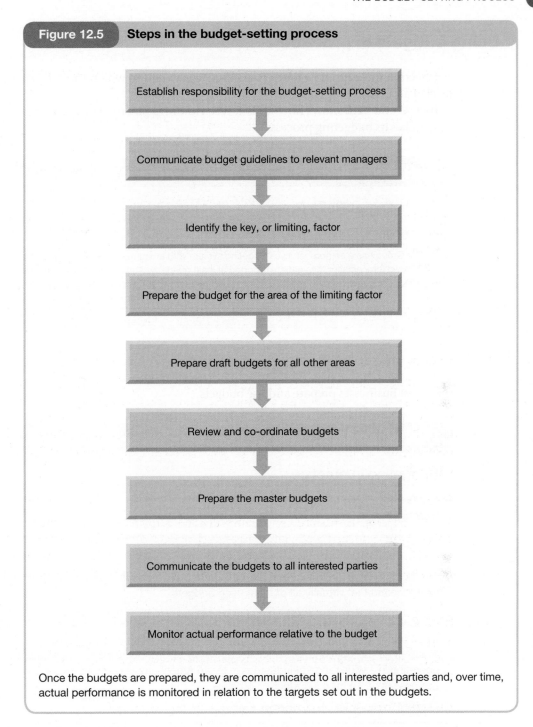

Once the budgets are prepared, they are communicated to all interested parties and, over time, actual performance is monitored in relation to the targets set out in the budgets.

Where the established budgets are proving to be unrealistic, it is usually helpful to revise them. They may prove to be unrealistic because certain assumptions made when the budgets were first set have turned out to be incorrect. This may occur where managers (budget-setters) have made poor judgements or where the environment has changed unexpectedly. Unrealistic budgets are of little value and revising them may be the only logical option. Nevertheless, revising budgets should be regarded as exceptional and only undertaken after careful consideration.

Using budgets in practice

This section indicates how budgets are used, the extent to which they are used and their level of accuracy.

Real World 12.2 shows how Rolls-Royce Holdings plc, the UK engine manufacturer, undertakes its budgeting process.

Real World 12.2

Budgeting at Rolls-Royce

According to the annual report of Rolls-Royce:

> The Group has a comprehensive budgeting system with an annual budget approved by the Board. Revised forecasts for the year are reported at least quarterly. Actual results, at both a business and Group level, are reported monthly against budget and variances are kept under scrutiny.

Source: Rolls-Royce Holdings plc, Annual Report 2015, p. 67.

There is quite a lot of survey evidence that reveals the extent to which budgeting is used by businesses in practice. **Real World 12.3** reviews some of this evidence, which shows that most businesses prepare and use budgets.

Real World 12.3

Budgeting in practice

A survey of 41 UK manufacturing businesses found that 40 of the 41 surveyed prepared budgets.

Source: Dugdale, D., Jones, C. and Green, S. (2006) *Contemporary Management Accounting Practices in UK Manufacturing*, CIMA Publication, Elsevier.

Another survey of UK businesses, but this time businesses involved in the food and drink sector, found that virtually all of them used budgets.

Source: Abdel-Kader, M. and Luther, R. (2004) *An Empirical Investigation of the Evolution of Management Accounting Practices*, Working paper No. 04/06, University of Essex, October.

A survey of the opinions of senior finance staff at 340 businesses of various sizes and operating in a wide range of industries in North America revealed that 97 per cent of those businesses had a formal budgeting process.

Source: BPM Forum (2008) *Perfect how you project*.

On the other hand, a survey of seven small and four medium-sized UK businesses found that not all of the small ones had a formal budgeting process, though all of the medium-sized ones did.

Source: Lucas, M., Prowle, M. and Lowth, G. (2013) *Management Accounting Practices of UK Small-medium-sized Enterprises*, CIMA, July 2013, p. 6.

Although these four surveys relate to UK and North American businesses, they provide some idea of what is likely also to be the practice elsewhere in the developed world.

Real World 12.4 gives some insight about the accuracy of budgets.

Real World 12.4

Budget accuracy

The survey of senior finance staff of North American businesses, mentioned in Real World 12.3, asked them to compare the actual revenues with the budgeted revenues for 2007. Figure 12.6 shows the results.

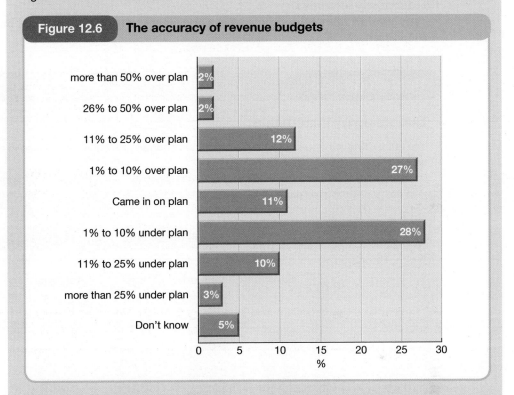

Figure 12.6   The accuracy of revenue budgets

We can see that only 66 per cent of revenue budgets were accurate within 10 per cent. The survey revealed that budgets for expenses were generally more accurate, with 74 per cent being accurate within 10 per cent.

Source: BPM Forum (2008) *Perfect how you project.*

Incremental and zero-base budgeting

Budget setting is often done on the basis of what happened last year, with some adjustment for changes in any factors expected to affect the forthcoming budget period (for example, inflation). This approach is known as **incremental budgeting** and is often used for **discretionary budgets,** such as research and development and staff training. With this type of budget, the **budget holder** (the manager responsible for the budget) is allocated a sum of money to be spent in the area of activity concerned. Such budgets are referred to as 'discretionary' because the sum allocated is normally at the discretion of senior management. These budgets are very common in local and central government (and in other public bodies), but are also used in commercial businesses to cover the types of activity mentioned.

Discretionary budgets are often found in areas where there is no clear relationship between inputs (resources applied) and outputs (benefits). They contrast with, say, a raw materials usage budget in a manufacturing business. Here the amount of material used and, therefore, the amount of funds involved, are clearly related to the level of production and, ultimately, to sales volumes. Discretionary budgets can easily eat up funds, with no clear benefit being derived. It is often only proposed periodic increases in these budgets that are closely scrutinised.

Real World 12.5 provides some idea of the extent to which incremental budgeting is used in practice.

Real World 12.5

Budgeting by increments

The 2009 CIMA survey showed that incremental budgeting is quite widely used in practice, as is shown by Figure 12.7.

It seems reasonable to presume that where businesses use an incremental approach, it is in the context of discretionary budgets.

| Figure 12.7 | The use of incremental budgeting |

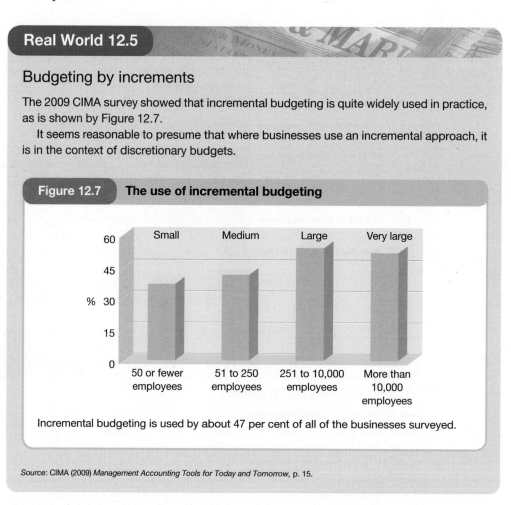

Incremental budgeting is used by about 47 per cent of all of the businesses surveyed.

Source: CIMA (2009) *Management Accounting Tools for Today and Tomorrow*, p. 15.

Zero-base budgeting (ZBB) rests on the philosophy that all spending needs to be justified. Thus, when establishing, say, the training budget each year, it is not automatically accepted that a particular training course should be financed in the future simply because it was undertaken this year. The training budget will start from a zero base (that is no resources at all) and will only be increased above zero if a good case can be made for the scarce resources of the business to be allocated to this activity. Senior management will need to be convinced that any proposed activities represent 'value for money'.

ZBB encourages managers to adopt a more questioning approach to their areas of responsibility. To justify the allocation of resources, managers are forced to think carefully about particular activities and how they are undertaken. With the increasing computerisation of production for both goods and services, an increasing portion of the total cost of businesses is in areas where the relationship between inputs and outputs is opaque. The commitment of resources, therefore, is discretionary rather than clearly linked to production. Hence, ZBB is increasingly relevant to managing costs, just as are some of the techniques discussed in Chapter 11.

Activity (12.9)

Can you think of any disadvantages of using ZBB?

The principal problems with ZBB are:

- It is time-consuming and therefore expensive to undertake.
- It can lead to a concentration on cost cutting at the expense of seeing the wider picture.
- Managers whose sphere of responsibility is subjected to ZBB can feel threatened by it.

The benefits of a ZBB approach can be gained to some extent – perhaps at not too great a cost – by using the approach on a selective basis. For example, a particular budget area could be subjected to ZBB-type scrutiny only every third or fourth year. Where ZBB is used more frequently, there is the danger that managers will use the same arguments each year to justify their activities. The process will simply become a mechanical exercise and the benefits will be lost. As mentioned earlier, the areas most likely to benefit from ZBB involve discretionary spending, such as training, advertising and research and development.

Where junior managers and other employees feel threatened by this form of budgeting, ZBB should be applied with sensitivity. However, in the quest for cost control and value for money, ZBB can result in tough decisions being made.

Real World 12.6 is an extract from an article written by three management consultants who are with McKinsey and Company, the leading management consultancy. The writers have had experience of establishing ZBB systems with various clients, resulting in significant operating cost savings.

Real World 12.6

Not zero cost savings

Zero-based budgeting can drive significant and sustainable savings, but it is much more than simply building a budget from zero. World-class ZBB programs build a culture of cost management through unprecedented cost visibility, a unique governance model, accountability at all levels of the organization, aligned incentives, and a rigorous and routine process. ZBB frees up unproductive costs and allows those savings to be taken to the bottom line or redirected to more productive areas that will drive future growth.

Source: Extract from Callaghan, S., Hawke, K. and Mignerey, C. (2014) *Five myths (and realities) about zero-based budgeting,* McKinsey and Company, www.mckinsey.com/insight/corporate_finance, October.

Real World 12.7 gives some impression of how much ZBB is used in practice.

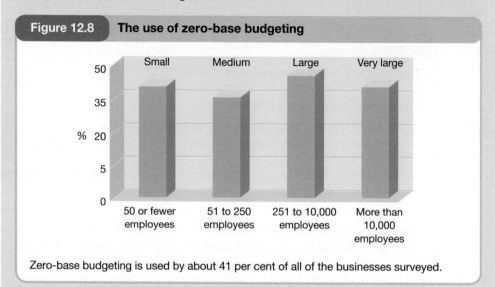

Real World 12.7

Too low for zero

A significant proportion of UK businesses use ZBB in practice, according to the 2009 CIMA survey. The detail is shown in Figure 12.8.

| Figure 12.8 | The use of zero-base budgeting |

Zero-base budgeting is used by about 41 per cent of all of the businesses surveyed.

A separate survey of 406 North American businesses reveals that, although the popularity of ZBB there had been lower than in the UK, the technique has rapidly grown in popularity recently. The proportion of North American businesses using ZBB jumped from 10 per cent in 2014 to 38 per cent by 2016. Major US food manufacturers seem to have led the way with this increase; Campbell Soup, Kellogg and Kraft Heinz have recently taken up the technique.

Sources: CIMA (2009) *Management Accounting Tools for Today and Tomorrow*, p. 15 and McLaughlin, T. (2017) *Back to zero: Companies use 1970s budget tool to cut costs as they hunt for growth*, Reuter Business News, uk.reuter.com, 30 January.

Preparing budgets

We shall now look in some detail at how the various budgets used by the typical business are prepared, starting with the cash budget and then looking at the others.

The cash budget

It is helpful for us to start with the cash budget because:

● It is a key budget (some people see it as a 'master budget' along with the budgeted income statement and budgeted statement of financial position); most economic aspects of a business are reflected in cash sooner or later. This means that, for a typical business, the cash budget reflects the whole business more comprehensively than any other single budget.

- A very small, unsophisticated business (for example, a corner shop) may feel that full-scale budgeting is not appropriate to its needs, but almost certainly it should prepare a cash budget as a minimum.

Since budgets are normally used only for internal purposes, their format is a matter of management choice and will vary from one business to the next. However, all managers, irrespective of the business, use budgets for similar purposes and so there is some consistency of approach. In most businesses, the cash budget will probably possess the following features:

1 The budget period would be broken down into sub-periods, typically months.
2 The budget would be in columnar form, with one column for each month.
3 Receipts of cash would be identified under various headings and a total for each month's receipts shown.
4 Payments of cash would be identified under various headings and a total for each month's payments shown.
5 The surplus of total cash receipts over payments, or of payments over receipts, for each month would be identified.
6 The running cash balance would be identified. This would be achieved by taking the balance at the end of the previous month and adjusting it for the surplus or deficit of receipts over payments for the current month.

Typically, all of the pieces of information in points 3 to 6 in this list would be useful to management for one reason or another.

Probably the best way to deal with this topic is through an example.

Example 12.1

Vierra Popova Ltd is a wholesale business. The budgeted income statements for each of the next six months are as follows:

	Jan £000	Feb £000	Mar £000	Apr £000	May £000	June £000
Sales revenue	52	55	55	60	55	53
Cost of goods sold	(30)	(31)	(31)	(35)	(31)	(32)
Salaries and wages	(10)	(10)	(10)	(10)	(10)	(10)
Electricity	(5)	(5)	(4)	(3)	(3)	(3)
Depreciation	(3)	(3)	(3)	(3)	(3)	(3)
Other overheads	(2)	(2)	(2)	(2)	(2)	(2)
Total expenses	(50)	(51)	(50)	(53)	(49)	(50)
Profit for the month	2	4	5	7	6	3

The business allows all of its customers one month's credit (this means, for example, that cash from sales made during January will be received in February). Sales revenue during December totalled £60,000.

The business plans to maintain inventories at their existing level until March. During that month they are to be reduced by £5,000. Inventories will remain at this lower level indefinitely. Inventories purchases are made on one month's credit.

Example 12.1 *continued*

December purchases totalled £30,000. Salaries, wages and 'other overheads' are paid in the month concerned. Electricity is paid quarterly in arrears in March and June. The business plans to buy and pay for a new delivery van in March. This will cost a total of £15,000, but an existing van will be traded in for £4,000 as part of the deal.

The business expects to have £12,000 in cash at the beginning of January.

The cash budget for the six months ending in June will look as follows:

	Jan £000	Feb £000	Mar £000	Apr £000	May £000	June £000
Receipts						
Trade receivables (Note 1)	60	52	55	55	60	55
Payments						
Trade payables (Note 2)	(30)	(30)	(31)	(26)	(35)	(31)
Salaries and wages	(10)	(10)	(10)	(10)	(10)	(10)
Electricity	–	–	(14)	–	–	(9)
Other overheads	(2)	(2)	(2)	(2)	(2)	(2)
Van purchase	–	–	(11)	–	–	–
Total payments	(42)	(42)	(68)	(38)	(47)	(52)
Cash surplus for the month	18	10	(13)	17	13	3
Opening balance (Note 3)	12	30	40	27	44	57
Closing balance	30	40	27	44	57	60

Notes:

1 The cash receipts from trade receivables lag a month behind sales because customers are given a month in which to pay for their purchases. So, December sales will be paid for in January and so on.
2 For inventories to remain constant at the end of each month, the business must replace exactly the amount that has been used. In most months, the purchases of inventories will, therefore, equal the cost of goods sold. During March, however, the business plans to reduce its inventories by £5,000. This means that inventories purchases will be lower than inventories usage in that month. The payments for inventories purchases lag a month behind purchases because the business expects to be allowed a month to pay for what it buys.
3 Each month's cash balance is the previous month's figure plus the cash surplus (or minus the cash deficit) for the current month. The balance at the start of January is £12,000 according to the information provided just before the cash budget (above).
4 Depreciation does not give rise to a cash payment. In the context of profit measurement (in the income statement), depreciation is a very important aspect. Here, however, we are interested only in cash.

Activity 12.10

Looking at the cash budget of Vierra Popova Ltd, what conclusions do you draw and what possible course of action do you recommend regarding the cash balance over the period concerned?

Given the size of the business, there is a fairly large cash balance that seems to be increasing. Management might consider:

- putting some of the cash into an income-yielding deposit;
- increasing the investment in non-current (fixed) assets;
- increasing the investment in current assets;
- paying a dividend to the owners; and
- repaying borrowings.

You may have thought of others.

Activity 12.11

Vierra Popova Ltd (Example 12.1) now wishes to prepare its cash budget for the second six months of the year. The budgeted income statements for each month of the second half of the year are as follows:

	July £000	Aug £000	Sept £000	Oct £000	Nov £000	Dec £000
Sales revenue	57	59	62	57	53	51
Cost of goods sold	(32)	(33)	(35)	(32)	(30)	(29)
Salaries and wages	(10)	(10)	(10)	(10)	(10)	(10)
Electricity	(3)	(3)	(4)	(5)	(6)	(6)
Depreciation	(3)	(3)	(3)	(3)	(3)	(3)
Other overheads	(2)	(2)	(2)	(2)	(2)	(2)
Total expenses	(50)	(51)	(54)	(52)	(51)	(50)
Profit for the month	7	8	8	5	2	1

The business will continue to allow all of its customers one month's credit.

It plans to increase inventories from the 30 June level by £1,000 during each month until, and including, September. During the following three months, inventories levels will be decreased by £1,000 each month.

Inventories purchases, which had been made on one month's credit until the June payment, will, starting with the purchases made in June, be made on two months' credit.

Salaries, wages and 'other overheads' will continue to be paid in the month concerned. Electricity is paid quarterly in arrears in September and December.

At the end of December, the business intends to pay off part of some borrowings. This payment is to be such that it will leave the business with a cash balance of £5,000 with which to start next year.

Prepare the cash budget for the six months ending in December. (Remember that any information you need that relates to the first six months of the year, including the cash balance that is expected to be brought forward on 1 July, is given in Example 12.1.)

→

Activity 12.11 continued

The cash budget for the six months ended 31 December is:

	July £000	Aug £000	Sept £000	Oct £000	Nov £000	Dec £000
Receipts						
Trade receivables	53	57	59	62	57	53
Payments						
Trade payables (Note 1)	–	(32)	(33)	(34)	(36)	(31)
Salaries and wages	(10)	(10)	(10)	(10)	(10)	(10)
Electricity	–	–	(10)	–	–	(17)
Other overheads	(2)	(2)	(2)	(2)	(2)	(2)
Borrowings repayment (Note 2)	–	–	–	–	–	(131)
Total payments	(12)	(44)	(55)	(46)	(48)	(191)
Cash surplus for the month	41	13	4	16	9	(138)
Opening balance	60	101	114	118	134	143
Closing balance	101	114	118	134	143	5

Notes:

1 There will be no payment to suppliers (trade payables) in July because the June purchases will be made on two months' credit and will therefore be paid in August. The July purchases, which will equal the July cost of sales figure plus the increase in inventories made in July, will be paid for in September and so on.

2 The borrowings repayment is simply the amount that will cause the balance at 31 December to be £5,000.

Preparing other budgets

Although each budget will have its own particular features, many will follow the same sort of pattern as the cash budget. That is, they will show inflows and outflows during each month and the opening and closing balances in each month.

Example 12.2

To illustrate some of the other budgets, we shall continue to use the example of Vierra Popova Ltd that we considered in Example 12.1. To the information given there, we need to add the fact that the inventories balance at 1 January was £30,000.

Trade receivables budget

This would normally show the planned amount owed to the business by credit customers at the beginning and at the end of each month, the planned total credit sales revenue for each month and the planned total cash receipts from credit customers (trade receivables). The layout would be something like this:

	Jan £000	Feb £000	Mar £000	Apr £000	May £000	June £000
Opening balance	60	52	55	55	60	55
Sales revenue	52	55	55	60	55	53
Cash receipts	(60)	(52)	(55)	(55)	(60)	(55)
Closing balance	52	55	55	60	55	53

The opening and closing balances represent the amount that the business plans to be owed (in total) by credit customers (trade receivables) at the beginning and end of each month, respectively.

Trade payables budget

Typically this shows the planned amount owed to suppliers by the business at the beginning and at the end of each month, the planned credit purchases for each month and the planned total cash payments to trade payables. The layout would be something like this:

	Jan £000	Feb £000	Mar £000	Apr £000	May £000	June £000
Opening balance	30	30	31	26	35	31
Purchases	30	31	26	35	31	32
Cash payment	(30)	(30)	(31)	(26)	(35)	(31)
Closing balance	30	31	26	35	31	32

The opening and closing balances represent the amount planned to be owed (in total) by the business to suppliers (trade payables), at the beginning and end of each month, respectively.

Inventories budget

This would normally show the planned amount of inventories to be held by the business at the beginning and at the end of each month, the planned total inventories purchases for each month and the planned total monthly inventories usage. The layout would be something like this:

	Jan £000	Feb £000	Mar £000	Apr £000	May £000	June £000
Opening balance	30	30	30	25	25	25
Purchases	30	31	26	35	31	32
Inventories used	(30)	(31)	(31)	(35)	(31)	(32)
Closing balance	30	30	25	25	25	25

The opening and closing balances represent the amount of inventories, at cost, planned to be held by the business at the beginning and end of each month, respectively.

A *raw materials inventories budget,* for a manufacturing business, would follow a similar pattern, with the 'inventories usage' being the cost of the inventories put into

> **Example 12.2** *continued*
>
> production. A *finished inventories budget* for a manufacturer would also be similar to the one shown above, except that 'inventories manufactured' would replace 'purchases'. A manufacturing business would normally prepare both a raw materials inventories budget and a finished inventories budget. Both of these would typically be based on the full cost of the inventories (that is, including overheads). There is no reason, however, why the inventories should not be valued on a variable cost, or direct cost, basis if this would provide more useful information.
>
> The inventories budget will normally be expressed in financial terms, but may also be expressed in physical terms (for example, units of production, kilograms or metres) for individual inventories' items.

Note how the trade receivables, trade payables and inventories budgets in Example 12.2 link to one another, and to the cash budget for the same business shown in Example 12.1. Note particularly that:

- the purchases figures in the trade payables budget and in the inventories budget are identical;
- the cash payments figures in the trade payables budget and the trade payables figures in the cash budget are identical; and
- the cash receipts figures in the trade receivables budget and the trade receivables figures in the cash budget are identical.

Other values would link different budgets in a similar way. For example, the row of sales revenue figures in the trade receivables budget would be identical to the sales revenue figures that will be found in the sales budget. This is how the linking (co-ordination), which was discussed earlier in this chapter, is achieved.

Activity 12.12

Have a go at preparing the trade receivables budget for Vierra Popova Ltd for the six months from July to December (see Activity 12.11).

The trade receivables budget for the six months ended 31 December is:

	July £000	Aug £000	Sep £000	Oct £000	Nov £000	Dec £000
Opening balance (Note 1)	53	57	59	62	57	53
Sales revenue (Note 2)	57	59	62	57	53	51
Cash receipts (Note 3)	(53)	(57)	(59)	(62)	(57)	(53)
Closing balance (Note 4)	57	59	62	57	53	51

Notes:

1. The opening trade receivables figure is the previous month's sales revenue figure (sales are on one month's credit).
2. The sales revenue is the current month's figure.
3. The cash received each month is equal to the previous month's sales revenue figure.
4. The closing balance is equal to the current month's sales revenue figure.

Note that if we knew any three of the four figures each month, we could deduce the fourth.

This budget could be set out in any manner that would have given the sort of information that management would require in respect of planned levels of trade receivables and associated transactions.

Activity 12.13

Have a go at preparing the trade payables budget for Vierra Popova Ltd for the six months from July to December (see Activity 12.11). (*Hint*: Remember that the trade payables settlement period alters from the June purchases onwards.)

The trade payables budget for the six months ended 31 December is:

	July £000	Aug £000	Sept £000	Oct £000	Nov £000	Dec £000
Opening balance	32	65	67	70	67	60
Purchases	33	34	36	31	29	28
Cash payments	–	(32)	(33)	(34)	(36)	(31)
Closing balance	65	67	70	67	60	57

This, again, could be set out in any manner that would have given the sort of information that management would require in respect of planned levels of trade payables and associated transactions.

Activity-based budgeting

Activity-based budgeting (ABB) extends the principles of activity-based costing discussed in Chapter 11 to the budgeting process. Under a system of ABB, the first step is usually to determine the sales budget. This is, of course, the same starting point as under conventional budgeting. The next step is to identify the activities needed to achieve the budgeted sales, along with their cost drivers. For each activity, a budgeted cost driver rate is established, which is then multiplied by the estimated usage of the cost driver (as determined by the sales budget). This final calculation provides the activity budget for the period.

The following example should help to make the ABB process clear.

Example 12.3

Danube Ltd produces two products, the Gamma and the Delta. The sales budget for next year shows that 60,000 units of Gamma and 80,000 units of Delta are expected to be sold. Each type of product spends time in the finished goods stores, which has been identified as a cost-driving activity.

Example 12.3 *continued*

Both products are of roughly similar size and have very similar storage needs. It is felt, therefore, that the period spent in the stores ('product weeks') is the cost driver. It is estimated that Product Gamma will spend an average of two weeks in the stores before being sold; for Product Delta, the average period is five weeks.

To derive the activity budget for the finished goods stores, the estimated total usage of the cost driver must be calculated. This will be the total number of 'product weeks' that the products are in store.

Product		Product weeks
Delta	60,000 × 2 weeks =	120,000
Gamma	80,000 × 5 weeks =	400,000
		520,000

The budgeted rate for the cost driver, based on figure calculated using ABC, has been set at £1.50 per product week.

The number of product weeks will then be multiplied by the budgeted rate for the cost driver to derive the activity budget figure. That is:

$$520,000 \times £1.50 = £780,000$$

A similar process will be carried out for the other cost-driving activities identified.

Note that budgets are prepared according to the various activities carried out. (In the case of Example 12.3 above, it was finished goods stores.) They are not prepared along functional lines, as occurs under the conventional approach. Under ABB, each activity has a cost pool and there is a separate budget for each cost pool.

Through the application of ABC principles, the factors that cause costs are known and there is a direct linking of costs with output. This means that ABB should provide a better understanding of future resource needs and more accurate budgets. It should also provide a better understanding of the effect on budgeted costs of changes in the usage of the cost driver because of the explicit relationship between cost drivers, activities and costs.

Control should be improved within an ABB environment for two reasons:

- By developing more accurate budgets, managers can be provided with demanding yet realistic targets.
- ABB should ensure that costs are closely linked to responsibilities. Managers who have control over particular cost drivers will become accountable for the costs that are caused. An important principle of effective budgeting is that those responsible for meeting a particular budget (budget holders) should have control over the events that affect performance in their area.

As with ABC, a system of ABB can be costly to implement and to run. A careful weighing of costs and benefits should therefore be carried out before considering its adoption. Furthermore, it is only feasible to adopt ABB if the business is also adopting a system of ABC. ABB and traditional absorption costing do not fit well together.

Real World 12.8 provides some indication of the extent to which ABB is used in practice.

Real World 12.8

Quite a lot of activity

The 2009 CIMA survey showed that ABB is used by a significant proportion of businesses in practice, as shown in Figure 12.9.

Figure 12.9　The use of activity-based budgeting

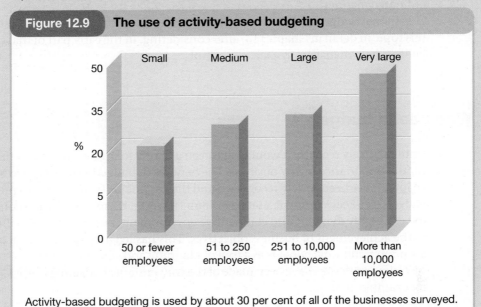

Activity-based budgeting is used by about 30 per cent of all of the businesses surveyed.

Unsurprisingly, the percentages that use ABB almost precisely match the proportion of the same survey sample that use activity-based costing. It is logical that businesses that use an activity-based approach to deriving their costs should also apply the same approach to holding managers responsible for the costs that are incurred, through the budgets.

Source: CIMA (2009) *Management Accounting Tools for Today and Tomorrow*, p. 15.

Non-financial measures in budgeting

The efficiency of internal operations and customer satisfaction levels have become of critical importance to businesses striving to survive in an increasingly competitive environment. As we saw in Chapter 11, non-financial performance indicators have an important role to play in assessing performance in such key areas as customer/supplier delivery times, set-up times, defect levels and customer satisfaction levels.

There is no reason why budgeting need be confined to financial targets and measures. Non-financial targets and measures can also be brought into the budgeting process. They can then be reported alongside the financial ones.

Budgets and management behaviour

All accounting reports are intended to affect human behaviour. In the case of budgets, it is the behaviour of managers that is the focus of interest. We have seen that budgets try to encourage managers to work towards the business's objectives and to do this in a co-ordinated manner.

Whether budgets are effective is of crucial importance to a business. We shall examine this topic in detail in Chapter 13, after considering, in the early part of that chapter, how budgets help managers to exercise control.

Who needs budgets?

Until relatively recently it would have been a heresy to suggest that budgeting was not of central importance to any business. The benefits of budgeting, mentioned earlier in this chapter, have been widely recognised and the vast majority of businesses prepare annual budgets (see Real World 12.3 on page 486). However, there is increasing concern that, in today's highly dynamic and competitive environment, budgets may actually be harmful to the achievement of business objectives. This has led a small number of businesses to abandon traditional budgets as a tool of planning and control.

Various criticisms have been made of the conventional budgeting process. It is claimed, for example, that:

- Budgets cannot deal with a fast-changing environment and they are often out of date before the start of the budget period.
- They focus too much management attention on the achievement of short-term financial targets. Instead, managers should focus on the things that create value for the business (for example, innovation, building brand loyalty, responding quickly to competitive threats and so on).
- They reinforce a 'command and control' structure that concentrates power in the hands of senior managers and prevents junior managers from exercising autonomy. This is particularly true where a top-down approach that allocates budgets to managers is being used. Where managers feel constrained, attempts to retain and recruit able managers can be difficult.
- Budgeting takes up an enormous amount of management time that could be better used. In practice, budgeting can be a lengthy process that may involve much negotiation, reworking and updating. However, this may add little to the achievement of business objectives.
- Budgets are based around business functions (sales, marketing, production and so on). To achieve the business's objectives, however, the focus should be on business processes that cut across functional boundaries and reflect the needs of the customer.
- They encourage incremental thinking by employing a 'last year plus x per cent' approach to planning. This can inhibit the development of 'break out' strategies that may be necessary in a fast-changing environment.

- They can protect costs rather than lower costs, particularly in the area of discretionary budgets. In some cases, a fixed budget for an activity, such as research and development, is allocated to a manager. If the amount is not spent, the budget may be taken away and, in future periods, the budget for this activity may be either reduced or eliminated. Such a response to unused budget allocations may encourage managers to spend the whole of the budget, irrespective of need, in order to protect the allocations they receive.
- They promote 'sharp' practice among managers. In order to meet budget targets, managers may try to negotiate lower sales targets or higher cost allocations than they feel is really necessary. This helps them to build some 'slack' into the budgets and so meeting the budget becomes easier (see reference 4 at the end of the chapter).

Although some believe that many of the problems identified can be solved by better budgeting systems such as activity-based budgeting and zero-base budgeting and by taking a more flexible approach, others believe that a more radical solution is required.

Real World 12.9 is taken from a question and answer column written by John Timpson. He was the chief executive of a very successful high street shoe-repairing and key-cutting business with over 800 branches (and expanding) throughout the UK. His answer to a question about budgeting echoes some of the criticisms of conventional budgeting that we have just considered. The answer appeared in the *Daily Telegraph.*

Real World 12.9

Cobblers

A long time ago I learnt that having a lot of figures doesn't mean you are better informed – it just makes life more complicated.

In the 1980s, we set budget sales figures for every shop every week, our Finance Director insisting that individual shop numbers added up to his company budget. It was a tortuous process that took weeks of area management time and although head office hoped the plan would provide the perfect incentive, it made no difference to our performance. Sales never seemed to follow our forecast – our customers clearly didn't know how much they were expected to spend! I scrapped the budgetary process and for the last 20 years we have compared branch performance with last year – it has saved us a lot of bother.

Life at Timpson has little to do with budgets and we don't have KPIs [key performance indicators]. We have bought several loss making companies and found that every one of them was monitoring minute detail from Head Office – Sketchley, the dry cleaners, were keen on keeping a count of their 'supercrease' sales; Max Spielmann, the photo chain, kept an eye on the average price of picture frames; and shoe repairers Mr Minit was controlling costs so closely that they recorded every shop's expenditure on postage stamps. While management concentrated on the detail they seemed to miss out on the big picture. Instead of studying their computers they should have visited more shops to talk to the colleagues who met their customers.

Of the few figures I receive, the most important is the bank balance compared with the same day last year. It gives me a daily health check on our business. I get a daily report on all the new shops we have opened in the last three months and a weekly sales report for the company, in total, and by department. We revise our profit forecast every week and

Real World 12.9 *continued*

produce management accounts every month, but I seldom look beyond the front page summary.

The only time I ask for detail is when we are introducing a new service – like our current growth in portraits, locksmith work and complicated car keys. If you know which shops are successful you can pass their secret around the rest of the business.

With little to look at it is easy to see how the company is doing and I have plenty of time left to visit our branches and discover what is really going on.

Source: Timpson, J. (2011) The management column, *Daily Telegraph Business*, 5 June.

Beyond conventional budgeting

In recent years, a few businesses have abandoned budgeting, although they still recognise the need for forward planning. No one seriously doubts that there must be appropriate systems in place to steer a business towards its objectives. It is claimed, however, that the systems adopted should reflect a broader, more integrated approach to planning. The new systems that have been implemented are often based around a 'leaner' financial planning process that is more closely linked to other measurement and reward systems. Emphasis is placed on the use of rolling forecasts and key performance indicators (such as market share, customer satisfaction and innovations) that identify both monetary and non-monetary targets to be achieved both over the long term and in the short term. These are often very demanding ('stretch') targets, based on benchmarks that have been set by world-class businesses.

The new 'beyond budgeting' model promotes a more decentralised, participative approach to managing the business. It is claimed that the traditional hierarchical management structure, where decision making is concentrated at the higher levels of the hierarchy, encourages a culture of dependency where meeting the budget targets set by senior managers is the key to managerial success. This traditional structure is replaced by a network structure where decision making is devolved to 'front-line' managers. A more open, questioning attitude among employees is encouraged by the new structure. There is a sharing of knowledge and best practice; protective behaviour by managers is discouraged. In addition, rewards are linked to targets based on improvement in relative performance rather than to meeting the budget. It is claimed that this new approach allows greater adaptability to changing conditions, increases performance and increases motivation among staff.

Figure 12.10 sets out the main differences between the traditional and 'beyond budgeting' planning models.

Real World 12.10 looks at the management planning systems at Toyota, the well-known Japanese motor vehicle business. Toyota does not use conventional budgets.

| Figure 12.10 | The traditional planning model versus the 'beyond budgeting' planning model |

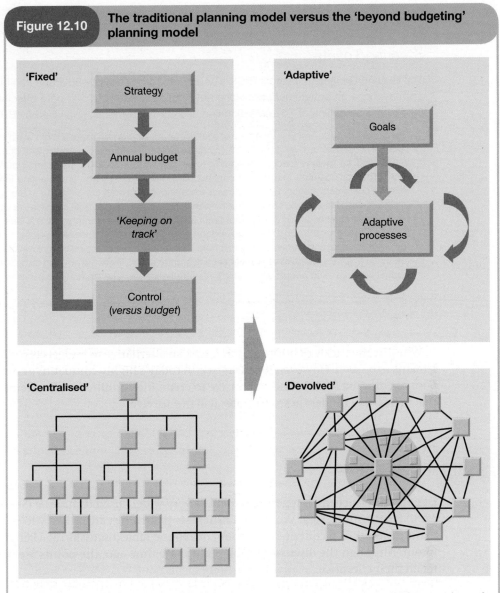

The traditional model is based on the use of fixed targets, which determine the future actions of managers. The 'beyond budgeting' model, on the other hand, is based on the use of stretch targets that can be adapted. The traditional hierarchical management structure is replaced by a network structure.

Source: Beyond budgeting, www.bbrt.org.

Real World 12.10

Steering Toyota

The Beyond Budgeting Institute (BBI) is at the forefront of those who argue that budgeting systems have an adverse effect on the ability of businesses to compete effectively. The following is an outline of Toyota's planning and control systems, published by BBI:

> Despite incurring its first loss in many decades (not even Toyota can make a profit when the market suddenly collapses by over 30 per cent) Toyota remains the best managed manufacturing company in the world. Its Toyota Production System is legendary and spawned the lean manufacturing movement. The management focus is on continuously improving systems and meeting internal and external customers' needs. Everyone has a voice and is expected to contribute to the continuous improvement of their work. Medium-term operational goals aimed at best practice are set at every level. Planning takes place at the plant/team level and happens monthly within a clear strategic framework (12 month rolling forecasts support capacity planning). Knowledge about current performance is visual and immediate (for example, throughput, downtime, inventory levels). Resources are made available just-in-time to meet each customer order. There are no fixed targets, no annual budget contracts and people are trusted with information to make the right decisions.

Source: BBI, *Toyota – A World Class manufacturing model,* www.bbrt.org/beyond-budgeting, accessed 17 May 2017.

Whether the trickle of businesses that seek an alternative to budgets turns into a flood remains to be seen. However, it is clear that in today's highly competitive environment a business must be flexible and responsive to changing conditions. Management systems that in any way hinder these attributes will not survive.

Long live budgets!

Despite the criticisms, budgeting remains a very widely used technique (See Real World 12.3.) Furthermore, **Real World 12.11** suggests that things are unlikely to change much in the near future. It contains an account of a round table discussion at a Better Budgeting forum. Although the discussion took place some time ago, the points are well put and retain their relevance.

Real World 12.11

Alive and kicking

A Better Budgeting forum was attended by representatives of 32 large organisations, including BAA (the airport operator), the BBC, Ford Motors, Sainsbury (the supermarket business) and Unilever (the household goods group).

The report of the forum discussions said:

> If you were to believe all that has been written in recent years, you'd be forgiven for thinking that budgeting is on its way to becoming extinct. Various research reports allude to the widespread dissatisfaction with the bureaucratic exercise in cost cutting that budgeting is accused of having become. Budgets are pilloried as being out of touch with the needs of modern business and accused of taking too long, costing too much and encouraging all sorts of perverse behaviour.
>
> Yet if there was one conclusion to emerge from the day's discussions it was that budgets are in fact alive and well. Not only did all the organisations present operate a formal budget but all bar two had no interest in getting rid of it. Quite the opposite – although aware of the problems it can cause,

the participants by and large regarded the budgeting system and the accompanying processes as indispensable.

Later in the report, in what could have been a reference to the use of 'rolling forecasts' among businesses that claim to have abandoned budgeting (see Real World 12.10, relating to Toyota), it said:

It quickly became obvious that, as one participant put it, 'one man's budget is another man's rolling forecast'. What people refer to when they talk about budgeting could in reality be very different things.

This presumably meant that businesses that abandon 'budgets' reintroduce them under another name.

Source: The Chartered Institute of Management Accountants and The Faculty of Finance and Management, Institute of Chartered Accountants in England and Wales (2004) *Better Budgeting*, March.

Activity 12.14

John Timpson (see Real World 12.9) denies having a budgetary process for his business. From what he says, do you agree?

Although the business may no longer have a full budgeting system in place, there are still benchmarks and targets. It can be argued that these constitute a rudimentary budgeting system. John Timpson compares branch performance with the previous year and the bank balance with the same day in the previous year. This is presumably because he sees last year's figures as some sort of benchmark or budget. Furthermore, he mentions 'profit forecasts', which may well suggest a target, or budget, to be achieved.

Real World 12.12 provides survey evidence of senior finance staff that indicates considerable support for budgets. Nevertheless, many recognise that budgeting is not always well managed and acknowledge some of the criticisms of budgets mentioned earlier.

Real World 12.12

Problems with budgets

The survey of the opinions of senior finance staff at 340 businesses of various sizes and operating in a wide range of industries in North America that was mentioned earlier (see Real World 12.3) showed that 86 per cent of those surveyed regarded the budget process as either 'essential' or 'very important'. However,

- 66 per cent thought that budgeting in their business was not agile or flexible enough;
- 59 per cent were not very confident that budget targets would be met in the following year;
- 67 per cent felt that their business devoted inappropriate amounts of time to budgeting (51 per cent felt it was too much and 16 per cent too little);
- 76 per cent felt that their businesses used inappropriate software in the budgeting process (generally using a spreadsheet rather than custom-designed software).

Source: BPM Forum (2008) *Perfect how you project.*

Despite the undoubted problems with budgeting, and the way in which it is often carried out, the 'beyond budgeting' approach is not popular in practice, as revealed by **Real World 12.13**.

Real World 12.13

Not going into the beyond

The 2009 CIMA survey showed that the 'beyond budgeting' philosophy is little followed in practice, as is shown by Figure 12.11.

Figure 12.11	The use of the 'beyond budgeting' philosophy

The 'beyond budgeting' philosophy is followed by only about 3 per cent of all of the businesses surveyed.

Source: CIMA (2009) *Management Accounting Tools for Today and Tomorrow*, p. 15.

A survey of 588 management accountants based in Canada and the USA, working in businesses of a large range of sizes and activities, indicated that budgets are overwhelmingly regarded as key tools in management. The results may be summarised as follows:

Percentage of businesses where the budget was regarded as:

	%
'more helpful than harmful'	28
'good value'	27
'very good value'	20
'excellent value'	7

Thus, 82 per cent of businesses regarded budgeting as broadly beneficial.

Only 5 per cent of management accountants surveyed worked in organisations where managers were considering abandoning budgeting. The survey revealed that steps had recently been taken, or were to be taken, to overcome some of the criticisms identified by the 'beyond budgeting' advocates.

Source: Libby, T. and Lindsay, R. (2010) Beyond budgeting or budgeting reconsidered? A survey of North-American budgeting practice, *Management Accounting Research*, vol. 21, no. 1, pp. 56–75.

A survey of 40 managers in UK businesses showed that all of their businesses used budgets, with only 5 per cent expressing serious doubt about their usefulness. Like the survey of Canadian and US management accountants, this study showed that the nature of budgeting was changing to overcome perceived problems.

Source: Dugdale, D. and Lyne, S. (2010) Budgeting practice and organisational structure, Chartered Institute of Management Accountants, *Research*, vol. 6, no. 4, April.

Activity 12.15

Do you think that the continuing popularity of traditional budgeting is the result of habit and an unwillingness to try a different approach?

It might be true that businesses are simply following the traditional approach without giving serious consideration to an alternative approach. This, however, does not seem likely, particularly for large, well-managed, businesses. A great deal of thought has probably been given to the alternative, but the traditional approach has, presumably, been viewed as having more to commend it.

Maintaining a system of budgeting is very costly, yet in this era where there is acute pressure to bear down on costs, budgeting remains very popular. It is very unlikely that businesses would blindly continue with such a costly activity unless it was considered worth it.

Self-assessment question 12.1 pulls together the points made in this chapter about preparing budgets.

Self-assessment question 12.1

Antonio Ltd, which makes and sells one standard product, has planned production and sales for the next nine months as follows:

	Production units	Sales units
May	350	350
June	400	400
July	500	400
August	600	500
September	600	600
October	700	650
November	750	700
December	750	800
January	750	750

Self-assessment question 12.1 *continued*

During the period, the business plans to advertise so as to generate these increases in sales. Payments for advertising of £1,000 and £1,500 will be made in July and October, respectively.

The selling price per unit will be £20 throughout the period. Forty per cent of sales are normally made on two months' credit. The other sixty per cent are settled within the month of the sale.

Raw materials will be held for one month before they are taken into production. Purchases of raw materials will be on one month's credit (buy one month, pay the next). The cost of raw materials is £8 per unit of production.

Other direct production expenses, including labour, are £6 per unit of production. These will be paid in the month concerned.

Various production overheads, which at present are £1,800 a month and are expected to continue at that level until the end of June, are expected to rise to £2,000 each month from 1 July to 31 October. They are expected to rise again from 1 November to £2,400 a month and to remain at that level for the foreseeable future. These overheads include a steady £400 each month for depreciation. Overheads are planned to be paid eighty per cent in the month of production and twenty per cent in the following month.

To help to meet the planned increased production, a new item of plant will be bought and delivered in August. The cost of this item is £6,600; the contract with the supplier will specify that this will be paid in three equal amounts in September, October and November.

The raw materials inventories level is planned to be enough for 500 units of production on 1 July. The balance at the bank on the same day is planned to be £7,500.

Required:

(a) Draw up the following for the six months ending 31 December:
1 A raw materials inventories budget, showing both physical quantities and financial values.
2 A trade payables budget.
3 A cash budget.

(b) The cash budget reveals a potential cash deficiency during October and November. Can you suggest any ways in which a modification of plans could overcome this problem?

The solution to this question can be found at the back of the book on pp. 778–780.

Summary

The main points of this chapter may be summarised as follows:

A budget is a short-term business plan, expressed in financial or in physical terms.

● Budgets are the short-term means of working towards the business's objectives.
● They are usually prepared for a one-year period with sub-periods of a month.
● There is usually a separate budget for each key area.

Periodic and continual budgets

● Periodic budgets are prepared for a particular period (usually one year).
● Continual (rolling) budgets are continually updated, thereby ensuring, that there are budgets for a full planning period.

Uses of budgets

- Promote forward thinking.
- Help co-ordinate the various aspects of the business.
- Motivate performance.
- Provide the basis of a system of control.
- Provide a system of authorisation.

The budget-setting process

- Establish who will take responsibility.
- Communicate guidelines.
- Identify key factor.
- Prepare budget for key factor area.
- Prepare draft budgets for all other areas.
- Review and co-ordinate.
- Prepare master budgets (income statement and statement of financial position).
- Communicate the budgets to interested parties.
- Monitor performance relative to budget.

Incremental budgeting and zero-base budgeting (ZBB)

- Incremental budgets are often based on those of previous periods, with some adjustment for factors affecting the forthcoming period.
- ZBB rests on the philosophy that all spending must be justified.
- ZBB promotes a more questioning approach in order to achieve a more efficient use of resources.

Preparing budgets

- There is no standard style – practicality and usefulness are the key issues.
- They are usually prepared in columnar form, with a column for each month (or similarly short period).
- Each budget must link (co-ordinate) with others.

Activity-based budgeting (ABB)

- ABB extends the principles of ABC to budgeting.
- Budgets are based on the cost-driving activity rather than a business function.
- Can result in more accurate budgets and closer links between costs and management responsibilities.

Criticisms of budgets

- Cannot deal with rapid change.
- Focus on short-term financial targets, rather than value creation.
- Encourage a 'top-down' management style.
- Can be time-consuming.
- Based around traditional business functions and do not cross boundaries.
- Encourage incremental thinking (last year's figure, plus x per cent).

- Protect rather than lower costs.
- Promote 'sharp' practice among managers.
- Budgeting is still widely regarded as useful and extensively practised despite the criticisms and the costliness of a traditional budgeting system.
- Even businesses that claim to have abandoned budgets use planning and control devices that appear to be budgets by another name.

Key terms

For definitions of these terms, see Appendix B.

budget *p. 472*
forecast *p. 475*
periodic budget *p. 475*
continual budget *p. 475*
rolling budget *p. 476*
limiting factor *p. 477*
master budget *p. 477*
control *p. 480*

management by exception *p. 481*
budget committee *p. 483*
budget officer *p. 483*
incremental budgeting *p. 487*
discretionary budget *p. 487*
budget holder *p. 487*
zero-base budgeting (ZBB) *p. 488*
activity-based budgeting (ABB) *p. 497*

References

1 PWC (2010) *Breaking the cycle: The case for eliminating the budget,* PWC.

2 O'Mahoney, J. and Lyon, J. (2015) *Planning, budgeting and forecasting: An eye to the future,* KPMG/ACCA.

3 Durfee, D. (2006) Alternative budgeting, *CFO Magazine,* June.

4 Teach, E. (2014) No time for budgets, *CFO Magazine,* 27 May.

Further reading

If you would like to explore the topics covered in this chapter in more depth, we recommend the following:

Atkinson, A., Kaplan, R., Matsumura, E. and Young, S.M. (2013) *Management Accounting,* 6th edn, Pearson, Chapter 10.

Bhimani A., Horngren, C., Datar, S. and Rajan, M. (2015) *Management and Cost Accounting,* 6th edn, Pearson, Chapter 14.

Drury, C. (2015) *Management and Cost Accounting,* 9th edn, Cengage Learning EMEA, Chapter 15.

Hilton, R. and Platt, D. (2014) *Managerial Accounting,* McGraw-Hill Higher Education, Chapter 9.

Review questions

Solutions to these questions can be found at the back of the book on pp. 795–796.

12.1 Define a budget. How is a budget different from a forecast?

12.2 What were the five uses of budgets that were identified in the chapter?

12.3 What do budgets have to do with control?

12.4 What is a budget committee? What purpose does it serve?

Exercises

Exercises with coloured numbers have solutions given at the back of the book on pp. 826–828.

Basic-level exercises

12.1 Prolog Ltd is a small wholesaler of high-specification personal computers. It has in recent months been selling 50 machines a month at a price of £2,000 each. These machines cost £1,600 each. A new model has just been launched and this is expected to offer greatly enhanced performance. Its selling price and cost will be the same as for the old model. From the beginning of January, sales are planned to increase at a rate of 20 machines each month until the end of June, when sales will amount to 170 units a month. Sales are planned to continue at that level thereafter. Operating costs including depreciation of £2,000 a month are planned as follows:

	Jan	Feb	Mar	Apr	May	June
Operating costs (£000)	6	8	10	12	12	12

Prolog expects to receive no credit for operating costs. Additional shelving for storage will be bought, installed and paid for in April, costing £12,000. Tax of £25,000 is due at the end of March. Prolog anticipates that trade receivables will amount to two months' sales revenue. To give its customers a good level of service, Prolog plans to hold enough inventories at the end of each month to fulfil anticipated demand from customers in the following month. The computer manufacturer, however, grants one month's credit to Prolog. Prolog Ltd's statement of financial position is:

Statement of financial position at 31 December

	£000
ASSETS	
Non-current assets	80
Current assets	
Inventories	112
Trade receivables	200
Cash	–
	312
Total assets	392

	£000
EQUITY AND LIABILITIES	
Equity	
Share capital (25p ordinary shares)	10
Retained profit	177
	187
Current liabilities	
Trade payables	112
Taxation	25
Overdraft	68
	205
Total equity and liabilities	392

Required:

(a) Prepare a cash budget for Prolog Ltd showing the cash balance or required overdraft for the six months ending 30 June.

(b) State briefly what further information a banker would require from Prolog Ltd before granting additional overdraft facilities for the anticipated expansion of sales.

12.2 You have overheard the following statements:

(a) 'A budget is a forecast of what is expected to happen in a business during the next year.'

(b) 'Monthly budgets must be prepared with a column for each month so that you can see the whole year at a glance, month by month.'

(c) 'Budgets are OK but they stifle all initiative. No manager worth employing would work for a business that seeks to control through budgets.'

(d) 'Activity-based budgeting is an approach that takes account of the planned volume of activity in order to deduce the figures to go into the budget.'

(e) 'Any sensible person would start with the sales budget and build up the other budgets from there.'

Required:

Critically discuss these statements, explaining any technical terms.

Intermediate-level exercises

12.3 A nursing home, which is linked to a large hospital, has been examining its budgetary control procedures, with particular reference to overhead costs.

The level of activity in the facility is measured by the number of patients treated in the budget period. For the current year, the budget stands at 6,000 patients and this is expected to be met.

For months 1 to 6 of this year (assume 12 months of equal length), 2,700 patients were treated. The actual variable overhead costs incurred during this six-month period are as follows:

Expense	£
Staffing	59,400
Power	27,000
Supplies	54,000
Other	8,100
Total	148,500

The hospital accountant believes that the variable overhead costs will be incurred at the same rate during months 7 to 12 of the year.

Fixed overheads are budgeted for the whole year as follows:

Expense	£
Supervision	120,000
Depreciation/financing	187,200
Other	64,800
Total	372,000

Required:

(a) Present an overheads budget for the final six-month period of the year (one budget). You should show each expense. What is the total overhead cost for each patient that would be incorporated into any statistics?

(b) The nursing home actually treated 3,800 patients during the final six months of the year, the actual variable overheads were £203,300 and the actual fixed overheads were £190,000. In summary form, examine how well the nursing home exercised control over its overheads.

(c) Interpret your analysis and point out any limitations or assumptions.

12.4 Linpet Ltd is to be incorporated on 1 June. The opening statement of financial position of the business will then be as follows:

	£
Assets	
Cash at bank	60,000
Share capital	
£1 ordinary shares	60,000

During June, the business intends to make payments of £40,000 for a leasehold property, £10,000 for equipment and £6,000 for a motor vehicle. The business will also purchase initial trading inventories costing £22,000 on credit.

The business has produced the following estimates:

1 Sales revenue for June will be £8,000 and will increase at the rate of £3,000 a month until, and including, September. In October, sales revenue will rise to £22,000, and in subsequent months it will be maintained at this figure.

2 The gross profit percentage (that is, (gross profit/sales) × 100) on goods sold will be 25 per cent.

3 There is a risk that supplies of trading inventories will be interrupted towards the end of the accounting year. The business therefore intends to build up its initial level of inventories (£22,000) by purchasing £1,000 of inventories each month in addition to the monthly purchases necessary to satisfy monthly sales requirements. All purchases of inventories (including the initial inventories) will be on one month's credit.

4 Sales revenue will be divided equally between cash and credit sales. Credit customers are expected to pay two months after the sale is agreed.

5 Wages and salaries will be £900 a month. Other overheads will be £500 a month for the first four months and £650 a month thereafter. Both types of expense will be payable when incurred.

6 80 per cent of sales revenue will be generated by salespeople who will receive 5 per cent commission on sales revenue. The commission is payable one month after the sale is agreed.

7 The business intends to purchase further equipment in November for £7,000 cash.

8 Depreciation will be provided at the rate of 5 per cent a year on property and 20 per cent a year on equipment. (Depreciation has not been included in the overheads mentioned in point 5 above.)

Required:

(a) State why a cash budget is required for a business.

(b) Prepare a cash budget for Linpet Ltd for the six-month period to 30 November.

12.5 Lewisham Ltd manufactures one product line – the Zenith. Plans over the next few months are as follows:

1 *Sales demand*

	Units
July	180,000
August	240,000
September	200,000
October	180,000

Each Zenith will sell for £3.

2 *Receipts from sales.* Payments from credit customers are expected to be 70 per cent during the month of sale, and 28 per cent during the following month. The remaining trade receivables are expected to go bad (that is, to be uncollectable).

  Credit customers who pay in the month of sale are entitled to deduct a 2 per cent discount from the invoice price.

3 *Finished goods inventories.* These are expected to be 40,000 units at 1 July. The business's policy is that, in future, the inventories at the end of each month should equal 20 per cent of the following month's planned sales requirements.

4 *Raw materials inventories.* These are expected to be 40,000 kg on 1 July. The business's policy is that, in future, the inventories at the end of each month should equal 50 per cent of the following month's planned production requirements. Each Zenith requires 0.5 kg of the raw material, which costs £1.50/kg. Raw materials purchases are paid in the month after purchase.

5 *Labour and overheads.* The direct labour cost of each Zenith is £0.50. The variable overhead element of each Zenith is £0.30. Fixed overheads, including depreciation of £25,000, total £47,000 a month. All labour and overheads are paid during the month in which they arise.

6 *Cash in hand.* At 1 August the business plans to have a bank balance (in funds) of £20,000.

Required:
Prepare the following budgets:

(a) Finished goods inventories budget (expressed in units of Zenith) for each of the three months July, August and September.
(b) Raw materials inventories budget (expressed in kilograms of the raw material) for the two months July and August.
(c) Cash budget for August and September.

Advanced-level exercises

12.6 Daniel Chu Ltd, a new business, will start production on 1 April, but sales will not start until 1 May. Planned sales for the next nine months are as follows:

	Sales units
May	500
June	600
July	700
August	800
September	900
October	900
November	900
December	800
January	700

The selling price of a unit will be a consistent £100 and all sales will be made on one month's credit. It is planned that sufficient finished goods inventories for each month's sales should be available at the end of the previous month.

Raw materials purchases will be such that there will be sufficient raw materials inventories available at the end of each month precisely to meet the following month's planned production. This planned policy will operate from the end of April. Purchases of raw materials will be on one month's credit. The cost of raw material is £40 a unit of finished product.

The direct labour cost, which is variable with the level of production, is planned to be £20 a unit of finished production. Production overheads are planned to be £20,000 each month, including £3,000 for depreciation. Non-production overheads are planned to be £11,000 a month, of which £1,000 will be depreciation.

Various non-current (fixed) assets costing £250,000 will be bought and paid for during April. Except where specified, assume that all payments take place in the same month as the cost is incurred.

The business will raise £300,000 in cash from a share issue in April.

Required:
Draw up the following for the six months ending 30 September:

(a) A finished inventories budget, showing just physical quantities.
(b) A raw materials inventories budget showing both physical quantities and financial values.
(c) A trade payables budget.
(d) A trade receivables budget.
(e) A cash budget.

12.7 Brown and Jeffreys, a West Midlands business, makes one standard product for use in the motor trade. The product, known as the Fuel Miser, for which the business holds the patent, when fitted to the fuel system of production model cars has the effect of reducing petrol consumption.

Part of the production is sold direct to a local car manufacturer, which fits the Fuel Miser as an optional extra to several of its models. The rest of the production is sold through various retail outlets, garages and so on.

Brown and Jeffreys assemble the Fuel Miser, but all three components are manufactured by local engineering businesses. The three components are codenamed A, B and C. One Fuel Miser consists of one of each component.

The planned sales for the first seven months of the forthcoming accounting period, by channels of distribution and in terms of Fuel Miser units, are as follows:

	Jan	Feb	Mar	Apr	May	June	July
Manufacturers	4,000	4,000	4,500	4,500	4,500	4,500	4,500
Retail and so on	2,000	2,700	3,200	3,000	2,700	2,500	2,400
	6,000	6,700	7,700	7,500	7,200	7,000	6,900

The following further information is available:

1 There will be inventories of finished units at 1 January of 7,000 Fuel Misers.
2 The inventories of raw materials at 1 January will be:
   A 10,000 units
   B 16,500 units
   C 7,200 units
3 The selling price of Fuel Misers is to be £10 each to the motor manufacturer and £12 each to retail outlets.
4 The maximum production capacity of the business is 7,000 units a month. There is no possibility of increasing this.

5   Assembly of each Fuel Miser will take 10 minutes of direct labour. Direct labour is paid at the rate of £7.20 an hour during the month of production.

6   The components are each expected to cost the following:

A £2.50

B £1.30

C £0.80

7   Indirect costs are to be paid at a regular rate of £32,000 each month.

8   The cash at the bank at 1 January will be £2,620.

The planned sales volumes must be met and the business intends to pursue the following policies *for as many months as possible,* consistent with meeting the sales targets:

● Finished inventories at the end of each month are to equal the following month's total sales to retail outlets and half the total of the following month's sales to the motor manufacturer.

● Raw materials at the end of each month are to be sufficient to cover production requirements for the following month. The production for July will be 6,800 units.

● Suppliers of raw materials are to be paid during the month following purchase. The payment for January will be £21,250.

● Customers will pay in the month of sale, in the case of sales to the motor manufacturer, and the month after sale, in the case of retail sales. Retail sales during December were 2,000 units at £12 each.

Required:

Prepare the following budgets in monthly columnar form, both in terms of money and units (where relevant), for the six months of January to June inclusive:

(a)   Sales budget.*

(b)   Finished inventories budget (valued at direct cost).†

(c)   Raw materials inventories budget (one budget for each component).†

(d)   Production budget (direct costs only).*

(e)   Trade receivables budget.†

(f)   Trade payables budget.†

(g)   Cash budget.†

Notes:

* The sales and production budgets should merely state each month's sales or production in units and in money terms.

† The other budgets should all seek to reconcile the opening balance of inventories, trade receivables, trade payables or cash with the closing balance through movements of the relevant factors over the month.

CHAPTER  13

Accounting for control

Introduction

Associated British Foods Group plc, the food processor (including Ovaltine and Ryvita) and retailer (Primark), states in its 2016 annual report (p. 62):

> All operations prepare annual operating plans and budgets which are updated regularly. Performance against budget is monitored at operational level and centrally, with variances being reported promptly. The cash position at group and operational level is monitored constantly and variances from expected levels are investigated thoroughly.

This raises important issues such as the way in which performance is monitored, the nature of variances, why the business should identify them, how they should be reported and what action the business should take where variances occur. These issues provide the focus for the chapter. We shall see that the procedures at Associated British Foods are widely adopted throughout the business world.

This chapter develops some of the themes that were discussed in Chapter 12. We shall see how a budget can be used to help control a business and how, by collecting information on actual performance and comparing it with the budget, it is possible to identify those activities that are in control and those that are not.

We shall take a look at standard costing and its relationship with budgeting. We shall see that a budget is often constructed from standards. Like budgets, standards provide targets against which actual performance can be measured. Finally, we shall explore the behavioural aspects of budgets and standards. We shall assess their value as a motivational device and consider the ways in which managers use them in practice.

Learning outcomes

When you have completed this chapter, you should be able to:

● discuss the role and limitations of budgets for performance evaluation and control;

● undertake variance analysis and discuss possible reasons for the variances calculated;

● explain the nature, role and limitations of standard costing; and

● discuss the issues that should be taken into account when designing an effective system of budgetary control.

Budgeting for control

In Chapter 12, we saw that budgets can provide a useful basis for exercising control over a business. Control involves making events conform to a plan and, since a budget is a short-term plan, making events conform to it is an obvious way to try to control the business. We also saw that, for most businesses, the routine is as shown in Figure 13.1.

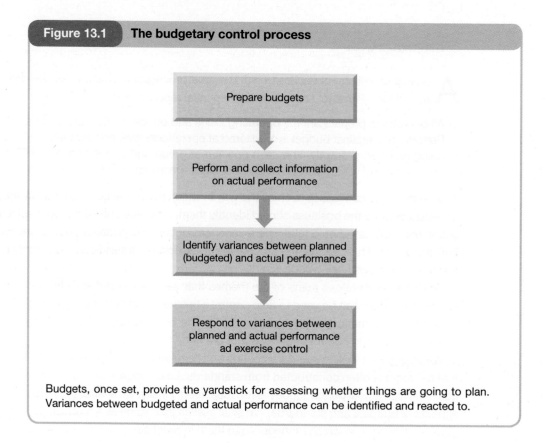

Figure 13.1   The budgetary control process

Prepare budgets

↓

Perform and collect information on actual performance

↓

Identify variances between planned (budgeted) and actual performance

↓

Respond to variances between planned and actual performance ad exercise control

Budgets, once set, provide the yardstick for assessing whether things are going to plan. Variances between budgeted and actual performance can be identified and reacted to.

If plans are drawn up sensibly, we have a basis for exercising control over the business. We must, however, measure actual performance in the same terms as those in which the budget is stated. Unless we do this, proper comparison is not possible.

Exercising control involves identifying where and why things did not go according to plan and then seeking ways to correct them for the future. One reason why things may not have gone according to plan is that the budget targets were unachievable. In this case, it may be necessary to revise the budgets for future periods.

This last point does not imply that budget targets can simply be ignored if the going gets tough. Rather, it means that they should be adaptable. Unrealistic budget targets cannot form a basis for exercising control and little can be gained by sticking with them.

Real World 13.1 discusses how one budget, which was revised in the light of cost overruns, was still too ambitious.

Real World 13.1

Digging itself out of a hole

DiamondCorp plc owns, and is now developing, the Lace diamond mine in South Africa. An update on progress by the business revealed that the tunnelling budget had been revised. Nevertheless, tunnelling costs were exceeding the revised budget. The company stated:

> Tunnel development costs to date are averaging Rand 39,135/metre against a revised budget of Rand 37,000/metre. The over spend continues to be the result of increased operating costs on the company's underground mining fleet. However, cost saving initiatives, including the introduction of chains to the tyres of the underground loaders and computerisation of maintenance scheduling, are starting to show a positive impact which should be reflected in improvements in the cost per metre rate going forward. The overall mine development expenditure is within budget.

Source: DiamondCorp plc (2014), Lace Diamond mine Project Update, www.24hgold.com, 30 October.

Providing there is an adequate system of budgetary control, decision making and responsibility can be delegated to junior management. However, senior management can still retain control by using the system to discover which junior managers are meeting budget targets. This enables a *management-by-exception* environment to be created where senior management can focus on areas where things are *not* going according to plan (the exceptions – it is to be hoped). Junior managers who are performing to budget can be left to get on with their jobs.

Types of control

The control process just outlined is known as **feedback control.** Its main feature is that steps are taken to get operations back on track as soon as there is a signal that they have gone wrong. This is similar to the thermostatic control that is a feature of most central heating systems. The thermostat incorporates a thermometer that senses when the temperature has fallen below a pre-set level (analogous to the budget). The thermostat then takes action to correct matters by activating the heating device that restores the required minimum temperature. Figure 13.2 depicts the stages in a feedback control system using budgets.

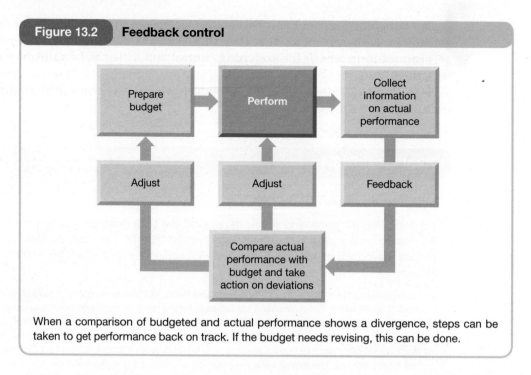

Figure 13.2 **Feedback control**

When a comparison of budgeted and actual performance shows a divergence, steps can be taken to get performance back on track. If the budget needs revising, this can be done.

There is an alternative type of control, known as **feedforward control.** Here predictions are made as to what can go wrong and steps are then taken to avoid any undesirable outcome. Budgets can also be used to exert this type of control. It involves preparing a budget and then comparing it with a forecast of actual outcomes in order to identify potential problems. For example, a cash budget may be compared with a forecast of actual cash flows. Where significant deviations from budget are revealed, corrective action may be taken before the problems arise. Figure 13.3 depicts the stages in a feedforward control system using budgets.

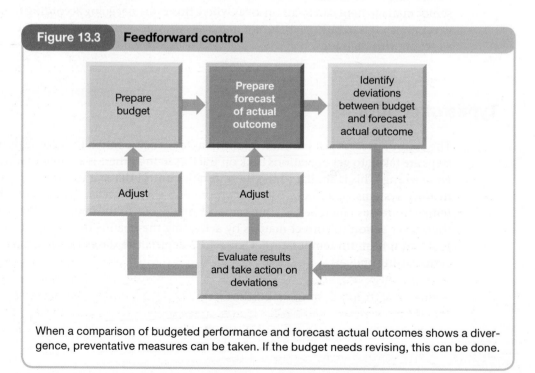

Figure 13.3 **Feedforward control**

When a comparison of budgeted performance and forecast actual outcomes shows a divergence, preventative measures can be taken. If the budget needs revising, this can be done.

Feedforward controls are proactive and try to anticipate problems beforehand, whereas feedback controls react to existing problems. To put it another way, feedforward controls are preventative, whereas feedback controls are remedial. As it is better to avoid problems rather than have to solve them, feedforward controls are preferable. However, they require timely and accurate predictions of actual outcomes, which are not always available.

Activity 13.1

The act of preparing budgets may lead directly to feedforward control. Can you think how preparing budgets may help to anticipate problems? Use the cash budget as an example.

During the preparation of a cash budget, it may become clear that it is unrealistic and needs amendment. It may reveal that there will be insufficient cash at particular times during the budget period. By identifying the future cash shortage, spending commitments in the budget may be revised.

Variances from budget

We saw in Chapter 1 that the key financial objective of a business is to increase the wealth of its owners (shareholders). Since profit is the net increase in wealth from business operations, the most important budget target to meet is the profit target. We shall therefore take this as our starting point when comparing the budget with the actual results. Example 13.1 shows the budgeted and actual income statements for Baxter Ltd for the month of May.

Example 13.1

The following are the budgeted and actual outcomes for Baxter Ltd, a manufacturing business, for the month of May:

	Budget	Actual
Output (production and sales)	1,000 units	900 units
	£	£
Sales revenue	100,000	92,000
Raw materials	(40,000) (40,000 metres)	(36,900) (37,000 metres)
Labour	(20,000) (2,500 hours)	(17,500) (2,150 hours)
Fixed overheads	(20,000)	(20,700)
Operating profit	20,000	16,900

From these figures, it is clear that the budgeted profit was not achieved. As far as May is concerned, this is a matter of history. However, the business (or one or more aspects of it) is out of control. Managers must discover where things went wrong during May and try to ensure that these mistakes are not repeated in later months. It is not enough to know that things went wrong overall. We need to know precisely where and why. To achieve this, we must compare the budgeted and actual figures for the various items (sales revenue, raw materials and so on) in the statement shown above.

Activity (13.2)

Can you see any problems in comparing the various items (sales revenue, raw materials and so on) for the budget with the actual performance of Baxter Ltd in an attempt to draw conclusions as to which aspects were out of control?

The problem is that the actual level of output was not as budgeted. In fact it was 10 per cent lower than budget. This means that we cannot, for example, say that there was a labour cost saving of £2,500 (that is, £20,000 − £17,500) and conclude that all is well in that area.

Flexing the budget

One practical way to overcome our difficulty is to 'flex' the budget to what it would have been had the planned level of output been 900 units rather than 1,000 units. **Flexing a budget** simply means revising it, based on a different volume of output.

To flex the budget, we need to know which revenues and costs are fixed and which are variable relative to the volume of output. Once we know this, flexing is a simple operation. We shall assume that sales revenue, materials cost and labour cost vary strictly with volume. Fixed overheads, by definition, will not. Whether, in real life, labour cost does vary with the volume of output is not so certain, but it will serve well enough as an assumption for our purposes. If labour cost is actually fixed, we can simply take this into account in the flexing process.

On the basis of our assumptions regarding the behaviour of revenues and costs, the flexed budget would be as follows:

	Flexed budget
Output (production and sales)	900 units
	£
Sales revenue	90,000
Raw materials	(36,000) (36,000 metres)
Labour	(18,000) (2,250 hours)
Fixed overheads	(20,000)
Operating profit	16,000

This is simply the original budget, with the sales revenue, raw materials and labour cost figures scaled down by 10 per cent (the same factor as the actual output fell short of the budgeted one).

Putting the original budget, the flexed budget and the actual outcome for May together gives us the following:

	Original budget	Flexed budget	Actual
Output (production and sales)	1,000 units	900 units	900 units
	£	£	£
Sales revenue	100,000	90,000	92,000
Raw materials	(40,000)	(36,000) (36,000 m)	(36,900) (37,000 m)
Labour	(20,000)	(18,000) (2,250 hr)	(17,500) (2,150 hr)
Fixed overheads	(20,000)	(20,000)	(20,700)
Operating profit	20,000	16,000	16,900

Flexible budgets allow us to make a more valid comparison between the budget (using the flexed figures) and the actual results. Key differences, or *variances,* between budgeted and actual results for each aspect of the business's activities can be calculated. In the rest of this section we consider some of these variances.

Sales volume variance

Let us begin by dealing with the shortfall in sales volume. By flexing the budget, as we just did, it may seem as if we are saying that it does not matter that the business failed to achieve the budgeted sales volume. We simply revise the budget and carry on as if all is well. However, losing sales volume clearly does matter. A sales volume shortfall normally means losing profit. The first point we must pick up, therefore, is the profit shortfall arising from the loss of sales of 100 units of the product.

Activity 13.3

What will be the loss of profit arising from the sales volume shortfall, assuming that everything except sales volume was as planned?

The answer is simply the difference between the original and flexed budget profit figures. The only difference between these two profit figures is the volume of sales; everything else was the same. (That is to say that the flexing was carried out assuming that the per-unit sales revenue, raw material cost and labour cost were all as originally budgeted.) This means that the figure for the loss of profit due to the volume shortfall, taken alone, is £4,000 (that is, £20,000 − £16,000).

When we considered the relationship between cost, volume and profit in Chapter 9, we saw that selling one unit fewer will result in the loss of one unit's contribution to profit. The contribution is sales revenue less variable cost. We can see from the original budget that the unit sales revenue is £100 (that is, £100,000/1,000), raw material cost is £40 a unit (that is, £40,000/1,000) and labour cost is £20 a unit (that is, £20,000/1,000). Thus the contribution is £40 a unit (that is, £100 − (£40 + £20)).

If 100 units of sales are lost, £4,000 (that is, 100 × £40) of contributions, and therefore profit, are forgone. Incidentally, this is an alternative means of finding the sales volume variance, to that of calculating the difference between the original and flexed budget profit figures. Once we have produced the flexed budget, however, it is generally easier to simply compare the two profit figures.

The difference between the original and flexed budget profit figures is called the **sales volume variance**.

In this case, it is an **adverse variance** because, taken alone, it has the effect of making the actual profit lower than the budgeted profit. A variance that has the effect of increasing profit beyond the budgeted profit is known as a **favourable variance**. We can therefore say that a **variance** is the effect of one factor (taken alone) on the budgeted profit. Shortly we shall consider other forms of variance, some of which may be favourable and some adverse. The difference between the sum of all the various favourable and adverse variances will represent the difference between the budgeted and actual profit. This is shown in Figure 13.4.

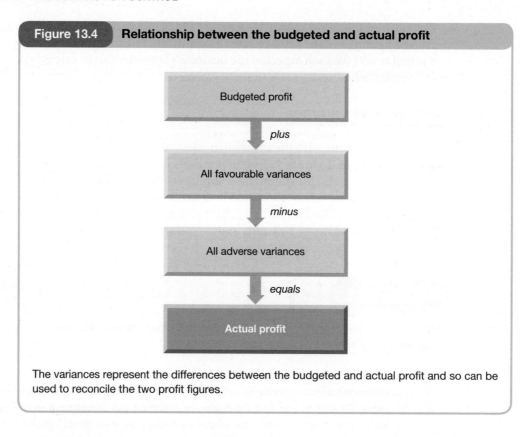

Figure 13.4 Relationship between the budgeted and actual profit

The variances represent the differences between the budgeted and actual profit and so can be used to reconcile the two profit figures.

When calculating a particular variance, such as that for sales volume, we assume that all other factors went according to plan.

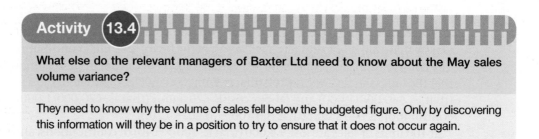

Activity 13.4

What else do the relevant managers of Baxter Ltd need to know about the May sales volume variance?

They need to know why the volume of sales fell below the budgeted figure. Only by discovering this information will they be in a position to try to ensure that it does not occur again.

Who should be held accountable for this sales volume variance? The answer is probably the sales manager, who should know precisely why this has occurred. This is not the same as saying, however, that it was the sales manager's fault. The problem may have been that the business failed to produce the budgeted quantities so that not enough items were available to sell. Nevertheless, the sales manager should know the reason for the problem.

The budget and actual figures for Baxter Ltd for June are given in Activity 13.5 and will be used as the basis for a series of activities that provide an opportunity to calculate and assess the variances. We shall continue to use the May figures, however, for explaining the variances.

Note that the business had budgeted for a higher level of output for June than it did for May.

Activity 13.5

The following are the budgeted and actual income statements for the month of June:

	Budget for June	Actual for June
Output (production and sales)	1,100 units	1,150 units
	£	£
Sales revenue	110,000	113,500
Raw materials	(44,000) (44,000 metres)	(46,300) (46,300 metres)
Labour	(22,000) (2,750 hours)	(23,200) (2,960 hours)
Fixed overheads	(20,000)	(19,300)
Operating profit	24,000	24,700

Try flexing the June budget, comparing it with the original June budget and so find the sales volume variance.

	Flexed budget
Output (production and sales)	1,150 units
	£
Sales revenue	115,000
Raw materials	(46,000) (46,000 metres)
Labour	(23,000) (2,875 hours)
Fixed overheads	(20,000)
Operating profit	26,000

The sales volume variance is £2,000 (favourable) (that is, £26,000 − £24,000). It is favourable because the original budget profit was lower than the flexed budget profit. This arises from more sales actually being made than were budgeted.

For the month of May, we have already identified one reason why the budgeted profit of £20,000 was not achieved and that the actual profit was only £16,900. This was the £4,000 loss of profit (adverse variance) that arose from the sales volume shortfall. Now that the budget is flexed, we can compare the other factors, like with like, and reach further conclusions about May's trading.

We can see that May's sales revenue, raw materials, labour and fixed overheads figures all differ between the flexed budget and the actual results. This means that the adverse sales volume variance was not the only problem area. To gain further information relating to each of the revenue and cost items mentioned, we need to calculate further variances. We shall now do this.

Sales price variance

Starting with the sales revenue figure, we can see that, for May, there is a difference of £2,000 (favourable) between the flexed budget and the actual figures. This can only arise from higher prices being charged than were envisaged in the original budget, because any variance arising from the volume difference has already been 'stripped out' in the flexing process. This price difference is known as the **sales price variance.** Higher sales prices will, all other things being equal, mean more profit. So there is a favourable variance.

When senior management is trying to identify the reason for a sales price variance, the sales manager should normally be able to provide this. As we shall see later in the chapter, favourable variances of significant size will normally be investigated.

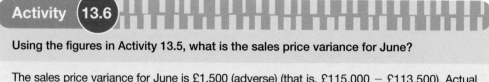

Activity 13.6

Using the figures in Activity 13.5, what is the sales price variance for June?

The sales price variance for June is £1,500 (adverse) (that is, £115,000 − £113,500). Actual sales prices, on average, must have been lower than those budgeted. The actual price averaged £98.70 (that is, £113,500/1,150) whereas the budgeted price was £100. Selling output at a lower price than that budgeted will have an adverse effect on profit, hence an adverse variance.

The sales variances for May are summarised in Figure 13.5.

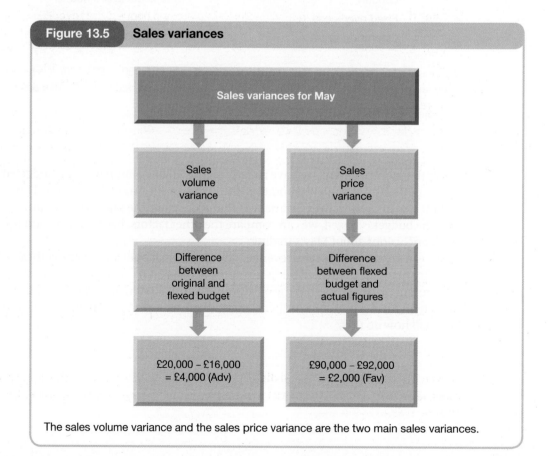

Figure 13.5 **Sales variances**

The sales volume variance and the sales price variance are the two main sales variances.

Let us now move on to look at the cost variances, starting with materials variances.

Materials variances

In May, there was an overall or **total direct materials variance** of £900 (adverse) (that is, £36,900 − £36,000). It is adverse because the actual material cost was higher than the budgeted one, which has an adverse effect on operating profit.

Who should be held accountable for this variance? The answer depends on whether the difference arises from excess usage of the raw material, in which case it is the production manager, or whether it is a higher-than-budgeted cost per metre being paid, in which case it is the buying manager. Fortunately, we can go beyond this total variance to examine the effect of changes in both usage and cost.

We can see from the figures that in May there was a 1,000 metre excess usage of the raw material (that is, 37,000 metres − 36,000 metres). All other things being equal, this alone would have led to a profit shortfall of £1,000, since clearly the budgeted cost per metre is £1. The £1,000 (adverse) variance is known as the **direct materials usage variance.** Normally, this variance would be the responsibility of the production manager.

Activity 13.7

Using the figures in Activity 13.5, what was the direct material usage variance for June?

The direct material usage variance for June was £300 (adverse) (that is, (46,300 metres − 46,000 metres) × £1). It is adverse because more material was used than was budgeted, for an output of 1,150 units. Excess usage of material will tend to reduce profit.

The other aspect of direct materials is their cost. The **direct materials price variance** simply takes the actual cost of materials used and compares it with the budgeted cost, given the quantity used. In May, the actual cost of direct materials used was £36,900, whereas the budgeted cost of the 37,000 metres was £37,000. Thus we have a favourable variance of £100. Paying less than the budgeted cost will have a favourable effect on profit, hence a favourable variance.

Activity 13.8

Using the figures in Activity 13.5, what was the direct materials price variance for June?

The direct materials price variance for June was zero (that is, £46,300 − (46,300 × £1)).

As we have just seen, the total direct materials variance is the sum of the usage variance and the price variance. The relationship between the direct materials variances for May is shown in Figure 13.6.

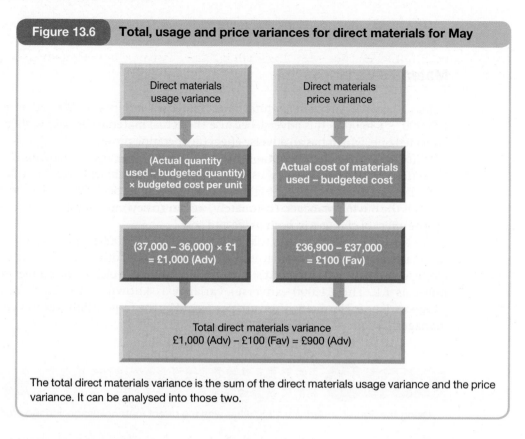

Figure 13.6 Total, usage and price variances for direct materials for May

The total direct materials variance is the sum of the direct materials usage variance and the price variance. It can be analysed into those two.

Labour variances

Direct labour variances are similar in form to those for direct materials. The **total direct labour variance** for May was £500 (favourable) (that is, £18,000 − £17,500). It is favourable because £500 less was spent on labour than was budgeted for the actual level of output achieved.

Again, this total variance is not particularly helpful and needs to be analysed further into its usage and cost elements. We should bear in mind that the number of hours used to complete a particular quantity of output is the responsibility of the production manager, whereas the responsibility for the rate of pay lies primarily with the human resources manager.

The **direct labour efficiency variance** compares the number of hours budgeted for the achieved level of production with the actual number of hours taken. It then costs this difference at the budgeted hourly rate. For May, the budgeted hourly rate is £8 as the original budget shows that 2,500 hours were budgeted to cost £20,000. Thus, the variance is (2,250 hours − 2,150 hours) × £8 = £800 (favourable). It is favourable because fewer hours were worked than budgeted for the actual level of output. Working more quickly tends to increase profit.

Activity 13.9

Using the figures in Activity 13.5, what was the direct labour efficiency variance for June?

The direct labour efficiency variance for June was £680 (adverse) (that is, (2,960 hours − 2,875 hours) × £8). It is adverse because the work took longer than the budget allowed and so will have an adverse effect on profit.

The **direct labour rate variance** compares the actual cost of the hours worked with their budgeted cost. For 2,150 hours worked in May, the budgeted cost would be £17,200 (that is, 2,150 × £8). So, the direct labour rate variance is £300 (adverse) (that is, £17,500 − £17,200).

Activity 13.10

Using the figures in Activity 13.5, what was the direct labour rate variance for June?

The direct labour rate variance for June was £480 (favourable) (that is, (2,960 × £8) − £23,200). It is favourable because a lower rate was paid than budgeted. Paying a lower wage rate will have a favourable effect on profit.

The relationship between the direct labour variances for May is shown in Figure 13.7.

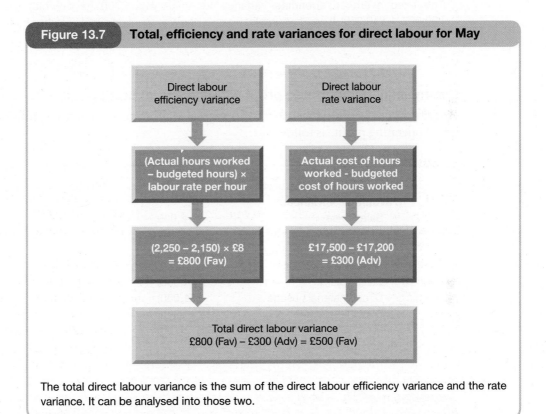

Figure 13.7   Total, efficiency and rate variances for direct labour for May

The total direct labour variance is the sum of the direct labour efficiency variance and the rate variance. It can be analysed into those two.

Fixed overhead variance

The final area is that of overheads. In our example, we have assumed that all of the overheads are fixed. Variable overheads certainly exist in practice, but they have been omitted here simply to restrict the amount of detail. Variances involving variable overheads are similar in style to labour and material variances.

The **fixed overhead spending variance** is simply the difference between the flexed (or original – they will be the same) budget and the actual figures. For May, this was £700 (adverse) (that is, £20,700 − £20,000). It is adverse because more overheads cost was actually incurred than was budgeted. This will lead to less profit. In theory, this is the responsibility of whoever controls overheads expenditure.

In practice, overheads can be a very slippery area and one that is notoriously difficult to control. Overheads, both fixed and variable, are made up of more than one type of cost. Typically, they include such things as rent, administrative costs, management salaries, cleaning, electricity and so on. Each item mentioned could be separately budgeted and the actual figures recorded. Individual spending variances can then be identified for each overhead item to reveal problem areas.

Activity 13.11

Using the figures in Activity 13.5, what was the fixed overhead spending variance for June?

The fixed overhead spending variance for June was £700 (favourable) (that is, £20,000 − £19,300). It was favourable because less was spent on overheads than budgeted, thereby having a favourable effect on profit.

Reconciling the budgeted profit with the actual profit

We are now in a position to reconcile the original May budgeted operating profit with the actual operating profit, as follows:

	£	£
Budgeted operating profit		20,000
Favourable variances		
Sales price	2,000	
Direct materials price	100	
Direct labour efficiency	800	2,900
Adverse variances		
Sales volume	(4,000)	
Direct materials usage	(1,000)	
Direct labour rate	(300)	
Fixed overhead spending	(700)	(6,000)
Actual operating profit		16,900

Activity 13.12

If you were the chief executive of Baxter Ltd, what attitude would you take to the overall difference between the budgeted profit and the actual one?
How would you react to the individual variances shown above?

You would probably be concerned about how large the variances are and their direction (favourable or adverse). In particular you may have thought of the following:

● The overall adverse profit variance is £3,100 (that is £20,000 − £16,900). This represents 15.5 per cent of the budgeted profit (that is £3,100/£20,000 × 100%) and you (as chief executive) would almost certainly see it as significant and worrying.

- The £4,000 adverse sales volume variance represents 20 per cent of budgeted profit and would be a particular cause of concern.
- The £2,000 favourable sales price variance represents 10 per cent of budgeted profit. Since this is favourable it might be seen as a cause for celebration rather than concern. On the other hand, it means that Baxter Ltd's output was, on average, sold at prices 10 per cent above the planned price. This could have been the cause of the worrying adverse sales volume variance. The business may have sold fewer units because it charged higher prices.
- The £100 favourable direct materials price variance is very small in relation to budgeted profit – only 0.5 per cent. It would be unrealistic to expect the actual figures to hit the precise budgeted figures each month and so this is unlikely to be regarded as significant. The direct materials usage variance, however, represents 5 per cent of the budgeted profit. The chief executive may feel this is cause for concern.
- The £800 favourable direct labour efficiency variance represents 4 per cent of budgeted profit. Although it is a favourable variance, the reasons for it may be worth investigating. The £300 adverse direct labour rate variance represents only 1.5 per cent of the budgeted profit and may not be regarded as significant.
- The £700 fixed overhead adverse variance represents 3.5 per cent of budgeted profit. The chief executive may feel that this is too low to cause real concern.

The chief executive will now need to ask some questions as to why things went so badly wrong in several areas and what can be done to improve future performance.

We shall shortly come back to the dilemma as to which variances to investigate and which to accept.

Activity 13.13

Using the figures in Activity 13.5, reconcile the original operating profit figure for June with the actual June figure.

	£	£
Budgeted operating profit		24,000
Favourable variances		
Sales volume	2,000	
Direct labour rate	480	
Fixed overhead spending	700	3,180
Adverse variances		
Sales price	(1,500)	
Direct materials usage	(300)	
Direct labour efficiency	(680)	(2,480)
Actual operating profit		24,700

Activity (13.14)

The following are the budgeted and actual income statements for Baxter Ltd for the month of July:

	Budget	Actual
Output (production and sales)	1,000 units	1,050 units
	£	£
Sales revenue	100,000	104,300
Raw materials	(40,000) (40,000 metres)	(41,200) (40,500 metres)
Labour	(20,000) (2,500 hours)	(21,300) (2,600 hours)
Fixed overheads	(20,000)	(19,400)
Operating profit	20,000	22,400

Produce a reconciliation of the budgeted and actual operating profit, going into as much detail as possible with the variance analysis.

The original budget, the flexed budget and the actual outcome are as follows:

	Original budget	Flexed budget	Actual
Output (production and sales)	1,000 units	1,050 units	1,050 units
	£	£	£
Sales revenue	100,000	105,000	104,300
Raw materials	(40,000)	(42,000) (42,000 m)	(41,200) (40,500 m)
Labour	(20,000)	(21,000) (2,625 hr)	(21,300) (2,600 hr)
Fixed overheads	(20,000)	(20,000)	(19,400)
Operating profit	20,000	22,000	22,400

Reconciliation of the budgeted and actual operating profits for July

	£	£
Budgeted operating profit		20,000
Favourable variances:		
Sales volume (22,000 − 20,000)	2,000	
Direct materials usage ((42,000 − 40,500) × £1)	1,500	
Direct labour efficiency ((2,625 − 2,600) × £8)	200	
Fixed overhead spending (20,000 − 19,400)	600	4,300
Adverse variances:		
Sales price (105,000 − 104,300)	(700)	
Direct materials price ((40,500 × £1) − 41,200)	(700)	
Direct labour rate ((2,600 × £8) − 21,300)	(500)	(1,900)
Actual operating profit		22,400

Real World 13.2 shows how two UK-based businesses, the engine manufacturer Rolls-Royce Holdings plc and the food ingredients business Tate and Lyle plc, use variance analysis to exercise control over their operations. Many businesses explain in their annual reports how they operate systems of budgetary control.

Real World 13.2

Variance analysis in practice

Controlling the engines

In its 2016 annual report, Rolls-Royce Holdings plc states:

> The Group has a comprehensive budgeting system with an annual budget approved by the Board. Revised forecasts for the year are reported at least quarterly. Actual results, at both a business and Group level, are reported monthly against budget and variances are kept under scrutiny.

Refined controls

Tate and Lyle plc makes it clear that it too uses budgets and variance analysis to help keep control over its activities. The 2015 annual report states that there is:

> A comprehensive planning and budgeting system for all items of expenditure with an annual budget approved by the Board. Performance is reported monthly against budget and prior year results; significant variances are investigated.

The boards of directors of these businesses will not seek explanations of variances arising at each department, but they will be looking at figures for the businesses as a whole or the results for major divisions of them.

Equally certainly, department managers will receive a monthly (or perhaps more frequent) report of variances arising within their area of responsibility alone.

Sources: Rolls-Royce Holdings plc Annual Report 2016, p. 64; Tate & Lyle plc Annual Report 2015, p. 51.

Real World 13.3 gives some indication of the importance of flexible budgeting in practice.

Real World 13.3

Flexing the budgets

A survey of the UK food and drinks industry provides us with an indication of the importance attached by management accountants to flexible budgeting. The survey asked those in charge of the management accounting function to rate the importance of flexible budgeting by selecting one of three possible categories – 'not important', 'moderately important' or 'important'. Figure 13.8 sets out the results, from the sample of 117 respondents.

Real World 13.3 *continued*

| Figure 13.8 | Degree of importance attached to flexible budgeting |

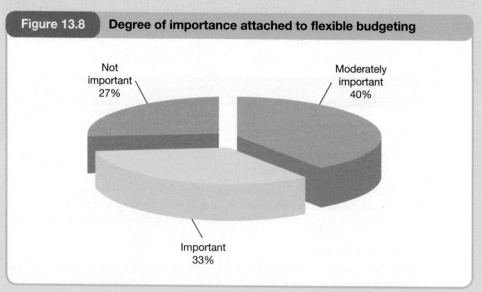

Respondents were also asked to state the frequency with which flexible budgeting was used within the business, using a five-point scale ranging from 1 (never) through to 5 (very often). Figure 13.9 sets out these results.

| Figure 13.9 | Frequency of use of flexible budgets |

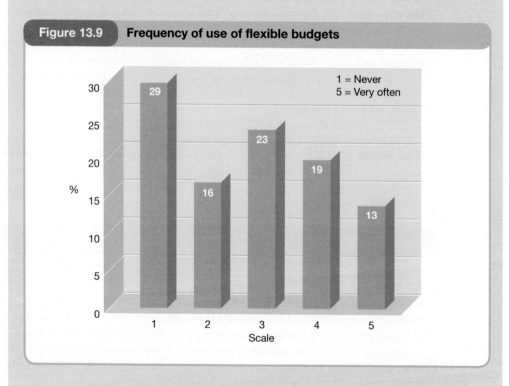

We can see that, while flexible budgeting is regarded as important by a significant proportion of management accountants and is being used in practice, not all businesses use it.

Source: Taken from information appearing in Abdel-Kader, M. and Luther, R. (2004) *An Empirical Investigation of the Evolution of Management Accounting Practices*, Working paper No. 04/06, University of Essex, October.

Reasons for adverse variances

Adverse variances may occur simply because the budgets against which performance is being measured are unachievable. If this is the case, budgets will not provide a useful means of exercising control. There are other reasons, however, that may lead to actual performance deviating from budgeted performance.

Activity 13.15

The variances that we have considered are:

- sales volume;
- sales price;
- direct materials usage;
- direct materials price;
- direct labour efficiency;
- direct labour rate; and
- fixed overhead spending.

Assuming that the budget targets are reasonable, jot down possible reasons for *adverse* variances arising for each of the above.

The reasons that we thought of included the following:

Sales volume
- Poor performance by sales staff.
- Deterioration in market conditions between the time the budget was set and the actual event.
- Lack of goods or services to sell as a result of some production problem.

Sales price
- Poor performance by sales staff.
- Deterioration in market conditions between the time the budget was set and the actual event.

Direct materials usage
- Poor performance by production department staff, leading to high rates of scrap.
- Substandard materials, leading to high rates of scrap.
- Faulty machinery, causing high rates of scrap.

Direct materials price
- Poor performance by the buying department staff.
- Using higher quality material than was planned.
- Change in market conditions between the time when the budget was set and the actual event.

Labour efficiency
- Poor supervision.
- A low skill grade of worker taking longer to do the work than envisaged for a higher skill grade.
- Low-grade materials, leading to high levels of scrap and wasted labour time.
- Problems with a customer for whom a service is being rendered.

Activity 13.15 *continued*

- Problems with machinery, leading to labour time being wasted.
- Dislocation of materials supply, leading to workers being unable to proceed with production.

Labour rate
- Poor performance by the human resources department.
- Using a higher grade of worker than planned.
- Change in labour market conditions between the time the budget was set and the actual event.

Fixed overheads
- Poor supervision of overheads.
- General increase in costs of overheads not taken into account in the budget.

Note that different variances may have the same underlying cause. For example, the purchase of low quality, cheaper materials may result in an unfavourable direct materials usage variance, a favourable direct materials price variance and an unfavourable direct labour efficiency variance.

Variance analysis in service industries

Although we have used the example of a manufacturing business to explain variance analysis, this does not imply that variance analysis is irrelevant for service-sector businesses. It is simply that manufacturing businesses usually have all of the variances found in practice. Service businesses, for example, may not have material variances.

Next plc, the well-known retailer, uses budgets and variance analysis to help manage its business, according to its 2016 annual report. It is probably the case that most major service-sector businesses use some form of variance reporting to help them keep control of their affairs.

Non-operating profit variances

There are many areas of business where a budget will be used, but where any variances will not have a direct effect on operating profit. The variances will often, however, have an indirect effect and, sometimes, a profound one. The cash budget, for example, sets out planned receipts, payments and the resultant cash balance for the period. If this budget turns out to be wrong because of, say, unforeseen expenditures, there may be unplanned cash shortages and accompanying costs. These costs may be limited to interest incurred on borrowing. If, however, borrowing cannot cover the cash shortage, the consequences could be more serious, such as lost profits from projects that are abandoned due to lack of funds.

Control must, therefore, be exercised over areas such as cash management, to try to avoid adverse **non-operating-profit variances.**

Investigating variances

It is unreasonable to expect budget targets to be met precisely each month and so variances will usually arise. Discovering the reasons for these variances can be costly. Information will usually have to be produced and examined and discussions with appropriate members of staff carried out. Sometimes, activities may have to be brought to a halt to discover what went wrong. Since small variances are almost inevitable, and investigating variances can be expensive, managers need some guiding principle concerning which variances to investigate and which to accept.

Activity 13.16

What principle do you feel should guide managers when deciding whether to spend money investigating a particular variance? (*Hint*: Think back to Chapter 1)

When deciding whether to produce accounting information, there should be a consideration of both benefit and cost. The benefit likely to be gained from knowing why a variance arose needs to be weighed against the cost of obtaining that knowledge.

There are difficulties in implementing this principle, however, as both the value of the benefit and the cost of investigation may be difficult to assess in advance of the investigation.

The following practical guidelines for investigating variances, which try to take some account of benefit and cost, may be adopted by managers:

- Significant *adverse* variances should normally be investigated, as a continuation of the underlying problem could be very costly. What 'significant' means must ultimately be a matter of managerial judgement. It may be decided, for example, that variances above a threshold of a percentage of the budgeted figure (say, 5 per cent) or a fixed financial amount (say, £1,000) are considered significant.
- Significant *favourable* variances should probably be investigated. Although they may not cause such immediate concern as adverse variances, they still indicate that things are not going according to plan. If actual performance is significantly better than planned, it may mean that the budget target is unrealistically low.
- Insignificant variances, though not triggering immediate investigation, should be kept under review. For each aspect of operations, the cumulative sum of variances, over a series of control periods, should be zero, with small adverse variances in some periods being compensated for by small favourable ones in others. This is because small variances caused by random factors will not necessarily recur and they are as likely to be favourable as adverse. Where a variance is caused by systemic (non-random) factors, which recur over time, the cumulative sum of the periodic variances will not be zero

but an increasing figure. Even though the individual variances may be insignificant, the cumulative effect of these variances may not. Thus, an investigation may well be worthwhile, particularly if the variances are adverse. Example 13.2 looks at this review process.

While these guidelines may be of some help, managers must be flexible. They may, for example, decide against investigating a significant variance where the cost of correcting the potential causes is expected to be very high. They may calculate that it would be cheaper to live with the problem and so adjust the budget.

To illustrate the cumulative effect of relatively small systemic variances, let us consider Example 13.2.

Example 13.2

Indisurers Ltd finds that the variances for direct labour efficiency for processing motor insurance claims, since the beginning of the year, are as follows:

	£		£
January	250 (adverse)	July	200 (adverse)
February	150 (favourable)	August	150 (favourable)
March	50 (favourable)	September	230 (adverse)
April	200 (adverse)	October	150 (favourable)
May	220 (adverse)	November	50 (favourable)
June	80 (favourable)	December	260 (adverse)

The average total cost of labour performing this task is about £12,000 a month. Management believes that none of these variances, taken alone, is significant given the monthly labour cost. The question is, are they significant when taken together? If we add them together, taking account of the signs, we find that we have a net adverse variance for the year of £730. Of itself this, too, is probably not significant, but we should expect the cumulative total to be close to zero where the variances are random. We might feel that a pattern is developing and, given long enough, a net adverse variance of significant size might build up.

Investigating the labour efficiency might be worth doing. Finding the cause of the variance would put management in a position to correct a systemic fault, which could lead to future cost savings. (Note that 12 periods are probably not enough to reach a statistically sound conclusion on whether the variances are random or not, but it provides an illustration of the point.)

Plotting the cumulative variances, from month to month, as in Figure 13.10, makes it clear what is happening as time proceeds.

| Figure 13.10 | The cumulative variances for labour efficiency in motor insurance claim handling at Indisurers Ltd |

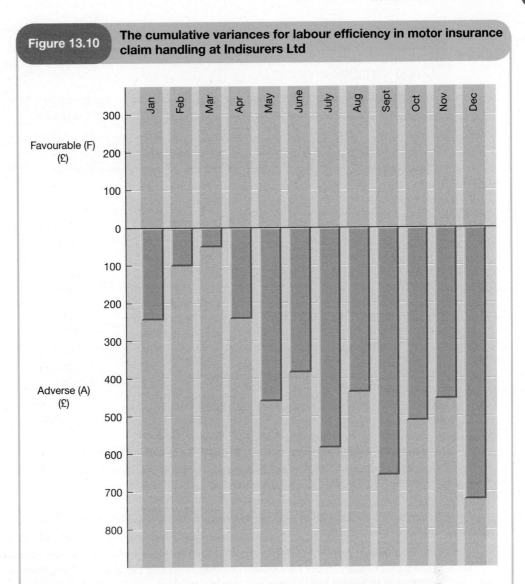

Starting at zero at the beginning of January, each month the cumulative variance is plotted. This is the sum taking account of positive and negative signs. The January figure is £250 (A). The February one is £100 (A) (that is £250 (A) plus £150 (F)) and so on. The graph seems to show an overall trend of adverse variances, but with several favourable variances involved.

Variance analysis in practice

Real World 13.4 provides some evidence concerning the use of variance analysis.

Real World 13.4

Using variance analysis

The CIMA survey, mentioned in previous chapters, examined the extent to which the use of variance analysis varies with business size. Figure 13.11 shows the results.

Figure 13.11 **Variance analysis and business size**

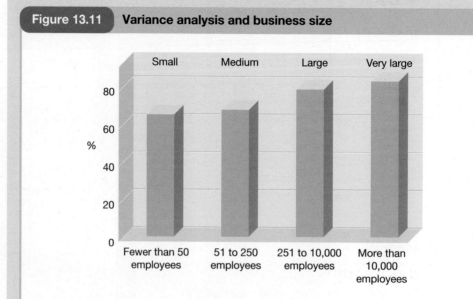

The use of this approach increases in line with the size of the business.

Source: Figure adapted from CIMA (2009) *Management Accounting Tools for Today and Tomorrow*, p. 12.

The survey also indicated that variance analysis was the most widely used of a variety of costing tools examined (which included the techniques covered in previous chapters). Overall, more than 70 per cent of respondents used this technique.

The CIMA survey indicated that there is a tendency for smaller businesses to be less likely to use variance analysis. This was supported by the survey of seven small and four medium-sized UK businesses, which we met earlier in the chapter, that found that none of these 11 businesses used variance analysis.

Source: CIMA (2009) 'Management accounting tools for today and tomorrow', p.12.

Compensating variances

There may be superficial appeal in the idea of **compensating variances.** These are linked favourable and adverse variances, which are traded off against each other. A sales manager, for example, may suggest that more units of a particular service could be sold if prices were lowered and that, overall, this would result in increased profits. This suggestion would lead to a favourable sales volume variance, but also to an adverse sales price variance. On the face of it, provided that the former is greater than the latter, all would be well.

Activity 13.17

Can you think of a reason why the sales manager should not go ahead with the price reduction?

The change in policy will have ramifications for other areas of the business, including:

- the need to supply more of the service: staff and other resources may not be available to accommodate this increase; and/or
- the need to provide more finance: increased levels of activity will lead to an increased need for funds to pay, for example, additional staff costs.

Trading off variances in this way is, therefore, not normally acceptable without a more far-reaching consultation and revision of plans.

Standard quantities and costs

We have already seen that a budget is a business plan for the short term – typically one year – that is expressed mainly in financial terms. A budget is typically constructed from standards. **Standard quantities and costs** (or revenues) are those planned for an individual unit of input or output and provide the building blocks for budgets.

We can say about Baxter Ltd's operations (see Example 13.1 on page 521) that:

- the standard selling price is £100 for one unit of output;
- the standard marginal cost for one manufactured unit is £60;
- the standard raw materials cost is £40 for one unit of output;
- the standard raw materials usage is 40 metres for one unit of output;
- the standard raw materials price is £1 a metre (that is, for one unit of input);
- the standard labour cost is £20 for one unit of output;
- the standard labour time is 2.50 hours for one unit of output; and
- the standard labour rate is £8 an hour (that is, for one unit of input).

Standards, like the budgets to which they are closely linked, represent targets against which actual performance can be measured. They also provide the basis for variance analysis, which, as we have seen, helps managers to identify where deviations from planned, or standard, performance have occurred and the extent of those deviations. To maintain their usefulness for planning and control purposes, they should be subject to frequent review and, where necessary, revision.

Real World 13.5 provides some evidence on the frequency of updating standards in practice.

Real World 13.5

Keeping up standards

KPMG, the accountancy firm, conducted interviews with senior financial officers of 12 large international manufacturing businesses covering pharmaceuticals, industrials and consumer goods. A key finding was that increasing economic volatility was leading to more frequent updates of standards. Most of the businesses updated standards annually. However, one updated on a quarterly basis, but another had not updated for two years because of the costs and time involved.

Source: KPMG (2010) *Standard costing: insights from leading companies,* February.

Standards may be applied to a wide variety of products or services. A firm of accountants, for example, may set standard costs per hour for each grade of staff (audit manager, audit senior, trainee and so on). When planning a particular audit of a client business, it can decide the standard hours that each grade of staff should spend on the audit and, using the standard cost per hour for each grade, it can derive a standard cost or 'budget' for the job as a whole. These standards can subsequently be compared with the actual hours and hourly rates.

Setting standards

When setting standards various matters have to be considered. We shall now explore some of the more important of these.

Who sets the standards?

Standards often result from the collective effort of various individuals including management accountants, industrial engineers, human resource managers, production managers and other employees. The manager responsible for achieving a particular standard will usually have some involvement and may provide specialised knowledge. This involvement, however, provides the risk that 'slack' may be built into the standard in order to make it easier to achieve. The same problem was mentioned earlier in relation to budgets.

How is information gathered?

Setting standards involves gathering information concerning how much material should be used, how much machine time should be required, how much direct labour time should be spent and so on. Two possible ways of collecting information for standard setting are available.

Activity 13.18

Can you think what these possible ways are?

The first is to examine the particular processes and tasks involved in producing the product or service and to develop suitable estimates. Standards concerning material usage, machine time and direct labour hours may be established by carrying out dummy production runs, time-and-motion studies and so on. This will require close collaboration between the management accountant, industrial engineers and those involved in the production process.

The second approach is to collect information relating to past costs, times and usage for the same, or similar, products and to use this information as a basis for predicting the future. This information may have to be adjusted to reflect changes in price, changes in the production process and so on.

Where the product or service is entirely new, or involves entirely new processes, the first approach will probably have to be used, even though it is usually more costly.

What kind of standards should be used?

There are basically two types of standards that may be used: **ideal standards** and **practical standards.** Ideal standards, as the name suggests, assume perfect operating conditions where there is no inefficiency due to lost production time, defects and so on. The objective of setting ideal standards, which are attainable in theory at least, is to encourage employees to strive towards excellence. Practical standards, also as the name suggests, do not assume ideal operating conditions. Although they demand a high level of efficiency, account is taken of possible lost production time, defects and so on. They are designed to be challenging yet achievable.

There are two major difficulties with using ideal standards.

- They do not provide a useful basis for exercising control. Unless the standards set are realistic, any variances computed are extremely difficult to interpret.
- They may not achieve their intended purpose of motivating managers; indeed, the opposite may occur. As we shall see a little later, the evidence suggests that where managers regard a target as beyond their grasp, it is likely to have a demotivating effect.

Given these problems, it is not surprising that practical standards seem to enjoy more widespread support than ideal standards. Nevertheless, by taking account of wastage, lost production time and so on, there is a risk that they will entrench operating inefficiencies.

The learning-curve effect

Where an activity undertaken by direct workers has been unchanged for some time, and the workers are experienced at performing it, the standard labour time will normally stay unchanged. However, where a new activity is introduced, or new workers are involved with performing an existing activity, a **learning-curve** effect will normally occur. This is shown in Figure 13.12.

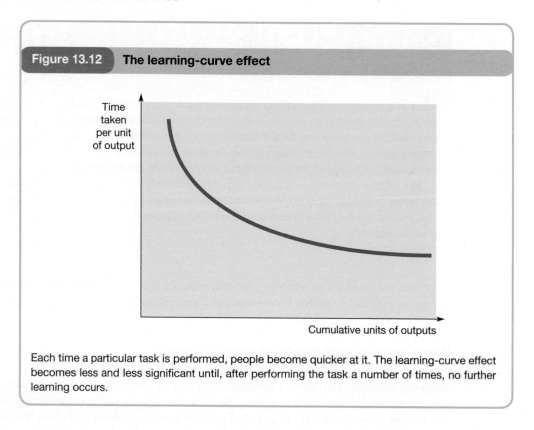

Figure 13.12 **The learning-curve effect**

Each time a particular task is performed, people become quicker at it. The learning-curve effect becomes less and less significant until, after performing the task a number of times, no further learning occurs.

The first unit of output takes a relatively long time to produce. As experience is gained, the worker takes less time to produce each successive unit of output. The rate of reduction in the time taken will, however, decrease as experience is gained. Thus, for example, the reduction in time taken between the first and second unit produced will be much greater than the reduction between, say, the ninth and the tenth. Eventually, the rate of reduction in time taken will reduce to zero so that each unit will take as long as the preceding one. At this point, where the curve in Figure 13.12 becomes horizontal (the bottom right of the graph), the learning-curve effect will have been eliminated and a steady, long-term standard time for the activity will have been established.

The learning-curve effect seems to have little to do with whether workers are skilled or unskilled; if they are unfamiliar with the task, the learning-curve effect will arise. Practical experience shows that learning curves show remarkable regularity and, therefore, predictability from one activity to another.

The learning-curve effect applies equally well to activities involved with providing a service (such as dealing with an insurance claim, in an insurance business) as to manufacturing-type activities (like upholstering an armchair by hand, in a furniture-making business).

Clearly, the learning-curve effect must be taken into account when setting standards, and when interpreting any adverse labour efficiency variances, where a new process and/or new staff are involved.

Other uses for standard costing

We have already seen that standards can play a valuable role in performance evaluation and control. However, standards relating to costs, usages, selling prices and so on may also be used for other purposes such as:

- measuring operating efficiency;
- product-sourcing decisions;
- determining the cost of inventories and work in progress for income measurement purposes; and
- determining the cost of items for use in pricing decisions.

This does not mean that standards are regarded as the primary measure in all cases. When making decisions about operating efficiency, product sourcing or pricing, they may be used as a secondary measure.

Real World 13.6 provides some information on the use of standards for decision making.

Real World 13.6

Standard practice

The KPMG survey, mentioned in Real World 13.5 (page 542), found that some of the 12 manufacturing businesses in the study had moved away from using standard costing as the key measure of operating effectiveness and for product-sourcing decisions. Instead, they relied on other operating and financial measures.

Source: KPMG (2010) *Standard costing: insights from leading companies*, February.

Some problems

Although standards and variances may be useful for decision-making purposes, they have limited application. Many business and commercial activities do not have direct relationships between inputs and outputs, as is the case with, say, the number of direct labour hours worked and the number of products manufactured. Many expenses of modern business are in areas such as human resource development, advertising, maintenance of equipment and research and development, where the expense is discretionary and there is no direct link to the level of output.

There are also potential problems when applying **standard costing** techniques. These include the following:

- Standards can quickly become out of date as a result of both changes in the production process and price changes. When standards become outdated, performance can be adversely affected. For example, a human resources manager who finds it impossible to meet targets on rates of pay for labour, because of general labour cost rises, may have less incentive to minimise costs.

- Factors may affect a variance for which a particular manager is accountable but over which the manager has no control. When assessing the manager's performance, these uncontrollable factors should be taken into account, but there is always a risk that they will not.

- In practice, creating clear lines of demarcation between the areas of responsibility of various managers may be difficult. In this case, one of the prerequisites of effective standard costing is lost.

- Once a standard has been met, there is no incentive for employees to improve the quality or quantity of output further. There are usually no additional rewards for doing so, only additional work. Indeed, employees may have a disincentive for exceeding a standard as managers may then view it as too loose and, therefore, in need of tightening. However, simply achieving a standard, and no more, may not be enough in highly competitive and fast-changing markets. To compete effectively, a business may need to strive for continuous improvement and standard costing techniques may impede this process.

- Standard costing may create incentives for managers and employees to act in undesirable ways. It may, for example, encourage the build-up of excess inventories, leading to significant storage and financing costs. This problem can arise where there are opportunities for discounts on bulk purchases of materials, which the purchasing manager then exploits to achieve a favourable direct materials price variance. One way to avoid this problem might be to impose limits on the level of inventories held.

Activity (13.19)

Can you think of another example of how a manager may achieve a favourable direct materials price variance but in doing so would create problems for a business?

A manager may buy cheaper, but lower quality, materials. Although this may lead to a favourable price variance, it may also lead to additional inspection and reworking costs and, perhaps, lost sales.

To avoid this problem, the manager may be required to buy material of a particular quality or from particular sources.

A final example of the perverse incentives created by standard costing relates to labour efficiency variances. Where these variances are calculated for individual employees, and form the basis for their rewards, there is little incentive for them to work co-operatively. Co-operative working may, however, be in the best interests of the business. To avoid this problem, some businesses calculate labour efficiency variances for groups of employees rather than individual employees. This, however, creates the risk that some individuals will become 'free riders' and will rely on the more conscientious employees to carry the load.

Activity (13.20)

How might the business try to eliminate the 'free-rider' problem just mentioned?

One way would be to carry out an evaluation, perhaps by the group members themselves, of individual contributions to group output, as well as evaluating group output as a whole.

Real World 13.7 indicates that, despite the problems mentioned above, standard costing is used by businesses.

Real World 13.7

Standard usage

The CIMA survey, mentioned previously, examined the extent to which the use of standard costing varies with business size. Figure 13.13 shows the results.

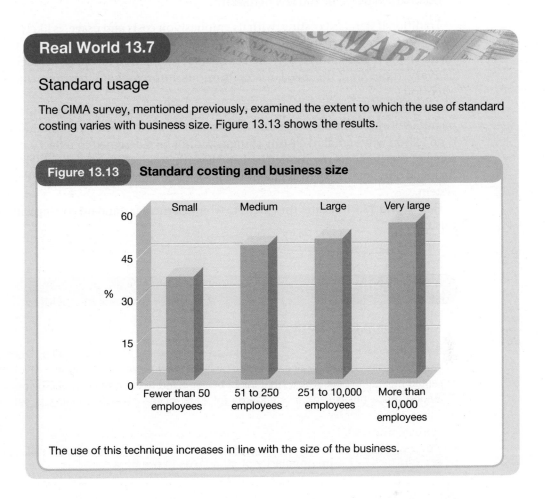

Figure 13.13   Standard costing and business size

The use of this technique increases in line with the size of the business.

The new business environment

The traditional standard costing approach was developed during an era when business operations were characterised by few product lines, long production runs and heavy reliance on direct labour. More recently, the increasingly competitive environment and the onward march of technology have changed the business landscape. Now, many business operations are characterised by a wide range of different products, shorter product life cycles (leading to shorter production runs) and automated production processes. The effect of these changes has resulted in:

- a need for more frequent development of standards to deal with frequent changes to the product range;
- a change in the focus for control – where manufacturing systems are automated, for example, direct labour becomes less important than direct materials; and

- a decline in the importance of monitoring from cost and usage variances – where manufacturing systems are automated, deviations from standards relating to costs and usage become less frequent and less significant.

Traditional standard costing, with its emphasis on costs and usage, is likely to take on less importance for businesses with highly automated production systems. Other elements of the production process such as quality, production levels, product cycle times, delivery times and the need for continuous improvement become the focus of attention.

This does not mean, however, that a standards-based approach is not useful for the new manufacturing environment. It can still provide valuable control information and there is no reason why standard costing systems cannot be redesigned to reflect a concern for some of the elements mentioned earlier. Nevertheless, other measures, including non-financial ones, may help to augment the information provided by the standard costing system.

Real World 13.8 indicates the extent to which particular standard costing variances are calculated.

Real World 13.8

Maintaining standards

Senior financial managers of 33 UK businesses were asked about their costing systems. It emerged that standard costing was used by 30 of the businesses concerned, which represented most of the businesses that might be expected to use this method. The popularity among these businesses of standards for each of the main cost items is set out in Figure 13.14.

Figure 13.14	The popularity of standards in practice

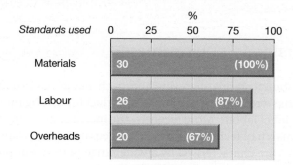

Standards for materials were used by all businesses in the survey that used standard costing. Standards for labour were used by nearly all businesses.

Source: Figure adapted from CIMA (2009) *Management Accounting Tools for Today and Tomorrow*, p. 12.

Despite the popularity of materials standards, the study found that four businesses calculated the total direct materials variance only and that only two-thirds of businesses calculated both the direct materials price and usage variances. For labour standards, the variance analysis is even less complete. The study found that 15 businesses calculated the total direct labour variance only and a mere one-third of businesses calculated both the direct labour and efficiency variances. It seems, therefore, that standard costing was not extensively employed by the businesses.

Source: Figure based on information in Dugdale, D., Jones, C. and Green, S. (2006) *Contemporary Management Accounting Practices in UK Manufacturing*, CIMA Research Publication, Vol.1, No. 13.

Making budgetary control effective

It should be clear from what we have seen of **budgetary control** that a system, or a set of routines, must be put in place to enable the potential benefits to be gained. Most businesses that operate successful budgetary control and standard costing systems tend to share common features. These include the following:

- *A serious attitude taken to the system.* This should apply to all levels of management, right from the very top. For example, senior managers need to make clear to subordinates that they take notice of the monthly variance reports and base some of their actions and decisions upon them.
- *Clear demarcation between areas of managerial responsibility.* It needs to be made clear which manager is responsible for each business area. In this way, accountability can be ascribed for an area that seems to be going out of control.
- *Budget targets that are challenging yet achievable.* Setting unachievable targets is likely to have a demotivating effect. Managers may be permitted to participate in establishing their own targets to help create a sense of ownership. This, in turn, may increase levels of commitment and motivation. We shall consider this in more detail shortly.
- *Established data collection, analysis and reporting routines.* These should take the actual results and the budget figures and use them to calculate and report the variances. This should be part of the business's regular accounting information system, so that the required reports are automatically produced each month.
- *Reports aimed at individual managers, rather than general-purpose documents.* This avoids managers having to read through many pages of reports to find the part that is relevant to them.
- *Fairly short reporting periods.* These would typically be one month long, so that things cannot go too far wrong before they are picked up.
- *Timely variance reports.* Reports should be produced and made available to managers shortly after the end of the relevant reporting period. If it is not until the end of June that a manager is informed that the performance in May was below the budgeted level, it is quite likely that the performance for June will be below target as well. Reports on the performance in May ideally need to emerge in early June.
- *Action being taken to get operations back under control if they are shown to be out of control.* A budget report will not change things by itself. Managers need to take action to try to ensure that the reporting of significant adverse variances leads to action to put things right for the future.

Behavioural issues

Budgets are prepared with the objective of affecting the attitudes and behaviour of managers. The point was made in Chapter 12 that budgets are intended to motivate managers; research evidence generally shows that budgets can be effective in achieving this. More specifically, the research shows:

● The existence of budgets can improve job satisfaction and performance. Where a manager's role might otherwise be ill-defined or ambiguous, budgets can bring structure and certainty. Budgets provide clear, quantifiable, targets to be pursued. This can be reassuring to managers and can increase their level of commitment.

● Demanding, yet achievable, budget targets tend to motivate better than less demanding targets. It seems that setting the most demanding targets that are acceptable to managers is a very effective way to motivate them.

● Unrealistically demanding targets tend to have an adverse effect on managers' performance. Once managers begin to view the budget targets as being too difficult to achieve, their level of motivation and performance declines. The relationship between the level of performance and the perceived degree of budget difficulty is shown in Figure 13.15.

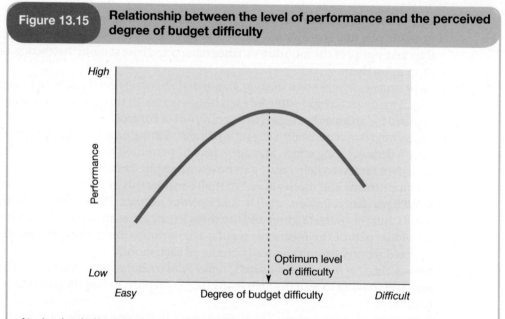

Figure 13.15 **Relationship between the level of performance and the perceived degree of budget difficulty**

At a low level of budget difficulty, performance also tends to be low as managers do not find the targets sufficiently motivating. However, as the degree of difficulty starts to increase, managers rise to the challenge and improve their performance. Beyond a certain point, managers see the budgets as being too difficult to achieve and so motivation and performance decline.

● The participation of managers in setting their targets tends to improve motivation and performance. This is probably because those managers feel a sense of commitment to the targets and a moral obligation to achieve them.

It has been suggested that allowing managers to set their own targets will lead to slack (that is, easily achievable) targets being introduced. This would make achievement of the target that much easier. On the other hand, in an effort to impress, a manager may select a target that is not really achievable. These points imply that care must be taken in the extent to which managers have unfettered choice of their own targets.

Conflict can occur in the budget-setting process, as different groups may well have different agendas. For example, junior managers may be keen to build slack into their budgets while their senior managers may seek to impose unrealistically demanding budget targets. Sometimes, such conflict can be constructive and can result in better decisions being made. To resolve the conflict over budget targets, negotiations may have to take place and other options may have to be explored. This may lead to a better understanding by all parties of the issues involved and final agreement may result in demanding, yet achievable, targets.

The impact of management style

There has been a great deal of discussion among experts on the way in which managers use information generated by the budgeting system and the impact of its use on the attitudes and behaviour of subordinates (that is, the staff). A pioneering study by Hopwood (see reference 1 at the end of the chapter) examined the way that managers, working within a manufacturing environment, used budget information to evaluate the performance of subordinates. He argued that three distinct styles of management could be observed. These are:

- *Budget-constrained style.* This management style focuses rigidly on the ability of subordinates to meet the budget. Other factors relating to the performance of subordinates are not given serious consideration even though they might include improving the long-term effectiveness of the area for which the subordinate has responsibility.
- *Profit-conscious style.* This management style uses budget information in a more flexible way and often in conjunction with other data. The main focus is on the ability of each subordinate to improve long-term effectiveness.
- *Non-accounting style.* In this case, budget information plays no significant role in the evaluation of a subordinate's performance.

Activity 13.21

How might a manager respond to information that indicates a subordinate has not met the budget targets for the period, assuming the manager adopts:

(a) a budget-constrained style?
(b) a profit-conscious style?
(c) a non-accounting style?

(a) A manager adopting a budget-constrained style is likely to take the budget information very seriously. This may result in criticism of the subordinate and, perhaps, some form of sanction.
(b) A manager adopting a profit-conscious style is likely to take a broader view when examining the budget information and so will take other factors into consideration (for example, factors that could not have been anticipated at the time of preparing the budgets), before deciding whether criticism or a sanction is justified.
(c) A manager adopting a non-accounting style will regard the failure to meet the budget as being relatively unimportant and so no action may be taken.

Hopwood found that subordinates working for a manager who adopts a budget-constrained style had unpleasant experiences. They suffered higher levels of job-related stress and had poorer working relationships, with both their colleagues and their manager, than those whose manager adopted one of the other two styles. Hopwood also found that the subordinates of a budget-constrained style of manager were more likely to manipulate the budget figures, or to take other undesirable actions, to ensure the budgets were met.

Reservations about the Hopwood study

Although Hopwood's findings are interesting, subsequent studies have cast doubt on their universal applicability. Later studies confirm that human attitudes and behaviour are complex and can vary according to the particular situation. For example, it has been found that the impact of different management styles on such factors as job-related stress and the manipulation of budget figures seems to vary. It is likely to depend on such factors as the level of independence enjoyed by the subordinates and the level of uncertainty associated with the tasks to be undertaken.

It seems that where there is a high level of interdependence between business divisions, subordinate managers are more likely to feel that they have less control over their performance. This is because the performance of staff in other divisions could be an important influence on the final outcome. In such a situation, rigid application of the budget could be viewed as being unfair and may lead to undesirable behaviour. However, where managers have a high degree of independence, the application of budgets as a measure of performance is likely to be more acceptable. In this case, the managers are likely to feel that the final outcome is much less dependent on the performance of others.

Later studies have also shown that where a subordinate is undertaking a task that has a high degree of uncertainty concerning the outcome (for example, developing a new product), budget targets are unlikely to be an adequate measure of performance. In such a situation, other factors and measures should be taken into account in order to derive a more complete assessment of performance. However, where a task has a low degree of uncertainty concerning the outcome (for example, producing a standard product using standard equipment and an experienced workforce), budget measures may be regarded as more reliable indicators of performance. Thus, it appears that a budget-constrained style is more likely to work where subordinates enjoy a fair amount of independence and where the tasks set have a low level of uncertainty concerning their outcomes.

Failing to meet the budget

The existence of budgets gives senior managers a ready means to assess the performance of their subordinates (that is, junior managers). If a subordinate fails to meet a budget, the relevant senior manager must handle this carefully. Adverse variances may imply that the subordinate needs help. If this were the case, a harsh, critical approach would have a demotivating effect and would be counterproductive.

Real World 13.9 gives some indication of the effects of the **behavioural aspects of budgetary control** in practice.

Real World 13.9

Behavioural problems

A survey indicated that there is a large degree of participation in setting budgets by those who will be expected to perform to the budget (the budget holders).

The survey also showed that senior managers have greater influence in setting the targets than their junior manager budget holders. Where there is a conflict between the cost estimates submitted by the budget holders and their senior managers, in 40 per cent of respondent businesses the senior manager's view would prevail without negotiation. In nearly 60 per cent of cases, however, a reduction would be negotiated between the budget holder and the senior manager. The general philosophy of the businesses that responded to the survey, regarding budget holders influencing the setting of their own budgets, is:

- 23 per cent of respondents believe that budget holders should not have too much influence since they will seek to obtain easy budgets (build in slack) if they do;
- 69 per cent of respondents take an opposite view.

The general view on how senior managers should judge their subordinates is:

- 46 per cent of respondent businesses think that senior managers should judge junior managers mainly on their ability to achieve the budget;
- 40 per cent think otherwise.

Although this research is not very recent (1993), in the absence of more recent evidence it provides some feel for budget setting in practice.

Source: Drury, C., Braund, S., Osborne, P. and Tayles, M. (1993) *A Survey of Management Accounting Practices in UK Manufacturing Companies*, Chartered Association of Certified Accountants.

Budgets and innovation

We saw in Chapter 12 that budgets are often criticised for reinforcing a 'command and control' structure that concentrates power in the hands of senior managers and prevents junior managers from exercising autonomy. It has been argued that this can deter innovation and can leave subordinates feeling constrained and frustrated. There is no compelling evidence, however, to support this view. **Real World 13.10** discusses some research that explored the possible tension between budgetary control and innovative behaviour.

Real World 13.10

Not guilty

A research project was carried out within a large multinational business, which is referred to as 'Astoria' by researchers to preserve its anonymity. The business employs a broadly traditional budgeting system even though it is subject to rapid technological change and operates within a highly competitive environment. Interviews with 25 managers, drawn from

Real World 13.10 *continued*

different functional areas, were conducted to see whether the budgeting process stifled innovation in any way. The researchers concluded:

> . . . we found little evidence to suggest that managers at Astoria were deterred from engaging in innovative activities simply because they had budget responsibilities. Of course, the amount of resources available to them may have presented a sort of boundary, but they didn't see the presence of budgetary targets as a constraint. The closest we came to finding any suggestion that budgets might inhibit innovation was a comment from one manager who remarked that 'everybody has a sandpit to play in. My sandpit financially is my control plan. If I stay within it, I'm free to play.' More generally, managers considered that, if they felt restricted in pursuing innovation, it was the degree of general empowerment they had that mattered. One manager went so far as to say that he felt 'constrained in some ways by not having enough hours in the day'. Our findings suggest that, although much of the accounting literature argues that budgets may deter innovation, this seems far from the truth.

Source: Marginson, D. and Ogden, S. (2005) Budgeting and innovation, *Financial Management*, April, pp. 29–31.

Self-assessment question (13.1)

Toscanini Ltd makes a standard product, which is budgeted to sell at £4.00 a unit, in a competitive market. It is made by taking a budgeted 0.4 kg of material, budgeted to cost £2.40/kg, and having it worked on by hand by an employee, paid a budgeted £8.00/hour, for a budgeted 6 minutes. Monthly fixed overheads are budgeted at £4,800. The output for May was budgeted at 4,000 units.

The actual results for May were as follows:

	£
Sales revenue (3,500 units)	13,820
Materials (1,425 kg)	(3,420)
Labour (345 hours)	(2,690)
Fixed overheads	(4,900)
Actual operating profit	2,810

No inventories of any description were held at the beginning or end of the month.

Required:

(a) Deduce the budgeted profit for May and reconcile it, through variances, with the actual profit in as much detail as the information provided will allow.

(b) State which manager should be held accountable, in the first instance, for each variance calculated.

(c) Assuming that the budget was well set and achievable, suggest at least one feasible reason for each of the variances that you identified in (a), given what you know about the business's performance for May.

(d) If it were discovered that the actual total world market demand for the business's product was 10 per cent lower than estimated when the May budget was set, explain how and why the variances that you identified in (a) could be revised to provide information that would be potentially more useful.

The solution to this question can be found at the back of the book on pp. 780–781.

Summary

The main points of this chapter may be summarised as follows:

Controlling through budgets

- Budgets can act as a system of both feedback and feedforward control.
- To exercise control, budgets can be flexed to match actual volume of output.

Variance analysis

- Variances may be favourable or adverse according to whether they result in an increase to, or a decrease from, the budgeted profit figure.
- Budgeted profit plus all favourable variances less all adverse variances equals actual profit.
- Commonly calculated variances:
  - Sales volume variance = difference between the original budget and the flexed budget profit figures.
  - Sales price variance = difference between actual sales revenue and actual volume at the standard sales price.
  - Total direct materials variance = difference between the actual direct materials cost and the direct materials cost according to the flexed budget.
  - Direct materials usage variance = difference between actual usage and budgeted usage, for the actual volume of output, multiplied by the standard materials cost.
  - Direct materials price variance = difference between the actual materials cost and the actual usage multiplied by the standard materials cost.
  - Total direct labour variance = difference between the actual direct labour cost and the direct labour cost according to the flexed budget.
  - Direct labour efficiency variance = difference between actual labour time and budgeted time, for the actual volume of output, multiplied by the standard labour rate.
  - Direct labour rate variance = difference between the actual labour cost and the actual labour time multiplied by the standard labour rate.
  - Fixed overhead spending variance = difference between the actual and budgeted spending on fixed overheads.
- Significant and/or persistent variances should normally be investigated to establish their cause. However, the costs and benefits of investigating variances must be considered.
- Trading off favourable variances against linked adverse variances should not be automatically acceptable.
- Not all activities can usefully be controlled through traditional variance analysis.

Standard costing

- Standards are budgeted physical quantities and financial values for one unit of inputs and outputs.
- There are two types of standards: ideal standards and practical standards.
- Information necessary for developing standards can be gathered by analysing the task or by using past data.
- There tends to be a learning-curve effect: routine tasks are performed more quickly with experience.

- Standards can be useful in providing data for income measurement, pricing decisions, product sourcing and efficiency measurement.

- Standards have their limitations, particularly in modern manufacturing environments; however, they are still widely used.

Effective budgetary control

- Good budgetary control requires establishing systems and routines to ensure such things as a clear distinction between individual managers' areas of responsibility; prompt, frequent and relevant variance reporting; and senior management commitment.

- There are behavioural aspects of control relating to management style, participation in budget setting and the failure to meet budget targets that should be taken into account by senior managers.

- The view that budgetary control stifles initiative is not well supported by the evidence.

Key terms

For definitions of these terms, see Appendix B.

feedback control *p. 519*	**direct labour efficiency variance** *p. 528*
feedforward control *p. 520*	**direct labour rate variance** *p. 529*
flexing a budget *p. 522*	**fixed overhead spending**
flexible budget *p. 523*	**variance** *p. 529*
sales volume variance *p. 523*	**non-operating-profit variance** *p. 537*
adverse variance *p. 523*	**compensating variance** *p. 540*
favourable variance *p. 523*	**standard quantities and costs** *p. 541*
variance *p. 523*	**ideal standard** *p. 543*
sales price variance *p. 526*	**practical standard** *p. 543*
total direct materials variance *p. 527*	**learning curve** *p. 543*
direct materials usage	**standard costing** *p. 545*
variance *p. 527*	**budgetary control** *p. 549*
direct materials price variance *p. 527*	**behavioural aspects of budgetary**
total direct labour variance *p. 528*	**control** *p. 552*

Reference

1 Hopwood, A.G. (1972) An empirical study of the role of accounting data in performance evaluation, *Empirical Research in Accounting,* a supplement to the *Journal of Accounting Research,* pp. 15–82.

Further reading

If you would like to explore the topics covered in this chapter in more depth, we recommend the following:

Atkinson, A., Kaplan, R., Matsamura, E. and Young, S.M. (2013) *Management Accounting: Information for Decision Making and Strategy Execution,* 6th edn, Pearson, Chapters 9 and 11.

Bhimani, A., Horngren, C., Datar, S. and Rajan, M. (2015) *Management and Cost Accounting,* 6th edn, Pearson, Chapters 14–16.

Drury, C. (2015) *Management and Cost Accounting,* 9th edn, Cengage Learning EMEA, Chapters 16–18.

Hilton, R. and Platt, D. (2014) *Managerial Accounting,* McGraw-Hill Higher Education, Chapters 10 and 11.

Review questions

Solutions to these questions can be found at the back of the book on pp. 796–797.

13.1 Explain what is meant by feedforward control and distinguish it from feedback control.

13.2 What is meant by a variance? What is the point in analysing variances?

13.3 What is the point in flexing the budget in the context of variance analysis? Does flexing imply that differences between budget and actual in the volume of output are ignored in variance analysis?

13.4 Should all variances be investigated to find their cause? Explain your answer.

Exercises

Solutions to exercises with coloured numbers can be found at the back of the book on pp. 830–832.

Basic-level exercises

13.1 You have recently overheard the following remarks:
  (a) 'A favourable direct labour rate variance can only be caused by staff working more efficiently than budgeted.'
  (b) 'Selling more units than budgeted, because the units were sold at less than standard price, automatically leads to a favourable sales volume variance.'
  (c) 'Using below-standard materials will tend to lead to adverse materials usage variances but cannot affect labour variances.'
  (d) 'Higher-than-budgeted sales could not possibly affect the labour rate variance.'
  (e) 'An adverse sales price variance can only arise from selling a product at less than standard price.'

Required:
Are these remarks true or false? Critically assess each remark, explaining any technical terms.

13.2 You have recently overheard the following remarks:

(a) 'When calculating variances, we ignore differences of volume of output, between original budget and actual, by flexing the budget. If there were a volume difference, it is water under the bridge by the time that the variances come to be calculated.'

(b) 'It is very valuable to calculate variances because they will tell you what went wrong.'

(c) 'All variances should be investigated to find their cause.'

(d) 'Research evidence shows that the more demanding the target, the more motivated the manager.'

(e) 'Most businesses do not have feedforward controls of any type, just feedback controls through budgets.'

Required:

Critically assess these remarks, explaining any technical terms.

Intermediate-level exercises

13.3 Pilot Ltd makes a standard product, which is budgeted to sell at £5.00 a unit. It is made by taking a budgeted 0.5 kg of material, budgeted to cost £3.00 a kilogram, and having it worked on by hand by an employee, paid a budgeted £10.00 an hour, for a budgeted $7\frac{1}{2}$ minutes. Monthly fixed overheads are budgeted at £6,000. The output for March was budgeted at 5,000 units. The actual results for March were as follows:

	£
Sales revenue (5,400 units)	26,460
Materials (2,830 kg)	(8,770)
Labour (650 hours)	(6,885)
Fixed overheads	(6,350)
Actual operating profit	4,455

No inventories existed at the start or end of March.

Required:

(a) Deduce the budgeted profit for March and reconcile it with the actual profit in as much detail as the information provided will allow.

(b) State which manager should be held accountable, in the first instance, for each variance calculated.

13.4 Antonio plc makes Product X, the standard costs of which are:

	£
Sales revenue	31
Direct labour (1 hour)	(11)
Direct materials (1 kg)	(10)
Fixed overheads	(3)
Standard profit	7

The budgeted output for March was 1,000 units of Product X; the actual output was 1,100 units, which was sold for £34,950. There were no inventories at the start or end of March.

The actual production costs were:

	£
Direct labour (1,075 hours)	12,210
Direct materials (1,170 kg)	11,630
Fixed overheads	3,200

Required:
Calculate the variances for March as fully as you are able from the available information and use them to reconcile the budgeted and actual profit figures.

Advanced-level exercises

13.5 Bradley-Allen Ltd makes one standard product. Its budgeted operating statement for May is as follows:

		£	£
Sales (volume and revenue):	800 units		64,000
Direct materials:	Type A	(12,000)	
	Type B	(16,000)	
Direct labour:	Skilled	(4,000)	
	Unskilled	(10,000)	
Fixed overheads:		(12,000)	
			(54,000)
Budgeted operating profit			10,000

The standard costs were as follows:

Direct materials:	Type A	£50/kg
	Type B	£20/m
Direct labour:	Skilled	£10/hour
	Unskilled	£8/hour

During May, the following occurred:

1 950 units were sold for a total of £73,000.
2 310 kg (costing £15,200) of type A material were used in production.
3 920 metres (costing £18,900) of type B material were used in production.
4 Skilled workers were paid £4,628 for 445 hours.
5 Unskilled workers were paid £11,275 for 1,375 hours.
6 Fixed overheads cost £11,960.

There were no inventories of finished production or of work in progress at either the beginning or end of May.

Required:

(a) Prepare a statement that reconciles the budgeted to the actual profit of the business for May, through variances. Your statement should analyse the difference between the two profit figures in as much detail as possible.
(b) Explain how the statement in (a) might be helpful to managers.

13.6   Mowbray Ltd makes and sells one product, the standard costs of which are as follows:

	£
Direct materials (3 kg at £2.50/kg)	(7.50)
Direct labour (15 minutes at £9.00/hr)	(2.25)
Fixed overheads	(3.60)
Full cost	(13.35)
Selling price	20.00
Standard profit margin	6.65

The monthly production and sales are planned to be 1,200 units.

The actual results for May were as follows:

	£	
Sales revenue	18,000	
Direct materials	(7,400)	(2,800 kg)
Direct labour	(2,300)	(255 hr)
Fixed overheads	(4,100)	
Operating profit	4,200	

There were no inventories at the start or end of May. As a result of poor sales demand during May, the business reduced the price of all sales by 10 per cent.

Required:
Calculate the budgeted profit for May and reconcile it to the actual profit through variances, going into as much detail as is possible from the information available.

13.7   Brive plc has the following standards for its only product:

Selling price:	£110/unit
Direct labour:	1 hour at £10.50/hour
Direct material:	3 kg at £14.00/kg
Fixed overheads:	£27.00/unit, based on a budgeted output of 800 units/month

During May, there was an actual output of 850 units and the operating statement for the month was as follows:

	£
Sales revenue	92,930
Direct labour (890 hours)	(9,665)
Direct materials (2,410 kg)	(33,258)
Fixed overheads	(21,365)
Operating profit	28,642

There were no inventories of any description at the beginning and end of May.

Required:
Prepare the original budget and a budget flexed to the actual volume. Use these to compare the budgeted and actual profits of the business for the month, going into as much detail with your analysis as the information given will allow.

PART 3

Financial management

Part 3 examines the area of 'business finance' or 'financial management'. In broad terms, this part is concerned with decisions regarding the raising and investment of funds. Businesses can be seen, from an economic perspective, as entities that raise funds from investors (broadly, shareholders and lenders) and then use those funds to make investments (typically in equipment and other assets). These are important decision areas, often involving large sums of money and long time horizons. The ultimate objective of these decisions is to make the owners of the business more wealthy.

Chapter 14 considers how a business may determine whether proposed investments in long-term assets are worthwhile. We describe the various decision-making techniques available and examine their strengths and weaknesses. Although our focus is on investment proposals concerning buildings, equipment, motor vehicles and so on, the decision-making techniques discussed can be used when considering proposals to acquire shares in a business, or other 'financial' assets.

Chapter 15 deals with how businesses may raise the funds required to make investments. Here we review the main forms of funding available. We shall see how various factors, such as the size of the business, the period for which the funds are required and the degree of risk that businesses are prepared to take, will influence the form in which funds are raised.

Chapter 16 considers the management of working capital. Working capital is made up of the short-term assets and claims of the business. It consists of inventories, trade receivables, cash and trade payables. Businesses often invest large amounts of finance in working capital and so it needs to be managed carefully. In this chapter, each element of working capital is reviewed along with the various techniques that can be used in its management.

CHAPTER 14

Making capital investment decisions

Introduction

This chapter looks at how businesses should assess proposed investments in new plant, machinery, buildings and other long-term assets. This is a very important area; expensive and far-reaching consequences can flow from bad investment decisions.

We shall also consider some of the practical aspects that should be taken into account when evaluating investment proposals. Finally, we shall discuss the ways that managers can oversee capital investment projects and how control may be exercised throughout the life of a project.

Learning outcomes

When you have completed this chapter, you should be able to:

● explain the nature and importance of investment decision making;

● identify and evaluate the four main investment appraisal methods found in practice;

● discuss the popularity and use of the four main investment appraisal methods in practice; and

● explain the methods used to monitor and control investment projects.

The nature of investment decisions

The essential feature of investment decisions is *time*. Investment involves making an outlay of something of economic value, usually cash, at one point in time, which is expected to yield economic benefits to the investor at some other point in time. Usually, the outlay precedes the benefits. Furthermore, the outlay is typically a single large amount while the benefits arrive as a series of smaller amounts over a fairly protracted period.

Investment decisions tend to be of profound importance to the business because:

- *Large amounts of resources are often involved.* Many investments made by businesses involve laying out a significant proportion of their total resources (see Real World 14.2). If mistakes are made with the decision, the effects on the businesses could be significant, if not catastrophic.
- *Relatively long timescales are involved.* There is usually more time for things to go wrong between the decision being made and the end of the project in comparison with many business decisions.
- *It is often difficult and/or expensive to bail out of an investment once it has been undertaken.* Investments made by a business are often specific to its needs. A hotel business, for example, may invest in a new, custom-designed hotel complex. If the business found, after having made the investment, that room occupancy rates were significantly lower than projected, the only course of action might be to sell the complex. The specialist nature of the complex may, however, lead to it having a rather limited resale value. This could mean that the amount recouped from the investment is much less than it had originally cost.

Real World 14.1 gives an illustration of a major investment by a well-known business operating in the UK.

Real World 14.1

Brittany Ferries launches an investment

Brittany Ferries, the cross-Channel ferry operator, is having an additional ferry built. The ferry is costing the business an amount thought to be well in excess of £200 million and will be used on the Portsmouth to Caen route from 2019. Although Brittany Ferries is a substantial business, this level of expenditure is significant. Clearly, the business believes that acquiring the new ferry will be profitable for it, but how would it have reached this conclusion? Presumably the anticipated future benefits from carrying passengers and freight as well as the costs of labour, fuel and maintenance will have been major inputs to the decision.

Source: www.brittany-ferries.co.uk.

The issues raised by Brittany Ferries' investment will be the main subject of this chapter.

Real World 14.2 indicates the level of annual net investment for a number of randomly selected, well-known UK businesses. We can see that the scale of investment varies from one business to another. (It also tends to vary from one year to another for a particular business.) In nearly all of these businesses the scale of investment was significant.

Real World 14.2

The scale of investment by UK businesses

	Expenditure on additional non-current assets as a percentage of:	
	Annual sales revenue	End-of-year non-current assets
British Sky Broadcasting plc (television)	8.9	8.3
Go-Ahead Group plc (transport)	3.4	25.7
J D Wetherspoon plc (pub operator)	7.8	14.9
Marks and Spencer plc (stores)	5.8	8.7
Ryanair Holdings plc (airline)	18.6	19.0
Severn Trent Water plc (water and sewerage)	23.5	5.4
Vodafone plc (telecommunications)	29.2	11.3
Wm Morrison Supermarkets plc (supermarkets)	2.3	4.6

Source: Annual reports of the businesses concerned for the financial year ending in 2016.

Real World 14.2 considers only expenditure on non-current assets, but business investment typically requires a significant outlay on current assets to support it (additional inventories, for example). This suggests that the real scale of investment is even greater than indicated above.

Activity 14.1

When managers are making decisions involving capital investments, what should the decision seek to achieve?

Investment decisions must be consistent with the objectives of the particular organisation. For a private-sector business, maximising the wealth of the owners (shareholders) is normally assumed to be the key financial objective.

Investment appraisal methods

Given the importance of investment decisions, it is essential that proper screening of investment proposals takes place. An important part of this screening process is to ensure that appropriate methods of evaluation are used. Research shows that there are basically four methods used by businesses to evaluate investment opportunities. These are:

- accounting rate of return (ARR);
- payback period (PP);
- net present value (NPV); and
- internal rate of return (IRR).

It is possible to find businesses that use variants of these four methods. It is also possible to find businesses, particularly smaller ones, that do not use any formal appraisal method but rely instead on the 'gut feeling' of their managers. Most businesses, however, seem to use one (or more) of these four methods.

We will assess the effectiveness of each of these methods, but we shall see that only one of them (NPV) is a wholly logical approach. The other three all have flaws. This raises the question as to why we should be examining the flawed methods. The answer is that, despite these flaws, all four of the methods are fairly widely used by managers in practice, as we shall see later in the chapter.

To help in examining each of the methods, it might be useful to see how each of them would cope with a particular investment opportunity. Let us consider Example 14.1.

Example 14.1

Billingsgate Battery Company has carried out research that shows there is a market for a standard service that it has recently developed.

Providing the service would require investment in a machine that would cost £100,000, payable immediately. Sales of the service would take place throughout the next five years. At the end of that time, it is estimated that the machine could be sold for £20,000.

Inflows and outflows from sales of the service would be expected to be:

Time		£000
Immediately	Cost of machine	(100)
1 year's time	Operating profit before depreciation	20
2 years' time	Operating profit before depreciation	40
3 years' time	Operating profit before depreciation	60
4 years' time	Operating profit before depreciation	60
5 years' time	Operating profit before depreciation	20
5 years' time	Disposal proceeds from the machine	20

Note that, broadly speaking, the operating profit before deducting depreciation (that is, before non-cash items) equals the net amount of cash flowing into the business. Broadly, apart from depreciation, all of this business's expenses cause cash to flow out of the business. Sales revenues tend to lead to cash flowing in. Expenses tend to lead to it flowing out. For the time being, we shall assume that working capital – which is made up of inventories, trade receivables and trade payables – remains constant. This means that operating profit before depreciation will tend to equal the net cash inflow.

To simplify matters, we shall assume that the cash from sales and for the expenses of providing the service are received and paid, respectively, at the end of each year. This is unlikely to be true in real life. Money will be paid to employees (for salaries and wages) on a weekly or a monthly basis. Customers will pay within a month or two of buying the service. Making the assumption, however, probably does not lead to a serious distortion. It is a simplifying assumption, that is often made in real life, and will make things more straightforward. Nevertheless, we should be clear that there is nothing about any of the four methods that *demands* that this assumption be made.

Having set up the example, let us now go on to consider how each of the appraisal methods works.

Accounting rate of return (ARR)

The first of the four methods that we shall consider is the **accounting rate of return (ARR)**. This method takes the average accounting operating profit that the investment will generate and expresses it as a percentage of the average investment made over the life of the project. In other words:

$$\text{ARR} = \frac{\text{Average annual operating profit}}{\text{Average investment to earn that profit}} \times 100\%$$

We can see from the equation that, to calculate the ARR, we need two pieces of information about the particular project:

- the annual average operating profit; and
- the average investment.

In our example, the average annual operating profit *before depreciation* over the five years is £40,000 (that is, £000(20 + 40 + 60 + 60 + 20)/5). Assuming 'straight-line' depreciation (that is, equal annual amounts), the annual depreciation charge will be £16,000 (that is, £(100,000 − 20,000)/5). Therefore, the average annual operating profit *after depreciation* is £24,000 (that is, £40,000 − £16,000).

The average investment over the five years can be calculated as follows:

$$\text{Average investment} = \frac{\text{Cost of machine + Disposal value*}}{2}$$

$$= \frac{£100,000 + £20,000}{2}$$

$$= £60,000$$

* Note: To find the average investment we are simply adding the value of the amount invested at the beginning and end of the investment period together and dividing by two.

The ARR of the investment, therefore, is:

$$\text{ARR} = \frac{£24,000}{£60,000} \times 100\% = 40\%$$

The following decision rules apply when using ARR:

- For any project to be acceptable, it must achieve a target ARR as a minimum.
- Where there are competing projects that all seem capable of exceeding this minimum rate (that is, where the business must choose between more than one project), the one with the higher (or highest) ARR should be selected.

To decide whether the 40 per cent return is acceptable, we must compare this percentage return with the minimum rate required by the business.

Activity 14.2

Chaotic Industries is considering an investment in a fleet of 10 delivery vans to take its products to customers. The vans will cost £15,000 each, which will be payable immediately. The annual running costs are expected to total £50,000 for each van (including the driver's salary). The vans are expected to operate successfully for six years, at the end of which period they will all be sold, with disposal proceeds expected to be £3,000 a van. At present, the business outsources transport, for all of its deliveries, to a commercial carrier. The carrier is expected to charge a total of £530,000 each year for the next six years to undertake the deliveries.

What is the ARR of buying the vans? (Note that cost savings are as relevant a benefit from an investment as are net cash inflows.)

The vans will save the business £30,000 a year (that is, £530,000 − (£50,000 × 10)), before depreciation, in total. Therefore, the inflows and outflows will be:

Time		£000
Immediately	Cost of vans (10 × £15,000)	(150)
1 year's time	Saving before depreciation	30
2 years' time	Saving before depreciation	30
3 years' time	Saving before depreciation	30
4 years' time	Saving before depreciation	30
5 years' time	Saving before depreciation	30
6 years' time	Saving before depreciation	30
6 years' time	Disposal proceeds from the vans (10 × £3,000)	30

The total annual depreciation expense (assuming a straight-line method) will be £20,000 (that is, (£150,000 − £30,000)/6). Therefore, the average annual saving, *after depreciation,* is £10,000 (that is, £30,000 − £20,000).

The average investment will be

$$\text{Average investment} = \frac{£150,000 + £30,000}{2}$$

$$= £90,000$$

and the ARR of the investment is

$$\text{ARR} = \frac{£10,000}{£90,000} \times 100\%$$

$$= 11.1\%$$

ARR and ROCE

We saw in Chapter 7 that **return on capital employed (ROCE)** is a widely-used measure of economic performance. It expresses the business's operating profit as a percentage of the value of the assets used to generate it. Both ROCE and ARR take the same approach to measuring business performance. They both relate operating profit to the cost of assets used to generate that profit. ROCE, however, assesses the performance of the entire business *after* it has performed, while ARR assesses the performance of a particular investment *before* it has performed.

Given the link between the two measures, the target ARR could be based on overall ROCE previously achieved. It could also be based on the industry-average ROCE.

The link between ARR and ROCE may be used to support a case for adopting ARR as the appropriate method of investment appraisal. As already mentioned, ROCE is a widely-used measure of performance. Furthermore, we saw in Chapter 7 that some businesses express their financial objective in terms of a target ROCE. It may seem sensible, therefore, to use a method of investment appraisal that is consistent with this measure. A secondary argument in support of ARR is that it provides a result expressed percentage terms, which many managers seem to prefer.

Problems with ARR

ARR suffers from a major defect as a means of assessing investment opportunities. To illustrate this defect, consider Activity 14.3.

Activity 14.3

A business is evaluating three competing projects whose profits are shown below. All three involve investment in a machine that is expected to have no residual value at the end of the five years. Note that all the projects have the same total operating profits after depreciation over the five years.

Time		Project A £000	Project B £000	Project C £000
Immediately	Cost of machine	(160)	(160)	(160)
1 year's time	Operating profit after depreciation	20	10	160
2 years' time	Operating profit after depreciation	40	10	10
3 years' time	Operating profit after depreciation	60	10	10
4 years' time	Operating profit after depreciation	60	10	10
5 years' time	Operating profit after depreciation	20	160	10

What defect in the ARR method would prevent it from distinguishing between these competing projects? (*Hint*: The defect is not concerned with the ability of the decision maker to forecast future events, though this too can be a problem. Try to remember the essential feature of investment decisions, which we identified at the beginning of this chapter.)

In this example, each project has the same total operating profit over the five years (£200,000) and the same average investment of £80,000 (that is, £160,000/2). This means that each project will give rise to the same ARR of 50 per cent (that is, £40,000/£80,000).

Thus, ARR fails to distinguish between them even though they are not of equal merit. This is because ARR fails to take into account the time factor and, therefore, the cost of financing the project.

To maximise the wealth of the owners, a manager faced with a choice between the three projects set out in Activity 14.3 should select Project C. This is because most of the benefits arise within 12 months of making the initial investment. Project A would rank second and Project B would be a poor third. Any appraisal technique that is not capable of distinguishing between these three situations is seriously flawed. We shall look at why timing is so important later in the chapter.

There are further problems associated with the ARR method, which are now discussed.

Use of average investment

Using the average investment in calculating ARR can lead to daft results. Example 14.2 illustrates the kind of problem that can arise.

> ### Example 14.2
>
> George put forward an investment proposal to his boss. The business uses ARR to assess investment proposals using a minimum 'hurdle' rate of 27 per cent. Details of the proposal were:
>
> | | |
> |---|---|
> | Cost of equipment | £200,000 |
> | Estimated residual value of equipment | £40,000 |
> | Average annual operating profit before depreciation | £48,000 |
> | Estimated life of project | 10 years |
> | Annual straight-line depreciation charge | £16,000 (that is, (£200,000 − £40,000)/10) |
>
> The ARR of the project will be:
>
> $$\text{ARR} = \frac{48,000 - 16,000}{(200,000 + 40,000)/2} \times 100\% = 26.7\%$$
>
> The boss rejected George's proposal because it failed to achieve an ARR of at least 27 per cent. Although George was disappointed, he realised that there was still hope. In fact, all that the business had to do was to give away the piece of equipment at the end of its useful life rather than sell it. The residual value of the equipment then became zero and the annual depreciation charge became ([£200,000 − £0]/10) = £20,000 a year. The revised ARR calculation was then:
>
> $$\text{ARR} = \frac{48,000 - 20,000}{(200,000 + 0)/2} \times 100\% = 28\%$$

Use of accounting profit

We have seen that ARR is based on accounting profit. When measuring performance over the whole life of a project, however, it is cash flows rather than accounting profits that are important. Cash is the ultimate measure of the economic wealth generated by an investment. This is because it is cash that is used to acquire resources and for distribution to owners. Accounting profit is more appropriate for reporting achievement on a periodic basis. It is a useful measure of productive effort for a relatively short period, such as a year or half year. It is really a question of 'horses for courses'.

Target ARR

We saw earlier a target ARR, against which to assess investment opportunities, must be chosen. This cannot be objectively determined and so will depend on the judgement of managers. The target ARR may therefore vary both over time and between businesses.

Competing investments

The ARR method can create problems when considering competing investments of different size. Consider Activity 14.4.

Activity 14.4

Sinclair Wholesalers plc is currently considering opening a new sales outlet in Coventry. Two possible sites have been identified for the new outlet. Site A has an area of 30,000 square metres. It will require an average investment of £6 million and will produce an average operating profit of £600,000 a year. Site B has an area of 20,000 square metres. It will require an average investment of £4 million and will produce an average operating profit of £500,000 a year.

What is the ARR of each investment opportunity? Which site would you select and why?

The ARR of Site A is £600,000/£6m = 10 per cent The ARR of Site B is £500,000/£4m = 12.5 per cent. Site B, therefore has the higher ARR. In terms of the absolute operating profit generated, however, Site A is the more attractive. If the ultimate objective is to increase the wealth of the shareholders of Sinclair Wholesalers plc, it would be better to choose Site A even though the percentage return is lower. It is the absolute size of the return rather than the relative (percentage) that is important. This is a general problem of using comparative measures, such as percentages, when the objective is measured in absolute terms, such as an amount of money.

Real World 14.3 illustrates how using percentage measures can lead to confusion.

Real World 14.3

Increasing road capacity by sleight of hand

During the 1970s, the Mexican government wanted to increase the capacity of a major four-lane road. It came up with the idea of repainting the lane markings so that there were six narrower lanes occupying the same space as four wider ones had previously done. This increased the capacity of the road by 50 per cent (that is, $^2/_4 \times 100$). A tragic outcome of the narrower lanes was an increase in deaths from road accidents. A year later the Mexican government had the six narrower lanes changed back to the original four wider ones. This reduced the capacity of the road by 33 per cent (that is, $^2/_6 \times 100$). The Mexican government reported that, overall, it had increased the capacity of the road by 17 per cent (that is, 50% − 33%), despite the fact that its real capacity was identical to that which it had been originally. The confusion arose because each of the two percentages (50 per cent and 33 per cent) is based on different bases (four and six).

Source: Based on information in Gigerenzer, G. (2003) Reckoning with Risk, Penguin.

According to its 2016 annual report, Next plc, the fashion and household retailer, uses ARR in assessing its investments in new retail space.

Payback period (PP)

Another approach to appraising possible investments is the **payback period (PP)**. This is the time taken for an initial investment to be repaid out of the net cash inflows from a project. As the PP method takes time into account and it deals with cash, rather than accounting profit, it appears, at first glance, to overcome two key weaknesses of the ARR method.

Let us consider PP in the context of the Billingsgate Battery Company example. We should recall that the project's cash flows are:

Time		£000
Immediately	Cost of machine	(100)
1 year's time	Operating profit before depreciation	20
2 years' time	Operating profit before depreciation	40
3 years' time	Operating profit before depreciation	60
4 years' time	Operating profit before depreciation	60
5 years' time	Operating profit before depreciation	20
5 years' time	Disposal proceeds	20

Note that all of these figures are amounts of cash to be paid or received (we saw earlier that operating profit before depreciation is a rough measure of the cash flows from the project).

The payback period can be derived by calculating the cumulative cash flows as follows:

Time		Net cash flows £000	Cumulative net cash flows £000
Immediately	Cost of machine	(100)	(100)
1 year's time	Operating profit before depreciation	20	(80) (−100 + 20)
2 years' time	Operating profit before depreciation	40	(40) (−80 + 40)
3 years' time	Operating profit before depreciation	60	20 (−40 + 60)
4 years' time	Operating profit before depreciation	60	80 (20 + 60)
5 years' time	Operating profit before depreciation	20	100 (80 + 20)
5 years' time	Disposal proceeds	20	120 (100 + 20)

We can see that the cumulative cash flows become positive at the end of the third year. If the cash flows had arisen evenly over the year, the precise payback period would be:

$$2 \text{ years} + (^{40}/_{60}) \text{ years} = 2^2/_3 \text{ years}$$

where the top part of the fraction (40) represents the cash flow needed at the beginning of the third year to repay the initial outlay and the bottom part (60) represents the projected cash flow during the third year.

The following decision rules apply when using PP:

- For a project to be acceptable it should have a payback period no longer than a maximum payback period set by the business.
- If there were two (or more) competing projects whose payback periods were all shorter than the maximum payback period requirement, the project with the shorter (or shortest) payback period should be selected.

If, for example, the Billingsgate Battery Company had a maximum acceptable payback period of four years, the project would be undertaken. A project with a payback period longer than four years would not be acceptable.

Activity 14.5

What is the payback period of the Chaotic Industries project from Activity 14.2?

The inflows and outflows are expected to be:

Time		Net cash flows £000	Cumulative net cash flows £000
Immediately	Cost of vans	(150)	(150)
1 year's time	Saving before depreciation	30	(120) (−150 + 30)
2 years' time	Saving before depreciation	30	(90) (−120 + 30)
3 years' time	Saving before depreciation	30	(60) (−90 + 30)
4 years' time	Saving before depreciation	30	(30) (−60 + 30)
5 years' time	Saving before depreciation	30	0 (−30 + 30)
6 years' time	Saving before depreciation	30	30 (0 + 30)
6 years' time	Disposal proceeds from the vans	30	60 (30 + 30)

The payback period here is five years; that is, it is not until the end of the fifth year that the vans will pay for themselves out of the savings that they are expected to generate.

The logic of using PP is that projects that can recoup their cost quickly are economically more attractive than those with longer payback periods. In other words, it emphasises liquidity.

The PP method has certain advantages. It is quick and easy to calculate and it can be easily understood by managers.

Problems with PP

PP is an improvement on ARR as it uses cash flows (rather than accounting flows) and takes some account of the timing of cash flows. It is not, however, a complete answer to the problem. To understand why this is the case, consider the following cash flows arising from three competing projects.

Time		Project 1 £000	Project 2 £000	Project 3 £000
Immediately	Cost of machine	(200)	(200)	(200)
1 year's time	Operating profit before depreciation	70	20	70
2 years' time	Operating profit before depreciation	60	20	100
3 years' time	Operating profit before depreciation	70	160	30
4 years' time	Operating profit before depreciation	80	30	200
5 years' time	Operating profit before depreciation	50	20	440
5 years' time	Disposal proceeds	40	10	20

Activity (14.6)

Can you see from the above why PP is not a complete answer to the problem concerning the timing of cash flows?

The PP for each project is three years and so all three projects would be regarded as equally acceptable. This conclusion does not, however, take full account of the timing of cash flows. It does not distinguish between those projects that pay back a significant amount early within the three-year payback period and those that do not.

The PP method also ignores cash flows after the payback period. Managers concerned with increasing owners' wealth would prefer Project 3 because the cash inflows are received earlier. Most of the initial cost of making the investment has been repaid by the end of the second year. Furthermore, the cash inflows over the life of the project are greater in total.

The cumulative cash flows of each project in Activity 14.6 are set out in Figure 14.1.

Figure 14.1   The cumulative cash flows of each project in Activity 14.6

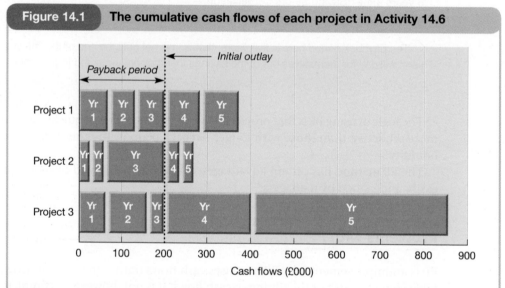

The payback method of investment appraisal would view Projects 1, 2 and 3 as being equally attractive. In doing so, the method completely ignores the fact that Project 3 provides most of the payback cash earlier in the three-year period and goes on to generate large benefits in later years.

Some additional points concerning the PP method are now considered.

Relevant information

We saw earlier that the PP method is simply concerned with how quickly the initial investment can be recouped. While this neatly avoids the practical problems of forecasting cash flows over a long period, it means that not all relevant information may be taken into account. Cash flows arising beyond the payback period are ignored.

Risk

By favouring projects with a short payback period, the PP method provides a way of dealing with risk. However, it offers a fairly crude approach to the problem. It deals only with the risk that the project will end earlier than expected. This is only one of many risk areas. For example, what about the risk that the demand for the product may be less than expected? There are more systematic approaches to dealing with risk, such sensitivity analysis, which we discussed in Chapter 8.

Wealth maximisation

Although the PP method takes some note of the timing of project costs and benefits, it is not concerned with maximising the wealth of the business owners. Rather, it favours projects that pay for themselves quickly.

Required payback period

Managers must select a maximum acceptable payback period. When doing so they confront a similar problem to the one arising when setting a target ARR. No objective basis can be used to determine this period: it is simply a matter of judgement.

Real World 14.4 is a short extract from a *Financial Times* article that discusses the increasing use of robots by Chinese manufacturers and the rapid decline in their payback period.

Real World 14.4

It's payback time

Every year, the amount of time it takes for a company's investment in a robot to pay off — known as the "payback period" — is narrowing sharply, making it more attractive for small Chinese companies and workshops to invest in automation. The payback period for a welding robot in the Chinese automotive industry, for instance, dropped from 5.3 years to 1.7 years between 2010 and 2015, according to calculations by analysts at Citi. By 2017, the payback period is forecast to shrink to just 1.3 years.

Source: Extract from Bland, B. (2016) China's robot revolution, ft.com, 6 June. © The Financial Times Limited 2016. All Rights Reserved.

Net present value (NPV)

From what we have seen so far, it seems that to make sensible investment decisions, we need a method of appraisal that both:

- considers all of the costs and benefits of each investment opportunity; and
- makes a logical allowance for the timing of those costs and benefits.

The third of the four methods of investment appraisal, the **net present value (NPV)** method, provides us with exactly this.

Consider the Billingsgate Battery (Example 14.1), whose cash flows are:

Time		£000
Immediately	Cost of machine	(100)
1 year's time	Operating profit before depreciation	20
2 years' time	Operating profit before depreciation	40
3 years' time	Operating profit before depreciation	60
4 years' time	Operating profit before depreciation	60
5 years' time	Operating profit before depreciation	20
5 years' time	Disposal proceeds	20

Given a financial objective of maximising owners' wealth, it would be easy to assess this investment if all cash inflows and outflows were to occur immediately. It would then simply be a matter of adding up the cash inflows (total £220,000) and comparing them with the cash outflows (£100,000). This would lead us to conclude that the project should go ahead because the owners would be better off by £120,000. It is, of course, not as easy as this because time is involved. The cash outflow will occur immediately, whereas the cash inflows will arise at different points in the future.

Why does time matter?

Time is an important issue because people do not normally see an amount paid out now as equivalent in value to the same amount being received in a year's time. Thus, if we were offered £100 in one year's time in exchange for paying out £100 now, we would not be interested, unless we wished to do someone a favour.

Activity 14.7

Why would you see £100 to be received in a year's time as not equal in value to £100 to be paid immediately? (There are basically three reasons.)

The reasons are:

- interest lost;
- risk; and
- inflation.

We shall now take a closer look at these three reasons in turn.

Interest lost

If we are to be deprived of the opportunity to spend our money for a year, we could equally well be deprived of its use by placing it on deposit in a bank or building society. By doing this, we could have our money back at the end of the year along with some interest earned. This interest, which is forgone by not placing our money on deposit, represents an *opportunity cost*. As we saw in Chapter 8, an opportunity cost occurs where one course of action deprives us of the opportunity to derive benefit from an alternative action.

An investment must exceed the opportunity cost of the funds invested if it is to be worthwhile. Therefore, if Billingsgate Battery Company sees putting the money in the bank on deposit as the alternative to investment in the machine, the return from investing in the machine must be better than that from investing in the bank. If this is not the case, there is no reason to buy the machine.

Risk

All investments expose their investors to risk. Thus, when Billingsgate Battery Company buys a machine on the strength of estimates made before its purchase, it must accept that things may not turn out as expected.

Activity (14.8)

Can you identify the kind of risks that the business may face by buying a machine?

We came up with the following:

- The machine might not work as well as expected; it might break down, leading to loss of the business's ability to provide the service.
- Sales of the service may not be as buoyant as expected.
- Labour costs may prove to be higher than expected.
- The sale proceeds of the machine could prove to be less than were estimated.

You may have thought of others.

As we saw in Chapter 8, it is important to remember that the purchase decision must be taken *before* any of these things are known. It is only after the machine has been purchased that we find out whether, for example, the forecast level of sales is going to be achieved. We can study reports and analyses of the market. We can commission sophisticated market surveys and advertise widely to promote sales. All these may give us more confidence in the likely outcome. Ultimately, however, we must decide whether to accept the risk that things will not turn out as expected in exchange for the opportunity to generate wealth.

We saw in Chapter 1 that people normally expect greater returns in exchange for taking on greater risk. Examples of this in real life are not difficult to find. One such example is that banks tend to charge higher rates of interest to borrowers whom the bank perceives as more risky. Those who can offer good security for a loan and who can point to a regular source of income tend to be charged lower rates of interest.

Going back to Billingsgate Battery Company's investment opportunity, it is not enough to say that we should buy the machine providing the expected returns are higher than those from investing in a bank deposit. We should expect much greater returns than the bank deposit interest rate because of the much greater risk involved. The logical equivalent of investing in the machine would be an investment that is of similar risk. Determining how risky a particular project is and, therefore, how large the **risk premium** should be, however, is a difficult task.

Inflation

If we are to be deprived of £100 for a year, when we come to spend that money it will not buy the same amount of goods and services as it would have done a year earlier. Generally, we will not be able to buy as many tins of baked beans or pairs of jeans or bus tickets as before. This is because of the loss in the purchasing power of money, or **inflation,** which tends to occur over time. Investors will expect to be compensated for this loss of purchasing power. This will be on top of a return that takes account of what could be gained from an alternative investment of similar risk.

In practice, interest rates observable in the market tend to take inflation into account. This means that rates offered to building society and bank depositors normally include an allowance for the expected rate of inflation.

What should managers do?

To summarise, managers seeking to increase the wealth of the business owners should invest only where the owners will be adequately compensated for the loss of interest, for the loss in the purchasing power of money invested and for the risk that the expected returns may not materialise. This normally involves investigating whether the proposed investment will yield a return greater than the basic rate of interest (which will normally include an allowance for inflation) plus an appropriate risk premium.

These three factors (interest lost, risk and inflation) are set out in Figure 14.2.

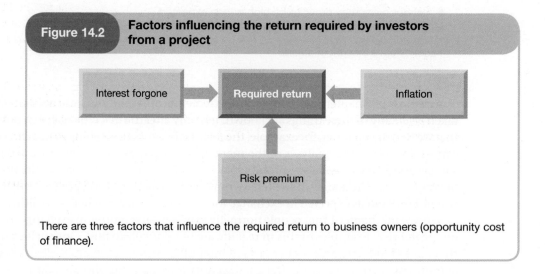

Figure 14.2 **Factors influencing the return required by investors from a project**

There are three factors that influence the required return to business owners (opportunity cost of finance).

Dealing with the time value of money

We have seen that money has a time value. That is, £100 received today is not regarded as equivalent in value to £100 received at some future date. We cannot, therefore, simply compare the cash inflows with cash outflows for an investment where they arise at different points in time. Each of these cash flows must be expressed in similar terms. Only then can a direct comparison be made.

To illustrate how this can be done, let us now return to the Billingsgate Battery Company example. The cash flows expected from this investment are:

Time		£000
Immediately	Cost of machine	(100)
1 year's time	Operating profit before depreciation	20
2 years' time	Operating profit before depreciation	40
3 years' time	Operating profit before depreciation	60
4 years' time	Operating profit before depreciation	60
5 years' time	Operating profit before depreciation	20
5 years' time	Disposal proceeds	20

Let us assume that, instead of making this investment, the business could make an alternative investment with similar risk and obtain a return of 20 per cent a year.

Activity 14.9

We now know that the Billingsgate Battery Company could invest its money at a rate of 20 per cent a year. What is the present (immediate) value of the expected first year receipt of £20,000? In other words if, instead of having to wait a year for the £20,000 and, therefore, being deprived of the opportunity to invest it at 20 per cent, the business could have some money now, what sum would be equivalent to getting £20,000 in one year's time?

The business should be happy to accept a lower amount if this amount could be received immediately rather than waiting a year. This is because it could invest the amount at 20 per cent (in the alternative project). Logically, it should be prepared to accept an amount that, with a year's income, will grow to £20,000. If we call this amount PV (for present value), we can say:

$$PV + (PV \times 20\%) = £20,000$$

that is, the amount plus income from investing the amount for the year equals the £20,000. If we rearrange this equation, we find:

$$PV \times (1 + 0.2) = £20,000$$

(Note that 0.2 is the same as 20 per cent, but expressed as a decimal.) Further rearranging gives:

$$PV = £20,000/(1 + 0.2) = £16,667$$

Thus, managers of Billingsgate Battery Company, who have the opportunity to invest at 20 per cent a year, should not mind whether they have £16,667 now or £20,000 in a year's time. In other words, £16,667 represents the *present value* of £20,000 to be received in one year's time.

We can make a statement about the PV of a particular cash flow. It is:

PV of the cash flow of year n = actual cash flow of year n divided by $(1 + r)^n$

where n is the year of the cash flow (that is, how many years into the future) and r is the opportunity financing cost expressed as a decimal (instead of as a percentage).

If we derive the present value (PV) of each of the cash flows associated with Billingsgate's machine investment, we can easily make the direct comparison between the cost of making the investment (£100,000) and the subsequent benefits to be derived in years 1 to 5.

We have already seen how this works for the £20,000 inflow for year 1. For year 2, the calculation would be:

$$\text{PV of year 2 cash flow (that is, £40,000)} = £40,000/(1 + 0.2)^2 = £40,000/(1.2)^2$$

$$= £40,000/(1.44) = £27,778$$

Thus, the present value of the £40,000 to be received in two years' time is £27,778.

Activity 14.10

See if you can show that the Billingsgate Battery Company would view £27,778, receivable now, as equally acceptable to receiving £40,000 in two years' time, assuming that there is a 20 per cent investment opportunity.

To answer this activity, we simply apply the principles of *compounding*. Income earned is reinvested and then added to the initial investment to derive the future value. Thus:

	£
Amount available for immediate investment	27,778
Income for year 1 (20% × 27,778)	5,556
	33,334
Income for year 2 (20% × 33,334)	6,667
	40,001

(The extra £1 is only a rounding error.)

Since the business can turn £27,778 into £40,000 in two years, these amounts are equivalent. We can say that £27,778 is the present value of £40,000 receivable after two years (given a 20 per cent cost of finance).

The act of reducing the value of a cash flow, to take account of the period between the present time and the time that the cash flow is expected, is known as **discounting**. Discounting, in effect, charges the project with the cost of financing it. Ignoring this financing cost would be to overlook a significant cost of undertaking the project.

Calculating the net present value

Now let us calculate the present values of all of the cash flows associated with the Billingsgate Battery machine project and, from them, the *net present value (NPV)* of the project as a whole.

The relevant cash flows and calculations are:

Time	Cash flow £000	Calculation of PV	PV £000
Immediately (time 0)	(100)	$(100)/(1 + 0.2)^0$	(100.00)
1 year's time	20	$20/(1 + 0.2)^1$	16.67
2 years' time	40	$40/(1 + 0.2)^2$	27.78
3 years' time	60	$60/(1 + 0.2)^3$	34.72
4 years' time	60	$60/(1 + 0.2)^4$	28.94
5 years' time	20	$20/(1 + 0.2)^5$	8.04
5 years' time	20	$20/(1 + 0.2)^5$	8.04
Net present value (NPV)			24.19

Note that $(1 + 0.2)^0 = 1$.

Once again, we must decide whether the machine project is acceptable to the business. To help us, the following decision rules for NPV should be applied:

- If the NPV is positive the project should be accepted; if it is negative the project should be rejected.
- If there are two (or more) competing projects that have positive NPVs, the project with the higher (or highest) NPV should be selected.

In this case, the NPV is positive, so we should accept the project and buy the machine. The reasoning behind this decision rule is quite straightforward. Investing in the machine will make the business, and its owners, £24,190 better off than they would be by taking up the next best available opportunity. The total benefits from investing in this machine are worth a total of £124,190 today. Since the business can 'buy' these benefits for just £100,000 today, the investment should be made. If, however, the present value of the benefits were below £100,000, it would be less than the cost of 'buying' those benefits and the opportunity should, therefore, be rejected.

Activity 14.11

What is the *maximum* the Billingsgate Battery Company should be prepared to pay for the machine, given the potential benefits of owning it?

The business would logically be prepared to pay up to £124,190 since the wealth of the owners of the business would be increased up to this price – although the business would prefer to pay as little as possible.

Using present value tables

To deduce each PV in the Billingsgate Battery Company project, we took the relevant cash flow and multiplied it by $1/(1 + r)^n$. There is a slightly different way to do this. Tables exist that show values of this **discount factor** for a range of values of r and n. Such a table appears at the end of this book in Appendix F on page 851. Take a look at it.

Look at the column for 20 per cent and the row for one year. We find that the factor is 0.833. This means that the PV of a cash flow of £1 receivable in one year is £0.833. So the present value of a cash flow of £20,000 receivable in one year's time is £16,660 (that is, 0.833 × £20,000). This is the same result, ignoring rounding errors, as we found earlier by using the equation.

Activity 14.12

What is the NPV of the Chaotic Industries project from Activity 14.2, assuming a 15 per cent opportunity cost of finance (discount rate)? (Use the present value table in Appendix F, page 851.)

Remember that the net cash inflows and outflow are expected to be:

Time		£000
Immediately	Cost of vans	(150)
1 year's time	Saving before depreciation	30
2 years' time	Saving before depreciation	30
3 years' time	Saving before depreciation	30
4 years' time	Saving before depreciation	30
5 years' time	Saving before depreciation	30
6 years' time	Saving before depreciation	30
6 years' time	Disposal proceeds from the vans	30

The calculation of the NPV of the project is as follows:

Time	Cash flows £000	Discount factor (15%)	Present value £000
Immediately	(150)	1.000	(150.00)
1 year's time	30	0.870	26.10
2 years' time	30	0.756	22.68
3 years' time	30	0.658	19.74
4 years' time	30	0.572	17.16
5 years' time	30	0.497	14.91
6 years' time	30	0.432	12.96
6 years' time	30	0.432	12.96
		NPV =	**(23.49)**

Activity 14.13

How would you interpret this result?

The project has a negative NPV. This means that the present values of the benefits from the investment are worth less than the initial outlay. Any amount up to £126,510 (the present value of the benefits) would be worth paying, but not £150,000.

The present value table in Appendix F shows how the value of £1 diminishes as its receipt goes further into the future. Assuming an opportunity cost of finance of 20 per cent a year, £1 to be received immediately, obviously, has a present value of £1. However, as the time before it is to be received increases, the present value diminishes significantly, as is shown in Figure 14.3.

| Figure 14.3 | Present value of £1 receivable at various times in the future, assuming an annual financing cost of 20 per cent |

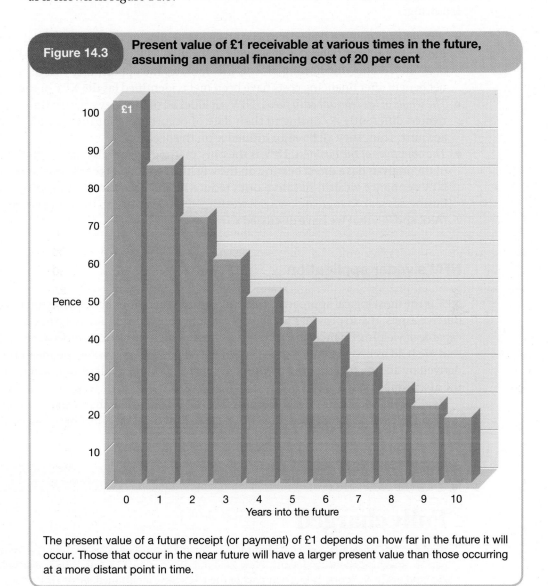

The present value of a future receipt (or payment) of £1 depends on how far in the future it will occur. Those that occur in the near future will have a larger present value than those occurring at a more distant point in time.

The discount rate and the cost of capital

We have seen that the appropriate discount rate to use in NPV assessments is the opportunity cost of finance. This is, in effect, the cost to the business of the finance needed to fund the investment. It will normally be the cost of a mixture of funds (shareholders' funds and borrowings) employed by the business and is often referred to as the **cost of capital.** We shall refer to it in this way from now on.

Why NPV is better

From what we have seen, NPV offers a better approach to appraising investment opportunities than either ARR or PP. This is because it fully takes account of each of the following:

- *The timing of the cash flows.* By discounting the various cash flows associated with each project according to when they are expected to arise, NPV takes account of the time value of money. As the discounting process incorporates the opportunity cost of capital, the net benefit after financing costs have been met is identified (as the NPV of the project).
- *The whole of the relevant cash flows.* NPV includes all of the relevant cash flows. They are treated differently according to their date of occurrence, but they are all taken into account. Thus, they all have an influence on the decision.
- *The objectives of the business.* NPV is the only method of appraisal in which the output of the analysis has a direct bearing on the wealth of the owners of the business. Positive NPVs enhance wealth; negative ones reduce it. Since we assume that private-sector businesses seek to increase owners' wealth, NPV is superior to the other two methods (ARR and PP) that we have discussed so far.

NPV's wider application

NPV is the most logical approach to making business decisions about investments in productive assets. It also provides the basis for valuing any economic asset, that is, any asset capable of yielding financial benefits. This includes such things as equity shares and loans that are held as investments. In fact, when we talk of *economic value,* we mean the value derived by adding together the discounted (present) values of all future cash flows from the asset concerned.

Real World 14.5 is an extract from a *Financial Times* article that discusses a telecoms takeover in New Zealand where the NPV has been used to assess its financial viability.

Real World 14.5

Fully charged

Flight of the Conchords, a sitcom about Kiwis adrift among New Yorkers ignorant of their nation, spawned the wry slogan: "New Zealand: it's not part of Australia". Nor is New Zealand's Sky Network Television part of the UK's Sky, mentioned above. But the group is set to become a subsidiary of deal-hungry telecoms group Vodafone through a NZ$3.4 billion merger, which, for readability, we'll convert to US$2.4bn.

British companies have been hanging back from mergers and acquisitions ahead of the Brexit vote. Vodafone is going ahead with this deal, though in a place about as far as you can get from Nigel Farage without boarding a spaceship.

Telephone air time is increasingly commodified. There is fierce competition in pay TV. The combination of SNT and Voda's New Zealand operations is expected to yield cost and capital expenditure synergies (benefits) with a net present value of $295 million.

Source: Extract from Guthrie, J. (2016) Kiwi combo, Lombard, ft.com, 9 June. © The Financial Times Limited 2016. All Rights Reserved.

Internal rate of return (IRR)

This is the last of the four major methods of investment appraisal found in practice. It is closely related to the NPV method in that both involve discounting future cash flows. The **internal rate of return (IRR)** of an investment is the discount rate that, when applied to its projected future cash flows, will produce an NPV of precisely zero. In essence, it represents the yield from a particular investment opportunity.

Activity 14.14

We should recall that, when we discounted the cash flows of the Billingsgate Battery Company machine project at 20 per cent, we found that the NPV was a positive figure of £24,190 (see page 581). What does the NPV of the machine project tell us about the rate of return that the investment will yield for the business (that is, the project's IRR)?

As the NPV is positive when discounting at 20 per cent, it implies that the project's rate of return is more than 20 per cent. The fact that the NPV is pretty large implies that the actual rate of return is quite a lot above 20 per cent. Normally, we should expect increasing the discount rate to reduce NPV, because the higher the discount rate the lower the discounted figure.

IRR cannot usually be calculated directly. Iteration (trial and error) is the approach normally adopted. Doing this manually, however, is fairly laborious. Fortunately, computer spreadsheet packages can do this with ease.

Despite it being laborious, we shall now derive the IRR for the Billingsgate Battery project manually to illustrate how it works. We shall increase the size of the discount rate to reduce NPV, because a higher discount rate gives a lower discounted figure.

Let us try a higher rate, say, 30 per cent and see what happens.

Time	Cash flow £000	Discount factor 30%	PV £000
Immediately (time 0)	(100)	1.000	(100.00)
1 year's time	20	0.769	15.38
2 years' time	40	0.592	23.68
3 years' time	60	0.455	27.30
4 years' time	60	0.350	21.00
5 years' time	20	0.269	5.38
5 years' time	20	0.269	5.38
		NPV	(1.88)

By increasing the discount rate from 20 per cent to 30 per cent, we have reduced the NPV from £24,190 (positive) to £1,880 (negative). Since the IRR is the discount rate that will give us an NPV of exactly zero, we can conclude that the IRR of Billingsgate Battery Company's machine project is very slightly below 30 per cent. Further trials could lead us to the exact rate, but there is probably not much point, given the likely inaccuracy of the cash flow estimates. For most practical purposes, it is good enough to say that the IRR is about 30 per cent.

The relationship between the NPV and the IRR is shown graphically in Figure 14.4 using the information relating to the Billingsgate Battery Company.

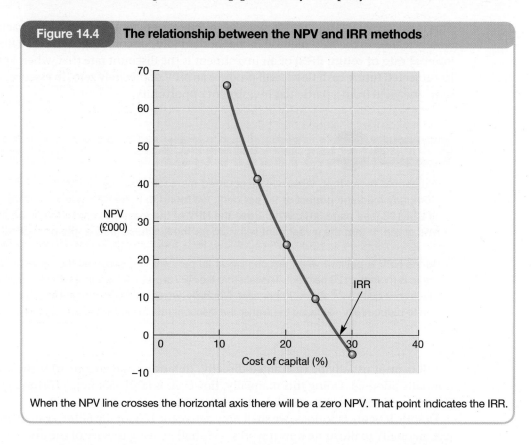

| Figure 14.4 | **The relationship between the NPV and IRR methods** |

When the NPV line crosses the horizontal axis there will be a zero NPV. That point indicates the IRR.

In Figure 14.4, if the cost of capital (discount rate) is equal to zero, the NPV will be the sum of the net cash flows. In other words, no account is taken of the time value of money. However, as the discount rate increases there is a corresponding decrease in the NPV of the project. When the NPV line crosses the horizontal axis there will be a zero NPV. That point represents the IRR.

Activity 14.15

What is the internal rate of return of the Chaotic Industries project from Activity 14.2? (Hint: Remember that you already know the NPV of this project at 15 per cent (from Activity 14.12).)

Since we know that, at a 15 per cent discount rate, the NPV is a relatively large negative figure, our next trial should use a lower discount rate, say 10 per cent:

Time	Cash flows	Discount factor (10% – from the table)	Present value
	£000		£000
Immediately	(150)	1.000	(150.00)
1 year's time	30	0.909	27.27
2 years' time	30	0.826	24.78
3 years' time	30	0.751	22.53

4 years' time	30	0.683	20.49
5 years' time	30	0.621	18.63
6 years' time	30	0.564	16.92
6 years' time	30	0.564	16.92
		NPV	(2.46)

This figure is close to zero NPV. However, the NPV is still negative and so the precise IRR will be a little below 10 per cent.

We could undertake further trials to derive the precise IRR. If done manually, this can be quite time consuming. We can, however, get an acceptable approximation to the answer fairly quickly by first calculating the change in NPV arising from a 1 per cent change in the discount rate. This is achieved by taking the difference between the two trials (that is, 15 per cent and 10 per cent) that have already been carried out (in Activities 14.12 and 14.15):

Trial	Discount factor %	Net present value £000
1	15	(23.49)
2	10	(2.46)
Difference	5	21.03

The change in NPV for every 1 per cent change in the discount rate will be:

$$(21.03/5) = 4.21$$

The amount by which the IRR would need to fall below the 10 per cent discount rate, in order to achieve a zero NPV would therefore be:

$$(2.46/4.21) \times 1\% = 0.58\%$$

The IRR is therefore:

$$(10.00 - 0.58) = 9.42\%$$

To say that the IRR is about 9 or 10 per cent, however, is near enough for most purposes.

Note that this approach to obtaining a more accurate figure for IRR assumes a straight-line relationship between the discount rate and NPV. We can see from Figure 14.4 that this assumption is not strictly correct. Over a relatively short range, however, this simplifying assumption is not usually a problem and so we can still arrive at a reasonable approximation using the approach taken. As most businesses have software packages to derive a project's IRR, it is not usually necessary to make the calculations just described.

The following decision rules are applied when using IRR:

- For any project to be acceptable, it must meet a minimum IRR requirement. This is often referred to as the *hurdle rate* and, logically, this should be the opportunity cost of capital.
- Where there are competing projects, the one with the higher (or highest) IRR should be selected.

Activity (14.16)

Assume that a project has an IRR that exceeds the business's cost of capital. Why might it be helpful to consider how much it exceeds it by?

It may help us to make some judgement about the riskiness of the project, as far as the projected cost of capital is concerned. We should be able to see how far this figure could rise in practice before the project would become unfavourable (assuming all of the other inputs to the project appraisal turned out to be as projected).

Real World 14.6 illustrates how the French energy business, EDF, used IRR in assessing a deal to build a nuclear power station in the UK.

Real World 14.6

IRR for EDF

The deal for EDF to build the Hinkley Point nuclear plant in the UK could either be the salvation, or the ruin, of the French state-owned group.

Jean-Bernard Lévy, the chief executive of EDF, told journalists the decision was "a big moment" for securing the future of EDF and also signified the "relaunch of nuclear in Europe", which should also benefit the group.

The British government confirmed on Thursday that EDF will be paid £92.50 per megawatt hour for the electricity generated by Hinkley Point C for 35-years, more than double the current rate for wholesale electricity prices.

According to the company this will deliver a 9 per cent internal rate of return over the 60 years lifespan on the £18 billion project.

The fixed price offered by the UK compares to the French market, which is being deregulated, leaving the company to sell an ever-increasing share of its electricity at market prices.

Source: Extract from Stothard, M. (2016) Hinkley Point is risk for overstretched EDF, warn critics, ft.com, 15 September. © The Financial Times Limited 2016. All Rights Reserved.

Real World 14.7 gives some examples of IRRs sought in practice.

Real World 14.7

Rates of return

IRRs for investment projects can vary considerably. Here are a few examples of the expected or target returns from investment projects of large businesses.

- GlaxoSmithKline plc, the leading pharmaceuticals business, is generating an annual IRR from investments in new products of 13 per cent.
- Next plc, the fashion retailer, requires an annual IRR of 30 per cent when appraising online advertising campaigns.

- Carillion plc, a facilities management and construction business, seeks a 15 per cent IRR on new public/private partnership projects.
- Rentokil Initial plc, the business services provider, has an after-tax required IRR of 15 per cent for any takeover targets that it may be considering.
- Gresham House plc, the investment management business, targets a minimum of 15 per cent IRR.
- Marks and Spencer plc, the stores chain, has targeted a 'hurdle' internal rate of return of 12 to 15 per cent on a new investment programme.

These values seem surprisingly high. A study of returns made by all of the businesses listed on the London Stock Exchange between 1900 and 2014 showed an average annual return of 5.3 per cent. This figure is the real return (that is, ignoring inflation). It would probably be fair to add at least 3 per cent to it to compare it with the targets for the businesses listed above. Also, the targets for five of the businesses are probably pre-tax (the businesses do not specify, except Rentokil Initial). In that case, it is probably reasonable to add about a third to the average Stock Exchange returns. This would give us around 11 per cent per year. This would be roughly in line with the Marks and Spencer target. The targets for the other businesses, however, seem rather ambitious – particularly ambitious in the case of Rentokil Initial, given that it's an after-tax rate. Their rate is for takeover targets, which they may regard as being particularly risky. Next's target is also high, though it relates to advertising campaigns.

Sources: GlaxoSmithKline plc, Annual Report 2015, p. 24; Next plc, Annual Report 2016, p. 13; Carillion plc, Annual Report 2014; Rentokil Initial plc, www.rentokil-initial.com, accessed 23 September 2016; Gresham House plc, www.greshamhouse.com, accessed 23 September 2016; Press release on 2012 annual results, Marks and Spencer plc, 22 May 2012; Dimson, E., Marsh, P. and Staunton, M. (2015) *Credit Suisse Global Investments Returns Yearbook.*

Problems with IRR

IRR has certain key attributes in common with NPV. All cash flows are taken into account and their timing is logically handled. The main problem of IRR, however, is that it does not directly address the question of wealth generation. It can, therefore, lead to the wrong decision being made. This is because the IRR approach will always rank a project with, for example, an IRR of 25 per cent above that of a project with an IRR of 20 per cent. Although accepting the project with the higher percentage return will often generate more wealth, this may not always be the case. This is because IRR completely ignores the *scale of investment.*

With a 15 per cent cost of capital, £15 million invested at 20 per cent for one year will make us wealthier by £0.75 million (that is, $15 \times (20 - 15)\% = 0.75$). With the same cost of capital, £5 million invested at 25 per cent for one year will make us only £0.5 million (that is, $5 \times (25 - 15)\% = 0.50$). IRR does not recognise this point.

Activity 14.17

Which other investment appraisal method ignores the scale of investment?

We saw earlier that the ARR method suffers from this problem.

Competing projects do not usually show such large differences in scale and so IRR and NPV normally give the same signal. However, as NPV will always give the correct signal, it is difficult to see why any other method should be used.

A further problem with the IRR method is that it has difficulty handling projects with unconventional cash flows. In the examples studied so far, each project has a negative cash flow arising at the start of its life and then positive cash flows thereafter. In some cases, however, a project may have both positive and negative cash flows at future points in its life. Such a pattern of cash flows can result in there being more than one IRR, or even no IRR at all. This can make the IRR method difficult to use, although it should be said that this problem is also quite rare in practice.

Some practical points

When undertaking an investment appraisal, there are several practical points to bear in mind:

- *Past costs.* As with all decisions, we should take account only of relevant costs in our analysis. Only costs that vary with the decision should be considered, as we discussed in Chapter 8. This means that all past costs should be ignored, as they cannot vary with the decision. A business may incur costs (such as development costs and market research costs) before the evaluation of an opportunity to launch a new product. As those costs have already been incurred, they should be disregarded, even though the amounts may be substantial and relate directly to the project. Costs that have already been committed but not yet paid should also be disregarded. Where a business has entered into a binding contract to incur a particular cost, it becomes in effect a past cost even though payment may not be due until some point in the future.

- *Common future costs.* It is not only past costs that do not vary with the decision; some future costs may also be the same. For example, the cost of raw materials may not vary with the decision whether to invest in a new piece of manufacturing plant or to continue to use existing plant.

- *Opportunity costs.* Opportunity costs arising from benefits forgone must be taken into account. For example, when considering a decision concerning whether to continue to use a machine already owned by the business, the realisable value of the machine might be an important opportunity cost.

- *Taxation.* Owners will be interested in the after-tax returns generated from the business. Profits from the project will be taxed, the capital investment may attract tax relief and so on. As the rate of tax is often significant, taxation becomes an important consideration when making investment decisions. Unless tax is formally taken into account, the wrong decision could easily be made. This means that both the amount and the timing of tax outflows should be reflected in the cash flows for the project.

- *Cash flows not profit flows.* We have seen that for the NPV, IRR and PP methods, it is cash flows rather than profit flows that are relevant to the assessment of investment projects. Nevertheless, some proposals may contain only data relating to profits over the investment period. These will need to be adjusted in order to derive the cash flows. As mentioned earlier, operating profit before non-cash items (such as depreciation) provides an approximation to the cash flows for the period. We should, therefore, work back to this figure.

- *Working capital adjustment.* When the data are expressed in profit rather than cash flow terms, some adjustment for changes in working capital may also be needed. Launching a new product, for example, may give rise to an increase in the net investment made in working capital (trade receivables and inventories less trade payables). This would normally require an immediate outlay of cash, which should be shown as a cash outflow in the NPV calculations. However, at the end of the life of the project, the additional working capital will be released. This divestment results in an effective inflow of cash at the end of the project. This should be shown in the NPV calculations at the point at which it is received.

- *Year-end assumption.* In the examples and activities considered so far, we have assumed that cash flows arise at the end of the relevant year. This simplifying assumption is used to make the calculations easier. As we saw earlier, this assumption is unrealistic, as money will have to be paid to employees on a weekly or monthly basis, credit customers will pay within a month or two of the sale and so on. Nevertheless, it is probably not a serious distortion. It is perfectly possible to deal more precisely with the timing of the cash flows if required.

- *Interest payments.* When using discounted cash flow techniques (NPV and IRR), interest payments should not be taken into account in deriving cash flows for the period. Discounting already takes account of the costs of financing. To include interest charges in deriving cash flows for the period would therefore be double counting.

- *Other factors.* Investment decision making must not be viewed as simply a mechanical exercise. The results derived from a particular investment appraisal method will be only one input to the decision-making process. There may be broader issues connected to the decision that have to be taken into account but which may be difficult or impossible to quantify.

The reliability of the forecasts and the validity of the assumptions used in the evaluation will also have a bearing on the final decision.

Activity (14.18)

The directors of Manuff (Steel) Ltd are considering closing one of the business's factories. There has been a reduction in the demand for the products made at the factory in recent years. The directors are not optimistic about the long-term prospects for these products. The factory is situated in an area where unemployment is high.

The factory is leased with four years of the lease remaining. The directors are uncertain whether the factory should be closed immediately or at the end of the period of the lease. Another business has offered to sublease the premises from Manuff (Steel) Ltd at a rental of £40,000 a year for the remainder of the lease period.

The machinery and equipment at the factory cost £1,500,000. The value at which they appear in the statement of financial position is £400,000. In the event of immediate closure, the machinery and equipment could be sold for £220,000. The working capital at the factory is £420,000. It could be liquidated for that amount immediately, if required. Alternatively, the working capital can be liquidated in full at the end of the lease period. Immediate closure would result in redundancy payments to employees of £180,000.

If the factory continues in operation until the end of the lease period, the following operating profits (losses) are expected:

	Year 1 £000	Year 2 £000	Year 3 £000	Year 4 £000
Operating profit (loss)	160	(40)	30	20

Activity 14.18 *continued*

These figures are derived after deducting a charge of £90,000 a year for depreciation of machinery and equipment. The residual value of the machinery and equipment at the end of the lease period is estimated at £40,000.

Redundancy payments are expected to be £150,000 at the end of the lease period if the factory continues in operation. The business has an annual cost of capital of 12 per cent. Ignore taxation.

(a) Determine the relevant cash flows arising from a decision to continue operations until the end of the lease period rather than to close immediately.

(b) Calculate the net present value of continuing operations until the end of the lease period, rather than closing immediately.

(c) What other factors might the directors take into account before making a final decision on the timing of the factory closure?

(d) State, with reasons, whether or not the business should continue to operate the factory until the end of the lease period.

Your answer should be:

(a) Relevant cash flows

	Years				
	0	*1*	*2*	*3*	*4*
	£000	*£000*	*£000*	*£000*	*£000*
Operating cash flows (Note 1)		250	50	120	110
Sale of machinery (Note 2)	(220)				40
Redundancy costs (Note 3)	180				(150)
Sublease rentals (Note 4)		(40)	(40)	(40)	(40)
Working capital invested (Note 5)	(420)				420
Net cash flows	(460)	210	10	80	380

Notes:

1 Each year's operating cash flows are calculated by adding back the depreciation charge for the year to the operating profit for the year. In the case of the operating loss, the depreciation charge is deducted.

2 In the event of closure, machinery could be sold immediately. As a result, an opportunity cost of £220,000 is incurred if operations continue.

3 By continuing operations, there will be a saving in immediate redundancy costs of £180,000. However, redundancy costs of £150,000 will be paid in four years' time.

4 By continuing operations, the opportunity to sublease the factory will be forgone.

5 Immediate closure would mean that working capital could be liquidated. By continuing operations, this opportunity is forgone. However, working capital can be liquidated in four years' time.

(b)

	Years				
	0	*1*	*2*	*3*	*4*
Discount rate 12 %	1.000	0.893	0.797	0.712	0.636
Present value (£000)	(460.0)	187.5	8.0	57.0	241.7
Net present value (£000)	34.2				

(c) Other factors that may influence the decision include:

- *The overall strategy of the business.* The business may need to set the decision within a broader context. It may be necessary to manufacture the products at the factory because they are an integral part of the business's product range. The business may wish to avoid redundancies in an area of high unemployment for as long as possible.
- *Flexibility.* A decision to close the factory is probably irreversible. If the factory continues, however, there may be a chance that the prospects for the factory will brighten in the future.
- *Creditworthiness of sub-lessee.* The business should investigate the creditworthiness of the sub-lessee. Failure to receive the expected sublease payments would make the closure option far less attractive.
- *Accuracy of forecasts.* The forecasts made by the business should be examined carefully. Inaccuracies in the forecasts or any underlying assumptions may change

(d) The NPV of the decision to continue operations rather than close immediately is positive. Hence, shareholders would be better off if the directors took this course of action. The factory should therefore continue in operation rather than close down. This decision is likely to be welcomed by employees and would allow the business to maintain its flexibility.

The main methods of investment appraisal are summarised in Figure 14.5.

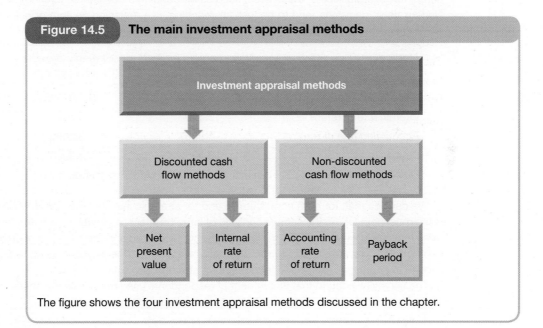

Figure 14.5   **The main investment appraisal methods**

The figure shows the four investment appraisal methods discussed in the chapter.

Investment appraisal in practice

Many surveys have been conducted in the UK, and elsewhere in the world, into the methods of investment appraisal used by businesses. They have revealed the following:

- Businesses tend to use more than one method to assess each investment decision.
- The discounting methods (NPV and IRR) have become increasingly popular over time. NPV and IRR are now the most popular of the four methods.
- PP continues to be popular and, to a lesser extent, so does ARR. This is despite the severe theoretical shortcomings of both of these methods.
- Larger businesses rely more heavily on discounting methods than smaller businesses and tend to use more of the four methods.

Real World 14.8 shows the results of a survey of a number of UK manufacturing businesses concerning their use of investment appraisal methods.

Real World 14.8

A survey of UK business practice

Senior financial managers at 83 of the UK's largest manufacturing businesses were asked about the investment appraisal methods used to evaluate both 'strategic' and 'non-strategic' projects. Strategic projects are broadly defined as those that aim to increase or change the competitive capabilities of a business, such as introducing a new manufacturing process. Non-strategic decisions tend to be less far-reaching, like replacing an item of plant in an existing and continuing activity.

Method	Non-strategic projects Mean score	Strategic projects Mean score
Net present value	3.6829	3.9759
Internal rate of return	3.3293	3.7073
Accounting rate of return	1.9867	2.2667
Payback	3.4268	3.6098

Response scale 1 = never, 2 = rarely, 3 = often, 4 = mostly, 5 = always

We can see that, for both non-strategic and for strategic investments, the NPV method is the most popular. As the sample consists of large businesses (nearly all with annual total sales revenue in excess of £100 million), a fairly sophisticated approach to evaluation might be expected. Nevertheless, for non-strategic investments, the payback method comes second in popularity. It drops to third place for strategic projects.

The survey also found that 98 per cent of respondents used more than one method and 88 per cent used all four methods of investment appraisal.

Source: Based on information in Alkaraan, F. and Northcott, D. (2006) Strategic capital investment decision-making: A role for emergent analysis tools? A study of practice in large UK manufacturing companies, *The British Accounting Review*, 38, p. 159.

A survey of large businesses in five leading industrialised countries, including the UK, also shows considerable support for the NPV and IRR methods. There is less support for the payback method but, nevertheless, it still seems to be fairly widely used. **Real World 14.9** sets out some key findings.

Real World 14.9

A multinational survey of business practice

A survey of investment and financing practices in five different countries was carried out by Cohen and Yagil. This survey, based on a sample of the largest 300 businesses in each country, revealed the following concerning the popularity of three of the investment appraisal methods discussed in this chapter.

Frequency of the use of investment appraisal techniques

	USA	UK	Germany	Canada	Japan	Average
IRR	4.00	4.16	4.08	4.15	3.29	3.93
NPV	3.88	4.00	3.50	4.09	3.57	3.80
PP	3.46	3.89	3.33	3.57	3.52	3.55

Response scale 1 = never, 2 = rarely, 3 = often, 4 = mostly, 5 = always

Key findings of the survey include the following:

- IRR is more popular than NPV in all countries, except Japan. The difference between the two methods, however, is not statistically significant.
- Managers of UK businesses use investment appraisal techniques the most, while managers of Japanese businesses use them the least. This may be related to business traditions within each country.
- There is a positive relationship between business size and the popularity of the IRR and NPV methods. This may be related to the greater experience and understanding of financial theory of managers of larger businesses. A more recent survey (by Lucas, Prowle and Lowth) of some much smaller UK businesses indicated that none of them carried out any investment appraisal. This adds emphasis to the size/sophistication relationship in this context.

Sources: Cohen, G. and Yagil, J. (2007) *A multinational survey of corporate financial policies*, Working Paper, Haifa University; Lucas, M., Prowle, M. and Lowth, G. (2013) *Management Accounting Practices of UK Small-medium-sized Enterprises,* CIMA, July.

Activity 14.19

Earlier in the chapter, we discussed the limitations of the PP method. Can you explain why it is still a reasonably popular method of investment appraisal among managers?

There seem to be several possible reasons:

- PP is easy to understand and use.
- It can avoid the problems of forecasting far into the future.
- It gives weight to early cash flows when there is greater certainty concerning the accuracy of their predicted value.
- It emphasises the importance of liquidity. Where a business has liquidity problems, a short payback period for a project is likely to appear attractive.

The popularity of PP may suggest a lack of sophistication on the part of managers concerning investment appraisal. This criticism is most often made against managers of smaller businesses. This point is borne out by both of the surveys discussed in Real World 14.9 which found that smaller businesses are much less likely to use discounted cash flow methods (NPV and IRR) than larger ones. Other surveys have tended to reach a similar conclusion.

IRR may be popular because it expresses outcomes in percentage terms rather than in absolute terms. This form of expression seems to be preferred by managers, despite the problems of percentage measures that we discussed earlier. This may be because managers are used to using percentage figures as targets (for example, return on capital employed).

Real World 14.10 shows extracts from the 2016 annual report of a well-known business: Rolls-Royce plc, the builder of engines for aircraft and other purposes.

Real World 14.10

The use of NPV at Rolls-Royce

In its 2016 annual report and accounts, Rolls-Royce plc stated that:

> The Group subjects all major investments and capital expenditure to a rigorous examination of risks and future cash flows to ensure that they create shareholder value. All major investments, including the launch of major programmes, require Board approval.
>
> The Group has a portfolio of projects at different stages of their life cycles. Discounted cash flow analysis of the remaining life of projects is performed on a regular basis.

Source: Rolls-Royce Holdings plc Annual Report 2016, p. 185.

Rolls-Royce indicates that it uses NPV (the report refers to creating shareholder value and to discounted cash flow, which strongly imply NPV). It is interesting to note that Rolls-Royce not only assesses new projects but also reassesses existing ones. This must be a sensible commercial approach. Businesses should not continue with existing projects unless those projects have a positive NPV based on future cash flows. Just because a project seemed to have a positive NPV before it started, and at early stages in its life, does not mean that this will persist, in the light of changing circumstances. Activity 14.18 (page 591) considered a decision to close down a project.

Investment appraisal and strategic planning

So far, we have tended to view investment opportunities as unconnected, independent, events. In practice, however, successful businesses are those that set out a clear strategic framework for the selection of investment projects in the way described in Chapter 12. Unless this framework is in place, it may be difficult to identify those projects that are likely to generate a positive NPV. The best investment projects are usually those that match the business's internal strengths (for example, skills, experience, access to finance) with the opportunities available. In areas where this match does not exist, other businesses, for which the match does exist, will have a distinct competitive advantage. This means that they can provide the product or service at a better price and/or quality.

Setting out the framework just described is an essential part of *strategic planning.* In practice, strategic plans often have a time span of around five years. It involves asking 'where do we want our business to be in five years' time and how can we get there?' It will set the appropriate direction, in terms of products, markets, financing and so on, to ensure that the business is best placed to generate profitable investment opportunities.

Real World 14.11 shows how one large business made an investment that fitted its strategic objectives.

Real World 14.11

Windows are a good fit

CRH plc, the Irish building materials business, bought the California-based glazing business C J Laurence Co. Inc. for $1.3 billion in August 2015.

CRH will become the world's third largest building materials group, partly as a result of this and other acquisitions. The business already has a major presence in the USA and Canada, which is why CRH's management described CJ Laurence as an 'exceptional strategic fit' for it. This means that CRH believes that the acquisition represented a good deal. That may not have been true, however, for another purchaser, paying the same price, for whom there was not that degree of strategic fit.

FT   *Source*: Information taken from Grant, J. (2015) CRH adds CR Laurence to acquisitions tally for $1.3bn, ft.com, 27 August. © The Financial Times Limited 2015. All Rights Reserved.

Risk and investment

As we saw in Chapter 8, all business activities are risky. This means that consideration of risk is an important aspect of financial decision making. As was mentioned at the start of this chapter, risk is a particularly important issue in the context of investment decisions, because:

- large amounts of resources are often involved;
- relatively long timescales tend to be involved; and
- it is often difficult and/or expensive to bail out of an investment once it has been undertaken.

Various methods for dealing with risk have been proposed and we considered one of these, sensitivity analysis, in Chapter 8. Undertaking sensitivity analysis for an investment project, appraised on the basis on NPV, will follow the approach discussed in that chapter. Two additional factors, however, the cost of capital and the life of the project, have to be considered.

Activity **14.20**

When undertaking sensitivity analysis, how would we calculate the cost of capital figure that would produce an NPV for a project of precisely zero (that is, the 'break-even' cost of capital)?

We saw earlier in the chapter that calculating the IRR, which involves trial and error, will provide this cost of capital figure.

Identifying the break-even project life can be achieved by adopting a similar approach to that used in calculating the payback period. In other words, we calculate the point in time when future discounted cash inflows equal the initial cash outflows. It is at this point that the project will 'break even'.

Real World 14.12 describes a feasibility study of a silver mining project. It incorporated sensitivity analysis to test the robustness of the estimated NPV of the project.

Real World 14.12

A sensitive subject

In 2016, Silver Bear Resources Inc released the findings of a feasibility study for the Vertikalny Central deposit of the Mangazeisky Silver Project in the Republic of Sakha (Yakutia), Russia. As part of the study, sensitivity analysis was carried out, on key variables using an NPV discount rate of 5 per cent. This revealed that the silver price was the most sensitive variable, followed by the exchange rate, operating costs and capital expenditure costs.

Figure 14.6 below shows the sensitivity of each of these key variables in a diagrammatic form. The NPV of the project is shown on the vertical axis and the percentage change in the base case (most likely outcome) is shown on the horizontal axis.

Figure 14.6   NPV sensitivity analysis of the Mangazeisky Silver Project

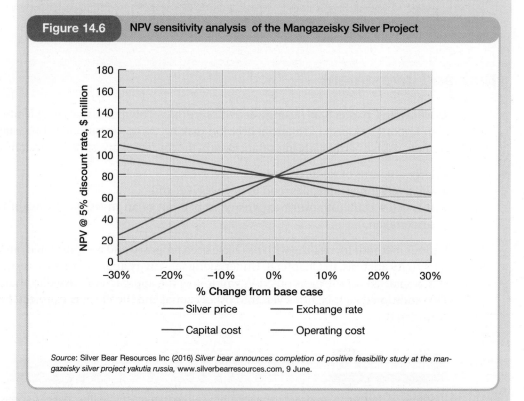

Source: Silver Bear Resources Inc (2016) *Silver bear announces completion of positive feasibility study at the mangazeisky silver project yakutia russia*, www.silverbearresources.com, 9 June.

We can see from the figure, for example, that a fall in the silver price of 30 per cent would take the NPV of the project close to zero whereas a 30 per cent rise in the price would almost double the NPV of the project, when compared to the base case.

Presenting the sensitivity analysis in this way may make it more accessible to those who lack a good grasp of finance.

Managing investment projects

So far, we have been concerned with the process of carrying out calculations to help choose among already identified investment opportunities. While this is important, it is only *part* of the process of investment decision making. There are other important aspects that managers must also consider.

It is possible to see the investment process as a sequence of five stages, each of which is set out in Figure 14.7.

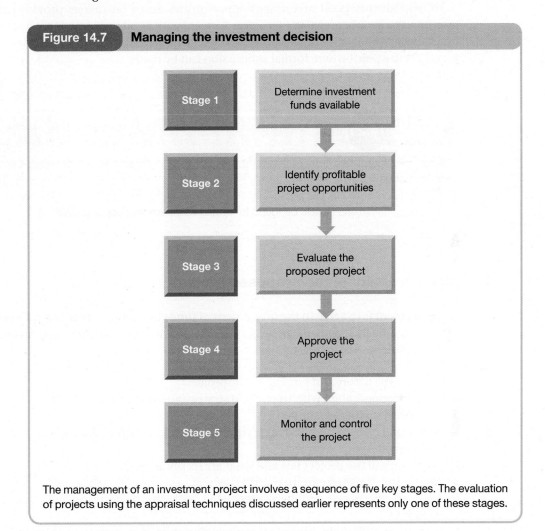

Figure 14.7   Managing the investment decision

The management of an investment project involves a sequence of five key stages. The evaluation of projects using the appraisal techniques discussed earlier represents only one of these stages.

Stage 1: Determine investment funds available

The amount of funds available for investment may be limited by the external market for funds or by internal management. In practice, it is the business's own senior managers that are more likely to impose limits, perhaps because they lack confidence in the business's ability to handle higher levels of investment. In either case, however, it may mean that the funds will not be sufficient to finance all of the potentially profitable investment opportunities available. This shortage of investment funds is known as **capital rationing.** When it arises, managers are faced with the task of deciding on the most profitable use of those funds available.

Stage 2: Identify profitable project opportunities

A vital part of the investment process is the search for profitable investment opportunities. The business should adopt a systematic approach to identifying feasible projects. To maintain a competitive edge, this should be a normal part of the planning process. The search process will usually involve scanning the environment for changes in technology, customer demand, market conditions and so on. Gathering the information needed may take some time, particularly for unusual or non-routine investment opportunities.

To help identify good investment opportunities, some businesses provide financial incentives to members of staff who come forward with good investment proposals. Even unrefined proposals may be welcome. Resources can then be invested to help develop the proposals to a point where formal submission can be made.

Activity 14.21

It can be argued that the sequence of these first two stages can be reversed. Can you figure out why?

In theory, finance can always be found for profitable investment opportunities.

Stage 3: Evaluate the proposed project

If management is to agree to the investment of funds in a project, that project's proposal must be rigorously screened. For larger projects, this will involve providing answers to a number of questions, including:

- What are the nature and purpose of the project?
- Does the project align with the overall strategy and objectives of the business?
- How much finance is required?
- What other resources (such as expertise, workspace and so on) are required for successful completion of the project?
- How long will the project last and what are its key stages?
- What is the expected pattern of cash flows?
- What are the major problems associated with the project and how can they be overcome?
- What is the NPV of the project? If capital is rationed, how does the NPV of this project compare with that of other opportunities available?
- Have risk and inflation been taken into account in the appraisal process and, if so, what are the results?

The ability and commitment of those responsible for proposing and managing the project will be vital to its success. This means that, when evaluating a new project, one consideration will be the quality of those proposing it. Senior managers may decide not to support a project that appears profitable on paper if they lack confidence in the ability of key managers to see it through to completion.

Stage 4: Approve the project

Once the managers responsible for investment decision making are satisfied that the project should be undertaken, formal approval can be given. However, a decision on a project may be postponed if senior managers need more information from those proposing the project, or if revisions are required to the proposal. Proposals may be rejected if they are considered unprofitable or likely to fail. Before rejecting a proposal, however, the implications of not pursuing the project must be carefully considered. Failure to pursue a particular project may impact such areas as market share, staff morale and existing business operations.

Approval may be authorised at different levels of the management hierarchy according to the nature of the investment and the amount of finance needed. For example, a plant manager may be given authority to invest in new equipment up to a maximum of, say, £500,000. For amounts above this figure, authority may be required from more senior management.

Stage 5: Monitor and control the project

Making a decision to invest does not automatically cause the investment to be made or mean that things will progress smoothly. Managers will need to manage the project actively through to completion. This, in turn, will require further information gathering.

Much of the control of a project would be through the routine budgetary control procedures that we met in Chapters 12 and 13. Management should also receive progress reports at regular intervals concerning the project. These should provide information relating to the actual cash flows for each stage of the project, which can then be compared against the forecast figures. Reasons for significant variations should be ascertained and corrective action taken where possible. Any changes in the expected completion date of the project or any expected variations in future cash flows from budget should be reported immediately. In extreme cases, managers may even abandon the project if circumstances appear to have changed dramatically for the worse.

Key non-financial measures may also be used to monitor performance. Measures may include wastage rates, physical output, customer satisfaction scores and so on. Certain types of projects, such as construction and civil engineering projects, may have 'milestones' (that is particular stages of completion) to be reached by certain dates. Progress towards each milestone should be monitored carefully and early warning should be given of any problems that may thwart their achievement. Project management techniques (for example, critical path analysis) should be employed wherever possible and their effectiveness monitored.

An important part of the control process is a **post-completion audit** of the project. This is, in essence, a review of the project performance to see if it lived up to expectations and whether any lessons can be learned. In addition to an evaluation of financial costs and benefits, non-financial measures of performance such as the ability to meet deadlines and levels of quality achieved will often be examined.

Adopting post-completion audits should encourage the use of more realistic estimates at the initial planning stage. Where over-optimistic estimates are used in an attempt to secure project approval, the managers responsible should be held accountable at the post-completion stage. **Real World 14.13** provides some evidence of a need for greater realism.

Real World 14.13

Looking on the bright side

McKinsey and Co, the management consultants, surveyed 2,500 senior managers world-wide. The managers were asked their opinions on investments made by their businesses in the previous three years. The general opinion was that estimates for the investment decision inputs had been too optimistic. For example, sales levels had been overestimated in about 50 per cent of cases, but underestimated in less than 20 per cent of cases. It is not clear whether the estimates were sufficiently inaccurate to call into question the decision that had been made.

The survey went on to ask about the extent to which investments made seemed, in the light of the actual outcomes, to have been mistakes. Managers felt that 19 per cent of investments that had been made should not have gone ahead. On the other hand, they felt that 31 per cent of rejected projects should have been taken up. Managers also felt that 'good money was thrown after bad' in that existing investments that were not performing well were continuing to be supported in a significant number of cases.

Source: Based on information in *How companies spend their money*, A McKinsey Global Survey, www.theglobalmarketer.com, 2007.

Other studies confirm a tendency among managers to use over-optimistic estimates when preparing investment proposals (see reference 1 at the end of the chapter). It seems that sometimes this is done deliberately in an attempt to secure project approval. Where over-optimistic estimates are used, the managers responsible may well find themselves accountable at the post-completion audit stage. Such audits, however, can be difficult and time-consuming to carry out. The likely benefits must, therefore, be weighed against the costs involved. Senior management may conclude that only projects above a certain size should be subject to a post-completion audit.

Real World 14.14 provides some indication of the extent that post-completion audits are used by businesses.

Real World 14.14

Looking back

The CIMA survey, mentioned in earlier chapters, examined the extent to which post-completion audits are used in practice. The results for all businesses surveyed, as well as for very large businesses (that is, with more than 10,000 employees), are set out in Figure 14.8.

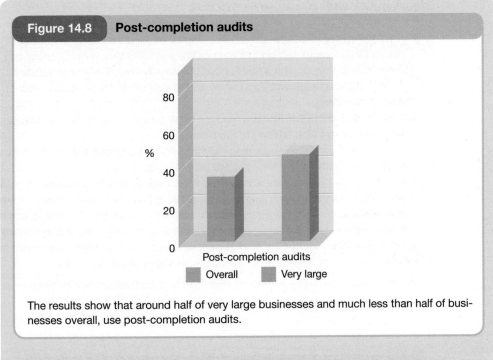

Figure 14.8   Post-completion audits

The results show that around half of very large businesses and much less than half of businesses overall, use post-completion audits.

We can see that larger businesses are more likely to use this technique. These businesses are likely to undertake more and bigger investment projects and have more finance staff to monitor business performance and so the results are not surprising.

Source: Adapted from figure in *Management Accounting Tools for Today and Tomorrow*, CIMA, July 2009, p. 18.

Real World 14.15 describes how one large retailer, Kingfisher plc, goes about monitoring and controlling its investment projects. Kingfisher sells do-it-yourself goods notably through the B and Q chain of stores.

Real World 14.15

Getting a grip

The 2016 annual report of Kingfisher plc reveals that the business invested £333 million during the year 2015/16. According to the report, to monitor and control this vast level of expenditure, the following procedures are adopted:

> The Group has a rigorous approach to capital allocation and authorisation, including an annual strategic planning and capital allocation process, an annual budget process, a project by project capital approval process and a bi-annual post-investment review process.

The annual report expanded on this approach, as follows:

● An annual strategic planning process based on detailed medium term plans for all businesses for the next three years. This process drives the key strategic capital allocation decisions and the output is reviewed by the Board;

Real World 14.15 *continued*

- A capital approval process through a capital expenditure committee, attended by the Group Chief Executive, Group Finance Director, CEO Group Productivity and Development, Group Property Director, Group General Counsel. The committee is delegated to review all projects above £0.75 million and to sign off the projects between £0.75 million and £15.0 million;
- Projects above £15.0 million are required to be approved by the Board. All projects above £0.75 million are also notified to the Board;
- Clear investment criteria including KEP (Kingfisher economic profit*) and NPV and challenging hurdle rates for IRR and DPB (discounted payback);
- An annual post-investment review process to undertake a full assessment of all projects above £0.75 million which were completed in the last two to four years. The findings of this exercise are considered by both the capital expenditure committee and the Board and used to inform the assumptions for similar project proposals going forward; and
- An annual review of KEP by store is performed which drives plans to improve the returns of weaker stores, and develop lessons from higher returning stores.

*Kingfisher economic profit is a measure of economic profit generated that is particular to Kingfisher.

Source: Kingfisher plc Annual Reports 2015/16, p. 28 and 2013/14, p. 25, www.kingfisher.co.uk.

Self-assessment question 14.1

Beacon Chemicals plc is considering buying some equipment to produce a chemical named X14. The new equipment's capital cost is estimated at £100 million. If its purchase is approved now, the equipment can be bought and production can commence by the end of this year. £50 million has already been spent on research and development work. Estimates of revenues and costs arising from the operation of the new equipment are:

	Year 1	Year 2	Year 3	Year 4	Year 5
Sales price (£/litre)	100	120	120	100	80
Sales volume (million litres)	0.8	1.0	1.2	1.0	0.8
Variable cost (£/litre)	50	50	40	30	40
Fixed cost (£m)	30	30	30	30	30

If the equipment is bought, sales of some existing products will be lost resulting in a loss of contribution of £15 million a year, over the life of the equipment.

The accountant has informed you that the fixed cost includes depreciation of £20 million a year on the new equipment. It also includes an allocation of £10 million for fixed overheads. A separate study has indicated that if the new equipment were bought, additional overheads, excluding depreciation, arising from producing the chemical would be £8 million a year. Production would require additional working capital of £30 million.

For the purposes of your initial calculations ignore taxation.

Required:

(a) Deduce the relevant annual cash flows associated with buying the equipment.
(b) Deduce the payback period.

(c) Calculate the net present value using a discount rate of 8 per cent.

(d) How sensitive is the NPV calculated in (c) to the estimate of the annual loss of contribution from the existing products? Comment on the sensitivity.

(*Hint*: You should deal with the investment in working capital by treating it as a cash outflow at the start of the project and an inflow at the end.)

The solution to this question can be found at the back of the book on p. 782.

Summary

The main points of this chapter may be summarised as follows:

Accounting rate of return (ARR) is the average accounting profit from the project expressed as a percentage of the average investment.

- Decision rule – projects with an ARR above a defined minimum are acceptable; the greater the ARR, the more attractive the project becomes.

- Conclusion on ARR:
  - does not relate directly to shareholders' wealth – can lead to illogical conclusions;
  - takes almost no account of the timing of cash flows;
  - ignores some relevant information and may take account of some irrelevant;
  - relatively simple to use;
  - much inferior to NPV.

Payback period (PP) is the length of time that it takes for the cash outflow for the initial investment to be repaid out of resulting cash inflows.

- Decision rule – projects with a PP up to a defined maximum period are acceptable; the shorter the PP, the more attractive the project.

- Conclusion on PP:
  - does not relate to shareholders' wealth;
  - ignores inflows after the payback date;
  - takes little account of the timing of cash flows;
  - ignores much relevant information;
  - does not always provide clear signals and can be impractical to use;
  - much inferior to NPV, but it is easy to understand and can offer a liquidity insight, which might be the reason for its widespread use.

Net present value (NPV) is the sum of the discounted values of the net cash flows from the investment.

- Money has a time value.

- Decision rule – all positive NPV investments enhance shareholders' wealth; the greater the NPV, the greater the enhancement and the greater the attractiveness of the project.

- PV of a cash flow = cash flow $\times 1/(1 + r)^n$, assuming a constant discount rate.

- Discounting brings cash flows at different points in time to a common valuation basis (their present value), which enables them to be directly compared.

- Conclusion on NPV:
  - relates directly to shareholders' wealth objective;
  - takes account of the timing of cash flows;
  - takes all relevant information into account;
  - provides clear signals and is practical to use.

Internal rate of return (IRR) is the discount rate that, when applied to the cash flows of a project, causes it to have a zero NPV.

- Represents the average percentage return on the investment, taking account of the fact that cash may be flowing in and out of the project at various points in its life.
- Decision rule – projects that have an IRR greater than the cost of capital are acceptable; the greater the IRR, the more attractive the project.
- Cannot normally be calculated directly; a trial and error approach is usually necessary.
- Conclusion on IRR:
  - does not relate directly to shareholders' wealth. Usually gives the same signals as NPV but can mislead where there are competing projects of different size;
  - takes account of the timing of cash flows;
  - takes all relevant information into account;
  - problems of multiple IRRs when there are unconventional cash flows;
  - inferior to NPV.

Use of appraisal methods in practice

- All four methods identified are widely used.
- The discounting methods (NPV and IRR) show a steady increase in usage over time.
- Many businesses use more than one method.
- Larger businesses seem to be more sophisticated in their choice and use of appraisal methods than smaller ones.

Investment appraisal and strategic planning

- It is important that businesses invest in a strategic way so as to play to their strengths.

Dealing with risk

- Risk is particularly important for investment projects because they tend to involve large amounts of finance, can be long lasting and expensive to bail out of.
- Sensitivity analysis can be a useful way of forming an impression about the riskiness of a project.

Managing investment projects

- Determine investment funds available – dealing, if necessary, with capital rationing problems.
- Identify profitable project opportunities.
- Evaluate the proposed project.
- Approve the project.
- Monitor and control the project – using a post-completion audit approach.

Key terms

For definitions of these terms, see Appendix B.

accounting rate of return (ARR) *p. 567*
return on capital employed
   (ROCE) *p. 568*
payback period (PP) *p. 571*
net present value (NPV) *p. 575*
risk *p. 577*
risk premium *p. 577*

inflation *p. 578*
discounting *p. 580*
discount factor *p. 581*
cost of capital *p. 583*
internal rate of return (IRR) *p. 585*
capital rationing *p. 599*
post-completion audit *p. 601*

Reference

1 Linder, S. (2005) *Fifty Years of Research on Accuracy of Capital Expenditure Project Estimates: A Review of the Findings and Their Validity,* Otto Beisham Graduate School of Management, April 2005.

Further reading

If you would like to explore the topics covered in this chapter in more depth, we recommend the following:

Arnold, G. (2013) *Corporate Financial Management,* 5th edn, Pearson, Chapters 2–4.

Drury, C. (2015) *Management and Cost Accounting,* 9th edn, South Western Cengage Learning, Chapters 13 and 14.

McLaney, E. (2017) *Business Finance: Theory and Practice,* 11th edn, Pearson, Chapters 4–6.

Pike, R., Neale, B. and Linsley, P. (2015) *Corporate Finance and Investment,* 8th edn, Pearson, Chapters 3–7.

Review questions

Solutions to these questions can be found at the back of the book on pp. 797–798.

14.1 Why is the net present value method of investment appraisal considered to be theoretically superior to other methods that are found in practice?

14.2 The payback period method has been criticised for not taking the time value of money into account. Could this limitation be overcome? If so, would this method then be preferable to the NPV method?

14.3 Research indicates that the IRR method is extremely popular even though it has shortcomings when compared to the NPV method. Why might managers prefer to use IRR rather than NPV when carrying out discounted cash flow evaluations?

14.4 Why are cash flows rather than profit flows used in the IRR, NPV and PP methods of investment appraisal?

Exercises

Solutions to exercises with coloured numbers can be hand at the back of the book on pp. 832–836.

Basic-level exercises

14.1 The directors of Mylo Ltd are currently considering two mutually exclusive investment projects. Both projects are concerned with the purchase of new plant. The following data are available for each project:

	Project	
	1	2
	£000	£000
Cost (immediate outlay)	100	60
Expected annual operating profit (loss):		
Year 1	29	18
2	(1)	(2)
3	2	4
Estimated residual value of the plant after 3 years	7	6

The business has an estimated cost of capital of 10 per cent. It uses the straight-line method of depreciation for all non-current (fixed) assets when calculating operating profit. Neither project would increase the working capital of the business. The business has sufficient funds to meet all investment expenditure requirements.

Required:

(a) Calculate for each project:
   1 the net present value;
   2 the approximate internal rate of return;
   3 the payback period.
(b) State, with reasons, which, if any, of the two investment projects the directors of Mylo Ltd should accept.

14.2 Arkwright Mills plc is considering expanding its production of a new yarn, code name X15. The plant is expected to cost £1 million and have a life of five years and a nil residual value. It will be bought, paid for and ready for operation on 31 December Year 0. £500,000 has already been spent on development costs of the product; this has been charged in the income statement in the year it was incurred.

   The following results are projected for the new yarn:

	Year 1	Year 2	Year 3	Year 4	Year 5
	£m	£m	£m	£m	£m
Sales revenue	1.2	1.4	1.4	1.4	1.4
Costs, including depreciation	(1.0)	(1.1)	(1.1)	(1.1)	(1.1)
Profit before tax	0.2	0.3	0.3	0.3	0.3

Tax is charged at 20 per cent on annual profits (before tax and after depreciation) and paid one year in arrears. Depreciation of the plant has been calculated on a straight-line basis. Additional working capital of £0.6 million will be required at the beginning of the project and released at the end of Year 5. You should assume that all cash flows occur at the end of the year in which they arise.

Required:

(a) Prepare a statement showing the incremental cash flows of the project relevant to a decision concerning whether or not to proceed with the construction of the new plant.
(b) Compute the net present value of the project using a 10 per cent discount rate.
(c) Compute the payback period to the nearest year. Explain the meaning of this term.

Intermediate-level exercises

14.3 Dirk plc has recently created a new male fragrance 'Sirocco' at a total development cost of £0.4 million. The business is now considering producing the fragrance, which will require an immediate outlay for new equipment of £10.5 million. Estimates relating to production of the fragrance are:

	Year 1	Year 2	Year 3	Year 4
Sales price (£/per bottle)	9.0	8.0	6.0	6.0
Sales volume (bottles)	1.0m	1.2m	1.2m	0.5m
Variable cost (£/per bottle)	1.0	1.0	1.0	1.4
Fixed cost (£)	4.5m	4.5m	4.5m	4.5m

The fixed cost includes depreciation of £2.5 million a year for the new equipment that is needed. This equipment will be sold at the end of the four years of production and the sales proceeds will reflect the residual value. Fixed cost also includes an allocation of £0.3 million to represent a 'fair share' of general business overheads.

If the project goes ahead, sales of an existing male fragrance, 'Mistral', will decline, resulting in a loss of contribution of £0.8 million per year for the next three years.

Producing the new fragrance will require an immediate outlay for working capital of £1.8 million, which can be released at the end of the production period.

Dirk plc has a cost of capital of 8 per cent.

Required:

(a) Calculate for the investment project:
  1 the net present value;
  2 the approximate internal rate of return.
(b) Briefly comment on the results of your calculations in (a).

14.4 Newton Electronics Ltd has incurred expenditure of £5 million over the past three years researching and developing a miniature hearing aid. The hearing aid is now fully developed. The directors are considering which of three mutually exclusive options should be taken to exploit the potential of the new product. The options are:

1 The business could manufacture the hearing aid itself. This would be a new departure, since the business has so far concentrated on research and development projects. However, the business has manufacturing space available that it currently rents to another business for £100,000 a year. This space will not continue to be leased if the decision is to manufacture. The business would have to purchase plant and equipment costing £9 million and invest £3 million in working capital immediately for production to begin.

A market research report, for which the business paid £50,000, indicates that the new product has an expected life of five years. Sales of the product during this period are predicted as:

Predicted sales for the year ended 30 November

	Year 1	Year 2	Year 3	Year 4	Year 5
Number of units (000s)	800	1,400	1,800	1,200	500

The selling price per unit will be £30 in the first year but will fall to £22 in the following three years. In the final year of the product's life, the selling price will fall to £20. Variable production costs are predicted to be £14 a unit. Fixed production costs (including depreciation) will be £2.4 million a year. Marketing costs will be £2 million a year.

The business intends to depreciate the plant and equipment using the straight-line method and based on an estimated residual value at the end of the five years of £1 million. The business has a cost of capital of 10 per cent a year.

2 Newton Electronics Ltd could agree to another business manufacturing and marketing the product under licence. A multinational business, Faraday Electricals plc, has offered to undertake the manufacture and marketing of the product. In return it will make a royalty payment to Newton Electronics Ltd of £5 per unit. It has been estimated that the annual number of sales of the hearing aid will be 10 per cent higher if the multinational business, rather than if Newton Electronics Ltd, manufactures and markets the product.

3 Newton Electronics Ltd could sell the patent rights to Faraday Electricals plc for £24 million, payable in two equal instalments. The first instalment would be payable immediately and the second at the end of two years. This option would give Faraday Electricals the exclusive right to manufacture and market the new product.

Ignore taxation.

Required:

(a) Calculate the net present value (as at the beginning of Year 1) of each of the options available to Newton Electronics Ltd.

(b) Identify and discuss any other factors that Newton Electronics Ltd should consider before arriving at a decision.

(c) State, with reasons, what you consider to be the most suitable option.

14.5 C. George (Controls) Ltd manufactures a thermostat that can be used in a range of kitchen appliances. The manufacturing process is, at present, semi-automated. The equipment used cost £540,000 and has a carrying amount (as shown on the statement of financial position) of £300,000. Demand for the product has been fairly stable at 50,000 units a year in recent years.

The following data, based on the current level of output, have been prepared in respect of the product:

	Per unit	
	£	£
Selling price		12.40
Labour	(3.30)	
Materials	(3.65)	
Overheads: Variable	(1.58)	
Fixed	(1.60)	
		(10.13)
Operating profit		2.27

Although the existing equipment is expected to last for a further four years before it is sold for an estimated £40,000, the business has recently been considering purchasing new equipment that would completely automate much of the production process. The new equipment would cost £670,000 and would have an expected life of four years, at the end of which it would be sold for an estimated £70,000. If the new equipment is purchased, the old equipment could be sold for £150,000 immediately.

The assistant to the business's accountant has prepared a report to help assess the viability of the proposed change, which includes the following data:

	Per unit	
	£	£
Selling price		12.40
Labour	(1.20)	
Materials	(3.20)	
Overheads: Variable	(1.40)	
Fixed	(3.30)	
		(9.10)
Operating profit		3.30

Depreciation charges will increase by £85,000 a year as a result of purchasing the new machinery; however, other fixed costs are not expected to change.

In the report the assistant wrote:

The figures shown above that relate to the proposed change are based on the current level of output and take account of a depreciation charge of £150,000 a year in respect of the new equipment. The effect of purchasing the new equipment will be to increase the operating profit to sales revenue ratio from 18.3 per cent to 26.6 per cent. In addition, the purchase of the new equipment will enable us to reduce our inventories level immediately by £130,000.

In view of these facts, I recommend purchase of the new equipment.

The business has a cost of capital of 12 per cent. Ignore taxation.

Required:

(a) Prepare a statement of the incremental cash flows arising from the purchase of the new equipment.
(b) Calculate the net present value of the proposed purchase of new equipment.
(c) State, with reasons, whether the business should purchase the new equipment.
(d) Explain why cash flow, rather than profit, projections are used to assess the viability of proposed capital expenditure projects.

Advanced-level exercises

14.6 The accountant of your business has recently been taken ill through overwork. In his absence his assistant has prepared some calculations of the profitability of a project, which are to be discussed soon at the board meeting of your business. His workings, which are set out below, include some errors of principle. You can assume that there are no arithmetical errors.

Year	0	1	2	3	4	5
	£000	£000	£000	£000	£000	£000
Sales revenue		450	470	470	470	470
Less Costs						
Materials		126	132	132	132	132
Labour		90	94	94	94	94
Overheads		45	47	47	47	47
Depreciation		120	120	120	120	120
Working capital	180					
Interest on working capital		27	27	27	27	27
Write-off of development costs	—	30	30	30		—
Total costs	180	438	450	450	420	420
Operating profit/(loss)	(180)	12	20	20	50	50

$$\frac{\text{Total profit (loss)}}{\text{Cost of equipment}} = \frac{(£28,000)}{£600,000} = \text{Return on investment (4.7\%)}$$

You ascertain the following additional information:

1. The cost of equipment includes £100,000, being the carrying value of an old machine. If it were not used for this project, it would be scrapped with a zero net realisable value. New equipment costing £500,000 will be purchased on 31 December Year 0. You should assume that all other cash flows occur at the end of the year to which they relate.
2. The development costs of £90,000 have already been spent.
3. Overheads have been costed at 50 per cent of direct labour, which is the business's normal practice. An independent assessment has suggested that incremental overheads are likely to amount to £30,000 a year.
4. The business's cost of capital is 12 per cent.

Ignore taxation.

Required:

(a) Prepare a corrected statement of the incremental cash flows arising from the project. Where you have altered the assistant's figures you should attach a brief note explaining your alterations.
(b) Calculate:
   1. the project's payback period;
   2. the project's net present value as at 31 December Year 0.
(c) Write a memo to the board advising on the acceptance or rejection of the project.

14.7 Simtex Ltd has invested £120,000 to date in developing a new type of shaving foam. The shaving foam is now ready for production and it has been estimated that the business will sell 160,000 cans a year of the new product over the next four years. At the end of four years, the product will be discontinued and probably replaced by a new product.

The shaving foam is expected to sell at £6 a can and the variable cost is estimated at £4 per can. Fixed cost (excluding depreciation) is expected to be £300,000 a year. (This figure includes £130,000 of the existing general overheads of the business that will be apportioned to this new product.)

To manufacture and package the new product, equipment costing £480,000 must be acquired immediately. The estimated value of this equipment in four years' time is £100,000.

The business calculates depreciation using the straight-line method (equal amounts each year). It has an estimated cost of capital of 12 per cent.

Required:

(a) Deduce the net present value of the new product.
(b) Calculate by how much each of the following must change before the new product is no longer profitable:
    1 the discount rate;
    2 the initial outlay on new equipment;
    3 the net operating cash flows;
    4 the residual value of the equipment.
(c) Should the business produce the new product?

CHAPTER 15

Financing a business

Introduction

In this chapter, we shall examine various aspects of financing a business. We begin by considering the main sources of finance available. Some of these sources have already been touched upon when we discussed the financing of limited companies in Chapter 4. We shall now look at these in more detail as well as discussing other sources of finance that have not yet been mentioned. The factors to be taken into account when choosing an appropriate source of finance are also considered.

Following our consideration of the main sources of finance, we shall examine how long-term finance may be raised. We shall take a look at various aspects of the capital markets, including the ways in which share capital may be issued, the role of the Stock Exchange and the financing of smaller businesses.

Learning outcomes

When you have completed this chapter, you should be able to:

- identify the main sources of finance available to a business and explain the advantages and disadvantages of each;

- outline the ways in which share capital may be issued;

- explain the role and nature of the Stock Exchange; and

- discuss the ways in which smaller businesses may seek to raise finance.

The main objective of financing policy

Managers should aim to raise finance in such a way that the wealth of the business and its owners is maximised. To do this, the sources of finance selected should combine cost and risk in a way that minimises the overall cost of capital. The value of a business represents the sum of the discounted future cash flows that it generates, where the discount rate is the business's cost of capital. By minimising the cost of capital, the discount rate is minimised, which means, in turn, that the value of the business will be maximised.

Sources of finance

When considering the various sources of finance available to a business, it is useful to distinguish between *internal* and *external* sources of finance. By internal sources we mean sources that do not require the agreement of anyone beyond the directors and managers of the business. Thus, retained earnings are considered an internal source because directors have the power to retain earnings without the agreement of the shareholders, whose earnings they are. Finance raised from the issue of new shares, on the other hand, is an external source because it requires the agreement of potential shareholders.

Within each of these two categories (internal and external), we can further distinguish between *long-term* and *short-term* sources of finance. There is no set definition concerning each of these terms, but most see long-term sources as those providing finance for at least one year. Short-term sources are, therefore, those providing finance for up to one year. As we shall see, sources of finance that are considered short-term when first raised often end up being used by the business for long periods.

We shall begin the chapter by considering the various sources of internal finance available. We then go on to consider the various sources of external finance. This is probably the appropriate order since businesses tend to look first to internal sources before going outside for new funds.

Internal sources of finance

Internal sources of finance usually have the advantage that they are flexible. They may also be obtained quickly; this is particularly true of working capital sources. The main internal sources of funds are summarised in Figure 15.1 and are described below.

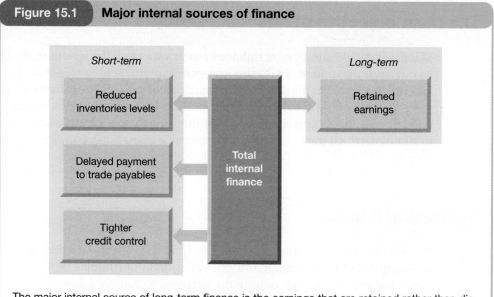

Figure 15.1 **Major internal sources of finance**

The major internal source of long-term finance is the earnings that are retained rather than distributed to shareholders. The major internal sources of short-term finance involve reducing the level of trade receivables and inventories and increasing the level of trade payables.

Internal sources of long-term finance

Retained earnings

Earnings that are retained within the business, rather than distributed to shareholders in the form of dividends, represent much the most important source of new finance for UK businesses in terms of value of funds raised.

Activity 15.1

Are retained earnings a free source of finance for the business? Explain.

No. This is because they have an opportunity cost to shareholders. If shareholders receive a dividend, they can use the cash to make other income-yielding investments. If the business retains the cash, shareholders are deprived of this potential income.

In view of the opportunity cost involved, shareholders will expect a rate of return from retained earnings that is equivalent to what they would receive had the funds been invested in another opportunity with the same level of risk.

Although the reinvestment of earnings incurs a cost to the business, it may be preferable to raise finance from equity (ordinary share) investors in this way rather than by an issue of shares. No issue costs are incurred and the amount raised is certain, once the earnings have been generated. Where new shares are issued, issue costs tend to be substantial and the success of the issue may be uncertain, as we shall see later in the chapter.

In addition, any new shares issued to outside investors will result in existing shareholders suffering some dilution of control.

Retaining earnings may be an easier option than asking investors to subscribe to a new share issue. These earnings are already held by the business and so there is no delay in receiving the funds. Moreover, there is often less scrutiny when earnings are retained for reinvestment purposes compared to when new shares are issued. Investors tend to examine closely the reasons for any new share issue. A problem with the use of earnings as a source of finance, however, is that their timing and future level cannot always be reliably determined.

It would be wrong to gain the impression that businesses either retain their entire earnings or pay them all out as dividends. Larger businesses, for example, tend to pay dividends but normally pay out no more than 50 per cent of their earnings.

Dividend policy

The directors of profitable businesses can decide the amount of dividends to be paid to shareholders. This raises the question of how large each year's dividend should be. The traditional view is that dividend payments should be maximised. The belief is that the higher the dividend payments, the more attractive the ordinary shares will become. This, in turn, will lead to higher share prices and to wealthier shareholders. Since the 1950s, however, this traditional view has been subject to increasing challenge.

The main thrust of the critics' argument is that, since the business is owned by the shareholders, why should transferring some of the business's assets to shareholders through a cash dividend make them better off? What shareholders are gaining, through the dividend, they are losing through their business being less well off. Funds handed to shareholders as dividends means less being retained within the business for investment in wealth-generating projects.

An alternative, more modern, view is that funds should be retained providing they generate higher returns than the shareholders could earn from reinvesting any dividends received in other investment opportunities with the same level of risk. Where the directors cannot generate higher returns, shareholders would be worse off. Thus, only those earnings that can be invested at a rate at least as high as the shareholders' opportunity cost of funds should be retained. The residue should be paid as a dividend.

Not all businesses follow the more modern view on dividend policy. One that does, however, is Asos plc (the online fashion and beauty retailer). ASOS was formed in 2004. The business has yet to pay a dividend, despite being profitable for every year up to the time of writing. **Real World 15.1** is an extract from the business's 2016 annual report.

Real World 15.1

Dividends out of fashion

The Board has again decided not to declare a dividend. We generate a high return on invested capital and currently have no shortage of places to invest our surplus cash to improve our customer proposition. We believe the right thing to do is to keep growing the business by focusing on our customers.

Source: Asos plc, 2016 Annual Report, p. 3.

Internal sources of short-term finance

The major internal forms of short-term finance are

- tighter credit control;
- reducing inventories levels; and
- delaying payments to trade payables (suppliers).

These are shown in Figure 15.1.

We saw in Chapter 6, in the context of statements of cash flows, that increases and decreases in these working capital items will have a direct and rapid effect on cash. Having funds tied up in trade receivables and inventories and failing to take advantage of free credit from suppliers cause a financing opportunity cost. This is because those funds could be used for profit-generating activities or for returning funds to shareholders or lenders.

Tighter credit control

By exerting tighter control over amounts owed by credit customers, a business may be able to reduce the funds tied up. It is important, however, to weigh the benefits of tighter credit control against the likely costs in the form of lost customer goodwill and lost sales.

To remain competitive, a business must take account of the needs of its customers and the credit policies adopted by rival businesses.

Reducing inventories levels

This internal source of funds may prove attractive to a business. However, it must ensure that there are sufficient inventories available to meet likely future production and sales demand. Failure to do so may well result in costly dislocation of production, lost customer goodwill and/or lost sales revenue.

The nature and condition of the inventories held will determine whether it is possible to exploit this form of finance. A business may have excessive inventories as a result of poor buying decisions. This may mean that a significant proportion of inventories held is slow moving or obsolete and cannot, therefore, be liquidated easily.

Delaying payment to trade payables

By providing a period of credit, suppliers are in effect offering their customers interest-free loans. If the business delays payment, the period of the 'loan' is extended and funds are retained within the business. This can be highly beneficial for a business, although it is not always the case. If a business fails to pay within the agreed credit period, there may be significant costs: for example, it may face difficulties buying on credit because of its reputation as a slow payer.

Activity 15.2 concerns the cash flow benefit of more efficient management of the working capital elements.

Activity (15.2)

Trader Ltd is a wholesaler of imported washing machines. The business is partly funded by a bank overdraft and the bank is putting pressure on Trader Ltd to reduce this as soon as possible.

Sales revenue is £14.6 million a year and is all on credit. Purchases and cost of sales are roughly equal at £7.3 million a year. Current investment in the relevant working capital elements is:

	£m
Inventories	1.5
Trade receivables	3.8
Trade payables	0.7

Trader Ltd's accountant believes that much of the overdraft could be eliminated through better control of working capital. As a result, she has investigated and bench-marked several successful businesses that are similar to Trader Ltd and found the following averages:

	Days
Average inventories turnover period	22
Average settlement period for trade receivables	57
Average settlement period for trade payables	55

How much cash could Trader Ltd generate if it were able to bring its ratios into line with those of similar businesses?

The cash that could be generated is as follows:

	£m	£m
Inventories		
Current level	1.5	
Target level: $^{22}/_{365} \times 7.3 =$	0.4	1.1
Trade receivables		
Current level	3.8	
Target level: $^{57}/_{365} \times 14.6 =$	2.3	1.5
Trade payables		
Current level	0.7	
Target level: $^{55}/_{365} \times 7.3 =$	1.1	0.4
Total		3.0

Some further points

The sources of finance just described are short-term insofar that they can be reversed at short notice. For example, a reduction in the level of trade receivables can be reversed within a couple of weeks. Typically, however, once a business has established a reduced receivables settlement period, a reduced inventories holding period and/or an expanded payables settlement period, it will tend to maintain these new levels.

In Chapter 16, we shall see how these three elements of working capital may be managed. We shall also see that, for many businesses, funds invested in working capital items are vast and, in many cases, excessive. There is often considerable scope for generating funds through more efficient management of working capital.

External sources of finance

The main external sources of long-term and short-term finance are summarised in Figure 15.2.

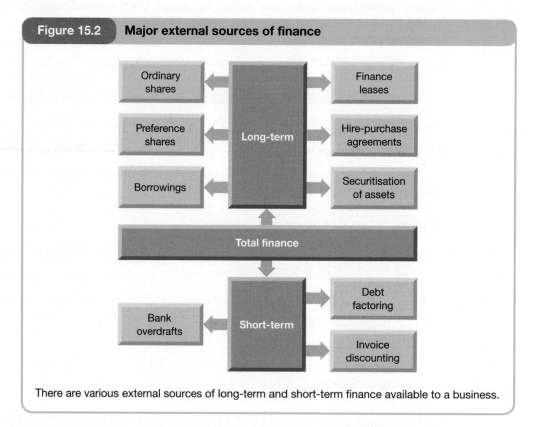

Figure 15.2 **Major external sources of finance**

There are various external sources of long-term and short-term finance available to a business.

External sources of long-term finance

The major external sources of long-term finance are:

- ordinary shares;
- preference shares;
- borrowing;

- finance leases (including sale-and-leaseback arrangements);
- hire-purchase agreements; and
- securitisation of assets.

We shall now look at each of these sources in turn.

Ordinary shares

Ordinary (equity) shares represent the risk capital of a business and form the backbone of a business's financial structure. There is no fixed rate of dividend. Furthermore, ordinary shareholders will receive a dividend only if profits available for distribution still remain after other investors (preference shareholders and lenders) have received their dividend or interest payments. If the business is wound up, the ordinary shareholders will receive any proceeds from asset disposals only after lenders and creditors and, in some cases preference shareholders, have received their entitlements. Because of the high risks associated with this form of investment, ordinary shareholders will normally expect a relatively high rate of return.

Although ordinary shareholders' potential losses are limited to the amount that they have invested or agreed to invest, the potential returns from their investment are unlimited. After preference shareholders and lenders have received their returns, all the remaining profits will accrue to the ordinary shareholders. Thus, while their 'downside' risk is limited, their 'upside' potential is not. Ordinary shareholders control the business through their voting rights, which give them the power to elect the directors and to remove them from office.

From the business's perspective, ordinary shares can be an effective form of financing compared to borrowing. It is possible to avoid paying a dividend, whereas it is not usually possible to avoid interest payments.

Activity **15.3**

From the business's point of view, ordinary shares represent a less risky form of financing than borrowing. Why is this?

It is because the obligation to make interest payments and capital repayments could put the business in financial jeopardy. There is no such risk with ordinary shares.

Preference shares

Preference shares offer investors a lower level of risk than ordinary shares. Provided there are sufficient profits available, preference shares will normally receive a fixed rate of dividend each year and will also receive the first slice of any dividend paid. If the business is wound up, preference shareholders may be given priority over the claims of ordinary shareholders. (The business's own particular documents of incorporation will state the precise rights of preference shareholders in this respect.)

Activity 15.4

Would you expect the returns to preference shares to be higher or lower than those to ordinary shares?

Preference shareholders will be offered a lower level of return than those that ordinary share-holders expect to earn. This is because of the lower level of risk associated with this form of investment (preference shareholders have priority over ordinary shareholders regarding divi-dends and, perhaps, capital repayment).

Preference shareholders are not usually given voting rights, although these may be granted where the preference dividend is in arrears. Both preference shares and ordinary shares are, in effect, redeemable. The business is allowed to buy back the shares from shareholders at any time.

Activity 15.5

Would you expect the market price of ordinary shares or of preference shares to be the more volatile? Why?

The share price, which reflects the expected future returns from the share, will normally be less volatile for preference shares than for ordinary shares. The dividends of preference shares tend to be fairly stable over time, and there is usually an upper limit on the returns that can be received.

Preference shares are no longer an important source of new finance. A major reason for this is that dividends paid to preference shareholders, like those paid to ordinary share-holders, are not fully allowable against taxable profits, whereas loan interest is an allow-able expense. From the business's point of view, preference shares and loans are quite similar, so the tax treatment of loan interest is an important issue. Furthermore, in recent years, interest rates on borrowing have been at historically low levels.

Borrowing

Most businesses rely on borrowings as well as share capital to finance operations. Lenders enter into a contract with the business in which the interest rate, dates of interest pay-ments, capital repayments and security for the loan are clearly stated. If a business is suc-cessful, lenders will not benefit beyond the fact that their claim will become more secure. If, on the other hand, the business experiences financial difficulties, there is a risk that the agreed interest payments and capital repayments will not be made. To protect themselves against this risk, lenders often seek some form of **security** from the business. This may take the form of assets pledged either by a **fixed charge** on particular assets held by the business, or by a **floating charge**, which 'hovers' over the whole of the business's assets. A floating charge will only fix on particular assets in the event that the business defaults on its obligations.

Activity (15.6)

What do you think is the advantage for the business of having a floating charge rather than a fixed charge on its assets?

A floating charge on assets will allow the managers of the business greater flexibility in their day-to-day operations than a fixed charge. Individual assets can be sold without reference to the lenders.

Not all assets are acceptable to lenders as security. To be acceptable, they must normally be non-perishable, easy to sell and of high and stable value. (Property normally meets these criteria and so is often favoured by lenders.) In the event of default, lenders have the right to seize the assets pledged and to sell them. Any surplus from the sale, after lenders have been paid, will be passed to the business. In some cases, security offered may take the form of a personal guarantee by the owners of the business or, perhaps, by some third party. This most often occurs with small businesses.

Lenders may seek further protection through the use of **loan covenants.** These are obligations, or restrictions, on the business that form part of the loan contract. Covenants may impose:

- the right of lenders to receive regular financial reports concerning the business;
- an obligation to insure the assets being offered as security;
- a restriction on the right to make further borrowings (for example, issue further loan notes) without prior permission of the existing lenders;
- a restriction on the right to sell certain assets held;
- a restriction on dividend payments and/or payments made to directors; and
- minimum levels of liquidity and/or maximum levels of financial gearing.

Any breach of these covenants can have serious consequences. Lenders may demand immediate repayment of the loan in the event of a material breach.

Real World 15.2 comprises extracts from an article that describes how one well-known Japanese manufacturer, Toshiba, has recently struggled to generate profits, which, in turn, has led to it breaching its loan covenants. This could result in the various banks, to which it owes money, requiring immediate repayment. It could also lead to the Tokyo Stock Exchange refusing to allow its members to deal in Toshiba's shares.

Real World 15.2

Toshiba in trouble

Toshiba shares plunged as much as 13 per cent on Wednesday as the troubled conglomerate scrambled to convince lenders to extend a loan violation waiver amid fears that one of Japan's biggest industrial names could be delisted from the Tokyo Stock Exchange. Amid new allegations of management failure, friction with the auditors and possible accounting irregularities, Toshiba shares fell to a fresh low as Kazutoshi Inano, the chairman of the Japan Securities and Dealers Association, publicly questioned whether Toshiba "has functioning governance in place". Toshiba on Wednesday asked for a further waiver for a loan covenant violation from its lenders — the four large national banks, which between them lend the company around Y600 billion, and dozens of other regional banks and trust banks.

Real World 15.2 *continued*

When the extent of Toshiba's problems emerged in late December, the company asked that group of lenders for a one month waiver, which was granted in January.

Toshiba investors warned that it has become harder for Toshiba to present a convincing argument that it has a viable recovery plan in place. One of the sternest tests could come in March when the Tokyo Stock Exchange, which has had Toshiba on "stock on alert" status since its $1.3 billion accounting scandal in 2015, decides whether the company has improved internal controls. "Previously I thought that delisting was a probability, but based on the chaos we saw yesterday, I now think it is a likelihood and a likelihood that is going up every day."

Source: Extracts from Lewis, L. (2017) Toshiba shares plummet on new fears over future of business, ft.com, 15 February.
© The Financial Times Limited 2017. All Rights Reserved.

Loan covenants and the availability of security can lower the risk for lenders and can make the difference between a successful and an unsuccessful loan issue. They can also lower the cost of borrowing as the rate of return that lenders require will depend on the perceived level of risk to which they are exposed.

It is possible for a business to make a loan note issue that is subordinated to (that is, ranked below) other borrowings already in existence. Holders of subordinated loan notes will not receive interest payments or capital repayments until the claims of more senior loan holders (that is, lenders ranked above them) are met. Any restrictive covenants imposed by senior lenders, concerning the issue of further borrowing, often ignore the issue of **subordinated loans** as it poses no real threat to their claims. Subordinated lenders normally expect to receive a higher return than senior lenders because of the higher risks.

Activity 15.7

Would you expect the returns to lenders to be higher or lower than those to preference shares?

Investors are usually prepared to accept a lower rate of return from loans. This is because they normally view them as being less risky than preference shares. Lenders have priority over any claims from preference shareholders and will usually have security for their loans.

The risk/return characteristics of loan, preference share and ordinary share finance are shown graphically in Figure 15.3. Note that, from the viewpoint of the business (the existing shareholders), the level of risk associated with each form of finance is in reverse order. Thus, borrowing is the most risky because it exposes shareholders to the legally enforceable obligation to make regular interest payments and, usually, repayment of the amount borrowed.

| Figure 15.3 | The risk/return characteristics of sources of long-term finance |

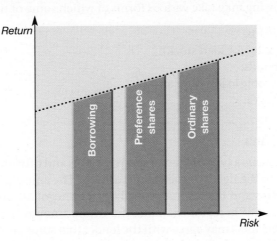

From an investor's perspective, borrowing is normally the least risky and ordinary shares the most risky.

Activity 15.8

What factors might a business take into account when deciding between preference shares and borrowing as a means of raising new finance?

The main factors are as follows:

- Preference shares have a higher rate of return than loans. From the investor's point of view, preference shares are more risky. The amount invested cannot be secured and the return is paid after the returns paid to lenders.
- A business has a legal obligation to pay interest on borrowings and to make capital repayments at the agreed dates. It will usually make every effort to meet its obligations, as failure to do so can have serious consequences. Failure to pay a preference dividend, on the other hand, is less important. There is no legal obligation to pay if profits are not available for distribution. Failure to pay a preference dividend may therefore prove to be an embarrassment and nothing more. It may, however, make it difficult to persuade investors to take up future preference share issues.
- Interest on borrowings can be fully deducted from profits for taxation purposes, whereas preference dividends cannot. As a result, the cost of servicing borrowings is, £ for £, usually rather less for a business than the cost of servicing preference shares.
- Borrowing may result in managers having to accept some restrictions on their freedom of action. Loan agreements often contain covenants that can be onerous. However, no such restrictions can be imposed by preference shareholders.

A further point is that any preference shares issued form part of the permanent capital base of the business. If they are redeemed, UK law requires that they be replaced, either by a new issue of shares or by a transfer from revenue reserves, so that the business's capital base stays intact. Borrowings, however, are not viewed, in law, as part of the business's permanent capital base and, therefore, there is no legal requirement to replace any that have been redeemed.

Borrowing may take various forms of which some of the more important are:

- term loans;
- loan notes (or loan stock);
- Eurobonds;
- convertible loan notes; and
- mortgages.

Term loans

A **term loan** is a type of loan offered by banks and other financial institutions that can be tailored to the needs of the client business. The amount of the loan, time period, repayment terms and interest rate are all open to negotiation and agreement – which can be very useful. Where, for example, the whole amount borrowed is not required immediately, a business may agree with the lender that sums are drawn only when required. This means that interest will be paid only on amounts actually drawn and there is no need to pay interest on amounts borrowed that are not yet needed. Term loans tend to be cheap to set up (from the borrower's perspective) and can be quite flexible as to conditions. For these reasons, they tend to be popular in practice.

Loan notes (or loan stock)

Another form of long-term borrowing is *loan notes* (or *loan stock*). Loan notes are frequently divided into units (rather like share capital), and investors are invited to purchase the number of units they require. Loan notes may be redeemable or irredeemable. The loan notes of public limited companies are often traded on the Stock Exchange. Their listed value will fluctuate according to the fortunes of the business, movements in interest rates, and so on.

Loan notes are usually referred to as **bonds** in the USA and, increasingly, in the UK.

Real World 15.3 consists of extracts from an article that describes how Microsoft Corporation, the US-based software provider, made a massive bond issue, perhaps timed to beat the possibility of a rise in general interest rates.

Real World 15.3

Macro borrowings for Microsoft

Microsoft borrowed $17 billion on Monday in what is the largest corporate bond sale of the year so far, as the US technology company joins a rush to tap debt markets ahead of expected interest rate rises later this year. The deal ranked among the largest ever corporate debt sales not to finance a takeover and follows a bumper start to the year for bond offerings. Companies, governments and their agencies have borrowed more than $600 billion in 2017, the strongest start to a year since 2013.

The deal comes just six months after Microsoft borrowed almost $20 billion to fund its purchase of social network LinkedIn, which was the fifth-largest corporate bond on record at the time.

"It has been an extraordinary month," said Peter Burger, the head of HSBC's debt syndicate in the Americas. "What companies are seeing is that market conditions may change. While we have a very supportive bond market in January, they want to take advantage of it." The prospect of rising interest rates in 2017 has raised question marks over whether the rapid rate of issuance can continue and if debt sales in the first half of the year will be front loaded.

Source: Extracts from Platt, E. and Hale, T. (2017) Microsoft issues biggest bond of the year in debt market boom, ft.com, 30 January. © The Financial Times Limited 2017. All Rights Reserved.

Activity 15.9

Would you expect the market price of ordinary shares or of loan notes to be the more volatile? Why?

Price movements will normally be much less volatile for loan notes than for ordinary shares. The price of loan notes and ordinary shares will reflect the expected future returns from each. Interest from loan notes is fixed by contract over time. Returns from ordinary shares, on the other hand, are very much less certain.

Activity 15.10

Would you expect the returns on loan notes to be higher or lower than those of ordinary shares?

Loan note holders will expect to receive a lower level of return than ordinary shareholders. This is because of the lower level of risk associated with this form of investment (loan interest is fixed by contract and security will often be available).

Eurobonds

Eurobonds are unsecured loan notes denominated in a currency other than the home currency of the business that issued them. They are issued by listed businesses (and other large organisations) in various countries, and the finance is raised on an international basis. They are often denominated in US dollars, but many are issued in other major currencies. They are bearer bonds (that is, the owner of the bond is not registered and the holder of the bond certificate is regarded as the owner) and interest is normally paid, without deduction of tax, on an annual basis.

Eurobonds are part of an international capital market that is not restricted by regulations imposed by authorities in particular countries. This partly explains why the cost of servicing eurobonds is usually lower than the cost of similar domestic bonds. Numerous banks and other financial institutions throughout the world have created a market for the purchase and sale of eurobonds. These bonds are made available to financial institutions, which may retain them as an investment or sell them to clients.

The extent of borrowing, by UK businesses, in currencies other than sterling has expanded greatly in recent years. Businesses are often attracted to eurobonds because of the size of the international capital market. Access to a wider pool of potential investors can increase the chances of a successful issue.

Real World 15.4 provides an example of eurobond financing by a well-known business.

Real World 15.4

Something worth watching?

ITV plc, the broadcasting and online business, has various Eurobonds in issue. As at 15 February 2017, Eurobonds with the following maturity dates and interest (coupon) rates were outstanding:

Maturity (date due)	Eurobond €m	Coupon %
September 2022	600	2.125
December 2023	500	2.000

Source: Adapted from itvplc.com/investors/debt_ir.

Deep discount bonds

A business may issue redeemable loan notes that offer a rate of interest below the market rate. In some cases, the loan notes may have a zero rate of interest. These loans are issued at a discount to their redeemable value and are referred to as **deep discount bonds.** Thus, loan notes may be issued at, say, £80 for every £100 of nominal value. Although lenders will receive little or no interest during the period of the loan, they will receive a £20 gain when it is finally redeemed at the full £100. The effective rate of return over the life of their loan (known as the redemption yield) can be quite high and often better than returns from other forms of lending with the same level of risk.

Deep discount bonds may have particular appeal to businesses with short-term cash flow problems. They receive an immediate injection of cash and there are no significant cash outflows associated with the loan notes until the maturity date. From an investment perspective, the situation is reversed. Deep discount bonds are likely to appeal to investors that do not have short-term cash flow needs since a large part of the return is received on maturity of the loan. However, deep discount bonds can often be traded on the London Stock Exchange, which will not affect the borrower but will enable the lender to sell the bonds and so obtain cash.

Convertible loan notes

Convertible loan notes (or convertible bonds) give investors the right to convert loan notes into ordinary shares at a specified price and at a given future date (or range of dates). The share price specified, which is known as the *exercise price,* will normally be higher than the market price of the ordinary shares at the time of the loan notes issue. In effect, the investor swaps the loan notes for a particular number of shares. The investor remains a lender to the business and will receive interest on the amount of the loan notes, until such time as the conversion takes place. There is no obligation to convert to ordinary shares. This will be done only if the market price of the shares at the conversion date exceeds the agreed conversion price.

An investor may find this form of investment a useful 'hedge' against risk (that is, it can reduce the level of risk). This may be particularly useful when investment in a new business is being considered. Initially, the investment will be in the form of loan notes, and regular interest payments will be received. If the business is successful, the investor can then convert the investment into ordinary shares.

A business may also find this form of financing useful. If the business is successful, the loan notes become self-liquidating (that is, no cash outlay is required to redeem them) as investors will exercise their option to convert. It may also be possible to offer a lower rate of interest on the loan notes because of the expected future benefits arising from conversion. There will be, however, some dilution of control and, possibly, a dilution of earnings for existing shareholders if holders of convertible loan notes exercise their option to convert. (Dilution of earnings available to shareholders will not automatically occur as a result of the conversion of borrowings to share capital. There will be a saving in interest charges that will have, at least a partially, offsetting effect.)

Real World 15.5 outlines a convertible loan note (bond) issued by J Sainsbury plc, the major UK supermarket business.

Real World 15.5

Convertible groceries

J Sainsbury plc has borrowings of £450 million by way of convertible bonds. The bonds have an annual 1.25 per cent interest rate, but may be converted into fully paid-up ordinary Sainsbury shares. They can be converted at any time up to 21 November 2019 at a price of £3.21 a share. The conversion share price was about 36 per cent above the share price on the date of the issue of the bonds (November 2014) and continuously above it from the issue date until the time of writing.

The convertible bond represents about 20 per cent of Sainsbury's borrowings.

Source: J Sainsbury plc 2016 Annual Report, p.12.

Convertibles are an example of a **financial derivative.** This is any form of financial instrument, based on equity or loans, which can be used by investors to increase their returns or reduce risk.

Mortgages

A **mortgage** is a form of loan that is secured on an asset, typically land and property. Financial institutions such as banks, insurance businesses and pension funds are often prepared to lend to businesses on this basis. The mortgage may be over a long period (20 years or more).

Interest rates

Interest rates may be either floating or fixed. A **floating interest rate** means that the rate of return will rise and fall with market rates of interest. (However, a condition of a floating rate loan can be that there would be a maximum and/or a minimum rate of interest payable.) The market value of floating loan notes is likely to remain fairly stable over time.

The converse will normally be true for loans with a **fixed interest rate.** Interest payments will remain unchanged with rises and falls in market rates of interest. This means that the value of the loan notes will fall when interest rates rise, and will rise when interest rates fall.

Activity 15.11

Why do you think the value of fixed-interest loan notes will rise and fall with rises and falls in interest rates?

This is because investors will be prepared to pay less for loan notes that pay a rate of interest below the market rate of interest and will be prepared to pay more for loan notes that pay a rate of interest above the market rate of interest.

Movements in interest rates can be a significant issue for businesses that have high levels of borrowing. A business with a floating rate of interest may find that rate rises will place real strains on cash flows and profitability. Conversely, a business that has a fixed rate of interest will find that, when rates are falling, it will not enjoy the benefits of lower interest charges.

Finance leases

When a business needs a particular asset, such as a piece of equipment, instead of buying it direct from a supplier, the business may arrange for a bank (or other financial institution) to buy it and then lease it to the business. The financial institution that owns the asset, and then leases it to the business, is known as a 'lessor'. The business that leases the asset from the bank and then uses it is known as the 'lessee'.

A **finance lease**, as such an arrangement is known, is in essence a form of lending. This is because, had the lessee borrowed the funds and then used them to buy the asset itself, the effect would be much the same. The lessee would have use of the asset, but would also have a financial obligation to the lender – just as with a leasing arrangement.

With finance leasing, legal ownership of the asset remains with the lessor. However, the lease agreement transfers to the lessee virtually all the rewards and risks associated with the item being leased. The finance lease agreement will cover a substantial part of the life of the leased item and, often, cannot be cancelled. **Real World 15.6** gives an example of the use of finance leasing by a large international business.

Real World 15.6

Leased assets take off

Many airline businesses use finance leasing as a means of acquiring new aeroplanes. This includes International Airlines Group (IAG), the business that owns British Airways and Iberia. At 31 December 2016, the carrying amount of IAG's fleet of planes was made up roughly 57 per cent leased and 43 per cent owned outright.

Source: Based on information in International Airlines Group Annual Report 2016, p. 123.

A finance lease can be contrasted with an **operating lease**, where the rewards and risks of ownership stay with the owner and where the lease is short-term. An example of an operating lease is where a builder hires some earth-moving equipment for a week to carry out a particular job.

Over the years, some important benefits associated with finance leasing have disappeared. Changes in the tax laws mean that it is no longer quite such a tax-efficient form of financing, and changes in accounting disclosure requirements make it no longer possible to conceal this form of 'borrowing' from investors. Nevertheless, the popularity of finance leases has continued. Other reasons must, therefore, exist for businesses to adopt this form of financing. These reasons are said to include the following:

- *Ease of borrowing.* Leasing may be obtained more easily than other forms of long-term finance. Lenders normally require some form of security and a profitable track record before making advances to a business. However, a lessor may be prepared to lease assets to a new business without a track record and to use the leased assets as security for the amounts owing.
- *Cost.* Leasing agreements may be offered at reasonable cost. As the asset leased is used as security, standard lease arrangements can be applied and detailed credit checking of lessees may be unnecessary. This can reduce administration costs for the lessor and thereby help in providing competitive lease rentals.
- *Flexibility.* Leasing can help provide flexibility where there are rapid changes in technology. If an option to cancel can be incorporated into the lease, the business may be able to exercise this option and invest in new technology as it becomes available. This will help the business to avoid the risk of obsolescence. Avoiding this risk will come at a cost to the lessee, however, because the risk is passed to the lessor, who will require this increased risk to be rewarded.
- *Cash flows.* Leasing, rather than buying an asset outright, means that large cash outflows can be avoided. The leasing option allows cash outflows to be smoothed out over the asset's life. In some cases, it is possible to arrange for low lease payments to be made in the early years of the asset's life, when cash inflows may be low, and for these to increase over time as the asset generates higher cash flows.

These benefits are summarised in diagrammatic form in Figure 15.4.

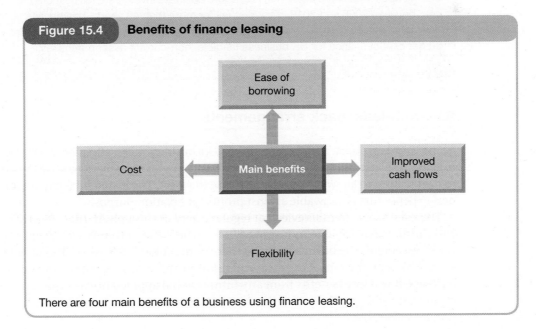

Figure 15.4   Benefits of finance leasing

There are four main benefits of a business using finance leasing.

Real World 15.7 provides some impression of the importance of finance leasing over recent years.

Real World 15.7

A new lease of life in the UK

Figure 15.5 charts the changes in the value of finance leasing in the UK over the years 2007 to 2015.

| Figure 15.5 | **Asset finance (new business) provided by FLA members, 2007–2015** |

Asset finance to businesses provided through finance leasing suffered a significant decline as a result of the economic recession. Business investment fell by more than 20 per cent between 2008 and 2010, the worst fall for more than 40 years. This decline seems to have been reversed with five consecutive years of growth. Finance leasing provides about 30 per cent of finance for UK business tangible, non-current asset purchases.

Source: Finance and Leasing Association (FLA) Annual Review 2016, p. 17, www.fla.org.uk.

Sale-and-leaseback arrangements

A **sale-and-leaseback** arrangement involves a business raising finance by selling an asset to a financial institution. The sale is accompanied by an agreement to lease the asset back to the business to allow it to continue to use the asset. The lease rental payment is a business expense that is allowable against profits for taxation purposes.

There are usually rental reviews at regular intervals throughout the period of the lease, and the amounts payable in future years may be difficult to predict. At the end of the lease agreement, the business must either try to renew the lease or find an alternative asset. Although the sale of the asset will result in an immediate injection of cash for the business, it will lose benefits from any future capital appreciation on the asset. Where a capital gain arises on the sale of the asset to the financial institution, a liability for taxation may also arise.

Activity (15.12)

Can you think which type of asset is often subject to a sale-and-leaseback arrangement?

Property is often the asset that is subject to such an arrangement.

Many of the well-known UK high street retailers (for example, Boots, Debenhams, Marks and Spencer, Tesco and Sainsbury) have sold off their store sites under sale-and-leaseback arrangements.

Sale-and-leaseback arrangements can be used to help a business focus on its core areas of competence. In recent years, many hotel businesses have entered into sale-and-leaseback arrangements to enable them to become hotel operators rather than a combination of hotel operators and owners.

Real World 15.8 explains how a leading UK hotel operator raised funds through the sale-and-leaseback of some of its hotel sites.

Real World 15.8

Rooms for sale and leaseback

Whitbread plc, the owner of the Premier Inn chain (as well as Costa coffee and a number of restaurant chains), entered into sale and leaseback arrangements for two of its central London hotels, early in 2017.

The business sold (and leased back) its 339-room Premier Inn in Westminster for £101.825 million to M and G Investments on a 25-year lease arrangement. It also entered into a similar arrangement with Aviva Investors for its 326-room Premier Inn in West Smithfield for £102.86 million.

Whitbread intends to use the proceeds of these deals to finance 'new growth opportunities in the UK and Germany'.

Source: Whitbread plc press release, Whitbread plc announces the sale and leaseback of two prime London sites, 12 January 2017.

Hire purchase

Hire purchase is a form of credit used to acquire an asset. Under the terms of a hire-purchase (HP) agreement, a customer pays for the asset by instalments over an agreed period. Normally, the customer will pay an initial deposit (down payment) and then make instalment payments at regular intervals, perhaps monthly, until the balance outstanding has been paid. The customer will usually take possession of the asset after payment of the initial deposit, although legal ownership of the asset will not be transferred until the final instalment has been paid. HP agreements will often involve three parties:

● the supplier;
● the customer; and
● a financial institution.

Although the supplier will deliver the asset to the customer, the financial institution will buy the asset from the supplier and then enter into an HP agreement with the customer. This intermediary role played by the financial institution enables the supplier to receive immediate payment for the asset but allows the customer a period of extended credit.

Figure 15.6 sets out the main steps in the hire purchase process.

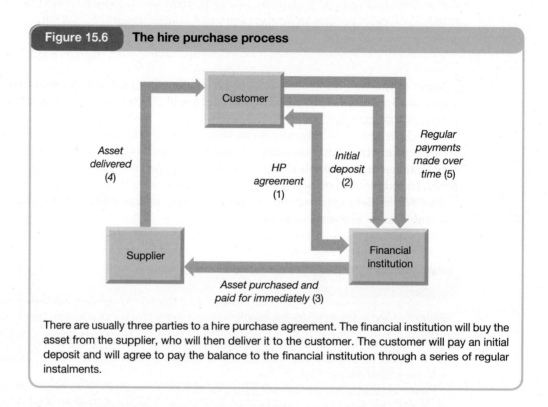

| Figure 15.6 | The hire purchase process |

There are usually three parties to a hire purchase agreement. The financial institution will buy the asset from the supplier, who will then deliver it to the customer. The customer will pay an initial deposit and will agree to pay the balance to the financial institution through a series of regular instalments.

HP agreements are, perhaps, most commonly associated with private consumers acquiring large household items or cars. Nevertheless, it is also a significant form of financing for businesses.

HP agreements are similar to finance leases insofar as they allow a customer to obtain immediate possession of the asset without paying its full cost. Under the terms of an HP agreement, however, the customer will eventually become the legal owner of the asset, whereas under the terms of a finance lease, ownership will stay with the lessor.

Real World 15.9 shows the extent to which one large UK business depends on hire purchase to finance its main assets.

Real World 15.9

Getting there by instalments

Stagecoach Group plc, the transport business, reported in its 2016 annual report, passenger service vehicles with a carrying amount of £776.6 million, of which £90.5 million related to assets purchased under HP agreements. This amounts to around 12 per cent of the total. Also, around 5 per cent of the £776.6 million was funded by finance leases.

Source: Stagecoach Group plc, Annual Report 2016, p. 89.

Securitisation

Securitisation involves bundling together illiquid financial or physical assets of the same type so as to provide financial backing for an issue of bonds. 'Illiquid' in this sense means not readily able to be sold. This financing method was first used by US banks, which bundled together residential mortgage loans to provide asset backing for bonds issued to investors. (Mortgage loans held by a bank are financial assets that provide future cash flows in the form of interest receivable and, usually, repayment of the amount of the loan.)

Securitisation has spread beyond the banking industry and has now become an important source of finance for businesses in a wide range of industries. Future cash flows from a variety of illiquid assets are now used as backing for bond issues, including:

- credit card receipts;
- water industry charges;
- receipts from former students in respect of their borrowings;
- rental income from university accommodation;
- ticket sales for football matches;
- royalties from music copyright;
- consumer instalment contracts; and
- beer sales to pub tenants.

The effect of securitisation is to capitalise future cash flows arising from illiquid assets. This capitalised amount is sold to investors, through the financial markets, to raise finance for the business holding these assets. Purchasers of securities bonds are, in effect, buying a share of the future cash flows from the assets concerned, in much the same way as the buyer of any bond or equity share.

Securitisation usually involves setting up a special-purpose vehicle (SPV) to acquire the assets from the business wishing to raise finance. This SPV will then arrange the issue of bonds to investors. Income generated from the securitised assets is received by the SPV and used to meet the interest payable on the bonds. When the bonds mature, the funds for repayment may come from either:

- receipts from the securitised assets (so long as the maturity dates are similar);
- the issue of new bonds; or
- surplus income generated by the securitised assets.

To reassure investors about the quality of the bonds, the securitised assets may be of a higher value than the value of the bonds (this is known as *overcollateralisation*). Alternatively, some form of credit insurance can be available from a third party, such as a bank.

The main elements of the securitisation process are set out in Figure 15.7.

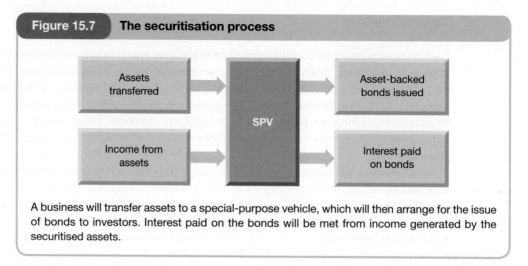

| Figure 15.7 | The securitisation process |

A business will transfer assets to a special-purpose vehicle, which will then arrange for the issue of bonds to investors. Interest paid on the bonds will be met from income generated by the securitised assets.

Securitisation may also be used to help manage risk. Where, for example, a bank has lent a lot of funds to a particular industry, its industry exposure can be reduced by bundling together some of the outstanding loan contracts and making a securitisation issue. This means that those who invested in the securitised bonds will bear the risk relating to the loan contracts concerned and not the bank.

Securitisation and the financial crisis

Securitising mortgage loan repayments became popular among US mortgage lenders during the early years of the 2000s. Where this approach was adopted, the monthly repayments due to be made by the relevant mortgage borrowers were 'securitised' and sold to many of the major banks, particularly in the USA. Unfortunately, many of the mortgage loans were made to people on low incomes who were not good credit risks (sub-prime loans). When the borrowers started to default on their obligations, it became clear that the securities, now owned by the banks, were worth much less than the banks had paid the mortgage lenders for them. This led to the so-called 'sub-prime' crisis that triggered the worldwide economic problems that emerged during 2008. There is, however, no inherent reason for securitisation to be the cause of such a problem and it is unfortunate that the practice is linked with the sub-prime crisis. It can be a perfectly ethical and practical way for a business to raise finance.

External sources of short-term finance

Short-term, in this context, is usually taken to mean up to one year. The major external sources of short-term finance (as were shown in Figure 15.2) are:

- bank overdrafts;
- debt factoring; and
- invoice discounting.

We shall now discuss each of these.

Bank overdrafts

A **bank overdraft** enables a business to maintain a negative balance on its bank account. It represents a very flexible form of borrowing as the size of an overdraft can (subject to bank approval) be increased or decreased more or less instantaneously. It is relatively inexpensive to arrange and interest rates are often very competitive, though often higher than those for a term loan. As with all loans, the rate of interest charged will vary according to how creditworthy the customer is perceived, by the bank, to be. An overdraft is fairly easy to arrange – sometimes it can be agreed by a telephone call to the bank. In view of these advantages, it is not surprising that an overdraft is an extremely popular form of short-term finance.

Banks prefer to grant overdrafts that are self-liquidating, that is, the funds are used in such a way as to extinguish the overdraft balance by generating cash inflows. The banks may ask the business to provide a projected cash flow statement or a cash budget to see when the overdraft is projected to be repaid and how much finance is required. They may also require some form of security on amounts advanced.

One potential drawback with this form of finance is that it is repayable on demand. This may pose problems for a business that is illiquid. However, many businesses operate for many years using an overdraft, simply because the banks remain confident of their ability to repay and the arrangement suits the business. Thus, bank overdrafts, though in theory regarded as short-term, can, in practice, become a source of long-term finance.

Debt factoring

Debt factoring is a service offered by financial institutions (known as factors), many of which are subsidiaries of commercial banks. It involves the factor taking over the trade receivables collection for a business. In addition to operating normal credit control procedures, a factor may offer to undertake credit investigations and advise on the creditworthiness of the business. It may also offer protection for approved credit sales. Two main forms of factoring agreement exist:

- *Recourse factoring,* where the factor assumes no responsibility for bad debts arising from credit sales.
- *Non-recourse factoring,* where, for an additional fee, the factor assumes responsibility for bad debts up to an agreed amount.

The factor is usually prepared to make an advance to the business of up to around 80 per cent of approved trade receivables (although it can sometimes be as high as 90 per cent). This advance is usually paid immediately after the goods have been supplied to the customer. The balance of the debt, less any deductions for fees and interest, will be paid after an agreed period or when the debt is collected. The charge made for the factoring service is based on total sales revenue and is often around 2 or 3 per cent of sales revenue. Any advances made to the business by the factor will attract a rate of interest similar to the rate charged on bank overdrafts.

Debt factoring is, in effect, outsourcing trade receivables collection to a specialist subcontractor. Many businesses find a factoring arrangement very convenient. It can result in savings in credit management costs and can create more certain cash flows. It can also release the time of key personnel for more profitable ends. This may be important for smaller businesses that rely on the talent and skills of a few key individuals. In addition, the level of finance available will rise spontaneously with the level of sales. There is a possibility, however, that a factoring arrangement may be viewed as an indication that the business is experiencing financial difficulties. This may have an adverse effect on the confidence of customers, suppliers and staff. For this reason, some businesses try to conceal the factoring arrangement by collecting outstanding debts on behalf of the factor.

Not all businesses will find factoring arrangements the answer to their financing needs. Factoring agreements may not be possible to arrange for very small businesses (those with total sales revenue of, say, less than £100,000) because of the high set-up costs. In addition, businesses engaged in certain sectors where trade disputes are part of the business culture, such as building contractors, may find that factoring arrangements are simply not available.

Figure 15.8 shows the factoring process diagrammatically.

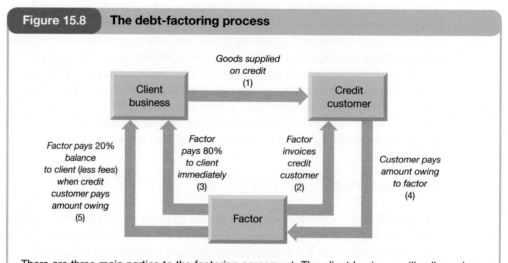

Figure 15.8   **The debt-factoring process**

There are three main parties to the factoring agreement. The client business will sell goods on credit and the factor will take responsibility for invoicing the customer and collecting the amount owing. The factor will then pay the client business the invoice amount, less fees and interest, in two stages. The first stage typically represents 80 per cent of the invoice value and will be paid immediately after the goods have been delivered to the customer. The second stage will represent the balance outstanding and will usually be paid when the customer has paid the factor the amount owing.

When considering a factoring agreement, it is necessary to identify and carefully weigh the costs and likely benefits arising. Example 15.1 illustrates how this may be done.

Example 15.1

Balkan Ltd has annual credit sales revenue of £50 million of which bad debts account for £0.2 million. The average settlement period for trade receivables is 80 days, which is causing some strain on the liquidity of the business.

Balkan Ltd is considering whether to use a factoring business to improve its liquidity position. The factor will advance an equivalent to 80 per cent of trade receivables (where the trade receivables figure is based on an average settlement period of 30 days) at an interest rate of 10 per cent. In addition, the factor will collect the trade receivables and will charge a fee of 3 per cent of total sales revenue for doing so. The remaining 20 per cent of the trade receivables will be paid to Balkan Ltd when the factor receives the cash. If the factor service is used, it is expected that the average settlement period for trade receivables will be reduced to 30 days, bad debts will be eliminated and credit administration savings of £320,000 will be gained.

The business currently has an overdraft of £10.0 million at an interest rate of 11 per cent a year.

In evaluating the factoring arrangement, it is useful to begin by considering the cost of the existing arrangements:

Existing arrangements

	£000
Bad debts written off each year	200
Interest cost of average receivables outstanding ((£50m × 80/365) × 11%)	1,205
Total cost of existing arrangement	1,405

The cost of the factoring arrangement can now be compared with this:

Factoring arrangement

	£000
Factoring fee (£50m × 3%)	1,500
Interest on factor loan (assuming 80% advance and reduction in average credit period) ((£40m × 30/365) × 10%)	329
Interest on overdraft (remaining 20% of receivables financed in this way) ((£10m × 30/365) × 11%)	90
	1,919
Savings in credit administration	(320)
Total cost of factoring	1,599

The net additional cost of using factoring would be £194,000 (that is, £1,599,000 less £1,405,000). Obviously, all other things being equal, the business would continue with the existing arrangements.

Invoice discounting

Invoice discounting involves a factor or other financial institution providing a loan based on a proportion of the face value of a business's credit sales outstanding. The amount advanced is usually 75 to 80 per cent of the value of the approved sales invoices outstanding. The business must agree to repay the advance within a relatively short period – perhaps 60 or 90 days. Responsibility for collecting the trade receivables outstanding remains with the business and repayment of the advance is not dependent on the trade receivables being collected. Invoice discounting will not result in such a close relationship developing between the business and the financial institution as occurs with factoring. It may be a short-term arrangement, whereas debt factoring usually involves a longer-term arrangement.

Invoice discounting is a much more important source of funds to businesses than factoring (see Real World 15.10). There are three main reasons for this:

- It is a confidential form of financing which the business's customers will know nothing about.
- The service charge for invoice discounting is only about 0.2 to 0.3 per cent of sales revenue compared to 2.0 to 3.0 per cent, around 10 times as much, for factoring.
- If customers know that a debt factor is collecting the amount due, this may cause customers to lose confidence in the business and its ability to continue to supply.

Real World 15.10 shows the relative importance of invoice discounting and factoring.

Real World 15.10

The popularity of invoice discounting and factoring

Figure 15.9 charts the relative importance of invoice discounting and factoring in terms of the value of client sales revenue.

Figure 15.9 **Client sales revenue (UK sales): invoice discounting and factoring, 2009–2015**

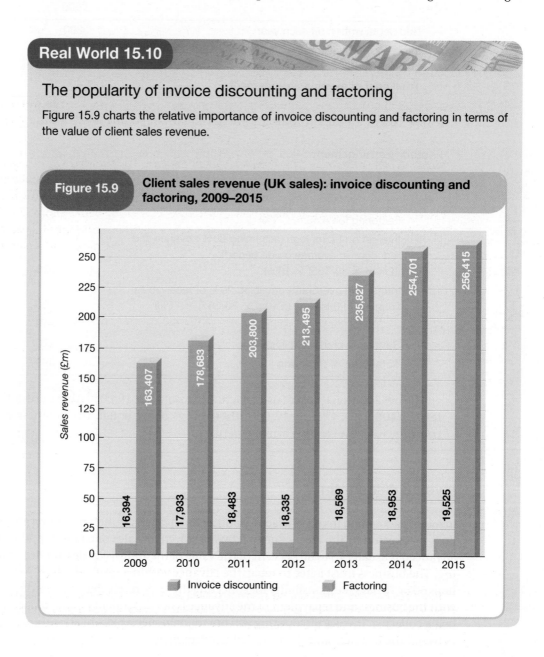

	Invoice discounting	Factoring
2009	16,394	163,407
2010	17,933	178,683
2011	18,483	203,800
2012	18,335	213,495
2013	18,569	235,827
2014	18,953	254,701
2015	19,525	256,415

Throughout the period, invoice discounting has been massively more important than factoring. Since 2009, the level of factoring has broadly increased by about 19 per cent. At the same time, the level of invoice discounting has increased quite strongly (about 57 per cent over the five years). The flatness of the UK economy over the earlier part of this period implies a clear increase in popularity of both of these funding approaches, particularly in the case of invoice discounting.

Source: Chart constructed from data published by the Asset Based Finance Association (www.abfa.org.uk).

Factoring and invoice discounting are forms of **asset-based finance** because the assets of receivables are, in effect, used as security for the cash advances received by the business.

Long-term versus short-term borrowing

Where it is clear that some form of borrowing is required to finance the business, a decision must be made as to whether long-term or short-term borrowing is more appropriate. There are many factors to be taken into account, which include the following:

- *Matching.* The business may attempt to match the type of borrowing with the nature of the assets held. Thus, long-term borrowing may be used to finance assets that form part of the permanent operating base of the business. These normally include non-current assets and a certain level of current assets. This leaves assets held for a short period, such as current assets used to meet seasonal increases in demand, to be financed by short-term borrowing, which tends to be more flexible in that funds can be raised and repaid at short notice. Figure 15.10 shows this funding division graphically.

| **Figure 15.10** | **Short-term and long-term financing requirements** |

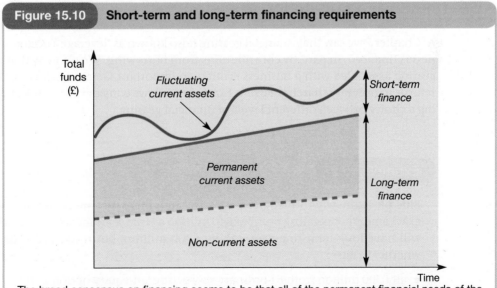

The broad consensus on financing seems to be that all of the permanent financial needs of the business should come from long-term sources. Only that part of current assets that fluctuates in the short term, probably on a seasonal basis, should be financed from short-term sources.

A business may wish to match the period of borrowing exactly with the asset life. This may not be possible, however, because of the difficulty of predicting the life of many assets.

- *Flexibility.* Short-term borrowing may be used as a means of postponing a commitment to long-term borrowing. Short-term borrowing does not usually incur a financial penalty for early repayment, whereas this may arise if long-term borrowing is repaid early.
- *Refunding risk.* Short-term borrowing has to be renewed more frequently than long-term borrowing. This may create problems for the business if it is in financial difficulties or if there is a shortage of funds available for borrowing.
- *Interest rates.* Interest payable on long-term borrowing is often higher than for short-term borrowing, as lenders require a higher return where their funds are locked up for a long period. This fact may make short-term borrowing a more attractive source of finance for a business. However, there may be other costs associated with borrowing (arrangement fees, for example) to be taken into account. The more frequently borrowings are renewed, the higher these costs will be.

Activity (15.13)

Some businesses may take up a less cautious financing position than that shown in Figure 15.10 and others may take up a more cautious one. How would the diagram differ under each of these options?

A less cautious position would mean relying on short-term finance to help fund part of the permanent capital base. A more cautious position would mean relying on long-term finance to help finance the fluctuating assets of the business.

Gearing and the financing decision

In Chapter 7 we saw that financial gearing (also known as 'leverage') occurs when a business is financed, in part, by contributions from borrowing. We also saw that the level of gearing associated with a business is often an important factor in assessing the risk and returns to ordinary shareholders. In Example 15.2, we consider the implications of making a choice between different levels of financial gearing.

Example 15.2

Blue plc is a newly-formed business. Although there is some uncertainty as to the exact amount, operating profit of £40 million a year seems most likely. The business will have long-term finance totalling £300 million, but it has yet to be decided whether to raise:

- all £300 million from £1 ordinary shares (the 'all-equity option'); or
- £150 million from £1 ordinary shares and £150 million from the issue of secured loan notes paying interest at 10 per cent a year (the 'geared option').

The rate of corporation tax is 20 per cent.

It is useful to look at the outcomes, under each financing option, for the shareholders for a range of possible operating profits.

All-equity option

	£m	£m	£m	£m	£m
Operating profit	20.00	30.00	40.00	50.00	60.00
Interest	–	–	–	–	–
Profit before taxation	20.00	30.00	40.00	50.00	60.00
Taxation (20%)	(4.00)	(6.00)	(8.00)	(10.00)	(12.00)
Profit for the year	16.00	24.00	32.00	40.00	48.00
Earnings per share	£0.053	£0.080	£0.107	£0.133	£0.160

Geared option

	£m	£m	£m	£m	£m
Operating profit	20.00	30.00	40.00	50.00	60.00
Interest	(15.00)	(15.00)	(15.00)	(15.00)	(15.00)
Profit before taxation	5.00	15.00	25.00	35.00	45.00
Taxation (20%)	(1.00)	(3.00)	(5.00)	(7.00)	(9.00)
Profit for the year	4.00	12.00	20.00	28.00	36.00
Earnings per share	£0.027	£0.080	£0.133	£0.187	£0.240

Activity 15.14

What do you notice about the earnings per share (EPS) values for each of the two financing options, in the light of different possible operating profits?

The obvious point is that, with the geared option, the EPS values are more sensitive to changes in the level of operating profit. An increase in £10 million from the most likely operating profit of £40 million will increase EPS with the geared option by 41 per cent (from £0.133 to £0.187). With the all-equity option, the increase is only 24 per cent (from £0.107 to £0.133).

Activity 15.15

Given that a £40 million operating profit is the most likely, what advice would you give the shareholders as to the better financing option?

The geared option will give the shareholders £0.025 more EPS and so appears to be more attractive. If the operating profit proves to be greater than £40 million, shareholders would be still better off than under the all-equity option. If, however, the operating profit falls below £40 million, the reduction in EPS would be much more dramatic under the geared option.

Note in Example 15.2 that, with an operating profit of £30 million, the EPS figures are the same irrespective of the financing option chosen (£0.080). This is because the rate of return (operating profit/long-term investment) is 10 per cent. This is the same as the interest rate for the loan notes. Where a business is able to generate a rate of return greater than the interest rate on the borrowings, the effect of gearing is to increase EPS. Where the opposite is the case, the effect of gearing is to decrease EPS.

Activity 15.16

In Chapter 9, we came across *operating gearing*. Is this the same thing as *financial gearing*?

No. Operating gearing is the relationship between fixed and variable costs in the total cost of some activity. Financial gearing is the relationship between the amount of equity and the amount of fixed return finance in the long-term funding of a business.

Activity 15.17

If a business's main activity has high operating gearing, would we expect it also to have high financial gearing?

A business with high operating gearing will find that its operating profit is particularly sensitive to changes in the level of sales revenue. A business with high financial gearing will find that its profit after interest is particularly sensitive to changes in the level of operating profit. Thus, returns to shareholders in a business that has both high operating gearing and high financial gearing will be highly sensitive to changes in the level of sales revenue. To avoid this degree of sensitivity, a business whose activities have high operating gearing will not usually have high financial gearing.

Financial gearing: the traditional approach

The traditional view of financial gearing seems to be that an element of it is a good thing. This is because borrowing rates tend to be lower than the rates of return expected by shareholders. Borrowing part of the long-term financing needs of the business, therefore, lowers the overall cost of capital and so increases the value of the business. This increase in value of the business would normally accrue only to the shareholders. This is because the amount of interest due to lenders and the amount owed by the business to its lenders tend to be fixed; they are not usually related to the profitability of the business. Thus, provided that shareholders are confident that the business can earn a rate of return higher than the interest rate on borrowing, the value of the business will increase, merely by borrowing. The fact that interest payments attract tax relief makes borrowing even cheaper. There is convincing evidence to show that rates of return to businesses tend to be higher than interest rates (see reference 1 at the end of the chapter).

The traditional approach, however, takes the view that the benefits of financial gearing are limited. Beyond a certain level, the advantages diminish so there is a point at which the business's overall cost of capital is at a minimum and the value of the business (and the shareholders' wealth) is at a maximum.

A challenge to the traditional approach

As with dividend policy, the traditional approach to gearing has been challenged. It seems illogical that, in Example 15.2, at an operating profit of £40 million (the most likely outcome), shareholders could be 24 per cent better off (EPS of £0.133 compared to £0.107) simply as a result of borrowing. This 'something for nothing' outcome seems to defy economic logic. This has led to an alternative, more modern, more analytical, view that this benefit is illusory. Although financial gearing can lead to increased returns to shareholders, it comes at a price. That price is increased risk. When judging the value of a share, investors look both at potential returns and the level of risk. In Example 15.2, we saw that returns to shareholders are more risky with gearing. The alternative view is that the gain from the cheap loan finance is exactly matched by a loss of share value due to increased risk.

The tax element of gearing, however, is beneficial to shareholders. If we look at the £40 million operating profit case in Example 15.2, we can see that the business would pay £8 million in corporation tax with the all-equity option, but only £5 million with the geared option. This £3 million is a direct, annual transfer of wealth from the tax authority to the shareholders as a result of gearing. It is a real benefit but accounts for only part of the difference between the two EPS figures. The remainder of the difference, the modernists argue, is valueless because the additional EPS is exactly matched by the additional risk.

Activity 15.18

The fact that the tax effect of gearing has a real benefit might lead to the conclusion that businesses should take on very high levels of borrowing. What would stop a business from doing this?

High levels of gearing give rise to high levels of commitment to make cash payments of interest, and eventually to redeem the borrowing. These commitments expose the business to significant risk. If operating profits (and accompanying cash inflows) fall below the projected level, the business may be forced into liquidation. Apart from anything else, this will tend to make potential lenders avoid the business.

Being forced into liquidation has a significant cost to the business, so sensible financial gearing policy tends to try to balance the benefit from the tax relief on interest with the potential cost of going bust. This is known as the 'trade-off theory' of financial gearing, which is illustrated in Figure 15.11.

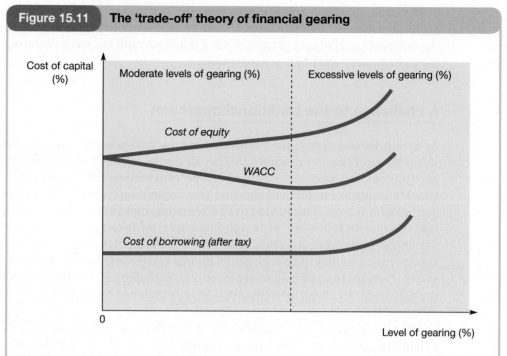

Figure 15.11   **The 'trade-off' theory of financial gearing**

As the level of gearing increases, the cost of equity rises to reflect the additional risk that gearing engenders. Despite this, the tax-deductibility of interest means that the weighted average cost of capital (WACC) decreases. Once the level of gearing reaches a level that is considered as being excessive, the risk of forced liquidation causes the cost both of equity and of borrowing to increase with further elements of borrowing. This leads to a rise in WACC.

The figure shows the cost of equity, the cost of borrowing and the average of these two, weighted according to how much of each there is in the financial structure. This average, the weighted average cost of capital (WACC), is the effective cost of capital for the business as a whole. These three are plotted against the level of financial gearing. At a zero level of gearing, the cost of equity is at a minimum because there is no risk arising from financial gearing. As borrowing becomes an increased part of the total long-term finance, the cost of equity increases but, because of the tax-deductibility of interest, WACC decreases. At the point where the level of gearing stops being moderate and starts being excessive, the cost of both equity and borrowing start to increase sharply and, with them, WACC. Logically businesses should seek to have their gearing level as indicated by the dotted line. At this point, the benefit of the tax relief on loan interest is balanced by the cost of a potential forced liquidation. WACC is at a minimum and the value of the business at a maximum.

Note in Figure 15.11 that if it were not for the tax relief, the cost of borrowing line would have been higher. This would have led to the increase in the cost of equity (due to increased perceptions of risk) exactly balancing the apparent cheapness of the cost of borrowing. The net effect would be that WACC would have remained constant at all moderate levels of gearing.

Activity 15.19

If shareholders gain from the business borrowing up to a reasonable level of financial gearing, who loses?

The gain to the shareholders arises only from the tax-deductibility of interest payable on borrowings, so it is other taxpayers who lose.

Financial gearing: the evidence

The formal research evidence strongly shows that businesses tend to follow the 'trade-off' theory. This evidence is discussed in the further reading recommendations at the end of this chapter. The informal evidence is also quite powerful. Most businesses are financially geared, but few of them are very highly geared.

Raising long-term finance

We shall now consider ways in which long-term finance may be raised by a business. We begin by looking at various forms of share issue and then go on to examine the role of capital markets.

Share issues

A business may issue shares in a number of ways. These may involve direct appeals to investors or the use of financial intermediaries. The most common methods of share issues are set out in Figure 15.12.

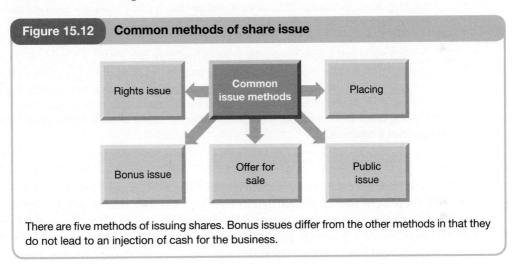

Figure 15.12   Common methods of share issue

There are five methods of issuing shares. Bonus issues differ from the other methods in that they do not lead to an injection of cash for the business.

We shall now discuss each of these methods in turn.

Rights issues

As we saw in Chapter 4, a **rights issue** can be made by established businesses that seek to raise additional funds by issuing new shares to their existing shareholders. Company law gives existing shareholders the first right of refusal to buy any new shares issued by a company, so the new shares would be offered to shareholders in proportion to their existing holding. Only where the existing shareholders agree to waive their right could the shares be offered to the investing public generally.

Rights issues are a fairly common form of share issue. During 2016, they accounted for approximately 37 per cent of all finance raised from share issues by businesses already listed on the London Stock Exchange (see reference 2 at the end of the chapter). The business (in effect, the existing shareholders) would typically prefer that existing shareholders buy the shares through a rights issue, irrespective of the legal position. This is for two reasons:

- Ownership (and, therefore, control) of the business remains in the same hands; there is no 'dilution' of control.
- Issue costs (advertising, complying with various company law requirements) tend to be lower where new shares are offered to existing shareholders. It is estimated that the average cost of a rights issue is between 2 and 3 per cent of the funds raised. A lot of the cost is fixed and so this percentage will be higher for smaller rights issues and lower for larger rights issues (see reference 3 at the end of the chapter). This compares with up to 4 per cent for an issue to the public (see reference 4 at the end of the chapter).

To encourage existing shareholders to take up their 'rights' to buy new shares, they are offered at a price below the current market price of existing shares. The new shares are typically offered at between 30 and 40 per cent below the current pre-rights price (see reference 5 at the end of the chapter).

Activity 15.20

In Chapter 4 (Example 4.2, page 134) the point was made that issuing new shares at below their current value is to the benefit of new shareholders and to the detriment of existing ones. In view of this, does it matter that rights issues are always made below the current value of the shares?

The answer is that it does not matter *in these particular circumstances,* because the existing shareholders and the new shareholders are exactly the same people. Moreover, the shareholders will hold the new shares in the same proportion as they currently hold the existing shares. Thus, shareholders will gain on the new shares exactly as much as they lose on the existing ones: in the end, no one is better or worse off as a result of the rights issue being made at a discount.

Shareholders cannot be compelled to buy the new shares. Not only that, but they can sell their right to buy the particular number of shares that they are entitled to buy to another potential investor. They can even choose to take up part of their rights (by buying some of the new shares that they are entitled to buy) and sell the remainder of the rights.

Calculating the value of the rights offer received by shareholders is quite straightforward, as shown in Example 15.3.

Example 15.3

Shaw Holdings plc has 20 million ordinary shares of 50p in issue. These shares are currently valued on the Stock Exchange at £1.60 per share. The directors have decided to make a one-for-four issue (that is, one new share for every four shares held) at £1.30 per share.

The first step in the valuation process is to calculate the price of a share following the rights issue. This is known as the *ex-rights price,* and is simply a weighted average of the price of shares before the rights issue and the price of the rights issue shares.

In this example, we have a one-for-four rights issue. The theoretical ex-rights price is therefore calculated as follows:

	£
Price of four shares before the rights issue (4 × £1.60)	6.40
Price of taking up one rights share	1.30
	7.70

$$\text{Theoretical ex-right price} = \frac{£7.70}{5} = \underline{1.54}$$

As the price of each share, in theory, should be £1.54 following the rights issue, and the price of a rights share is £1.30, the value of the rights offer will be the difference between the two:

$$£1.54 - 1.30 = 0.24 \text{ per share}$$

Market forces will usually ensure that the actual and theoretical price of rights shares will be fairly close.

Activity 15.21

An investor with 2,000 shares in Shaw Holdings plc (see Example 15.3) has contacted you for investment advice. She is undecided whether to take up the rights issue, sell the rights or allow the rights offer to lapse.

Calculate the effect on the net wealth of the investor of each of the options being considered.

Before the rights issue, the position of the investor was:

	£
Value of shares (2,000 × £1.60)	3,200

If she takes up the rights issue, she will be in the following position:

	£
Value of holding after rights issue ((2,000 + 500) × £1.54)	3,850
Cost of buying the rights shares (500 × £1.30)	(650)
	3,200

If the investor sells the rights, she will be in the following position:

	£
Value of holding after rights issue (2,000 × £1.54)	3,080
Sale of rights (500 × £0.24)	120
	3,200

If the investor lets the rights offer lapse, she will be in the following position:

	£
Value of holding after rights issue (2,000 × £1.54)	3,080

As we can see, the first two options should leave her in the same position concerning net wealth as before the rights issue. Before the rights issue, she had 2,000 shares worth £1.60 each, or £3,200 in total. However, she will be worse off if she allows the rights offer to lapse than under the other two options.

In practice, businesses will typically sell the rights on behalf of those investors who seem to be allowing them to lapse. It will then pass on the proceeds in order to ensure that they are not worse off as a result of the issue.

When considering a rights issue, the directors must first consider the amount of funds needing to be raised. This will depend on the future plans and needs of the business. The directors must then decide on the issue price of the rights shares. Normally, this decision is not critical. In Example 15.3, the business made a one-for-four issue with the price of the rights shares set at £1.30. However, it could have raised the same amount by making a one-for-two issue with the rights price at £0.65, a one-for-one issue with the price at £0.325, and so on. The issue price that is finally decided upon will not affect the value of the underlying assets of the business or the proportion of the underlying assets and earnings to which each shareholder is entitled. The directors must try to ensure that the issue price is not above the current market price of the shares, however, or the issue will be unsuccessful.

Real World 15.11 describes how Laird plc, the UK-based electronics and technology business, used a rights issue to help with its funding problem.

Real World 15.11

By rights . . .

In February 2017, Laird plc announced its intention to raise £185 million through a four-for-five rights issue. The issue was to be made at £0.85 per new share, a discount of 51.4 per cent on the market share price immediately preceding the announcement of the issue.

Laird, which has been through an adverse period of trading, planned to use the majority of the new funds to reduce its borrowing and thereby avoid breaching covenants linked to its borrowing.

Source: Based on information contained on the Laird plc website (www.laird-plc.com).

Offers for sale and public issues

An **offer for sale** usually involves a business that trades as a public limited company selling a new issue of shares to a financial institution known as an *issuing house*. However, shares that are already in issue may also be sold to an issuing house. In this case, existing shareholders agree to sell all or some of their shares to the issuing house. The issuing house will, in turn, sell the shares, purchased from either the business or its shareholders, to the public. It will publish a prospectus that sets out details of the business and the type of shares to be sold, and investors will be invited to apply for shares. The advantage of this type of issue, from the business's viewpoint, is that the sale proceeds of the shares are certain.

A **public issue** involves the business making a direct invitation to the public to purchase its shares. Typically, this is done through newspaper advertisements and the internet. The shares may, once again, be either a new issue or those already in issue. An offer for sale and a public issue will both result in a widening of share ownership in the business.

In practical terms, the net effect on the business is much the same whether there is an offer for sale or a public issue. As we have seen, the costs of a public issue can be very large. Some share issues by Stock Exchange listed businesses arise from the initial listing of the business, often known as an *initial public offering (IPO)*. Other share issues are undertaken by businesses that are already listed and are seeking additional finance from investors; these are usually known as *seasoned equity offerings (SEOs)*.

Setting a share price

When making an issue of shares, the business or the issuing house will usually set a price for the shares. This may not be an easy task, however, particularly where the market is volatile or where the business has unique characteristics. One way of dealing with this pricing problem is to make a **tender issue** of shares. This involves the investors determining the price at which the shares are issued. Although the business (or issuing house) may publish a reserve price to help guide investors, it will be up to the individual investor to determine the number of shares to be purchased and the price that should be paid. Once the offers from investors have all been received and recorded, a price at which all the shares can be sold will be established (known as the *striking price*). Investors who have made offers at, or above, the striking price will be issued shares at the striking price; offers received below the striking price will be rejected. Note that all of the shares will be issued at the same price irrespective of the prices actually offered by individual investors.

Although this form of issue is adopted occasionally, it is not popular with investors, and is therefore not in widespread use.

Private placings

A **private placing** does not involve an invitation to the public to subscribe for shares. Instead the shares are 'placed' with selected investors, such as large financial institutions. This can be a quick and relatively cheap way of raising funds, because savings can be made in advertising and legal costs. However, it can result in the ownership of the business being concentrated in a few hands.

Real World 15.12 describes how a placing was used by a major UK online estate agent to expand its activities.

Real World 15.12

Purple patch

In February 2017, UK-based Purplebricks Group plc announced its intention to raise £50 million through a placing. The business intends to use the funds to expand its estate agency business in the USA.

Purplebricks is a leading UK online estate agent. It is listed on the London Stock Exchange's 'junior' market, the Alternative Investment Market, which we shall discuss shortly.

Source: Information taken from Travers Smith LLP (2017) *£50m placing by Purplebricks Group*, www.traverssmith.com, 24 February.

Placings are used by both newly-listed and more seasoned listed businesses. During 2016, 95 per cent of the total finance raised from shares issued by businesses that were newly listed on the London Stock Exchange came from placings. This was a much higher percentage than in recent years. Placings are also popular for seasoned offerings, accounting for around 50 per cent of total issues by such businesses during 2016. It used to be the case that once a business has made its IPO, the rights issue route tended to be preferred for further equity fundraising. This seems decreasingly the case with rights only accounting for around 37 per cent of funds raised during 2016 (see reference 2 at the end of the chapter).

Unlisted businesses may also make this form of issue.

Bonus issues

We should recall from Chapter 4 that a bonus issue is not a means of raising finance. It is simply converting one part of the equity (reserves) into another (ordinary shares). No cash changes hands; this benefits neither the business nor the shareholders.

The role of the Stock Exchange

Earlier we considered the various forms of long-term capital that are available to a business. In this section, we shall consider the role that the Stock Exchange plays in providing finance for businesses. The Stock Exchange acts as both an important *primary* and *secondary* capital market for businesses. As a primary market, its function is to enable businesses to raise new finance. As a secondary market, its function is to enable investors to sell their securities (including shares and loan notes) with ease. Thus, it provides a 'second-hand' market where shares and loan notes already in issue may be bought and sold.

In order to issue shares or loan notes through the Stock Exchange, or for existing shares and loan notes to be bought and sold through the Stock Exchange, a business must become 'listed'. To obtain a listing, a business must meet fairly stringent requirements concerning size, profit history, information disclosure and so on.

Advantages of a listing

The secondary market role of the Stock Exchange means that shares and other financial claims are easily transferable. Investors are not obliged to use the Stock Exchange as the means of transferring shares in a listed business. There is no reason why an existing shareholder in a particular business should not sell the shares directly to another potential shareholder, outside the Stock Exchange. The problem here is that the two parties need to identify one another. Using the facility offered by the Stock Exchange is usually the most convenient way of buying or selling shares.

The Stock Exchange can be a useful vehicle for a successful entrepreneur wishing to realise the value of the business that has been built up. By successfully floating (listing) the shares on the Stock Exchange, and thereby making the shares available to the public, the entrepreneur will be in a position to realise the value of the shares held. Thus the entrepreneur can turn the 'paper' value of some, or all, of the shares into cash.

The Stock Exchange is often cited as an example of an **efficient capital market.** This is a market where share prices at all times rationally reflect all available, relevant information. It implies that any new information coming to light which bears on a particular business and its share price will be taken into account quickly and rationally, in terms of size and direction of share price movement. This helps to promote the tendency for the price quoted for a share to reflect its true worth at that particular time.

Activity 15.22

What benefits might a listed business gain from this tendency?

If it is generally accepted that shares can easily be sold for prices that tend to reflect their true worth, investors will have more confidence to invest. The business may benefit from this greater investor confidence by finding it easier to raise long-term finance and by obtaining this finance at a lower cost, as investors will view their investment as being less risky.

In a secondary capital market, such as the Stock Exchange, share prices are observed by large numbers of people, many of them skilled and experienced. Nearly all of these people observe the market because of that great motivator – financial gain. Information on the business comes to these observers in a variety of ways. The business itself provides financial statements, press releases and leaks (deliberate or otherwise). Information on the industry and economy, in which the business operates, is also relevant. This information will emerge from a variety of sources.

Where observers spot what they consider to be an irrational price, in the light of their assessment of future projected dividends, they try to take advantage of it, or advise others to do so. For example, an investment analyst employed by an insurance business might assess the worth of a share in Tesco plc at £2.00 but note that the current share price is £1.80. The analyst may therefore contact the investment manager to advise the purchase of some of these shares on the basis that they are currently underpriced and there are gains to be made. Prices are set in the Stock Exchange by forces of supply and demand. The increase in demand from large-scale buying will increase the share price. Our analyst, however, will be just one of many who are constantly comparing the market price of Tesco shares with their own assessments of the shares' worth.

The market price of the shares at all times represents the consensus view. If people feel strongly that this price is irrational, they will take steps to gain from their beliefs: the greater they perceive the irrationality to be, the more dramatic the steps that they will take.

Activity 15.23

If a capital market is price-efficient, does this mean that the current market price of a share in a particular business is the correct price?

No. A share price is based on expectations concerning its future returns. No one can know for certain what those future returns will be.

Price-efficiency does not imply perfect powers of prediction on the part of investors. All it means is that the current price of a share is the best estimate of its future returns on the basis of the available evidence.

An enormous amount of research has been undertaken on the pricing efficiency of most of the world's capital markets. Although there are anomalies, evidence from mature capital markets (including the London Stock Exchange) tends to conclude that:

1 the price of a share in any particular business fully, rationally and very rapidly takes account of all relevant *publicly* available information that relates to that business and its shares; and

2 any information that is only *privately* available is not necessarily taken into account in the share price.

This means that it is not possible for investors to make systematic gains from trading on the basis of any information that is publicly available. On the other hand, relevant information that is known only, say, to a director of a particular business, but will become publicly known later, may enable that person to gain from trading in the shares.

Activity 15.24

If we look at a graph of the price of a share in a particular business plotted against time, we often find that it jumps up and down. This is similar to the effect that we get if we plot a graph of a series of random numbers.
   Does this mean that share prices are random and arbitrary?

The share price movements mentioned above occur because new information does not arise in a gradual or systematic way but in a random, unexpected way. The share price movements will, however, be a rational and timely response to the new information coming to light.

Disadvantages of a listing

A Stock Exchange listing can have certain disadvantages for a business. These include:

- Strict rules are imposed on listed businesses, including requirements for levels of financial disclosure additional to those already imposed by International Financial Reporting Standards (for example, the listing rules require that half-yearly financial reports are published).
- Financial analysts, financial journalists and others monitor closely the activities of listed businesses, particularly larger ones. Such scrutiny may not be welcome, particularly if the business is dealing with sensitive issues or is experiencing operational problems.
- It is often suggested that listed businesses are under pressure to perform well over the short term. This pressure may detract from undertaking projects that will yield benefits only in the longer term. If the market becomes disenchanted with the business, and the price of its shares falls, this may make it vulnerable to a takeover bid from another business.
- The costs of obtaining and retaining a listing are huge and this may be a real deterrent for some businesses. To make an initial public offering, a business will rely on the help of various specialists such as lawyers, accountants and bankers. As we have seen, this represents a significant cost to the business.

Although there are over 900 UK businesses listed on the main market of the London Stock Exchange, in terms of equity market value, the market is dominated by just a few large ones, as is shown in **Real World 15.13**.

Real World 15.13

Listing to one side

At 31 December 2016, there were 928 businesses that had a London Stock Exchange Main Market listing. Just 163 of these (17.6 per cent) accounted for 86.7 per cent of their total equity market value.

A total of 266 businesses (28.7 per cent of listed businesses) accounted for 92.7 per cent of total equity market value.

Source: London Stock Exchange (2016) Market Statistics, Table 8 (December).

Real World 15.14 provides an analysis of the ownership of shares in UK listed businesses at the end of 2014.

Real World 15.14

Sharing things out

At the end of 2014, the proportion of shares of UK listed businesses held by various investors was as shown in Figure 15.13.

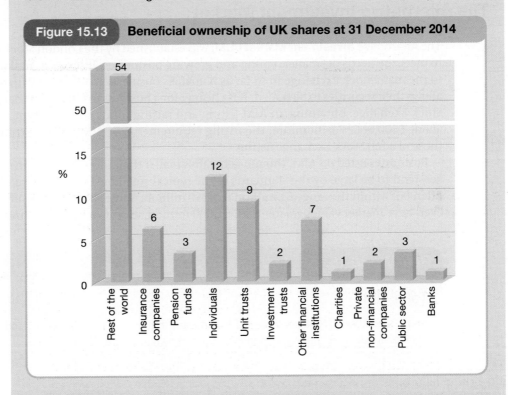

Figure 15.13 Beneficial ownership of UK shares at 31 December 2014

A striking feature of the ownership of UK shares is the extent of overseas ownership. At the end of 2014, this accounted for 54 per cent of the total; in 1963 it was 7 per cent and in 1998, still only 31 per cent. This overseas investors ownership of shares in UK businesses is broadly mirrored by the extent to which UK investors own shares of businesses based elsewhere in the world. It reflects the high level of the globalisation of business.

Real World 15.14 *continued*

Another striking feature is the extent to which large financial institutions now dominate the ownership of UK listed shares. In 1963, individuals owned 58 per cent of those UK shares owned by UK investors. By the end of 2014, it was only 25 per cent, though it had been even lower in recent past years.

Information on the types of overseas investors that own UK shares is not available, but it seems reasonable to speculate that the make-up is broadly similar to that of UK investors. This is to say that individuals probably make up a relatively small part of the total and professionally managed funds make up the bulk of it.

Source: Office for National Statistics (2015) *Ownership of UK Quoted Shares: 2014*, 2 September.

Going private

Such are the disadvantages of a stock market listing that many businesses have 'de-listed'. This has obviously denied them the advantages of a listing, but it has avoided the disadvantages.

The Alternative Investment Market

The **Alternative Investment Market (AIM)** was established by the London Stock Exchange to meet the needs of smaller, young and growing businesses. It serves a similar function to the main Stock Exchange in so far as it enables businesses to raise new finance and it allows their securities to be traded. It is cheaper for a business to enter AIM than the main Stock Exchange: obtaining an AIM listing and raising funds costs the typical business about £500,000. Furthermore, the listing requirements of AIM are less stringent than those of a full Stock Exchange listing.

Businesses listed on AIM, though generally smaller than those listed on the main market, tend to be large by the standards of the typical small business. Their market values often fall within the range £1 million to £250 million. Some AIM listed businesses, however, have market values greater than £1,000 million, as shown by **Real World 15.15**.

Real World 15.15

Take AIM

At 31 December 2016, there were 957 businesses that had shares that were listed on AIM. Their distribution according to market value is shown in Figure 15.14.

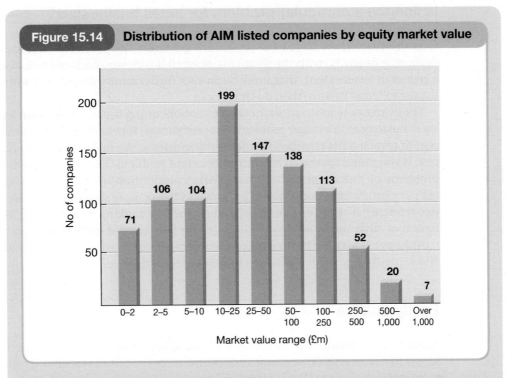

Figure 15.14   Distribution of AIM listed companies by equity market value

It seems that only about one in three AIM listed businesses have a market capitalisation greater than £50 million. The most popular range is £10 million to £25 million.

Source: London Stock Exchange (2016) *AIM Factsheet*, December.

AIM listed businesses are generally smaller and younger than those on the main Stock Exchange and so they tend to be higher-risk investments. Nevertheless, there are many investors who are attracted to this market.

AIM listed businesses include Fevertree Drinks plc, the soft drinks provider, Majestic Wine plc, the wine retailer, Asos plc and Boohoo.com plc, the online fashion retailers, and Purplebricks Group plc, the online estate agents that we met in Real World 15.12.

Providing long-term finance for the small business

Although the Stock Exchange and AIM provide an important source of long-term finance for larger businesses, they are not really suitable for smaller businesses. In practice, the costs of obtaining and retaining a listing are high, even with AIM. Thus, small businesses must look elsewhere for help in raising long-term finance. The more important sources of finance available specifically for small businesses are venture capital, business angels and government assistance. Each of these is discussed below. We will first consider, however, the extent to which small businesses experience difficulties in raising finance as this has been a source of much concern.

Is finance a particular problem for small businesses?

Over the years, there have been several UK government-sponsored enquiries that have dealt, at least partly, with the financing of small businesses. Each of these discovered, to a greater or lesser extent, that small businesses find it more difficult and more expensive to raise external finance than do larger ones.

The evidence tends to show, however, that obtaining finance is not seen by owners of small businesses as a major problem. A recent survey, for example, found that only 5 per cent of respondents regarded financing difficulties as the main obstacle to business success. It was ranked as the eighth most important problem. This placed it well behind the problems of 'the economy' (13 per cent), 'competition' (12 per cent) and 'taxation' (11 per cent), which respondents indicated as being more significant barriers to success (see reference 6 at the end of the chapter). The low ranking for financing difficulties is typical of other survey evidence relating to the problems of small businesses.

Although it may not be their biggest problem, there is no doubt that it remains difficult and expensive for small businesses to raise external finance.

Equity finance

Raising equity finance can be difficult for small businesses. For this reason they may be forced to rely heavily on personal savings and, once the business is up and running, internally generated equity finance (retained earnings).

Exit routes

A particular problem faced by small businesses in their quest for equity capital is the absence of an 'exit route'. Generally, investors require some way of liquidating their investment before they commit any funds. Three possible exit routes that may be used are:

1 *Share buyback.* A business may buy back the shares from the shareholder. However, this requires surplus cash that is not needed for further investment. This is not usually a very attractive option for the business. One of the key advantages of issuing equity is that it does not have to be redeemed.
2 *Share listing.* A business may obtain a listing on the Stock Exchange. The Alternative Investment Market (see above) may be appropriate, but it is still only larger businesses within the small business sector that can exploit this route.
3 *Business sale.* The business may be sold to another business or to a management team.

For very small businesses, however, none of the above is a likely possibility. Finding equity backing can, therefore, be a real problem. As already mentioned, the personal savings of owners and ploughed-back profits are the only significant sources of equity finance. We shall look briefly at the evidence on how small businesses raise finance, in practice, later in the chapter.

Venture capital

Venture capital is the name given to equity finance provided to support new, expanding and entrepreneurial businesses. Venture capitalists usually prefer to take a close interest in the business concerned. This could involve taking part in decisions made by the business. Much venture capital comes from institutional investors, such as pension funds and insurance companies. It also comes, however, from individual investors, in many cases taking advantage of tax incentives available.

Venture capitalists tend to be attracted to fast-expanding, often high-tech, businesses. They look for high returns, perhaps 25 to 35 per cent per year, a relatively short-term involvement (up to five years) and an exit route. They tend to take equity holdings of up to 40 per cent of the equity, typically involving investments of more than £1 million.

Despite the valuable role played by venture capital, however, not many small businesses use it.

Business angels

Whereas venture capital is provided by organisations specialising in such investments, **business angels** are typically individual investors who make investments, usually equity investments, in small businesses. There are estimated to be about 18,000 business angels active in the UK. Most investments made by business angels seem to be of amounts between £10,000 and £750,000, with an average amount of £47,000. Some 90 per cent of the investments made are of amounts less than £100,000. Typically, business angels take up to 40 per cent of the equity, though the average amount is only 8 per cent (see reference 7 at the end of the chapter). Business angels seek a close interest in the business. A National Business Angels Network has been established in the UK that puts potential angels in contact with businesses needing finance. The investors appearing in the BBC television programme *Dragons' Den* are business angels.

Crowdfunding

Crowdfunding involves raising funds from a large number of investors (the crowd). Each investor will normally pledge a relatively small sum. Crowdfunding has been around for very many years, but the internet has made it a more feasible way of raising equity. It is particularly relevant to small businesses for whom the more traditional approaches to equity financing are not available.

Typically, the small business requiring equity capital will approach a crowdfunding 'platform' (such as Crowdcube in the UK). In essence, the business sets out its plans and financial requirements, which the 'platform' puts on its website. Investors are invited to pledge funds in amounts, typically as little as £10, to buy a share or shares in the small business. The 'platform' charges the small business a commission, based on the amount of funds raised. Crowdfunding is becoming part of the established small-business funding environment and is expanding rapidly.

Real World 15.16 is extracts from a *Financial Times* article that discusses the origins and practices relating to crowdfunding.

Real World 15.16

Crowding around

For something that is considered a very "now" way of raising money, crowdfunding has its roots in something very old school: prog rock. It is generally acknowledged that modern crowdfunding was invented by Marillion, a band better known for "Kayleigh" (and a generation of girls bearing the name) than for technological innovation. In 1997, short of cash to make its next album, the band emailed its 6,000-strong database of fans asking if they would buy the album in advance. Some 12,000 advance orders later, the album was made and the idea of offering perks in return for speculatively stumping up cash was born. Two decades on and crowdfunding is part of the financial landscape for start-ups that want either to raise cash additional to venture capital funding, or to get a nifty idea off the ground. The main platforms are Kickstarter and Indiegogo, but there are many others . . .

Christian Smith, founder of TrackR, which makes Bluetooth tracking tags for items from keys to pets, harnessing what he calls "crowd GPS" to locate lost items, used Indiegogo to raise more than $1.75 million in 2014 to fund the business. Meanwhile he has another Indiegogo campaign under way for further product development which has raised more than $210,000 so far.

Building an audience before launching is important, he says. "You want to be in conversation with hundreds or thousands of people before you launch. If you can understand what they're interested in and get them interested in what's brewing, then people will be more interested when you do launch." The "conversation" part of this is key. Being well known can propel your project to undreamed of heights.

Exploding Kittens is a card game created by computer game designers Elan Lee, Shane Small, and Matthew Inman, founder of the hugely popular online comic The Oatmeal. The game launched last year looking for a modest $10,000. The immediate buzz on Twitter drove supporters straight to the crowdfunding page. Eight minutes later, Exploding Kittens had exceeded its goal and when the project closed less than a month later, it had raised $8.8 million. By the time the game shipped in the summer, it had become the most backed Kickstarter of all time, with 219,382 supporters.

However, there are also spectacular failures. Zano, a mini-drone, raised more than £2 milliion from 12,000 backers, yet failed to get off the ground when its creators could not make it work. To its credit, Kickstarter, which says "active governance is important to our platform; trust is important", commissioned Mark Harris, a freelance journalist, to write a comprehensive postmortem of the Zano project, giving Harris complete editorial freedom.

Failures inevitably dent confidence in crowdfunding, yet the big successes mean it is nonetheless an attractive way of raising capital. So what is the lesson for entrepreneurs? If you have done your homework, have a clear strategy for engagement, well-defined manufacturing processes in place and a project that catches the imagination, then you stand a good chance of hitting your target while avoiding the need to give venture capital funders a stake in your business.

And what of TrackR? Problems with delivery soured the relationship with its backers, though Smith says: "We did our best to be very open with what was happening on the engineering side." He warns: "A lot of problems you'll face are unexpected." But the TrackR devices are in some ways a metaphor for crowdfunding itself. The tags work by checking in with other people's phones running the app, which is great if you leave your phone in a New York restaurant. However, TrackR clearly has yet to catch on in west London, as the app could not locate my cat. And there's the thing: crowdsourcing has to tap into enough of the right people to be really effective.

FT

Source: Extracts from Bevan, K. (2016) How to get the most from crowdfunding — and the risks to avoid, ft.com, 22 May.
© The Financial Times Limited 2016. All Rights Reserved.

Non-equity finance

Small businesses often rely for debt-type finance on some of the same sources as do larger ones, including bank overdrafts, term loans, hire purchase and leasing. There are, however, a few other sources that tend to apply more exclusively to smaller businesses.

Credit cards

Here the small business uses a credit card to make payments for items that might otherwise require an immediate cash payment, but settle at a later date. If the amount due to the credit card provider is settled at the end of the month, normally no interest or fees will be charged to the business. It is, of course, the supplier of the goods or services that is charged for the credit card provider's commission. Where the small business does not settle its credit card obligation at the end of the credit-free period, interest charges to the business arise and at quite high rates.

Peer-to-peer lending

Peer-to-peer lending, sometimes known as *crowdlending,* is the non-equity equivalent of crowdfunding discussed earlier. It operates on a very similar basis to crowdfunding in that a commercial 'platform' acts as the online interface between potential borrowers and potential lenders, where the latter may each provide very small amounts of loan finance.

Some peer-to-peer loans are made to private individuals to fund personal spending, such as buying a car. Much of it, however, relates to small businesses seeking to raise funds to finance their activities. Like crowdfunding, its widespread use is fairly recent, but it is becoming an increasingly important source of finance.

Government assisted loan finance

The UK government assists small businesses through the Enterprise Finance Guarantee (EFG) (formerly the Small Firms Loan Guarantee Scheme). This aims to help small businesses that have viable business plans, but lack the security to enable them to borrow. The scheme, which is available for businesses with annual sales revenue of up to £41 million, guarantees:

- 75 per cent of the amount borrowed, for which the borrower pays a premium of 2 per cent on the outstanding borrowing as a contribution towards the running of the scheme; and
- loans ranging from £1,000 to £1.2 million for a maximum period of 10 years.

In 2013, the UK government set up the British Business Bank (BBB). Its aim is to support economic growth by bringing together public and private funds so as to create a more effective and efficient finance market for small and medium sized businesses. As well as taking new initiatives, the Bank has taken over existing commitments of the UK government in the area of financing smaller businesses. The finance can be either in the form of loans or equity finance of the venture capital/business angel type.

In November 2014, the UK government increased its commitment to both EFG and BBB by pledging additional public finance to each of them. EFG is now managed by BBB.

In addition to other forms of financial assistance, such as government grants and tax incentives for investors to buy shares in small businesses, the government also helps by providing information concerning the sources of finance available.

Evidence on small business financing

It seems that the original owners of smaller businesses provide the vast majority of equity finance. Finance raised from outsiders tends to be through loans of various types. There is a dearth of published information, however, on the degree to which small businesses are financed by their owners, on the one hand, and lenders of various types, on the other. Nevertheless, lenders would usually be unwilling to provide funds, or even to allow trade credit, unless the owners provided a substantial buffer.

Survey information on where small businesses look for loan finance is rather more evident. **Real World 15.17** shows the sources of non-equity finance currently used by the average small UK business.

Real World 15.17

Small business funding

Bank finance, such as overdrafts and loans, is the main source of external finance for small businesses, as the pie chart in Figure 15.15 shows.

Figure 15.15 **External financing of small businesses, 2012–2014**

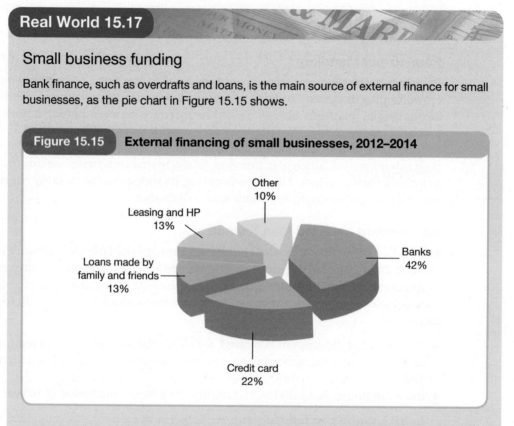

The bulk of finance is provided by financing institutions (banks and credit card businesses). Loans from family and friends also play a part along with leasing and HP finance. It is striking what a large proportion of the funding came from credit card funding (22 per cent). Presumably, this is used mainly to finance working capital and the debt is paid off before interest becomes payable.

Although venture capital is undoubtedly an important source of finance for some businesses, overall it is relatively insignificant (1 per cent – included in 'Other' in Figure 15.15).

Source: British Business Bank (2015) *Small Business Finance Markets 2014*.

Islamic finance

The increasing economic importance of those who follow the Islamic faith has led to greater attention being paid to their needs concerning the financing of businesses. Many of these individuals are citizens of Islamic states, but many others are nationals of the USA and Western European countries, particularly the UK and France.

A key feature of Islamic finance is the belief, based on the teachings of the Islamic holy book (the Quran), that charging pure interest is wrong. This stems from the notion that it is immoral to gain income (in the form of interest) merely because money has been lent. Sharia law, which guides Islamic practice, is not at all against free enterprise capitalism; it is the lack of risk taking that is the problem. Sharia is, however, also hostile to pure speculation. It is probably fair to say that Sharia looks favourably on profits earned through hard work and enterprise, but shuns gains from pure financing and speculation.

We can see that normal interest-bearing loans to businesses, such as term loans and loan notes, are contrary to Sharia law. All investors, not just equity investors, are required to bear part of the risk associated with operating the business. In recent years, special types of bonds have emerged to meet this requirement. This has enabled Tesco plc, the supermarket business, to make an issue of Sharia-compliant bonds in Malaysia.

Sharia law also forbids investing in businesses that contravene Islamic principles, such as those that produce alcoholic drinks, pornography and tobacco. This is not, however, different in essence from ethical investing practised by many non-Islamic investors, for example the Church of England.

Self-assessment question (15.1)

Helsim Ltd is a wholesaler and distributor of electrical components. The most recent draft financial statements of the business included the following:

Income statement for the year

	£m	£m
Sales revenue		14.2
Cost of sales		
Opening inventories	3.2	
Purchases	8.4	
	11.6	
Closing inventories	(3.8)	(7.8)
Gross profit		6.4
Administration expenses		(3.0)
Distribution expenses		(2.1)
Operating profit		1.3
Finance costs		(0.8)
Profit before taxation		0.5
Tax		(0.2)
Profit for the period		0.3

→

Self-assessment question 15.1 *continued*

Statement of financial position as at the end of the year

	£m
ASSETS	
Non-current assets	
Property, plant and equipment	
Land and buildings	3.8
Equipment	0.9
Motor vehicles	0.5
	5.2
Current assets	
Inventories	3.8
Trade receivables	3.6
Cash at bank	0.1
	7.5
Total assets	12.7
EQUITY AND LIABILITIES	
Equity	
Share capital	2.0
Retained earnings	1.8
	3.8
Non-current liabilities	
Loan notes (secured on property)	3.5
Current liabilities	
Trade payables	1.8
Short-term borrowings	3.6
	5.4
Total equity and liabilities	12.7

Notes:

1 Land and buildings are shown at their current market value. Equipment and motor vehicles are shown at cost less accumulated depreciation.
2 No dividends have been paid to ordinary shareholders for the past three years.

In recent months, trade payables have been pressing for payment. The chief executive officer has therefore decided to reduce the level of trade payables to an average of 40 days outstanding. To achieve this, he has decided to approach the bank with a view to increasing the overdraft (the short-term borrowings comprise only a bank overdraft). The business is currently paying 10 per cent a year interest on the overdraft.

Required:

(a) Comment on the liquidity position of the business.
(b) Calculate the amount of finance required to reduce trade payables, from the level shown on the statement of financial position, to an average of 40 days outstanding.
(c) State, with reasons, how you consider the bank would react to the proposal to grant an additional overdraft facility.
(d) Identify four sources of finance (internal or external, but excluding a bank overdraft) that may be suitable to finance the reduction in trade payables, and state, with reasons, which of these you consider the most appropriate.

The solution to this question can be found at the back of the book on pp.783–784.

Summary

The main points in this chapter may be summarised as follows:

Sources of finance

- Long-term finance is for at least one year whereas short-term finance is for a shorter period.
- External sources of finance require the agreement of outside parties, whereas internal sources do not.
- The higher the risk associated with a source of finance, the higher the expected return from investors.

Internal sources of finance

- Retained earnings are by far the most important source of new long-term finance (internal or external) for UK businesses.
- Retained earnings are not a free source of finance, as investors will require returns similar to those from ordinary shares.
- Dividend policy should be based on the principle that the directors should retain such funds that can be invested at above the rate of the shareholders opportunity cost of capital.
- Internal sources of short-term finance include tighter control of trade receivables, reducing inventories levels and delaying payments to trade payables.

External sources of finance

- External sources of long-term finance include ordinary shares, preference shares, borrowings, leases, hire-purchase agreements and securitisation.
- From an investor's perspective, ordinary shares are normally the most risky form of investment and provide the highest expected returns to investors. Borrowings (loans) are normally the least risky and provide the lowest expected returns to investors.
- Loans are relatively low-risk because lenders usually have security for their loan. Loan covenants can further protect lenders.
- Types of loans include term loans, convertible loan notes, mortgages, eurobonds and deep discount bonds.
- Convertible loan notes offer the right of conversion to ordinary shares at a specified date and a specified price.
- Interest rates may be floating or fixed.
- A finance lease is really a form of lending that gives the lessee the use of an asset over most of its useful life in return for regular payments.
- A sale-and-leaseback arrangement involves the sale of an asset to a financial institution accompanied by an agreement to lease the asset back to the business.
- Hire purchase is a form of credit to acquire an asset. Under the terms of a hire-purchase agreement, a customer pays for an asset by instalments over an agreed period.
- Securitisation involves bundling together similar, illiquid assets to provide backing for the issue of bonds.
- External sources of short-term finance include bank overdrafts, debt factoring and invoice discounting.

- Bank overdrafts are flexible and cheap but are repayable on demand.
- Debt factoring and invoice discounting use trade receivables as a basis for borrowing, with the latter more popular because of cost and flexibility.
- When choosing between long-term and short-term borrowing, important factors include matching the type of borrowing to the type of assets, flexibility, refunding risk and interest rates.

Financial gearing

- Most businesses have some fixed-return element in their long-term financial structures.
- Financial gearing increases the risk to shareholders.
- Gearing is beneficial to shareholders because interest payments to lenders are tax-deductible.
- Sensible financial gearing policy should probably seek to strike a balance between the tax deductibility of interest payments and the cost of the business being forced into liquidation.

Share issues

- Share issues that involve the payment of cash by investors can take the form of a rights issue, public issue, offer for sale or a private placing.
- A rights issue is made to existing shareholders. Most share issues are of this type as the law requires that shares that are to be issued for cash must first be offered to existing shareholders. Rights issue costs are relatively low.
- A public issue involves a direct issue to the public and an offer for sale involves an indirect issue to the public.
- A private placing is an issue of shares to selected investors.
- A bonus issue of shares does not involve the receipt of cash in exchange for the shares issued.

The Stock Exchange

- The Stock Exchange is an important primary and secondary market in capital for large businesses. However, obtaining a Stock Exchange listing can have certain drawbacks for a business.
- The Stock Exchange is broadly seen as an efficient capital market. This means that new information that becomes publicly available is quickly and rationally reflected in share prices. This leads to share prices representing the best estimate of the 'true' value of shares, on the basis of publicly-known information.

The Alternative Investment Market (AIM)

- AIM is another important primary and secondary market managed by the London Stock Exchange for smaller, growing businesses. It tends to be a cheaper way for a business to become listed.

Small businesses

- Venture capital is long-term capital for small or medium-sized businesses that are not listed on the Stock Exchange. These businesses often have higher levels of risk but provide the venture capitalist with the prospect of higher levels of return.

- Business angels are wealthy individuals who are willing to invest in businesses at either an early stage or expansion stage of development.
- Crowdfunding, where a large number of investors contribute small amounts of equity finance, is becoming increasingly important.
- Peer-to-peer lending, where a large number of lenders contribute small amounts of finance, is also becoming increasingly important.
- The government assists small businesses through guaranteeing loans and by providing grants and tax incentives.
- The British Business Bank has been set up by the government to support small businesses in their quest for funding by bringing together public and private funds.

Islamic finance

- The teachings of the Islamic faith are hostile to investors receiving pure interest on amounts that are lent to businesses and where risk is not shared; they are also hostile to investors making purely speculative gains.
- Special types of investment vehicles have been devised to try to ensure that returns to all investors are compliant with Sharia law.

Key terms

For definitions of these terms, see Appendix B.

References

1 Dimson, E., Marsh, P. and Staunton, M. (2017) *Credit Suisse Global Investments Returns Yearbook.*

2 London Stock Exchange, Main Market Factsheet, December 2016, Table 3.

3 Association of British Insurers (2013) Encouraging equity investment, p. 36.

4 Association of British Insurers (2013) Encouraging equity investment, p. 24.

5 Association of British Insurers (2013) Encouraging equity investment, p. 32.

6 Department for Business, Innovation and Skills (2015) *Small Business Survey,* April.

7 Burn-Callander, R. (2016) Campaign seeks to generate an extra £1bn of angel capital in UK over next three years, *The Daily Telegraph,* 23 March.

Further reading

If you would like to explore the topics discussed in this chapter in more depth, we recommend the following:

Arnold, G. (2012) *Corporate Financial Management,* 5th edn, Pearson, Chapters 11 and 12.

Brealey, R. and Myers, S. (2013) *Principles of Corporate Finance, Global edition,* 11th edn, McGraw-Hill Education, Chapters 13–19 and 23–25.

Hillier, D., Clacher I., Ross, S., Westerfield, R. and Jordan, B. (2014) *Fundamentals of Corporate Finance,* 2nd European edn, McGraw-Hill Education, Chapters 14–16.

McLaney, E. (2017) *Business Finance: Theory and Practice,* 11th edn, Pearson, Chapters 8, 9, 11 and 12.

Pike, R., Neale, B. and Linsley, P. (2015) *Corporate Finance and Investment,* 8th edn, Pearson, Chapters 15 and 16.

Review questions

Solutions to these questions can be found at the back of the book on pp. 798–799.

15.1 What are the potential disadvantages of raising finance through a sale-and-leaseback arrangement?

15.2 Why might a business that has a Stock Exchange listing revert to being unlisted?

15.3 Distinguish between an offer for sale and a public issue of shares.

15.4 Distinguish between invoice discounting and factoring.

Exercises

Solutions to exercises with **coloured numbers** can be found at the back of the book on pp. 838–841.

Basic-level exercises

15.1 Provide reasons why a business may decide to:
(a) lease rather than buy an asset which is to be held for long-term use;
(b) use retained earnings to finance growth rather than issue new shares; and
(c) repay long-term borrowings earlier than the specified repayment date.

15.2 H. Brown (Portsmouth) Ltd produces a range of central heating systems for sale to builders' merchants. As a result of increasing demand for the business's products, the directors have decided to expand production. The cost of acquiring new plant and machinery and the increase in working capital requirements are planned to be financed by a mixture of long-term and short-term borrowing.

Required:

(a) Discuss the major factors that should be taken into account when deciding on the appropriate mix of long-term and short-term borrowing necessary to finance the expansion programme.
(b) Discuss the major factors that a lender should take into account when deciding whether to grant a long-term loan to the business.
(c) Identify three conditions that might be included in a long-term loan agreement.

Intermediate-level exercises

15.3 Devonian plc has the following equity as at 30 November Year 4:

	£m
Ordinary shares 25p fully paid	50.0
General reserve	22.5
Retained earnings	25.5
	98.0

In the year to 30 November Year 4, the operating profit (profit before interest and taxation) was £40 million and it is expected that this will increase by 25 per cent during the forthcoming year. The business is listed on the London Stock Exchange and the share price as at 30 November Year 4 was £2.10.

The business wishes to raise £72 million in order to re-equip one of its factories and is considering two possible financing options. The first option is to make a 1-for-5 rights issue at a discount price of £1.80 per share. The second option is to borrow long-term at an interest rate of 10 per cent a year. If the first option is taken, it is expected that the price/earnings (P/E) ratio will remain the same for the forthcoming year. If the second option is taken, it is estimated that the P/E ratio will fall by 10 per cent of its Year 4 value by the end of the forthcoming year.

Assume a tax rate of 20 per cent.

Required:

(a) Assuming a rights issue of shares is made, calculate:
   1 the theoretical ex-rights price of an ordinary share in Devonian plc; and
   2 the value of the rights for each original ordinary share.
(b) Calculate the price of an ordinary share in Devonian plc in one year's time assuming:
   1 a rights issue is made; and
   2 the required funds are borrowed.
   Comment on your findings.
(c) Explain why rights issues are usually made at a discount.
(d) From the business's viewpoint, how critical is the pricing of a rights issue likely to be?

15.4 Raphael Ltd is a small engineering business that has annual sales revenue of £2.4 million, all of which is on credit. In recent years, the business has experienced credit control problems. The average settlement period for trade receivables has risen to 50 days even though the stated policy of the business is for payment to be made within 30 days. In addition, 1.5 per cent of sales are written off as bad debts each year.

The business has recently been in talks with a factor, which is prepared to make an advance to the business equivalent to 80 per cent of trade receivables, based on the assumption that customers will, in future, adhere to a 30-day settlement period. The interest rate for the advance will be 11 per cent a year. The trade receivables are currently financed through a bank overdraft, which has an interest rate of 12 per cent a year. The factor will take over the credit control procedures of the business and this will result in a saving to the business of £18,000 a year. However, the factor will make a charge of 2 per cent of sales revenue for this service. The use of the factoring service is expected to eliminate the bad debts incurred by the business.

Required:

Calculate the net cost of the factor agreement to the business and state whether the business should take advantage of the opportunity to factor its trade receivables.

Advanced-level exercises

15.5 Russell Ltd installs and services heating and ventilation systems for commercial premises. The business's most recent statement of financial position and income statement are as follows:

Statement of financial position

	£000
ASSETS	
Non-current assets	
Property, plant and equipment	741.8
Current assets	
Inventories at cost	293.2
Trade receivables	510.3
	803.5
Total assets	1,545.3

	£000
EQUITY AND LIABILITIES	
Equity	
£1 ordinary shares	400.0
General reserve	50.2
Retained earnings	382.2
	832.4
Non-current liabilities	
Borrowings – 12% loan notes (repayable in 5 years' time)	250.0
Current liabilities	
Trade payables	199.7
Taxation	128.0
Borrowings – bank overdraft	135.2
	462.9
Total equity and liabilities	1,545.3

Income statement for the year

	£000
Sales revenue	5,207.8
Operating profit	542.0
Interest payable	(30.0)
Profit before taxation	512.0
Taxation	(128.0)
Profit for the year	384.0
Note:	
Dividend paid during the year	153.6

The business wishes to invest in more machinery and equipment to enable it to cope with an upsurge in demand for its services. An additional operating profit of £120,000 a year is expected if an investment of £600,000 is made in plant and machinery.

The directors are considering an offer from venture capitalists to finance the expansion programme. The finance will be made available immediately through either

● an issue of £1 ordinary shares at a premium on nominal value of £3 a share; or
● an issue of £600,000 10 per cent loan notes at nominal value.

The directors wish to maintain the same dividend payout ratio in future years as in past years whichever method of finance is chosen.

Required:
(a) For each of the financing schemes:
    1 prepare a projected income statement for next year;
    2 calculate the projected earnings per share for next year; and
    3 calculate the projected level of gearing as at the end of next year.
(b) Briefly assess both of the financing schemes under consideration from the viewpoint of the existing shareholders.

15.6 Carpets Direct plc wishes to increase the number of its retail outlets in the south of England. The board of directors has decided to finance this expansion programme by raising the funds from existing shareholders through a 1-for-4 rights issue. The following is extracted from the most recent income statement of the business:

Income statement for the year ended 30 April

	£m
Sales revenue	164.5
Operating profit	12.6
Interest	(6.2)
Profit before taxation	6.4
Taxation	(1.9)
Profit for the year	4.5

A £2 million ordinary dividend had been paid in respect of the year.

The share capital consists of 120 million ordinary shares with a nominal value of £0.50 a share. These are currently being traded on the Stock Exchange at a price/earnings ratio of 22 times and the board of directors has decided to issue the new shares at a discount of 20 per cent on the current market value.

Required:

(a) Calculate the theoretical ex-rights price of an ordinary share in Carpets Direct plc.
(b) Calculate the price at which the rights in Carpets Direct plc are likely to be traded.
(c) Identify and evaluate, at the time of the rights issue, each of the options arising from the rights issue to an investor who holds 4,000 ordinary shares before the rights announcement.

(*Hint*: To answer part (a), first calculate the earnings per share and then use this and the P/E ratio to calculate the marker value per share.)

15.7 Gainsborough Fashions Ltd operates a small chain of fashion shops. In recent months the business has been under pressure from its suppliers to reduce the average credit period taken from three months to one month. As a result, the directors have approached the bank to ask for an increase in the existing overdraft for one year to be able to comply with the suppliers' demands. The most recent financial statements of the business are as follows:

Statement of financial position as at 31 May

	£000
ASSETS	
Non-current assets	
Property, plant and equipment	74
Current assets	
Inventories at cost	198
Trade receivables	3
	201
Total assets	275
EQUITY AND LIABILITIES	
Equity	
£1 ordinary shares	20
General reserve	4
Retained earnings	17
	41
Non-current liabilities	
Borrowings – loan notes repayable in just over one year's time	40
Current liabilities	
Trade payables	162
Accrued expenses	10
Borrowings – bank overdraft	17
Taxation	5
	194
Total equity and liabilities	275

Abbreviated income statement for the year ended 31 May

	£000
Sales revenue	74
Operating profit	38
Interest charges	(5)
Profit before taxation	33
Taxation	(10)
Profit for the year	23

A dividend of £23,000 was paid for the year.

Notes:

1 The loan notes are secured by personal guarantees from the directors.
2 The current overdraft bears an interest rate of 12 per cent a year.

Required:

(a) Identify and discuss the major factors that a bank would take into account before deciding whether to grant an increase in the overdraft of a business.

(b) State whether, in your opinion, the bank should grant the required increase in the overdraft for Gainsborought Fashions Ltd. You should provide reasoned arguments and supporting calculations where necessary.

Managing working capital

Introduction

This chapter considers the factors to be taken into account when managing the working capital of a business. Each element of working capital will be identified and the major issues surrounding them will be discussed. Working capital represents a significant investment for many businesses and so its proper management and control can be vital. We saw in Chapter 14 that an investment in working capital is typically an important aspect of many new investment proposals.

Learning outcomes

When you have completed this chapter, you should be able to:

- identify the main elements of working capital;

- discuss the purpose of working capital and the nature of the working capital cycle;

- explain the importance of establishing policies for the control of working capital; and

- explain the factors that have to be taken into account when managing each element of working capital.

What is working capital?

Working capital is usually defined as *current assets less current liabilities*. The major elements of current assets are:

- inventories;
- trade receivables; and
- cash (in hand and at bank).

The major elements of current liabilities are:

- trade payables; and
- bank overdrafts and other short-term borrowings.

The size and composition of working capital can vary between industries. For some types of business, the investment in working capital can be substantial. A manufacturing business, for example, will often be heavily invested in raw material, work in progress and finished goods. It will also normally sell its goods on credit, giving rise to trade receivables. A retailer, on the other hand, holds only one form of inventories (finished goods) and will normally sell its goods for cash rather than on credit. Many service businesses hold no inventories. Few, if any, businesses operate without a cash balance. In some cases, however, it is a negative one (a bank overdraft). Most businesses buy goods and/or services on credit, giving rise to trade payables.

The size and composition of working capital can also vary between businesses of similar size within the same industry. This usually reflects different attitudes towards the management of working capital and its individual elements which, in turn, is often linked to different attitudes towards risk.

Working capital represents a net investment in short-term assets. These assets are continually flowing into and out of the business and are essential for day-to-day operations. The various elements of working capital are interrelated and can be seen as part of a short-term cycle. For a manufacturing business, the working capital cycle can be depicted as shown in Figure 16.1.

Figure 16.1	**The working capital cycle**

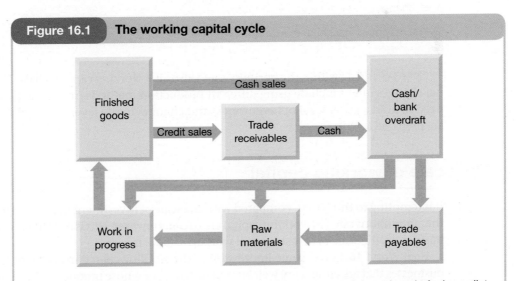

Cash is used to pay trade payables for raw materials, or raw materials are bought for immediate cash settlement. Cash is also spent on labour and other items that turn raw materials into work in progress and, finally, into finished goods. The finished goods are sold to customers either for cash or on credit. In the case of credit customers, there will be a delay before the cash is received from the sales. Receipt of cash completes the cycle.

For a retailer, the situation would be as in Figure 16.1 except that there will be only inventories of finished goods. There will be no work in progress or raw materials. For a purely service business, the working capital cycle would also be similar to that depicted in Figure 16.1 except that there would be no inventories of finished goods or raw materials. There may well be work in progress, however, since many forms of service take time to complete. A case handled by a firm of solicitors, for example, may take several months. During this period, costs will build up before the client is billed for them.

Managing working capital

The management of working capital is an essential part of the business's short-term planning process. Management must decide how much of each element should be held. As we shall see later, there are costs associated with holding either too much or too little of each element. Management must be aware of these costs, which include opportunity costs, in order to manage working capital effectively. Potential benefits must then be weighed against likely costs to arrive at the optimum investment.

The working capital needs of a business are likely to vary over time as a result of changes in the business environment. Managers must monitor these changes to ensure that the business retains an appropriate level of investment in working capital.

Activity 16.1

What kinds of changes in the business environment might lead to a decision to change the level of investment in working capital? Try to identify three possible changes that could affect the working capital needs of a business.

These may include the following:

- changes in interest rates;
- changes in market demand for the business's output;
- changes in the seasons; and
- changes in the state of the economy.

You may have thought of others.

Changes arising within the business could also alter working capital needs. These internal changes might include using different production methods (resulting, perhaps, in a need to hold a lower level of inventories) and changes in the level of risk that managers are prepared to take.

The scale of working capital

It is tempting to think that, compared with the scale of investment in non-current assets, the amounts invested in working capital are trivial. However, this is not the case. For many businesses, the scale of investment in working capital is vast.

Real World 16.1 gives some impression of the working capital investment for five UK businesses that are either very well known by name, or whose products are everyday commodities for most of us. These businesses were randomly selected, except that each one is high profile and from a different industry. For each business, the major items appearing on the statement of financial position are expressed as a percentage of the total investment by the providers of long-term finance (equity and non-current liabilities).

Real World 16.1

A summary of the statements of financial position of five UK businesses

Business:	Next plc	Ryanair Holdings plc	Babcock Int Group plc	Tesco plc	Severn Trent plc
Statement of financial position date:	30.1.16	31.3.16	31.3.16	27.2.16	31.3.16
Non-current assets	59	82	106	120	102
Current assets					
Inventories	42	–	3	10	–
Trade and other receivables	91	1	18	7	7
Other current assets	3	44	1	31	2
Cash and near cash	6	16	4	13	1
	142	61	26	61	10
Total assets	201	143	132	181	112
Equity and non-current liabilities	100	100	100	100	100
Current liabilities					
Trade and other payables	58	30	28	35	7
Other short-term liabilities	13	13	1	34	1
Overdrafts and short-term borrowings	30	–	3	12	4
	101	43	32	81	12
Total equity and non-current liabilities	201	143	132	181	112

The non-current assets, current assets and current liabilities are expressed as a percentage of the total long-term investment (equity plus non-current liabilities) of the business concerned. Next plc is a major retail and home shopping business. Ryanair is a leading airline. Babcock International Group plc is a large engineering and support business. Tesco plc is one of the UK's leading supermarkets. Severn Trent plc is an important supplier of water, sewerage services and waste management, mainly in the UK.

Source: Table constructed from information appearing in the financial statements for the year ended during 2016 for each of the five businesses concerned.

Real World 16.1 reveals quite striking differences in the make-up of the statement of financial position from one business to the next. Take, for example, the current assets and current liabilities. Although the totals for current assets are pretty large when compared with the total long-term investment, these percentages vary considerably between businesses. When looking at the mix of current assets, we can see that only Next, Babcock and Tesco, which produce and/or sell goods, hold some inventories. The other two businesses are service providers and so inventories are an insignificant item. We can also see that very few of the sales of Tesco, Ryanair and Severn Trent are on credit, as they have relatively little invested in trade receivables.

Note that Tesco's trade payables are much higher than its inventories. Since trade payables represent amounts due to suppliers of inventories, it means that Tesco receives the cash from a typical trolley load of groceries well in advance of paying for them. The relatively large 'Other current assets' and 'Other short-term liabilities' for Tesco arises from advances to and deposits from customers, respectively, that arise from the business's involvement in banking.

In the sections that follow, we shall consider each element of working capital separately and how they might be properly managed. Before doing so, however, it is worth looking at **Real World 16.2**, which suggests that there is considerable scope for improving working capital management among European businesses.

Real World 16.2

Working capital not working hard enough

According to a survey of 1,000 of Europe's largest businesses (excluding financial and auto manufacturing businesses), working capital is not as well managed as it could be. The survey, conducted in 2015 by Ernst and Young, suggests that larger European businesses had, in total, between €280 billion and €480 billion tied up in working capital that could be released through better management of inventories, trade receivables and trade payables. The potential for savings represents between 11 per cent and 19 per cent of the total working capital invested and between 4 per cent and 7 per cent of total sales. The lower figure of each range is calculated by comparing the results for each business with the results for the average for the industry, and the higher figure is calculated by comparing the results for each business with the upper quartile (that is the best performing 25 per cent of businesses) of the industry within which that business operates.

The report suggests that the higher figure for each range probably represents an ambitious target for savings as, across Europe, there are wide variations in payment terms, customer types, discount practices and so on.

The average investment (in days) for each of the five years to 2015, by the largest 1,000 European businesses, for each of the main elements of working capital is set out in Figure 16.2. As the figure shows, the working capital performance of businesses has not altered very much over the period. Within each average, however, some businesses have improved and some have deteriorated.

Figure 16.2	Average investment (in days) for the main working capital elements

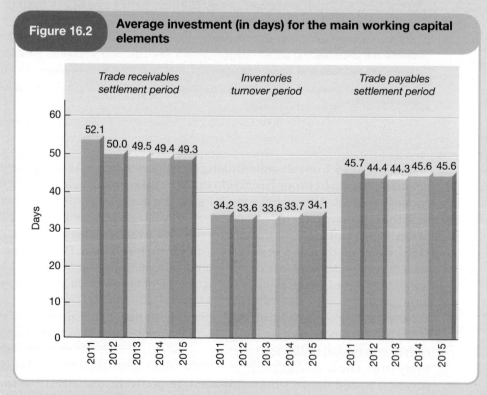

The survey results also showed that there are slightly lower levels of working capital held by large US businesses than by their European counterparts.

Source: Compiled from information in *All Tied Up: Working Capital Management Report 2015 and 2016*, Ernst and Young, www.ey.com.

Real World 16.2 focuses on the working capital problems of large businesses. For smaller businesses, however, these problems may be even more acute.

Activity 16.2

Why might smaller businesses carry more excess working capital than larger ones? Try to think of at least one reason.

Two possible reasons are:

1 Smaller businesses tend to be less well managed than larger ones. They often lack the resources to employ people with the same level of expertise as those employed by larger businesses.
2 Economies of scale may be a factor. For example, a business with twice the sales revenue of a competitor business would not normally need twice the level of inventories.

You may have thought of other reasons.

Managing inventories

A business may hold inventories for various reasons, the most common of which is to meet the immediate day-to-day requirements of customers and production. However, a business may hold more than is necessary for this purpose where there is a risk that future supplies may be interrupted or scarce. Similarly, if there is a risk that the cost of inventories will increase in the future, a business may decide to buy in large quantities.

Mining businesses and businesses that trade in commodities, such as precious metals, oil, coffee and so on, can benefit by holding large amounts of inventories when commodity prices are rising. When prices are falling, however, large inventories' holdings can be a burden. **Real World 16.3** describes how one business sought to reduce its inventories, valued at a massive $18 billion, during a recent downturn.

Real World 16.3

Inventories overload

Glencore plc, the Anglo-Swiss international commodity trading and mining business has been severely adversely affected by the falls in world prices of the commodities in which it trades. Despite these price reductions, the overall value of Glencore's inventories had stayed much the same, pointing to a large increase in the volumes of inventories held.

Real World 16.3 *continued*

The volume increase was accounted for by the fact that the business expected an increase in the price of oil and other commodities that it held. Such an increase would have been profitable for the business.

As things turned out, the anticipated increase in the world oil price failed to materialise meaning that it was sensible for Glencore to reduce inventories volumes.

Source: Information taken from McFarlane S. and Zhdannikov D. (2015), *Glencore shrinking its $18 bn commodity inventory mountain*, www.reuters.com, 29 October.

For some types of business, inventories held may represent a substantial proportion of total assets held. For example, a car dealership that rents its premises may have nearly all of its total assets in the form of inventories. Manufacturers also tend to invest heavily in inventories, as they typically need to hold three kinds of inventories: raw materials, work in progress and finished goods. Each form of inventories represents a particular stage in the production cycle.

For businesses with seasonal demand, the level of inventories held may vary greatly over the year. One such example might be greetings card manufacturers. For those businesses with fairly stable demand, the level of inventories held may vary little from one month to the next.

Businesses that hold inventories simply to meet the day-to-day requirements of their customers, and for production, will normally seek to minimise the amount of inventories held. This is because there are significant costs associated with holding inventories. These costs include:

- storage and handling costs;
- the cost of financing the inventories;
- the cost of pilferage and obsolescence; and
- the cost of opportunities forgone in tying up funds in this form of asset.

To gain some impression of the cost involved in holding inventories, **Real World 16.4** estimates the *financing* cost of inventories for five large businesses.

Real World 16.4

Inventories financing cost

The financing cost of inventories for each of five large businesses, based on their respective opportunity costs of capital, is calculated below.

Business	Type of operations	Cost of capital (a) %	Average inventories held* (b) £m	Financing cost of holding inventories (a) × (b) £m	Operating profit £m	Financing cost as a % of operating profit/(loss) %
Associated British Foods plc	Food producer	12.2	1,729	210	947	22.2

Business	Type of operations	Cost of capital	Average inventories held*	Financing cost of holding inventories	Operating profit	Financing cost as a % of operating profit/(loss)
		(a) %	(b) £m	(a) × (b) £m	£m	%
Babcock International Group plc	Engineering and business support	9.1	147.2	13.4	352.5	3.8
Go-ahead Group plc	Transport operator	8.8	18.1	1.6	117.4	1.4
Kingfisher plc	DIY retailer	7.4	1989	147.2	526	30.0
J Sainsbury plc	Supermarket	9.0	982.5	88.4	707	12.5

* Based on opening and closing inventories for the relevant financial period.

We can see that for three of the five businesses, inventories financing costs are significant in relation to their operating profits. The nature of their businesses requires Associated British Foods, Kingfisher and Sainsbury to invest heavily in inventories. Sainsbury, however, is likely to turn over its inventories more quickly than the other three. For Go-ahead, inventories financing costs are not significant. This is because it is a service provider with a much lower investment in inventories.

These figures do not take account of other costs of inventories' holding mentioned earlier, such as the cost of providing secure storage. As these other costs may easily outweigh the costs of finance, the total cost of maintaining inventories may be very high in relation to operating profits.

The five businesses were not selected because they have particularly high inventories' costs but simply because they are among the relatively few that publish their costs of capital.

Source: Annual reports of the businesses for the years ended during 2015 and 2016.

Given the potentially high cost of holding inventories, it may be tempting to think that a business should seek to hold few or no inventories. There are, however, costs that may arise when the level of inventories is too low.

Activity (16.3)

What costs might a business incur as a result of holding too low a level of inventories? Try to jot down at least three types of cost.

In answering this activity you may have thought of the following costs:

- loss of sales, from being unable to provide the goods required immediately;
- loss of customer goodwill, for being unable to satisfy customer demand;
- purchasing inventories at a higher price than might otherwise have been necessary to replenish inventories quickly;
- high transport costs incurred to ensure that inventories are replenished quickly;
- lost production due to shortage of raw materials; and
- inefficient production scheduling due to shortages of raw materials.

To help manage inventories, a number of procedures and techniques may be employed. We shall now consider the more important of these.

Budgeting future demand

Preparing appropriate budgets is one of the best ways to ensure that inventories will be available to meet future production and sales requirements. These budgets should deal with each product that the business buys, makes and/or sells. It is important that they are realistic, as they will determine future ordering and production levels. The budgets may be derived in various ways. They may be developed using statistical techniques, such as time series analysis, or may be based on the judgement of sales and marketing staff. We discussed budgets and budgeting, at some length, in Chapter 12.

Financial ratios

One ratio that we met in Chapter 7 that can be used to help monitor inventories levels is the average inventories turnover period ratio. This ratio is calculated as follows:

$$\text{Average inventories turnover period} = \frac{\text{Average inventories held}}{\text{Cost of sales}} \times 365$$

The ratio provides a picture of the average period for which inventories are held. This can be useful as a basis for comparison. The average inventories turnover period can be calculated for individual product lines, and for particular categories of inventories, as well as for inventories as a whole.

Recording and reordering systems

A sound system of recording inventories movements is a key element in managing inventories. There should be proper procedures for recording inventories purchases and usages. Periodic checks should be made to ensure that the amount of physical inventories held corresponds with what is indicated by the inventories' records.

There should also be clear procedures for the reordering of inventories. Authorisation for both the purchase and the issue of inventories should be confined to a few nominated members of staff. This should avoid problems of duplication and lack of co-ordination. To determine the point at which inventories should be reordered, information will be required concerning the **lead time** (that is, the time between the placing of an order and the receipt of the goods) and the likely level of demand.

Activity (16.4)

An electrical wholesaler sells a particular type of light switch. The annual demand for the light switch is 10,400 units and the lead time for orders is four weeks. Demand for the light switch is even throughout the year. At what level of inventories of the light switch should the business reorder, assuming that it is confident of the information given above?

The average weekly demand for the switch is 10,400/52 = 200 units. During the time between ordering new switches and receiving them, the quantity sold will be 4 × 200 units = 800 units. So the business should reorder no later than when the level held reaches 800 units. This should avoid running out of inventories.

For most businesses, there will be some uncertainty surrounding the level of demand, pattern of demand and lead time. To avoid the risk of running out of inventories, a buffer, or safety, inventories level may be maintained. The amount of buffer inventories is a matter of judgement. In forming this judgement, the following should be taken into account:

- the degree of uncertainty concerning the above factors;
- the likely costs of running out of the item concerned; and
- the cost of holding the buffer inventories.

The effect of holding a buffer will be to raise the inventories level at which an order for new inventories is placed (the reorder point).

Activity 16.5

Assume the same facts as in Activity 16.4, except that the business wishes to maintain buffer inventories of 300 units. At what level should the business reorder?

Reorder point = expected level of demand during the lead time *plus* the level of buffer
inventories

= 800 + 300

= 1,100 units

Carrying buffer inventories will increase the cost of holding inventories. This must, however, be weighed against the cost of running out of inventories, in terms of lost sales, production problems and so on.

Activity 16.6

Hora plc holds inventories of a particular type of motor car tyre, which is ordered in batches of 1,200 units. The supply lead times and usage rates for the tyres are:

	Maximum	Most likely	Minimum
Supply lead times	25 days	15 days	8 days
Daily usage	30 units	20 units	12 units

The business wishes to avoid the risk of running out of inventories.

At what minimum level of inventories should Hora plc place a new order, such that it can guarantee not to run out?

What is the size of the buffer inventories based on the most likely lead times and usages?

If Hora plc were to place an order based on the maximum lead time and usage, but only the minimum lead time and usage were actually to occur, what would be the level of inventories immediately following the delivery of the new inventories? What does this inventories figure represent?

→

Activity 16.6 *continued*

To be certain of avoiding running out of inventories, the business must assume a reorder point based on the maximum usage and lead time. This is 750 units (that is, 30 × 25).

The most likely usage during the lead time will be only 300 units (that is, 20 × 15). Thus, the buffer inventories based on most likely usage and lead time is 450 units (that is, 750 − 300).

The level of inventories when a new order of 1,200 units is received, immediately following the minimum supply lead time and minimum daily usage during the lead time, is 1,854 units (that is, 1,200 + 750 − (8 × 12)). This should represents the maximum inventories holding for the business.

Levels of control

Deciding on the appropriate level of inventories control to adopt requires a careful weighing of costs and benefits. This may lead to the implementation of different levels of control according to the nature of the inventories held. The **ABC system of inventories control** is based on the idea of selective levels of control. For example, a business may find it possible to divide its inventories into three broad categories: A, B and C. Each category will be based on the value of inventories held, as illustrated in Example 16.1.

Example 16.1

Alascan Products plc makes door handles and door fittings. It makes them in brass, in steel and in plastic. The business finds that brass fittings account for 10 per cent of the physical volume of the finished inventories that it holds, but these represent 65 per cent of the total value. These are treated as Category A inventories. There are sophisticated recording procedures, tight control is exerted over inventories movements and there is a high level of security where the brass inventories are stored. This is economically viable because these inventories represent a relatively small proportion of the total volume.

The business finds that steel fittings account for 30 per cent of the total volume of finished inventories and represent 25 per cent of the total value. These are treated as Category B inventories, with a lower level of recording and management control being applied.

The remaining 60 per cent of the volume of inventories is plastic fittings, which represent the least valuable items, accounting for only 10 per cent of the total value of finished inventories held. These are treated as Category C inventories, so the level of recording and management control would be lower still. Applying to these inventories the level of control that is applied to Category A or even Category B inventories would be uneconomic.

Categorising inventories in this way helps to direct management effort to the most important areas. It also helps to ensure that the costs of controlling inventories are proportionate to their value.

Figure 16.3 provides a graphical depiction of the ABC approach to inventories control.

| Figure 16.3 | ABC method of analysing and controlling inventories |

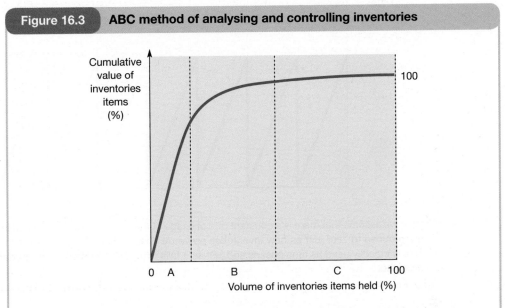

Category A contains inventories that, though relatively few in quantity, account for a large proportion of the total value. Category B inventories consists of those items that are less valuable but more numerous. Category C comprises those inventories items that are very numerous but relatively low in value. Different inventories' control rules would be applied to each category. For example, only Category A inventories would attract the more expensive and sophisticated controls.

Inventories management models

Economic order quantity

Decision models may be used to help manage inventories. The **economic order quantity (EOQ)** model is concerned with determining the quantity of a particular inventories item that should be ordered each time. In its simplest form, the EOQ model assumes that demand is constant. This implies that inventories will be depleted evenly over time to be replenished just at the point that they run out. These assumptions would lead to a 'saw-tooth' pattern to represent inventories movements, as shown in Figure 16.4.

> ### Figure 16.4 Patterns of inventories movements over time
>
>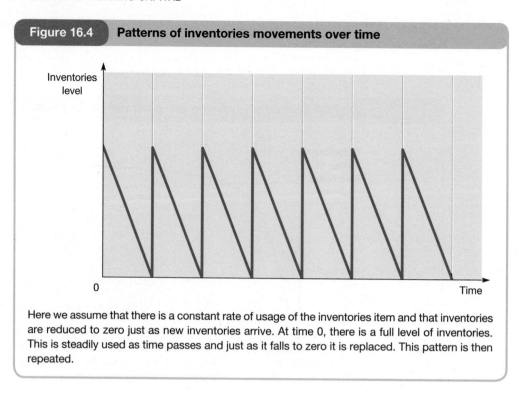
>
> Here we assume that there is a constant rate of usage of the inventories item and that inventories are reduced to zero just as new inventories arrive. At time 0, there is a full level of inventories. This is steadily used as time passes and just as it falls to zero it is replaced. This pattern is then repeated.

The EOQ model recognises that the key costs associated with inventories' management are the cost of holding the inventories and the cost of ordering them. The cost of holding inventories can be substantial. Management may, therefore, try to minimise the average amount of inventories held and, with it, the holding cost. It will, however, increase the number of orders placed during the period and so ordering costs will rise. The EOQ model seeks to calculate the optimum size of a purchase order that will balance both of these cost elements.

Figure 16.5 shows how, as the level of inventories and the size of inventories orders increase, the annual costs of placing orders will decrease because fewer orders will be placed. However, the cost of holding inventories will increase, as there will be higher average inventories levels. The total costs curve, which is based on the sum of holding costs and ordering costs, will fall until the point E, which represents the minimum total cost. Thereafter, total costs begin to rise. The EOQ model seeks to identify point E, at which total costs are minimised. This will represent half of the optimum amount that should be ordered on each occasion. Assuming, as we are doing, that inventories are used evenly over time and that they fall to zero before being replaced, the average inventories level equals half of the order size.

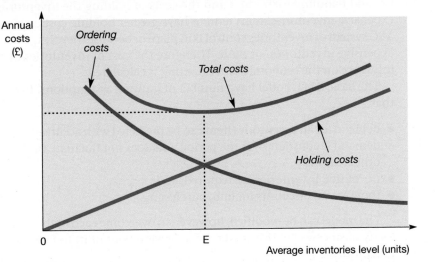

> **Figure 16.5** **Inventories holding and order costs**

Small inventories levels imply frequent reordering and high annual ordering costs. Small inventories levels also imply relatively low inventories holding costs. High inventories levels imply exactly the opposite. There is, in theory, an optimum order size that will lead to the sum of ordering and holding costs (total costs) being at a minimum.

The EOQ model, which can be used to derive the most economic order quantity, is:

$$EOQ = \sqrt{\frac{2DC}{H}}$$

where

D = the annual demand for the inventories item (expressed in units of the inventories item);
C = the cost of placing an order;
H = the cost of holding one unit of the inventories item for one year.

Activity 16.7

HLA Ltd sells 2,000 bags of cement each year. It has been estimated that the cost of holding one bag of cement for a year is £4. The cost of placing an order for new inventories is estimated at £250.

Calculate the EOQ for bags of cement.

Your answer to this activity should be as follows:

$$EOQ = \sqrt{\frac{2 \times 2,000 \times 250}{4}} = 500 \text{ bags}$$

This will mean that the business will have to order bags of cement four times each year (that is 2,000/500) in batches of 500 bags so that sales demand can be met.

Note that the cost of inventories, which is the price paid to the supplier, does not directly affect the EOQ model. It is concerned only with the administrative costs of placing and handling each order and the costs of holding the inventories. However, more expensive inventories items tend to have greater holding costs. This may be because an ABC system of inventories control is in place or because they tie up more finance than less expensive inventories, or both. Therefore the cost of inventories may have an indirect influence on the economic order size that is calculated.

The basic EOQ model has a number of limiting assumptions. In particular, it assumes that:

- demand for an inventories item can be predicted with accuracy;
- demand is constant over the period and does not fluctuate through seasonality or for other reasons;
- no 'buffer' inventories are required; and
- there are no discounts for bulk purchasing.

The model can be modified, however, to overcome each of these limiting assumptions. Many businesses use this model (or a development of it) to help in the management of inventories.

Activity 16.8

Petrov plc sells 10,000 tonnes of sand each year and demand is constant over time. The purchase cost of each tonne is £15 and the cost of placing and handling an order is estimated to be £32. The cost of holding 1 tonne of sand for one year is estimated to be £4. The business uses the EOQ model to determine the appropriate order quantity and holds no buffer inventories.

Calculate the total annual cost of trading in this product.

The total annual cost will be made up of three elements:

- the cost of purchases;
- the cost of ordering; and
- the cost of holding this item in inventories.

The *annual cost of purchases* is 10,000 × £15 = £150,000.

The *annual cost of ordering* is calculated as follows:

The EOQ is:

$$\text{EOQ} = \sqrt{\frac{2 \times 10,000 \times 32}{4}} = 400 \text{ tonnes}$$

This will mean that 10,000/400 = 25 orders will be placed each year. The annual cost of ordering is therefore 25 × £32 = £800.

The annual cost of holding inventories is calculated as follows:

The average quantity of inventories held will be half the optimum order size, as mentioned earlier. That is, 400/2 = 200 tonnes.

The annual holding cost is therefore 200 × £4 = £800

The total annual cost of trading in this product is therefore:

£150,000 + £800 + £800 = £151,600*

* Note that the annual ordering cost and annual holding cost are the same. This is no coincidence. If we look back at Figure 16.5 we can see that the economic order quantity represents the point at which total costs are minimised. At this point, annual order costs and annual holding costs are equal.

Enterprise resource planning systems

Enterprise resource planning (ERP) systems provide an automated and integrated approach to managing a business. They consist of a suite of software applications (modules) that record, report, analyse and interpret data for a range of business operations, including production, marketing, human resources, accounting and inventories management. These integrated software applications are supported by a common database, which is operated on a real-time (or near real-time) basis and which can be accessed remotely.

An ERP software application for the management of inventories will carry out a wide range of tasks such as:

- forecasting demand using statistical formulae;
- making reorder decisions based on forecast future demand;
- ordering the transfer of goods between locations;
- tracking and reporting inventories according to type, serial numbers and so on;
- providing real-time information concerning shipping costs, trends in inventories holdings, on-time deliveries and so on;
- allocating warehouse space for where goods are to be stored;
- helping inventories audits by setting tolerance levels for variations between actual and reported inventories held; and
- pricing inventories being shipped, to take account of required profit margins, bulk discounts and so on.

The software application will normally embed best practice within a particular industry, but may be customised to meet the needs of an individual business.

ERP inventories' management applications greatly enhance the quality, range and timeliness of information to managers. This can be of enormous benefit in driving efficiencies and in responding to changing circumstances. These applications can, however, be costly to introduce.

Just-in-time inventories management

In recent years, many businesses have tried to eliminate the need to hold inventories by adopting **just-in-time (JIT) inventories management.** This approach was originally used in the US defence industry during the Second World War, but was first used on a wide scale by Japanese manufacturing businesses. The essence of JIT is, as the name suggests, to have supplies delivered to the business just in time for them to be used in the production process or in a sale. By adopting this approach, the inventories holding cost can move from the business itself to the suppliers. On the other hand, a well-managed JIT system should lead to significantly lower inventories levels for all parties, leading to significant overall cost savings. A failure by a particular supplier to deliver on time, however, could cause enormous problems and costs to the business. Thus JIT may save cost, but it tends to increase risk.

For JIT to be successful, there needs to be a close relationship between a business and its suppliers. It is important that a business informs suppliers of its inventories' requirements in advance so that suppliers can schedule their own production to that of the business. Suppliers must then deliver materials of the right quality at the agreed times. Any delivery failures could lead to a dislocation of production and could be very costly. Successful JIT tends to require that suppliers are geographically near to the business.

Activity 16.9

Superlec plc makes electrical appliances. One of its major component suppliers is Technicalities Ltd. The two businesses have recently established a comprehensive JIT relationship.

Would you expect the inventories of Technicalites Ltd to:

- increase,
- reduce, or
- stay the same

as a result of the change of relationship?

The introduction of JIT by Superlec Ltd will pass the inventories holding problem to Technicalities Ltd. As a result, Technicalities inventories' holdings could increase. However, the close working relationship that a JIT relationship requires should lead to a reduction in the total amount of inventories held by the supplier. Knowing Superlec's inventories' requirements in advance should help Technicalities to schedule its own production and inventories to those requirements. It may encourage Technicalities to introduce a system of JIT from its own suppliers.

Adopting JIT will usually require re-engineering a business's production process in order to avoid the risk that production will be brought to a halt for any reason. Changes may, therefore, be made to the production layout and to working practices. To ensure that orders are quickly fulfilled, the production process must be flexible and responsive. Production flows may be redesigned and employees may be given greater responsibility to deal with unanticipated problems. Information systems must also be installed that both monitor and facilitate an uninterrupted production flow.

Although a business that applies JIT will not have to hold inventories, there may be other costs associated with this approach. For example, the close relationship necessary between the business and its suppliers may prevent the business from taking advantage of cheaper sources of supply that become available. Furthermore, where a supplier needs to hold inventories for the customer, it may try to recoup this additional cost through increased prices. The close relationship between customer and supplier, however, should enable the supplier to predict its customers' inventories needs. This means that suppliers can tailor their own production to that of the customer.

JIT is widely viewed as more than simply an inventories control system. The philosophy underpinning this approach is that of *total quality management.* This is concerned with eliminating waste and striving for excellence. There is an expectation that suppliers will always deliver inventories on time and that there will be no defects in the items supplied. There is also an expectation that, for manufacturers, the production process will operate at maximum efficiency. This means that there will be no production breakdowns and the queuing and storage times of products manufactured will be eliminated, as only time spent directly on processing the products is seen as adding value. While these expectations may be impossible to achieve, they can help to create a culture that is dedicated to the pursuit of excellence and quality.

A final point worth making is that successful implementation of a JIT system rests with the workforce. A more streamlined and efficient production flow will only be achieved if workers are well trained and fully committed to the pursuit of quality. They must be prepared to operate as part of a team and to adapt to changes in both the nature and pace of working practices. They must also be prepared to show initiative in dealing with problems arising in the production process.

Real World 16.5 shows how a very well-known business operating in the UK uses JIT to advantage.

Real World 16.5

JIT at Nissan

Nissan Motors UK limited, the UK manufacturing arm of the world-famous Japanese car business, has a plant in Sunderland in the north east of England. Here it operates a fairly well-developed JIT system. For example, Calsonic Kansei supplies car exhausts from a factory close to the Nissan plant. It makes deliveries to Nissan once every 30 minutes on average, so as to arrive exactly as the exhausts are needed in production. This is fairly typical of all of the 200 suppliers of components and materials to the Nissan plant.

Nissan used to have a comprehensive JIT system. More recently, however, Nissan has drawn back from its total adherence to JIT. By using only local suppliers, it had cut itself off from the opportunity to exploit low-cost suppliers, particularly those located in China. A change in policy has led the business to hold buffer inventories for certain items to guard against disruption of supply arising from sourcing parts from the Far East.

Sources: Information taken from Tighe, C. (2006) Nissan reviews just-in-time parts policy, *Financial Times*, 23 October; Ludwig, C. (2014) Local logistics and engineering partnership at Nissan Europe, *Automotive Logistics*, 5 February.

Managing trade receivables

Selling goods or services on credit will result in costs being incurred by a business. These costs include the costs of credit administration, of bad debts and of opportunities forgone to use the funds for other purposes. However, these costs must be weighed against the benefits of increased sales revenue resulting from the opportunity for customers to delay payment.

Selling on credit is the norm outside the retail industry. When a business offers to sell its goods or services on credit, it must have clear policies concerning:

- which customers should receive credit;
- how much credit should be offered;
- what length of credit it is prepared to offer;
- whether discounts will be offered for prompt payment;
- what collection policies should be adopted; and
- how the risk of non-payment can be reduced.

In this section, we consider each of these issues.

Which customers should receive credit and how much should they be offered?

A business offering credit runs the risk of not receiving payment for goods or services supplied. Therefore, care must be taken over the type of customer to whom credit facilities are offered and how much credit is allowed. When considering a proposal from a customer for the supply of goods or services on credit, a business should take into account a number of factors. The following **five Cs of credit** provide a useful checklist:

- *Capital.* The customer must appear to be financially sound before any credit is extended. Where the customer is a business, its financial statements should be examined. Particular regard should be given to the customer's likely future profitability and liquidity. In addition, any major financial commitments (such as outstanding borrowings, capital expenditure commitments and contracts with suppliers) should be taken into account.

- *Capacity.* The customer must appear to have the capacity to pay for the goods acquired on credit. The customer's payment record to date should be examined to provide important clues. To help further assess capacity, the type of business and the amount of credit required in relation to the customer's total financial resources should be taken into account.

- *Collateral.* On occasions, it may be necessary to ask for some kind of security for goods supplied on credit. When this occurs, the business must be convinced that the customer is able to offer a satisfactory form of security.

- *Conditions.* The state of the industry in which the customer operates, as well as the general economic conditions of the particular region or country, should be taken into account. The sensitivity of the customer's business to changes in economic conditions can also have an important influence on the ability of the customer to pay on time.

- *Character.* It is important to make some assessment of the customer's character. The willingness to pay will depend on the honesty and integrity of the individual with whom the business is dealing. Where the customer is a business, this will mean assessing the characters of its senior managers as well as their reputation within the industry. The selling business must feel confident that the customer will make every effort to pay any amounts owing.

To help assess the above factors, various sources of information are available. These include:

- *Trade references.* Some businesses ask potential customers to provide references from other suppliers that have extended credit to them. This can be extremely useful as long as the references provided are truly representative of the opinions of all the customer's suppliers. There is a danger that a potential customer will be selective when giving details of other suppliers, in an attempt to create a more favourable impression than is deserved.

- *Bank references.* It is possible to ask the potential customer for a bank reference. Although banks are usually prepared to supply references, their contents are not always very informative. The bank will usually charge a fee for providing a reference.

- *Published financial statements.* A limited company is obliged by law to file a copy of its annual financial statements with the Registrar of Companies. These are available for public inspection and can provide a useful insight into performance and financial position. Many companies also publish their annual financial statements on their websites or on computer-based information systems. A problem with the publicly-available financial statements is that they are often quite out of date by the time that they can first be examined by the potential supplier of credit.

- *The customer.* Interviews with the directors of the customer business and visits to its premises may be carried out to gain an impression of the way that the customer conducts its business. Where a significant amount of credit is required, the business may ask the customer for access to internal forecasts and other unpublished financial information to help assess the level of risk involved.

- *Credit agencies.* Specialist agencies exist to provide information that can be used to assess the creditworthiness of a potential customer. The information that a credit agency supplies may be gleaned from various sources, including the customer's financial statements and news items relating to the customer from both published and unpublished sources. The credit agencies may also provide a credit rating for the business. Agencies will charge a fee for their services.

- *Register of County Court Judgments.* Any money judgments given against the business or an individual in a county court will be maintained on the register for six years. This register is available for inspection by any member of the public for a small fee.
- *Other suppliers.* Similar businesses will often be prepared to exchange information concerning slow payers or defaulting customers through an industry credit circle. This can be a reliable and relatively cheap way of obtaining information.

Activity (16.10)

It was mentioned above that, although banks are usually prepared to supply references, their contents are not always very informative. Why might this be the case?

If a bank's customer is in financial difficulties, the bank may be unwilling to add to its problems by supplying a poor reference. It is worth remembering that the bank's loyalty is likely to be with its customer rather than the enquirer.

Once a customer is considered creditworthy, credit limits should be established. When doing so, the business must take account of its own financial resources and risk appetite. Unfortunately, there are no theories or models to guide a business when deciding on the appropriate credit limit to adopt; it is really a matter of judgement. Some businesses adopt simple 'rule of thumb' methods based on the amount of sales made to the customer (say, twice the monthly sales figure for the customer) or the maximum the business is prepared to be owed (say, a maximum of 20 per cent of its working capital) by all of its customers.

Length of credit period

A business must determine what credit terms it is prepared to offer its customers. The length of credit offered to customers can vary significantly between businesses. It may be influenced by such factors as:

- the typical credit terms operating within the industry;
- the degree of competition within the industry;
- the bargaining power of particular customers;
- the risk of non-payment;
- the capacity of the business to offer credit; and
- the marketing strategy of the business.

The last point may require some explanation. Credit policy can be a basis on which a business may compete for custom with its competitors. So if, for example, a business wishes to increase its market share, it may decide to be more generous in its credit policy in an attempt to stimulate sales. Potential customers may be attracted by the offer of a longer credit period. However, any such change in policy must take account of the likely costs and benefits arising. To illustrate this point, consider Example 16.2.

Example 16.2

Torrance Ltd produces a new type of golf putter. The business sells the putter to wholesalers and retailers and has an annual sales revenue of £600,000. The following data relate to each putter produced:

	£
Selling price	40
Variable cost	(20)
Fixed cost apportionment	(6)
Profit	14

The business's cost of capital is estimated at 10 per cent a year.

Torrance Ltd wishes to expand the sales volume of the new putter. It believes that offering a longer credit period can achieve this. The business's average trade receivables settlement period is currently 30 days. It is considering three options in an attempt to increase sales revenue. These are as follows:

	Option		
	1	*2*	*3*
Increase in average settlement period (days)	10	20	30
Increase in sales revenue (£)	30,000	45,000	50,000

To help the business to decide on the best option, the benefits of the various options should be weighed against their respective costs. Benefits will be represented by the increase in profit from the sale of additional putters. From the information supplied, we can see that the contribution to profit (that is, selling price (£40) less variable costs (£20)) is £20 a putter. This represents 50 per cent of the selling price. So, whatever increase occurs in sales revenue, the additional contribution to profit will be half of that figure. The fixed cost can be ignored in our calculations, as it will remain the same whichever option is chosen.

The increase in contribution under each option will therefore be:

	Option		
	1	*2*	*3*
50% of the increase in sales revenue (£)	15,000	22,500	25,000

The increase in trade receivables under each option will be as follows:

	Option		
	1	*2*	*3*
	£	£	£
Projected level of trade receivables:			
40 × £630,000/365 (Note 1)	69,041		
50 × £645,000/365		88,356	
60 × £650,000/365			106,849

	Option		
	1 £	2 £	3 £
Current level of trade receivables:			
30 × £600,000/365	(49,315)	(49,315)	(49,315)
Increase in trade receivables	19,726	39,041	57,534

The increase in receivables that results from each option will mean an additional finance cost to the business.

The net increase in the business's profit arising from the projected change is:

	Option		
	1 £	2 £	3 £
Increase in contribution (see above)	15,000	22,500	25,000
Increase in finance cost (Note 2)	(1,973)	(3,904)	(5,753)
Net increase in profits	13,027	18,596	19,247

The calculations show that Option 3 will be the most profitable one.

Notes:
1 If the annual sales revenue totals £630,000 and 40 days' credit is allowed (both of which will apply under Option 1), the average amount that will be owed to the business by its customers, at any point during the year, will be the daily sales revenue (that is, £630,000/365) multiplied by the number of days that the customers take to pay (that is 40).
Exactly the same logic applies to Options 2 and 3 and to the current level of trade receivables.
2 The increase in the finance cost for Option 1 will be the increase in trade receivables (£19,726) × 10 per cent. The equivalent figures for the other options are derived in a similar way.

Example 16.2 illustrates the broad approach that a business should take when assessing changes in credit terms. However, by extending the length of credit, other costs may be incurred. These may include bad debts and additional collections costs, which should also be taken into account in the calculations.

Real World 16.6 is an article that discusses how supermarkets have often been guilty of extending the credit period granted by its suppliers.

Real World 16.6

Credit where it's due

Supermarkets are still routinely mistreating suppliers by paying bills late, despite government pressure for grocers to clean up their act, a study has revealed. An analysis of thousands of invoices from small and medium-sized suppliers found that almost 70 per cent of payments made by supermarkets were late in 2015.

Real World 16.6 *continued*

On average, supermarkets settled bills 7.24 days beyond contractually agreed terms last year, according to research conducted by MarketInvoice, an online invoice finance company. The sector's payment performance was markedly worse than technology companies, banks and the broader FTSE 350 average. Banks paid supplier invoices only 0.3 days late.

The continued poor performance of large grocers comes despite the creation of the Groceries Code Adjudicator in 2013 to improve the treatment of suppliers. Anil Stocker, a co-founder of MarketInvoice, said: "That these bad payment practices are clearly sector-wide is a sign that something is very wrong in the supermarket industry."

Ian Cass, managing director of the Forum of Private Business, said: "Supermarkets get paid pretty much immediately for their products, so there is no excuse for paying late . . . I never thought I would hear myself state that anyone should follow the example of banks, but it is clear that is precisely what supermarkets should do."

MarketInvoice analysed almost 15,000 invoices during 2015, including 1,000 supermarket invoices. It also analysed more than 5,000 invoices filed between 2010 and 2014. It said that 14 per cent of invoices to supermarkets were paid more than two weeks later than agreed terms, and 7 per cent were more than a month late. This was on top of grocers' standard contractual payment terms, which can mean suppliers wait three months or more to be paid.

Source: Hurley, J. (2016) *Suppliers 'routinely kept waiting by supermarkets'*, www.thetimes.co.uk, 25 January.

An alternative approach to evaluating the credit decision

It is possible to view the credit decision as a capital investment decision. Granting trade credit involves an opportunity outlay of resources in the form of cash (which has been temporarily forgone) in the expectation that future cash flows will be increased (through higher sales) as a result. A business will usually have choices concerning the level of investment to be made in credit sales and the period over which credit is granted. These choices will result in different returns and different levels of risk. There is no reason in principle why the NPV investment appraisal method, which we considered in Chapter 14, should not be used to evaluate these choices. The NPV method takes into account both the time value of money and the level of risk involved.

Approaching the problem as an NPV assessment is not different in principle from the way that we dealt with the decision in Example 16.2. In both approaches, the time value of money is considered, but in Example 16.2 we did it by charging a financing cost on the outstanding trade receivables.

Cash discounts

To encourage prompt payment from its credit customers, a business may offer a **cash discount** (or discount for prompt payment). The size of any discount will be an important influence on whether a customer decides to pay promptly.

From the business's viewpoint, the cost of offering discounts must be weighed against the likely benefits in the form of a reduction both in the cost of financing trade receivables and in the amount of bad debts. Example 16.3 shows how this may be done.

Example 16.3

Williams Wholesalers Ltd currently asks its credit customers to pay by the end of the month after the month of delivery. In practice, customers take rather longer to pay – on average 70 days. Sales revenue amounts to £4 million a year and bad debts to £20,000 a year.

It is planned to offer customers a cash discount of 2 per cent for payment within 30 days. Williams estimates that 50 per cent of customers will accept this facility but that the remaining customers, who tend to be slow payers, will not pay until 80 days after the sale. At present, the business has an overdraft facility at an interest rate of 13 per cent a year. If the plan goes ahead, bad debts will be reduced to £10,000 a year and there will be savings in credit administration expenses of £6,000 a year.

Should Williams Wholesalers Ltd offer the new credit terms to customers?

Solution

The first step is to determine the reduction in trade receivables arising from the new policy.

		£	£
Existing level of trade receivables	(£4m × 70/365)		767,123
New level of trade receivables:	£2m × 80/365	438,356	
	£2m × 30/365	164,384	(602,740)
Reduction in trade receivables			164,383

The costs and benefits of offering the discount can be set out as follows:

	£	£
Cost and benefits of policy		
Cost of discount (£2m × 2%)		40,000
Less		
Interest saved on the reduction in trade receivables		
(£164,383* × 13%)	21,370	
Administration cost saving	6,000	
Cost of bad debts saved		
(20,000 − 10,000)	10,000	(37,370)
Net cost of policy		2,630

These calculations show that the business will be worse off by offering the new credit terms.

* It could be argued that the interest should be based on the amount expected to be received; that is the value of the trade receivables *after* taking account of the discount. Basing it on the expected receipt figure would not, however, alter the conclusion that the business should not offer the new credit terms.

Activity (16.11)

In practice, there is always the danger that a customer may be slow to pay and yet may still take the discount offered. Where the customer is important to the business, it may be difficult to insist on full payment. How might a business overcome this problem?

Instead of allowing customers to deduct a discount, customers who pay promptly can be rewarded separately, say on a three-monthly basis. The reward could be a cash payment to the customer or, perhaps, a credit note. The value of the reward would be equal to the cash discounts earned by each customer during the three months.

Debt factoring and invoice discounting

Trade receivables can, in effect, be turned into cash by either factoring them or having sales invoices discounted. Both are forms of asset-based finance, which involves a financial institution providing a business with an advance up to 80 per cent of the value of the trade receivables outstanding. These methods, which are fairly popular approaches to managing receivables, were discussed in Chapter 15.

Credit insurance

It is often possible for a supplier to insure its entire trade receivables, individual customer accounts or the outstanding balance relating to a particular transaction.

Collection policies

A business offering credit must ensure that receivables are collected as quickly as possible so that non-payment risk is minimised and operating cash flows are maximised. Various steps can be taken to achieve this, including the following.

Develop customer relationships

For major customers, it is often useful to cultivate a relationship with the key staff responsible for paying sales invoices. By so doing, the chances of prompt payment may be increased. For less important customers, the business should at least identify the key members of staff responsible for paying invoices, who can be contacted in the event of a payment problem.

Publicise credit terms

The credit terms of the business should be made clear in all relevant correspondence, such as order acknowledgements, invoices and statements. In early negotiations with the prospective customer, credit terms should be openly discussed and an agreement reached.

Issue invoices promptly

An efficient collection policy requires an efficient accounting system. Invoices (bills) must be sent out promptly to customers, as must monthly statements. Reminders must also be dispatched promptly to customers who are late in paying. If a customer fails to respond to a reminder, the accounting system should alert managers so that a stop can be placed on further deliveries.

Use financial ratios to monitor outstanding receivables

Managers can monitor the effectiveness of collection through the use of ratios. They can, for example, calculate the average settlement period for trade receivables ratio, which we met in Chapter 7. This ratio is calculated as follows:

$$\text{Average settlement period for trade receivables} = \frac{\text{Average trade receivables}}{\text{Credit sales}} \times 365$$

Although this ratio can be useful, it is important to remember that it produces an *average* figure for the number of days for which debts are outstanding. This average may be badly distorted by a few large customers who are very slow, or very fast, payers.

A further ratio that may be of assistance is the **trade receivables to sales ratio**. This ratio is calculated as follows:

$$\text{Trade receivables to sales} = \frac{\text{Trade receivables outstanding at end of the period}}{\text{Sales revenue for the period}}$$

In practice, this ratio is normally calculated on a monthly basis and can be used to detect trends. Since it uses the month-end figure as the numerator, it has a little more immediacy than a ratio calculated on an annual basis, as the average settlement period for trade receivables ratio (above) tends to be. Where, for example, the ratio is increasing each month, it means that trade receivables are growing faster than sales revenue.

Activity 16.12

Why might this trend be a cause of concern?

It suggests that the business is slow in collecting its receivables, which may signal future cash flow problems.

Where trade receivables exceed the current monthly sales revenue, the ratio will be greater than one. Calculating this ratio for seasonal businesses can be tricky as the ratio will tend to increase or decrease as the seasons change. Thus, making comparisons with similar months in previous years may be more useful in detecting trends.

Produce an ageing schedule of trade receivables

A more detailed and informative approach to monitoring receivables may be to produce an **ageing schedule of trade receivables**. Receivables are divided into categories according to the length of time they have been outstanding. An ageing schedule can be produced on a regular basis to help managers see the pattern of outstanding receivables. An example of an ageing schedule is set out in Example 16.4.

Example 16.4

Ageing schedule of trade receivables at 31 December

	Days outstanding				
Customer	1 to 30 days	31 to 60 days	61 to 90 days	More than 90 days	Total
	£	£	£	£	£
A Ltd	12,000	13,000	14,000	18,000	57,000
B Ltd	20,000	10,000	–	–	30,000
C Ltd	–	24,000	–	–	24,000
Total	32,000	47,000	14,000	18,000	111,000

This shows a business's trade receivables figure at 31 December, which totals £111,000. Each customer's balance is analysed according to how long the amount has been outstanding. (This business has just three credit customers.) To help focus management attention, accounts may be listed in order of size, with the largest debts first.

We can see from the schedule, for example, that A Ltd still has £14,000 outstanding for between 61 and 90 days (that is, arising from sales during October) and £18,000 outstanding for more than 90 days (that is, arising from sales during September or even before). This information can be very useful for credit control purposes.

Usually accounting software includes this ageing schedule as one of the routine reports available to managers. Such packages often have the facility to put customers 'on hold' when they reach their credit limits. Putting a customer on hold means that no further credit sales will be made to that customer until amounts owing from past sales have been settled.

Many businesses use ageing summaries to assess the effectiveness of their receivables collection processes. Increasingly, some of these businesses show the end-of-reporting period summary in their annual report. **Real World 16.7** is an extract from the annual report of Sky plc, the satellite broadcaster.

Real World 16.7

Analysing receivables

Sky plc, publishes an analysis of its trade receivables each year according to how long they are overdue. Figures for the previous year are also published for comparison purposes.

The ageing of the group's net trade receivables which are past due date but not impaired is as follows:

	2016 £m	2015 £m
Up to 30 days past due date	61	27
30 to 60 days past due date	14	8
60 to 120 days past due date	4	4
120+ days past due	3	1
	82	40

Seventy-six per cent of Sky's unimpaired trade receivables were still within due date (30 days) at the business's 2016 year-end.

Source: Sky plc Annual Report 2016, p. 100.

Identify the pattern of receipts

A slightly different approach to exercising control over receivables is to identify the pattern of receipts from credit sales on a monthly basis. This involves monitoring the percentage of credit sales that are paid in the month of sale and the percentage that is paid in subsequent months. To do this, credit sales for each month must be examined separately. Example 16.5 illustrates this.

Example 16.5

A business made credit sales of £250,000 in June. It received 30 per cent of that amount during June, 40 per cent during July, 20 per cent during August and 10 per cent during September. The pattern of credit sales receipts and amounts owing is:

Pattern of credit sales receipts

	Receipts from June credit sales £	Amounts received %	Amount outstanding from June sales at month end £	Amount outstanding %
June	75,000	30	175,000	70
July	100,000	40	75,000	30
August	50,000	20	25,000	10
September	25,000	10	0	0

This information can be used as a basis for control. Targets may be established for the pattern of cash received from credit sales. The actual pattern can then be compared with the target pattern of receipts to see whether there is any significant deviation (see Figure 16.6). Where this is the case, managers should consider corrective action.

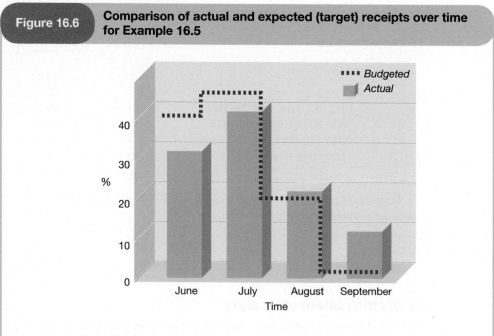

Figure 16.6   Comparison of actual and expected (target) receipts over time for Example 16.5

It can be seen that 30 per cent of the sales income for June is received in that month; the remainder is received in the following three months. The expected (target) pattern of cash receipts for June sales, which has been assumed, is also depicted. By comparing the actual and expected pattern of receipts, it is possible to see whether credit sales are being properly controlled and to decide whether corrective action is required.

Answer queries quickly

It is important for relevant staff to deal with customer queries on goods and services supplied quickly and efficiently. Payment is unlikely to be made by customers until their queries have been dealt with.

Deal with slow payers

A business making significant sales on credit will, almost inevitably, be faced with customers who do not pay. When this occurs, there should be established procedures for dealing with the problem. There should be a timetable for sending out reminders and for adding customers to a 'stop list' for future supplies. The timetable may also specify the point at which the unpaid amount is passed to a collection agency for recovery. These agencies often work on a 'no collection – no fee' basis. Charges for their services vary but can be up to 15 per cent of the amounts collected.

Legal action may also be considered against delinquent credit customers. The cost of such action, however, must be weighed against likely returns. There is little point, for example, in incurring large legal expenses to try to recoup amounts owing if there is evidence that the customer has no money. Where possible, an estimate of the cost of bad debts should be taken into account when setting prices for products or services.

As a footnote to our consideration of managing receivables, **Real World 16.8** outlines some of the excuses that long-suffering credit managers must listen to when chasing payment for outstanding debts.

Real World 16.8

It's in the post

It's been reported that businesses in the UK regularly experience late payment. A recent survey shows that the type of excuses given for this have changed little over the years despite the advance of online payment. Here are some of the most frequent excuses given:

1 We can't pay you until we have been paid by others ourselves
2 Our cheque is in the post to you
3 We have a dispute on the account so we can't pay you yet
4 We haven't received your invoice
5 We think there's an error in your invoice so can't make payment
6 We only pay by cheque and unfortunately our manager is away so the cheque can't be written

These are by no means the only excuses. Others regularly used include bereavement, the fact that there's nobody in the office at the moment, and that the company is changing bank accounts.

Source: Adapted from https://debtadvocate.co.uk/the-uk-top-10-excuses-for-late-payment/

Reducing the risk of non-payment

Efficient collection policies are important in reducing the risk of non-payment. There are, however, other ways in which a business can reduce this type of risk. Possibilities include:

- requiring customers to pay part of their sale value in advance of the goods being sent;
- agreeing to offset amounts owed for the purchase of goods against amounts due for goods supplied to the same business;
- requiring a third-party guarantee from a financially sound business such as a bank or parent company;
- making it a condition of sale that the legal title to the goods is not passed to the customer until the goods are paid for; and/or
- taking out insurance to cover the cost of any legal expenses incurred in recovering the amount owed. (Some customers may refuse to pay if they feel the business does not have the resources to pursue the debt through the courts.)

Managing cash

Why hold cash?

Most businesses hold a certain amount of cash. There are broadly three reasons why they do so.

Activity (16.13)

Can you think what these reasons may be? Try to think of at least one.

The three reasons are:

1 *To meet day-to-day commitments.* A business needs a certain amount of cash to pay for wages, overhead expenses, goods purchased and so on, when they fall due. Cash has been described as the lifeblood of a business. Unless it circulates through the business and is available to meet maturing obligations, the survival of the business will be put at risk. Simply being profitable is not enough to ensure survival.

2 *For precautionary purposes.* If future cash flows are uncertain, it would be prudent to hold a balance of cash. For example, a major customer that owes a large sum to the business may be in financial difficulties. This could lead to an expected large receipt not arriving. By holding cash, the business could retain its capacity to meet its obligations. Similarly, if there is some uncertainty concerning future outlays, a cash balance will be needed.

3 *To exploit opportunities.* A business may decide to hold cash to put itself in a position to exploit profitable opportunities as and when they arise. For example, it may enable the acquisition of a competitor business that suddenly becomes available at an attractive price.

How much cash should be held?

The amount of cash held tends to vary considerably between businesses. The decision as to how much cash a business should hold is a difficult one. Various factors can influence the final decision.

Activity (16.14)

Try to think of four possible factors that might influence the amount of cash that a business holds.

You may have thought of the following:

● *The nature of the business.* Some businesses, such as utilities (for example, water, electricity and gas suppliers), have cash flows that are both predictable and reasonably certain. This will enable them to hold lower cash balances. For some businesses, cash balances may vary greatly according to the time of year. A seasonal business may accumulate cash during the high season to enable it to meet commitments during the low season.

● *The opportunity cost of holding cash.* Where there are profitable opportunities in which to invest, it may not be wise to hold a large cash balance.

● *The level of inflation.* Holding cash during a period of rising prices will lead to a loss of purchasing power. The higher the level of inflation, the greater will be this loss.

● *The availability of near-liquid assets.* If a business has marketable securities or inventories that may easily be liquidated, high cash balances may not be necessary.

● *The availability of borrowing.* If a business can borrow easily (and quickly) there is less need to hold cash.

● *The cost of borrowing.* When interest rates are high, the option of borrowing becomes less attractive.

- *Economic conditions.* When the economy is in recession, businesses may prefer to hold cash so that they can be well placed to invest when the economy improves. In addition, during a recession, businesses may experience difficulties in collecting trade receivables. They may therefore hold higher cash balances than usual in order to meet commitments.
- *Relationships with suppliers.* Too little cash may hinder the ability of the business to pay suppliers promptly. This can lead to a loss of goodwill. It may also lead to discounts being forgone.

Controlling the cash balance

Several models have been developed to help control the cash balance of the business. One such model proposes the use of upper and lower control limits for cash balances and the use of a target cash balance. The model assumes that the business will invest in marketable investments that can easily be liquidated. These investments will be purchased or sold, as necessary, in order to keep the cash balance within the control limits.

The model proposes two upper and two lower control limits (see Figure 16.7). If the business exceeds either of the *outer* limits, the managers must decide whether, over the next few days, the cash balance is likely to return to a point within the *inner* control limits set. If this seems likely, then no action is required. If, however, it does not seem likely, managers should change the cash position by either buying or selling marketable investments. In Figure 16.8, we can see that the lower outer control limit has been breached for four days. If a four-day period is unacceptable, managers should sell marketable investments to replenish the cash balance.

Figure 16.7	Controlling the cash balance

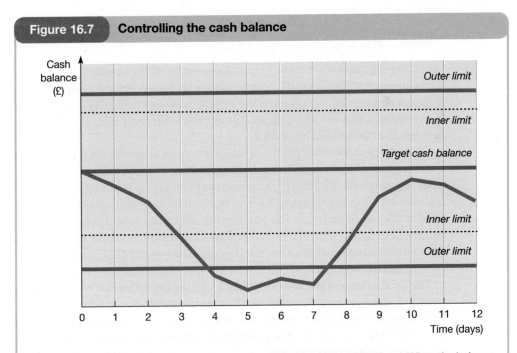

Management sets the upper and lower limits for the business's cash balance. When the balance goes beyond either of these limits, unless it is clear that the balance will return fairly quickly to within the limit, action will need to be taken. If the upper limit is breached, some cash will be placed on deposit or used to buy some marketable securities. If the lower limit is breached, the business will need to borrow some cash or sell some securities.

The model relies heavily on management judgement to determine where the control limits are set and the length of the period within which breaches of the control limits are acceptable. Past experience may be useful in helping managers decide on these issues. There are other models, however, that do not rely on management judgement. Instead, these use quantitative techniques to determine an optimal cash policy. One model proposed is the cash equivalent of the inventories economic order quantity model, discussed earlier in the chapter.

Cash budgets and managing cash

To manage cash effectively, it is useful for a business to prepare a cash budget. This is a very important tool for both planning and control purposes. Cash budgets were considered in Chapter 12 and so we shall not consider them again in detail. However, it is worth repeating that these statements enable managers to see how planned events are expected to affect the cash balance. The cash budget will identify periods when cash surpluses and cash deficits are expected.

When a cash surplus is expected to arise, managers must decide on the best use of the surplus funds. When a cash deficit is expected, managers must make adequate provision by borrowing, liquidating assets or rescheduling cash payments or receipts to deal with this. Cash budgets can help to control the cash held. Actual cash flows can be compared with the planned cash flows for the period. If there is a significant divergence between the planned cash flows and the actual cash flows, explanations must be sought and corrective action taken where necessary.

(To refresh your memory on cash budgets it would probably be worth looking back at Chapter 12, pages 490–491.)

Operating cash cycle

When managing cash, it is important to be aware of the **operating cash cycle (OCC)** of the business. For a business that purchases goods on credit for subsequent resale on credit, such as a wholesaler, it represents the period between the outlay of cash for the purchase of inventories and the ultimate receipt of cash from their sale. The OCC for this type of business is as shown in Figure 16.8.

Figure 16.8 shows that payment for inventories acquired on credit occurs some time after those inventories have been purchased. Therefore, no immediate cash outflow arises from the purchase. Similarly, cash receipts from credit customers will occur some time after the sale is made. There will be no immediate cash inflow as a result of the sale. The OCC is the period between the payment made to the supplier for the goods concerned and the cash received from the credit customer. Although Figure 16.8 depicts the position for a wholesaling business, the precise definition of the OCC can easily be adapted for other types of business.

The OCC is important because it has a significant influence on the financing requirements of the business. Broadly, the longer the cycle, the greater will be the financing requirements and the greater the financial risks. The business may therefore wish to reduce the OCC to the minimum period possible. A business with a short OCC is said to have 'good (or strong) cash flow'.

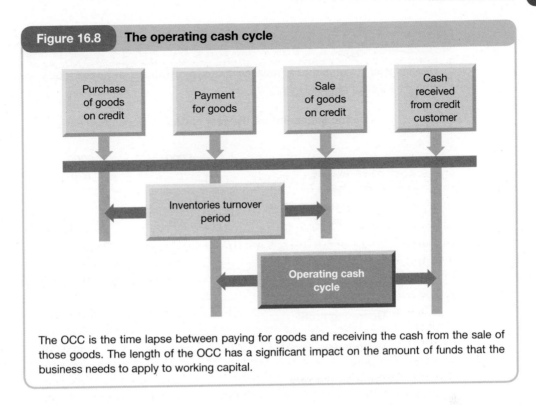

Figure 16.8   The operating cash cycle

The OCC is the time lapse between paying for goods and receiving the cash from the sale of those goods. The length of the OCC has a significant impact on the amount of funds that the business needs to apply to working capital.

For businesses that buy and sell goods on credit, the OCC can be deduced from their financial statements through the use of certain ratios. The calculations required are as shown in Figure 16.9.

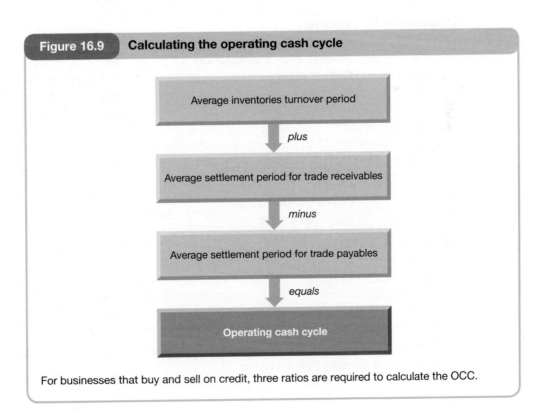

Figure 16.9   Calculating the operating cash cycle

For businesses that buy and sell on credit, three ratios are required to calculate the OCC.

Activity 16.15

The financial statements of Freezeqwik Ltd, a distributor of frozen foods, for the year ended 31 December last year are:

Income statement for the year ended 31 December last year

	£000	£000
Sales revenue		820
Cost of sales		
Opening inventories	142	
Purchases	568	
	710	
Closing inventories	(166)	(544)
Gross profit		276
Administration expenses		(120)
Distribution expenses		(95)
Operating profit		61
Financial expenses		(32)
Profit before taxation		29
Taxation		(7)
Profit for the year		22

Statement of financial position as at 31 December last year

	£000
ASSETS	
Non-current assets	
Property, plant and equipment	364
Current assets	
Inventories	166
Trade receivables	264
Cash	24
	454
Total assets	818
EQUITY AND LIABILITIES	
Equity	
Ordinary share capital	300
Retained earnings	352
	652
Current liabilities	
Trade payables	159
Taxation	7
	166
Total equity and liabilities	818

All purchases and sales are on credit. There has been no change in the level of trade receivables or payables over the period.

Calculate the length of the OCC for the business.

The OCC may be calculated as follows:

	Number of days
Average inventories turnover period:	
$\dfrac{\text{(Opening inventories + Closing inventories)/2}}{\text{Cost of sales}} \times 365 = \dfrac{(142 + 166)/2}{544} \times 365$	103
Average settlement period for trade receivables:	
$\dfrac{\text{Trade receivables}}{\text{Credit sales}} \times 365 = \dfrac{264}{820} \times 365$	118
Average settlement period for trade payables:	
$\dfrac{\text{Trade payables}}{\text{Credit purchases}} \times 365 = \dfrac{159}{568} \times 365$	(102)
OCC	119

We can see from the formula above that if a business wishes to reduce the OCC, it should do one or more of the following:

- reduce the average inventories turnover period;
- reduce the average settlement period for trade receivables; and/or
- increase the average settlement period for trade payables.

Activity 16.16

Assume that Freezeqwik Ltd (Activity 16.15) wishes to reduce its OCC by 30 days. Evaluate each of the options available to this business.

The average inventories turnover period for the business represents more than three months' sales requirements. Similarly, the average settlement period for trade receivables represent nearly four months' sales. Both periods seem quite long. It is possible that both could be reduced through greater operating efficiency. Improving inventories control and credit control procedures may achieve the required reduction in OCC without any adverse effect on future sales. If so, this may offer the best way forward.

The average settlement period for trade payables represents more than three months' purchases. Any decision to extend this period, however, must be given very careful consideration. It is quite long and may already be breaching the payment terms required by suppliers.

There is no reason why the 30 days reduction in the OCC could not come from a combination of altering all three of the periods involved (inventories, trade receivables and trade payables).

Before a final decision is made, full account must be taken of current trading conditions.

It seems to be quite common, in practice, for businesses to try to maintain the OCC at a particular target level. However, not all days in the OCC are of equal value. In Activity 16.14, for example, the operating cash cycle is 119 days. If the average settlement periods for both trade receivables and trade payables were increased by seven days, the OCC would remain at 119 days. The amount tied up in working capital, however, would not remain the same. Trade receivables would increase by £15,726 (that is, 7 × £820,000/365) and trade payables would increase by £10,893 (that is, 7 × £568,000/365). This means that there would be a net increase of £4,833 in working capital.

Real World 16.9 shows the average operating cash cycle for large European businesses.

Real World 16.9

Cycling along

The survey of working capital by Ernst and Young (see Real World 16.2, page 678) calculates the average operating cash cycle for the top 1,000 European businesses (excluding financial and auto manufacturing businesses). The results for the period 2002 to 2014 are set out in Figure 16.10.

Figure 16.10 **The average OCC of large European businesses for 2002 to 2014**

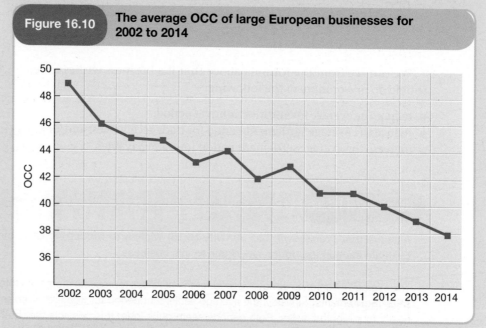

The average operating cash cycle has reduced by 21 per cent over the twelve years between 2002 and 2014, with each element of working capital making a contribution to this. The inventories holding period fell by 3 per cent and the trade receivables settlement period fell by 11 per cent, while the trade payables settlement period increased by 7 per cent.

Source: Adapted from figure in *All Tied Up: Working Capital Management Report 2014*, Ernst and Young, p. 7, www.ey.com.

Cash transmission

A business will normally wish to benefit from receipts from customers at the earliest opportunity. Where cash is received, the benefit is immediate. Where payment is made by cheque, however, there may be a delay before it is cleared through the banking system. The business must therefore wait before it can benefit from the amount paid in. In recent years, the CHAPS (Clearing House Automated Payments) system has helped to reduce the time that cheques spend in the banking system. It is now possible for cheques to be fast tracked so that they reach the recipient's bank account on the same day. Payment by cheque, however, is in decline. Increasingly, customers prefer to instruct their bank to make a direct transfer of the amount owed to the business's bank account. The transfer may be completed within hours and provides a more efficient form of cash transmission for both parties.

Setting up a standing order or a direct debit is another way of carrying out transfers between a customer's bank account and the business's bank account. In both cases, the transfer will then take place on an agreed date. Businesses providing services over time, such as insurance, satellite television and mobile phone services, often rely on this method of payment.

A final way in which a business may be paid promptly is through the use of a debit card. This allows the customer's bank account to be charged (debited) and the seller's bank account to be simultaneously increased (credited) with the sale price of the item. Many types of business, including retailers and restaurants, use this method. It is operated through computerised cash tills and is referred to as electronic funds transfer at point of sale (EFTPOS).

Bank overdrafts

As we saw in Chapter 15, bank overdrafts are simply bank current accounts that have a negative balance. They are a type of bank loan and can be a useful tool in managing the business's cash flow requirements.

Real World 16.10 shows how Mears Group plc managed to improve its cash flows through better management practices. Mears is an AIM-listed business that provides maintenance and improvements to social housing, as well as other support services. Most of its work is small scale (that is, involves lots of small jobs) and is outsourced to Mears by public-sector organisations. The businesses took part in a major survey of working capital management undertaken by REL Consulting.

Real World 16.10

Putting cash to work

The nature of the work undertaken by Mears tends to lead to the business undertaking thousands of relatively small value jobs. This leads to potential problems in managing working capital, particularly in the area of management and collection of trade receivables (debts). The business's finance director, Andrew Smith, makes the point that, for such a business, failure to manage trade receivables effectively could easily lead to the collapse of the business. Despite the difficulties, Mears proved to be one of the best performers in this area, as shown by the 2015 REL Working Capital Survey, having massively reduced the length of its operating cash cycle from its previous years results.

Real World 16.10 *continued*

Mears attributed its improvement in trade receivables management to the introduction of a new IT system, in the design of which, accountants had been heavily involved. The business has managed to promote a 'cash culture' where a particular job is only viewed as being completed once the cash for it has been received.

Source: Information taken from Crump, R., (2015) 'Debt is king: REL working capital survey 2015, Financial Director, 20 August.

Managing trade payables

Most businesses buy their goods and services on credit. Trade payables are the other side of the coin from trade receivables. In a trade credit transaction, one business's trade payable is another one's trade receivable. Trade payables are an important source of finance for most businesses. They have been described as a 'spontaneous' source, as they tend to increase in line with the increase in the level of activity achieved by a business.

There are potential costs associated with taking trade credit. A business that buys supplies on credit may incur additional administration and accounting costs resulting from the scrutiny and payment of invoices, maintaining and updating payables accounts and so on. Furthermore, customers who take credit may not be as well treated as those who pay immediately. When goods are in short supply, they may be given lower priority. They may also be less favoured in terms of delivery dates or in gaining access to technical support. Where credit is required, customers may even have to pay more. In most industries, however, trade credit is the norm. As a result, these disadvantages do not normally apply unless, perhaps, the credit facilities are being abused.

The benefits to be gained from taking credit usually outweigh any costs involved. In effect, it is an interest-free loan from suppliers. It can also provide a more convenient way of paying for goods and services than paying by cash. Furthermore, during a period of inflation, there is an economic gain from paying later rather than sooner for goods and services supplied.

Activity 16.17

Why might a supplier prefer a customer to take a period of credit rather than pay for the goods or services on delivery? (There are probably two reasons.)

1 Paying on delivery may not be administratively convenient for the seller. Most customers will take a period of credit, so the systems of the seller will be geared up to receive payment after a reasonable period of credit.
2 A credit period can allow any problems with the goods or service supplied to be resolved before payment is made. This might avoid the seller having to make refunds.

Delaying payment to suppliers may be a sign of financial problems. It may also, however, reflect an imbalance in bargaining power. It is not unusual for large businesses to delay payment to small suppliers, which are reliant on them for continuing trade. The UK government has encouraged large businesses to sign up to a 'Prompt Payment Code' to help small suppliers but, to date, this has achieved only limited success. As mentioned in Chapter 7, however, there are now plans to strengthen the Code.

Taking advantage of cash discounts

Where a supplier offers a discount for prompt payment, the business should give careful consideration to the possibility of paying within the discount period. Example 16.6 illustrates the cost of forgoing possible discounts.

Example 16.6

Hassan Ltd takes 70 days to pay for goods from its supplier. To encourage prompt payment, the supplier has offered the business a 2 per cent discount if payment for goods is made within 30 days. Hassan Ltd is not sure, however, whether it is worth taking the discount offered.

If the discount is taken, payment could be made on the last day of the discount period (that is, the 30th day). However, if the discount is not taken, payment will be made after 70 days. This means that, by not taking the discount, the business will receive an extra 40 days' (that is, 70 − 30) credit. The cost of this extra credit to the business will be the 2 per cent discount forgone. If we annualise the cost of this discount forgone, we have:

$$365/40 \times 2\% = 18.3\%*$$

We can see that the annual cost of forgoing the discount is very high. It may, therefore, be profitable for the business to pay the supplier within the discount period, even if it means that it will have to borrow in order to do so.

* This is an approximate annual rate. For the more mathematically minded, the precise rate is:

$$\{[(1 + 2/98)^{9.125}] - 1\} \times 100\% = 20.2\%$$

The key difference is that, in this calculation, compound interest is used, whereas in the first calculation, simple interest is used, which is not strictly correct.

Controlling trade payables

To help monitor the level of trade credit taken, management can calculate the **average settlement period for trade payables ratio**. As we saw in Chapter 7, this ratio is:

$$\text{Average settlement period for trade payables} = \frac{\text{Average trade payables}}{\text{Credit purchases}} \times 365$$

Once again, this provides an average figure, which could be misleading. A more informative approach would be to produce an ageing schedule for payables. This would look much the same as the ageing schedule for receivables described earlier in Example 16.4.

Managing working capital

As a footnote to our discussion about the management of working capital, we draw on the experience of two firms of management consultants. **Real World 16.11** is an extract from an article that makes the point that many businesses do not pay as much attention to it as they should since the rewards in liberating funds tied up are often huge. The article was written by two consultants with the international management consultants, McKinsey and Company.

Real World 16.11

Uncovering cash

Managing a company's working capital isn't the sexiest task. It's often painstakingly technical. It's hard to know how well a company is doing, even relative to peers; published financial data are too high level for precise benchmarking. And because working capital doesn't appear on the income statement, it doesn't directly affect earnings or operating profit—the measures that most commonly influence compensation (salaries, bonuses and so on). Although working capital management has long been a business-school staple, our research shows that performance is surprisingly variable, even among companies in the same industry.

That's quite a missed opportunity – and it has implications beyond the finance department. Working capital can amount to as much as several months' worth of revenues, which isn't trivial. Improving its management can be a quick way to free up cash. We routinely see companies generate tens or even hundreds of millions of dollars of cash impact within 60 to 90 days, without increasing sales or cutting costs. And the rewards for persistence and dedication to continuous improvement can be lucrative.

The global aluminum company Alcoa made working capital a priority in 2009 in response to the financial crisis and global economic downturn, and it recently celebrated its 17th straight quarter of year-on-year reduction in net working capital. Over that time, the company has reduced its net working capital cycle – the amount of time it takes to turn assets and liabilities into cash – by 23 days and unlocked $1.4 billion in cash. For distressed companies, that kind of improvement can be a lifeline. For healthy companies, the windfall can often be reinvested in ways that more directly affect value creation, such as growth initiatives or increased balance-sheet flexibility. Moreover, the process of improving working capital can also highlight opportunities in other areas, such as operations, supply-chain management, procurement, sales, and finance.

Of course, not all reductions in working capital are beneficial. Too little inventory can disrupt operations. Stretching supplier payment terms can leak back in the form of higher prices, if not negotiated carefully, or unwittingly send a signal of distress to the market. But managers who are mindful of such pitfalls can still improve working capital by setting incentives that ensure visibility, collecting the right data, defining meaningful targets, and managing ongoing performance.

Working capital is often undermanaged simply because of lack of awareness or attention. It may not be tracked or published in a way that is transparent and relevant to employees, or it may not be communicated as a priority. In particular, working capital is often underemphasized when the performance of a business—and of its managers—is evaluated primarily on income-statement measures such as earnings before interest, taxes, depreciation, and amortization (EBITDA) or earnings per share, which don't reflect changes in working capital.

What actions should managers take, beyond communicating that working capital is important? In our experience, the selection of metrics (measurements) to manage the business and measure performance is especially important, because different metrics will lead to different outcomes. For one manufacturing company, switching from EBITDA (earnings before interest, taxes, depreciation and amortisation) to free cash flow as a primary measure of performance had an immediate effect; managers began to measure cash flow at the plant level and then distributed inventory metrics to frontline supervisors. As a result, inventories quickly fell as managers, for the first time, identified and debated issues such as the right level of inventories and coordination among plants.

Source: Extract from Davies, R. and Merin, D. (2014) *Uncovering Cash and Insights From Working Capital*, McKinsey and Company, www.mckinsey.com, July.

Real World 16.12 sets out a 'health check' for businesses concerning the management of working capital. It was devised by REL Consulting, a firm of management consultants specialising in working capital management issues.

Real World 16.12

Working out whether working capital is working

The diagnostic check below takes the form of a series of questions, each with five possible answers. These answers attract a score from 0 to 4 according to the maturity level of the working capital management process: the higher the score, the more mature it is. The questions contain a few differences in terminology to that used in the chapter. These differences are as follows:

DSO (Days sales outstanding)   = Settlement period for trade receivables
DIO (Days inventory turnover)   = Inventory turnover period
DPO (Days payables outstanding) = Settlement period for trade payables
CCC (Cash conversion cycle)   = Operating cash cycle

What are the strengths and weaknesses of your current working capital processes?

1. How quickly do you collect cash?
   __ Less than 30 days (4)
   __ 31–45 days (3)
   __ 46–60 days (2)
   __ More than 61 days (1)
   __ Don't know (0)

2. What per cent of payments do you receive after the due date?
   __ Less than 5% (4)
   __ 6–10% (3)
   __ 11–20% (2)
   __ 21%+ (1)
   __ Don't know (0)

3. How quickly do you pay supplier invoices?
   __ Don't know (0)
   __ Less than 30 days (1)
   __ 31–45 days (2)
   __ 46–60 days (3)
   __ More than 61 days (4)

4. What proportion of supplier invoices are paid after the due date?
   __ 0–5%, (4)
   __ 6–10% (3)
   __ 11–20% (2)
   __ 21%+ (1)
   __ Don't know (0)

Real World 16.12 *continued*

5. How much inventory do you hold in days?
   __ Up to 30 days (4)
   __ 31–60 days (3)
   __ 61–90 days (2)
   __ More than 91 (1)
   __ Don't know (0)

6. What per cent of orders are delivered on time?
   __ 98–100% (4)
   __ 95–97% (3)
   __ 90–94% (2)
   __ Less than 90% (1)
   __ Don't know (0)

7. How quickly after month-end do you report the metrics of DSO, DIO, DPO & CCC?
   __ Within 5 days (4)
   __ 6–10 days (3)
   __ 11–15 days (2)
   __ >16 days (1)
   __ Do not report at all (0)

8. How standardised are your working capital metrics across the different reporting units?
   __ Fully standardised (4)
   __ Partly standardised (3)
   __ Only standard at Group level (2)
   __ Not at all standardised (1)
   __ Do not report at all (0)

9. How well trained are employees in working capital management?
   __ Fully trained with regular updates (4)
   __ Trained at least once (3)
   __ Ad hoc training (2)
   __ Access to relevant WC training materials on company intranet (1)
   __ No specific WC training (0)

10. Are the functional and individual responsibilities for working capital management documented and clearly assigned across the organisation?
   __ Fully documented and assigned for all levels in the organisation (4)
   __ Partially documented and assigned at C-suite (3)
   __ Partially documented and assigned within functional roles (2)
   __ Not documented but assigned on ad hoc basis (1)
   __ Not considered (0)

Source: REL Consulting, *The Working Capitalist–Spring 2016*, p. 8, www.relconsultancy.com.

Self-assessment question 16.1

Town Mills Ltd is a wholesale business. Extracts from the business's most recent financial statements are as follows:

Income statement for the year ended 31 May

	£000
Sales	903
Cost of sales	(652)
Gross profit	251
Other operating expenses	(109)
Operating profit	142
Interest	(11)
Profit before taxation	131
Taxation	(38)
Profit for the year	93

Statement of financial position as at 31 May

	£000
ASSETS	
Non-current assets	
Property, plant and equipment at cost	714
Accumulated depreciation	(295)
	419
Current assets	
Inventories	192
Trade receivables	202
	394
Total assets	813
EQUITY AND LIABILITIES	
Equity	
Ordinary share capital	200
Retained earnings	246
	446
Current liabilities	
Trade payables	260
Borrowings (all bank overdraft)	107
	367
Total equity and liabilities	813

The levels of trade receivables and trade payables increased by 10 per cent, by value, during the year ended 31 May. Inventories levels remained the same. The chief financial officer believes that inventories levels are too high and should be reduced.

Required:
(a) Calculate the average operating cash cycle (in days) during the year ended 31 May and explain to what use this value can be put and what limitations it has.
(b) Discuss whether there is evidence that the business has a liquidity problem.
(c) Explain the types of risk and cost that might be reduced by following the chief financial officer proposal to reduce inventories levels.

The answer to this question can be found at the back of the book on pp. 784–785.

Summary

The main points of this chapter may be summarised as follows.

Working capital

- Is the difference between current assets and current liabilities.
- That is, working capital = inventories + trade receivables + cash − trade payables − short term borrowings (including bank overdrafts).
- An investment in working capital cannot be avoided in practice – typically large amounts of finance are involved.

Inventories

- There are costs of holding inventories, which include:
  - lost interest;
  - storage cost;
  - insurance cost; and
  - obsolescence.
- There are also costs of not holding sufficient inventories, which include:
  - loss of sales and customer goodwill;
  - production dislocation;
  - loss of flexibility – cannot take advantage of opportunities; and
  - reorder costs – low inventories imply more frequent ordering.
- Practical points on inventories management include:
  - implement selective levels of control based on value (ABC);
  - identify optimum order size – models can help with this;
  - set inventories reorder levels;
  - use budgets;
  - keep reliable inventories records;
  - use accounting ratios (for example, inventories turnover period ratio);
  - establish systems for security of inventories and authorisation;
  - employ ERP applications to automate and integrate the recording and management of inventories; and
  - implement just-in-time (JIT) inventories management.

Trade receivables

- When assessing which customers should receive credit, the five Cs of credit can be used:
  - capital;
  - capacity;
  - collateral;
  - condition; and
  - character.
- The costs of allowing credit include:
  - lost interest;
  - lost purchasing power;
  - costs of assessing customer creditworthiness;
  - administration cost;

- bad debts; and
- cash discounts (for prompt payment).
- The costs of denying credit include loss of customer goodwill.
- Practical points on receivables management:
  - establish a policy;
  - assess and monitor customer creditworthiness;
  - establish effective administration of receivables;
  - establish a policy on bad debts;
  - consider cash discounts;
  - use financial ratios (for example, average settlement period for trade receivables ratio); and
  - use ageing summaries.

Cash

- The costs of holding cash include:
  - lost interest; and
  - lost purchasing power.
- The costs of holding insufficient cash include:
  - loss of supplier goodwill if unable to meet commitments on time;
  - loss of opportunities;
  - inability to claim cash discounts; and
  - costs of borrowing (should an obligation need to be met at short notice).
- Practical points on cash management:
  - establish a policy;
  - plan cash flows;
  - make judicious use of bank overdraft finance – it can be cheap and flexible;
  - use short-term cash surpluses profitably;
  - bank frequently; and
  - transmit cash promptly.
- Operating cash cycle (for a wholesaler) = average inventories' turnover period + average settlement period for trade receivables − average settlement period for trade payables.
  - An objective of working capital management is to limit the length of the operating cash cycle (OCC), subject to any risks that this may cause.

Trade payables

- The costs of taking credit include:
  - higher price than purchases for immediate cash settlement;
  - administrative costs; and
  - restrictions imposed by seller.
- The costs of not taking credit include:
  - lost interest-free borrowing;
  - lost purchasing power; and
  - inconvenience – paying at the time of purchase can be inconvenient.
- Practical points on payables management:
  - establish a policy;
  - exploit free credit as far as possible; and
  - use accounting ratios (for example, average settlement period for trade payables ratio).

Key terms

For definitions of these terms, see Appendix B.

working capital *p. 675*
lead time *p. 682*
ABC system of inventories control *p. 684*
economic order quantity (EOQ) *p. 685*
enterprise resource planning (ERP) system *p. 689*
just-in-time (JIT) inventories management *p. 689*

five Cs of credit *p. 692*
cash discount *p. 696*
trade receivables to sales ratio *p. 699*
ageing schedule of trade receivables *p. 699*
operating cash cycle (OCC) *p. 706*
average settlement period for trade payables ratio *p. 713*

Further reading

If you would like to explore the topics covered in this chapter in more depth, try the following:

Brigham, E. and Ehrdhart, M. (2016) *Financial Management: Theory and Practice,* 15th Edn, Cengage Learning Custom Publishing, Chapters 16 and 28.

Hillier, D., Clacher I., Ross, S., Westerfield, R. and Jordan, B. (2014) *Fundamentals of Corporate Finance,* 2nd European edn, McGraw-Hill Education, Chapter 17.

McLaney, E. (2017) *Business Finance: Theory and practice,* 11th edn, Pearson, Chapters 8, 9, 11 and 12.

Pike, R., Neale, B. and Linsley, P. (2015) *Corporate Finance and Investment,* 8th edn, Pearson, Chapters 13 and 14.

Sagner, J. (2014) *Working Capital Management: Applications and Case Studies,* Wiley Corporate F&A, Chapters 2–8.

Review questions

Solutions to these questions can be found at the back of the book on pp. 799–800.

16.1 Tariq is the credit manager of Heltex plc. He is concerned that the pattern of monthly cash receipts from credit sales shows that credit collection is poor compared with budget. Heltex's sales director believes that Tariq is to blame for this situation, but Tariq insists that he is not. Why might Tariq not be to blame for the deterioration in the credit collection period?

16.2 How might each of the following affect the level of inventories held by a business?

(a) An increase in the number of production bottlenecks experienced by the business.
(b) A rise in the business's cost of capital.
(c) A decision to offer customers a narrower range of products in the future.
(d) A switch of suppliers from an overseas business to a local business.
(e) A deterioration in the quality and reliability of bought-in components.

16.3 What are the reasons for holding inventories? Are these reasons different from the reasons for holding cash?

16.4 Identify the costs of holding:

(a) too little cash
(b) too much cash.

Exercises

Solutions to exercises with coloured numbers can be found at the back of the book on pp. 841–844.

Basic-level exercises

16.1 The chief executive officer of Sparkrite Ltd, a trading business, has just received summary sets of financial statements for last year and this year:

Income statements for years ended 30 September

	Last year		This year	
	£000	£000	£000	£000
Sales revenue		1,800		1,920
Cost of sales				
Opening inventories	160		200	
Purchases	1,120		1,175	
	1,280		1,375	
Closing inventories	(200)	(1,080)	(250)	(1,125)
Gross profit		720		795
Expenses		(680)		(750)
Profit for the year		40		45

Statements of financial position as at 30 September

	Last year £000	This year £000
ASSETS		
Non-current assets	950	930
Current assets		
Inventories	200	250
Trade receivables	375	480
Cash at bank	4	2
	579	732
Total assets	1,529	1,662
EQUITY AND LIABILITIES		
Equity		
Fully paid £1 ordinary shares	825	883
Retained earnings	509	554
	1,334	1,437
Current liabilities	195	225
Total equity and liabilities	1,529	1,662

The chief financial officer has expressed concern at the increase in inventories and trade receivables levels.

Required:

(a) Show, by using the data given, how you would calculate ratios that could be used to measure inventories and trade receivables levels during last year and this year.

(b) Discuss the ways in which the management of Sparkrite Ltd could exercise control over the levels of:

   1 inventories
   2 trade receivables.

16.2 Hercules Wholesalers Ltd has been particularly concerned with its liquidity position in recent months. The most recent income statement and statement of financial position of the business are as follows:

Income statement for the year ended 31 December last year

	£000	£000
Sales revenue		452
Cost of sales		
Opening inventories	125	
Purchases	341	
	466	
Closing inventories	(143)	(323)
Gross profit		129
Expenses		(132)
Loss for the year		(3)

Statement of financial position as at 31 December last year

	£000
ASSETS	
Non-current assets	
Property, plant and equipment	357
Current assets	
Inventories	143
Trade receivables	163
	306
Total assets	663
EQUITY AND LIABILITIES	
Equity	
Ordinary share capital	100
Retained earnings	158
	258
Non-current liabilities	
Borrowings – loans	120
Current liabilities	
Trade payables	145
Borrowings – bank overdraft	140
	285
Total equity and liabilities	663

The trade receivables and payables were maintained at a constant level throughout the year.

Required:

(a) Explain why Hercules Wholesalers Ltd is concerned about its liquidity position.

(b) Calculate the operating cash cycle for Hercules Wholesalers Ltd.

(c) State what steps may be taken to improve the operating cash cycle of the business.

Intermediate-level exercises

16.3 International Electric plc at present offers its customers 30 days' credit. Half of the customers, by value, pay on time. The other half takes an average of 70 days to pay. The business is considering offering a cash discount of 2 per cent to its customers for payment within 30 days.

The credit controller anticipates that half of the customers who now take an average of 70 days to pay (that is, a quarter of all customers) will pay in 30 days. The other half (the final quarter) will still take an average of 70 days to pay. The scheme will also reduce bad debts by £300,000 a year.

Annual sales revenue of £365 million is made evenly throughout the year. At present the business has a large overdraft (£60 million) with its bank at an interest cost of 12 per cent a year.

Required:

(a) Calculate the approximate equivalent annual percentage cost of a discount of 2 per cent, which reduces the time taken by credit customers to pay from 70 days to 30 days. (*Hint*: This part can be answered without reference to the narrative above.)

(b) Calculate the value of trade receivables outstanding under both the old and new schemes.

(c) How much will the scheme cost the business in discounts?

(d) Should the business go ahead with the scheme? State what other factors, if any, should be taken into account.

16.4 Your superior, the general manager of Plastics Manufacturers Limited, has recently been talking to the chief buyer of Plastic Toys Limited, which manufactures a wide range of toys for young children. At present, Plastic Toys is considering changing its supplier of plastic granules and has offered to buy its entire requirement of 2,000 kg a month from you at the going market rate, provided that you will grant it three months' credit on its purchases. The following information is available:

1 Plastic granules sell for £10 a kg, variable costs are £7 a kg and fixed costs £2 a kg.
2 Your own business is financially strong and has sales revenue of £15 million a year. For the foreseeable future it will have surplus capacity and it is actively looking for new outlets.
3 Extracts from Plastic Toys' financial statements:

	Year 1	Year 2	Year 3
	£000	£000	£000
Sales revenue	800	980	640
Operating profit (Profit (loss) before			
interest and tax)	100	110	(150)
Capital employed	600	650	575
Current assets			
Inventories	200	220	320
Trade receivables	140	160	160
	340	380	480
Current liabilities			
Trade payables	180	190	220
Overdraft	100	150	310
	280	340	530
Working capital	60	40	(50)

Required:
Advise your general manager on the acceptability of the proposal. You should give your reasons and do any calculations you consider necessary.

Advanced-level exercises

16.5 Mayo Computers Ltd has annual sales of £20 million. Bad debts amount to £100,000 a year. All sales made by the business are on credit and, at present, credit terms are negotiable by the customer. On average, the settlement period for trade receivables is 60 days. Trade receivables are financed by an overdraft bearing a 14 per cent rate of interest per year. The business is currently reviewing its credit policies to see whether more efficient and profitable methods could be employed. Only one proposal has so far been put forward concerning the management of trade credit.

The credit control department has proposed that customers should be given a 2.5 per cent discount if they pay within 30 days. For those who do not pay within this period, a maximum of 50 days' credit should be given. The credit department believes that 60 per cent of customers will take advantage of the discount by paying at the end of the discount period. The remainder will pay at the end of 50 days. The credit department believes that bad debts can be effectively eliminated by adopting the proposed policies and by employing stricter credit investigation procedures, which will cost an additional £20,000 a year. The credit department is confident that these new policies will not result in any reduction in sales revenue.

Required:
Calculate the net annual cost (savings) to the business of abandoning its existing credit policies and adopting the proposals of the credit control department. (*Hint*: To answer this question you must weigh the costs of administration and cash discounts against the savings in bad debts and interest charges.)

16.6 Boswell Enterprises Ltd is reviewing its trade credit policy. The business, which sells all of its goods on credit, has estimated that sales revenue for the forthcoming year will be £3 million under the existing policy. Credit customers representing 30 per cent of trade receivables are expected to pay one month after being invoiced and 70 per cent are expected to pay two months after being invoiced. These estimates are in line with previous years' figures.

At present, no cash discounts are offered to customers. However, to encourage prompt payment, the business is considering giving a 2.5 per cent cash discount to credit customers who pay in one month or less. Given this incentive, the business expects credit customers accounting for 60 per cent of trade receivables to pay one month after being invoiced and those accounting for 40 per cent of trade receivables to pay two months after being invoiced. The business believes that the introduction of a cash discount policy will prove attractive to some customers and will lead to a 5 per cent increase in total sales revenue.

Irrespective of the trade credit policy adopted, the gross profit margin of the business will be 20 per cent for the forthcoming year and three months' inventories will be held. Fixed monthly expenses of £15,000 and variable expenses (excluding discounts), equivalent to 10 per cent of sales revenue, will be incurred and will be paid one month in arrears. Trade payables will be paid in arrears and will be equal to two months' cost of sales. The business will hold a fixed cash balance of £140,000 throughout the year, whichever trade credit policy is adopted. Ignore taxation.

Required:

(a) Calculate the investment in working capital at the end of the forthcoming year under:
  1 the existing policy
  2 the proposed policy.
(b) Calculate the expected profit for the forthcoming year under:
  1 the existing policy
  2 the proposed policy.
(c) Advise the business as to whether it should implement the proposed policy.

(Hint: The investment in working capital will be made up of inventories, trade receivables and cash, *less* trade payables and any unpaid expenses at the year-end.)

16.7 Goliath plc is a food wholesaler. The most recent financial statements of the business are as follows:

Income statement for the year to 31 May

	£000	£000
Sales revenue		2,400.0
Cost of sales		
Opening inventories	550.0	
Purchases	1,450.0	
	2,000.0	
Closing inventories	(560.0)	(1,440.0)
Gross profit		960.0
Administration expenses		(300.0)
Selling expenses		(436.0)
Operating profit		224.0
Interest payable		(40.0)
Profit before taxation		184.0
Taxation (25%)		(46.0)
Profit for the period		138.0

Statement of financial position as at 31 May

	£000
Non-current assets	
Property, plant and equipment	456.4
Current assets	
Inventories	560.0
Trade receivables	565.0
Cash at bank	36.4
	1,161.4
Total assets	1,617.8
Equity	
£1 ordinary shares	200.0
Retained earnings	520.8
	720.8
Non-current liabilities	
Borrowings – loan notes	400.0
Current liabilities	
Trade payables	451.0
Taxation	46.0
	497.0
Total equity and liabilities	1,617.8

All sales and purchases are made on credit.

The business is considering whether to grant extended credit facilities to its customers. It has been estimated that increasing the settlement period for trade receivables by a further 20 days will increase the sales revenue of the business by 10 per cent. However, inventories will have to be increased by 15 per cent to cope with the increased demand. It is estimated that purchases will have to rise to £1,668,000 during the next year as a result of these changes. To finance the increase in inventories and trade receivables, the business will increase the settlement period taken from suppliers by 15 days and use a loan facility bearing a 10 per cent rate of interest for the remaining balance.

If the policy is implemented, bad debts are likely to increase by £120,000 a year and administration costs will rise by 15 per cent.

Required:

(a) Calculate the increase or decrease to each of the following that will occur in the forthcoming year if the proposed policy is implemented:
1 operating cash cycle (based on year-end figures)
2 net investment in inventories, trade receivables and trade payables
3 profit for the period.
(b) Should the business implement the proposed policy? Give reasons for your conclusion.

PART 4

Supplementary information

Part 4 provides information that is supplementary to the main text.

Appendix A takes the format of a normal textual chapter and describes the way in which financial transactions can be recorded, usually manually, in books of account. Generally, this is by means of the 'double-entry' system, described in basic terms in the appendix.

Appendix B gives definitions of the key terms highlighted throughout the main text and listed at the end of each chapter. The aim of the appendix is to provide a single location to check on the meanings of the major accounting terms used in this book and in the world of finance.

Appendices C, D and E give answers to some of the questions set in the course of the main text. Appendix C gives answers to the self-assessment questions, Appendix D gives the answers to the review questions and Appendix E gives answers to those of the exercises that are marked as having their answers provided in the book.

Appendix F is a table of present value factors that can be used to discount future cash flows.

APPENDIX  A

Recording financial transactions

Introduction

In Chapters 2 and 3, we saw how the financial transactions of a business may be recorded by making a series of entries on the statement of financial position and/or the income statement. Each of these entries had its corresponding 'double', meaning that both sides of the transaction were recorded. However, adjusting the financial statements for each transaction, by hand, can be pretty messy and confusing. Where there are many transactions, as there tends to be even for a fairly small business, it is pretty certain to result in mistakes.

For businesses whose accounting systems are on a computer, this problem is overcome because suitable software can deal with a series of 'plus' and 'minus' entries very reliably. Where the accounting system is not computerised, however, it would be helpful to have some more practical way of keeping accounting records. Such a system not only exists but, before the advent of the computer, was the routine way of keeping accounting records. In fact, the system had been in constant use for recording business transactions since medieval times. It is this system that is explained in this appendix. We should be clear that this system follows exactly the same rules as those that we have already met. Its distinguishing feature is that it provides those keeping accounting records, by hand, with a methodical approach that allows each transaction to be clearly identified and errors to be minimised.

Learning outcomes

When you have completed this appendix, you should be able to:

● explain the basic principles of double-entry bookkeeping;

● write up a series of business transactions and balance the accounts;

● extract a trial balance and explain its purpose; and

● prepare a set of financial statements from the underlying double-entry accounts.

The basics of double-entry bookkeeping

When we record accounting transactions by hand, we use a recording system known as **double-entry bookkeeping**. This system does not use plus and minus entries on the face of a statement of financial position and income statement to record a particular transaction, in the way described in Chapters 2 and 3. Instead, individual transactions are recorded in accounts. An **account** is simply a record of one or more transactions relating to a particular item, such as:

- cash at bank;
- property, plant and equipment;
- borrowings;
- sales revenue;
- rent payable; and
- equity.

A business may keep few or many accounts, depending on the size and complexity of its operations. Broadly, businesses tend to keep a separate account for each item that appears in either the income statement or the statement of financial position.

An example of an account, in this case the *cash at bank* account, is as follows:

Cash at bank

£ | £

We can see that an account, which has a T-shape (and is often known as a *T account*), has three main features:

- a title indicating the item to which it relates;
- a left-hand side, known as the **debit** side; and
- a right-hand side, known as the **credit** side.

One side of an account will record increases in the particular item and the other will record decreases. This is, of course, slightly different from the approach that we used when adjusting the financial statements. When adjusting the statement of financial position, for example, we put a reduction in an asset or claim in the same column as any increases, but with a minus sign against it. However, when T accounts are used, a reduction is shown on the opposite side of the account.

The side on which an increase or decrease is shown will depend on the nature of the item to which the account relates. For example, an account for an asset, such as cash at bank, will show increases on the left-hand (debit) side of the account and decreases on the right-hand (credit) side. However, for claims (that is, equity and liabilities) it is the other way around. An increase in equity or for a liability will be shown on the right-hand (credit) side and a decrease will be shown on the left-hand (debit) side of the relevant account.

To understand why this difference exists, we need to go back to the accounting equation that we first came across in Chapter 2.

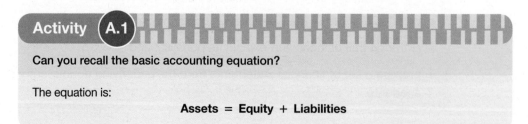

Activity A.1

Can you recall the basic accounting equation?

The equation is:

Assets = Equity + Liabilities

We can see that assets appear on one side of the equation and equity and liabilities appear on the other. Recording transactions in accounts simply expresses this difference in the recording process. Increases in assets are shown on the debit (left-hand) side of an account and increases in equity and liabilities are shown on the credit (right-hand) side of the account. We should recall the point made in Chapter 2 that each transaction has two aspects. Thus, when we record a particular transaction, two separate accounts will be affected. Recording transactions in this way is known as *double-entry bookkeeping*.

It is worth going through a simple example to see how transactions affecting statement of financial position items would be recorded under the double-entry bookkeeping system. Suppose a new business started on 1 January with the owner introducing initial equity of £5,000 in cash, which was put into a newly-opened business bank account. The cash introduced will appear in a separate *cash at bank* account. It represents an increase in an asset and so will be shown on the debit (left-hand) side of the account as follows:

Cash at bank

	£		£
1 January Equity	5,000		

The corresponding entry, which reflects the introduction of equity by the owner, will appear in a separate *equity* account. It represents an increase in equity and so will be shown on the credit (right-hand) side as follows:

Equity

	£		£
		1 January Cash at bank	5,000

It is usual to show, in each account by way of note, where the other side of the entry can be found. Thus, someone looking at the equity account will know that the £5,000 arose from an introduction of cash. This provides potentially useful information, partly because it establishes a 'trail' that can be followed when checking for errors. By including the date of the transaction, additional information is provided to the reader of the accounts.

Now suppose that, on 2 January, £600 of the cash in the bank is used to buy inventories. This would affect the *cash at bank* account as follows:

Cash at bank

	£		£
1 January Equity	5,000	2 January Inventories	600

This account, in effect, shows 'positive' cash of £5,000 and 'negative' cash of £600 a net amount of £4,400.

Activity A.2

As you know, we must record the other side of the transaction involving the acquisition of the inventories for £600. See if you can work out what to do in respect of the inventories and then record the transaction.

We must open a separate account for *inventories.* Since inventories are assets, an increase in it will appear on the debit (left-hand) side of the account, as follows:

Inventories

	£		£
2 January Cash at bank	600		

What we have seen so far highlights the key rule of double-entry bookkeeping: each left-hand entry must have a right-hand entry of equal size. Using the jargon, we can say that:

Every debit must have a credit.

It might be helpful at this point to make it absolutely clear that the words 'debit' and 'credit' are no more than accounting jargon for left and right, respectively. When used outside the context of accounting, people tend to use the word 'credit' to imply something good and 'debit' something undesirable. When used in accounting, however, the words 'debit' and 'credit' have no such implication. Each transaction requires both a debit entry and a credit entry. This is true whether the transaction is 'good', like receiving cash from a credit customer, or 'bad', like having to treat a credit customer's balance as worthless because the customer has gone bankrupt.

Recording trading transactions

The rules of double entry also extend to 'trading' transactions, which involve making revenues (sales and so on) and incurring expenses. To understand how these transactions are recorded, we should recall that in Chapter 3 the extended accounting equation was set out as follows:

$$\text{Assets} = \text{Equity} + (\text{Revenues} - \text{Expenses}) + \text{Liabilities}$$

This equation can be rearranged as follows:

$$\text{Assets} + \text{Expenses} = \text{Equity} + \text{Revenues} + \text{Liabilities}$$

We can see that increases in expenses are shown on the same side as assets. This means that they will be dealt with in the same way for recording purposes. Thus, an increase in an expense, such as wages, will be shown on the debit (left-hand) side of the *wages* account and a decrease will be shown on the credit (right-hand) side. Increases in revenues are shown on the same side as equity and liabilities and so will be dealt with in the same way. Thus, an increase in revenues, such as sales, will be shown on the credit (right-hand) side of the *sales revenue* account and a decrease will be shown on the debit (left-hand) side.

To summarise, therefore, we can say that:

- Debits (left-hand entries) represent increases in assets and expenses and decreases in equity, liabilities and revenues.
- Credits (right-hand entries) represent increases in equity, liabilities and revenues and decreases in assets and expenses.

Let us continue with our example by assuming that, on 3 January, the business paid £900 to rent business premises for the three months to 31 March. To record this transaction, we should normally open a *rent* account and make entries in this account and in the *cash at bank* account as follows:

Rent			
	£		£
3 January Cash at bank	900		

Cash at bank

	£		£
1 January Equity	5,000	2 January Inventories	600
		3 January Rent	900

The fact that assets and expenses are dealt with in the same way should not be altogether surprising as assets and expenses are closely linked. Most assets transform into expenses as they are 'used up'. Rent which, as here, is usually paid in advance is an asset when it is first paid. It represents the value to the business of being entitled to occupy the premises for the forthcoming period (until 31 March in this case). As the three months progress, this asset becomes an expense; it is 'used up'. The debit entry in the rent account does not necessarily represent either an asset or an expense; it could be a mixture of the two. Strictly, by the end of the day on which it was paid (3 January), £30 would have represented an expense for the three days; the remaining £870 would have been an asset. As each day passes, an additional £10 (that is, £900/90 (there are 90 days in January, February and March altogether)) will transform from an asset into an expense. As we have already seen, it is not necessary for us to make any adjustment to the rent account as the days pass.

Now let us assume that, on 5 January, the business sold inventories costing £200 for £300 on credit. When we can identify the cost of the inventories sold at the time of sale, we should deal with the sale and the cost of sales separately, with each having its own debits and credits.

First, let us deal with the sale. We need to open separate accounts for both sales revenue and trade receivables – which do not, as yet, exist.

Activity A.3

Can you work out what to do in respect of the sale? Show the entries in the relevant accounts.

The sale gives rise to an increase in revenue and so there is a credit entry in the *sales revenue* account. The sale also creates an asset of trade receivables and so there is debit entry in the *trade receivables* account.

The two accounts will, therefore, be as follows:

Sales revenue

	£		£
		5 January Trade receivables	300

Trade receivables

	£		£
5 January Sales revenue	300		

Let us now deal with the inventories sold. Since they have become the expense 'cost of sales', we need to reduce the figure on the inventories account by making a credit entry. We must also make a corresponding debit in a *cost of sales* account, opened for the purpose:

Inventories

	£		£
2 January Cash at bank	600	5 January Cost of sales	200

Cost of sales

	£		£
5 January Inventories	200		

We shall now look at other transactions for our hypothetical business for the remainder of January. They are as follows:

8 January	Bought some inventories on credit costing £800
11 January	Bought some office furniture for £600 cash
15 January	Sold inventories costing £600 for £900, on credit
18 January	Received £800 from trade receivables
21 January	Paid trade payables £500
24 January	Paid wages for the month £400
27 January	Bought inventories on credit for £800
31 January	Borrowed £2,000 from the Commercial Finance Company

We have to open several additional accounts to enable us to record all of these transactions. By the end of January, the set of accounts would appear as follows:

Cash at bank

	£		£
1 January Equity	5,000	2 January Inventories	600
18 January Trade receivables	800	3 January Rent	900
31 January Borrowings	2,000	11 January Office furniture	600
		21 January Trade payables	500
		24 January Wages	400

Equity

	£		£
		1 January Cash at bank	5,000

Inventories

	£		£
2 January Cash at bank	600	5 January Cost of sales	200
8 January Trade payables	800	15 January Cost of sales	600
27 January Trade payables	800		

Rent

	£		£
3 January Cash at bank	900		

Sales revenue

	£		£
		5 January Trade receivables	300
		15 January Trade receivables	900

Trade receivables

	£		£
5 January Sales revenue	300	18 January Cash at bank	800
15 January Sales revenue	900		

Cost of sales

	£		£
5 January Inventories	200		
15 January Inventories	600		

Trade payables

	£		£
21 January Cash at bank	500	8 January Inventories	800
		27 January Inventories	800

Office furniture

	£		£
11 January Cash at bank	600		

Wages

	£		£
24 January Cash at bank	400		

Borrowings

	£		£
		31 January Cash at bank	2,000

All of the transactions from 8 January onwards are similar to those up to that date, which have been discussed in detail. We should, therefore, be able to follow them using the date references as our guide.

Balancing accounts and the trial balance

Businesses keeping their accounts in the way that we have been following find it helpful to summarise their individual accounts periodically – perhaps weekly or monthly – for two reasons:

- to see at a glance how much is in each account (for example, to see how much cash the business has left); and
- to check the accuracy of the bookkeeping so far.

Let us look at the *cash at bank* account again:

Cash at bank

	£		£
1 January Equity	5,000	2 January Inventories	600
18 January Trade receivables	800	3 January Rent	900
31 January Borrowings	2,000	11 January Office furniture	600
		21 January Trade payables	500
		24 January Wages	400

Does this account tell us how much cash the business has at 31 January? The answer is partly yes and partly no.

We do not have a single figure showing the cash at bank **balance**, but we can easily deduce this by adding up the debit (receipts) column and deducting the sum of the credit (payments) column. It would be better, however, if the current balance were clearly shown.

To summarise, or *balance*, this account, we simply add up the column with the larger amount (in this case, the debit side) and put this total on both sides of the account. We then record, on the credit side (in this case), the figure that will make that side add up to the total appearing on both sides of the account. We cannot record this balancing figure just once, as that would contravene the double-entry rule. Thus, to preserve the double entry, we must also *carry down* this figure. This involves putting it on the other side of the same account below the totals, as follows:

Cash at bank

	£		£
1 January Equity	5,000	2 January Inventories	600
18 January Trade receivables	800	3 January Rent	900
31 January Borrowings	2,000	11 January Office furniture	600
		21 January Trade payables	500
		24 January Wages	400
		31 January Balance carried down	4,800
	7,800		7,800
1 February Balance brought down	4,800		

Note that the *balance carried down* (usually abbreviated to 'c/d') at the end of one period becomes the *balance brought down* ('b/d') at the beginning of the next. We can now see at a glance what the cash position is, without having to do any mental arithmetic.

Activity **A.4**

Try balancing the inventories account and then state what we know about the inventories position at the end of January.

The inventories account will be balanced as follows:

Inventories

	£		£
2 January Cash at bank	600	5 January Cost of sales	200
8 January Trade payables	800	15 January Cost of sales	600
27 January Trade payables	800	31 January Balance c/d	1,400
	2,200		2,200
1 February Balance b/d	1,400		

We can see that the business held inventories costing £1,400 at the end of January. We can also see the movements in inventories during January leading to this figure.

The remaining accounts can be balanced in a similar way. However, we need not balance accounts that have only one entry (for example, the equity account for our business at this point). This is because they are already in as summarised a form as possible. Following the balancing process, the remaining accounts will appear as shown below:

Equity

	£		£
		1 January Cash at bank	5,000

Rent

	£		£
3 January Cash at bank	900		

Sales revenue

	£		£
		5 January Trade receivables	300
31 January Balance c/d	1,200	15 January Trade receivables	900
	1,200		1,200
		1 February Balance b/d	1,200

Trade receivables

	£		£
5 January Sales revenue	300	18 January Cash at bank	800
15 January Sales revenue	900	31 January Balance c/d	400
	1,200		1,200
1 February Balance b/d	400		

Cost of sales

	£		£
5 January Inventories	200	31 January Balance c/d	800
15 January Inventories	600		
	800		800
1 February Balance b/d	800		

Trade payables

	£		£
21 January Cash at bank	500	8 January Inventories	800
31 January Balance c/d	1,100	27 January Inventories	800
	1,600		1,600
		1 February Balance b/d	1,100

Office furniture

	£		£
11 January Cash at bank	600		

Wages

	£		£
24 January Cash at bank	400		

Borrowings

	£		£
		31 January Cash at bank	2,000

Activity A.5

If we now make a list of all the accounts, showing each one's balance, and separately total the debit balances and the credit balances, what should we expect to find and why?

We should expect to find that these two totals are equal. This must, in theory, be true since every debit entry was matched by an opposite and equal-sized credit entry.

Let us see if our expectation in Activity A.5 works in our example, by listing the debit and credit balances in separate columns as follows:

	Debits	Credits
	£	£
Cash at bank	4,800	
Inventories	1,400	
Equity		5,000
Rent	900	
Sales revenue		1,200
Trade receivables	400	
Cost of sales	800	
Trade payables		1,100
Office furniture	600	
Wages	400	
Borrowings		2,000
	9,300	9,300

This listing is known as a **trial balance**. The fact that the totals for each column agree provides *some* indication that we have not made any recording, or bookkeeping, errors.

We cannot, however, have total confidence that there are no errors. Consider, for example, the transaction that took place on 3 January (paid rent for the month of £900). In each of the following cases, all of which are an incorrect treatment of the transaction, the trial balance would still have agreed:

- The transaction was completely omitted from the accounts, that is, no entries were made at all.
- The amount was misread as £9,000 but then (correctly) debited to the rent account and credited to cash at bank.
- The correct amount of £900 was (incorrectly) debited to cash at bank and credited to rent.

Nevertheless, a trial balance, where the totals agree, provides some assurance that the accounts have been correctly recorded.

Activity (A.6)

Why do you think the words 'debtor' and 'creditor' are used to describe those who owe money or are owed money by a business?

The answer simply is that debtors have a debit balance (that is, a balance brought down on the debit side) in the books of the business, whereas creditors have a credit balance.

Preparing the financial statements (final accounts)

Providing the trial balance totals agree and we are not aware of any errors in recording, the next stage is to prepare the income statement and statement of financial position. Preparing the income statement is simply a matter of going through the individual accounts, identifying those amounts that represent revenues and expenses of the period, and transferring them to the income statement, which is itself part of the double-entry system.

We shall now do this for the example that we have been using. The situation is complicated slightly for three reasons:

- As we know, the £900 rent paid during January relates to the three months January, February and March.
- The business's owner estimates that the electricity used during January is about £110. There is no bill yet from the electricity supply business because it normally bills customers only at the end of each three-month period.
- The business's owner believes that the office furniture should be depreciated by 20 per cent each year (straight-line).

These complications will require end-of-period adjustments to be made. This is easily handled, however, in the double-entry accounts. Let us see how it is done.

After completing the transfer to the income statement, the rent account will appear as follows:

Rent

	£		£
3 January Cash at bank	900	31 January Income statement	300
		Balance c/d	600
	900		900
1 February Balance b/d	600		

At 31 January, two months' rent is still unused and so £600 will be an asset of the business. This amount, which is carried down as a debit balance, will appear in the 31 January statement of financial position. The remaining £300 (representing January's rent) is an expense for the period. It is credited to the rent account and debited to a newly-opened income statement.

Let us now look at the electricity adjustment. After the transfer to the income statement, the electricity account will be as follows:

Electricity

	£		£
		31 January Income statement	110

As there has been no cash payment or other transaction recorded so far for electricity, an account has not yet been opened. It is, therefore, necessary to open one. We must debit the income statement with the £110 of electricity used during January and credit the electricity account with the same amount. At 31 January, this credit balance reflects the amount owed by this business to the electricity supplier. This balance will, once again, appear on the statement of financial position.

Finally, let us look at the adjustment required regarding the office furniture. The depreciation for the month will be $20\% \times £600 \times \frac{1}{12}$, that is £10. Normal accounting practice is to charge (debit) this to the income statement, with the corresponding credit appearing in a *Depreciation of office furniture* account. The latter entry will be as follows:

Depreciation of office furniture account

	£		£
		31 January Income statement	10

This £10 balance will be shown in the statement of financial position at 31 January. It is deducted from the office furniture asset, as we shall see shortly.

The balances on the following accounts represent straightforward revenue and expenses for the month of January:

- Sales revenue
- Cost of sales
- Wages.

The balances on these accounts will simply be transferred to the income statement.

To transfer balances to the income statement, we simply debit or credit the account concerned, such that any balance amount is eliminated, and make the corresponding credit or debit in the income statement. Take sales revenue, for example. The sales revenue account has a credit balance (because the balance represents a revenue). We must debit this account with £1,200 and credit the income statement with the same amount. So a credit balance on the sales revenue account becomes a credit entry in the income statement. For the three accounts, then, we have the following:

Sales revenue

	£		£
31 January Balance c/d	1,200	5 January Trade receivables	300
		15 January Trade receivables	900
	1,200		1,200
31 January Income statement	1,200	1 February Balance b/d	1,200

Cost of sales

	£		£
5 January Inventories	200		
15 January Inventories	600	31 January Balance c/d	800
	800		800
1 February Balance b/d	800	31 January Income statement	800

Wages

	£		£
24 January Cash at bank	400	31 January Income statement	400

The income statement will now be as follows:

Income statement

	£		£
31 January Cost of sales	800	31 January Sales revenue	1,200
31 January Rent	300		
31 January Wages	400		
31 January Electricity	110		
31 January Depreciation	10		

We must now transfer the balance on the income statement (a debit balance of £420).

Activity A.7

What does the balance on the income statement represent and to where should it be transferred?

The balance is either the profit or the loss for the period. In this case, it is a loss as the total expenses exceed the total revenue. This loss must be borne by the owner, and it must therefore be transferred to the equity account.

The two accounts will now appear as follows:

Income statement

	£		£
31 January Cost of sales	800	31 January Sales revenue	1,200
31 January Rent	300		
31 January Wages	400		
31 January Electricity	110		
31 January Depreciation	10	31 January Equity (loss)	420
	1,620		1,620

Equity

	£		£
31 January Income statement (loss)	420	1 January Cash at bank	5,000
31 January Balance c/d	4,580		
	5,000		5,000
		1 February Balance b/d	4,580

The final recording entry was to balance the equity account.

Now all of the balances remaining on accounts represent either assets or claims as at 31 January. These balances can now be used to produce a statement of financial position, as follows:

Statement of financial position as at 31 January

	£
ASSETS	
Non-current assets	
Property, plant and equipment	
Office furniture – cost	600
– depreciation	(10)
	590
Current assets	
Inventories	1,400
Prepaid expense	600
Trade receivables	400
Cash at bank	4,800
	7,200
Total assets	7,790
EQUITY AND LIABILITIES	
Owners' equity	4,580
Non-current liability	
Borrowings	2,000
Current liabilities	
Accrued expense	110
Trade payables	1,100
	1,210
Total equity and liabilities	7,790

The income statement could be written in a more stylish manner, for reporting to users, as follows:

Income statement for the month ended 31 January

	£
Sales revenue	1,200
Cost of sales	(800)
Gross profit	400
Rent	(300)
Wages	(400)
Electricity	(110)
Depreciation	(10)
Loss for the month	(420)

The ledger and its division

The book in which the accounts are traditionally kept is known as the **ledger**, and accounts are sometimes referred to as *ledger accounts*.

The ledger is often divided into separate sections. This is for three main reasons:

- Having all of the accounts in one book means that it is only possible for one person at a time to use the accounts, either to make entries or to extract information.
- It can allow specialisation, thereby allowing individual members of the accounts staff to focus on their own part of the system. This can lead to more accurate and efficient record keeping.
- It can lead to greater security, and so reduce the risk of fraud.

Activity A.8

Can you think how dividing the ledger into various sections could reduce the risk of fraud?

A different member of staff can be responsible for writing up each section so that no one has access to the entire set of accounts. It then becomes much more difficult to conceal irregular transactions. A withdrawal of cash, for example, could be recorded in one section with the corresponding entry appearing in another section of the ledger.

There are no universally accepted rules on the division of the ledger, but the following division is fairly common:

- *The cash book.* This tends to be all of the accounts relating to cash either loose (often known as *petty cash*) or in the bank.
- *The sales (or trade receivables) ledger.* This contains the accounts of all of the business's individual trade receivables.
- *The purchases (or trade payables) ledger.* This consists of the accounts of all of the business's individual trade payables.
- *The nominal ledger.* These accounts tend to be those of expenses and revenue, for example, sales revenue, purchases, wages, rent and so on.
- *The general ledger.* This contains the remainder of the business's accounts, mainly those to do with non-current assets and long-term finance.

Summary

The main points in this appendix may be summarised as follows:

Double-entry bookkeeping

- Double-entry bookkeeping is a system for keeping accounting records by hand, such that a relatively large volume of transactions can be handled effectively and accurately.
- There is a separate account for each item of asset, claim, expense and revenue.
- Each account is T-shaped.
- Left-hand (debit) side of the account records increases in assets and expenses and decreases in revenues, equity and liabilities.
- Right-hand (credit) side records increases in revenues, equity and liabilities and decreases in assets and expenses.

- There is an equal credit entry in one account for a debit entry in another.
- Double-entry bookkeeping is used to record day-to-day transactions.

Double-entry bookkeeping and financial statements

- Double-entry bookkeeping can be used to generate the income statement.
- The statement of financial position is a list of the of the accounts on which there is a net figure, or balance, after appropriate transfers have been made to the income statement.

Ledgers

- The accounts are traditionally kept in a *ledger,* a term that persists even with computerised accounting.
- The ledger is often broken down into separate sections, each containing particular types of account.

Key terms

For definitions of these terms, see Appendix B.

double-entry bookkeeping   *p. 730*
account   *p. 730*

debit   *p. 730*
credit   *p. 730*
balance   *p. 736*
trial balance   *p. 738*
ledger   *p. 742*

Further reading

If you would like to explore the topics covered in this appendix in more depth, we recommend the following:

Benedict, A. and Elliott, B. (2001) *Practical Accounting,* Financial Times Prentice Hall, 2nd edn, Chapters 2–5.

Fardon, M. (2013) *Computer Accounting Systems Tutorial,* Osborne Books, Chapters 1–12.

Thomas, A. and Ward, A. M. (2015) *Introduction to Financial Accounting,* 8th edn, McGraw-Hill, Chapters 7–10.

Wood, F. and Robinson, S. (2013) *Book-keeping and Accounts,* 8th edn, Pearson, Chapters 2–8.

Exercises

The solutions to all three of these exercises can be found at the back of the book on pp. 844–850.

A.1 In respect of each of the following transactions, state in which two accounts an entry must be made and whether the entry is a debit or a credit. (For example, if the transaction were buying inventories for cash, the answer would be debit the inventories account and credit the cash at bank account.)

(a) Bought inventories on credit.
(b) Owner made cash drawings.
(c) Paid interest on business borrowings.
(d) Bought inventories for cash.
(e) Received cash from a credit customer.
(f) Paid wages to employees.
(g) The owner received some cash from a credit customer, which was taken as drawings rather than being paid into the business's bank account.
(h) Paid a credit supplier.
(i) Paid electricity bill.
(j) Made cash sales.

A.2 (a) Record the following transactions in a set of double-entry accounts:

1 February	Lee (the owner) put £6,000 into a newly-opened business bank account to start a new business
3 February	Bought inventories for £2,600 for cash
5 February	Bought some equipment (non-current asset) for cash for £800
6 February	Bought inventories costing £3,000 on credit
9 February	Paid rent for the month of £250
10 February	Paid fuel and electricity for the month of £240
11 February	Paid general expenses of £200
15 February	Sold inventories for £4,000 in cash; the inventories had cost £2,400
19 February	Sold inventories for £3,800 on credit; the inventories had cost £2,300
21 February	Lee withdrew £1,000 in cash for personal use
25 February	Paid £2,000 to trade payables
28 February	received £2,500 from trade receivables

(b) Balance the relevant accounts and prepare a trial balance (making sure that it agrees).
(c) Prepare an income statement for the month and a statement of financial position at the month-end. Assume that there are no prepaid or accrued expenses at the end of the month and ignore any possible depreciation.

A.3 The following is the statement of financial position of David's business at 1 January of last year.

	£	£
ASSETS		
Non-current assets		
Property, plant and equipment		
Buildings		25,000
Fittings – cost	10,000	
– depreciation	(2,000)	8,000
		33,000
Current assets		
Inventories of stationery		140
Trading inventories		1,350
Prepaid rent		500
Trade receivables		1,840
Cash at bank		2,180
		6,010
Total assets		39,010
EQUITY AND LIABILITIES		
Owners' equity		25,050
Non-current liability		
Borrowings		12,000
Current liabilities		
Trade payables		1,690
Accrued electricity		270
		1,960
Total equity and liabilities		39,010

The following is a summary of the transactions that took place during the year:

1 Inventories were bought on credit for £17,220.
2 Inventories were bought for £3,760 cash.
3 Credit sales revenue amounted to £33,100 (cost £15,220).
4 Cash sales revenue amounted to £10,360 (cost £4,900).
5 Wages of £3,770 were paid.
6 Rent of £3,000 was paid. The annual rental amounts to £3,000.
7 Electricity of £1,070 was paid.
8 General expenses of £580 were paid.
9 Additional fittings were purchased on 1 January for £2,000. The cash for this was raised from additional borrowings of this amount. The interest rate is 10 per cent a year, the same as for the existing borrowings.
10 £1,000 of the borrowing was repaid on 30 June.
11 Cash received from trade receivables amounted to £32,810.
12 Cash paid to trade payables amounted to £18,150.
13 The owner withdrew £10,400 cash and £560 inventories for private use.

At the end of the year:

● The electricity bill for the last quarter of the year for £290 had not been paid.
● Trade receivables amounting to £260 were unlikely to be received.

- The value of stationery remaining was estimated at £150. Stationery is included in general expenses.
- The borrowings carried interest of 10 per cent a year and were unpaid at the year-end.
- Depreciation is to be taken at 20 per cent on the cost of the fittings owned at the year end. Buildings are not depreciated.

Required:

(a) Open ledger accounts and bring down all of the balances in the opening statement of financial position.

(b) Make entries to record the transactions 1 to 13 (above), opening any additional accounts as necessary.

(c) Open an income statement (part of the double-entry process, remember). Make the necessary entries for the bulleted list above and the appropriate transfers to the income statement.

(d) List the remaining balances in the same form as the opening statement of financial position (above).

APPENDIX B

Glossary of key terms

ABC system of inventories control A method of applying different levels of inventories control, based on the value of each category of inventories. *p. 684*

Absorption costing (or full costing) Deducing the total direct and indirect (overhead) costs of pursuing some activity or objective, in which a appropriate share of the total manufacturing/service provision overhead cost is included. *p. 373*

Account A section of a double-entry bookkeeping system that deals with one particular asset, claim, expense or revenue. *p. 730*

Accounting The process of identifying, measuring and communicating information to permit informed judgements and decisions by users of the information. *p. 2*

Accounting convention One of the generally accepted rules that accountants tend to follow when preparing financial statements. These have evolved over time to deal with practical problems rather than to reflect some theoretical ideal. *p. 60*

Accounting information system The system used within a business to identify, record, analyse and report accounting information. *p. 12*

Accounting rate of return (ARR) The average profit from an investment, expressed as a percentage of the average investment made. *p. 567*

Accruals accounting The system of accounting that follows the accruals convention. This is the system followed in drawing up the statement of financial position and the income statement. *p. 94*

Accruals convention The convention of accounting that asserts that profit is the excess of revenue over expenses, not the excess of cash receipts over cash payments. *p. 94*

Accrued expense An expenses that is outstanding (unpaid) at the end of a reporting period. *p. 91*

Acid test ratio A liquidity ratio that relates the liquid assets (usually defined as current assets less inventories) to the current liabilities. *p. 258*

Activity-based budgeting (ABB) A system of budgeting based on the philosophy of activity-based costing (ABC). *p. 497*

Activity-based costing (ABC) A technique for relating overheads to specific production or provision of a service. It is based on acceptance of the fact that overheads do not just occur but are caused by activities, such as holding products in stores, which 'drive' the costs. *p. 420*

Adverse variance A difference between planned and actual performance, usually where the difference will cause the actual profit to be lower than the budgeted profit. *p. 523*

Ageing schedule of trade receivables A report analysing receivables into categories, according to the length of time outstanding. *p. 699*

Allotted share capital *See* Issued share capital. *p. 138*

Allowance for trade receivables An amount set aside out of profit to provide for anticipated losses arising from debts (trade receivables) that may prove irrecoverable. *p. 113*

Alternative Investment Market (AIM) A stock market for the shares of smaller businesses. AIM is a junior market to the main London Stock Exchange market. It is cheaper for a business to enter and has a lighter regulatory regime. *p. 656*

Amortisation A measure of that portion of the cost (or fair value) of a non-current asset that has been consumed during a reporting period. The word 'amortisation' tends to be used where the particular non-current asset is an intangible one, whereas 'depreciation' is normally used with tangible assets. *p. 95*

Assets Resources held by a business that have certain characteristics, such as the potential to provide economic benefits. *p. 44*

Asset-based finance A form of finance where assets are used as security for cash advances to the business. Factoring and invoice discounting, where the security is trade receivables, are examples of asset-based financing. *p. 641*

Auditors Professionals whose main duty is to make a report to shareholders as to whether, in their opinion, the financial statements of a company show a true and fair view of performance and position and comply with statutory and financial reporting standard requirements. *p. 178*

AVCO *See* Weighted average cost. *p. 106*

Average inventories turnover period ratio An efficiency ratio that measures the average period for which inventories are held by a business. *p. 250*

Average settlement period for trade payables ratio An efficiency ratio that measures the average time taken for a business to pay its trade payables. *p. 252*

Average settlement period for trade receivables ratio An efficiency ratio that measures the average time taken for trade receivables to pay the amounts owing. *p. 251*

Bad debt An amount owed to the business that is considered to be irrecoverable. *p. 111*

Balance The net of the debit and credit totals in an account in a double-entry bookkeeping system. *p. 736*

Balanced scorecard A framework for translating the aims and objectives of a business into a series of key performance measures and targets. *p. 446*

Bank overdraft A flexible form of borrowing that allows an individual or business to have a negative current account balance. *p. 637*

Batch costing A technique for identifying full cost, where the production of many types of goods and services, particularly goods, involves producing a batch of identical or nearly identical units of output, but where each batch is distinctly different from other batches. *p. 396*

Behavioural aspects of budgetary control The effect on people's behaviour of the various aspects of using budgets as the basis for planning and controlling a business. *p. 552*

Benchmarking Identifying a successful business, or part of a business, and measuring the effectiveness of one's own business by comparison with this standard. *p. 438*

Benefit That outcome, resulting from a course of action, that helps a business to achieve its objectives. *p. 298*

Bond *See* Loan note. *p. 626.*

Bonus share Reserve that is converted into shares and issued 'free' to existing shareholders. *p. 136*

Break-even analysis The activity of deducing the break-even point of some activity by analysing the relationship between cost, volume and revenue. *p. 330*

Break-even chart A graphical representation of the cost and sales revenue of some activity, at various levels, that enables the break-even point to be identified. *p. 331*

Break-even point (BEP) A level of activity where revenue will exactly equal total cost, so there is neither profit nor loss. *p. 331*

Budget A financial plan for the short term, typically one year or less. *p. 472*

Budget committee A group of managers formed to supervise and take responsibility for the budget-setting process. *p. 483*

Budget holder An individual responsible for a particular budget. *p. 487*

Budget officer An individual, often an accountant, who is responsible for carrying out the technical tasks of the budget committee. *p. 483*

Budgetary control Using the budget as a yardstick against which the effectiveness of actual performance may be assessed. *p. 549*

Business angel An individual who supplies finance (usually equity finance) to start-up businesses or small businesses wishing to expand. Usually the amount of finance supplied falls between £10,000 and £750,000. *p. 659*

Business cycle The business cycle refers to the contraction and expansion in activity arising within an economy over time. *p. 345*

Business entity convention The convention that holds that, for accounting purposes, the business and its owner(s) are treated as quite separate and distinct. *p. 60*

Called-up share capital That part of a company's share capital for which the shareholders have been asked to pay the agreed amount. It is part of the claim of the owners against the business. *p. 138*

Capital rationing Where the amount of funds committed is insufficient for the investment opportunities available and decisions have to be made concerning the most profitable use of those funds. *p. 599*

Capital reserve A reserve that arise from an unrealised 'capital' profits or gains, or as a result of issuing new shares at a price above their nominal value, rather than from normal realised trading activities. *p. 134*

Carrying amount The difference between the cost (or fair value) of a non-current asset and the accumulated depreciation relating to the asset. The carrying amount is also referred to as the written-down value and the net book value. *p. 98*

Cash discount A reduction in the amount due for goods or services sold on credit in return for prompt payment. *p. 696*

Cash generated from operations (CGO) per ordinary share ratio An investment ratio that relates the cash generated from operations and available to ordinary shareholders to the number of ordinary shares. *p. 269*

Cash generated from operations (CGO) to maturing obligations ratio A liquidity ratio that compares the cash generated from operations to the current liabilities of the business. *p. 259*

Claims Obligations on the part of a business to provide cash or some other benefit to outside parties. *p. 44*

Committed cost A cost incurred that has not yet been paid, but which must, under some existing contract or obligation, be paid. *p. 303*

Comparability The quality that helps users to identify similarities and differences between items of information. It enhances the usefulness of accounting information. *p. 8*

Compensating variances The situation where two linked variances, one adverse and the other favourable, are of equal size, and therefore cancel each other out. *p. 540*

Conceptual framework The main concepts, or principles, that underpin accounting, which can help in identifying best practice and in developing accounting rules. *p. 175*

Consistency convention The accounting convention that holds that, when a particular method of accounting is selected to deal with a transaction, this method should be applied consistently over time. *p. 111*

Consolidated financial statements *See* Group financial statements. *p. 148*

Consolidating Changing the nominal value of shares to a higher figure (from, say, £0.50 to £1.00) and then reducing the number of shares in issue so that each shareholder has the same total nominal value of shares as before. *p. 133*

Continual budget A budget that is continually being updated so that there is always a budget for a full planning period. (Also known as a 'rolling budget'.) *p. 475*

Contribution margin ratio The contribution from an activity expressed as a percentage of the sales revenue. *p. 336*

Contribution per unit Sales revenue per unit less variable cost per unit. *p. 336*

Control Compelling events to conform to plan. *p. 480*

Convertible loan note A loan note that give investors the right to convert it into ordinary shares at a specified price and a given future date (or range of dates). *p. 628*

Corporate governance Matters concerned with directing and controlling a company. *p. 183*

Corporate governance statement A statement normally contained within the annual financial reports of a public listed company that describes various aspects of how the business is directed and controlled. The statement will include various matters such as a description of how the board operates, the names of senior directors and a description of key board committees. *p. 186*

Corporation tax Taxation that a limited company is liable to pay on its profits. *p. 129*

Cost An amount of resources, usually measured in monetary terms, sacrificed to achieve a particular objective. *p. 298*

Cost allocation Assigning cost to cost centres according to the amount of cost that has been incurred in each centre. *p. 388*

Cost apportionment Dividing cost between cost centres on a basis that is considered to reflect fairly the cost incurred in each centre. *p. 388*

Cost behaviour The manner in which cost alters with changes in the level of activity. *p. 375*

Cost–benefit analysis Methodically weighing the cost of pursuing some objective against the benefits that it likely to generate to enable a decision to be made as to whether to proceed. *p. 298*

Cost centre Some area, object, person or activity for which elements of cost are separately collected. *p. 386*

Cost driver An activity that cause cost. *p. 421*

Cost of capital The cost to a business of finance needed to fund its investments. *p. 583*

Cost of sales The cost of the goods sold during a period. Cost of sales can be derived by adding the opening inventories held to the inventories purchases for the period and then deducting the closing inventories held. *p. 82*

Cost-plus pricing An approach to pricing output that is based on full cost plus a percentage profit loading. *p. 383*

Cost pool The sum of the overhead costs that are seen as being caused by the same cost driver. *p. 421*

Cost unit The objective for which the cost is being deduced, usually a product or service. *p. 368*

Creative accounting Adopting accounting policies to achieve a particular view of performance and position that preparers would like users to see rather than what is a true and fair view. *p. 190*

Credit An entry made in the right-hand side of an account in double-entry bookkeeping. *p. 730*

Crowdfunding Raising equity funds, typically by small businesses, from a large number of investors often with each investor providing a relatively small sum. A commercial crowdfunding platform usually provides an internet interface between potential investors and the business. *p. 659*

Current asset An asset that is held for the short term. This includes cash itself and other assets that are held for sale or consumption in the normal course of a business's operating cycle. *p. 54*

Current liability A liability that is expected to be settled within the normal course of the business's operating cycle or within 12 months of the statement of financial position date, or which are held primarily for trading purposes, or for which the business does not have the right to defer settlement beyond 12 months of the statement of financial position date. *p. 56*

Current ratio A liquidity ratio that relates the current assets of the business to the current liabilities. *p. 258*

Debenture *See* Loan note. *p. 138*

Debit An entry made in the left-hand side of an account in double-entry bookkeeping. *p. 730*

Debt factoring A service offered by a financial institution (a factor) that involves the factor taking over the management of the trade receivables of the business. The factor is often prepared to make an advance to the business, based on the amount of trade receivables outstanding. *p. 637*

Deep discount bond A redeemable bond (loan note) offering a rate of interest below the market rate and issued at a discount to its redeemable value. *p. 628*

Depreciation A measure of that portion of the cost (or fair value) of a non-current asset that has been consumed during a reporting period. *p. 95*

Direct cost A cost that can be identified with a specific cost unit, to the extent that the effect of the cost can be measured in respect of that cost unit. *p. 372*

Direct labour efficiency variance The difference between the actual direct labour hours worked and the number of direct labour hours according to the flexed budget (budgeted direct labour hours for the actual output). This figure is multiplied by the budgeted direct labour rate for one hour. *p. 528*

Direct labour rate variance The difference between the actual cost of the direct labour hours worked and the direct labour cost allowed (actual direct labour hours worked at the budgeted labour rate). *p. 529*

Direct materials price variance The difference between the actual cost of the direct material used and the direct materials cost allowed (actual quantity of material used at the budgeted direct material cost). *p. 527*

Direct materials usage variance The difference between the actual quantity of direct materials used and the quantity of direct materials according to the flexed budget (budgeted usage for actual output). This quantity is multiplied by the budgeted direct materials cost for one unit of the direct materials. *p. 527*

Direct method An approach to deducing the cash flows from operating activities, in a statement of cash flows, by analysing the business's cash records. *p. 213*

Director An individual appointed (normally by being elected by the shareholders) to act as part of the most senior level of management of a company (board of directors). *p. 130*

Directors' report A report containing information of a financial and non-financial nature that the directors must produce as part of the annual financial report to shareholders. *p. 187*

Discount factor The rate applied to future cash flows to derive the present value of those cash flows. *p. 581*

Discounting Applying the discount factor to a project's cash flows to take account of the time period involved and the cost of capital. It is, in effect, charging the project with the cost of financing it *p. 580*

Discretionary budget A budget based on a sum allocated at the discretion of senior management. *p. 487*

Discriminate function (in financial distress assessment) A boundary line, produced by multiple discriminate analysis, which can be used to identify those businesses that are likely to suffer financial distress and those that are not. *p. 278*

Dividend The transfer of assets (usually cash) made by a company to its shareholders. *p. 132*

Dividend cover ratio An investment ratio that relates the earnings available for dividends to the dividend announced, to indicate how many times the former covers the latter. *p. 266*

Dividend payout ratio An investment ratio that relates the dividends announced for the period to the earnings available for dividends that were generated in that period. *p. 265*

Dividend yield ratio An investment ratio that relates the cash return from a share to its current market value. *p. 266*

Double-entry bookkeeping A system for recording financial transactions where each transaction is recorded twice, once as a debit and once as a credit. *p. 730*

Dual aspect convention The accounting convention that holds that each transaction has two aspects and that each aspect must be recorded in the financial statements. *p. 63*

Earnings per share (EPS) An investment ratio that relates the earnings generated by the business during a period, and available to shareholders, to the number of shares in issue. *p. 266*

Economic order quantity (EOQ) The quantity of inventories that should be bought with each order so as to minimise the sum of inventories ordering and carrying costs. *p. 685*

Economic value added (EVA®) A measure of business performance that concentrates on wealth generation. It is based on economic profit rather than accounting profit and takes full account of the cost of financing. *p. 456*

Economies of scale Cost savings per unit that result from undertaking a large volume of activities; they are due to factors such as division and specialisation of labour and discounts from bulk buying. *p. 343*

Efficient capital market A capital market (for example, a Stock Exchange) whose prices rapidly and rationally take account of all relevant information. *p. 652*

Enterprise resource planning (ERP) system An automated and integrated approach to managing a business through a suite of software applications (modules) that record, report, analyse and interpret data for a range of business operations. These operations include production, marketing, human resources, accounting and inventories management. *p. 689*

Equity The owners' claim on the business. In the case of a limited company, it comprises the sum of shares and reserves. *p. 48*

Eurobond A form of long-term borrowing where the finance is raised on an international basis. Eurobonds are issued in a currency that is not that of the country in which the bonds are issued. *p. 627*

Expense A measure of the outflow of assets (or increase in liabilities) incurred as a result of endeavouring to generate revenue. *p. 82*

Fair value The value ascribed to an asset as an alternative to historic cost. It is usually the current market values (that is, the exchange values in an arm's-length transaction). *p. 68*

Faithful representation The ability of information to be relied on to represent what it purports to represent. This is regarded as a fundamental quality of useful accounting information. *p. 7*

Favourable variance The difference between planned and actual performance, usually where the difference will cause the actual profit to be higher than the budgeted profit. *p. 523*

Feedback control A form of control where actual performance is compared with planned performance and where action is taken to deal with any future divergences between the two. *p. 519*

Feedforward control A form of control where forecast future performance is compared with planned performance and where action is taken to deal with divergences between the two. *p. 520*

Final accounts The income statement, statement of cash flows and statement of financial position taken together. *p. 43*

Finance The study of how businesses raise funds and select appropriate investments. *p. 2*

Finance lease A financial arrangement where the asset title remains with the owner (the lessor) but the lease agreement transfers virtually all the rewards and risks to the business (the lessee). *p. 630*

Financial accounting The identification, measurement and communication of accounting information for external users (those users other than the managers of the business). *p. 14*

Financial derivative Any form of financial instrument, based on equity or borrowings, which can be used by investors either to increase their returns or to decrease their exposure to risk. *p. 629*

Financial gearing The existence of fixed-payment-bearing sources of finance (for example, borrowings) in the capital structure of a business. *p. 260*

First in, first out (FIFO) A method of inventories costing that deals with issues of inventories as if the inventories acquired earliest are used (in production or sales) first. *p. 106*

Five Cs of credit A checklist of factors to be taken into account when assessing the creditworthiness of a customer. *p. 692*

Fixed asset *See* Non-current asset. *p. 54*

Fixed charge Where specific assets are pledged as security for a loan. *p. 622*

Fixed cost A cost that stays the same when changes occur to the volume of activity. *p. 325*

Fixed interest rate An interest rate on borrowings that will remain unchanged over the period of the loan, irrespective of rises and falls in market rates of interest. *p. 630*

Fixed overhead spending variance The difference between the actual fixed overhead cost and the fixed overhead cost, according to the flexed (and the original) budget. *p. 529*

Flexible budget A budget that is adjusted to reflect the actual level of output achieved. *p. 523*

Flexing a budget Revising a budget to what it would have been had the planned level of output been different. *p. 522*

Floating charge Where the whole of a business's assets, or a group of assets, is pledged as security for a loan. The charge will fix on specific assets only if the business defaults on its obligations. *p. 622*

Floating interest rate An interest rate on borrowings that will rise and fall with market rates of interest. *p. 629*

Forecast A prediction of future outcomes or of the future state of the environment. *p. 475*

Full cost The total amount of resources, usually measured in monetary terms, sacrificed to achieve a particular objective. *p. 368*

Full costing *See* Absorption costing. *p. 368*

Fully paid share Share on which the shareholder has paid the full issue price. *p. 138*

Gearing ratio A ratio that relates long-term fixed-return finance (such as borrowings) to the total long-term finance of the business. *p. 263*

Going concern convention The accounting convention that holds that a business is assumed to continue operations for the foreseeable future, unless there is reason to believe otherwise. In other words, it is assumed that there is no intention, or need, to liquidate the business. *p. 62*

Goodwill An intangible, non-current asset that lacks a clear and separate identity. The term is often used to cover various positive attributes such as the quality of products, the skill of employees and the relationship with customers. *p. 64*

Gross profit The amount remaining (if positive) after the cost of sales has been deducted from trading revenue. *p. 84*

Gross profit margin ratio A profitability ratio that expresses the gross profit as a percentage of the sales revenue for a period. *p. 248*

Group financial statement Financial accounting statement that combines the performance, position and cash flows of a group of companies under common control. Also known as a 'consolidated financial statement'. *p. 148*

High-low method An approach to distinguishing between the fixed and variable elements of a cost by looking at just two sets of past data. *p. 329*

Hire purchase A method of acquiring an asset by paying the purchase price by instalments over a period. Normally, control of the asset will pass as soon as the hire-purchase contract is signed and the first instalment is paid, whereas ownership will pass on payment of the final instalment. *p. 633*

Historic cost What was paid for an asset when it was originally acquired. *p. 299*

Historic cost convention The accounting convention that holds that assets should be recorded at their historic (acquisition) cost. *p. 60*

Holding company *See* Parent company. *p. 148*

Ideal standard Standard that assumes perfect operating conditions where there is no inefficiency due to lost production time, defects and so on. The objective of setting ideal standards is to encourage employees to strive towards excellence. *p. 543*

Impairment loss The loss to be reported following an assessment that the value of an asset has been diminished as a result of a change in some fundamental factor relating to the asset, such as the market for the service provided by the asset suddenly collapsing. It should not be confused with depreciation (amortisation), which is concerned with routine loss of value through usage of the asset or passage of time. *p. 70*

Income statement A financial statement (also known as 'profit and loss account') that measures and reports the profit (or loss) the business has generated during a period. It is derived by deducting from total revenue for a period, the total expenses associated with that revenue. *p. 40*

Incremental budgeting Constructing budgets on the basis of what happened in the previous period, with some adjustment for expected changes in the forthcoming budget period. *p. 487*

Indirect cost (or overheads) The element of production cost (of a product or service) that cannot be directly measured in respect of a particular cost unit – that is, all production cost except direct cost. *p. 372*

Indirect method An approach to deducing the cash flows from operating activities, in a statement of cash flows, by analysing the business's other financial statements. *p. 213*

Inflation An increase in the general price of goods and services resulting in a corresponding decline in the purchasing power of money. *p. 578*

Intangible asset An asset that does not have a physical substance (for example, patents, goodwill and trade receivables). *p. 47*

Interest cover ratio A gearing ratio that divides the operating profit (that is, profit before interest and taxation) by the interest payable for a period. *p. 264*

Internal rate of return (IRR) The discount rate for an investment that will have the effect of producing a zero NPV. *p. 585*

International Accounting Standard *See* International Financial Reporting Standard. *p. 166*

International Financial Reporting Standard Transnational accounting rule that has been adopted, or developed, by the International Accounting Standards Board and which should be followed in preparing the published financial statements of listed limited companies. *p. 166*

Invoice discounting Where a financial institution provides a loan based on a proportion of the face value of a business's credit sales outstanding. *p. 639*

Irrelevant cost A cost that is not relevant to a particular decision. *p. 300*

Issued share capital That part of the share capital that has been issued to shareholders. Also known as 'allotted share capital'. *p. 138*

Job costing A technique for identifying the full cost per cost unit, where each cost unit is not identical to other cost units produced. *p. 371*

Just-in-time (JIT) inventories management A system of inventories management that aims to have supplies delivered just in time for their required use in production or sales. *p. 689*

Kaizen costing An approach to cost control where an attempt is made to control cost by trying continually to make cost savings, often only small ones, from one time period to the next during the production stage of the product life cycle. *p. 435*

Last in, first out (LIFO) A method of inventories costing that deals with inventories issues as if the most recently acquired inventories are used (in production or sales) first. *p. 106*

Lead time The time lag between placing an order for goods or services and their delivery to the required location. *p. 682*

Learning curve The curved line on a graph that represents the tendency for people to carry out tasks more quickly as they become more experienced in doing them. *p. 543*

Ledger The book in which accounts are traditionally kept. *p. 742*

Liability A claim of an individual and organisation, apart from the owner(s), that has arisen from past transactions or events, such as supplying goods or lending money to the business. *p. 48*

Limited company A form of business unit that is granted a separate legal existence from that of its owners. The owners of this type of business are liable for debts only up to the amount that they have agreed to invest. *p. 21*

Limited liability The restriction of the legal obligation of shareholders to meet all of the company's debts. *p. 126*

Limiting factor Some aspect of the business (for example, lack of sales demand) that will prevent it achieving its objectives to the maximum extent. *p. 477*

Loan covenant A conditions contained within a loan agreement that are designed to help protect the lenders. *p. 623*

Loan note Long-term borrowings usually made by limited companies. *p. 138*

Loan stock *See* Loan note. *p. 138*

Management accounting The identification, measurement and communication of accounting information for the managers of a business. *p. 14*

Management by exception A system of control, based on a comparison of planned and actual performance, that allows managers to focus on areas of poor performance rather than dealing with areas where performance is satisfactory. *p. 481*

Margin of safety The extent to which the planned level of output or sales lies above the break-even point. *p. 337*

Marginal analysis The activity of decision making through analysing variable cost and revenue, ignoring fixed cost. *p. 349*

Marginal cost The additional cost of producing one more unit. This is often the same as the variable cost. *p. 349*

Master budget A summary of individual budgets, usually consisting of a budgeted income statement, a budgeted statement of financial position and a cash budget. *p. 477*

Matching convention The accounting convention that holds that, when measuring income, expenses should be matched to revenue, which they helped generate, in the same reporting period as that in which the revenue was realised. *p. 90*

Materiality The quality of accounting information such that its omission or misrepresentation will alter the decisions that users make. The threshold of materiality will vary from one business to the next. *p. 7*

Materiality convention The accounting convention that states that, where the amounts involved are immaterial, only what is expedient should be considered. *p. 94*

Mortgage A loan secured on property. *p. 629*

Multiple discriminate analysis (MDA) A statistical technique that can be used to predict financial distress; it involves using an index based on a combination of two or more financial ratios. *p. 278*

Net book value *See* Carrying amount. *p. 98*

Net present value (NPV) A method of investment appraisal based on the present value of all relevant cash flows associated with an investment. *p. 575*

Nominal value The face value of a share in a company. Also called par value. *p. 131*

Non-controlling interest That part of the net assets of a subsidiary company that is financed by shareholders other than the parent company. (Formerly known as 'minority interest'.) *p. 149*

Non-current asset An asset held that does not meet the criteria of a current asset. They are held for the long-term operations of the business rather than continuously circulating within the business. A non-current asset can be seen as one of the tools of the business. They are also known as 'fixed assets'. *p. 54*

Non-current liability A liability of the business that is not a current liability. *p. 56*

Non-operating-profit variance A difference between budgeted and actual performance that does not lead directly to differences between budgeted and actual operating profit. *p. 537*

Offer for sale An issue of shares that involves a public limited company (or its shareholders) selling the shares to a financial institution that will, in turn, sell the shares to the public. *p. 650*

Operating cash cycle (OCC) The period between the outlay of cash to buy supplies and the ultimate receipt of cash from the sale of goods. *p. 706*

Operating gearing (operational gearing) The relationship between the total fixed and the total variable elements of cost for some activity. *p. 340*

Operating lease An arrangement where a business hires an asset, usually for a short time. Hiring an asset under an operating lease tends to be seen as an operating, rather than a financing, decision. *p. 631*

Operating profit The profit achieved during a period after all operating expenses have been deducted from revenues from operations. Financing expenses are deducted after the calculation of operating profit. *p. 84*

Operating profit margin ratio A profitability ratio that expresses the operating profit as a percentage of the sales revenue for the period. *p. 247*

Opportunity cost The cost incurred when one course of action prevents an opportunity to derive some benefit from another course of action. *p. 299*

Ordinary share A portion of ownership of a company owned by those who are due the benefits of the company's activities after all other stakeholders have been satisfied. *p. 132*

Outlay cost A cost that involves the spending of money or some other transfer of assets. *p. 300*

Outsourcing Subcontracting activities to (sourcing goods or services from) organisations outside of the business. *p. 354*

Overhead absorption (recovery) rate The rate at which overheads are charged to cost units (jobs), usually in a job costing system. *p. 377*

Overheads *See* Indirect cost. *p. 372*

Overtrading The situation arising where a business is operating at a level of activity that cannot be supported by the amount of finance that has been committed. *p. 273*

Paid-up share capital That part of the share capital of a company that has been called and paid. *p. 138*

Par value *See* Nominal value. *p. 131*

Parent company A company that has a controlling interest in another company. *p. 148*

Partnership A form of business unit where there are at least two individuals, but usually no more than 20, carrying on a business with the intention of making a profit. *p. 21*

Past cost A cost that has been incurred in the past. *p. 300*

Payback period (PP) The time taken for the initial outlay for an investment to be repaid from its future net cash inflows. *p. 571*

Peer-to-peer lending Lending where a commercial 'platform' acts as the online interface between potential borrowers and potential lenders, where the latter may each provide very small amounts of loan finance. *p. 661*

Periodic budget A budget developed on a one-off basis to cover a particular planning period. *p. 475*

Post-completion audit A review of the performance of an investment project to see whether lessons can be drawn from the way in which the project was appraised and carried out. *p. 601*

Practical standard Standard that does not assume perfect operating conditions. Although demanding a high level of efficiency, account is taken of possible lost production time, defects and so on. Designed to be challenging yet achievable. *p. 543*

Preference share A shares of a company that entitle their owners to the first part of any dividend that the company may pay. *p. 132*

Prepaid expense An expense that has been paid in advance at the end of the reporting period. *p. 93*

Price/earnings (P/E) ratio An investment ratio that relates the market value of a share to the earnings per share. *p. 269*

Private limited company A limited company for which the directors can restrict the ownership of its shares. *p. 127*

Private placing An issue of shares that involves a limited company arranging for the shares to be sold to the clients of particular issuing houses or stockbrokers, rather than to the general investing public. *p. 651*

Process costing A technique for deriving the full cost per unit of output, where the units of output are exactly similar or it is reasonable to treat them as being so. *p. 370*

Product cost centre Some area, object, person or activity for which cost is separately collected, in which cost units have cost added. *p. 387*

Profit The increase in wealth attributable to the owners of a business that arises through business operations. *p. 81*

Profit before taxation The result when all of the appropriately matched expenses of running a business have been deducted from the revenue for the year, but before the taxation charge is deducted. *p. 145*

Profit for the period The result when all of the appropriately matched expenses of running a business have been deducted from the revenue for the year and then, in the case of a limited company, the taxation charge deducted. *p. 84*

Profit–volume (PV) chart A graphical representation of the contributions (revenue less variable cost) of some activity, at various levels, which enables the break-even point, and the profit at various activity levels, to be identified. *p. 342*

Property, plant and equipment Those non-current assets that have a physical substance (for example, plant and machinery, motor vehicles). *p. 54*

Prudence convention The accounting convention that holds that caution should be exercised when making accounting judgements. It normally involves reporting actual and expected losses immediately but reporting profits when they arise. *p. 61*

Public issue An issue of shares that involves a public limited company (plc) making a direct invitation to the public to buy shares in the company. *p. 650*

Public limited company A limited company for which the directors cannot restrict the ownership of its shares. *p. 127*

Quality cost The cost of establishing procedures that promote the quality of output, either by preventing quality problems in the first place or by dealing with them when they occur. *p. 442*

Reducing-balance method A method of calculating depreciation that applies a fixed percentage rate of depreciation to the carrying amount of an asset in each period. *p. 98*

Relevance The ability of accounting information to influence decisions. Relevance is regarded as a fundamental characteristic of useful accounting information. *p. 7*

Relevant cost A cost that is relevant to a particular decision. *p. 300*

Relevant range The range of output within which a particular business is expected to operate. *p. 344*

Reporting period The time span for which a business prepares its financial statements. *p. 51*

Reserve Part of the owners' claim (equity) of a limited company that has arisen from profits and gains, to the extent that these have not been distributed to the shareholders or reduced by losses. *p. 131*

Residual value The amount for which a non-current asset is expected to be sold when the business has no further use for it. *p. 97*

Return on capital employed ratio (ROCE) A profitability ratio that expresses the operating profit (that is, profit before interest and taxation) as a percentage of the long-term funds (equity and borrowings) invested in the business. *p. 245*

Return on ordinary shareholders' funds ratio (ROSF) A profitability ratio that expresses the profit for the period available to ordinary shareholders as a percentage of the funds that they have invested. *p. 244*

Revenue A measure of the inflow of assets (for example, cash or amounts owed to a business by credit customers), or a reduction in liabilities, arising as a result of trading operations. *p. 81*

Revenue reserve Part of the owners' claim (equity) of a company that arises from realised profits and gains, including after-tax trading profits and gains from disposals of non-current assets. *p. 132*

Rights issue An issue of shares for cash to existing shareholders on the basis of the number of shares already held. *p. 647*

Risk The extent and likelihood that what is projected to occur will not actually occur. *p. 312*

Risk premium The additional return required for investing in a risky project. *p. 577*

Rolling budget *See* Continual budget. *p. 476*

Sale-and-leaseback An agreement to sell an asset (usually property) to another party and simultaneously to lease the asset back in order to continue using the asset. *p. 632*

Sales price variance The difference between the actual sales revenue figure for the period and the sales revenue figure as shown in the flexed budget. *p. 526*

Sales revenue per employee ratio An efficiency ratio that relates the sales revenue generated during a period to the number of employees of the business. *p. 254*

Sales revenue to capital employed ratio An efficiency ratio that relates the sales revenue generated during a period to the capital employed. *p. 254*

Sales volume variance The difference between the operating profit as shown in the original budget, and the operating profit as shown in the flexed budget for the period. *p. 523*

Scenario building Creating a model of a business decision, usually on a computer spreadsheet, enabling the decision maker to look at the effect of different assumptions on the decision outcome. *p. 315*

Securitisation Bundling together illiquid physical or financial assets of the same type to provide backing for issuing interest-bearing securities such as bonds. *p. 635*

Security Assets pledged or guarantees given to provide lenders with some protection against default. *p. 622*

Segmental financial reports Financial reports that break down the overall results of a business according to its different types of business operations. *p. 179*

Semi-fixed (semi-variable) cost A cost that has an element of both fixed and variable cost. *p. 328*

Sensitivity analysis An examination of the key variables affecting a decision (for example, an investment project) to see how changes in each input might influence the outcome. *p. 313*

Service cost centre Some area, object, person or activity for which cost is collected separately, in which cost units do not have cost added, because service cost centres render services, only to product cost centres and to other service cost centres. *p. 387*

Share Portion of the ownership, or equity, of a company. *p. 6*

Share premium account A capital reserve reflecting any amount, above the nominal value of shares, that is paid for those shares when they are issued by a company. *p. 135*

Sole proprietorship A form of business unit where an individual is operating a business on his or her own account. *p. 20*

Splitting Changing the nominal value of shares to a lower figure (from, say, £1.00 to £0.50) and then issuing sufficient shares so that each shareholder has the same total nominal value of shares as before. *p. 133*

Standard costing Using standard quantities and costs to derive variances. Effectively, another name for variance analysis. *p. 545*

Standard quantities and costs Planned quantities and costs (or revenue) for individual units of input or output. Standards are the building blocks used to produce the budget. *p. 541*

Statement of cash flows A statement that shows a business's sources and uses of cash for a period. *p. 40*

Statement of changes in equity A financial statement, required by IAS 1, which shows the effect of gains/losses and capital injections/withdrawals on the equity base of a company. *p. 173*

Statement of comprehensive income A financial statement that extends the conventional income statement to include other gains and losses that affect shareholders' equity. *p. 171*

Statement of financial position A statement that shows the assets of a business and the claims on those assets. It is also known as a 'balance sheet'. *p. 40*

Stepped fixed cost A fixed cost that does not remain fixed over all levels of output but which changes in steps as a threshold level of output is reached. *p. 327*

Stock Exchange A market where 'second-hand' shares may be bought and sold and new capital raised. *p. 129*

Straight-line method A method of accounting for depreciation that allocates the amount to be depreciated evenly over the useful life of the asset. *p. 97*

Strategic management Setting a course to achieve the business's objectives, taking account of the commercial and economic environment in which the business operates. *p. 26*

Strategic report A report designed to provide a fair review of the company's business. Directors of all but the smallest companies are legally obliged to produce a strategic report, which is required to be a balanced and comprehensive analysis of financial performance for the year and financial position at the end of the year. The report must also describe the principal risks and uncertainties facing the company. *p. 188*

Subordinated loan A form of loan where the lender's claim is ranked below those of other loans already in existence. *p. 624*

Sunk cost A cost that has been incurred in the past; the same as a past cost. *p. 303*

Sunk cost fallacy Pursuing a particular course of action because of the money, time and effort previously invested in it while failing to consider whether it is rational to do so. *p. 304*

Takeover The acquisition of control of one company by another, usually as a result of acquiring a majority of the ordinary shares of the former. *p. 150*

Tangible asset An asset that has a physical substance (for example, plant and machinery, motor vehicles). *p. 47*

Target costing An approach to deriving product costs where the business starts with the projected selling price and from it deduces the target cost per unit that is required for the business to meet its profit objectives. *p. 433*

Tender issue A public issue of shares or loan notes (by a public limited company) where potential investors are invited to state a bid price rather than the company setting the price for the securities. *p. 651*

Term loan Finance provided by financial institutions, for example banks and insurance companies, under a contract indicating the interest rate and date of payments of interest and repayment of the loan. *p. 626*

Timeliness The provision of accounting information in time for users to make use of it in their decision making. This quality enhances the usefulness of accounting information. *p. 8*

Total direct labour variance The difference between the actual direct labour cost and the direct labour cost according to the flexed budget (budgeted direct labour hours for the actual output). *p. 528*

Total direct materials variance The difference between the actual direct materials cost and the direct materials cost according to the flexed budget. *p. 527*

Total life-cycle costing An approach to costing that takes account of all the costs to be incurred during the entire life of a product or service. *p. 430*

Total quality management (TQM) A philosophy concerned with providing products that meet, or exceed, customers' requirements all of the time. *p. 440*

Trade payable An amount owed to a supplies from whom the business has received goods or services on credit. *p. 56*

Trade receivable An amount owed by a customer to whom the business has provided goods or services on credit. *p. 47*

Trade receivables to sales ratio Trade receivables outstanding at the end of the period divided by the sales revenue for the period. *p. 699*

Transfer price The price at which goods or services are sold, or transferred, between divisions of the same business. *p. 181*

Trial balance A totalled list of the balances on each of the accounts in a double-entry bookkeeping system. *p. 738*

UK Corporate Governance Code A code of practice for companies that are listed on the London Stock Exchange that deals with corporate governance matters. *p. 184*

Understandability The quality that enables accounting information to be understood by those for whom the information is primarily compiled. This quality enhances the usefulness of accounting information. *p. 8*

Univariate analysis A statistical technique that can be used to help predict financial distress, which involves the use of a single ratio as a predictor. *p. 277*

Value chain analysis Analysing each activity undertaken by a business to identify any that do not add value to the output of goods or services. *p. 437*

Value driver A factor that creates wealth, such as employee satisfaction, customer loyalty and the level of product innovation. *p. 445*

Variable cost A cost that varies according to the volume of activity. *p. 325*

Variable (marginal) costing An approach to costing in which only those costs that vary with the level of output are included in the product cost. *p. 404*

Variance The financial effect, usually on the budgeted profit, of the particular factor under consideration being more or less than budgeted. *p. 523*

Venture capital Long-term finance provided by certain institutions to small and medium-sized businesses in order to exploit relatively high-risk opportunities. *p. 659*

Verifiability The quality that provides assurance to users that the information provided faithfully represents what it is supposed to represent. It enhances the quality of accounting information. *p. 8*

Weighted average cost (AVCO) An approach to inventories costing which assumes that inventories entering the business lose their separate identity and any issues of inventories reflect the weighted average cost of the inventories held. *p. 106*

Working capital Current assets less current liabilities. *p. 215*

Work in progress Partially completed production of an object or service. *p. 371*

Written-down value *See* Carrying amount. *p. 98*

Zero-base budgeting (ZBB) An approach to budgeting, based on the philosophy that all spending needs to be justified annually and that each budget should start as a clean sheet. *p. 488*

APPENDIX  C

Solutions to self-assessment questions

Chapter 2

2.1 **Simonson Engineering**

(a) The statement of financial position should be set out as follows:

Simonson Engineering
Statement of financial position as at 30 September 2017

	£
ASSETS	
Non-current assets	
Property, plant and equipment	
Property	72,000
Plant and machinery	25,000
Fixtures and fittings	9,000
Motor vehicles	15,000
	121,000
Current assets	
Inventories	45,000
Trade receivables	48,000
Cash in hand	1,500
	94,500
Total assets	215,500
EQUITY AND LIABILITIES	
Equity	
Closing balance*	120,500
Non-current liabilities	
Long-term borrowings	51,000
Current liabilities	
Trade payables	18,000
Short-term borrowings	26,000
	44,000
Total equity and liabilities	215,500

*The equity is calculated as follows:

	£
Opening balance	117,500
Profit	18,000
	135,500
Drawings	(15,000)
Closing balance	120,500

(b) The statement of financial position shows:
 - The biggest investment in assets is property, followed by trade receivables and inventories. These combined account for more than 76 per cent of the value of assets held.
 - The investment in current assets accounts for 44 per cent of the total investment in assets.
 - The total long-term finance is divided 70 per cent equity and 30 per cent long-term borrowings. There is, therefore, not excessive reliance on long-term borrowings.
 - The current assets (which are cash or near cash) cover the current liabilities (which are maturing obligations) by a ratio of more than 2:1.

(c) The revised statement of position will be as follows:

Simonson Engineering
Statement of financial position as at 30 September 2017

	£
ASSETS	
Non-current assets	
Property, plant and equipment	
Property	115,000
Plant and machinery	25,000
Motor vehicles	15,000
Fixtures and fittings	9,000
	164,000
Current assets	
Inventories	38,000
Trade receivables	48,000
Cash in hand	1,500
	87,500
Total assets	251,500
EQUITY AND LIABILITIES	
Equity	
Closing balance	156,500
Non-current liabilities	
Long-term borrowings	51,000
Current liabilities	
Trade payables	18,000
Short-term borrowings	26,000
	44,000
Total equity and liabilities	251,500

Chapter 3

3.1   TT and Co.

Statement of financial position as at 31 December 2016

ASSETS	£
Delivery van (12,000 − 2,500)	9,500
inventories (143,000 + 12,000 − 74,000 − 16,000)	65,000
Trade receivables (152,000 − 132,000 − 400)	19,600
Cash at bank (50,000 − 25,000 − 500 − 1,200 − 12,000 − 33,500 − 1,650 − 12,000 + 35,000 + 132,000 − 121,000 − 9,400)	750
Prepaid expenses (5,000 + 300)	5,300
Total assets	100,150
EQUITY AND LIABILITIES	
Equity (50,000 + 26,900)	76,900
Trade payables (143,000 − 121,000)	22,000
Accrued expenses (630 + 620)	1,250
Total equity and liabilities	100,150

Income statement for the year ended 31 December 2016

	£
Sales revenue (152,000 + 35,000)	187,000
Cost of goods sold (74,000 + 16,000)	(90,000)
Gross profit	97,000
Rent	(20,000)
Rates (500 + 900)	(1,400)
Wages (33,500 + 630)	(34,130)
Electricity (1,650 + 620)	(2,270)
Bad debts	(400)
Van depreciation ((12,000 − 2,000)/4)	(2,500)
Van expenses	(9,400)
Profit for the year	26,900

The statement of financial position could now be rewritten in a more stylish form as follows:

Statement of financial position as at 31 December 2016

	£
ASSETS	
Non-current assets	
Property, plant and equipment	
Delivery van at cost	12,000
Accumulated depreciation	(2,500)
	9,500
Current assets	
Inventories	65,000
Trade receivables	19,600
Prepaid expenses	5,300
Cash	750
	90,650
Total assets	100,150
EQUITY AND LIABILITIES	
Equity	
Closing balance	76,900
Current liabilities	
Trade payables	22,000
Accrued expenses	1,250
	23,250
Total equity and liabilities	100,150

Chapter 4

4.1 Dev Ltd

(a) The summarised statement of financial position of Dev Ltd, immediately following the rights and bonus issue, is as follows:

Statement of financial position

	£000
Net assets (235 + 40 (cash from the rights issue))	275
Equity	
Share capital: 180,000 shares @ £1 ((100 + 20) + 60)	180
Share premium account (30 + 20 − 50)	–
Revaluation reserve (37 − 10)	27
Retained earnings	68
	275

Note that the bonus issue of £60,000 is taken from capital reserves (reserves unavailable for dividends) as follows:

	£000
Share premium account	50
Revaluation reserve	10
	60

More could have been taken from the revaluation reserve and less from the share premium account without making any difference to dividend payment possibilities.

(b) There may be pressure from a potential lender for the business to limit its ability to pay dividends. This would place lenders in a more secure position because the maximum buffer, or safety margin, between the value of the assets and the amount owed by the business is maintained. It is not unusual for potential lenders to insist on some measure to lock up shareholders' funds in this way as a condition of granting the loan.

(c) The summarised statement of financial position of Dev Ltd, immediately following the rights and bonus issue, assuming a minimum dividend potential objective, is as follows:

Statement of financial position

	£000
Net assets (235 + 40 (cash from the rights issue))	275
Equity	
Share capital: 180,000 shares @ £1 ((100 + 20) + 60)	180
Share premium account (30 + 20)	50
Revaluation reserve	37
Retained earnings (68 − 60)	8
	275

(d) Before the bonus issue, the maximum dividend was £68,000. Now it is £8,000. Thus the bonus issue has had the effect of locking up an additional £60,000 of the business's assets in terms of the business's ability to pay dividends.

(e) Before the issues, Lee had 100 shares worth £2.35 (£235,000/100,000) each or £235 in total. Lee would be offered 20 shares in the rights issue at £2 each or £40 in total. After the rights issue, Lee would have 120 shares worth £2.2917 (£275,000/120,000) each or £275 in total.

The bonus issue would give Lee 60 additional shares. After the bonus issue, Lee would have 180 shares worth £1.5278 (£275,000/180,000) each or £275 in total.

None of this affects Lee's wealth. Before the issues, Lee had £235 worth of shares and £40 more in cash. After the issues, Lee has the same total wealth but all £275 is in the value of shares held.

(f) The things that we know about the company are as follows:
- It is a private (as opposed to a public) limited company, for it has 'Ltd' (limited) as part of its name, rather than plc (public limited company).
- It has made an issue of shares at a premium, almost certainly after it had traded successfully for a period. (There is a share premium account. It would be unlikely that the original shares, issued when the company was first formed, would have been issued at a premium.)
- Certain of the assets in the statement of financial position have been upwardly revalued by at least £37,000. (There is a revaluation reserve of £37,000. This, however, may be what is left after a bonus issue took part of the reserve.)
- The company has traded at an aggregate profit (though there could have been losses in some years), net of tax and any dividends paid. (There is a positive balance on retained earnings.)

Chapter 5

5.1 (a) 1 Dividends paid during a reporting period *can* be shown on the face of that period's statement of changes in equity, but they can equally correctly be shown by way of a note.

2 IAS 1 provides support for three key accounting conventions – accruals, going concern and consistency. It does not specifically support the historic cost convention.

3 IAS 1 does not permit bank overdrafts to be offset against positive bank balances when preparing the statement of financial position. For the sake of relevance they should be shown separately.

(b) **Dali plc**

A striking feature of the segmental reports is that the car parts segment generates the highest revenue – more than the other two segments combined. Nevertheless, it is the aircraft parts segment that generates the highest profit. We can use some simple ratios at this point to help evaluate performance.

We can start by considering the profit generated in relation to the sales revenue for each operating segment. We can see from the table below that the boat parts segment generates the most profit in relation to sales revenue. Around 21 per cent, or £0.21 in every £1, of profit is derived from the sales revenue generated. The total revenue for this segment, however, is much lower than for the other two segments. Although the car parts segment generates the most revenue, less than 6 per cent, or £0.06 in every £1, of profit is derived from the sales revenue generated. It is worth noting that the aircraft parts segment suffered a large impairment charge during the year, which had a significant effect on profits. The reasons for this impairment charge should be investigated.

We can also compare the profit generated with the net assets employed (that is, total assets less total liabilities) for each segment. We can see from the table below that the boat parts segment produces the best return on net assets employed by far: around 82 per cent, that is, £0.82 for every £1 invested. Once again, the car parts segment produces the worst results with a return of less than 24 per cent.

The relatively poor results from the car parts segment may simply reflect the nature of the market in which it operates. Compared with car parts segments of other businesses, it may be doing very well. Nevertheless, the business may still wish to consider whether future investment would not be better directed to those areas where greater profits can be found.

The investment in non-current assets during the period in relation to the total assets held is much higher for the boat parts segment. This may reflect the faith of the directors in the potential of this segment.

The depreciation charge as a percentage of segment assets seems to be high for all of the operating segments – but particularly for the car parts division. This should be investigated as it may suggest poor buying decisions.

Table of key results

	Car parts	Aircraft parts	Boat parts
Total revenue	£360m	£210m	£85m
Segment profit	£20m	£24m	£18m
Net assets (assets less liabilities)	£85m	£58m	£22m
Segment profit as a percentage of sales revenue	5.6%	11.4%	21.2%
Segment profit as a percentage of net assets employed	23.5%	41.4%	81.8%
Total assets	£170m	£125m	£44m
Expenditure on non-current assets	£28m	£23m	£26m
Depreciation	£80m	£55m	£15m
Depreciation as a percentage of segment assets	47.1%	44.0%	34.1%

Chapter 6

6.1   Touchstone plc

Statement of cash flows for the year ended 31 December 2016

	£m
Cash flows from operating activities	
Profit before taxation (after interest) (see Note 1 below)	60
Adjustments for:	
Depreciation	16
Interest expense (Note 2)	4
	80
Increase in trade receivables (26 − 16)	(10)
Decrease in trade payables (38 − 37)	(1)
Decrease in inventories (25 − 24)	1
Cash generated from operations	70
Interest paid	(4)
Taxation paid (Note 3)	(12)
Dividend paid	(18)
Net cash from operating activities	36
Cash flows from investing activities	
Payments to acquire tangible non-current assets (Note 4)	(41)
Net cash used in investing activities	(41)
Cash flows from financing activities	
Issue of loan notes (40 − 20)	20
Net cash used in financing activities	20
Net increase in cash and cash equivalents	15
Cash and cash equivalents at 1 January 2016	
Cash	4
Cash and cash equivalents at 31 December 2016	
Cash	4
Treasury bills	15
	19

To see how this relates to the cash of the business at the beginning and end of the year it can be useful to provide a reconciliation as follows:

Analysis of cash and cash equivalents during the year ended 31 December 2016

	£m
Cash and cash equivalents at 1 January 2016	4
Net cash inflow	15
Cash and cash equivalents at 31 December 2016	19

Notes:

1 This is simply taken from the income statement for the year.
2 Interest payable expense must be taken out, by adding it back to the profit before taxation figure. We subsequently deduct the cash paid for interest payable during the year. In this case, the two figures are identical.
3 Companies pay 50 per cent of their tax during their accounting year and the other 50 per cent in the following year. Thus the 2016 payment would have been half the tax on the 2015 profit (that is, the figure that would have appeared in the current liabilities at the end of 2015), plus half of the 2016 tax charge (that is, $4 + (\frac{1}{2} \times 16) = 12$).

4 Since there were no disposals, the depreciation charges must be the difference between the start and end of the year's non-current asset values, adjusted by the cost of any additions:

	£m
Carrying amount at 1 January 2016	147
Additions (balancing figure)	41
	188
Depreciation (6 + 10)	(16)
Carrying amount at 31 December 2016	172

Chapter 7

7.1 Ali plc and Bhaskar plc

(a) To answer this question, you may have used the following ratios:

	Ali plc	Bhaskar plc
Return on ordinary shareholders' funds ratio	$\dfrac{99.9}{687.6} \times 100 = 14.5\%$	$\dfrac{104.6}{874.6} \times 100 = 12.0\%$
Operating profit margin ratio	$\dfrac{151.3}{1{,}478.1} \times 100 = 10.2\%$	$\dfrac{166.9}{1{,}790.4} \times 100 = 9.3\%$
Inventories turnover period ratio	$\dfrac{592.0}{1{,}018.3} \times 12 = 7.0$ months	$\dfrac{403.0}{1{,}214.9} \times 12 = 4.0$ months
Settlement period for trade receivables ratio	$\dfrac{176.4}{1{,}478.1} \times 12 = 1.4$ months	$\dfrac{321.9}{1{,}790.4} \times 12 = 2.2$ months
Current ratio	$\dfrac{853.0}{422.4} = 2.0$	$\dfrac{816.5}{293.1} = 2.8$
Acid test ratio	$\dfrac{(853.0 - 592.0)}{422.4} = 0.6$	$\dfrac{(816.5 - 403.0)}{293.1} = 1.4$
Gearing ratio	$\dfrac{190}{(687.6 + 190)} \times 100 = 21.6\%$	$\dfrac{250}{(874.6 + 250)} \times 100 = 22.2\%$
Interest cover ratio	$\dfrac{151.3}{19.4} = 7.8$ times	$\dfrac{166.9}{27.5} = 6.1$ times
Earnings per share	$\dfrac{99.9}{320} = 31.2$p	$\dfrac{104.6}{250} = 41.8$p
Price/earnings ratio	$\dfrac{650}{31.2} = 20.8$ times	$\dfrac{820}{41.8} = 19.6$ times

(*Note*: It is not possible to use any average ratios because only the end-of-year figures are provided for each business.)

Ali plc seems more effective than Bhaskar plc at generating returns for shareholders, as indicated by the higher ROSF ratio. This may be partly caused by Ali plc's higher operating profit margin.

Both businesses have a very high inventories turnover period; this probably needs to be investigated. This ratio is particularly high for Ali plc. Both may suffer from poor inventories management.

Ali plc has a lower settlement period for trade receivables than Bhaskar plc. This may suggest that Bhaskar plc needs to exert greater control over trade receivables.

Ali plc has a much lower current ratio and acid test ratio than Bhaskar plc. The acid test ratio of Ali plc is substantially below 1.0: this may suggest a liquidity problem.

The gearing ratio of each business is quite similar. Neither business seems to have excessive borrowing. The interest cover ratio for each business is also similar. The ratios indicate that both businesses have good profit coverage for their interest charges.

Earnings per share is significantly higher for Bhaskar plc than for Ali plc. However, the P/E ratio for Bhaskar plc is slightly lower. This latter ratio suggests that the market considers Ali plc has slightly better prospects than Bhaskar plc.

To draw better comparisons between the two businesses, it would be useful to calculate other ratios from the financial statements. It would also be helpful to calculate ratios for both businesses over (say) five years as well as key ratios of other businesses operating in the same industry.

(b) The Altman Z-score model is as follows:

$$Z = 0.717a + 0.847b + 3.107c + 0.420d + 0.998e$$

where

a = Working capital/Total assets

b = Accumulated retained profits/Total assets

c = Operating profit/Total assets

d = Book (statement of financial position) value of ordinary and preference shares/ Total liabilities at book (statement of financial position) value

e = Sales revenue/Total assets

For Ali plc, the Z-score is:

$$0.717[(853.0 - 422.4)/1,300.0] + 0.847(367.6/1,300.0) + 3.107(151.3/1,300.0)$$

$$+0.420[320.0/(190.0 + 422.4)] + 0.998(1,478.1/1,300.0) = \underline{2.193}$$

For Bhaskar plc, the Z-score is:

$$0.717[(816.5 - 293.1)/1,417.7] + 0.847(624.6/1,417.7) + 3.107(166.9/1,417.7)$$

$$+0.420[250.0/(250.0 + 293.1)] + 0.998(1,790.4/1,417.7) = \underline{2.457}$$

(c) The Z-scores for these two businesses are quite close, with Bhaskar looking slightly safer. They are both in the 'zone of ignorance' category of businesses and, therefore, difficult to classify (a Z-score between 1.23 and 4.14). This is quite unusual since the Altman model is able confidently to classify 91 per cent of businesses. Clearly, these two businesses fall into the remaining 9 per cent.

It is questionable whether the Altman model is strictly applicable to UK businesses, since it was derived from data relating to US businesses that had failed. On the other hand, it probably provides a useful insight.

Chapter 8

8.1 JB Limited

(a)

	£	
Material M1 400 × 3 @ £5.50	6,600	The original cost is irrelevant since any inventories used will need to be replaced
Material P2 400 × 2 @ £2.00 (that is, £3.60 − £1.60)	1,600	The best alternative use of this material is as a substitute for P4 – an effective opportunity cost of £2.00/kg
Part number 678 400 × 1 @ £50	20,000	
Labour		
Skilled 400 × 5 @ £12	24,000	The effective cost is £12/hour
Semi-skilled 400 × 5 @ £10	20,000	
Overheads	3,200	It is only the additional cost which is relevant; the method of apportioning total overheads is not relevant
Total relevant cost	75,400	
Potential revenue		
400 @ £200	80,000	

Clearly, on the basis of the information available it would be beneficial for the business to undertake the contract.

(b) The net financial benefit of undertaking the contract is £4,600 (that is £80,000 − £75,400).
  1 For the project not to be financially viable, the cost of Material M1 would have to increase by a total of £4,600 from its projected cost of £6,600, an increase of around 70 per cent.
  2 With the skilled labour rate, the cost of this factor would have to increase by £4,600, from £20,000, an increase of 23 per cent.

(c) There are many possible answers to this part of the question, including:
  ● If Material P2 had not already been held, it may not have been possible to buy it in at a price that would still produce a beneficial outcome. The business may, therefore, be uneasy about accepting a price under the particular conditions that apply, which would not be accepted under other conditions.
  ● Will the replacement for the skilled worker be capable of doing the work to the required standard?
  ● Is JB Limited confident that the additional semi-skilled employee can be made redundant at the end of this contract without cost to the business?
  ● The sensitivities of all of the other factors could also be established to try to assess the riskiness of JB Limited undertaking this contract.

Chapter 9

9.1 Khan Ltd

(a) The break-even point, if only the Alpha service were provided, would be:

$$\frac{\text{Fixed costs}}{\text{Sales revenue per unit} - \text{Variable cost per unit}} = \frac{\text{\pounds}40{,}000}{\text{\pounds}30 - \text{\pounds}(15 + 6)} = 4{,}445 \text{ units (per year)}$$

(Strictly it is 4,444.44, but 4,445 is the smallest number of units of the service that must be provided to avoid a loss.)

(b)

	Alpha	Beta	Gamma
Selling price	30	39	20
Variable materials	(15)	(18)	(10)
Variable production cost	(6)	(10)	(5)
Contribution	9	11	5
Staff time (hr/unit)	2	3	1
Contribution/staff hour	£4.50	£3.67	£5.00
Order of priority	2nd	3rd	1st

(c)

	Hours	Contribution	
			£
Provide:			
5,000 Gamma using	5,000	generating (that is, 5,000 × £5 =)	25,000
2,500 Alpha using	5,000	generating (that is, 2,500 × £9 =)	22,500
	10,000		47,500
		Fixed cost	(40,000)
		Profit	7,500

This leaves a demand for 500 units of Alpha and 2,000 units of Beta unsatisfied.

Chapter 10

10.1 Hector and Co. Ltd

(a) Job costing basis

		£
Materials: Metal wire	1,000 × 2 × £2.20*	4,400
Fabric	1,000 × 0.5 × £1.00*	500
Labour: Skilled	1,000 × (10/60) × £12.00	2,000
Unskilled	1,000 × (5/60) × £7.50	625
Indirect cost	1,000 × (15/60) × (50,000/12,500)	1,000
Total cost		8,525
Profit loading	12.5% thereof	1,066
Total tender price		9,591

*In the traditional approach to full costing, historic costs of materials tend to be used. It would not necessarily have been incorrect to have used the 'relevant' (opportunity) costs here.

(b) Minimum contract price (relevant cost basis)

		£
Materials: Metal wire	1,000 × 2 × £2.50 (replacement cost)	5,000
Fabric	1,000 × 0.5 × £0.40 (scrap value)	200
Labour: Skilled	(there is no effective cost of skilled staff)	–
Unskilled	1,000 × 5/60 × £7.50	625
Minimum tender price		5,825

The difference between the two prices is partly that the relevant costing approach tends to look to the future, partly that it considers opportunity costs, and partly that the job-costing basis total has a profit loading.

Chapter 11

11.1 **Psilis Ltd**

(a) Full cost (present basis)

	Basic		Super	
	£		£	
Direct labour (all £10/hour)	40.00	(4 hours)	60.00	(6 hours)
Direct material	15.00		20.00	
Overheads	18.20	(£4.55* × 4)	27.30	(£4.55* × 6)
	73.20		107.30	

*Total direct labour hours worked = (40,000 × 4) + (10,000 × 6) = 220,000 hours. Overhead recovery rate = £1,000,000/220,000 = £4.55 per direct labour hour.

Thus the selling prices are currently:

Basic :   £73.20 + 25% = £91.50

Super: £107.30 + 25% = £134.13

(b) Full cost (activity cost basis)
Here, the cost of each cost-driving activity is apportioned between total production of the two products.

Activity	Cost	Basis of apportionment	Basic		Super	
	£000		£000		£000	
Machine set-ups	280	Number of set-ups	56	(20/100)	224	(80/100)
Quality inspection	220	Number of inspections	55	(500/2,000)	165	(1,500/2,000)
Sales order processing	240	Number of orders processed	72	(1,500/5,000)	168	(3,500/5,000)
General production	260	Machine hours	182	(350/500)	78	(150/500)
Total	1,000		365		635	

The overheads per unit are:

$$\text{Basic:} \quad \frac{£365{,}000}{40{,}000} = £9.13$$

$$\text{Super:} \quad \frac{£635{,}000}{10{,}000} = £63.50$$

Thus, on an activity basis the full costs are as follows:

	Basic		Super	
	£		£	
Direct labour (all £10/hour)	40.00	(4 hours)	60.00	(6 hours)
Direct material	15.00		20.00	
Overheads	9.13		63.50	
Full cost	64.13		143.50	
Current selling price	91.50		134.13	

(c) It seems that the Supers are being sold for less than they cost to produce. If the price cannot be increased, there is a very strong case for abandoning this product. At the same time, the Basics are very profitable to the extent that it may be worth considering lowering the price to attract more sales revenue.

   The fact that the overhead costs can be related to activities and, more specifically, to products does not mean that abandoning Super production would lead to immediate overhead cost savings. For example, it may not be possible or desirable to dismiss machine-setting staff overnight. It would certainly rarely be possible to release factory space occupied by machine setters and make immediate cost savings. Nevertheless, in the medium term it is possible to avoid these costs, and it may be sensible to do so.

(d) Three major differences between the cost-plus approach and the target costing approach to pricing are as follows:
   - With the cost-plus approach, the price of a product is determined by its cost, whereas, with the target costing approach, it is the other way around.
   - With the cost-plus approach, cost efficiencies are normally achieved after the product is developed, whereas, with the target costing approach, cost efficiencies are built into the design process.
   - With the cost-plus approach, cost management is not driven by the demands of the market, whereas, with the target costing approach, cost management is market-driven.

(e) Three non-financial measures that could act as lead indicators concerning the internal business processes of a laptop manufacturer are:
   - number of new products brought to market;
   - percentage of customers requiring after-sales service; and
   - time taken to process new orders.

(f) It is difficult for these different approaches to coexist in a highly competitive economy. The pursuit of shareholder value may be necessary in order to secure funds and for managers to secure their jobs. A stakeholder approach, which is committed to satisfying the needs of a broad group of constituents, may be difficult to sustain in such an environment.

   It has been suggested that other stakeholders have been seriously adversely affected by the pursuit of shareholder value. It is claimed that the application of various techniques to improve shareholder value such as hostile takeovers, cost-cutting and large management incentive bonuses have badly damaged the interests of certain stakeholders such as employees and local communities. However, a commitment to shareholder value must take account of the needs of other stakeholders if it is to deliver long-term benefits.

(g) If businesses are overcapitalised it is probably because insufficient attention is given to the amount of capital that is required. Management incentive schemes that are geared towards generating a particular level of profits or achieving a particular market share without specifying the level of capital invested can help create such a problem. EVA® can help by highlighting the cost of capital, through the capital charge.

Chapter 12

12.1 Antonio Ltd

(a) 1 Raw materials inventories budget for the six months ending 31 December (physical quantities):

	July Units	Aug Units	Sept Units	Oct Units	Nov Units	Dec Units
Opening inventories (current month's production)	500	600	600	700	750	750
Purchases (balance figure)	600	600	700	750	750	750
	1,100	1,200	1,300	1,450	1,500	1,500
Issues to production (from question)	(500)	(600)	(600)	(700)	(750)	(750)
Closing inventories (next month's production)	600	600	700	750	750	750

Raw material inventories budget for the six months ending 31 December (in financial terms), that is, the physical quantities × £8:

	July £	Aug £	Sept £	Oct £	Nov £	Dec £
Opening inventories	4,000	4,800	4,800	5,600	6,000	6,000
Purchases	4,800	4,800	5,600	6,000	6,000	6,000
	8,800	9,600	10,400	11,600	12,000	12,000
Issues to production	(4,000)	(4,800)	(4,800)	(5,600)	(6,000)	(6,000)
Closing inventories	4,800	4,800	5,600	6,000	6,000	6,000

2 Trade payables budget for the six months ending 31 December:

	July £	Aug £	Sept £	Oct £	Nov £	Dec £
Opening balance (current month's payment)	4,000	4,800	4,800	5,600	6,000	6,000
Purchases (from raw materials inventories budget)	4,800	4,800	5,600	6,000	6,000	6,000
	8,800	9,600	10,400	11,600	12,000	12,000
Payments	(4,000)	(4,800)	(4,800)	(5,600)	(6,000)	(6,000)
Closing balance (next month's payment)	4,800	4,800	5,600	6,000	6,000	6,000

3 Cash budget for the six months ending 31 December:

	July £	Aug £	Sept £	Oct £	Nov £	Dec £
Inflows						
Trade receivables (40% of sales revenue of two months previous)	2,800	3,200	3,200	4,000	4,800	5,200
Cash sales revenue (60% of current month's sales revenue)	4,800	6,000	7,200	7,800	8,400	9,600
Total inflows	7,600	9,200	10,400	11,800	13,200	14,800
Outflows						
Payables (from payables budget)	(4,000)	(4,800)	(4,800)	(5,600)	(6,000)	(6,000)
Direct costs	(3,000)	(3,600)	(3,600)	(4,200)	(4,500)	(4,500)
Advertising	(1,000)	–	–	(1,500)	–	–
Overheads: 80%	(1,280)	(1,280)	(1,280)	(1,280)	(1,600)	(1,600)
20%	(280)	(320)	(320)	(320)	(320)	(400)
New plant			(2,200)	(2,200)	(2,200)	
Total outflows	(9,560)	(10,000)	(12,200)	(15,100)	(14,620)	(12,500)
Net inflows/(outflows)	(1,960)	(800)	(1,800)	(3,300)	(1,420)	2,300
Balance c/f	5,540	4,740	2,940	(360)	(1,780)	520

The cash balances carried forward are deduced by subtracting the deficit (net outflows) for the month from (or adding the surplus for the month to) the previous month's balance.

Note how budgets are linked; in this case, the inventories budget to the trade payables budget and the payables budget to the cash budget.

(b) The following are possible means of relieving the cash shortages revealed by the budget:

- Make a higher proportion of sales on a cash basis.
- Collect the money from credit customers more promptly, for example during the month following the sale.
- Hold lower levels of inventories, both of raw materials and of finished goods.
- Increase the trade payables payment period.
- Delay the payments for advertising.
- Obtain more credit for the overhead costs; at present only 20 per cent are on credit.
- Delay the payments for the new plant.

A combination of two or more of these ways might be used.

Chapter 13

13.1 Toscanini Ltd

(a)

	Budget			Actual	
	Original	Flexed		Actual	
Output (units) (production and sales)	4,000	3,500		3,500	
	£	£		£	
Sales revenue	16,000	14,000		13,820	
Raw materials	(3,840)	(3,360)	(1,400 kg)	(3,420)	(1,425 kg)
Labour	(3,200)	(2,800)	(350 hr)	(2,690)	(345 hr)
Fixed overheads	(4,800)	(4,800)		(4,900)	
Operating profit	4,160	3,040		2,810	

	£	
Sales volume variance (4,160 − 3,040)	(1,120)	(A)
Sales price variance (14,000 − 13,820)	(180)	(A)
Materials price variance (1,425 × 2.40) − 3,420	0	
Materials usage variance [(3,500 × 0.4) − 1,425] × £2.40	(60)	(A)
Labour rate variance (345 × £8) − 2,690	70	(F)
Labour efficiency variance [(3,500 × 0.10) − 345] × £8	40	(F)
Fixed overhead spending variance (4,800 − 4,900)	(100)	(A)
Total net variances	(1,350)	(A)
Budgeted profit	4,160	
Less Total net variance	1,350	
Actual profit	2,810	

(b) Manager to be held accountable:

Sales volume variance	Sales manager
Sales price variance	Sales manager
Materials usage variance	Production manager
Labour rate variance	Human resources manager
Labour efficiency variance	Production manager
Fixed overhead spending variance	Various, depending on the nature of overheads

(c) Feasible explanations include the following:

Sales volume variance	Unanticipated fall in demand would account for 400 × £2.24 = £896 of this variance (£2.24 is the budgeted contribution per unit). Ineffective marketing probably caused the remainder, though a lack of availability of the finished product to sell could be a reason.
Sales price variance	Ineffective selling seems the only logical reason.
Materials usage variance	Inefficient usage of material, perhaps because of poor performance by labour, or substandard materials.
Labour rate variance	Less overtime worked or lower production bonuses paid as a result of lower volume of activity.
Labour efficiency variance	More effective working.
Fixed overheads spending variance	Ineffective control of overheads.

(d) Clearly, not all of the sales volume variance can be attributed to poor marketing, given a 10 per cent reduction in demand.

It will probably be useful to distinguish between that part of the variance that arose from the shortfall in general demand (a planning variance) and a volume variance, which is more fairly attributable to the manager concerned. Thus accountability will be more fairly imposed.

	£
Planning variance (10% × 4,000) × £2.24 (£2.24 is the budgeted contribution per unit)	896
'Revised' sales volume variance [4,000 − (10% × 4,000) − 3,500] × £2.24	224
Original sales volume variance	1,120

Chapter 14

14.1 Beacon Chemicals plc

(a) Relevant cash flows are as follows:

	Year 0 £m	Year 1 £m	Year 2 £m	Year 3 £m	Year 4 £m	Year 5 £m
Sales revenue		80	120	144	100	64
Loss of contribution		(15)	(15)	(15)	(15)	(15)
Variable cost		(40)	(50)	(48)	(30)	(32)
Fixed cost (Note 1)		(8)	(8)	(8)	(8)	(8)
Operating cash flows		17	47	73	47	9
Working capital	(30)					30
Capital cost	(100)					
Net relevant cash flows	(130)	17	47	73	47	39

Notes:
1. Only the elements of fixed cost that are incremental to the project (only existing because of the project) are relevant. Depreciation is irrelevant because it is not a cash flow.
2. The research and development cost is irrelevant since it has been spent irrespective of the decision on X14 production.

(b) The payback period is as follows:

	Year 0 £m	Year 1 £m	Year 2 £m	Year 3 £m
Cumulative cash flows	(130)	(113)	(66)	7

Thus the equipment will have repaid the initial investment by the end of the third year of operations. The payback period is, therefore, three years.

(c) The net present value is as follows:

	Year 0	Year 1	Year 2	Year 3	Year 4	Year 5
Discount factor (8%)	1.00	0.926	0.857	0.794	0.735	0.681
Present value (£m)	(130)	15.74	40.28	57.96	34.55	26.56
Net present value (£m)	45.09	(That is, the sum of the present values for years 0 to 5.)				

(d) To have the effect of reducing the NPV to zero, the additional loss of contribution would have to be such that its present value would be £45.09 million. As the loss of contribution arises in each year (1 to 5), letting A = the additional loss of contribution:

$$45.09 = (A \times 0.926) + (A \times 0.857) + (A \times 0.794) + (A + 0.735) + (A + 0.681)$$

$$A = 45.09/3.993$$

$$A = £11.29 \text{ million}$$

This means that the loss of contribution would have to move from £15 million to £26.29 million – an increase of 75 per cent – before a possible misestimation of this value would, taken alone, cause the project to be wealth destructive. In other words, the potential success of the project is not very sensitive to the estimate of the loss of contribution.

Chapter 15

15.1 **Helsim Ltd**

(a) The liquidity position may be assessed by using the liquidity ratios discussed in Chapter 7:

$$\text{Current ratio} = \frac{\text{Current assets}}{\text{Current liabilities}}$$

$$= \frac{£7.5\text{m}}{£5.4\text{m}}$$

$$= 1.4$$

$$\text{Acid test ratio} = \frac{\text{Current assets (excluding inventories)}}{\text{Current liabilities}}$$

$$= \frac{£3.7\text{m}}{£5.4\text{m}}$$

$$= 0.7$$

These ratios reveal a fairly weak liquidity position. The current ratio seems quite low and the acid test ratio very low. This latter ratio suggests that the business does not have sufficient liquid assets to meet its maturing obligations. It would, however, be useful to have details of the liquidity ratios of similar businesses in the same industry in order to make a more informed judgement. The bank overdraft represents 67 per cent of the current liabilities and 40 per cent of the total liabilities of the business. The continuing support of the bank is therefore important to the ability of the business to meet its commitments.

(b) The finance required to reduce trade payables to an average of 40 days outstanding is calculated as follows:

	£m	
Trade payables at the date of the statement of financial position	1.80	
Trade payables outstanding based on 40 days' credit:		
40/365 × £8.4m (that is, credit purchases)	(0.92)	
Finance required	0.88	(say £0.9m)

(c) The bank may not wish to provide further finance to the business. The increase in overdraft will reduce the level of trade payables but will increase the risk exposure of the bank. The additional finance invested by the bank will not generate further funds (it will not increase profit) and will not therefore be self-liquidating. The information available implies that the business would not be able to offer any security for further loans. The loan notes (£3.5 million) are secured on the property (market value £3.8 million). On top of that, there is already an overdraft (£3.6 million). The profits of the business will be reduced and the interest cover ratio, based on the profits generated last year, would reduce to about 1.6* times if the additional overdraft were granted (based on interest charged at 10 per cent each year). This is very low and means that only a small decline in profits would leave interest charges uncovered.

*Existing bank overdraft (3.6) + extension of overdraft to cover reduction in trade payables (0.9) + loan notes (3.5) = £8.0m. Assuming a 10 percent interest rate means a yearly interest payment of £0.8m. The operating profit was £1.3m. Interest cover would be 1.63 (that is, 1.3/0.8).

(d) A number of possible sources of finance might be considered. Four possible sources are as follows:

- *Issue ordinary (equity) shares.* This option may be unattractive to investors. The return on equity is fairly low at 7.9 per cent (that is, profit for the year (0.3)/equity (3.8)) and there is no evidence that the profitability of the business will improve. If profits remain at their current level, the effect of issuing more equity will be to reduce further the returns to equity.

- *Make other borrowings.* This option may also prove unattractive to investors. The effect of making further borrowings will have a similar effect to that of increasing the overdraft. The profits of the business will be reduced and the interest cover ratio will decrease to a low level. The gearing ratio of the business is already quite high at 48 per cent (that is, loan notes (3.5)/(loan notes + equity (3.5 + 3.8)) and it is not clear what security would be available for the loan. The gearing ratio would be much higher if the overdraft were to be included.

- *Chase trade receivables.* It may be possible to improve cash flows by reducing the level of credit outstanding from customers. At present, the average settlement period is 93 days (that is, (trade receivables (3.6)/sales revenue (14.2)) × 365), which seems quite high. A reduction in the average settlement period by approximately a quarter would generate the funds required. However, it is not clear what effect this would have on sales.

- *Reduce inventories.* This appears to be the most attractive of the four options. At present, the average inventories holding period is 178 days (that is, (closing inventories (3.8)/cost of sales (7.8)) × 365), which seems very high. A reduction in this period by less than a quarter would generate the funds required.

Chapter 16

16.1   Town Mills Ltd

(a) Operating cash cycle

	Days
Inventories holding period: 192/652 × 365	107
Trade receivables period: 202 × (105/110)/903 × 365 (Note 1)	78
	185
Trade payables period:	
260 × (105/110)/652 × 365 (Notes 1 and 2)	(139)
Operating cash cycle	46

Notes:

1 Since the closing level of trade receivables/payables was 10 per cent higher at the end of the year than at the start, the average balance would be 105/110 of the end of year balance.

2 Since inventories were the same at both ends of the year, purchases equal cost of sales.

Knowledge of the length of the operating cash cycle (OCC) enables the business to monitor it over time, perhaps relative to other businesses or some target. It is not possible to draw any helpful conclusion from looking at just one figure; there needs to be a basis of comparison.

A problem with using the 'bottom line' figure for the OCC is that values within it are not equivalent. In the case of Town Mills, one day's sales are worth £2,474, whereas one day's purchases or inventories holding are worth £1,786. So, whilst an extra day of trade receivables period coupled with an extra day of trade payables period would leave the OCC unchanged at 46 days, it would involve an additional £700 or so of investment in working capital.

(b) As mentioned in (a) knowledge of the number of days of the OCC tells us little without some basis of comparison.

The acid test (quick assets) ratio for this company is very low at 0.55:1 (trade receivables divided by trade payables plus overdraft). Where the inventories are fairly fast-moving with a short trade receivables period, this may not be a worry but, as it stands, this is a concern.

The current ratio is close to 1:1, which looks low, but it is not possible to say too much without a comparison with similar businesses, or this business over time.

A glance at Real World 16.1 (page 677) indicates that there are some successful businesses, that no one is accusing of having liquidity problems, that operate at very low acid-test and current ratios.

The level of the overdraft looks worrying. It represents almost 20 per cent of the total financing of the business, according to statement of financial position values. The statement of financial position may well understate the value of equity, but it still seems a lot of short-term finance that could be recalled instantly, which in practice probably means a couple of months.

A term loan may be a better arrangement than an overdraft.

The level of trade payables also seems high, compared with trade receivables. This too could be a problem. It depends on the relative market positions of Town Mills and its suppliers.

Overall, the liquidity does not look strong and probably needs to be reviewed. It is not possible to be too dogmatic on this with very limited bases of comparison.

(c) The types of risk and cost that might be associated with high inventories levels of a wholesaler include:

- *Financing cost.* Inventories normally need to be financed. Usually buying on free trade credit covers some of this. In the case as Town Mills, at present at least, trade payables are greater than the value of inventories. The credit is linked to purchases not inventories levels so, if inventories levels were to be reduced, the level of payables need not be lessened.
- *Storage costs.* These are likely to be less where inventories are lower. The degree of significance of these costs is likely to depend on the nature of the inventories. Those with a high value and/or those needing special treatment are typically more expensive to store than other inventories.
- *Insurance cost.* This is likely to be subject to the same considerations as storage cost, of which it can be seen as being part.
- *Obsolescence cost.* The more inventories held, the greater the risk that it will lose value either through physical deterioration or through becoming obsolete. A spare part for a machine no longer used may be in perfect condition and, in principle, still as capable of being used. If the machine is no longer being used, the spare part may be worthless.

Solutions to review questions

Chapter 1

1.1 The economic cost of providing accounting information should be less than the expected economic benefit from having the information available. In other words, there should be a net economic benefit from producing it. If this is not the case, it should not be produced. There are obvious problems, however, in determining the precise value of the benefit. There are also problems in determining the costs involved. Hence, making a judgement about whether to provide additional accounting information is far from straightforward.

Economics is not the only issue to consider, particularly in the context of financial accounting. Social and other factors may well be involved. It can be argued, for example, that society has a right to certain information about a large business, even though this information may not have any direct economic value to society.

1.2 The main users of financial information for a university and the way in which they are likely to use this information may be summed up as follows:

Students	Whether to enrol on a course of study. This would probably involve an assessment of the university's ability to continue to operate and to provide the resources that fulfil students' needs.
Other universities and colleges	How best to compete against the university. This might involve using the university's performance in various aspects as 'benchmarks' when evaluating their own performance. These aspects may include costs incurred, student fee income generated and new investments made in facilities.
Employees	Whether to take up or to continue in employment with the university. Employees might assess this by considering the ability of the university to continue to provide employment and to reward employees adequately for their labour.
Government/funding authority	How efficient and effective the university is in undertaking its various activities. What additional funding the university may need.
Local community representatives	Whether to allow/encourage the university to expand its premises. To assess this, the university's ability to continue to provide employment for the community, to use community resources and to help fund environmental improvements may be considered.
Suppliers	Whether to continue to supply the university at all; also whether to supply on credit. This would involve an assessment of the university's ability to pay for any goods and services supplied.

| Lenders | Whether to lend money to the university and/or whether to require repayment of any existing loans. To assess this, the university's ability to meet its obligations to pay interest and to repay the principal would be considered. |
| Board of governors and managers (faculty deans and so on) | Whether the performance of the university requires improvement. Performance to date would be compared with earlier plans or some other 'benchmark' to decide whether action needs to be taken. Whether there should be a change in the university's future direction. In making such decisions, management will need to look at the university's ability to perform, its resources and at the opportunities available to it. |

We can see that the users of accounting information and their needs are similar to those of a private-sector business.

1.3 Many businesses are far too large and complex for managers to see and assess everything that is happening within their areas of responsibility merely by personal observation. Nevertheless, managers need information on all matters within their control. Management accounting reports can help provide much of the information that is needed. These reports can, therefore, act as the eyes and ears of the managers, by bringing matters to their attention.

1.4 Since we can never be sure what is going to happen in the future, the best that we can often do is to make judgements on the basis of past experience. Thus information concerning performance in the recent past may well be a useful source on which to base judgements about possible future performance.

Chapter 2

2.1 The owner seems unaware of the business entity convention in accounting. This convention requires a separation of the business from the owner(s) of the business for accounting purposes. The business is regarded as a separate entity and the statement of financial position is prepared from the perspective of the business rather than that of the owner. As a result, funds invested in the business by the owner are regarded as a claim that the owner has on the business. In the standard layout of the statement of financial position, this claim will be shown alongside other claims on the business from outsiders.

2.2 A statement of financial position does not show what a business is worth, for two major reasons:

1 Only those items that can be measured reliably in monetary terms are shown on the statement of financial position. Thus, things of value such as the reputation for product quality, skills of employees and so on will not normally appear in the statement of financial position.

2 The historic cost convention results in assets often being recorded at their outlay (acquisition) cost rather than their current value. For certain assets, the difference between historic cost and current value may be significant.

2.3 The accounting equation expresses the relationship between a business's assets, liabilities and equity. For the standard layout, it is:

Assets (current and non-current) = Equity + Liabilities (current and non-current)

For the alternative layout mentioned in the chapter, the equation is:

$$\text{Assets (current and non-current)} - \text{Liabilities (current and non-current)} = \text{Equity}$$

2.4   Some object to the idea of humans being treated as assets for inclusion on the statement of financial position. It is seen as demeaning for humans to be listed alongside inventories, plant and machinery and other assets. Others argue, however, that humans are often the most valuable resource of a business and that placing a value on this resource will help bring to the attention of managers the importance of nurturing and developing this 'asset'.

Humans are likely to meet the criterion of an asset relating to the right to potential economic benefits, otherwise there would be little point in employing them. The criterion relating to control is, however, more problematic. A business cannot control humans in the same way as most other assets, but it can control the rights to their employment services. This makes it possible to argue that this criterion can be met.

The criterion concerning whether the value of humans (or their services) can be measured with any degree of certainty poses the major difficulty. Apart from the unusual circumstances relating to professional footballers mentioned in the chapter, humans defy reliable measurement.

Chapter 3

3.1   When preparing the income statement, it is not always possible to determine accurately the expenses that need to be matched to the sales revenue for the period. It is perhaps only at some later point that the true position becomes clear. Nevertheless, we must try to include all relevant expenses and so estimates of the future have to be made. These estimates may include accrued expenses, depreciation charges and bad debts incurred. The income statement would lose much of its usefulness if we were to wait for all uncertainties to become clear.

3.2   Depreciation attempts to allocate the cost or fair value, less any residual value, of an asset over its useful life. Depreciation does not attempt to measure the fall in value of the asset during a particular accounting period. Thus, the carrying amount of the asset appearing on the statement of financial position normally represents the unexpired part of its cost, or fair value, rather than its current market value.

3.3   The convention of consistency aims to provide some uniformity in the application of accounting policies. In certain areas, there may be more than one method of accounting for an item, for example inventories. The convention of consistency states that, having decided on a particular accounting policy, a business should continue to apply the policy in successive periods. While this policy helps to ensure that more valid comparisons can be made of business performance *over time*, it does not ensure that valid comparisons can be made *between businesses*. Different businesses may still consistently apply different accounting policies.

3.4   An expense is that element of the cost incurred that is used up during the reporting period. An asset is that element of cost which is carried forward on the statement of financial position and which will normally be used up in future periods. Thus, both assets and expenses arise from costs being incurred. The major difference between the two is the period over which the benefits (arising from the costs incurred) accrue.

Chapter 4

4.1 Both companies and individuals are required to meet their debts to the full extent of their available assets. Thus, their liability is limited only by the extent of their assets. It is the shareholders of a limited company that enjoy greater protection. Their liability for the unsatisfied debts of a company is limited to the amount that they paid or have pledged to pay for their shares.

This contrasts with the position of the owner, or part owner, of an unincorporated business. Here all of the individual's assets could be used to meet the unsatisfied debts of the business. Thus, while there is a difference between the position of a shareholder and that of a sole proprietor or partner, there is no difference between the position of the company itself and that of a sole proprietor or partner.

4.2 A private limited company may place restrictions on the transfer of its shares. (There is therefore an opportunity to control who becomes a shareholder.) A public company cannot impose such restrictions.

A public limited company must have authorised share capital of at least £50,000. There is no minimum for a private limited company.

A public limited company may offer its shares and loan notes to the general public; a private company cannot make such an offer.

4.3 A reserve is that part of the equity (owners' claim) of a company that is not share capital. Reserves represent gains or surpluses that enhance the claim of the shareholders above the nominal value of their shares. Revenue reserves arise from realised profits and gains, such as ploughed-back trading profits. Capital reserves arise from issuing shares at a premium or from unrealised profits and gains (for example, the upward revaluation of non-current assets).

4.4 A preference share represents part of the ownership of the company. Holders of preference shares are entitled to the first part of any dividend paid by a company.

(a) Holders of preference shares are normally entitled to dividends up to a predetermined maximum value. Dividends to ordinary shareholders have no predetermined maximum. The priority awarded in receiving dividends means that preference shares are seen as less risky than ordinary shares. Ordinary shareholders are the primary risk takers and are given voting rights. Preference shareholders do not normally have voting rights.

(b) Loan notes represent borrowings for the company. Loan note holders normally have a contract that specifies the rate of interest, interest payment dates and redemption date. The loan notes are often secured on the company's assets. Preference shareholders have no such contract. The claims of preference shareholders are ranked below those of loan note holders in the event that the company is liquidated.

Chapter 5

5.1 Accounting is an evolving subject. It is not static and so the conceptual framework that is laid down at any particular point in time may become obsolete as a result of changes in our understanding of the nature of accounting information and its impact on users and changes in the economic and social environment within which accounting is used. We must accept, therefore, that accounting principles will continue to evolve and that existing ones must be frequently reviewed.

5.2 There are various problems associated with the measurement of business segments. These include:

- the definition of a segment;
- the treatment of inter-segmental transactions, such as sales; and
- the treatment of expenses and assets that are shared between segments.

There is no single correct method of dealing with these problems and variations will arise in practice. This, in turn, will hinder comparisons between businesses.

5.3 Accounting rules are important for the purpose of comparability, both over time and between businesses. They also help to ensure that unscrupulous directors do not exploit their position and portray an unrealistic view of financial health.

5.4 The main methods of creative accounting are misstating revenues, massaging expenses, misstating assets, concealing 'bad news' and inadequate disclosure.

Chapter 6

6.1 Cash is normally required in the settlement of claims. Employees, contractors, lenders and suppliers expect to be paid in cash. When businesses fail, it is their inability to find the cash to pay claimants that actually drives them under. These factors lead to cash being the pre-eminent business asset. It is studied carefully to assess the ability of a business to survive and/or to take advantage of commercial opportunities.

6.2 With the direct method, the business's cash records are analysed for the period concerned. The analysis reveals the amounts of cash, in total, that have been paid and received in respect of each category of the statement of cash flows. This is not difficult in principle, or in practice if it is done by computer, as a matter of routine.

The indirect method takes the approach that, while the profit (loss) for the reporting period is not equal to the net inflow (outflow) of cash from operations, they are fairly closely linked to the extent that appropriate adjustment of the profit (loss) for the period figure will produce the correct cash flow figure. The adjustment is concerned with the depreciation charge for, and movements in, relevant working capital items over the period.

6.3 (a) *Cash flows from operating activities.* This would normally be positive, even for a business with small profits or even losses. The fact that depreciation is not a cash flow tends to lead to positive cash flows in this area in most cases.

(b) *Cash flows from investing activities.* Normally this would be negative since many non-current assets wear out or become obsolete and need to be replaced in the normal course of business. This means that, typically, old non-current assets generate less cash on their disposal than must be paid to replace them.

(c) *Cash flows from financing activities.* Businesses tend either to expand or to fail. In either case, this is likely to mean that, over the years, more finance will be raised than will be redeemed.

6.4 There are several possible reasons for this, including the following:

- Changes in inventories, trade receivables and trade payables. For example, an increase in trade receivables during a reporting period would mean that the cash received from credit sales would be less than the credit sales revenue for the same period.

- Cash may have been spent on new non-current assets or received from disposals of old ones; these would not directly affect profit.
- Cash may have been spent to redeem or repay a financial claim or received as a result of the creation, or the increase of, a claim. These would not directly affect profit.
- Tax charged in the income statement is not normally the same as the tax paid during the same reporting period.

Chapter 7

7.1 The fact that a business operates on a low operating profit margin indicates that only a small operating profit is being produced for each £1 of sales revenue generated. However, this does not necessarily mean that the ROCE will be low. If the business is able to generate sufficient sales revenue during a period, the operating profit may be very high even though the operating profit per £1 of sales revenue is low. If the overall operating profit is high, this can lead, in turn, to a high ROCE, since it is the total operating profit that is used as the numerator (top part of the fraction) in this ratio. Many businesses (including supermarkets) pursue a strategy of 'low margin, high sales revenue'.

7.2 The statement of financial position is drawn up at a single point in time – usually the end of the reporting period. As a result, the figures shown on the statement represent the position at that single point in time and may not be representative of the position during the period. Wherever possible, average figures (perhaps based on monthly figures) should be used. However, an external user may only have access to the opening and closing statements of financial position for the year and so a simple average based on these figures may be all that it is possible to calculate. Where a business is seasonal in nature or is subject to cyclical changes, this simple averaging may not be sufficient.

7.3 In view of the fact that Z-scores are derived from information that is published by the businesses themselves, it is difficult to say that Z-scores should not be made publicly available. Indeed, many of those connected with a business – shareholders, lenders, employees and so on – may find this information extremely valuable for decision making. Nevertheless, there is a risk that a poor Z-score will lead to a loss of confidence in the business among investors and suppliers which may, in turn, prevent the business from taking corrective action as lines of credit and investment will be withdrawn.

7.4 The P/E ratio may vary between businesses within the same industry for the following reasons:

- *Accounting policies.* Differences in the methods used to compute profit (for example, inventories valuation and depreciation) can lead to different profit figures and, therefore, different P/E ratios.
- *Different prospects.* One business may be regarded as having a much brighter future due to factors such as the quality of management, the quality of products, or location. This will affect the market price investors are prepared to pay for the share and hence will also affect the P/E ratio.
- *Different asset structure.* The business's underlying asset base may be much higher and this may affect the market price of the shares.

Chapter 8

8.1   The three attributes of a relevant cost are:

1   It must relate to the objective(s) that the decision is intended to work towards. In most businesses this is taken to be wealth enhancement. This means that any information relating to the decision that does not impact on wealth enhancement is irrelevant. (In practice, however, a business may have other objectives in addition to wealth enhancement.)
2   It must relate to the future. A past cost is always irrelevant.
3   It must differ between the options under consideration. Where a cost is the same irrespective of the options being considered, it is irrelevant.

8.2   A sunk cost is a past and, therefore, an irrelevant cost. This is because decisions relate to the future. Thus, for example, the cost of an item of inventories already bought is a sunk cost. It is irrelevant in any decision involving the use of this item because the sunk cost is the same irrespective of the decision made.

An opportunity cost is the cost of being deprived of the next best option to the one under consideration. For example, where using an hour of a worker's time on Activity A deprives the business of the opportunity to use that time in the next most profitable activity, Activity B, the benefit lost from Activity B is an opportunity cost of pursuing Activity A.

8.3   A committed cost is similar to a past cost in that an irrevocable decision has been made to incur the cost. This might be because the business has entered into a binding contract, for example to rent some accommodation for the next two years. This type of cost is effectively, therefore, a past cost even though payment (for rent, in our example) has yet to be made. Since the business cannot avoid a committed cost, it cannot be a relevant cost.

8.4   These two factors – raw materials cost and sales volume – are not necessarily equally risky for the business. It may be that the probability of unexpected raw material price rises is very low because, for example, there are many competing suppliers and there is no shortage of the particular raw materials. At the same time, predictions of sales volume may be very susceptible to error because, for example, it is a new product whose market potential is highly uncertain.

On the other hand, supplies of the particular raw material may be uncertain, which could lead to unpredicted price rises. At the same time, the business may be able to enter into binding contracts for the sale of the product.

Chapter 9

9.1   A fixed cost is one that is the same irrespective of the level of activity or output. Typical examples of costs that are fixed include rent of business accommodation, salaries of supervisory staff and insurance. A variable cost is one that varies with the level of activity or output. Examples include raw materials and power for machinery. It also includes labour where payment is made according to the level of output.

Note that it is in relation to the level of activity that costs are fixed. These costs are affected by inflation and the time period involved.

For a particular product or service, knowing which costs are fixed and which are variable helps managers to predict the total cost for a given level of activity. It also helps them to focus only on variable costs where a short-term decision does not alter the fixed costs.

9.2 The BEP is the break-even point, that is, the level of activity, measured either in units of output or in value of sales revenue, at which the sales revenue exactly covers all of the costs, both fixed and variable.

BEP is calculated as

$$\text{Fixed costs/(sales revenue per unit} - \text{variable costs per unit)}$$

which may alternatively be expressed as

$$\text{Fixed costs/Contribution per unit}$$

Thus break-even will occur when the contributions for the period are sufficient to cover the fixed costs for the period.

The BEP can be used to compare with the planned level of activity. This can help in assessing the riskiness of the activity.

9.3 Operating gearing refers to the proportion of fixed cost in relation to the total cost of some activity. Where the fixed cost forms a relatively high proportion of the total cost (at the business's normal level of activity), we say that the activity has high operating gearing.

Typically, high operating gearing is present in environments where there is a relatively high level of mechanisation (that is, capital-intensive environments). These environments tend to have relatively high fixed costs, such as depreciation and maintenance, together with relatively low variable costs.

High operating gearing means that changes in the level of activity have an accentuated effect on operating profit. For example, a 20 per cent decrease in output of a particular service will lead to a greater than 20 per cent decrease in operating profit (assuming no cost or price changes).

9.4 In the face of a restricting scarce resource, profit will be maximised by using the scarce resource on output where the contribution per unit of the scarce resource is maximised.

This means that the contribution per unit of the scarce resource (for example, hour of scarce labour or unit of scarce raw material) for each competing product or service needs to be identified. It is then a question of allocating the scarce resource to the product or service that provides the highest contribution per unit of the particular scarce resource.

The logic of this approach is that the scarce resource is allocated to the activity that uses it most effectively, in terms of contribution and, therefore, profit.

Chapter 10

10.1 In process costing, the total production cost for a period is divided by the number of completed units of output for the period to deduce the full cost per unit. Where there is work in progress at the beginning and/or the end of the period complications arise.

The problem is that some of the completed output incurred cost in the preceding period. Similarly, some of the cost incurred in the current period leads to completed production in the subsequent period. Account needs to be taken of these facts, if reliable full cost information is to be obtained.

Making the necessary adjustment involves calculating the equivalent units of production that the work in progress represents. This is the equivalent amount of completed units that could have been made given the effort and resources invested.

10.2 The only reason for distinguishing between direct and indirect costs is to help to deduce the full cost of a unit of output in a job-costing environment. In this environment, the products or services provided are quite distinct. Where all units of output are identical, or near identical, a process-costing approach will be taken. This means that an average cost can be applied to each identical unit. This avoids the need to separately identify direct and indirect costs.

Direct cost forms that part of the total cost of pursuing some activity that can be identified with, and measured in respect of, that particular activity. Examples of direct cost items in a typical job-costing environment include direct labour and direct materials. Indirect cost is the remainder of the cost of pursuing some activity.

10.3 The notion of direct and indirect cost is concerned only with the extent to which particular elements of cost can be identified with, and measured in respect of, a particular cost unit, usually a product or service. The distinction between the two costs is made exclusively for the purpose of calculating the full cost of some cost unit, where each cost unit produced is different. Thus, it is typically in the context of job costing, or some variant of it, that the distinction between direct and indirect cost is useful.

The notion of variable and fixed cost is concerned entirely with how costs behave in the face of changes in the volume of output. By distinguishing between fixed and variable cost, predictions can be made as to the total cost incurred at different levels of volume and/or the changes to total cost that occur if the volume of output is reduced or increased.

Thus the notions of direct and indirect cost, on the one hand, and of variable and fixed cost, on the other, are not related. In practice, some elements of direct cost are variable, while some are fixed. The same is true for indirect cost.

10.4 Full cost includes all of the cost of pursuing the cost objective, including a 'fair' share of the overheads. This means that, if the business were to sell its output at a price exactly equal to the full cost (which includes both manufacturing and non-manufacturing cost), the sales revenues for the period would exactly cover all of the cost. In other words, the business would break even.

Chapter 11

11.1 ABC is a means of dealing with charging overheads to units of output to derive full cost in a multi-product (job-or-batch costing) environment.

The traditional approach tends to accept that once identifiable direct cost, normally labour and materials, has been taken out, all of the remaining cost (overheads) must be treated as a common cost and applied to jobs using some formula, typically on the basis of direct labour hours.

ABC takes a much more questioning approach to overheads. It follows the philosophy that overheads do not occur for no reason, but they must be driven by activities. For example, a particular type of product may take up a disproportionately large part of supervisors' time. If that product were not made, in the long run, the supervision cost could be cut (fewer supervisors would be needed). Whereas the traditional approach would just accept that supervisory salaries are an overhead, which needs to be apportioned along with other overheads, ABC would seek to charge that part of the supervisors' salaries which is driven by the particular type of product to that product.

11.2 One criticism is on the issue of the cost/benefit balance. It is claimed that the work necessary to analyse activities and identify the cost drivers tends to be more expensive than is justified by the increased quality of the full cost information that emerges.

Linked to this is the belief of many that full cost information is of rather dubious value for most purposes, irrespective of how the full cost information is deduced. Many argue that full cost information is flawed by the fact that it takes no account of opportunity cost.

ABC enthusiasts would probably argue that deducing better quality full cost information is not the only benefit that is available, if the overhead cost drivers can be identified. Knowing what drives the costs can enable management to exercise more control over them.

11.3   The four main areas in the balanced scorecard are:

1   *Finance.* In this area, targets for measures such as return on capital employed will be stated.
2   *Customer.* Here the market/customers that the business will aim for is established, as will be targets for such things as measures of customer satisfaction and rate of growth in customer numbers.
3   *Internal business process.* Here the processes that are vital to the business will be identified. This might include levels of innovation, types of operation and after-sales service.
4   *Learning and growth.* In this area issues relating to growing the business and development of staff are identified and targets set.

11.4   The three phases of the product life cycle are:

- The *pre-production phase.* This is the period that precedes production of the product or service. During this phase, research and development – both of the product or service and of the market – is conducted.
- The *production phase* comes next, the one in which the product is made and sold or the service is rendered to customers.
- The *post-production phase* comes last. During this phase, costs may be incurred to correct faults that arose with products or services sold (after-sales service).

Target costing can be applied at the pre-production phase. Careful planning at this phase of the product's life can prevent future manufacturing costs from becoming 'locked in'. Thus, having determined a target price for the product, costs may be managed through redesign and so on to ensure that the total costs incurred allow room for an acceptable profit to be made. Kaizen costing aims to reduce the manufacturing cost of a particular product to below that of the previous period. Hence it is employed at the production phase.

Chapter 12

12.1   A budget can be defined as a financial plan for a future period of time. Thus it sets out the intentions which management has for the period concerned. Achieving the budget plans should help to achieve the long-term plans of the business. Achievement of the long-term plans should mean that the business is successfully working towards its strategic objectives and mission.

A budget differs from a forecast in that a forecast is a statement of what is expected to happen without the intervention of management, perhaps because they cannot intervene (as with a weather forecast). A plan is an intention to achieve.

Normally, management would take account of reliable forecasts when making its plans.

12.2   1   Budgets tend to promote forward thinking and the possible identification of short-term problems. Managers must plan and the budgeting process forces them to do so. In doing so, they are likely to encounter potential problems. If the potential problems can be identified early enough, solutions might be easily found.

2 Budgets can be used to help co-ordination between various sections of the business. It is important that the plans of one area of the business fit in with those of other areas; a lack of co-ordination could have disastrous consequences. Having formal statements of plans for each aspect of the business enables a check to be made that plans are complementary.

3 Budgets can motivate managers to better performance. It is believed that people are motivated by having a target to aim for. Provided that the inherent goals are achievable, budgets can provide an effective motivational device.

4 Budgets can provide a basis for a system of control. Having a plan against which actual performance can be measured provides a potentially useful tool of control.

5 Budgets can provide a system of authorisation. Many managers have 'spending' budgets such as research and development, staff training and so on. For these managers, the size of their budget defines their authority to spend.

12.3 Control can be defined as 'compelling things to occur as planned'. This implies that control can only be achieved if a plan exists. Budgets are financial plans. This means that, if actual performance can be compared with the budget (plan) for each aspect of the business, divergences from plan can be spotted. Steps can then be taken to bring matters back under control where they are going out of control.

12.4 A budget committee is a group of senior staff that is responsible for the budget preparation process within an organisation. The existence of the committee places the budget responsibility clearly with an identifiable group of people. This group can focus on the tasks involved.

Chapter 13

13.1 Feedforward controls try to anticipate what is likely to happen in the future and then assist in making the actual outcome match the desired outcome. They contrast with feedback controls, which simply compare actual to planned outcomes after the event. Feedforward controls are therefore more proactive.

13.2 A variance is the effect on budgeted profit of the particular cost or revenue item being considered. It represents the difference between the budgeted profit and the actual profit assuming everything, except the item under consideration, had gone according to budget. From this it must be the case that

Budgeted profit + favourable variances − unfavourable variances = actual profit

The purpose of analysing variances is to identify whether, and if so where, things are not going according to plan. If this can be done, it may be possible to find out the cause of things going out of control. If this can be discovered, it may then be possible to put things right for the future.

13.3 Where the budgeted and actual volumes of output do not coincide it is impossible to make valid comparison of 'allowed' and actual costs and revenues. Flexing the original budget to reflect the actual output level enables a more informative comparison to be made.

Flexing certainly does not mean that output volume differences do not matter. Flexing will show (as the difference between flexed and original budget profits) the effect on profit of output volume differences.

13.4 Deciding whether variances should be investigated involves the use of judgement. Often management will set a threshold of significance, for example 5 per cent of the budgeted figure for each variance relating to revenue or cost items. All variances above this threshold would then be investigated. Even where variances are below the threshold, any sign of a systemic variance, shown, for example, by an increasing cumulative total for the factor, should be investigated.

Knowledge of the cause of a particular variance may well put management in a position to take actions that will be beneficial to the business in the future. Investigating variances, however, is likely to be relatively expensive in staff time. A judgement needs to be made on whether the value or benefit of knowing the cause of the variance will be justified by the cost of this knowledge. As with most investigations of this type, it is difficult to judge the value of the knowledge until after the variance has been investigated.

Chapter 14

14.1 NPV is usually considered the best method of assessing investment opportunities because it takes account of:

- *The timing of the cash flows.* By *discounting* the various cash flows associated with each project according to when it is expected to arise, it recognises the fact that cash flows do not all occur simultaneously. Associated with this is the fact that, by discounting, using the opportunity cost of finance, the net benefit, after financing costs have been met, is identified (as the NPV).
- *The whole of the relevant cash flows.* NPV includes all of the relevant cash flows irrespective of when they are expected to occur. It treats them differently according to their date of occurrence, but they are all taken into account in the NPV and all can have an influence on the decision.
- *The objectives of the business.* NPV is the only method of appraisal where the output of the analysis has a direct bearing on the wealth of the owners of the business. (Positive NPVs enhance wealth; negative ones reduce it.) Since most private-sector businesses seek to increase their owners' wealth, NPV clearly is the best approach to use.

NPV provides clear decision rules concerning acceptance/rejection of projects and the ranking of projects. It is fairly simple to use, particularly with the availability of modern computer software that takes away the need for routine calculations to be done manually.

14.2 The payback period method, in its original form, does not take account of the time value of money. However, it would be possible to modify the payback method to accommodate this requirement. Cash flows arising from a project could be discounted, using the cost of finance as the appropriate discount rate, in the same way as in the NPV and IRR methods. The discounted payback approach is used by some businesses (for example Kingfisher plc – see Real World 14.15, page 603) and represents an improvement on the original approach described in the chapter. However, it still retains the other flaws of the original payback approach that were discussed. For example, it ignores relevant data after the payback period. Thus, even in its modified form, the PP method cannot be regarded as superior to NPV.

14.3 The IRR method does appear to be similar in popularity to the NPV method among practising managers. The main reasons for this appear to be as follows:

- A preference for a percentage return ratio rather than an absolute figure as a means of expressing the outcome of a project. This preference may reflect the fact that other financial goals of the business are often set in terms of ratios, for example return on capital employed.

- A preference for ranking projects in terms of their percentage return. Managers feel it is easier to rank projects on the basis of percentage returns (though NPV outcomes should be just as easy for them). We saw in the chapter that the IRR method could provide misleading advice on the ranking of projects and the NPV method was preferable for this purpose.

14.4 Cash flows are preferred to profit flows because cash is the ultimate measure of economic wealth. Cash is used to acquire resources and for distribution to shareholders. When cash is invested in a project, an opportunity cost is incurred, as the cash cannot be used in other investment projects. Similarly, when positive cash flows are generated by the project, the cash can be used to reinvest in other projects.

Profit, on the other hand, is relevant to reporting the productive effort for a period. This measure of effort may have only a tenuous relationship to cash flows for a period. The conventions of accounting may lead to the recognition of gains and losses in one period and the relevant cash inflows and outflows occurring in another period.

Chapter 15

15.1 A sale-and-leaseback arrangement may have the following disadvantages:

- There may be a tax liability arising on the sale of the asset.
- The future cost of the lease payments may be difficult to predict.
- Lease payments may become a burden over time as a result of upward reviews.
- Where property is being used in a sale-and-leaseback arrangement, the business may have to relocate its operations at the end of the lease period if a new lease agreement cannot be reached.
- The business will not benefit from any future increases in value of the asset.

15.2 A listed business may wish to revert to unlisted status for a number of possible reasons. These include:

- *Cost.* A Stock Exchange listing can be costly, as the business must adhere to certain administrative regulations and financial disclosures.
- *Scrutiny.* Listed companies are subject to close scrutiny by analysts and this may not be welcome if the business is engaged in sensitive negotiations or controversial business activities.
- *Takeover risk.* An unwelcome bidder may purchase the shares of the business and this may result in a takeover.
- *Investor profile.* If the business is dominated by a few investors who wish to retain their interest in the business and do not wish to raise further equity by public issues, the benefits of a listing are few.

15.3 An offer for sale involves an issuing house buying the shares in the business and then, in turn, selling the shares to the public. The issue will be advertised by the publication of a prospectus, which will set out details of the business and the issue price of the shares (or reserve price if a tender issue is being made). The shares issued by the issuing house may be either new shares or shares that have been purchased from existing shareholders. A public issue is where the business undertakes direct responsibility for issuing shares to the public. If an issuing house is employed, it will usually be in the role of adviser and administrator of the issue. However, the issuing house may also underwrite the issue. A public issue runs the risk that the shares will not be taken up and is a less popular form of issue for businesses.

15.4 Invoice discounting is a service offered to businesses by a financial institution that is prepared to advance a sum equivalent to 80 per cent, or so, of outstanding trade receivables. The amount advanced is usually payable within 60 to 90 days. The business will retain responsibility for collecting the amounts owing from credit customers and the advance must be repaid irrespective of whether the trade receivables have been collected.

Factoring is a service that is also offered to businesses by financial institutions. In this case, the factor will take over the business's sales and trade receivables records and will undertake to collect trade receivables on behalf of the client business. The factor will also be prepared to make an advance of 80 per cent, or so, of approved trade receivables that is repayable from the amounts received from customers. The service charge for invoice discounting is up to 0.5 per cent of sales revenue, whereas the service charge for factoring is up to 3 per cent of sales revenue. This difference explains, in part, why businesses have shown a preference for invoice discounting rather than factoring in recent years. However, the factor provides additional services, as explained.

Chapter 16

16.1 Although the credit manager is responsible for ensuring that receivables pay on time, Tariq may be right in denying blame. Various factors may be responsible for the situation described which are beyond the control of the credit manager. These include:

- a downturn in the economy leading to financial difficulties among credit customers;
- decisions by other managers within the business to liberalise credit policy in order to stimulate sales;
- an increase in competition among suppliers offering credit, which is being exploited by customers;
- disputes with customers over the quality of goods or services supplied; and
- problems in the delivery of goods leading to delays.

You may have thought of others.

16.2 The level of inventories held will be affected in the following ways:

(a) An increase in production bottlenecks is likely to result in an increase in raw materials and work in progress being processed within the plant. Therefore, inventories levels should rise.

(b) A rise in the cost of capital will make holding inventories more expensive. This may, in turn, lead to a decision to reduce inventories levels.

(c) The decision to reduce the range of products should result in a lower level of inventories being held. It would no longer be necessary to hold certain items in order to meet customer demand.

(d) Switching to a local supplier may reduce the lead time between ordering an item and receiving it. This should, in turn, reduce the need to carry such high levels of the particular item.

(e) A deterioration in the quality of bought-in items may result in the purchase of higher quantities of inventories in order to take account of the defective element in inventories acquired. It may also lead to an increase in the inspection time for items received. This too would lead to a rise in inventories levels.

16.3 Inventories are held:

- to meet customer demand;
- to avoid the problems of running out of inventories; and
- to take advantage of profitable opportunities (for example, buying a product that is expected to rise steeply in price in the future).

The first reason may be described as transactionary, the second precautionary and the third speculative. They are, in essence, the same reasons why a business holds cash.

16.4 (a) The costs of holding too little cash are:

- failure to meet obligations when they fall due which can damage the reputation of the business and may, in the extreme, lead to the business being wound up;
- having to borrow and thereby incur interest charges; and
- an inability to take advantage of profitable opportunities.

(b) The costs of holding too much cash are:

- failure to use the funds available for more profitable purposes; and
- loss of value during a period of inflation.

APPENDIX  E

Solutions to selected exercises

Chapter 2

2.1   Paul

Statement of cash flows for Thursday

	£
Opening balance (from Wednesday)	59
Cash from sale of wrapping paper	47
Cash paid to purchase wrapping paper	(53)
Closing balance	53

Income statement for Thursday

	£
Sales revenue	47
Cost of goods sold	(33)
Profit	14

Statement of financial position as at Thursday evening

	£
Cash	53
Inventories of goods for resale (23 + 53 − 33)	43
Total assets	96
Equity	96

2.2   Paul (*continued*)

Equity

	£
Cash introduced by Paul on Monday	40
Profit for Monday	15
Profit for Tuesday	18
Profit for Wednesday	9
Profit for Thursday	14
Total business wealth (total assets)	96

Thus the equity, all of which belongs to Paul as sole owner, consists of the cash he put in to start the business plus the profit earned each day.

2.3   Helen

Income statement for day 1

	£
Sales revenue (70 × £0.80)	56
Cost of sales (70 × £0.50)	(35)
Profit	21

Statement of cash flows for day 1

	£
Cash introduced by Helen	40
Cash from sales	56
Cash for purchases (80 × £0.50)	(40)
Closing balance	56

Statement of financial position as at end of day 1

	£
Cash balance	56
Inventories of unsold goods (10 × £0.50)	5
Total assets	61
Equity	61

Income statement for day 2

	£
Sales revenue (65 × £0.80)	52.0
Cost of sales (65 × £0.50)	(32.5)
Profit	19.5

Statement of cash flows for day 2

	£
Opening balance	56.0
Cash from sales	52.0
Cash for purchases (60 × £0.50)	(30.0)
Closing balance	78.0

Statement of financial position as at end of day 2

	£
Cash balance	78.0
Inventories of unsold goods (5 × £0.50)	2.5
Total assets	80.5
Equity	80.5

Income statement for day 3

	£
Sales revenue ((20 × £0.80) + (45 × £0.40))	34.0
Cost of sales (65 × £0.50)	(32.5)
Profit	1.5

Statement of cash flows for day 3

	£
Opening balance	78.0
Cash from sales	34.0
Cash for purchases (60 × £0.50)	(30.0)
Closing balance	82.0

Statement of financial position as at end of day 3

	£
Cash balance	82.0
Inventories of unsold goods	–
Total assets	82.0
Equity	82.0

2.6 Crafty Engineering

(a) **Statement of financial position as at 30 June last year**

	£000
ASSETS	
Non-current assets	
Property, plant and equipment	
Property	320
Equipment and tools	207
Motor vehicles	38
	565
Current assets	
Inventories	153
Trade receivables	185
	338
Total assets	903
EQUITY AND LIABILITIES	
Equity (which is the missing figure)	441
Non-current liabilities	
Long-term borrowings (loan from Industrial Finance Company)	260
Current liabilities	
Trade payables	86
Short-term borrowings	116
	202
Total equity and liabilities	903

(b) The statement of financial position reveals a large investment in non-current assets. It represents more than 60 per cent of the total investment in assets (565/903). The nature of the business may require a heavy investment in non-current assets. The current assets exceed the current liabilities by a large amount (approximately 1.7 times). Hence, there is no obvious sign of a liquidity problem. However, the statement of financial position reveals that the business has no cash balance and is therefore dependent on the continuing support of short-term borrowing to meet maturing obligations.

When considering the long-term financing of the business, we can see that about 37 per cent (that is, 260/(260 + 441)) of total long-term finance is supplied by borrowings and about 63 per cent (that is, 441/(260 + 441)) by the owners. This level of long-term borrowing seems high but not excessive. However, we need to know more about the ability of the business to service the borrowing (that is, make interest payments and repayments of the amount borrowed) before a full assessment can be made.

Chapter 3

3.1 **Comments**

(a) Equity does increase as a result of the owners introducing more cash into the business, but it will also increase as a result of the owners introducing other assets (for example, a motor car) and by the business generating revenue by trading. Similarly, equity decreases not only as a result of withdrawals of cash by owners but also by withdrawals of other assets (for example, inventories for the owners' personal use) and through the business incurring trading expenses. Generally speaking, equity will alter more as a result of trading activities than for any other reason.

(b) An accrued expense is not one that relates to next year. It is one that needs to be matched with the revenue of the reporting period under review, but that has yet to be met in terms of cash payment. As such, it will appear on the statement of financial position as a current liability.

(c) The purpose of depreciation is not to provide for asset replacement. It is an attempt to allocate the cost, or fair value, of the asset (less any residual value) over its useful life. Depreciation provides a measure of the amount of a non-current asset that has been consumed during a period. This amount is then charged as an expense for the period. Depreciation is a book entry (the outlay of cash occurs when the asset is purchased) and does not normally entail setting aside a separate amount of cash for asset replacement. Even if this were done, there would be no guarantee that sufficient funds would be available at the end of the asset's life for its replacement. Factors such as inflation and technological change may mean that the replacement cost is higher than the original cost of the asset.

(d) In the short term, the current value of a non-current asset may exceed its original cost. However, nearly all non-current assets wear out over time through being used to generate wealth. This will be the case for buildings. Thus, some measure of depreciation is needed to reflect the fact that the asset is being consumed. Some businesses revalue their buildings upwards where the current value is significantly higher than the original cost. Where this occurs, the depreciation charge should be based on the revalued amount, which will result in higher depreciation charges.

3.3 The generation of profit combined with downward movement in cash may arise for various reasons, including the following:

- the purchase for cash during the period of assets (for example, motor cars and inventories) which were not all consumed during the period and so will not affect expenses as much as cash;
- the payment of an outstanding liability (for example, borrowings), which will have an effect on cash but not on expenses in the income statement;
- the withdrawal of cash by the owners from the equity invested, which will not affect the expenses in the income statement;
- the generation of revenue on credit where the cash has yet to be received. This will increase the sales revenue for the period but will not increase the cash balance until a later time.

3.4 **Missing values**

(a) Rent payable – expense for period	£9,000
(b) Rates and insurance – expense for period	£6,000
(c) General expenses – paid in period	£7,000
(d) Interest (on borrowings) payable – prepaid	£500
(e) Salaries – paid in period	£6,000
(f) Rent receivable – received during period	£3,000

3.7   Nikov and Co.

An examination of the income statements for the two years reveals a number of interesting points, which include:

- an increase in sales revenue and gross profit of 9.9 per cent in 2016;
- the gross profit expressed as a percentage of sales revenue remaining at 70 per cent;
- an increase in salaries of 7.2 per cent;
- an increase in selling and distribution costs of 31.2 per cent;
- an increase in bad debts of 392.5 per cent;
- a decline in profit for the year of 39.3 per cent; and
- a decline in the profit for the year as a percentage of sales revenue from 13.3 per cent to 7.4 per cent.

We can see that the business has enjoyed an increase in sales revenue and gross profits, but this has failed to translate to an increase in profit for the year because of the significant rise in overheads. The increase in selling costs during 2016 suggests that the increase in sales revenue was achieved by greater marketing effort, and the huge increase in bad debts suggests that the increase in sales revenue may be attributable to selling to less creditworthy customers or to a weak debt-collection policy. There appears to have been a change of policy in 2016 towards sales, and this has not been successful overall as the profit for the year has shown a dramatic decline.

Chapter 4

4.1 Limited companies can no more set a limit on the amount of debts they will meet than can individuals. They must meet their debts up to the limit of their assets, just as we as individuals must. In the context of owners' claim, 'reserves' mean part of the owners' claim against the assets of the company. These assets may or may not include cash. The legal ability of the company to pay dividends is not related to the amount of cash held.

Preference shares do not carry a guaranteed dividend. They simply guarantee that the preference shareholders have a right to the first slice of any dividend that is paid. Shares of many companies can, in effect, be bought by one investor from another through the Stock Exchange. Such a transaction has no direct effect on the company, however. These are not new shares being offered by the company, but 'second-hand' (that is, existing) shares that are being sold between investors.

4.2 (a) The first part of the quote is incorrect. Bonus shares should not, of themselves, increase the value of the shareholders' wealth. This is because reserves, which belong to the shareholders, are used to create bonus shares. Thus, each shareholder's stake in the company has not changed.

(b) This statement is incorrect. Shares can be issued at any price, provided that it is not below the nominal value of the shares. Once the company has been trading profitably for a period, the shares will be worth more than their nominal value: that is, the amount at which they were issued when the company was first formed. In such circumstances, issuing shares at above their nominal value would not only be legal, but essential to preserve the wealth of existing shareholders relative to new shareholders.

(c) This statement is incorrect. From a legal perspective, the maximum dividend payable is based on the amount of a company's revenue reserves. This amount represents any after-tax profits or gains realised that have not been eroded through, for example, payments of previous dividends. From a legal perspective, cash availability is not an issue. It would be perfectly legal for a company to borrow funds in order to pay a dividend – although whether this would be commercially prudent is another question.

(d) This statement is partly incorrect. Companies do indeed have to pay tax on their profits. Depending on their circumstances, shareholders might also have to pay tax on their dividends.

4.4 **Iqbal Ltd**

Year	Maximum dividend £	
2013	0	No profit exists out of which to pay a dividend.
2014	0	There remains a cumulative loss of £7,000. Since the revaluation represents a gain that has not been realised, it cannot be used to justify a dividend.
2015	13,000	The cumulative net realised gains are derived as (−£15,000 + £8,000 + £15,000 + £5,000).
2016	14,000	The realised profits and gains for the year.
2017	22,000	The realised profits and gains for the year.

4.6 **Pear Limited**

Statement of financial position as at 30 September 2017

	£000
ASSETS	
Non-current assets	
Property, plant and equipment	
Cost (1,570 + 30)	1,600
Depreciation (690 + 12)	(702)
	898
Current assets	
Inventories	207
Trade receivables (182 + 18 − 4)	196
Cash at bank	21
	424
Total assets	1,322
EQUITY AND LIABILITIES	
Equity	
Share capital	300
Share premium account	300
Retained earnings (104 + 41 − 25)	120
	720
Non-current liabilities	
Borrowings – 10% loan (repayable 2018)	300
Current liabilities	
Trade payables	88
Other payables (20 + 30 + 15 + 2)	67
Taxation	17
Dividend approved	25
Borrowings – bank overdraft	105
	302
Total equity and liabilities	1,322

Income statement for the year ended 30 September 2017

	£000
Revenue (1,456 + 18)	1,474
Cost of sales	(768)
Gross profit	706
Salaries	(220)
Depreciation (249 + 12)	(261)
Other operating costs (131 + (2% × 200) + 2)	(137)
Operating profit	88
Interest payable (15 + 15)	(30)
Profit before taxation	58
Taxation (58 × 30%)	(17)
Profit for the year	41

Chapter 5

5.3 **I. Ching (Booksellers) plc**

Statement of comprehensive income for the year ended 31 May 2017

	£000
Revenue	943
Cost of sales	(460)
Gross profit	483
Distribution expenses	(110)
Administrative expenses	(212)
Other expenses	(25)
Operating profit	136
Finance charges	(40)
Profit before tax	96
Taxation	(24)
Profit for the year	72
Other comprehensive income	
Revaluation of property, plant and equipment	20
Foreign currency translation differences for foreign operations	(15)
Tax on other comprehensive income	(1)
Other comprehensive income for the year, net of tax	4
Total comprehensive income for the year	76

5.4 **Manet plc**

Statement of changes in equity for the year ended 31 May 2017

	Share capital £m	Share premium £m	Revaluation reserve £m	Translation reserve £m	Retained earnings £m	Total £m
Balance as at 1 June 2016	250	50	120	15	380	815
Changes in equity for the year						
Dividends (Note 1)					(80)	(80)
Total comprehensive income for the year (Note 2)	–	–	30	(5)	160	185
Balance at 31 May 2017	250	50	150	10	460	920

Notes:

1 Dividends have been shown in the statement rather than in the notes. Either approach is acceptable.

2 The effect of each component of comprehensive income on each component of shareholder equity must be shown. The revaluation gain and loss on exchange translation are each transferred to a specific reserve and the profit for the year is transferred to retained earnings.

5.5 (a) The 'comply or explain' approach means that companies listed on the London Stock Exchange are expected to comply with the requirements of the UK Corporate Governance Code or the directors must give the shareholders good reason why they do not. Failure to do one or the other can lead to the company's shares being suspended from listing.

An advantage of this approach is that it provides a company with a degree of flexibility over its governance procedures. Where, for example, a company is dealing with a crisis situation, the board of directors may feel that a single, strong leader is required. It may, therefore, be decided that one person will occupy the roles of both chairman and chief executive. Although this is contrary to the UK Code, shareholders may agree, given the particular circumstances, to merging the two roles.

A disadvantage is that when applying the UK Code there is an element of subjectivity involved. The UK Code requires, for example, that the directors establish a satisfactory dialogue with shareholders. This may, however, be interpreted in different ways and so it may be difficult to establish whether compliance has really occurred. It may also be difficult to make comparisons between companies.

(b) Preparing a strategic report may present a problem for accountants. For information to be credible to all interested parties, accountants should be as neutral as possible in measuring and reporting the financial performance and position of the business. The strategic report requires some interpretation of results and there is always a risk of bias, or at least the perception of bias among some users, in what items are reported and how they reflect on business performance. The board of directors is charged with running the business and it is logical that the directors accept full responsibility for preparing the report. This should be made clear to users.

5.7 Turner plc

We can see from the table below that the software segment generates the highest revenue, but also generates the lowest profit. We can use some simple ratios at this point to help evaluate segmental performance. We can start by considering the profit generated in relation to the sales revenue for each operating segment. We can see from the table below that the engineering segment generates the most profit in relation to sales revenue. Around 23 per cent, or £0.23 in every £1, of profit is derived from the sales revenue generated. However, for the software segment, only 4 per cent, or £0.04 in every £1, of profit is derived from the sales revenue generated.

We can also compare the profit generated with the net assets employed (that is, total assets less total liabilities) for each segment. We can see from the table below that the electronics segment produces the best return on net assets employed: around £0.65 for every £1 invested. Once again, the software segment produces the worst results.

The reasons for the relatively poor results from the software segment need further investigation. There may be valid reasons; for example, it may be experiencing severe competitive pressures. The results for this segment, however, are not disastrous: it is making a profit. Nevertheless, the business may wish to re-evaluate its long-term presence in this market.

It is interesting to note that the software segment had the highest new investment in non-current assets during the period – as much as the other two segments combined. The reason for such a large investment in such a relatively poorly performing segment needs to be justified. It is possible that the business will reap rewards for the investment in the future; however, we do not have enough information to understand the reasons for the investment decision.

Depreciation charges in the software segment are significantly higher than for the other operating segments. This may be because the segment has more non-current assets, although we do not have a figure for the non-current assets held. The depreciation charge as a percentage of segment assets is also higher and the reasons for this should be investigated.

Table of key results

	Software	Electronics	Engineering
Total revenue	£250m	£230m	£52m
Segment profit	£10m	£34m	£12m
Net assets (assets less liabilities)	£85m	£52m	£30m
Segment profit as a percentage of sales revenue	4.0%	14.8%	23.1%
Segment profit as a percentage of net assets employed	11.8%	65.4%	40.0%
Expenditure on non-current assets	£22m	£12m	£10m
Total assets	£140m	£90m	£34m
Depreciation	£60m	£35m	£10m
Depreciation as a percentage of segment assets	42.9%	38.9%	29.4%

Chapter 6

6.1 (a) An increase in the level of inventories would, ultimately, have an adverse effect on cash.

(b) A rights issue of ordinary shares will give rise to a positive cash flow, which will be included in the 'financing' section of the statement of cash flows.

(c) A bonus issue of ordinary shares has no cash flow effect.

(d) Writing off some of the value of the inventories has no cash flow effect.

(e) A disposal for cash of a large number of shares by a major shareholder has no cash flow effect as far as the business is concerned.

(f) Depreciation does not involve cash at all. Using the indirect method of deducing cash flows from operating activities involves the depreciation expense in the calculation, but this is simply because we are trying to find out, from the profit before taxation (after depreciation) figure, what the profit before taxation *and* depreciation must have been.

6.3 **Torrent plc**

Statement of cash flows for the year ended 31 December 2016

	£m
Cash flows from operating activities	
Profit before taxation (after interest) (see Note 1 below)	170
Adjustments for:	
Depreciation (Note 2)	78
Interest expense (Note 3)	26
	274
Decrease in inventories (41 − 35)	6
Increase in trade receivables (145 − 139)	(6)
Decrease in trade payables (54 − 41)	(13)
Cash generated from operations	261
Interest paid	(26)
Taxation paid (Note 4)	(41)
Dividend paid	(60)
Net cash from operating activities	134
Cash flows from investing activities	
Payments to acquire plant and machinery	(67)
Net cash used in investing activities	(67)
Cash flows from financing activities	
Redemption of loan notes (250 − 150) (Note 5)	(100)
Net cash used in financing activities	(100)
Net decrease in cash and cash equivalents	(33)
Cash and cash equivalents at 1 January 2016	
Bank overdraft	(56)
Cash and cash equivalents at 31 December 2016	
Bank overdraft	(89)

To see how this relates to the cash of the business at the beginning and end of the year, it can be useful to provide a reconciliation as follows:

Analysis of cash and cash equivalents during the year ended 31 December 2016

	£m
Cash and cash equivalents at 1 January 2016	(56)
Net cash outflow	(33)
Cash and cash equivalents at 31 December 2016	(89)

Notes:

1   This is simply taken from the income statement for the year.

2   Since there were no disposals, the depreciation charges must be the difference between the start and end of the year's plant and machinery values, adjusted by the cost of any additions.

	£m
Carrying amount at 1 January 2016	325
Additions	67
Depreciation (balancing figure)	(78)
Carrying amount at 31 December 2016	314

3   Interest payable expense must be taken out, by adding it back to the profit before taxation figure. We subsequently deduct the cash paid for interest payable during the year. In this case, the two figures are identical.

4   Companies pay 50 per cent of their tax during their accounting year and 50 per cent in the following year. Thus the 2016 payment would have been half the tax on the 2015 profit (that is, the figure that would have appeared in the current liabilities at the end of 2015), plus half of the 2016 tax charge (that is, $23 + (\frac{1}{2} \times 36) = 41$).

5   It is assumed that the cash payment to redeem the loan notes was simply the difference between the two statement of financial position figures.
6   It seems that there was a bonus issue of ordinary shares during the year. These increased by £100m. At the same time, the share premium account balance reduced by £40m (to zero) and the revaluation reserve balance fell by £60m.

6.6   Blackstone plc

Statement of cash flows for the year ended 31 March 2017

	£m
Cash flows from operating activities	
Profit before taxation (after interest) (see Note 1)	1,853
Adjustments for:	
Depreciation (Note 2)	1,289
Interest expense (Note 3)	456
	3,598
Increase in inventories (2,410 − 1,209)	(1,201)
Increase in trade receivables (1,173 − 641)	(532)
Increase in trade payables (1,507 − 931)	576
Cash generated from operations	2,441
Interest paid	(456)
Taxation paid (Note 4)	(300)
Dividend paid	(400)
Net cash from operating activities	1,285
Cash flows from investing activities	
Proceeds of disposals	54
Payment to acquire intangible non-current asset	(700)
Payments to acquire property, plant and equipment	(4,578)
Net cash used in investing activities	(5,224)
Cash flows from financing activities	
Bank borrowings	2,000
Net cash from financing activities	2,000
Net decrease in cash and cash equivalents	(1,939)
Cash and cash equivalents at 1 April 2016	
Cash at bank	123
Cash and cash equivalents at 31 March 2017	
Bank overdraft	(1,816)

To see how this relates to the cash of the business at the beginning and end of the year it can be useful to provide a reconciliation as follows:

Analysis of cash and cash equivalents during the year ended 31 March 2017

	£m
Cash and cash equivalents at 1 April 2016	123
Net cash outflow	(1,939)
Cash and cash equivalents at 31 March 2017	1,816

Notes:
1   This is simply taken from the income statement for the year.
2   The full depreciation charge was that stated in Note 2 to the question (£1,251m), plus the deficit on disposal of the non-current assets. According to Note 2, these non-current assets had originally cost £581m and had been depreciated by £489m, giving a net carrying amount of £92m. They were sold for £54m, leading to a deficit on disposal of £38m. Thus the full depreciation expense for the year was £1,289m (that is, £1,251m + £38m).

3   Interest payable expense must be taken out, by adding it back to the profit before taxation figure. We subsequently deduct the cash paid for interest payable during the year. In this case, the two figures are identical.

4   Companies pay tax at 50 per cent during their accounting year and the other 50 per cent in the following year. Thus the 2017 payment would have been half the tax on the 2016 profit (that is, the figure that would have appeared in the current liabilities at 31 March 2016), plus half of the 2017 tax charge (that is, $105 + (^1/_2 \times 390) = 300$).

6.7   York plc

Statement of cash flows for the year ended 30 September 2017

	£m
Cash flows from operating activities	
Profit before taxation (after interest) (see Note 1)	10.0
Adjustments for:	
Depreciation (Note 2)	9.8
Interest expense (Note 3)	3.0
	22.8
Increase in inventories and trade receivables (122.1 − 119.8)	(2.3)
Increase in trade payables (82.5 − 80.0)	2.5
Cash generated from operations	23.0
Interest paid	(3.0)
Taxation paid (Note 4)	(2.3)
Dividend paid	(3.5)
Net cash from operating activities	14.2
Cash flows from investing activities	
Proceeds of disposals (Note 2)	5.2
Payments to acquire non-current assets	(20.0)
Net cash used in investing activities	(14.8)
Cash flows from financing activities	
Increase in long-term borrowings	3.0
Share issue (Note 5)	5.0
Net cash from financing activities	8.0
Net increase in cash and cash equivalents	7.4
Cash and cash equivalents at 1 October 2016	
Cash at bank	9.2
Cash and cash equivalents at 30 September 2017	
Cash at bank	16.6

To see how this relates to the cash of the business at the beginning and end of the year it can be useful to provide a reconciliation as follows:

Analysis of cash and cash equivalents during the year ended 30 September 2017

	£m
Cash and cash equivalents at 1 October 2016	9.2
Net cash inflow	7.4
Cash and cash equivalents at 30 September 2017	16.6

Notes:

1   This is simply taken from the income statement for the year.

2   The full depreciation charge was the £13.0m, less the surplus on disposal (£3.2m), both stated in Note 1 to the question. (According to the table in Note 4 to the question, the non-current assets disposed of had a net carrying value of £2.0m. To produce a surplus of £3.2m, they must have been sold for £5.2m.)

3 Interest payable expense must be taken out, by adding it back to the profit before taxation figure. We subsequently deduct the cash paid for interest payable during the year. In this case, the two figures are identical.

4 Companies pay 50 per cent of their tax during their accounting year and the other 50 per cent in the following year. Thus the 2017 payment would have been half the tax on the 2016 profit (that is, the figure that would have appeared in the current liabilities at 30 September 2016), plus half of the 2017 tax charge (that is, $1.0 + (\frac{1}{2} \times 2.6) = 2.3$).

5 This issue must have been for cash since it could not have been a bonus issue – the share premium is untouched and 'Reserves' had altered over the year only by the amount of the 2017 retained earnings (profit for the year, less the dividend). The shares seem to have been issued at their nominal value (par). This is a little surprising since the business has assets that seem to be above that value. On the other hand, if this was a rights issue, the low issue price would not have disadvantaged the existing shareholders since they were also the beneficiaries of the advantage of the low issue price.

Chapter 7

7.1 Three businesses

A plc operates a supermarket chain. The grocery business is highly competitive and, in order to generate high sales volumes, it is usually necessary to accept low operating profit margins. Thus, we can see that the operating profit margin of A plc is the lowest of the three businesses. The inventories turnover period of supermarket chains also tend to be quite low. They are often efficient in managing inventories, and most supermarket chains have invested heavily in inventories control and logistical systems over the years. The average settlement period for receivables is very low as most sales are for cash, although, when a customer pays by credit card, there is usually a small delay before the supermarket receives the amount due. A low inventories turnover period and a low average settlement period for receivables usually mean that the investment in current assets is low. Hence, the current ratio (current assets/current liabilities) is also low.

B plc is the holiday tour operator. We can see that the sales to capital employed ratio is the highest of the three. This is because tour operators do not usually require a large investment of capital: they do not need a large asset base in order to conduct their operations. The inventories turnover period ratio does not apply to B plc. It is a service business, which does not hold inventories for resale. We can see that the average settlement period for receivables is low. This may be because customers are invoiced near to the holiday date for any amounts outstanding and must pay before going on holiday. The lack of inventories held and low average settlement period for receivables leads to a very low current ratio.

C plc is the food manufacturing business. We can see that the sales to capital employed ratio is the lowest of the three. This is because manufacturers tend to invest heavily in both current and non-current assets. The inventories turnover period is the highest of the three. Three different kinds of inventories – raw materials, work in progress and finished goods – are held by manufacturers. The average receivables settlement period is also the highest of the three. Manufacturers tend to sell to other businesses rather than to the public and their customers will normally demand credit. A one-month credit period for customers is fairly common for manufacturing businesses, although customers may receive a discount for prompt payment. The relatively high investment in inventories and receivables usually results in a high current ratio.

7.2 Amsterdam Ltd and Berlin Ltd

The ratios for Amsterdam Ltd and Berlin Ltd reveal that the average settlement period for trade receivables for Amsterdam Ltd is three times that for Berlin Ltd. Berlin Ltd is therefore much quicker in collecting amounts outstanding from customers. On the other hand, there is not much difference between the two businesses in the time taken to pay trade payables.

It is interesting to compare the difference in the trade receivables and payables settlement periods for each business. As Amsterdam Ltd allows an average of 63 days' credit to its customers, yet pays suppliers within 50 days, it will require greater investment in working capital than Berlin Ltd, which allows an average of only 21 days to its customers but takes 45 days to pay its suppliers.

Amsterdam Ltd has a much higher gross profit margin than Berlin Ltd. However, the operating profit margin for the two businesses is identical. This suggests that Amsterdam Ltd has much higher overheads (as a percentage of sales revenue) than Berlin Ltd. The average inventories turnover period for Amsterdam Ltd is more than twice that of Berlin Ltd. This may be due to the fact that Amsterdam Ltd maintains a wider range of inventories in an attempt to meet customer requirements. The evidence therefore suggests that Amsterdam Ltd is the business that prides itself on personal service. The higher average settlement period for trade receivables is consistent with a more relaxed attitude to credit collection (thereby maintaining customer goodwill) and the high overheads are consistent with incurring the additional costs of satisfying customers' requirements. Amsterdam Ltd's high inventories levels are consistent with maintaining a wide range of inventories, with the aim of satisfying a range of customer needs.

Berlin Ltd has the characteristics of a more price-competitive business. Its gross profit margin is much lower than that of Amsterdam Ltd, that is, a much lower gross profit for each £1 of sales revenue. However, overheads have been kept low, the effect being that the operating profit margin is the same as Amsterdam Ltd's. The low average inventories turnover period and average settlement period for trade receivables are consistent with a business that wishes to minimise investment in current assets, thereby reducing costs.

7.6 **Genesis Ltd**

(a)
$$\text{Current ratio} = \frac{232}{550} = 0.42:1$$

$$\text{Acid test ratio} = \frac{104}{550} = 0.19:1$$

$$\text{Inventories turnover period} = \frac{128}{1,248} \times 365 = 37 \text{ days}$$

$$\text{Average settlement period for trade receivables} = \frac{104}{1,640} \times 365 = 23 \text{ days}$$

$$\text{Average settlement period for trade payables} = \frac{184}{1,260} \times 365 = 53 \text{ days}$$

It is difficult to make a judgement in the absence of any basis for comparison, but there is some suggestion that the business is overtrading. Both of the liquidity ratios look weak. The acid test ratio should probably be around 1:1. Customers are paying more than twice as quickly as suppliers are being paid. This suggests that pressure may be being applied to the former to pay quickly, perhaps with adverse results. It may also imply that payments to suppliers are being delayed because of a lack of available finance.

(b) Overtrading must be dealt with either by increasing the level of funding to match the level of activity, or by reducing the level of activity to match the funds available. The latter option may result in a reduction in operating profit in the short term but may be necessary to ensure long-term survival.

7.7 **Harridges Ltd**

(a)

	2016	2017
ROCE	$\frac{310}{1,600} = 19.4\%$	$\frac{350}{1,700} = 20.6\%$
ROSF	$\frac{155}{1,100} = 14.1\%$	$\frac{175}{1,200} = 14.6\%$
Gross profit margin	$\frac{1,040}{2,600} = 40\%$	$\frac{1,150}{3,500} = 32.9\%$
Operating profit margin	$\frac{310}{2,600} = 11.9\%$	$\frac{350}{3,500} = 10\%$
Current ratio	$\frac{735}{400} = 1.8$	$\frac{660}{485} = 1.4$
Acid test ratio	$\frac{485}{400} = 1.2$	$\frac{260}{485} = 0.5$
Trade receivables settlement period	$\frac{105}{2,600} \times 365 = 15$ days	$\frac{145}{3,500} \times 365 = 15$ days
Trade payables settlement period	$\frac{300}{1,560^*} \times 365 = 70$ days	$\frac{375}{2,350^*} \times 365 = 58$ days
Inventories turnover period	$\frac{250}{1,560} \times 365 = 58$ days	$\frac{400}{2,350} \times 365 = 62$ days
Gearing ratio	$\frac{500}{1,600} = 31.3\%$	$\frac{500}{1,700} = 29.4\%$

* Used because the credit purchases figure is not available.

(b) There has been a considerable decline in the gross profit margin during 2017. This fact, combined with the increase in sales revenue by more than a third, suggests that a price-cutting policy has been adopted in an attempt to stimulate sales. The resulting increase in sales revenue, however, has led to only a small improvement in ROCE and ROSF.

Despite a large cut in the gross profit margin, the operating profit margin has fallen by less than 2 per cent. This suggests that overheads may have been more tightly controlled during 2017. Certainly, overheads have not risen in proportion to sales revenue.

The current ratio has fallen a little and the acid test ratio has fallen by more than half. Although liquidity ratios tend to be lower in retailing than in manufacturing, the liquidity of the business should now be a cause for concern. However, this may be a passing problem. The business is investing heavily in non-current assets and is relying on internal funds to finance this growth. When this investment ends, the liquidity position may improve quickly.

The trade receivables period has remained unchanged over the two years, and there has been no significant change in the inventories turnover period in 2017. The gearing ratio seems quite low and provides no cause for concern given the profitability of the business.

Overall, the business appears to be financially sound. Although there has been rapid growth during 2017, there is no real cause for alarm provided that the liquidity of the business can be improved in the near future. In the absence of information concerning share price, it is not possible to say whether an investment should be made.

Chapter 8

8.1 Lombard Ltd

Relevant costs of undertaking the contract are:

	£
Equipment costs	200,000
Component X (20,000 × 4 × £5)	
(Any of these components used will need to be replaced.)	400,000
Component Y (20,000 × 3 × £8)	
(All of the required units will come from inventories and	
this will be an effective cost of the net realisable value.)	480,000
Additional costs (20,000 × £8)	160,000
	1,240,000
Revenue from the contract (20,000 × £80)	1,600,000

Thus, from a purely financial point of view, the project is acceptable. (Note that there is no relevant labour cost since the staff concerned will be paid irrespective of whether the contract is undertaken.)

8.2 Andrews and Co. Ltd

Minimum contract price:

			£
Materials	Steel core:	10,000 × £2.10	21,000
	Plastic:	10,000 × 0.10 × £0.10	100
Labour	Skilled:		–
	Unskilled:	10,000 × $^5/_{60}$ × £7.50	6,250
Minimum tender price			27,350

8.5 The local education authority

(a) One-off financial net benefits of closing:

	D only	A and B	A and C
Capacity reduction	800	700	800
	£m	£m	£m
Property developer (A)	–	14.0	14.0
Shopping complex (B)	–	8.0	–
Property developer (D)	9.0	–	–
Safety (C)	–	–	3.0
Adapt facilities	(1.8)	–	–
Total	7.2	22.0	17.0
Ranking based on total one-off benefits	3	1	2

(Note that all past costs of buying and improving the schools are irrelevant.)

Recurrent financial net benefits of closing:

	D only £m	A and B £m	A and C £m
Rent (C)	–	–	0.3
Administrators	0.2	0.4	0.4
Total	0.2	0.4	0.7
Ranking based on total of recurrent benefits	3	2	1

On the basis of the financial figures alone, closure of either A and B or A and C looks best. It is not possible to add the one-off and the recurring costs directly, but the large one-off cost saving associated with closing schools A and B makes this option look attractive. (In Chapter 14 we shall see that it is possible to combine one-off and recurring costs in a way that should lead to sensible conclusions.)

(b) The costs of acquiring and improving the schools in the past are past costs, or sunk costs, and, therefore, irrelevant. The costs of employing the chief education officer is a future cost, but irrelevant because it is not dependent on the options being considered.

(c) There are many other factors, some of a non-quantifiable nature. These include:

- accuracy of projections of capacity requirements;
- locality of existing schools relative to where potential pupils live;
- political acceptability of selling schools to property developers;
- importance of purely financial issues in making the final decision;
- the quality of the replacement sporting facilities compared with those at school D;
- political acceptability of staff redundancies;
- possible savings/costs of employing fewer teachers, which might be relevant if economies of scale are available by having fewer schools; and
- staff morale.

8.6 Rob Otics Ltd

(a) The minimum price for the proposed contract would be:

Materials	£
Component X (2 × 8 × £180)	2,880
This inventories item is in constant use by the business. This means that, though there are 10 units held, these will ultimately need to be replaced, as well as a further 6 units purchased. All of these will cost the new price.	
Component Y	0
The history of the components held in inventories is irrelevant because it applies irrespective of the decision made on this contract. Since the alternative to using the units on this contract is to scrap them, the relevant cost is zero.	
Component Z (75 + 32) × £20 − (75 × £25)	265
The relevant cost here is how much extra the business will pay the supplier as a result of undertaking the contract.	
Other miscellaneous items	250
Labour	
Assembly (25 + 24 + 23 + 22 + 21 + 20 + 19 + 18) × £48	8,256
The assembly labour cost is irrelevant because it will be incurred irrespective of which work the members of staff do. The relevant cost is based on the sales revenue per hour lost if the other orders are lost less the material cost per hour saved; that is £60 − £12 = £48.	
Inspection (8 × 6 × £12 × 150%)	864
Total	12,515

Thus the minimum price is £12,515.

(b) Other factors include:
- Competitive state of the market.
- The fact that the above figure is unique to the particular circumstances at the time – for example, having Component Y available but having no use for it. Any subsequent order might have to take account of an outlay cost.
- Breaking even (that is, just covering the costs) on a contract will not fulfil the business's objective.
- Charging a low price may cause marketing problems. Other customers may resent the low price for this contract. The current enquirer may also expect a similar price in future.

Chapter 9

9.1 Motormusic Ltd

(a) Break-even point = fixed cost/contribution per unit

$$= (80,000 + 60,000)/(60 - (20 + 14 + 12 + 3)) = 12,727.27 \text{ radios.}$$

This means that the business would need to sell 12,728 radios before it would break even.

These would have a sales value of £763,680 (that is, 12,728 × £60).

(b) The margin of safety is 7,272 radios (that is, 20,000 − 12,728). This margin would have a sales value of £436,320 (that is, 7,272 × £60).

9.3 Gandhi Ltd

(a) Given that the spare capacity could not be used by other services, the Standard service should continue to be offered. This is because it renders a positive contribution.

(b) The Standard service renders a contribution per unit of £15 (that is, £80 − £65), or £30 during the time it would take to render one unit of the Nova service. The Nova service would provide a contribution of only £25 (that is, £75 − £50).

The Nova service should, therefore, not replace the Standard service.

(c) Under the original plans, the following contributions would be rendered by the Basic and Standard services:

		£
Basic	11,000 × (£50 − £25) =	275,000
Standard	6,000 × (£80 − £65) =	90,000
		365,000

If the Basic were to take the Standard's place, 17,000 units (that is, 11,000 + 6,000) of them could be produced in total. To generate the same total contribution, each unit of the Standard service would need to provide £21.47 (that is, £365,000/17,000) of contribution. Given the Basic's variable cost of £25, this would mean a selling price of £46.47 each (that is, £21.47 + £25.00).

9.6 Products A, B and C

(a) Total time required on cutting machines is:

$$(2,500 \times 1.0) + (3,400 \times 1.0) + (5,100 \times 0.5) = 8,450 \text{ hours}$$

Total time available on cutting machines is 5,000 hours. Therefore, this is a limiting factor.

Total time required on assembling machines is:

$$(2,500 \times 0.5) + (3,400 \times 1.0) + (5,100 \times 0.5) = 7,200 \text{ hours}$$

Total time available on assembling machines is 8,000 hours. Therefore, this is not a limiting factor.

	A (per unit)	B (per unit)	C (per unit)
Selling price (£)	25	30	18
Variable materials (£)	(12)	(13)	(10)
Variable production cost (£)	(7)	(4)	(3)
Contribution (£)	6	13	5
Time on cutting machines	1.0 hour	1.0 hour	0.5 hour
Contribution per hour on cutting machines (£)	6	13	10
Order of priority	3rd	1st	2nd

Therefore, produce:

3,400 Product B using	3,400 hours
3,200 Product C using	1,600 hours
	5,000 hours

(b) Assuming that the business would make no saving in variable production cost by subcontracting, it would be worth paying up to the contribution per unit (£5) for Product C, which would therefore be £5 × (5,100 − 3,200) = £9,500 in total.

Similarly it would be worth paying up to £6 per unit for Product A – that is, £6 × 2,500 = £15,000 in total.

9.7 Darmor Ltd

(a) Contribution per hour of skilled labour of Product X is:

$$\frac{£(30 - 6 - 2 - 12 - 3)}{6/12} = £14$$

Given the scarcity of skilled labour, if the management is to be indifferent between the products, the contribution per skilled-labour-hour must be the same. Thus for Product Y the selling price must be:

$$£((14 \times (9/12)) + 9 + 4 + 25 + 7) = £55.50$$

(that is, the contribution plus the variable cost), and for Product Z the selling price must be:

$$£((14 \times (3/12)) + 3 + 10 + 14 + 7) = £37.50$$

(b) The business could pay up to £26 an hour (£12 + £14) for additional hours of skilled labour. This is the potential contribution per hour, before taking account of the labour rate of £12 an hour.

Chapter 10

10.1 Offending phrases and explanations

Offending phrase	Explanation
'Necessary to divide up the business into departments'	This can be done, but it will not always be of much benefit. Only in quite restricted circumstances will it give a significantly different job cost.
'Fixed costs (or overheads)'	This implies that fixed cost and overheads are the same thing. They are not really connected with one another. 'Fixed' is concerned with how cost behaves as the level of output is raised or lowered; 'overheads' are to do with the extent to which cost can be directly measured in respect of a particular unit of output. Although it is true that many overheads are fixed, not all are. For example, power for machinery.
	All of the other references to fixed and variable costs are wrong. The person should have referred to indirect and direct costs.
'Usually this is done on the basis of area'	Where overheads are apportioned to departments, they will be apportioned on some logical basis. For certain elements of cost, such as rent, the floor area may be the most logical. For others, such as machine maintenance cost, the floor area would be totally inappropriate.
'When the total fixed costs for each department have been identified, this will be divided by the number of hours that were worked'	Where overheads are dealt with on a departmental basis, they may be divided by the number of direct labour hours to deduce a recovery rate. However, this is only one basis of applying overheads to jobs. For example, machine hours or some other basis may be more appropriate to the particular circumstances involved.

10.4 Promptprint Ltd

(a) The plan (budget) may be summarised as:

	£	
Sales revenue	196,000	
Direct materials	(38,000)	
Direct labour	(32,000)	
Total indirect cost	(77,000)	(2,400 + 3,000 + 27,600 + 36,000 + 8,000)
Profit	49,000	

The job may be priced on the basis that both indirect cost and profit should be apportioned to it on the basis of direct labour cost, as follows:

	£	
Direct materials	4,000	
Direct labour	3,600	
Overheads	8,663	(£77,000 × 3,600/32,000)
Profit	5,513	(£49,000 × 3,600/32,000)
	21,776	

This answer assumes that variable overheads vary in proportion to direct labour cost.

Various other bases of charging overheads and profit loading the job could have been adopted. For example, materials cost could have been included (with direct labour) as the basis for profit loading, or even apportioning overheads.

(b) This part of the question is, in effect, asking for comments on the validity of 'full cost-plus' pricing. This approach can be useful as an indicator of the effective long-run cost of doing the job. On the other hand, it fails to take account of relevant opportunity cost as well as the state of the market and other external factors. For example, it ignores the price that a competitor printing business may quote.

(c) Revised estimates of direct material cost for the job:

	£	
Paper grade 1	1,500	(£1,200 × 125%) This item of inventories needs to be replaced
Paper grade 2	0	It has no opportunity cost value
Card	510	(£640 − £130: using the card on another job would save £640, but cost £130 to achieve that saving)
Inks and so on	300	This item of inventories needs to be replaced
	2,310	

10.5 (a) Charging overheads to jobs on a departmental basis means that overheads are collected 'product' cost centre (department) by 'product' cost centre. This involves picking up the overheads that are direct to each department and adding to them a share of overheads that are general to the business as a whole. The overheads of 'service' cost centres must then be apportioned to the product cost centres. At this point, all of the overheads for the whole business are divided between the 'product' cost centres, such that the sum of the 'product' cost centre overheads equals those for the whole business.

Dealing with overheads departmentally is believed to provide more accurate and useful information to decision makers, because different departments may have rather different overheads. Assigning overheads on a departmental basis takes this into account when calculating the cost of a job.

In theory, dealing with overheads on a departmental basis is more costly than on a business-wide basis. In practice, it possibly does not make too much difference to the cost of collecting the information. This is because, normally, businesses are divided into departments, and the costs are collected departmentally, as part of the normal routine.

(b) To make any difference to the job cost that will emerge as a result of dealing with overheads departmentally, rather than on a business-wide basis, the following *both* need to be the case:

- the overheads per unit of the basis of charging (for example direct labour hours) need to be different from one department to the next; and

- the proportion (but not the actual amounts) of total overheads that are charged to jobs must differ from one job to the next.

Assume, for the sake of argument, that direct labour hours are used as the basis of charging overheads in all departments. Also assume that there are three departments, A, B and C.

There will be no difference to the overheads charged to a particular job if the rate of overheads per direct labour hour is the same for all departments. Obviously, if the charging rate is the same in all departments, that same rate must also apply to the business taken as a whole.

Also, even where overheads per direct labour hour differ significantly from one department to another – if all jobs spend, say, about 20 per cent, of their time in Department A, 50 per cent in Department B and 30 per cent in Department C – it will not make any difference whether overheads are charged departmentally or overall.

These conclusions are not in any way dependent on the basis of charging overheads or even whether overheads are charged on the same basis in each department.

The points made above mean that, in practice, departmentalising overheads may not provide information that is significantly different from that when overheads are charged to jobs on a business-wide basis.

10.7 **Bookdon plc**

(a) To answer this question, we need first to allocate and apportion the overheads to product cost centres, as follows:

Cost	Basis of apportionment	Total	Department			
			Machine shop	Fitting section	Canteen	Machine maintenance section
		£	£	£	£	£
Allocated items:	Specific	90,380	27,660	19,470	16,600	26,650
Rent, rates, heat, light	Floor area	17,000	9,000	3,500	2,500	2,000
			(3,600/ 6,800)	*(1,400/ 6,800)*	*(1,000/ 6,800)*	*(800/ 6,800)*
Dep'n and insurance	Book value	25,000	12,500	6,250	2,500	3,750
			(150/300)	*(75/300)*	*(30/300)*	*(45/300)*
Canteen	Number of employees	–	10,800	8,400	(21,600)	2,400
			(18/36)	*(14/36)*		*(4/36)*
Machine maintenance section	Specified %	–	24,360	10,440		(34,800)
			(70%)	30%		
		132,380	84,320	48,060		

Note that the canteen overheads were reapportioned to the other cost centres first because the canteen renders a service to the machine maintenance section but does not receive a service from it.

Calculation of the overhead absorption (recovery) rates can now proceed:

1 Total budgeted machine hours are:

	Hours
Product X (4,200 × 6)	25,200
Product Y (6,900 × 3)	20,700
Product Z (1,700 × 4)	6,800
	52,700

Overhead absorption rate for the machine shop is:

$$\frac{£84,320}{52,700} = £1.60/\text{machine hour}$$

2 Total budgeted direct labour cost for the fitting section is:

	£
Product X (4,200 × £12)	50,400
Product Y (6,900 × £3)	20,700
Product Z (1,700 × £21)	35,700
	106,800

Overhead absorption rate for the fitting section is:

$$\frac{£48,060}{£106,800} \times 100\% = 45\% \text{ or } £0.45 \text{ per £ of direct labour cost}$$

(b) The cost of one unit of Product X is calculated as follows:

	£
Direct materials	11.00
Direct labour:	
Machine shop	6.00
Fitting section	12.00
Overheads:	
Machine shop (6 × £1.60)	9.60
Fitting section (£12 × 45%)	5.40
	44.00

Therefore, the cost of one unit of Product X is £44.00.

Chapter 11

11.1 Aires plc

The EVA® approach to determining shareholder value will be as follows:

Year	Opening capital invested (C) £m	Capital charge (12% × C) £m	Operating profit after tax £m	EVA® £m
1	64.0	7.7	12.0	4.3
2	48.0	5.8	12.0	6.2
3	32.0	3.8	12.0	8.2
4	16.0	1.9	12.0	10.1

11.2 The balanced scorecard

(a) The balanced scorecard has nothing to do with the statement of financial position. The former is a framework that translates the aims and objectives of a business into a series of key performance measures and targets. The latter is a statement of the assets of a business and the claims against it; it is sometimes known as the 'balance sheet'.

(b) The finance area of the balanced scorecard specifies financial targets for the future and is usually expressed in terms of financial ratios, such as return on capital employed. The income statement is a historic statement of revenues, the expenses matched against them and the resulting profit or loss.

(c) The balanced scorecard approach does not prescribe a particular set of objectives and targets. It is up to the business concerned to establish its own set of parameters.

(d) The balanced scorecard in no way downplays financial objectives and measures. Financial aspects are key issues in all areas of the balanced scorecard.

11.3 Kaplan plc

(a) The business makes each model of suitcase in a batch. The direct cost (materials and labour) will be recorded in respect of each batch. To this cost will be added a share of the overheads of the business for the period in which production of the batch takes place. The basis of the batch absorbing overheads is a matter of managerial judgement. A popular method is direct labour hours spent working on the batch, relative to total direct labour hours worked during the period. This is not the 'correct' way, however. There is no one correct way. If the activity is capital-intensive, some machine-hour basis of dealing with overheads might be more appropriate, though still not 'correct'. Overheads might be collected, cost centre by cost centre (department by department), and charged to the batch as it passes through each product cost centre. Alternatively, all of the overheads for the entire production facility might be totalled and the overheads dealt with more globally. It is only in restricted circumstances that overheads charged to batches will be affected by a decision to deal with them by cost centres, rather than globally.

Once the 'full cost' (direct cost plus a share of indirect cost) has been ascertained for the batch, the cost per suitcase can be established by dividing the batch cost by the number of suitcases in the batch.

(b) Whereas the traditional approach to dealing with overheads is just to accept that they exist and deal with them in a fairly broad manner, ABC takes a much more enquiring approach. ABC takes the view that overheads do not just 'occur', but that they are caused or 'driven' by 'activities'. It is a matter of finding out which activities are driving the cost and how much cost they are driving.

For example, a significant part of the cost of making suitcases of different sizes might be resetting machinery to cope with a batch of a different size from its predecessor batch. Where a particular model is made in very small batches, because it has only a small market, ABC would advocate that this model is charged directly with its machine-setting cost. The traditional approach would be to treat machine setting as a general overhead that the individual suitcases (irrespective of the model) might bear equally. ABC, it is claimed, leads to more accurate costing and thus to more accurate assessment of profitability.

(c) The other advantage of pursuing an ABC philosophy and identifying cost drivers is that, once the drivers have been identified, they are likely to become much more susceptible to being controlled. Thus it becomes more feasible for management to assess the benefit of certain activities against their cost.

11.5 Badger Ltd

(a) **Price using absorption costing**

Overhead absorption rate = total overheads/total direct labour hours = £280,000/ 4,000 = £70 per direct labour hour.

	Largeflo £	Smallflo £
Direct materials	16.00	15.00
Direct labour	8.00	8.00
Overheads: $\frac{1}{2} \times$ £70	35.00	35.00
Total cost	59.00	58.00
Mark-up of 35%	20.65	20.30
Price	79.65	78.30

(b) **Price using activity-based costing**

Cost driver rates:

Large machine	£96,000/480	=	£200 per hour
Small machine	£44,800/1,280	=	£35 per hour
Set-ups	£32,500/260	=	£125 per set-up
Ordering	£10,800/120	=	£90 per part
Handling	£45,600/380	=	£120 per movement
Other overheads	£50,300/4,000	=	£12.58 per direct labour hour

Prices for the two products:

		Largeflo £		*Smallflo* £
Direct materials		16.00		15.00
Direct labour		8.00		8.00
Large machine	(100 × £200)/1,000	20.00		–
Small machine			(25 × £35)/50	17.50
Set-ups	£125/1,000	0.13	(2 × £125)/50	5.00
Ordering		–	(3 × £90)/50	5.40
Handling	£120/1,000	0.12	(5 × £120)/50	12.00
Other overheads	$\frac{1}{2}$ × £12.58	6.29	$\frac{1}{2}$ × £12.58	6.29
Total cost		50.54		69.19
35% mark up		17.69		24.22
Price		68.23		93.41

(c) **Points for the management**

- Under the traditional approach, the prices are quite similar because the direct costs are quite similar, which also leads to a similar allocation of overheads (because these are absorbed on the basis of direct labour hours).
- With ABC there is quite a large price difference between the products. This is because the Smallflo product causes much more overhead cost than the Largeflo one and ABC reflects this fact.
- Management must seriously consider its pricing policy. If the traditionally based price is, in fact, the current selling price, the Smallflo product is earning only a small margin.
- If the market will not bear a higher price for Smallflo products, management may consider dropping them and concentrating its efforts on the Largeflo ones. Projected market demand for the two products will obviously have a major bearing on these considerations.

(d) **Practical problems of using ABC**

- Identifying the cost-driving activities and determining cost driver rates can be difficult and expensive. It is sometimes necessary to use arbitrary approaches to certain parts of the overheads, as with 'other overheads' in the Largeflo/Smallflo example above.
- The costs of introducing ABC may outweigh the benefits.
- Changing the culture in the way necessary to introduce ABC may pose difficulties. There may be resistance to a new approach.
- On a positive note, ABC may have benefits beyond cost determination and pricing. Careful analysis of costs and what drives them can provide a basis for exercising better control over costs.

Chapter 12

12.1   Prolog Ltd

(a) Cash budget for the six months to 30 June:

	Jan	Feb	Mar	Apr	May	June
	£000	£000	£000	£000	£000	£000
Receipts						
Credit sales revenue (Note 1)	100	100	140	180	220	260
Payments						
Trade payables (Note 2)	112	144	176	208	240	272
Operating expenses	4	6	8	10	10	10
Shelving				12		
Taxation			25			
	116	150	209	230	250	282
Cash flow	(16)	(50)	(69)	(50)	(30)	(22)
Opening balance	(68)	(84)	(134)	(203)	(253)	(283)
Closing balance	(84)	(134)	(203)	(253)	(283)	(305)

Notes:
1 Sales receipts will equal the month's sales revenue, but will be received two months later. For example, the January sales revenue = £2,000 × (50 + 20) = £140,000, to be received in March.
2 Payments to suppliers will equal the next month's sales requirements, payable the next month. For example, January purchases = £1,600 × (50 + 40) = £144,000, payable in February.

(b) A banker may require various pieces of information before granting additional overdraft facilities. These may include:

● security available for the loan;
● details of past profit performance;
● profit projections for the next 12 months;
● cash projections beyond the next six months to help assess the prospects of repayment;
● details of the assumptions underlying projected figures supplied;
● details of the contractual commitment between Prolog Ltd and its supplier;
● details of management expertise. Can they manage the expansion programme?
● details of the new machine and its performance in relation to competing models; and
● details of funds available from owners to finance the expansion.

12.3   Nursing home

(a) The rates per patient for the variable overheads, on the basis of experience during months 1 to 6, are as follows:

Expense	Amount for 2,700 patients £	Amount per patient £
Staffing	59,400	22
Power	27,000	10
Supplies	54,000	20
Other	8,100	3
	148,500	55

Since the expected level of activity for the full year is 6,000, the expected level of activity for the second six months is 3,300 (that is, 6,000 − 2,700).

Thus the budget for the second six months will be:

	£	
Variable element:		
Staffing	72,600	(3,300 × £22)
Power	33,000	(3,300 × £10)
Supplies	66,000	(3,300 × £20)
Other	9,900	(3,300 × £3)
	181,500	(3,300 × £55)

Fixed element:		
Supervision	60,000	6/12 of the annual figure
Depreciation/finance	93,600	ditto
Other	32,400	ditto
	186,000	(per patient = £56.36 (that is £186,000/3,300))
Total (second six months)	367,500	(per patient = £111.36 (that is £56.36 + £55.00))

(b) For the second six months, the actual activity was 3,800 patients. For a valid comparison with the actual outcome, the budget will need to be revised to reflect this activity.

	Actual costs £	Budget (3,800 patients) £	Difference £
Variable element	203,300	209,000 (3,800 × £55)	5,700 (saving)
Fixed element	190,000	186,000	4,000 (overspend)
Total	393,300	395,000	1,700 (saving)

(c) Relative to the budget, there was a saving of nearly 3 per cent on the variable element and an overspend of about 2 per cent on fixed costs. Without further information, it is impossible to deduce much more than this.

The differences between the budget and the actual may be caused by some assumptions made in framing the budget for 3,300 patients in the second part of the year. There may be some element of economies of scale in the variable costs; that is, the costs may not be strictly linear. If this were the case, basing a relatively large activity budget on the experi-ence of a relatively small activity period would tend to overstate the large activity budget. The fixed-cost budget was deduced by dividing the budget for 12 months by two. In fact, there could be seasonal factors or inflationary pressures at work that might make such a crude division of the fixed cost element unfair.

12.4 Linpet Ltd

(a) Cash budgets are extremely useful for decision-making purposes. They allow managers to see the likely effect on the cash balance of the plans that they have set in place. Cash is an important asset and it is necessary to ensure that it is properly managed. Failure to do so can have disastrous consequences for the business. Where the cash budget indicates a sur-plus balance, managers must decide whether this balance should be reinvested in the busi-ness or distributed to the owners. Where the cash budget indicates a deficit balance, managers must decide how this deficit should be financed or how it might be avoided.

(b) Cash budget for the six months to 30 November:

	June £	July £	Aug £	Sept £	Oct £	Nov £
Receipts						
Cash sales revenue (Note 1)	4,000	5,500	7,000	8,500	11,000	11,000
Credit sales revenue (Note 2)	–	–	4,000	5,500	7,000	8,500
	4,000	5,500	11,000	14,000	18,000	19,500
Payments						
Purchases (Note 3)	–	29,000	9,250	11,500	13,750	17,500
Overheads	500	500	500	500	650	650
Wages	900	900	900	900	900	900
Commission (Note 4)	–	320	440	560	680	880
Equipment	10,000	–	–	–	–	7,000
Motor vehicle	6,000	–	–	–	–	
Leasehold	40,000					
	57,400	30,720	11,090	13,460	15,980	26,930
Cash flow	(53,400)	(25,220)	(90)	540	2,020	(7,430)
Opening balance	60,000	6,600	(18,620)	(18,710)	(18,170)	(16,150)
Closing balance	6,600	(18,620)	(18,710)	(18,170)	(16,150)	(23,580)

Notes:
1 50 per cent of the current month's sales revenue.
2 50 per cent of sales revenue of two months previous.
3 To have sufficient inventories to meet each month's sales will require purchases of 75 per cent of the month's sales inventories figures (25 per cent is profit). In addition, each month the business will buy £1,000 more inventories than it will sell. In June, the business will also buy its initial inventories of £22,000. This will be paid for in the following month. For example, June's purchases will be (75% × £8,000) + £1,000 + £22,000 = £29,000, paid for in July.
4 This is 5 per cent of 80 per cent of the month's sales revenue, paid in the following month. For example, June's commission will be 5% × 80% × £8,000 = £320, payable in July.

12.5 **Lewisham Ltd**

(a) The finished goods inventories budget for the three months ending 30 September (in units of production) is:

	July '000 units	Aug '000 units	Sept '000 units
Opening inventories (Note 1)	40	48	40
Production (Note 2)	188	232	196
	228	280	236
Inventories sold (Note 3)	(180)	(240)	(200)
Closing inventories	48	40	36

(b) The raw materials inventories budget for the two months ending 31 August (in kg) is:

	July '000 kg	Aug '000 kg
Opening inventories (Note 1)	40	58
Purchases (Note 2)	112	107
	152	165
Production (Note 4)	(94)	(116)
Closing inventories	58	49

(c) The cash budget for the two months ending 30 September is:

	Aug £	Sept £
Inflows		
Receivables – current month (Note 5)	493,920	411,600
– preceding month (Note 6)	151,200	201,600
Total inflows	645,120	613,200
Outflows		
Payments to trade payables (Note 7)	168,000	160,500
Labour and overheads (Note 8)	185,600	156,800
Fixed overheads	22,000	22,000
Total outflows	375,600	339,300
Net inflows/(outflows)	269,520	273,900
Balance carried forward	289,520	563,420

Notes:

1 The opening balance is the same as the closing balance from the previous month.
2 This is a balancing figure.
3 This figure is given in the question.
4 This figure derives from the finished inventories budget. [July 188,000 × 0.5 = 94000]
5 This is 98 per cent of 70 per cent of the current month's sales revenue.
6 This is 28 per cent of the previous month's sales revenue.
7 This figure derives from the raw materials inventories budget. [July 112,000 × £1.50 = £168,000]
8 This figure derives from the finished invventories budget. [August £232,000 × £0.80 = £185,600]

Chapter 13

13.1   True or false

(a) A favourable direct labour rate variance can only be caused by something that leads to the rate per hour paid being less than standard. Normally, this would not be linked to efficient working. Where, however, the standard envisaged some overtime working, at premium rates, the actual labour rate may be below standard if efficiency has removed the need for the overtime.

(b) The statement is true. The action will lead to an adverse sales price variance and may well lead to problems elsewhere, but the sales volume variance must be favourable.

(c) It is true that below-standard materials could lead to adverse materials usage variances because there may be more than a standard amount of scrap. This could also cause adverse labour efficiency variances because working on materials that would not form part of the output would waste labour time.

(d) Higher-than-budgeted sales revenue could well lead to an adverse labour rate variance because producing the additional work may require overtime working at premium rates.

(e) The statement is true. Nothing else could cause such a variance.

13.2   Overheard remarks

(a) Flexing the budget identifies what the profit would have been, had the only difference between the original budget and the actual figures been concerned with the difference in volume of output. Comparing the original budget profit figure with that in the flexed budget reveals the profit difference (variance) arising solely from the volume difference (sales volume variance). Thus, flexing the budget does not mean at all that volume differences do not matter. Flexing the budget is the means of discovering the effect on profit of the volume difference.

In one sense, all variances are 'water under the bridge', to the extent that the past cannot be undone, and so it is impossible to go back to the last control period and put in a better performance. Identifying variances can, however, be useful in identifying where things went wrong, which should enable management to take steps to ensure that the same things do not to go wrong in the future.

(b) Variances will not tell you what went wrong. They should, however, be a great help in identifying the manager within whose sphere of responsibility things went wrong. That manager should know why it went wrong. In this sense, variances identify relevant questions, but not answers.

(c) Identifying the reason for variances may well cost money, usually in terms of staff time. It is a matter of judgement in any particular situation, of balancing the cost of investigation against the potential benefits. As is usual in such judgements, it is difficult, before undertaking the investigation, to know either the cost or the likely benefit.

In general, significant variances, particularly adverse ones, should be investigated. Persistent (over a period of months) smaller variances should also be investigated. It should not automatically be assumed that favourable variances can be ignored. They indicate that things are not going according to plan, possibly because the plans (budgets) are flawed.

(d) Research evidence does not show this. It seems to show that managers tend to be most motivated by having as a target the most difficult goals that they find acceptable.

(e) Budgets normally provide the basis of feedforward and feedback control. During a budget preparation period, potential problems (for example, an inventories shortage) might be revealed. Steps can then be taken to revise the plans in order to avoid the potential problem. This is an example of a feedforward control: potential problems are anticipated and eliminated before they can occur.

Budgetary control is a very good example of feedback control, where a signal that something is going wrong triggers steps to take corrective action for the future.

13.3 Pilot Ltd

(a)

	Original	Flexed		Actual	
	Budget				
Output (units)(production and sales)	5,000	5,400		5,400	
	£	£		£	
Sales revenue	25,000	27,000		26,460	
Raw materials	(7,500)	(8,100)	(2,700 kg)	(8,770)	(2,830 kg)
Labour	(6,250)	(6,750)	(675 hr)	(6,885)	(650 hr)
Fixed overheads	(6,000)	(6,000)		(6,350)	
Operating profit	5,250	6,150		4,455	

	£	
Sales volume variance (5,250 − 6,150)	900	(F)
Sales price variance (27,000 − 26,460)	(540)	(A)
Materials price variance (2,830 × 3) − 8,770	(280)	(A)
Materials usage variance [(5,400 × 0.5) − 2,830] × £3	(390)	(A)
Labour rate variance (650 × £10) − 6,885	(385)	(A)
Labour efficiency variance [(5,400 × 7.5/60) − 650] × £10	250	(F)
Fixed overhead spending variance (6,000 − 6,350)	(350)	(A)
Total net variances	(795)	(A)

	£
Budgeted profit	5,250
Less Total net variance	(795)
Actual profit	4,455

(b) Sales volume variance: sales manager; sales price variance: sales manager; materials price variance: buyer; materials usage variance: production manager; labour rate variance: human resources manager; labour efficiency variance: production manager; fixed overhead spending variance: various, depending on the nature of the overheads.

13.5 Bradley-Allen Ltd

(a)

	Original		Flexed		Actual
		Budget			
Output (units) (production and sales)	800		950		950
	£	£		£	
Sales revenue	64,000	76,000		73,000	
Raw materials – A	(12,000)	(14,250)	(285 kg)	(15,200)	(310 kg)
– B	(16,000)	(19,000)	(950 m)	(18,900)	(920 m)
Labour – skilled	(4,000)	(4,750)	(475 hr)	(4,628)	(445 hr)
– unskilled	(10,000)	(11,875)	(1,484 hr)	(11,275)	(1,375 hr)
Fixed overheads	(12,000)	(12,000)		(11,960)	
Operating profit	10,000	14,125		11,037	

Sales variances

Volume:	10,000 − 14,125 = £4,125	(F)
Price:	76,000 − 73,000 = £3,000	(A)

Direct materials A variances

Usage:	[(950 × 0.3) − 310] × £50 = £1,250	(A)
Price:	(310 × £50) − £15,200 = £300	(F)

Direct materials B variances

Usage:	[(950 × 1) − 920] × £20 = £600	(F)
Price:	(920 × £20) − £18,900 = £500	(A)

Skilled direct labour variances

Efficiency:	[(950 × 0.5) − 445] × £10 = £300	(F)
Rate:	(445 × £10) − £4,628 = £178	(A)

Unskilled direct labour variances

Efficiency:	[(950 × 1.5625) − 1,375] × £8 = £875	(F)
Rate:	(1,375 × £8) − £11,275 = £275	(A)

Fixed overhead variances

Spending:	(12,000 − 11,960) = £40	(F)

					£
Budgeted profit					10,000
Sales:	Volume		4,125	(F)	
	Price		(3,000)	(A)	1,125
Direct material A:	Usage		(1,250)	(A)	
	Price		300	(F)	(950)
Direct material B:	Usage		600	(F)	
	Price		(500)	(A)	100
Skilled labour:	Efficiency		300	(F)	
	Rate		(178)	(A)	122
Unskilled labour:	Efficiency		875	(F)	
	Rate		(275)	(A)	600
Fixed overheads:	Expenditure				40
Actual profit					11,037

(b) The statement in (a) is useful to management because it enables them to see where there have been failures to meet the original budget and to quantify the extent of such failures. This means that junior managers can be held accountable for the performance of their particular area of responsibility.

Chapter 14

14.1 Mylo Ltd

(a) The annual depreciation of the two projects is:

$$\text{Project 1: } \frac{(£100,000 − £7,000)}{3} = £31,000$$

$$\text{Project 2: } \frac{(£60,000 − £6,000)}{3} = £18,000$$

Project 1

1

	Year 0 £000	Year 1 £000	Year 2 £000	Year 3 £000
Operating profit/(loss) before depreciation		60	30	33
Capital cost	(100)			
Residual value				7
Net cash flows	(100)	60	30	40
Discount factor (10%)	1.000	0.909	0.826	0.751
Present value	(100.00)	54.54	24.78	30.04
Net present value	9.36			

2 Clearly the IRR lies above 10 per cent. Try 15 per cent:

	Year 0	Year 1	Year 2	Year 3
Discount factor (15%)	1.000	0.870	0.756	0.658
Present value (£000)	(100.00)	52.20	22.68	26.32
Net present value (£000)	1.20			

Thus the IRR lies a little above 15 per cent, perhaps around 16 per cent.

3 To find the payback period, the cumulative cash flows are calculated:

	Year 0 £000	Year 1 £000	Year 2 £000	Year 3 £000
Cumulative cash flows	(100)	(40)	(10)	30

Thus the payback will occur after three years if we assume year-end cash flows.

Project 2

1

	Year 0 £000	Year 1 £000	Year 2 £000	Year 3 £000
Operating profit/(loss) before depreciation)		36	16	22
Capital cost	(60)			
Residual value				6
Net cash flows	(60)	36	16	28
Discount factor (10%)	1.000	0.909	0.826	0.751
Present value	(60.00)	32.72	13.22	21.03
Net present value	6.97			

2 Clearly the IRR lies above 10 per cent. Try 15 per cent:

	Year 0	Year 1	Year 2	Year 3
Discount factor (15%)	1.000	0.870	0.756	0.658
Present value (£000)	(60.00)	31.32	12.10	18.42
Net present value (£000)	1.84			

Thus the IRR lies a little above 15 per cent, perhaps around 17 per cent.

3 The cumulative cash flows are:

	Year 0 £000	Year 1 £000	Year 2 £000	Year 3 £000
Cumulative cash flows	(60)	(24)	(8)	20

Thus, the payback will occur after three years (assuming year-end cash flows).

(a) Assuming that Mylo Ltd is pursuing a wealth-enhancement objective, Project 1 is preferable since it has the higher net present value. The difference between the two net present values is not significant, however.

14.3 **Dirk plc**

(a)1 Net relevant cash flows are:

	Year 0 £m	Year 1 £m	Year 2 £m	Year 3 £m	Year 4 £m
Sales revenue		9.0	9.6	7.2	3.0
Loss of contribution		(0.8)	(0.8)	(0.8)	
Variable cost		(1.0)	(1.2)	(1.2)	(0.7)
Fixed cost (Note 2)		(1.7)	(1.7)	(1.7)	(1.7)
Operating cash flows		5.5	5.9	3.5	0.6
Working capital	(1.8)				1.8
Capital cost (Note 3)	(10.5)				0.5
Net relevant cash flows	12.3	5.5	5.9	3.5	2.9

The NPV is:

	Year 0	Year 1	Year 2	Year 3	Year 4
Net relevant cash flows (£m)	(12.3)	5.5	5.9	3.5	2.9
Discount rate (8%)	1.000	0.926	0.857	0.794	0.735
Present value (£m)	(12.3)	5.1	5.1	2.8	2.1
NPV (£m)	2.8				

Notes:
1 The development cost of £0.4 million is irrelevant as it is a past cost.
2 Only that part of the fixed cost that arises as a direct result of the project is relevant. Depreciation is irrelevant as it is not a cash flow.
3 The residual value of the equipment is (£10.5m − (4 × £2.5m)) = £0.5m.

2 To calculate the IRR, a higher discount figure (12 per cent) will be applied.

	Year 0	Year 1	Year 2	Year 3	Year 4
Net relevant cash flows (£m)	(12.3)	5.5	5.9	3.5	2.9
Discount rate (12%)	1.000	0.893	0.797	0.712	0.636
Present value (£m)	(12.3)	4.9	4.7	2.5	1.8
NPV (£m)	1.6				

Trial	Discount rate %	Net present value £000
1	8	2.8
2	12	1.6
Difference	4	1.2

For every 1 per cent change in the discount rate, the change in NPV will be:

$$1.2/4 = 0.3$$

The increase in the 12 per cent discount rate necessary to achieve a zero NPV will be:

$$1.6/0.3 = 5.3\%$$

Thus the approximate IRR is:

$$(12.0 + 5.3) = 17.3\%$$

(b) The NPV of the project is positive and the IRR of the project exceeds the cost of capital. Acceptance of the project will therefore enhance shareholder wealth. The NPV, however, is not very high, and an analysis of the sensitivity of the key inputs to the decision may be useful to help assess the riskiness of the project.

14.4 Newton Electronics Ltd

(a)

Option 1

	Year 0 £m	Year 1 £m	Year 2 £m£m	Year 3 £m	Year 4 £m	Year 5 £m
Plant and equipment	(9.0)					1.0
Sales revenue		24.0	30.8	39.6	26.4	10.0
Variable cost		(11.2)	(19.6)	(25.2)	(16.8)	(7.0)
Fixed cost (excluding depreciation)		(0.8)	(0.8)	(0.8)	(0.8)	(0.8)
Working capital		(3.0)				3.0
Marketing cost		(2.0)	(2.0)	(2.0)	(2.0)	(2.0)
Lease		(0.1)	(0.1)	(0.1)	(0.1)	(0.1)
	(12.0)	9.9	8.3	11.5	6.7	4.1
Discount factor (10%)	1.000	0.909	0.826	0.751	0.683	0.621
Present value	(12.0)	9.0	6.9	8.6	4.6	2.5
Net present value	19.6					

Option 2

	Year 0	Year 1	Year 2	Year 3	Year 4	Year 5
Royalties (£m)	–	4.4	7.7	9.9	6.6	2.8
Discount factor (10%)	1.000	0.909	0.826	0.751	0.683	0.621
Present value (£m)	–	4.0	6.4	7.4	4.5	1.7
Net present value (£m)	24.0					

Option 3

	Year 0	Year 2
Instalments (£m)	12.0	12.0
Discount factor (10%)	1.000	0.826
Present value (£m)	12.0	9.9
Net present value (£m)	21.9	

(b) Before making a final decision, the board should consider the following factors:

- The long-term competitiveness of the business may be affected by the sale of the patents.
- At present, the business is not involved in manufacturing and marketing products. Would a change in direction be desirable?
- The business will probably have to buy in the skills necessary to produce the product itself. This will involve costs, and problems may be encountered. Has this been taken into account?
- How accurate are the forecasts made and how valid are the assumptions on which they are based?

(c) Option 2 has the highest net present value and is therefore the most attractive to share-holders. However, the accuracy of the forecasts should be checked before a final decision is made.

14.7 Simtex Ltd

(a) Net operating cash flows each year will be:

	£000
Sales revenue (160 × £6)	960
Variable cost (160 × £4)	(640)
Relevant fixed costs	(170)
	150

The estimated net present value of the new product can then be calculated:

	£000
Annual cash flows (150 × 3.038*)	456
Residual value of equipment (100 × 0.636)	64
	520
Initial outlay	(480)
Net present value	40

* This is the sum of the discount factors over four years (that is 0.893 + 0.797 + 0.712 + 0.636 = 3.038). Where the cash flows are constant, it is a quicker procedure than working out the present value of cash flows for each year and then adding them together.

(b) **1** Assume the discount rate is 18 per cent. The net present value of the project would be:

	£000
Annual cash flows (150 × 2.690*)	404
Residual value of equipment (100 × 0.516)	52
	456
Initial outlay	(480)
Net present value	(24)

> * That is 0.847 + 0.718 + 0.609 + 0.516 = 2.690.

Thus an increase of 6 per cent, from 12 per cent to 18 per cent, in the discount rate causes a fall from +40 to −24 in the net present value: a fall of 64, or 10.67 (that is, 64/6) for each 1 per cent rise in the discount rate. So a zero net present value will occur with a discount rate approximately equal to 12 + (40/10.67) = 15.75 percent. (This is, of course, the internal rate of return.)

This higher discount rate represents an increase of about 31 per cent on the existing cost of capital figure.

2 The initial outlay on equipment is already expressed in present-value terms and so, to make the project no longer viable, the outlay will have to increase by an amount equal to the net present value of the project (that is, £40,000) – an increase of 8.3 per cent on the stated initial outlay.

3 The change necessary in the annual net cash flows to make the project no longer profitable can be calculated as follows.

Let Y = change in the annual operating cash flows. Then Y × cumulative discount rates for a four-year period) − NPV = 0. This can be rearranged as:

$$Y \times \text{cumulative discount rates for a four-year period} = \text{NPV}$$

$$Y \times 3.038 = £40,000$$

$$Y = £40,000/3.038$$

$$= £13,167$$

In percentage terms, this is a decrease of 8.8 per cent on the estimated cash flows.

4 The change in the residual value required to make the new product no longer profitable can be calculated as follows:

Let V = change in the residual value. Then V × discount factor at end of four years) − NPV of product = 0. This can be rearranged as:

$$V \times \text{discount factor at end of four years} = \text{NPV of product}$$

$$V \times 0.636 = £40,000$$

$$V = £40,000/0.636$$

$$= £62,893$$

This is a decrease of 62.9 per cent in the residual value of the equipment.

(c) The net present value of the product is positive and so it will increase shareholder wealth. Thus, it should be produced. The sensitivity analysis suggests the initial outlay and the annual cash flows are the most sensitive variables for managers to consider.

Chapter 15

15.1 Financing issues

(a) This topic is dealt with in the chapter. The main benefits of leasing include ease of borrowing, reasonable cost, flexibility and avoidance of large cash outflows (which normally occur where an asset is purchased).

(b) This topic is also dealt with in the chapter. The main benefits of using retained profits include no dilution of control, no share issue costs, no delay in receiving funds and the tax benefits of capital appreciation over dividends.

(c) A business may decide to repay a loan earlier than required for various reasons including the following:

- A fall in interest rates may make the existing loan interest rates higher than current loan interest rates. Thus, the business may decide to repay the existing loan using finance from a cheaper loan.
- A rise in interest rates or changes in taxation policy may make loan financing more expensive than other forms of financing. This may make the business decide to repay the loan using another form of finance.
- The business may have surplus cash and may have no other profitable uses for the cash.
- The business may wish to reduce the level of financial risk by reducing the level of gearing.

15.2 H. Brown (Portsmouth) Ltd

(a) The main factors to take into account are:

- *Risk.* If a business borrows, there is a risk that at the maturity date for the repayment of the funds the business will not have sufficient funds to repay the amount owing and will be unable to find a suitable form of replacement borrowing. With short-term borrowings, the maturity dates will arrive more quickly and the type of risk outlined will occur at more frequent intervals.
- *Matching.* A business may wish to match the life of an asset with the maturity date of the borrowing. In other words, long-term assets will be purchased with long-term borrowed funds. A certain level of current assets, which form part of the long-term asset base of the business, may also be funded by long-term borrowing. Those current assets that fluctuate owing to seasonality and so on will be funded by short-term borrowing. This approach to funding assets will help reduce risks for the business.
- *Cost.* Interest rates for long-term borrowings may be higher than for short-term ones as investors may seek extra compensation for having their funds locked up for a long period. However, issue costs may be higher for short-term borrowings as there will be a need to refund at more frequent intervals.
- *Flexibility.* Short-term borrowings may be more flexible. It may be difficult to repay long-term ones before the maturity period.

(b) When deciding to grant a loan, a lender should consider the following factors:

- security;
- purpose of the loan;
- ability of the borrower to repay;
- loan period;
- availability of funds; and
- character and integrity of the senior managers.

(c) Loan conditions may include:
- the need to obtain permission before issuing further loans;
- the need to maintain a certain level of liquidity (perhaps measured by the current ratio) during the loan period; and
- a restriction on the level of dividends and directors' pay.

15.3   **Devonian plc**

(a)   **1**   *Ex-rights price*

	£
5 original shares @ £2.10 per share	10.50
1 rights share @ £1.80	1.80
	12.30
Theoretical ex-rights price (£12.30/6)	£2.05

   2   *Value of rights*

	£
Value of a share after the rights issue	2.05
Cost of a rights share	1.80
Value of rights	0.25
Value of rights attached to each original share (£0.25/5)	0.05

(b) **Share price in one year's time**

   1   *Rights issue*

We must first calculate the existing P/E ratio in order to determine the share price in one year's time. This can be done as follows:

	£m
Operating profit (Year 4)	40.0
Taxation (20%)	(8.0)
Profit for the year (available to shareholders)	32.0

Earnings per share (EPS)(£32.0m/200m) = £0.16

$$\text{P/E ratio} = \frac{\text{Share price}}{\text{EPS}}$$

$$= £2.10/£0.16$$

$$= 13.125 \text{ times}$$

	£m
Operating profit (Year 5)	50.0
Taxation (20%)	(10.0)
Profit for the year (available to ordinary shareholders)	40.0

Earnings per share (£40m/240m) = £0.167

Share price (Year 5) = EPS × P/E ratio

$$= £0.167 \times 13.125$$

$$= £2.19$$

2 Borrowing

	£m
Operating profit (Year 5)	50.0
Interest payable (£72m @ 10%)	(7.2)
	42.8
Taxation (20%)	(8.6)
Profit for the year (available to ordinary shareholders)	34.2

$$\text{Earnings per share } (£34.2\text{m}/200\text{m}) = £0.171$$

$$\text{Share price (Year 5)} = \text{EPS} \times \text{P/E ratio}$$

$$= £0.171 \times 11.813$$

$$= \underline{£2.02}$$

These calculations reveal that in one year's time the share price is expected to rise by more than 4 per cent above the current share price if a rights issue is made, whereas the share price will fall by more than 3 per cent if the business borrows the money. Given the additional financial risks attached to borrowing, it seems that a rights issue offers the better option – at least in the short term.

(c) If rights shares are issued at a discount, shareholders are encouraged to either take up the shares or sell the right to someone who will take them. Failure to do one of these will lead to a loss of wealth for the shareholder. (Since the discount offered on rights shares does not represent a real bonus to the shareholders, it can be quite large.)

(d) The price at which rights issues are made is not normally critical. It should, however, be low enough to ensure that, between setting the rights price and the date of the rights issue, the market price of existing shares will not fall below the rights issue price.

15.6 Carpets Direct plc

(a) The earnings per share (EPS) is:

$$\frac{\text{Profit after taxation}}{\text{Number of ordinary shares}} = \frac{£4.5 \text{ m}}{120 \text{ m}} = £0.0375$$

The current market value per share is:

$$\text{Earnings per share} \times \text{P/E} = £0.0375 \times 22 = £0.825$$

The rights issue price will be £0.825, less 20 per cent discount = £0.66.
The theoretical ex-rights price is:

	£
Original shares (4 @ £0.825)	3.30
Rights share (1 @ £0.66)	0.66
Value of five shares following rights issue	3.96

Therefore, the value of one share following the rights issue is:

$$\frac{£3.96}{5} = 79.2\text{p}$$

(b)

	p
Value of one share after rights issue	79.2
Cost of a rights share	(66.0)
Value of rights to shareholder	13.2

(c) *Taking up rights issue*

	£
Shareholding following rights issue ((4,000 + 1,000) × 79.2p)	3,960
Less Cost of rights shares (1,000 × 66p)	(660)
Shareholder wealth	3,300

Selling the rights

	£
Shareholding following rights issue (4,000 × 79.2p)	3,168
Add Proceeds from sale of rights (1,000 × 13.2p)	132
Shareholder wealth	3,300

Doing nothing

As the rights are neither purchased nor sold, the shareholder wealth following the rights issue will be:

	£
Shareholder wealth (4,000 × 79.2p)	3,168

We can see that the investor will have the same wealth under the first two options. However, if the investor does nothing, the rights offer will lapse and so the investor will lose the value of the rights and will be worse off.

Chapter 16

16.2 **Hercules Wholesalers Ltd**

(a) The business is probably concerned about its liquidity position because:
- it has a substantial overdraft, which together with its non-current borrowings means that it has borrowed an amount roughly equal to its equity (according to statement of financial position values);
- it has increased its investment in inventories during the past year (as shown by the income statement); and
- it has a low current ratio of 1.1:1 (that is, 306/285) and a low acid-test ratio of 0.6:1 (that is, 162/285).

(b) The operating cash cycle can be calculated as follows:

	Number of days
Average inventories holding period:	
$\dfrac{[(\text{Opening inventories} + \text{Closing inventories})/2]}{\text{Cost of inventories}} \times 365 = \dfrac{[(125 + 143)/2]}{323} \times 365$	= 151
Add Average settlement period for receivables:	
$\dfrac{\text{Trade receivables}}{\text{Credit sales revenue}} \times 365 = \dfrac{163}{452} \times 365$	= 132
	283
Less Average settlement period for payables:	
$\dfrac{\text{Trade payables}}{\text{Credit purchases}} \times 365 = \dfrac{145}{341} \times 365$	= 155
Operating cash cycle	128

(c) The business can reduce the operating cash cycle in a number of ways. The average inventories holding period seems quite long. At present, average inventories held represent about five months' inventories usage. Reducing the level of inventories held can reduce this period. Similarly, the average settlement period for receivables seems long at more than four months' sales revenue. Imposing tighter credit control, offering discounts, charging interest on overdue accounts and so on may reduce this. However, any policy decisions concerning inventories and receivables must take account of current trading conditions.

Extending the period of credit taken to pay suppliers would also reduce the operating cash cycle. For the reasons mentioned in the chapter, however, this option must be given careful consideration.

16.4 Plastics Manufacturers Ltd

Ratio analysis

Year	1	2	3
ROCE	16.7%	16.9%	(26.1%)
Operating profit margin	12.5%	11.2%	(23.4%)
Current ratio	1.2	1.1	0.9
Acid test ratio	0.5	0.5	0.3
Inventories' turnover period*	91 days	82 days	183 days
Average settlement period for trade receivables	64 days	60 days	91 days

* Using sales revenue figure rather than cost of sales, which is unavailable

These figures reveal that Year 3 was a disastrous one for Plastic Toys Ltd (PT). Sales revenue and profitability fell dramatically. The fall in sales revenue does not appear to have been anticipated as inventories levels rose dramatically in Year 3. The fall in profitability and increase in inventories has created a strain on liquidity that should cause acute concern. The liquidity ratios are very low and it seems the business is in a dangerous state. Extreme caution must therefore be exercised in any dealings with the business.

Before considering the proposal to supply, Plastics Manufacturers Ltd (PM) should establish why Plastic Toys Ltd wishes to change its suppliers. In view of the problems that it faces, there may well be problems with current suppliers. If three months' credit were to be granted, PM will be committed to supplying 6,000 kilos before payment is due. At a marginal cost of £7 a kilo, this means an exposure of £42,000. The risks of non-payment seem to be very high unless there is information concerning PT that indicates that its fortunes will improve in the near future. If PM is determined to supply the goods to PT then some kind of security should be required in order to reduce the risk to PM.

16.5 Mayo Computers Ltd

New proposals from credit control department

	£000	£000
Current level of investment in receivables		
(£20m × (60/365))		3,288
Proposed level of investment in receivables		
((£20m × 60%) × (30/365))	(986)	
((£20m × 40%) × (50/365))	(1,096)	(2,082)
Reduction in level of investment		1,206

The reduction in overdraft interest as a result of the reduction in the level of investment will be £1,206,000 × 10% = £120,600.

	£000	£000
Cost of cash discounts offered (£20m × 60% × 2.5%)		300

	£000	£000
Additional cost of credit administration		20
		320
Bad debt savings	(100)	
Interest charge savings (see above)	(121)	(221)
Net cost of policy each year		99

These calculations show that the business would incur additional annual cost if it implemented this proposal. It would therefore be cheaper to stay with the existing credit policy.

16.6 Boswell Enterprises Ltd

(a)

	Current policy		New policy	
	£000	£000	£000	£000
Trade receivables				
[(£3m × 1/12 × 30%) + (£3m × 2/12 × 70%)]		425.0		
[(£3.15m × 1/12 × 60%) + (£3.15m × 2/12 × 40%)]				367.5
Inventories				
{[£3m − (£3m × 20%)] × 3/12}		600.0		
{[£3.15m − (£3.15m × 20%)] × 3/12}				630.0
Cash (fixed)		140.0		140.0
		1,165.0		1,137.5
Trade payables				
[£3m − (£3m × 20%)] × 2/12]	(400.0)			
{[£3.15m − (£3.15m × 20%)] × 2/12}			(420.0)	
Accrued variable expenses				
[£3m × 1/12 × 10%]	(25.0)			
[£3.15m × 1/12 × 10%]			(26.3)	
Accrued fixed expenses	(15.0)	(440.0)	(15.0)	(461.3)
Investment in working capital		725.0		676.2

(b) The expected profit for the year:

	Current policy		New policy	
	£000	£000	£000	£000
Sales revenue		3,000.0		3,150.0
Cost of goods sold		(2,400.0)		(2,520.0)
Gross profit (20%)		600.0		630.0
Variable expenses (10%)	(300.0)		(315.0)	
Fixed expenses	(180.0)		(180.0)	
Discounts (£3.15m × 60% × 2.5%)	–	(480.0)	(47.3)	(542.3)
Profit for the year		120.0		87.7

(c) Under the proposed policy we can see that the investment in working capital will be slightly lower than under the current policy. However, profits will be substantially lower as a result of offering discounts. The increase in sales revenue resulting from the discounts will not be sufficient to offset the additional cost of making the discounts to customers. It seems that the business should, therefore, stick with its current policy.

Appendix A

A.1

	Account to be debited	Account to be credited
(a)	Inventories	Trade payables
(b)	Equity (or a separate drawings account)	Cash
(c)	Interest on borrowings	Cash
(d)	Inventories	Cash
(e)	Cash	Trade receivables
(f)	Wages	Cash
(g)	Equity (or a separate drawings account)	Trade receivables
(h)	Trade payables	Cash
(i)	Electricity (or heat and light)	Cash
(j)	Cash	Sales revenue

Note that the precise name given to an account is not crucial so long as it is clear to those who are using the information what each account deals with.

A.2   (a) and (b)

Cash at bank

		£			£
1 Feb	Equity	6,000	3 Feb	Inventories	2,600
15 Feb	Sales revenue	4,000	5 Feb	Equipment	800
28 Feb	Trade receivables	2,500	9 Feb	Rent	250
			10 Feb	Fuel and electricity	240
			11 Feb	General expenses	200
			21 Feb	Equity	1,000
			25 Feb	Trade payables	2,000
			28 Feb	Balance c/d	5,410
		12,500			12,500
1 Mar	Balance b/d	5,410			

Equity

		£			£
21 Feb	Cash at bank	1,000	1 Feb	Cash at bank	6,000
28 Feb	Balance c/d	5,000			
		6,000			6,000
			28 Feb	Balance b/d	5,000
28 Feb	Balance c/d	7,410	28 Feb	Income statement	2,410
		7,410			7,410
			1 Mar	Balance b/d	7,410

Inventories

		£			£
3 Feb	Cash at bank	2,600	15 Feb	Cost of sales	2,400
6 Feb	Trade payables	3,000	19 Feb	Cost of sales	2,300
			28 Feb	Balance c/d	900
		5,600			5,600
1 Mar	Balance b/d	900			

Equipment

		£			£
5 Feb	Cash at bank	800			

Trade payables

		£			£
25 Feb	Cash at bank	2,000	6 Feb	Inventories	3,000
28 Feb	Balance c/d	1,000			
		3,000			3,000
			1 Mar	Balance b/d	1,000

Rent

		£			£
9 Feb	Cash at bank	250	28 Feb	Income statement	250

Fuel and electricity

		£			£
10 Feb	Cash at bank	240	28 Feb	Income statement	240

General expenses

		£			£
11 Feb	Cash at bank	200	28 Feb	Income statement	200

Sales revenue

		£			£
28 Feb	Balance c/d	7,800	15 Feb	Cash at bank	4,000
			19 Feb	Trade receivables	3,800
		7,800			7,800
28 Feb	Income statement	7,800	28 Feb	Balance b/d	7,800

Cost of sales

		£			£
15 Feb	Inventories	2,400	28 Feb	Balance c/d	4,700
19 Feb	Inventories	2,300			
		4,700			4,700
28 Feb	Balance b/d	4,700	28 Feb	Income statement	4,700

Trade receivables

		£			£
19 Feb	Sales revenue	3,800	28 Feb	Cash at bank	2,500
			28 Feb	Balance c/d	1,300
		3,800			3,800
1 Mar	Balance b/d	1,300			

Trial balance as at 28 February

	Debits £	Credits £
Cash at bank	5,410	
Equity		5,000
Inventories	900	
Equipment	800	
Trade payables		1,000
Rent	250	
Fuel and electricity	240	
General expenses	200	
Sales revenue		7,800
Cost of sales	4,700	
Trade receivables	1,300	
	13,800	13,800

(c)

Income statement

		£			£
28 Feb	Cost of sales	4,700	28 February	Sales revenue	7,800
28 Feb	Rent	250			
28 Feb	Fuel and electricity	240			
28 Feb	General expenses	200			
28 Feb	Equity (profit)	2,410			
		7,800			7,800

Statement of financial position as at 28 February

	£
ASSETS	
Non-current assets	
Equipment	800
Current assets	
Inventories	900
Trade receivables	1,300
Cash at bank	5,410
	7,610
Total assets	8,410
EQUITY AND LIABILITIES	
Equity (owners' claim)	7,410
Current liabilities	
Trade payables	1,000
Total equity and liabilities	8,410

Income statement for the month ended 28 February

	£
Sales revenue	7,800
Cost of sales	(4,700)
Gross profit	3,100
Rent	(250)
Fuel and electricity	(240)
General expenses	(200)
Profit for the month	2,410

A.3 (a) and (b)

Buildings

		£			£
1 Jan	Balance b/d	25,000			

Fittings – cost

		£			£
1 Jan	Balance b/d	10,000	31 Dec	Balance c/d	12,000
31 Dec	Cash at bank	2,000			
		12,000			12,000
1 Jan	Balance b/d	12,000			

Fittings – depreciation

		£			£
31 Dec	Balance c/d	4,400	1 Jan	Balance b/d	2,000
			31 Dec	Income statement (£12,000 × 20%)	2,400
		4,400			4,400
			1 Jan	Balance b/d	4,400

General expenses

		£			£
1 Jan	Balance b/d	140	31 Dec	Income statement	570
31 Dec	Cash at bank	580		Balance c/d	150
		720			720
1 Jan	Balance b/d	150			

Inventories

		£			£
1 Jan	Balance b/d	1,350	31 Dec	Cost of sales	15,220
31 Dec	Trade payables	17,220		Cost of sales	4,900
	Cash at bank	3,760		Equity	560
				Balance c/d	1,650
		22,330			22,330
1 Jan	Balance b/d	1,650			

Cost of sales

		£			£
31 Dec	Inventories	15,220	31 Dec	Income statement	20,120
	Inventories	4,900			
		20,120			20,120

Rent

		£			£
1 Jan	Balance b/d	500	31 Dec	Income statement	3,000
31 Dec	Cash at bank	3,000		Balance c/d	500
		3,500			3,500
1 Jan	Balance b/d	500			

Trade receivables

		£			£
1 Jan	Balance b/d	1,840	31 Dec	Cash at bank	32,810
31 Dec	Sales revenue	33,100		Income statement	260
				(bad debt)	
				Balance c/d	1,870
		34,940			34,940
1 Jan	Balance b/d	1,870			

Cash at bank

		£			£
1 Jan	Balance b/d	2,180	31 Dec	Inventories	3,760
31 Dec	Sales revenue	10,360		Wages	3,770
	Borrowings	2,000		Rent	3,000
	Trade receivables	32,810		Electricity	1,070
				General expenses	580
				Fittings	2,000
				Borrowings	1,000
				Trade payables	18,150
				Equity	10,400
				Balance c/d	3,620
		47,350			47,350
1 Jan	Balance b/d	3,620			

Equity

		£			£
31 Dec	Inventories	560	1 Jan	Balance b/d	25,050
	Cash at bank	10,400		Income statement (profit)	10,900
	Balance c/d	24,990			
		35,950			35,950
			1 Jan	Balance b/d	24,990

Borrowings

		£			£
30 June	Cash at bank	1,000	1 Jan	Balance b/d	12,000
31 Dec	Balance c/d	13,000		Cash at bank	2,000
		14,000			14,000
			1 Jan	Balance b/d	13,000

Trade payables

		£			£
31 Dec	Cash at bank	18,150	1 Jan	Balance b/d	1,690
	Balance c/d	760	31 Dec	Inventories	17,220
		18,910			18,910
			1 Jan	Balance b/d	760

Electricity

		£			£
31 Dec	Cash at bank	1,070	1 Jan	Balance b/d	270
31 Dec	Balance c/d	290	31 Dec	Income statement	1,090
		1,360			1,360
			1 Jan	Balance b/d	290

Sales revenue

		£			£
31 Dec	Income statement	43,460	31 Dec	Trade receivables	33,100
				Cash at bank	10,360
		43,460			43,460

Wages

		£			£
31 Dec	Cash at bank	3,770	31 Dec	Income statement	3,770

Interest on borrowings

		£			£
			31 Dec	Income statement	
				((6/12 × 14,000) +	
				(6/12 × 13,000)) × 10%	1,350

(c)

Income statement for the year to 31 December

		£			£
31 Dec	Cost of sales	20,120	31 Dec	Sales revenue	43,460
	Depreciation	2,400			
	General expenses	570			
	Rent	3,000			
	Bad debts (Trade receivables)	260			
	Electricity	1,090			
	Wages	3,770			
	Interest on borrowings	1,350			
	Profit (Equity)	10,900			
		43,460			43,460

(d)

Statement of financial position as at 31 December last year

	£	£
ASSETS		
Non-current assets		
Property, plant and equipment		
Buildings		25,000
Fittings – cost	12,000	
– depreciation	(4,400)	7,600
		32,600
Current assets		
Inventories of stationery		150
Inventories		1,650
Prepaid rent		500
Trade receivables		1,870
Cash at bank		3,620
		7,790
Total assets		40,390
EQUITY AND LIABILITIES		
Equity (owners' claim)		24,990
Non-current liabilities		
Borrowings		13,000
Current liabilities		
Trade payables		760
Accrued electricity		290
Accrued interest on borrowings		1,350
		2,400
Total equity and liabilities		40,390

Present value table

Present value of £1, that is, $1/(1 + r)^n$

where r = discount rate

n = number of periods until payment

Periods (n)	Discount rates (r)										
	1%	2%	3%	4%	5%	6%	7%	8%	9%	10%	
1	0.990	0.980	0.971	0.962	0.952	0.943	0.935	0.926	0.917	0.909	1
2	0.980	0.961	0.943	0.925	0.907	0.890	0.873	0.857	0.842	0.826	2
3	0.971	0.942	0.915	0.889	0.864	0.840	0.816	0.794	0.772	0.751	3
4	0.961	0.924	0.888	0.855	0.823	0.792	0.763	0.735	0.708	0.683	4
5	0.951	0.906	0.863	0.822	0.784	0.747	0.713	0.681	0.650	0.621	5
6	0.942	0.888	0.837	0.790	0.746	0.705	0.666	0.630	0.596	0.564	6
7	0.933	0.871	0.813	0.760	0.711	0.665	0.623	0.583	0.547	0.513	7
8	0.923	0.853	0.789	0.731	0.677	0.627	0.582	0.540	0.502	0.467	8
9	0.914	0.837	0.766	0.703	0.645	0.592	0.544	0.500	0.460	0.424	9
10	0.905	0.820	0.744	0.676	0.614	0.558	0.508	0.463	0.422	0.386	10
11	0.896	0.804	0.722	0.650	0.585	0.527	0.475	0.429	0.388	0.350	11
12	0.887	0.788	0.701	0.625	0.557	0.497	0.444	0.397	0.356	0.319	12
13	0.879	0.773	0.681	0.601	0.530	0.469	0.415	0.368	0.326	0.290	13
14	0.870	0.758	0.661	0.577	0.505	0.442	0.388	0.340	0.299	0.263	14
15	0.861	0.743	0.642	0.555	0.481	0.417	0.362	0.315	0.276	0.239	15

					Discount rates (r)						
Periods (n)	11%	12%	13%	14%	15%	16%	17%	18%	19%	20%	
1	0.901	0.893	0.885	0.877	0.870	0.862	0.855	0.847	0.840	0.833	1
2	0.812	0.797	0.783	0.769	0.756	0.743	0.731	0.718	0.706	0.694	2
3	0.731	0.712	0.693	0.675	0.658	0.641	0.624	0.609	0.593	0.579	3
4	0.659	0.636	0.613	0.592	0.572	0.552	0.534	0.516	0.499	0.482	4
5	0.593	0.567	0.543	0.519	0.497	0.476	0.456	0.437	0.419	0.402	5
6	0.535	0.507	0.480	0.456	0.432	0.410	0.390	0.370	0.352	0.335	6
7	0.482	0.452	0.425	0.400	0.376	0.354	0.333	0.314	0.296	0.279	7
8	0.434	0.404	0.376	0.351	0.327	0.305	0.285	0.266	0.249	0.233	8
9	0.391	0.361	0.333	0.308	0.284	0.263	0.243	0.225	0.209	0.194	9
10	0.352	0.322	0.295	0.270	0.247	0.227	0.208	0.191	0.176	0.162	10
11	0.317	0.287	0.261	0.237	0.215	0.195	0.178	0.162	0.148	0.135	11
12	0.286	0.257	0.231	0.208	0.187	0.168	0.152	0.137	0.124	0.112	12
13	0.258	0.229	0.204	0.182	0.163	0.145	0.130	0.116	0.104	0.093	13
14	0.232	0.205	0.181	0.160	0.141	0.125	0.111	0.099	0.088	0.078	14
15	0.209	0.183	0.160	0.140	0.123	0.108	0.095	0.084	0.074	0.065	15

					Discount rates (r)						
Periods (n)	21%	22%	23%	24%	25%	26%	27%	28%	29%	30%	
1	0.826	0.820	0.813	0.806	0.800	0.794	0.787	0.781	0.775	0.769	1
2	0.683	0.672	0.661	0.650	0.640	0.630	0.620	0.610	0.601	0.592	2
3	0.564	0.551	0.537	0.524	0.512	0.500	0.488	0.477	0.466	0.455	3
4	0.467	0.451	0.437	0.423	0.410	0.397	0.384	0.373	0.361	0.350	4
5	0.386	0.370	0.355	0.341	0.328	0.315	0.303	0.291	0.280	0.269	5
6	0.319	0.303	0.289	0.275	0.262	0.250	0.238	0.277	0.217	0.207	6
7	0.263	0.249	0.235	0.222	0.210	0.198	0.188	0.178	0.168	0.159	7
8	0.218	0.204	0.191	0.179	0.168	0.157	0.148	0.139	0.130	0.123	8
9	0.180	0.167	0.155	0.144	0.134	0.125	0.116	0.108	0.101	0.094	9
10	0.149	0.137	0.126	0.116	0.107	0.099	0.092	0.085	0.078	0.073	10
11	0.123	0.112	0.103	0.094	0.086	0.079	0.072	0.066	0.061	0.056	11
12	0.102	0.092	0.083	0.076	0.069	0.062	0.057	0.052	0.047	0.043	12
13	0.084	0.075	0.068	0.061	0.055	0.050	0.045	0.040	0.037	0.033	13
14	0.069	0.062	0.055	0.049	0.044	0.039	0.035	0.032	0.028	0.025	14
15	0.057	0.051	0.045	0.040	0.035	0.031	0.028	0.025	0.022	0.020	15

Index

Page entries in **bold** refer to terms defined in the Glossary